REVEL enables students to read and interact with course material on the devices they use, **anywhere** and **anytime**. Responsive design allows students to access REVEL on their tablet devices, with content displayed clearly in both portrait and landscape view.

Highlighting, **note taking**, and a **glossary** personalize the learning experience. Educators can add **notes** for students, too, including reminders or study tips

REVEL's variety of **writing** activities and assignments develop and assess concept **mastery** and **critical thinking**.

Superior assignability and tracking

REVEL's assignability and tracking tools help educators make sure students are completing their reading and understanding core concepts.

REVEL allows educators to indicate precisely which readings must be completed on which dates. This clear, detailed schedule helps students stay on task and keeps them motivated throughout the course.

REVEL lets educators monitor class assignment completion and individual student achievement. It offers actionable information that helps educators intersect with their students in meaningful ways, such as points earned on quizzes and time on task.

Strategic Communication in Business and the Professions

EIGHTH EDITION

Dan O'Hair
University of Kentucky

Gustav W. Friedrich
Rutgers University

Lynda Dee Dixon
Bowling Green State University

PEARSON

Boston   Columbus   Hoboken   Indianapolis   New York   San Francisco   Amsterdam
Cape Town   Dubai   London   Madrid   Milan   Munich   Paris   Montréal   Toronto
Delhi   Mexico City   São Paulo   Sydney   Hong Kong   Seoul   Singapore   Taipei   Tokyo

Editor-in-Chief: Ashley Dodge
Managing Editor: Amber Mackey
Program Manager: Carly Czech
Sponsoring Editor: Priya Christopher
Editorial Assistant (Program Support): Casseia Lewis
Editorial Assistant (Customer Support): Pauline Kitele
Senior Marketing Coordinator: Susan Osterlitz
Editorial Project Manager: Patrick Walsh, iEnergizer Aptara®, Ltd.
Development Editor: Trish Nealon, iEnergizer Aptara®, Ltd.
Asset Development Project Management: LearningMate Solutions, Ltd.
Senior Operations Supervisor: Mary Fischer
Operations Specialist: Mary Ann Gloriande
Associate Director of Design: Blair Brown
Interior Design: Kathryn Foot
Cover Director: Maria Lange
Cover Designer: Heather Marshall, Lumina Datamatics, Inc.
Cover Image: Denniro/Shutterstock
Director of Digital Studio: Sacha Laustsen
Digital Studio Project Manager: Liz Roden Hall
Full-Service Project Management and Composition: Jogender Taneja, iEnergizer Aptara®, Ltd.
Printer/Binder: Manufactured in the United States by RR Donnelley
Cover Printer: Manufactured in the United States by RR Donnelley

Credits and acknowledgments borrowed from other sources and reproduced, with permission, in this textbook appear on appropriate page within.

Many of the designations by manufacturers and seller to distinguish their products are claimed as trademarks. Where those designations appear in this book, and the publisher was aware of a trademark claim, the designations have been printed in initial caps or all caps.

Library of Congress Cataloging-in-Publication Data

O'Hair, Dan.
  Strategic communication in business and the professions/Dan O'Hair, Gustav W. Friedrich, Lynda Dee Dixon.—8th edition.
    pages cm
  ISBN 978-0-13-401168-4—ISBN 0-13-401168-6
  1. Communication in organizations. 2. Communication in management. 3. Business communication. 4. Intercultural communication. I. Friedrich, Gustav W. II. Dixon, Lynda Dee. III. Title.
  HD30.3.O35 2016
  658.4′5—dc23
                                                                            2015011554

10 9 8 7 6 5 4 3 2 1

ISBN-10:   0-134-12803-6
ISBN-13: 978-0-134-12803-0

Brief Contents

Contents

Preface

The eighth edition of *Strategic Communication in Business and the Professions* represents our combined effort to produce a text that enables students to address daily professional challenges through the lens of communication skills. We know well that business and professional worlds consistently evolve as they adapt to change. As a result, students must stay knowledgeable of new advances in order to excel in their careers. This Revel edition alerts students to recent changes and challenges. Included are vivid discussions and examples of situations where ideas and loyalties have shifted in the global marketplace, work habits have changed, employees' private and public lives are seen in new light, technologies are more sophisticated, and cultural diversity has more impact than ever.

In the workplace, a person's ability to express thoughts and ideas efficiently and articulately to others across all domains and barriers, from one-on-one interactions through conflict management to large-scale presentations, is the backbone of a successful business model. Consequently, competent communication is one of the most important foundations of career success. The goal of *Strategic Communication* is to develop fundamental communication tools for students as they prepare to enter the business and professional worlds.

Meeting the needs of college-level courses that focus on oral communication within an organizational context has been the primary goal of this text over all of its editions. While crafting a well-written proposal is an important business communication skill, many students discover that presentations, personal interviews, and group meetings represent their first—and sometimes their biggest—communication challenges. *Strategic Communication in Business and the Professions* emphasizes the most essential skills in business and professional communication:

- Adapting to changes in the business or professional environment
- Embracing cultural diversity
- Thinking critically
- Promoting ethical communication
- Listening
- Communicating in managerial and leadership roles
- Managing conflict
- Communicating in teams and groups
- Making public presentations.

Students and instructors alike will find that *Strategic Communication in Business and the Professions* thoroughly integrates communication theory and practice. Our goal is to help instructors teach students to recognize the basic similarities among all forms of communication. Throughout a typical business day, one form of communication leads to another, can impact another, or cannot exist without another. Understanding how communication is interconnected leads to a better understanding of business itself. A broad and in-depth knowledge of communication theory and practice provides students with the skills and tools they need to overcome any challenge.

The Model of Strategic Communication

Our Model of Strategic Communication, which has been integrated into all chapters of this textbook, provides students with an easy-to-use framework for mastering oral communication skills. Introduced in Chapter 2, the model emphasizes that effective communicators must master four basic skills. They are:

- Set goals
- Understand the communication situation and the audience
- Demonstrate competence
- Manage anxiety effectively.

As in previous editions, we integrate these four essential elements throughout the text within the strategic model. We have taken special care in this edition to introduce new examples and provide more opportunities for application. By practicing the skills of effective communicators, students can approach any communication situation with confidence. In continually exercising this skill set, students will have their own pool of experiences to reference when faced with a communicative challenge. Our strategic approach helps students *understand, remember,* and *use* essential communication skills in any business or professional setting.

New to This Edition

The eighth edition of *Strategic Communication in Business and the Professions* takes into consideration:

- Current environment and business practices
- New and updated research and examples from contemporary organizations

- Trends in communication technology
- Clear viewpoints on communication variables
- Increased emphasis on problem-solving
- An even more robust strategic communication framework.

REVEL™

Educational technology designed for the way today's students read, think, and learn.

When students are engaged deeply, they learn more effectively and perform better in their courses. This simple fact inspired the creation of **REVEL**: an immersive learning experience designed for the way today's students read, think, and learn. Built in collaboration with educators and students nationwide, **REVEL** is the newest, fully digital way to deliver respected Pearson content.

REVEL enlivens course content with media interactives and assessments—integrated directly within the authors' narrative—that provide opportunities for students to read about and practice course material in tandem. This immersive **educational technology** boosts student engagement, which leads to better understanding of concepts and improved performance throughout the course.

Learn more about REVEL

Features of the Edition

Our text is designed for introductory business and organizational communication classes. To help students master the basics, features in each chapter emphasize the following:

Relevant Real-World Examples

- *Practicing Business Communication* is a recurring feature that examines communication practices in a range of businesses, broadening student awareness of communication tools in use. To describe how business and professional communication works today, the companies profiled range from small businesses to global corporations.
- *Strategic Scenarios* open each chapter, setting the stage by presenting a hypothetical situation with a problem similar to one students could easily face as they make the transition from the classroom to the world of work. Students are asked to be alert for solutions as they read the chapter. Then, at the end of the chapter in the *Strategic Scenario Wrap Up*, students revisit the situation for a possible solution and a chance to further extend learning.

Critical Thinking

- *What Do You Think?* and *What Would You Do?* journal exercises give students the opportunity to think through and write about communication situations and problems that they may eventually encounter.
- *Think Critically* journal exercises, which conclude each *Practicing Business Communication* feature, encourage students to examine the connections between concepts in the text and communication in actual companies and organizations.

Focus on Ethical and Unbiased Communication

- *Ethical Issues* challenge students to think critically about the role ethics take in business communication.
- *Diversity coverage.* United States demographics continue to evolve, and this edition has particularly strong coverage on how to refine communication skills with diversity in mind.

Effective In-Chapter Learning Aids

- *Learning Objectives* allow students to know what they are expected to master in each chapter.
- *Chapter Summaries* are presented in a bullet-point format to help readers identify and focus on essentials within the chapter.
- *Key Terms* show instant definitions for easy reference.
- *Shared Writing* assessments promote debate and discussion and further test understanding of concepts.

Available Instructor Resources

The following resources are available for instructors. These can be downloaded at http://www.pearsonhighered.com/irc. Login required.

- **PowerPoint**—provides a core template of the content covered throughout the text. Can easily be added to customize for your classroom.
- **Instructor's Manual**—includes a description, in-class discussion questions, and a research assignment for each chapter.
- **Test Bank**—includes additional questions beyond the REVEL in multiple choice and open-ended—short and essay response—formats.
- **MyTest**—an electronic format of the Test Bank to customize in-class tests or quizzes. Visit: http://www.pearsonhighered.com/mytest.

Acknowledgments

We would like to express our gratitude to the extremely helpful and supportive editorial, production, and marketing teams at Pearson.

We have benefited greatly from the participation and assistance of many people throughout our work on this edition. Allen R. Bean, Southeast Community College; Wendy Bjorklund, St. Cloud State University; Suzanne Buck, University of Houston; Cory Cunningham, University of Oklahoma; Kim Gatz, Northern Illinois University; Dr. Brendan B. Kelly, University of West Florida; John Parrish, Tarrant County College; Santo Trapani, LaGuardia Community College; Naomi Warren, University of Southern California.

We would also like to acknowledge the contribution of our families whose influence deeply benefited this new edition: for D.O., they are Mary, John, Erica, Jonathan, and Anders; for G.W.F., they are Betty Turock, the person he loves and shares his life with, and Bruce Friedrich and Alka Chanda, his son and wife whose life choices he admires; for L.D.D., they are Chick Stuhlman, Ryan Glenn, and Margo Bilinski with their super spouses and perfect children.

D.O., G.W.F., L.D.D.

Chapter 1
Communication in Organizations

 ## Learning Objectives

1.1 Recognize the importance of competent communication skills in today's information age

1.2 Review the elements of an effective interactive communication process

1.3 Report some of the reasons why communication may fail

1.4 Examine the structure of an organization in relation to its communication techniques

Strategic Scenario: A Business Evolves

Kate Hullison and Jeremy Sandusky were relaxing after work one day during happy hour. Both worked for online businesses, Jeremy as a software designer and Kate as a mid-level manager. They liked the type of work they did, but both really wanted to work for themselves. All they needed was a sound business plan, some guts, and a venture capitalist who believed in their ideas. After honing the details of their business strategy, they found a venture capitalist in DaKysha Masaal, who wanted to invest in a start-up.

Their new business began as a consulting company for other Internet businesses and quickly grew to seven employees (DaKysha, Kate, Jeremy, and four others). They managed themselves without much hierarchy or bureaucracy in part because they were small but more so because that is the way they liked it—especially Jeremy.

Rapid growth caused the ranks of their employees to swell to fifty-five, forcing them to move out of their comfortable digs in a converted apartment complex into a high-rise office building. The way that DaKysha, Kate, and Jeremy organized and managed their work and employees changed quickly as well. More structure, hierarchy, meetings, plans, and, as Jeremy puts it, "administrivia" have become the norm. DaKysha and Kate seem to thrive on the excitement of success that the company is experiencing, but Jeremy feels differently. He now finds himself in the same type of organization he left for the start-up—except now he is one of the bosses. His communication with others has expanded 100-fold, and he doesn't feel prepared for the responsibility. It seems to him that his interactions with others are different, more formal—exactly why he left his old company in the first place.

As you read through the chapter, think about the issues involved with managing, organizing, and communicating in various types of organizations. At the end of the chapter, we will revisit this scenario and discuss some solutions.

1.1: Overview

Communication in Organizations

1.1 **Recognize the importance of competent communication skills in today's information age**

What does your Facebook wall say about your business savvy? Does your Twitter feed provide you with professional advice? Is your technology quotient (TQ) up to snuff? We ask these questions in a business and professional communication course because communication technology plays a role, front and center, in our professional lives. Advances in communication technology may have blurred any lines there once were between work and daily life, and yet strategic business communication has specific, measurable goals and qualities. Are you up to the task?

Surveys of businesses confirm what we have been hearing for years: employers are looking for people who possess competent communication skills.[1] Oral presentations and report briefings, interviews, small-group communication, listening, and leadership are just a few of the communication activities you will perform in the real world. Your career success depends on your ability to communicate effectively within an organization.

Over the years, studies of working professionals have uncovered the value, and continuing necessity, of effective communication to business success. Without exception, these executives have reported that communication, especially the practice of good oral skills, is a key component of success in the business world. Interestingly, these executives have indicated that college courses (rather than in-house training or input from outside consultants) provide the best oral communication training. Furthermore, executives who hire college graduates believe that the importance of oral communication skills for career success is going to increase. In distressed economic times, communication is all the more important.[2] Thus, our goal is to integrate you into a successful career by providing you with the information necessary to become an effective organizational communicator.

The increasing importance of communication skills grows out of one feature of the present time: the amount of information that must be transmitted, consumed, analyzed, returned, or discarded. The information age of the present is considerably different from the industrial age of years past. Played out on the global stage, today's information age supports an organizational style that emphasizes constant, interactive management of knowledge among organizations and individuals, without geographical boundaries. Given that the amount of human knowledge *doubles* every year, organizational styles must focus on how to empower employees with information.

The shift in the value and volume of knowledge in the marketplace means a shift in the criteria that determine business success. Successful companies today integrate new technologies without alienating employees, handle information so efficiently that they are not swamped by data, and actively seek to enhance their communication through technology. None of this can be accomplished unless employees—from the president to the shipping clerk—know how to communicate effectively.

Communication skills are central to promoting excellence now and in the coming years.[3]

⊗ **Creative Insights**

Creative insight is the ability to ask the right questions. Asking tough questions may not be the most pleasant task, but such inquiries are necessary if a business is to deal with a dynamic work force and economy.

⊗ **Sensitivity**

Sensitivity means a business practices the Golden Rule with its workers: "Do unto others as you would have them do unto you." In communication, it means paying attention to the needs of others, listening empathetically, and monitoring others' reactions when you speak.

⊗ **Vision**

Vision means being able to imagine the future. Leaders of organizations must have a clear picture of where their organizations are going in turbulent times. In a more everyday sense, business speech should have a point—such as an idea, response, or vision to convey—that the speaker focuses on making in the talk or presentation.

⊗ **Shared Meaning**

Shared meaning concerns how you engage others. Can you connect to your listeners on their level and they on yours? Do you understand their perspective? Do you have common language?

⊗ **Integrity**

Integrity builds trust and confidence in relationships. If people trust you, they will believe what you say. If that trust has been damaged, and people don't believe what you say, it won't matter how well you communicate your point.

Globalization, the trend toward conducting business with and in foreign countries, is a fact of life. We live in an international marketplace, where the Internet places foreign businesses, services, and interactions with business-people at our fingertips. Globalization today means that every business, no matter how big or small, operates within a worldwide community. International trade, immigration, and the flow of information in real time have created a diverse work force, requiring communication skills that can bridge cultural gaps and reach far-flung locations. Businesses have to adapted to varied communication media: email, document transfer, Web communication, social networking, and more advanced forms. The global employee is skilled at using media, flexible and adaptive to rapidly changing communication technologies, and culturally aware. International organizations employ a dynamic communication rhetoric, focusing primarily on cultural adaptation and long-distance technological implementation. Each of the five communication skills implicitly include effective cultural communication. They also depend upon the interactive communication process.

1.2: The Interactive Communication Process

1.2 **Review the elements of an effective interactive communication process**

The essence of communication in all contexts is that people exchange messages to accomplish goals and objectives. Because people bring different goals, backgrounds, styles, habits, and preferences to the process, truly effective communication is **interactive:** each person takes part in the communication, listens, and responds to the others. Each element of the communication process contributes to making communication interactive. The cultures of the sender and the receiver affect all areas of interactive communication. Figure 1.1 diagrams the interactive communication process, and a brief explanation follows.

Figure 1.1 Interactive Communication Process

Shared meaning is the mutual understanding that results when the sender and all intended receivers interpret the message in the same way.

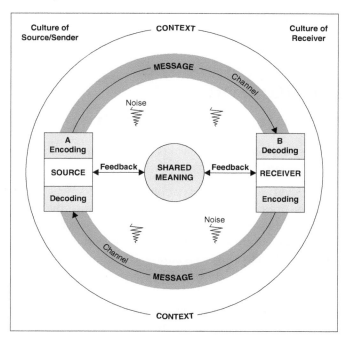

Messages are the content of communication with others—the ideas people wish to share. Messages may be expressed verbally—in spoken (oral) or written form—or nonverbally through gestures, posture, facial expressions, and even clothing. The **source** creates the message. Sometimes referred to as the sender, the source determines what type of message is to be sent and the best way to send it. When deciding how and what to send, a sender practicing interactive communication takes into account the needs of those who will be receiving the message.

Encoding is the physical process of organizing elements of the message for transmission to the receivers. In oral communication, encoding is the act of choosing and vocalizing words or sounds. In nonverbal communication, encoding means gesturing, smiling or nodding, and so on. Effective interactive communicators continually monitor the verbal and nonverbal cues from their audience to improve the accuracy and meaning of the messages they intend to send. Adding visual aids to written messages and friendly gestures to spoken messages make them more understandable and accessible, as do graphics in a computer-generated message. Emojis allow you to "smile" at someone by simply typing **:-)** on your keyboard, for example.

The **channel** is the medium that carries a message once it is encoded by a source. Channels include live meetings, which range from personal one-on-one interactions and group meetings to online chat sessions, telephone calls, and videoconferencing. In other, non-live communication channels, such as letters, memos, emails, faxes, and some Web communication, the parties don't interact simultaneously. Texting can be seen as an interesting hybrid; with senders and receivers simultaneously active it functions like a phone call, but since texts are not reliably received and responded to in real-time, texting is therefore a non-live channel. There is no question that channels affect the communication process.

The destination of the message is the **receiver**. The receipt of the message is the primary determinant of whether communication ever takes place. In other words, messages become communication only when a receiver picks up the message. Receivers include *all* persons who pick up the message, regardless of whether they were the sender's intended targets. "Sidestream listening"—where some receivers get messages inadvertently—can create problems, particularly in terms of breached confidentiality.

Fast-moving communication technology increases the chance that unintended receivers will pick up messages, but the risk has always been there. Examples range from old school indiscretions, such as overheard conversations in the break room or a forgotten paper memo at the copy machine or printer, to the classic misdirected email, to the modern malady of having data-heavy computer files broken into by hackers. And we know that one must be especially careful with messages posted on the Web since these messages are public and can be traced back to the sender.

The counterpart of encoding, **decoding** is the process that receivers go through to make sense of the message. Decoding is influenced by many factors, including cultural background, listening abilities, and attitudes toward the source or channel.

Feedback is any response, verbal or nonverbal, that a receiver makes to a message. Most senders seek feedback during the communication process because it lets them know whether the message has been understood correctly. Feedback can take the form of a verbal or nonverbal responses. Verbal responses include a listener's spoken questions or replies through email, phone calls or texts, or an organized forum such as a status meeting or quality circle; nonverbal responses can include a listener nodding in agreement on one hand or a puzzled facial expression on the other.

Noise is anything that interferes with communication. The common definition of *noise* is distracting sounds that prevent people from hearing or making themselves heard, but noise may take several forms. Noise is a more encompassing phenomenon than this description suggests. It includes psychological distractions such as nervousness or tension, emotional distractions such as extreme happiness or sadness, and physiological distractions such as fatigue or illness. Bias and prejudice are forms of psychological noise because bias against a speaker can interfere with a listener's reception of a message. All of these affect the quality of the message sent and received. Noise can occur at any point in the communication process.

Context is the situation or setting in which communication occurs. Whenever communication takes place, it does so within a context. Context can influence the content, the quality, and the effectiveness of a communication event. This may include the *physical context*, or the actual physical place (office, conference room, cafeteria) in which communication occurs; the *chronological context*, or the time/date at which an interaction takes place (after work hours, during a peak business cycle, first thing in the morning); the *cultural context*, or the ethnic/national and/or organizational backgrounds of the people communicating (New Englanders and Southwesterners, managers and staff, Native Americans and Asians); and the *social context*, or the social histories and relationships among communicators (age differences or similarities, out-of-the-office friendships, personality harmonies or conflicts). No matter what form it takes, context is an important and ever-present component of the communication process.

Notice the term **shared meaning** in the center of Figure 1.1. Shared meaning is the mutual understanding that results when the sender and all intended receivers interpret the message in the same way. It is the primary desired outcome of any communication. Even though sources and receivers nearly always try to share meaning with one another, they do not necessarily succeed in doing so. There are degrees, or stages, of shared meaning attained through this process.

> Imagine that you and your supervisor are in a crowded and noisy elevator. Your supervisor tells you the location, time, and agenda for an upcoming meeting, but because you can barely hear, you exit the elevator certain only of the location and time. You know enough to be able to get to the meeting, but your supervisor intended for you to know what was going to be discussed so that you could prepare some notes.

Shared meaning was not fully achieved in this example even though the meeting was held, it did not accomplish all that the supervisor expected. Communication is not an either/or concept; rather, varying degrees of communication are possible, depending on how the message is treated at each point. A great deal of communication can occur without the benefit of fully shared meaning, but enough information must be exchanged between sources and receivers so they can function together in a minimal fashion. Although business and professional communicators strive for shared meaning, there are many obstacles to achieving it.

1.3: Reasons for Communication Failure

1.3   Report some of the reasons why communication may fail

In your everyday communication with others, you have probably noticed that some messages, despite the best intentions of the sender, are not decoded by the receiver as expected. Errors are so common that one expert has likened communication to Murphy's Law—"If communication can fail, it will." "If you are sure that communication cannot fail, it necessarily will fail." "There is always someone who knows better than you what you meant by your message."[4] Errors can occur at any step in the communication process.

Interactive Communication Components

Context

Inadequate, poorly timed, or too much information can have an impact on decoding; the feedback loop may fail; a channel may be inappropriate; cultural or psychological factors may create too much noise; or a sender may simply be ineffectual.

1.3.1: Inadequate Information

One manager, Sarah, intentionally withholds information from her subordinates because she feels that they will be confused by "too much information." In fact, managers and employees frequently complain that they do not receive enough information to do their jobs effectively. In some cases, upper management provides too little information when issuing orders. In other cases, information is provided, but it is not the right type. In our example, Sarah is actually working at cross-purposes with her employees because they usually have to get needed information from other sources.

1.3.2: Information Overload

Khan owns and runs a successful used-car business. He believes it is good business to tell and text all his sales associates when new shipments of used cars arrive from various destinations. Khan, however, goes into great detail, even providing vital statistics about vehicles that are not yet on the lot.

Employees at all levels of an organization can be overwhelmed by information. To ensure that people get enough information, managers often overcompensate and provide employees with more information than necessary (especially in situations where they are not sure what is useful). To be safe, they, like Khan, send so much information that much of it winds up being ignored.

TECHNOLOGY TOOLS

How Much Email Do You Get at Work?

If you work full-time or even part-time, you already understand how taxing voluminous emails can be, especially when you're busy. Roughly 91 percent of all people who use the Internet are emailers. In the next couple of years, you will likely spend more than four hours per day dealing with fifty or more work-related email messages and by 2017 it is estimated that businesses will send over 127 billion emails a day. However, of the 57 million American workers who use email, most agree that the service is essential to their work and improves teamwork. Email has become an indispensable part of organizational communication.

(×) "What is the answer to this necessary burden?"

Experts recommend that you use folders to organize your messages. You can set up folders that will hold messages that are "urgent," those emails that need immediate attention; "aging," those messages that are a few weeks old; "copies," those emails where you were not the primary recipient; and "misc.," a catchall category for messages that don't fit elsewhere but should not be deleted. Most communications software can be configured to organize your messages in this way and to filter out junk email. Other suggestions include using two email accounts (one personal and one professional), avoiding mail distribution lists, and limiting how often you check incoming messages to two to three times a day.

Non–work-related emails have been a significant problem since day one. Almost everyone has received junk email, or spam. It is estimated that spam costs U.S. organizations billions, as companies have been forced to develop firewalls and other costly software to filter and delete junk email.

It is also important to be a competent emailer. Several tips can move you in that direction.

1. Make your subject line a summary of your message, not a description (instead of "Meeting," summarize by stating "Meeting Canceled Due to Budget").

2. Provide enough background in the beginning of the message to bring the reader up to speed. Instead of "Great, OK, we're good to go," say "In terms of the Herrington proposal from the last meeting, yes, great, we're good to go."

3. Reduce emails to less than one page.

4. Do not use email for coworkers who you know prefer to be reached in another way.

The burden of email includes relating to cultural differences, some quite serious. Irony, sarcasm, and humor are interpreted differently by people from different countries and organizational cultures. Formal banking institutions in Switzerland may not be amused by informal humor included in an email from Dallas, Texas.

SOURCES: D. Fallows (2007), "Spam 2007" Pew Internet: http://www.pewinternet.org/reports/2007/spam=2007. aspx (accessed May 20, 2009).

"Spam: How Much Do We Get?": http://www.silicon.com/news/165–500001/1/4618.html (accessed July 30, 2003).

"U.S. Workers Spared Junk Emails": http://news.bbc.co.uk/2/hi/technology/2558113.stm (accessed July 30, 2003).

"Managing the Email Explosion": http://CNN.com/2000/TECH/computing/09/06/e-mail.management.idg/index.html (accessed September 7, 2000).

S. Robbins (2004), "Tips for Mastering Email Overload": http://hbswk.hbs.edu/item.jhtml?id=4438&t=srobbins (accessed March 12, 2006).

The Radicati Group, Inc., "Email Statistics Report, 2013–2017": http://www.radicati.com/wp/wp-content/uploads/2013/04/Email-Statistics-Report-2013-2017-Executive-Summary.pdf

Adam Sobieski, "An Anti-Spam Hueristic": http://pubs.aeaweb.org/doi/pdfplus/10.1257/jep.26.3.87

1.3.3: Poor-Quality Information

Information that is readily available to employees may be of little use because of its poor quality. When Ryan asks Margaret, the in-house computer expert, for assistance and he gets a long, jargon-filled, disorganized response, both Ryan and Margaret have wasted time and are frustrated.

Other examples of poor-quality information include outdated, erroneous, misleading, overemphasized, and disorganized information. Many business blogs have become ineffective because they do not provide quality information.

1.3.4: Poor Timing

Having the right amount of information at the wrong time does little good. Sales reports, marketing figures, or consumer trends are of little value to decision makers if the information arrives too late to be used. Information timing is just as important as information quantity or quality.

For example, if you purchase a sound system on Saturday from one store and find out on Monday that the same system is on sale at another store, you have received information too late. Similarly, if information arrives too early, the receivers may set it aside for later use but then forget that they have it.

1.3.5: Lack of Feedback or Follow-up

Frequently a sender forwards a message with the expectation that the receiver will respond with feedback or a follow-up message. If the receiver does not recognize that a response is requested or does not bother to reply to the message, the sender is forced to waste time waiting for a follow-up or sending a second message asking for feedback. In either case, time and effort are wasted. Even with email, it is a good idea to reply to a sent message. This way the sender is assured that the message has been received. In one instance, Anniwake called Charlie to inform him about the next budget meeting. Charlie was not in, so his secretary took the message about the meeting. "Tell him to let me know" was the last thing Anniwake said to the secretary. Charlie did not respond, so Anniwake did not schedule Charlie's report for the meeting. When Charlie showed up expecting to make his report, both he and Anniwake were angry, blaming each other for the feedback error.

1.3.6: Problems with Channels

The communication channels that carry organizational messages include face-to-face conversation, telephone, email, letters, public speeches, memos, real-time video-conferencing, Skype, Facebook, Twitter, and company intranets. Problems can occur when senders use the wrong channels to convey information—for example, using the phone to notify an employee that he is not going to get a promotion or has been fired. Issues that are very personal and sensitive require face-to-face contact; any other channel would be inappropriate. Likewise, contacting ten people separately about a new dress code is an inefficient use of time and resources because they can be informed collectively by email or during a meeting.

1.3.7: Incompetent Communication

Some organizational members do not possess the communication skills necessary to be effective in today's professional world. For instance, a multimedia presentation will be ineffective if the presenter does not know how to use the equipment, experiences technical difficulties, or tries to liven up a dull topic merely by adding flashy graphics rather than by improving the content of the presentation. People who attend meetings unprepared waste others' time. People with poor listening skills frustrate those who have to repeat information for them. Those who make inappropriate grammatical or vocabulary choices embarrass themselves and those around them. Incompetent communicators hurt the organization they represent. This has especially been the case with hastily sent messages composed in a moment of anger.

1.3.8: Ineffective Goal Setting

One of the most important skills in effective communication is setting appropriate goals. When goals are too low, the communicator wastes the opportunity to influence, motivate, or inform the audience effectively. When goals are too high, the communicator becomes disappointed or disillusioned because the audience fails to grasp the message or simply dismisses what was said.

For example, after you make a C on the first two tests, a final grade of A for the course might be an unrealistic goal. More realistic goals would be to turn in all remaining assignments on time and to begin studying for the remaining tests at least one week before they are scheduled. What other examples of ineffective goal setting have you encountered?

1.3.9: Communication Anxiety

When communication situations cause you to feel nervous, stressed, or apprehensive, the effectiveness of your efforts is at risk. Anxiety can hamper the ability to think, talk, gesture, or even listen. Not all communication situations cause anxiety however; each person reacts differently. To minimize your own communication anxiety, recognize the situations in which you experience it and use the techniques described here to control your nervousness.

Some people may suffer communication anxiety surrounding certain technologies. For example, most people who have been exposed to email embrace it as efficient and helpful. However, a small percentage of people face anxiety when using newer technology, such as texting or webinars. The technology gap can be a serious problem for employees who have not adapted to all possible communication advances, but it cuts both ways. For example, what happens when an older worker chooses to default to more "traditional" methods of communicating, such as picking up the phone? A voice message may be left for a receiver who prefers texting and rarely checks voicemail. And does the younger, more tech-savvy worker perhaps have any issues about answering calls in real time, about being "on the spot"? On still another note, too much information can create communication anxiety for workers of any age. How do they pick out the important messages?

When communication failures occur in social situations, at worst the communicators wind up confused, embarrassed, or annoyed. But when communication fails within a business organization, the results can be much worse—inefficiency, loss of morale, decreased productivity, or job termination. The specter of such negative results highlights the importance of studying organizational communication, particularly when it is possible to do so before you join an organization.

The need for communication may arise anywhere, and technology should help you to facilitate communication, not create communication anxiety.

SOURCE: Danielescalise/Fotolia

1.3.10: Cultural Barriers

Cultural barriers may also contribute to communication failure. Biases and prejudices against cultures other than your own can interfere with listening to and understanding a message. An accent may influence your perception of a coworker or manager. Sometimes individuals are afraid to ask a sender who is from a different culture to repeat a message that is not understood. Sensitivity to diverse cultures and culturally different ways of communicating is essential for effective business communication.

1.4: Understanding Organizational Communication

1.4 **Examine the structure of an organization in relation to its communication techniques**

Organizational communication is the exchange of oral, written, and nonverbal messages among people working to accomplish common tasks and goals. This definition encompasses much of the activity that occurs at work. It includes such tasks as alerting workers to production goals, scheduling meetings within and between departments, planning how the company will communicate with its customers and respond to their messages, and producing in-house informational material about policies and goals. A good understanding of organizational communication provides you with options when you face tasks that need to be accomplished efficiently and effectively. When you understand how an organizational context affects communication, you will be in a much better position to achieve the goals you have set for yourself.

Communicating in organizations is not an easy task. Obstacles to effective communication are always present. Assumptions about what others are doing can be wrong ("I thought you were going to cover the *southeastern* sales territory this month!"), and closed communication channels can inhibit the exchange of messages ("I only want to hear good news about sales figures!"). Reluctance to receive new ideas and information—especially when they differ from your own ideas—can be detrimental to organizational goals ("I own this business, and I think I know best what it needs").

Many theories have been advanced to explain how organizations work, what relationship exists between management and labor, and what function, if any, communication performs in the working of an organization. Theories also explore how the structure of an organization relates to its communication techniques. These concepts, which sometimes overlap, have had significant, and in some cases continuing, influences on organizational practices.

1.4.1: Classical Theory

The classical school of thought includes theories that emphasize structure, rules, and control. Included in this category are scientific management theory and bureaucracy theory. Although developed near the turn of the twentieth century, many of the principles of classical theory are still in use.

SCIENTIFIC MANAGEMENT Frederick Taylor published *The Principles of Scientific Management* in 1911 and revolutionized the way managers thought about work in general and employees in particular.[5] Taylor had a great deal of respect for workers and was one of the first advocates of systematic training and development to improve workers' proficiency in their duties. He also encouraged organizations to match workers' abilities with the duties and responsibilities of their jobs. According to Taylor, four principles promote good management:

1. Development of a true science of work
2. Scientific selection of the worker
3. Scientific education and development of the worker
4. Friendly cooperation between management and labor.

From these principles grew a philosophy that advocates the goals of support for science, harmony, cooperation, maximum output, and employee development.

ⓧ Philosophy Based on Taylor's Principles

• Science, not rule of thumb, should be stressed.

• Harmony, not discord, should be encouraged.

• Cooperation, not individualism, should be advocated.

• Maximum output should be valued in place of restricted output.

• The development of workers and managers to their greatest efficiency and prosperity should be a priority.

BUREAUCRACY Max Weber, generally considered the father of the study of bureaucracy, worked to understand how authority and control were used in groups and organizations. His major contribution was a description of authority structures. He proposed three types: charismatic, traditional, and rational-legal.[6]

Weber's Authority Structures

Traditional authority

Remove card   1 of 3   Reset Deck

Rational-legal authority is the basis for bureaucracy (Weber is best known for this aspect of his theory). Government agencies, large corporations, and even the college or university you are now attending are good examples of bureaucracies. A bureaucratic structure enables organizations to define very clearly what behavior in employees is acceptable and expected. Bureaucratic authority structures concentrate a great deal of power at the top of a hierarchy. Successive, or lower, levels get their power from upper layers. Look at the typical hierarchical shown in Figure 1.2. Notice how each succeeding layer is dependent on and subservient to the previous level of authority.

Figure 1.2 Typical Organizational Chart
This "org chart" shows the hierarchical nature of many businesses, in which each layer of workers is dependent on and subservient to a higher level.

Bureaucracies adhere to formalized rules and policies that they put in place for themselves, and communication within a bureaucracy goes by the book. Workers cannot skip levels of authority when sending messages to superiors or inferiors—the message must pass through each layer on its journey to the receiver. Communication in a bureaucracy is highly routine. Procedures, probably written ones, regulate oral and written communication.

STRENGTHS AND WEAKNESSES OF CLASSICAL THEORY **Classical theory** describes an organization that functions like a machine.[7] Machines perform repetitious tasks in specific and unchanging ways that are determined by their structures. The classical theory of management is appropriate in an organization when the same product is produced time and again, precision is at a premium, and the human "machine" parts are compliant and behave as they have been designed to do.

Think of organizations with which you are familiar. Do any of them have these characteristics? It would not be surprising if your response is "no." Changes in the American work force—larger numbers of college graduates and white-collar workers and larger business organizations—have lessened the popularity of classical theory and few contemporary organizations rely strictly on its principles. The theory's views now seem overly mechanistic and impersonal, unsuited to the developing view of workers as human beings with needs rather than as faceless, impersonal parts of a business machine.

1.4.2: Humanistic Theory

A school of thought known as **humanistic theory** gained popularity in response to classical theory's mechanistic approach. It focused on the needs of labor rather than on the structure of management.

HUMAN RELATIONS THEORY In the late 1920s and early 1930s, a number of studies on productivity were conducted at the Western Electric Hawthorne plant in Cicero, Illinois, under the leadership of Elton Mayo, a Harvard professor.[8] One of the first studies examined the effect of lighting in the workplace on workers' productivity.

As researchers increased the lighting of the experimental group in the Hawthorne plant, productivity increased, not just in the experimental group but also in the control group (which did not get increased lighting). Furthermore, when the experimenters *reduced* the illumination for the experimental group, productivity *continued* to increase. The engineers at the plant were delighted but puzzled.

The researchers concluded that increases in productivity were the result not of the changes in lighting but rather of the special attention being paid to the workers. Thus, the researchers proved that technical factors are not the only influences on work efficiency. Human factors, they discovered, also affect the work of employees.

According to Mayo, "Social study should begin with careful observation of what may be described as communication: that is, the capacity of an individual to communicate his feelings and ideas to another, the capacity of groups to communicate effectively and intimately with each other."[9] Mayo's most important finding, which stood in stark contrast to classical theory, was that informal groups and camaraderie among workers; supervisors' demonstrated interest, encouragement, praise, and recognition; and the ability to form relationships on the job were more effective than economic incentives in increasing workers' productivity and morale.

HUMAN RESOURCES APPROACH Human relations theory came under criticism for focusing too narrowly on workers' happiness and for not taking into account that happy workers might be unproductive. A reevaluation of human relations began, based on one of the most influential motivational theory books ever written: *The Human Side of Enterprise* by Douglas McGregor.[10] This book struck a compromise between classical theory and human relations theory: McGregor suggested that productivity will increase if workers not only are happy but also are given the proper working conditions.

Are You Being Watched?

Ethical Issues

Surfing the Web and sending emails are pretty routine activities in the workplace. Many jobs require these kinds of communication tasks as part of an employee's duties. But what about personal emails and browsing the Internet for personal reasons, such as buying concert tickets or checking to see if you are still the high bidder on an auction? One estimate suggests that non–business-related Web surfing by employees costs U.S. firms $63 billion every year (that's $2,000 a second!). Many organizations have become so concerned about productivity losses from personal electronic communication at work that they have implemented surveillance processes to determine what employees are doing when they are on their computers. According to the American Management Association, three-fourths of employers use systems to monitor employees' Web site visits. About a third of these organizations monitor keystrokes as well. While most organizations have published policies on employee monitoring, 20 percent do not let employees know that monitoring is being conducted. Employee Internet management (EIM) is a growing software industry. This software can monitor email messages, Web surfing, software usage, computer idle-time, and even individual keystrokes. Currently, employees have very few privacy rights at the workplace. The courts tend to support the employers' sovereignty over company-owned computers and networks. An employer can legally monitor nearly everything involving workers' computers, and they can do it with no notification to employees whatsoever.

SOURCES: "Employee Monitoring: Is There Privacy in the Workplace?": http://www.privacyrights.org/fs/fs7-work.htm (accessed March 13, 2006).

"Trying to Measure Your Surfing at Work": http://www.cnn.com/2001/CAREER/trends/08/14/employee.net.use.idg/ (accessed July 31, 2003).

B. Petersen (May 26, 2008), "Employee Monitoring: It's Not Paranoia—You Really Are Being Watched!": http://www.pcmag.com/article2/0,2817,2308369,00.asp.

McGregor proposed two theories of motivation that have become part of everyday language in business, government, and even academia: theory X and theory Y. According to theory X, workers are unproductive and unmotivated and must be coerced through constant supervision to perform their tasks. According to theory Y, workers are creative and motivated persons who do not require coercion (except in rare circumstances) and, when given the chance, can perform exceedingly well. These theories have generated a great deal of debate between supporters of their competing viewpoints (see Table 1.1).

Table 1.1 Contrasting Viewpoints: Theory X and Theory Y

Theory X	Theory Y
1. Workers have an inherent dislike of work and will seek to avoid it if possible.	1. Activities and tasks at work are as natural as those at rest or play.
2. Most workers have to be coerced, forced, controlled, directed, and threatened to put out adequate effort on the job.	2. Control and coercion are not methods for obtaining adequate effort. Workers can and will exercise self-control to accomplish organizational objectives.
3. The average person prefers to be directed, likes to avoid responsibility, lacks motivation, and desires job security above all else.	3. The most significant reward for a worker is satisfying ego or self-actualization needs. The result of personal effort can be reward enough.
	4. Under the right conditions, the average worker may even seek responsibility.
	5. The ability to creatively and imaginatively solve organizational problems is widely distributed in the population. Creativity is not a managerial monopoly.
	6. The potential of the average worker is underdeveloped.

⊗ McGregor's X/Y theory

McGregor's X/Y theory continues to influence organizational theory even though it is not fully understood. The contrasting characteristics seem to stem in part from human nature and consequently are difficult to dismiss. As a number of managers told us, "Some people are theory Xers who have to be watched and supervised carefully; others are theory Yers whom you can leave alone." Of course, the same distinction can be applied to managers and supervisors. Think for a moment of organizations that fit a theory X profile. Were the employees lazy and unmotivated, causing management to constantly coerce and control them? Or were employees unmotivated because management did not trust them? What about theory Y organizations? Were the managers trusting, open-minded, and nurturing with workers, thereby causing them to be self-reliant and independent? Or did the workers demonstrate initiative, persistence, and reliability and thus lead management to think of employees more humanistically?

1.4.3: Systems Theory

The debate about organizations did not end with theories X and Y. Both classical and humanistic theories finally revealed a common shortcoming: neither considered the effect of the environment on organizational effectiveness. To fill this void, **systems theory** added a third element, the environment, to an equation that previously had contained only two: management and labor.

CONCEPTS OF SYSTEMS THEORY Systems theory draws heavily from the work conducted in botany by Ludwig von Bertalanfy.[11] Bertalanfy's research suggested that organizations are comparable to living organisms and have needs, desires, faults, shortcomings, and other features characteristic of living creatures, and that the parts of an organization and the parts of an organism are related in

a similar way. If one part of an organism breaks down (for example, if you catch a cold), the rest of the system is directly affected (by fatigue, aches, fever). Similarly, if one person on an organizational team is absent or fails to do her or his share of the work, the entire team suffers. In systems theory, this concept of relatedness is termed **interdependency.** If each member of a group is assigned a portion of a presentation, each member must participate for the presentation to succeed. If even one member fails to do her or his share of the work, then the overall quality of the presentation suffers.

The notion of interdependency gives rise to the concept of **synergy.** This is the phenomenon whereby the combined and integrated talents, energies, abilities, and knowledge of organizational members are greater than the sum of the isolated efforts of individuals. In other words, people who work in systems can learn from one another and be more creative because of their interactions with one another.

From these two concepts comes a third: **environment.** It includes the political, economic, and social characteristics of society that affect the way an organization operates. Classical theory did not recognize environment as a factor in workers' effectiveness. Even humanistic theories did not emphasize the strong influence that the environment has on an organization. Figure 1.3 illustrates the relationship of these concepts in systems theory.

Figure 1.3 Systems Theory
Systems theory uses the concepts of interdependency, synergy, and environment to explain organizational behavior.

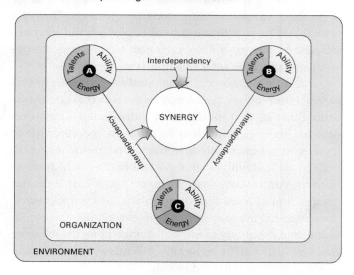

Consider the example of the fast-food industry. Decades ago few fast-food restaurants offered chicken sandwiches because customers apparently were satisfied with burgers and fries. Then people began to demand healthier and less fattening choices at fast-food restaurants. Fast-food companies that ignored the demands of health-conscious customers stood to lose a lot of business. So it is hardly surprising that today nearly all fast-food outlets offer (and strongly promote the health benefits of) salads, low-fat foods, and all-natural ingredients.

OPEN AND CLOSED SYSTEMS Organizations that attempt to respond to customer desires and needs are faced with a number of critical issues. What is the competition doing? What will suppliers be able to provide? What shape will the economy be in next year or the year after? Where can capital be raised? In terms of systems theory, responses to these issues are developed in either open systems or closed systems.

Open systems are systems that allow free movement of energy, information, ideas, data, people, and so on across organizational boundaries. **Closed systems** deliberately shut themselves off from the outside environment—sometimes with disastrous results, as markets expand and become more open, and as competition intensifies, leaving companies unable to keep up with the new business environment.

Open systems can take a variety of forms. Organizations may develop work groups that invite expert outsiders to discuss cutting-edge technology or invite representatives of several different departments to discuss new ideas for cooperation. They may encourage outside speakers at their meetings, hold open houses, or sponsor joint fundraising activities with the community.

Open systems encourage employees to take college courses, obtain advanced degrees, participate in special workshops outside the organization, volunteer in the community, or even collaborate with persons outside the organization. Open systems also embrace diversity among workers and learn from the cultural differences of their workers. The new knowledge generated by these activities not only helps the organization by providing additional expertise and ideas, but also improves morale among the work force.

Although closed systems generally are less conducive for communication, they can serve specific functions inside of organizations. Take for instance a research and development department, in which a closed system's discretion is critical in keeping inventions and trade secrets inside of a particular company. On the other hand, the public relations department of that same organization would desire an open system to garner trust and transparency.

WRITING PROMPT

We can apply organizational theories to real life. How might you describe the differences between two organizations you know, such as your school and your place of employment? Develop your own theory of organizations; what is ideal theory for you, and why?

▶ The response entered here will appear in the performance dashboard and can be viewed by your instructor.

Submit

1.4.4: Organizational Culture

Systems theory went far in explaining the dynamics of organizational communication and the reasons why some businesses are able to adapt to environmental change faster than others. But unanswered questions remained. One of the most significant was "Why would a communication system that is highly successful at one company be a failure at another?" The answer was provided in part by a relatively recent concept: organizational culture.

Organizational culture is "the social or normative glue that holds an organization together. It consists of values and beliefs that some groups or organizational members come to share."[12] Two best-selling books in the early 1980s—*Corporate Culture: The Rights and Rituals of Corporate Life* and *In Search of Excellence: Lessons from America's Best-Run Companies*—drew public attention to organizational or corporate culture.[13] Table 1.2 outlines the components of organizational cultures described in these two books.

Table 1.2 Organizational Cultures

Component	Description	Example
Values	Goals, ideals, and philosophies that an organization holds important	A company's mission statement
Rites and rituals	The activities and performances that illuminate the important issues of the organization	Annual picnic; quarterly sales meetings
Heroes	The noteworthy organizational members who have achieved success in advocating the culture of the organization	Bill Gates (Microsoft); Steve Jobs (Apple)
Communications	The networks that carry messages about work and social topics	Chain of command; grapevine
Norms	The task, social, and personal norms, standards, or ways of doing things in an organization	Allowing one casual dress day per week; parking lot privileges

Stories, myths, and legends	The retold experiences that function as important events in the history of the organization	The frequently repeated story of how the first Compaq computer was designed: the original founders met one day in a coffee shop and drew the first design on the back of a placemat
Climate	The feeling or general attitude formed by the way members interact with one another and with persons outside the organization (customers, suppliers, vendors)	Feeling good about the way people are treated

Hide All Cells   Show All Cells

Organizational culture provides a portrait of the actions, norms, motives, and philosophies that an organization values. In a sense, an analysis of organizational culture is an attempt to understand how organization members feel about themselves as a collective whole. *Shared meaning, shared understanding,* and *shared sense making* are all different ways of describing that culture. In talking about organizational culture, we are really talking about a process that allows people to see and understand particular events, actions, objects, or situations in distinctive ways. These patterns of understanding also provide a basis for making behavior sensible and meaningful.[14]

⊗ Example:

For example, part of your school's organizational culture includes rules about the graduation ceremony, sports rituals such as bonfires and mascots, and norms such as an identifiable hand signal as a logo or activities at the student union building. These norms, rituals, and activities help create the shared understanding among the students about what it means to be a part of their campus. Knowledge of an organization's—in this case, your school's—culture provides members with a sense of purpose. They come to realize their importance within the organization.

Organizational theories were designed as rational ways of managing workers and activities. Organizational culture, however, provides a useful framework for understanding the structure of an organization and how messages flow within it. Communication skills are essential in the information-rich environment of the modern organization. While it may be natural to simply talk or write on a personal level, *strategic* communication will help you develop the communication skills you will need to succeed in the world of business.

PRACTICING BUSINESS COMMUNICATION

IKEA

When a "build-up team" arrives on-site to open a new IKEA home furnishing outlet, it is fulfilling the management vision of the company's founder: "No method is more effective than a good example." Arriving at the store site anywhere from a year to a day prior to opening, experienced employees from IKEA's worldwide network of 240 stores in thirty-four countries assist new employees with operations and special events, speed up problem solving, and shorten the learning curve for their new coworkers.

IKEA's loose organizational structure and streamlined operations encourage employees to participate in decision making and to assume responsibility for the ideas they contribute to the business.

Ingvar Kamprad was just seventeen years old when he founded IKEA as a mail-order business in 1943. (The name is an acronym composed of his initials and the name of the farm and the village in Sweden where he grew up.) Early on, Kamprad distilled his philosophy into a business goal—"to create a better everyday life for many people"—a goal that translates into "freedom with responsibility" for IKEA employees.

⊗ A Networked Company

IKEA began using email soon after it was introduced as a workplace communication tool by MCI in the early 1980s. As a cost-cutting innovation at the time, email enabled IKEA coworkers around the world to communicate effectively without paper waste and costly international telephone service.

On IKEA's network today, coworkers, no matter where they work or travel, keep up-to-date with worldwide operations by accessing electronic bulletin boards and company databases. Because travel regularly connects employees to corporate management in Sweden and Denmark, the ability to stay in constant communication with coworkers while traveling is vital.

Throughout the year, IKEA store managers from around the world gather to meet with top management and to learn what's going on in product development. Just as travel and face-to-face communication are important for educating store managers about new IKEA products, so is sharing their expertise with coworkers when new stores open. Hence the concept of the build-up team.

⊗ Efficient Quality

By maximizing communication efficiency, IKEA minimizes costs and increases productivity. The company's philosophy is to produce "useful, attractive home furnishings at prices for every wallet." All IKEA products are first developed in Sweden under strict quality standards and are then introduced to visiting managers at informational presentations that serve to link each manager to corporate production and procedural goals.

At the retail level, furniture shopping at IKEA is a bare-bones process: customers buy items ranging from tableware to wicker furniture after viewing them on display at the store's "marketplace" of shops or in the annual full-color IKEA catalog. Shoppers then pick up their purchases—often unassembled—in an on-site, self-service warehouse. Employees are on hand to answer questions at storewide "Information Stations," but mostly they allow customers to shop or browse at their own pace, armed with "tools" (a catalog, tape measure, pencil, and shopping list) supplied by IKEA at each showroom entrance for making notes and taking measurements along the way. IKEA also provides free interior design assistance to customers.

As IKEA has grown to more than 262 stores in twenty-four countries worldwide, with more than 120,000 employees (about 13 percent of them are in North America), and as maintaining close communication among all coworkers has become more complex, Ingvar Kamprad's vision has served as a common resource for all IKEA coworkers. Managers act as "ambassadors," passing on the culture and the operations of the company to new employees, with everyone applying themselves to achieve the goal of satisfying customers.

WRITING PROMPT

Do you think it is important to maintain face-to-face communication in a large organization such as IKEA today, when so many remote communication alternatives are available? Why or why not? IKEA has achieved success by minimizing costs and improving productivity through a corporate culture that focuses on communication efficiency. Give some specific strategies that you, as a manager, can use to communicate IKEA's organizational culture to new employees.

  The response entered here will appear in the performance dashboard and can be viewed by your instructor.

Submit

Strategic Scenario Wrap-Up

Communication in Organizations

(X) Strategic Scenario

Kate Hullison and Jeremy Sandusky were relaxing after work one day during happy hour. Both worked for online businesses, Jeremy as a software designer and Kate as a mid-level manager. They liked the type of work they did, but both really wanted to work for themselves. All they needed was a sound business plan, some guts, and a venture capitalist who believed in their ideas. After honing the details of their business strategy, they found a venture capitalist in DaKysha Masaal, who wanted to invest in a start-up.

Their new business began as a consulting company for other Internet businesses and quickly grew to seven employees (DaKysha, Kate, Jeremy, and four others). They managed themselves without much hierarchy or bureaucracy in part because they were small but more so because that is the way they liked it—especially Jeremy.

Rapid growth caused the ranks of their employees to swell to fifty-five, forcing them to move out of their comfortable digs in a converted apartment complex into a high-rise office building. The way that DaKysha, Kate, and Jeremy organized and managed their work and employees changed quickly as well. More structure, hierarchy, meetings, plans, and, as Jeremy puts it, "administrivia" have become the norm. DaKysha and Kate seem to thrive on the excitement of success that the company is experiencing, but Jeremy feels differently. He now finds himself in the same type of organization he left for the start-up—except now he is one of the bosses. His communication with others has expanded 100-fold, and he doesn't feel prepared for the responsibility. It seems to him that his interactions with others are different, more formal—exactly why he left his old company in the first place.

As a company owner and executive manager, Jeremy must embrace the changes that come with the growth of his business. His two partners are not going to want to return to the past. Jeremy must use his own communication skills to discuss communication strategies.

He should meet with his colleagues Kate and DaKysha. Together they can clarify the company's evolving organizational structure. Jeremy might propose a discussion on how the structure could change and still remain efficient. He can also suggest that they find ways to streamline administrative tasks. The three can decide to seek feedback from the employees, as one option. If, for example, they discover that employees feel they are receiving more email than they can keep up with, the executives can then look for a solution, such as a company intranet or a Web-based system for internal communication, reserving email communication for clients. In addition, because Jeremy values a non-authoritarian atmosphere, he can always welcome suggestions from employees and make sure his door is open, literally and figuratively.

WRITING PROMPT

Jeremy's former position was software designer, Kate's was mid-level manager, and DaKysha's was investor. How, and why, might each partner see organizational communication differently?

  The response entered here will appear in the performance dashboard and can be viewed by your instructor.

Submit

Summary

Communication in Organizations

- An organization's success depends on **effective communication**.
- The **components of communication skills** include creative insight, sensitivity, vision, shared meaning, and integrity. These elements are essential in facing the challenges posed by globalization and diversity.
- The desired outcome of communication is **shared meaning** between sender and receiver.
- Several factors **prevent the achievement of shared meaning**: inadequate information, information overload, poor-quality information, poor timing, lack of feedback or follow-up, problems with channels, incompetent communication, ineffective goal setting, communication anxiety, and cultural barriers.
- Many theories have been advanced to explain **how organizations work.**
- **Classical theory** emphasizes structure, rules, and control.
- Classical theories include **Taylor's scientific management** theory and **Weber's bureaucracy theory**.
- **Humanistic theory** emphasizes camaraderie among workers, praise and recognition from supervisors, and relationship formation.
- The **human resources approach** suggests two theories of motivation for workers: theory X holds that workers must be coerced to be productive, and theory Y maintains that workers are motivated persons who do not require coercion.
- **Classical and humanistic theories** concentrate on management and labor.

- **Systems theory** adds the dimensions of interdependency, synergy, and environment; it distinguishes between two types of systems.
- **Open systems** allow free movement of information, ideas, and data across organizational boundaries.
- **Closed systems** shut themselves off from the outside environment.
- **Organizational culture** consists of the values and beliefs of an organization.
- An organization's culture tells how members feel about themselves as a **collective whole**. The components of this culture allow people to understand particular events, actions, or situations in distinctive ways, and they provide members with a sense of purpose.

SHARED WRITING: COMMUNICATION IN ORGANIZATIONS

Choose a student organization—a fraternity, sorority, political or religious club, or student government body—and examine its structure in terms of the organizational theories presented in the chapter. Write a brief report describing the structure. Include specific examples from the organization to support your ideas.

▶ A minimum number of characters is required to post and earn points. After posting, your response can be viewed by your class and instructor, and you can participate in the class discussion.

Post   0 characters | 140 minimum

Chapter 1 Quiz: Communication in Organizations

Chapter 2
The Model of Strategic Communication

 ## Learning Objectives

2.1 Enumerate the four areas of achieving competence in strategic communication

2.2 Describe the importance of situational knowledge

2.3 Identify the steps of the organizational goal-setting process in business communication

2.4 Express guidelines to achieving communication competence

2.5 Recount different causes for anxiety and the importance of managing anxiety in communication

Strategic Scenario: Executive Orders

Sam Klausner is one of four associate vice presidents for administration at Kempinik Industries in the Midwest. Sam was called into the executive suite to meet with CEO/president Joan Randall and Antonio Montegro, vice president for administration and his direct superior, to discuss a plan to reduce the work force. The company is in jeopardy of being bought by a fierce competitor if they do not quickly and substantially improve the bottom line. Since a large investment was made in automation earlier in the year, Ms. Randall and Mr. Montegro feel the time is right to reduce the enormous costs associated with employees. This means that 1,000 employees (about 25 percent of the company) will be let go.

The executives want Sam to develop a series of messages that clearly and accurately communicate their plans

for the massive layoff and to devise the best ways for carrying these messages to the work force. They stressed to Sam that the plans must be kept secret, because they do not want the best employees to be alarmed and quit, nor do they want the public (competitors, media) to know about the layoffs until the time is right. Sam is concerned about this responsibility, since he has a lot of friends in the company who will likely be laid off, many of whom have debts and families. Ms. Randall and Mr. Montegro want Sam to take a week to prepare his plan and report back to them on how he will implement this plan successfully.

As you read this chapter, think about the various tasks, and even dilemmas, that Sam faces with this new responsibility. At the end of the chapter, we will revisit this scenario and discuss some solutions.

2.1: Overview
The Model of Strategic Communication

2.1 **Enumerate the four areas of achieving competence in strategic communication**

With so many options to consider in the creation and transmission of messages today, communication must be planned carefully. To succeed, you need to know how to integrate

technology with communication skills and how to communicate with people who have diverse backgrounds and a wide range of goals and expectations. To make the most of your business career, you need to present yourself as a competent communicator; your communication skills will be your best selling point in job interviews, sales meetings, and company presentations. To be effective, communicate strategically. This approach, developed and applied both in the classroom and in the real world, is designed to maximize the opportunities for communication you will encounter now and after graduation. Managers, employees, students, or friends can use the model of strategic communication as a guideline for effective communication. The model can be employed in any situation to maximize your competency—a job interview, a business proposal for a client, or a class presentation.

Strategic communication means achieving your potential in four areas:

1. **SITUATIONAL KNOWLEDGE:** Information that you have (or can collect) about the requirements for successful communication in a particular context is situational knowledge. You greatly improve your chances of successful communication if you know what is appropriate and expected of you.

2. **GOAL SETTING:** Each communication situation can be approached as a goal-setting activity. You will be more likely to succeed in your communication if you set clear and appropriate goals for yourself.

3. **COMMUNICATION COMPETENCE:** When you plan communication strategically, you choose a number of factors—such as type of message, type of channel, and style of delivery—that demonstrate your understanding of the organization's values and needs. Communication competence also entails adapting correctly to situational demands. You will learn to make these choices consistently and correctly.

4. **ANXIETY MANAGEMENT:** Job interviews, meetings with superiors, and group problem-solving meetings are a few of the many situations that may cause anxiety on the job. Control of anxiety is a critical element in effective and strategic communication. You can learn to keep your nervousness at a level that energizes your communication without destroying its effectiveness.

These four components, as Figure 2.1 shows, provide a basis for developing communication skills within the context of the dynamic business environment.

Figure 2.1 Model of Strategic Communication
These four components provide a basis for developing solid communication skills within a business environment.

Over the years, many businesspeople, communications theorists, and teachers have advocated approaches to

business communication similar to the model of strategic communication. Elements of this model are evident in specific communication theories. For example, communicating competently allows a manager to provide the kind of special attention and feedback that, according to human relations theory, makes workers respond positively. These approaches are much talked about and even partially implemented in the workplace, yet they have not had the broad impact expected of them. The main reason for their limited success has to do with another important concept: environment.

Up through the 1970s, the environment of American business was relatively stable and insulated. Companies were largely homogeneous and tended to focus on domestic markets. There was no pressing need for American businesses to adopt flexible and open communication systems. Today, fierce competition within markets and industries, diversity on all levels, globalization, fast-moving technological advances, and instant access to information are standard within business and professional environments. As a result, there are complex demands on managers' time as organizations try to become more competitive by holding down costs without cutting back on products and services.

Work is being redefined today as all types of job descriptions become increasingly specialized and require knowledge of emerging technologies and comfort with customized information systems. Today employees can have quick access to information that was not available to top management and planners even five years ago. This competitive environment demands a new approach to on-the-job communication that provides efficiency (communication opportunities are not wasted for lack of planning) and flexibility (people at all levels can be encouraged and included in communication).

Strategic communication is effective because it helps you pinpoint the areas in which you excel and those in which you need to improve. This chapter uses the model to illustrate strategic communication in organizations. The four components of strategic communication—situational knowledge, goal setting, communication competence, and anxiety management—are the basis for understanding and improving your skills for interpersonal, group, and public communication. As each component of the model is discussed, you will be introduced to practical and straightforward methods for setting and achieving communication goals in a number of contexts.

2.2: Situational Knowledge

2.2 **Describe the importance of situational knowledge**

The first component of the model of strategic communication is **situational knowledge,** the information or facts you use in devising an effective communication strategy. In an organizational context, situational knowledge also refers to employees' awareness of the communication issues involved in their jobs. Communication can be different, depending on the type of organization where it is employed (classical versus humanistic). Having this type of situational knowledge can be helpful in knowing how to deal with people in those organizations.

You can increase your communication effectiveness by gathering a thorough knowledge of the person or people with whom you are communicating. In the following sections, you will learn how an organization's values and ethics, organizational structure, organizational learning, on-the-job training, politics, and communication climate build situational knowledge.

2.2.1: Values and Ethics

A key element in any communication activity is the values of the organization. **Values** are the principles and ideas that people or organizations strongly believe in and consider important. When people are in doubt about decisions, they frequently rely on deep-seated values to help them make the right choice. In organizations, reliance on shared values makes setting goals easier in the face of the competing ideas, desires, and objectives of individual employees.

VALUES How are shared values established in an organization? The process is difficult because values are fundamental and enduring and because each person has a particular personal value system. Despite these drawbacks, an organization has several choices when it comes to establishing values. Upper management can organize focus groups, small groups ranging from seven to twelve employees who meet to identify values they believe are vital to the organization. These lists of values are then circulated among all the focus groups for review and analysis. Next, a committee studies the values generated by the focus groups and arrives at a composite set that organizational members can vote on.

You can get a good idea about the values of an organization by examining its vision and mission statement. These statements are short descriptions of the purpose of organizations and the directions they try to take to achieve success. Many organizations post their vision and mission statements in several places so that employees know what the organization values. Take a look at the vision and mission statement of NPR, or National Public Radio. Did you get a sense of what it values?

The NPR Mission

The mission of NPR is to work in partnership with Member Stations to create a more informed public — one challenged and invigorated by a deeper understanding and appreciation of events, ideas, and cultures.

To accomplish our mission, we produce, acquire, and distribute programming that meets the highest standards of public service in journalism and cultural expression; we represent our members in matters of their mutual interest; and we provide satellite interconnection for the entire public radio system.

(x) Our Strategic Vision

In May 2014, the NPR Board of Directors adopted our strategic plan, which includes a declaration of NPR's strategic aspiration, four strategic priorities, and a description of the path forward toward achievement of this strategic plan, including aspirational outcomes and goals for the next three to five years for each of the priorities.

Courtesy of National Public Radio

Organizational values vary, depending on the nature of the business or profession. Values found in a large number of organizations include the following:

- Primacy of the customer
- Honesty and integrity
- Respect for other workers
- Importance of every person
- Maintenance of high professional standards
- Fair treatment
- Innovative thinking
- Quality service
- Creativity
- Reliance on ethical standards
- Profitable returns to shareholders

COMMUNICATION ETHICS The model of corporate America has seriously eroded in recent years.[1] Stakeholders no longer automatically trust organizational leaders and as a result investor relations must work harder on building relationships and trust and not just on increasing stock value.[2] In the late 1990s, a telecommunications firm called WorldCom had the world's largest Internet "backbone" network and was the second-largest long-distance provider in the United States. Between 1995 and 2000, WorldCom bought more than sixty other companies, including MCI for $37 billion. Despite all of this apparent success, in July 2002, WorldCom, facing $41 billion in debt, filed for bankruptcy, the largest bankruptcy in history.

During the investigation that followed, WorldCom was revealed as having a "culture of fraud." For several years profits fell below estimates. If investors knew about the decrease in earnings, the price of the stock would also decrease. Many of the people in positions of authority inside WorldCom had huge amounts of money to lose if the stock price were to drop. To appear as though they were meeting earning estimates and to maintain high stock prices, WorldCom falsified over $2 billion of revenue and ignored over $7 billion of expenses in earning reports for 1999 through 2002. This fraudulent communication of profits was finally uncovered in 2002, and the senior executives involved went on to face criminal charges. Although WorldCom has emerged from bankruptcy, this unethical behavior cost creditors and stockholders billions of dollars.[3]

An entire economic recession can be fed by industry leaders who engage in unethical communication practices, as the world learned in the last decade.[4–8]

⊗ **Bernie Madoff**

A non-executive chairman of the NASDAQ, Madoff was convicted of operating a Ponzi scheme, which has been called the largest investor fraud ever committed by a single person.

⊗ **Enron**

This case, which involved its founder and CEO Kenneth Lay and Jeffrey Skilling, included multiple instances of communicating fraud and concealing information about the performance of the company from stockholders, the government, and the public.

⊗ **General Motors**

The car company denied responsibility for a defect in its automobiles that caused deaths. In May 2009, GM engineers themselves reported there was a serious problem, but it took five years for GM to tell the public.

⊗ **Merrill Lynch**

Two high-ranking employees of this investment company were convicted of conspiracy and fraud for taking part in the bogus sale of barges associated with Enron transactions.

Because ethics and values do not become part of the overt discourse of the organization, the ethical framework used to make decisions often remains hidden from view. A general suggestion for ethical communicators is that they have a "well developed sense of social responsibility."[9] The following guidelines come in handy when uncertainty arises about ethical communication behavior.[10] Before you consider them, check out this example of ethical communication in businesses:

> Kent had been with his company for twenty-seven years and was disturbed to learn that he was being demoted, with a decrease in pay, because the company was merging with another company and his position was being eliminated. Kent was angry but could not resign because he was too old to get a similar job elsewhere. He began to take two-hour lunches, help himself to office supplies that he took home, and talk incessantly with coworkers about how unfairly the company

was treating him. When he was asked to relay information to others, he always delayed until the information was virtually useless, and he actually changed the tone or intent of the message. Before the merger, Kent had been one of the company's most trusted and loyal employees.

Consider these ethical guidelines, and apply them to Kent's case:

1. **MAINTAIN CANDOR.** Candor refers to truthfulness, honesty, and frankness in your communication with other people. Although revealing everything you know about a situation may not always be appropriate—for instance, providing all your information to adversaries during intense and sensitive negotiations will only compromise your position—it is usually wise and ethical to be as open and frank about information as possible. Others will take note and mirror your behavior, creating openness throughout the organization.

2. **KEEP MESSAGES ACCURATE.** When you are relaying information from one source to another, communicate the original message as accurately as possible. Ethical communicators do not take liberties with the messages they pass on.

3. **AVOID DECEPTION.** Ethical communicators are always vigilant in their quest to avoid deception—the fabrication, intentional distortion, or withholding of information—in their communication.

4. **BEHAVE CONSISTENTLY.** One of the most prevalent yet noticeable areas of unethical behavior is communicating one thing and doing another. You must always monitor your behavior to ensure that it matches what you say to others.

5. **KEEP CONFIDENCES.** When someone tells you something and expects you not to divulge that information to others, a sacred trust has been placed on you. Even if you then tell someone else and make her or him promise not to tell others, you cannot really expect that person to take you seriously. More often than not, the original information gets back to the source and the confidence that person placed in you is undermined.

6. **ENSURE TIMELINESS OF COMMUNICATION.** The timing of messages can be critical. When you delay sending messages so that others do not fully benefit, they can (rightly) assume that you have acted unethically.

7. **CONFRONT UNETHICAL BEHAVIOR.** To maintain a consistent ethical viewpoint, you must confront unethical behavior when you observe it. Public indictment of unethical persons may not be necessary, but it is important that people understand that your own tolerance for unethical behavior is low.

8. **CULTIVATE EMPATHIC LISTENING.** By lending a sensitive and empathic ear to those who are troubled by their own or others' unethical behavior, you can better understand and help to solve the problems associated with these acts. After all, many unethical acts are the result of circumstances that coworkers feel are beyond their control.

Although ethical behavior seems easy to recognize, ethics is a complex issue. It is often difficult to decide between conflicting guidelines. For example, if a coworker confides to you that she will be quitting in two weeks, and your supervisor asks you whether your soon-to-be-gone coworker would be capable of managing a long-term project, the guidelines of "keeping confidences" and "avoiding deception" are in direct conflict. Because of the complexity of human nature, situations such as this are not uncommon; therefore, maintaining ethical behavior can be difficult. In situations that require a choice, it may be wise to examine the outcomes and consequences of your actions, to maintain respect and empathy for others involved, and to maintain open communication. Openness in communication can help resolve ethical issues.

THE ADVANTAGE OF ETHICS Many experts do not expect substantial progress in the area of business ethics given the present state of affairs, but we are not so pessimistic. For one thing, more and more students are thinking about the issues of ethical behavior in organizations. Once employees realize the advantages of ethical behavior, progress is likely to be made. But what are the advantages of ethics in the professional world?

One advantage of ethics in the workplace is long-term integrity. Surveys report that all employees want to work for organizations with high ethical standards.[11] Organizations with leaders who are perceived as ethical both recruit and retain high performance employees, who value ethics in their workplace.[12]

Competent people are likely to search for organizations that maintain high ethical standards. They know that ethical practices are the only sure way to succeed in life. When competent people migrate toward ethical firms, everyone benefits because both competence and ethics are perpetuated. Indeed, it is quite easy to make the argument that competence and ethics go hand in hand. Those who understand how to succeed know that unethical behavior leads only to covert and clandestine activities that are time-consuming and unprofitable. Ethical firms therefore enjoy the advantage of employing greater numbers of competent professionals.

Furthermore, employee commitment is likely to be higher in ethical businesses. Employee commitment yields a number of benefits, including higher employee morale, less turnover, greater productivity, and enhanced

creativity. Although compromises on ethics may yield short-term benefits, over the long haul most unethical acts are eventually uncovered, contributing to a dishonorable, unscrupulous, and unprincipled professional atmosphere. Such an atmosphere perpetuates the myth that the only way to get ahead is by engaging in unethical behavior. But when leaders maintain high ethical standards, they can use their power for the good of the organization and its employees.

2.2.2: Organizational Structure

Each organization's ability to respond to challenges depends on its structure. **Organizational structure** consists of the actual environment where the organization is located. Some organizations occupy several floors in one office building; others have branch offices, resulting in employees being physically spread out. Departments within an organization may be contained in one location or split among several locations. An organization's physical structure has a strong effect on its communication style, as this example shows.

 Example:

College academic departments that concentrate faculty members on one floor create more frequent communication than do those that disperse faculty over several floors or several buildings. Organization members who are located away from their colleagues are likely to feel isolated and lonely.

Another organizational structure is the **virtual organization.** It is called *virtual* because a physical structure of this organization doesn't exist in one location—the organization is structured through telecommunications or remote connections. Virtual teams have become an integral part of organizations because of an increase in corporate restructuring, competition, and globalizations.[13] People in a virtual organization can do their work from a remote place (home, hotel room, car, airplane) using a computer, and Internet connection, and a phone service.

Sometimes organizations may be partially virtual if some of the employees work from home and communicate in the way previously described. These employees, called **telecommuters,** maintain regular communication with their organization through email, phones, fax, and the Internet. When you consider both the self-employed and non–self-employed, the work-at-home population grew 29.4% from 2005 to 2012. The rate of telecommuting among those who are not self-employed actually grew by 79.7%.[14]

There are three primary challenges that virtual teams face, which must be addressed in order for effective communication and productivity to be possible.[15] First, virtual teams lack face-to-face interaction and thus traditional nonverbal cues are often missing. New team members must be taught how to compensate by providing more detailed information, communicating more often, utilizing emoticons, and so on.[16] Second, it is difficult for virtual team members to build relationships with one another. Trust is essential for effective teamwork, and new members must be taught how to start off on the right foot to increase positive interpersonal perceptions.[17] Third, virtual teams face the challenge of accessing and leveraging unique knowledge of each member to achieve team goals. Team leaders must develop systems for sharing information so that relevant information does not slip through the cracks.[18]

Another way to understand structure is to look at the hierarchy, or pyramid of authority, a business maintains. **Tall organizations** have a large number of hierarchical levels. Banks, for example, are notorious for tall structures. At the top of the hierarchy is the board of directors, followed by the chief executive officer, the president, executive vice presidents, senior vice presidents, vice presidents, associate vice presidents, assistant vice presidents, cashiers, assistant cashiers, tellers, and finally bookkeepers. The chain of command in tall organizations usually requires subordinates who want to suggest any change to top management to first communicate with their boss, who then talks to her or his boss, who then contacts someone at the next level, and so on. In extreme instances, a message can take weeks or even months to make its way up the chain of command.

In contrast, **flat organizations** have few hierarchical levels. They place a large number of employees at the same level and do not rank most jobs as being "above" or "below" other jobs in the organization. The short chain of command in flat organizations allows a relatively rapid movement of messages throughout the organization. The modern trend in business is toward reducing the middle-level hierarchy and "flattening" the organization. Figure 2.2 contrasts a tall organization with a flat organization. The bottom line is that knowing about structure gives you an important piece of the situational knowledge necessary for effective communication.

Figure 2.2 Tall vs. Flat Organizations
A shorter chain of command, as in flatter hierarchies, allows for faster movement of messages throughout the organization.

2.2.3: Organizational Learning

To communicate effectively, people in business have traditionally thought it best to know as much as possible about an organization and its environment. Employees who monitor the organization and environment for new information are in the best position to make informed decisions about communication.[19] The more employees learn about the organization the less uncertainty and anxiety they will experience, which will lead to greater employee contributions, commitment to membership, and job satisfaction.[20] Southwest Airlines (SWA) is an organization that emphasizes learning among all employees. The SWA founder was known for promoting practices that helped his employees to learn but also to learn how to learn.[21]

The demands of the information age have altered how such monitoring takes place. Communication and Information Technologies (CITs) are computer-mediated technologies that facilitate two-way or multi-way communication among individuals. Many CITs are Internet or Web-based: blogs, webinars, online chats or instant messaging, videoconferences, database and calendar sharing, company intranets, and the ever-present email. Cellular communication also has speeded up communication tremendously via apps, text messaging, and more. Today there is much more information than can be analyzed piece by piece.

Because organizations are dynamic, or continually changing, it is necessary for all employees to continue learning. Socialization in organizations is an ongoing reciprocal process by which members simultaneously define their roles and attempt to influence the organization.[22]

Clearly, both new employees and workers dealing with large amounts of information for the first time need methods for learning about the organization without being overwhelmed. There are several ways to accomplish this goal, including adaptive learning, understanding organizational values, developing specific knowledge of the organization, and observing successes and failures.[23]

(x) **Adaptive Learning**

You can engage in **adaptive learning** by seeking to understand how goals, policies, procedures, and other people's actions conform to the dynamics of the workplace. Adaptation is a survival skill in today's organizations.

(x) Organizational Values

You can learn about the organization by **understanding organizational values**. Knowing and embracing organizational values will clarify your awareness of how and why organizations make the decisions they do.

(x) Specific Knowledge

Developing specific knowledge of the organization is another way to learn. You can cultivate awareness of the norms, policies, procedures, politics, and accepted behaviors that govern the workplace. A communication strategy benefits from knowledge about what rules and boundaries are in place; otherwise, the strategy can result in errors or violations of policy.

(x) Observation

You can learn by **observing successes and failures**. Essentially, you can learn a great deal about what works in an organization and what does not by assembling a track record of who succeeds and fails, and why.

TECHNOLOGY TOOLS

Tools for Business and Professional Productivity

Device	Description	Advantage
Blogs	Short for *Web logs*, blogs consist of content (opinions, viewpoints, relevant news) distributed by organizations for many purposes. CEOs may publish blogs to communicate with shareholders, customers, and employees.	Blogs provide a face for the organization. They usually allow the opportunity for feedback, which is essential for executives and managers who value input from the organization's environment.
Message Boards	Online boards provide the same function as physical message boards, with the added benefit of allowing users from across the globe to post their thoughts through the Internet.	Group leaders and businesses can create message boards to gather the individual thoughts and suggestions of group members, employees, and customers. Message board administrators may broach a subject and collect and analyze the response data for decision making.
RSS (Really Simple Syndication) Feeds	This technology allows organizational members to choose content areas that interest them and receive that content as a feed from newsgroups or other Web sites.	Organizational members do not have to search content manually; they can have RSS search certain domains, compile content, and send it to them.
SMART Board, IWB (Interactive whiteboard)	This large, interactive whiteboard acts as a touch screen when a computer's screen is projected on it. Special writing tools allow presenters to mark up areas of the board using digital ink and built-in sensors.	A technological upgrade from classic whiteboards and dry-erase boards, an interactive board provides direct touch screen interactivity with a computer. The presenter is not limited to a standing at a podium.
Smart Phones and Tablets	An advanced phone/minicomputer, the smart phone can connect to wi-fi networks as well as cellular and run a number of useful applications and software. All tablets have wi-fi capability, and many now have capacity for phone calls.	These devices can send emails, make calls, send messages, take photos, and connect to Web browsers via wi-fi or cellular networks. Productivity applications for a wide variety of professions are seemingly unlimited.
SMS (text messaging)	This efficient form of phone-to-phone or computer-to-computer messaging allows users to reach one or more recipients through short messages.	SMS has proven to be a useful business tool, a simple yet significant way to reach people quickly.
Social Networking	These Web sites allow users to create and customize profiles that can be seen by other users. Social networks facilitate worldwide communication through messages, wall-posts, and the formation of similar interest groups.	Used wisely and appropriately, social-networking sites can provide employers with beneficial information about potential new hires. A bank of contacts are one click away. Examples of social-networking sites include: Facebook (general), LinkedIn (business), livejournal (blogging), mixi (Japanese-based), MySpace (general), Netlog (European-based), Orkut (popular in India & Brazil), Skyrock (French-based), Sonico (Hispanic-based), Twitter (micro-blogging), V Kontakte (Russian-based), and Windows Live Spaces (blogging).
Teleconferencing	This technology allows a group of people to interact during the same phone conversation.	Teleconferencing is much less expensive and more instant than travel. Skype is an example—a partially free service used for making calls, instant messaging, file transferring, and videoconferencing over the Web.

(Continued)

Device	Description	Advantage
Twitter	This micro-social-networking service is accessed through the Web site and through SMS via phones. it allows users to become "followers" of certain individuals. Once somebody becomes a follower, the person will receive all status updates from the leader.	Twitter allows leaders to distribute immediate, brief status updates to all followers in a very simple way. Managers can update team members, and companies can provide timely product, service, legal, or stock info to customers/shareholders.
Videoconferencing	This technology is teleconferencing with a video component. It allows users to see one another and to view the presentation materials of participants.	Videoconferencing allows users to take advantage of nonverbal cues that are lost during a teleconference. It also facilitates visual inspection and review of material.
V-logs	Short for video logs, v-logs are similar to blogs but use video as the medium instead of written publication. V-logs are used by a wide variety of people for personal or business use. They can be especially useful in politics because politicians want viewers to recognize them.	V-logs provide the same advantages as blogs but can reach more viewers. Subtitles allow the v-log to be used by viewers with hearing and vision impairments. Viewers can associate a face with the words, which provides a more personal touch.
Web Conferencing/ Webinars	Web conferencing is used to conduct meetings online. Meeting attendees connect to each other through software or Web-based applications. Webinars are a form of Web conferencing where one person guides the conference while other members listen.	Group members can converse very easily from all over the world. This is a step up from teleconferencing because the written form of communication reduces the chance of interruption and textual displays are straightforward and clear.
Wiki	This Web site platform allows the user to edit content easily and without specific knowledge of technical computer languages.	These sites allow groups and individuals working on projects to access new information that has been posted by others and offer opportunities for editing and modifying the content quickly.
VoIP (Voice over Internet Protocol)	By merging telephones into an Internet connection, this technology is used to streamline auditory communications, thus eliminating the need for a traditional switched telephone network.	No traditional phone line, zero-charge access to features (such as conference calling, and so on) and charges by the megabyte rather than the minute all contribute to cost savings. Service is available anywhere a stable Internet connection exists.

2.2.4: On-the-Job Training

One of the first opportunities a new employee has to learn about an organization is likely to be an orientation program. The initial period of employment is referred to as "assimilation."[24] New workers coming into the organization are expected to assimilate the philosophies and operations of the workplace. Employee orientation programs provide important information about how the company operates, the chain of command, the relationships among departments, and so on. New employees can also gain knowledge through formal on-the-job training programs or through informal meetings with an immediate supervisor, handbooks, or conversations with coworkers. The "breaking-in" period is crucial because during this time employees learn how to deal with the various relationships in the organization.

Once new employees have mastered the various bits of knowledge about the company and the job, a "metamorphosis" occurs: they become functioning members of the organization. By this time, their situational knowledge has improved substantially.

Employees can continue to increase situational knowledge by finding out about and participating in performance appraisal interviews, career development activities such as seminars and workshops, and annual business meetings. Even the informal grapevine provides a forum through which new employees can gain knowledge of the organization. They should take advantage of ongoing training and educational opportunities, even when they are no longer new to the company.

On-the-job training can be informal or highly structured—from the simple advice of an experienced employee giving a newcomer a lesson in transferring a phone call to a week-long orientation session.
SOURCE: Shock/Fotolia

2.2.5: Politics

Knowledge of an organization is incomplete without awareness of the organization as a political entity. All organizations are political systems because they organize and distribute power, resources, and rewards in pursuit of specific goals. When new employees collect situational knowledge about an organization, they should consider the political climate that the organization maintains. Organizational politics is usually described as the exercise or negotiation of power.[25]

This negotiation, or "struggle," is a complex dynamic between power and resistance.[26] It is a continual dance between managers and employees. In other words, managers need employees to follow instructions in order for the organization to run smoothly. Yet, at the same time, managers need employees to maintain their individuality so that new ideas are continually pushing the organization to grow.[27] Individuals who understand this balance will ultimately have power within organizations as they position themselves according to their assessment of the circumstances.

Politics can be viewed from two perspectives: (1) as a set of negative and destructive behaviors that should be avoided or (2) as a group of important aspects of communication that must be accounted for in a strategic communication plan. Although frequently used in a negative sense, politics is not necessarily disastrous. For example, in your years in school, you may have found yourself in a situation in which you needed the support of faculty, alumni, parents, or administrators to achieve a goal you strongly believed in. Building cooperation among different groups and influencing people's opinions to support worthwhile goals or causes are political actions.

You may have little choice about whether to use politics, simply because business communication requires it. Even small details such as dressing appropriately and treating coworkers politely can be considered politics. The following political strategies are frequently employed in the workplace:[28]

- Controlling the agenda of a meeting so that only items of interest to you appear
- Building coalitions of "friendly" people
- Trading favors
- Adhering to policies thought desirable by powerful people
- Being sensitive to dress

Other political strategies include

- Associating with the "right" people
- Appearing at official functions and meetings
- Assuming seating positions at group meetings that display power

If you decide to use any of these strategies, consider the ethical consequences of your communication. One way to do this is by posing questions such as the following about the potential results of the decision you intend to make:[29]

- Who may be affected by my decision/action?
- Will my decision/action violate any commitments to these parties?
- What may be the negative consequences of my action?
- Will people be better or worse off in the long run?
- Would I be comfortable if my decision became company policy for others to use?

It is wise to take stock of the political atmosphere in the organization and to determine how your own political communication style fits in. This type of situational knowledge will be valuable as you try to influence others to accomplish your goals, as the following example indicates:

> Teresa, a recent graduate of Brugle College, has taken a job with a merchandising firm in a neighboring state. She is bright and generally perceptive when it comes to figuring out what other people are up to. Teresa was a bit shy at first but over time has become good friends with just about everyone. She prides herself on this accomplishment. She also has little trouble recognizing who has "real" power in the company and can therefore help to advance her career. She initially steered clear of the two political factions in the organization but managed to stay on amicable terms with members of both. Not until the two factions disagreed over whether to begin a recycling program did Teresa decide to affiliate with the side supporting the program. She believed recycling to be an important project and felt that in the long run the company's interests would be best served by the pro-recycling faction.

2.2.6: Communication Climate

Situational knowledge includes information on an organization's character. **Communication climate** is one aspect of character. Climate is a function of the interactions and social processes that occur in the workplace. Climate may change, depending on how communication changes in the organization.[30] Thus, although climate may be relatively stable, it is nevertheless subject to modification. The ideal communication climate has five dimensions: a supportive environment, participation, trust, openness, and high performance goals.[31]

Ideal Communication Climate

Remove card   1 of 5   Reset Deck

The ability of an organization to achieve an "ideal" climate depends on the knowledge it has of its own shortcomings. Recognition of this gap between the actual and the ideal is the first step in establishing a desirable climate. Of the five dimensions, openness is a particularly critical influence on climate.

OPENNESS **Openness** is a receiver-oriented concept: it focuses on being receptive and responsive to information from others. An open organization promotes communicative responsiveness among people at different levels of authority and responsibility. Being receptive and responsive to messages shows others that you are interested in what they have to say.

You can encourage openness in several ways. Ask questions that demonstrate a desire to communicate with other organizational members; they will probably appreciate your efforts and respond positively to you. Show genuine interest in discussions with others. Respond to others' communication actively. Feedback is one of the most important indications of an open organizational climate. [32] Consider the following communication strategies in organizations.

(X) Measures supporting open communication:

1. Managers provide genuine feedback to employees.
2. Co-workers ask for opinions and input from one another.
3. Leaders ask for input from those around them.
4. Managers provide time for mentoring and listening to feelings and ideas.
5. Co-workers engage in constructive discussion about new and old topics.
6. An air of open idea exchange is felt among organizational members.
7. Leaders ask for and engage in collaborative interchanges.
8. Participation is encouraged among co-workers.
9. Managers recognize others' positions/opinions and provide constructive feedback.
10. Information sharing is easily accomplished in the organization.

How many of the organizations that you have been associated with have had these characteristics? Often it is difficult to be receptive and responsive to people whom you do not like, trust, or respect. Nevertheless, openness, even if initially forced, can yield positive results.

Researchers studying organizational communication have described the potential advantages of open communication. Included among the advantages are improved organizational performance, enhanced job satisfaction, improved role clarity (understanding what your duties are), and increased information adequacy (having the right amount of information to do your job). [33] Open communication also encourages conscientious, open-minded, and innovative people to interact with and positively influence others. People respect those who are receptive and responsive to communication and can learn from their success in the organization.

Remember that tall and flat organizations have different communication styles. Because of the large number of hierarchical levels in a tall organization, openness can be difficult. The structure of tall organizations discourages

feedback and immediate responsiveness. In contrast, flat organizations allow rapid movement of messages, a situation more conducive to openness.

2.2.7: Benefits of Situational Knowledge

Situational knowledge is a significant component of our model of strategic communication for four reasons.

First, knowledge about the organization helps you to accomplish your personal and organizational goals. Knowing with whom to communicate and how enhances the possibility that your idea will be accepted.

Second, knowledge of an organization's reward system gives you an idea of what is valued and considered important. One of the biggest problems you will face as an employee is lack of information about the value of your contributions to the organization. This problem can be minimized when situational knowledge is high.

Third, situational knowledge allows for better coordination between you and other members of the organization. Recognizing and understanding the relative relationships among various people and units can save you time and effort.

Fourth, situational knowledge helps you grow as an employee. When you recognize the different paths to enhancing your career, you are in a good position to perform roles that could lead to promotions. When you know that you can grow, develop, and mature within an organization, you are likely to be loyal and remain with the company.

2.3: Goal Setting

2.3 **Identify the steps of the organizational goal-setting process in business communication**

Recall that goal setting is one of the four parts of the strategic model of communication. Once you feel knowledgeable about the organization's values, you will be able to work on appropriate goals for your communication. It is not enough simply to set positive-sounding goals ("I hope my department does better this quarter"). Research reveals that goals must be set with particular criteria in mind. In situations in which you must communicate to achieve objectives, it is usually best to set specific, rather than vague, goals. Specific goals enable communicators to map out the conditions that must be met for the goals to be reached. [34] In addition, organizations have found that performance is better when high goals, instead of low ones, are set. Therefore, setting specific and high goals is in your best interest when you anticipate a communication encounter. Consider the following example.

⊗ Limited Time + Limited Goal = ?

Bei Cai, head of distribution at Popular Ice Company, made an appointment to discuss budget problems with her boss, Harold Danzak. Bei planned to ask Harold for an increase in operating funds because the distribution department was having a tough time making ends meet. Bei and Harold occasionally bowled on the same team and went to the same church, so Bei felt pretty comfortable about the meeting. She did not plan out what she was going to say because she felt sure that Harold would see the situation her way.

When Bei arrived at Harold's office, she was kept waiting for almost thirty minutes. When Harold finally saw her, he told Bei that he had to catch a plane for Detroit in twenty minutes. He looked at Bei and said, "This is the worst year for budgets I have ever seen. Every department seems to need more funds to operate, and I don't have much to give. I can help only the departments that really show a need." Bei swallowed hard because she had planned to use the hour-long meeting to secure money from Harold on the basis of their friendship.

Bei's had come into the meeting with no data, hard facts, or specific goals. She did not even have a figure in mind for her budget increase request. She left the meeting with Harold encouraging her to keep up the hard work. Unfortunately, Bei left without any increase in her operating budget.

In the example, Bei's experience shows the importance of specific goals. Goals are valuable because they take set conditions into account and identify targets for communication. Specific goals allow you to plan your actions and behaviors in advance of the communication encounter. Bei should have set specific goals such as these:

- "I will present four points, each with supporting material."
- "I will prioritize my points so that if we run out of time, the most important ones will be covered."
- "I will show how our department is in genuine need of extra funds."
- "I will demonstrate how, with the increased funds, our department will be able to exceed its goals for next year and help the company achieve other goals."

By setting specific and high goals, Bei would have been in a better position for handling such a difficult situation. Nevertheless, sometimes flexible goals are a better alternative. The business and professional world is often uncertain, and setting highly specific goals may lead you to an inflexible position or give you an unfavorable reputation as a rigid or difficult person. Communicators must plan for some flexibility when the environment is uncertain so that they have some room to maneuver. In general, however, set goals in as many instances as possible, even if the goals have to be less specific than you would like.

PRACTICING BUSINESS COMMUNICATION

FedEx Corporation

Federal Express pioneered time-definite overnight shipping in 1973 and soon revolutionized the package transportation industry. Today, FedEx Corporation is a collaboratively managed network of independent companies—including FedEx Express; FedEx Ground, FedEx Freight, FedEx Custom Critical, and FedEx Kinko's Office and Print Services—that provides specialized solutions for shipping, printing, and trade throughout the world.

Founder, chairman, and chief executive officer Frederick W. Smith regards communication competence as part of the foundation of his business. At FedEx, communication is one of the most important skills managers use to accomplish their goals.

Strategic Communication in Action

The corporate philosophy that guides nearly 200,000 FedEx Express employees worldwide is "People—Service—Profit," or PSP. The PSP credo is based on a simple, powerful idea: if the company treats employees with dignity and respect, they in turn will provide excellent service.

Excellent service leads to satisfied customers, who will repeatedly entrust FedEx with their business. Repeat business increases company revenue and helps to keep FedEx profitable.

Does PSP work? The U.S. Department of Commerce thought so. In 1990, FedEx became the first service company to be awarded the prestigious Malcolm Baldrige National Quality Award. But for PSP to thrive, both upward and downward lines of communication in the organizational structure at FedEx must remain open and direct.

The five components of managerial communication competence concentrate on developing the communication skills of the company's managers. By turning these employee leaders into effective communicators, FedEx enhances company-wide communication.

Awareness The goal for FedEx Express managers is to understand what the company expects from them as communicators. Every manager attends the FedEx Leadership Institute in Memphis, Tennessee, for management training in such areas as conveying job responsibilities to employees, listening and offering feedback on employees' needs and concerns and on their performance, and ensuring open information flow between higher-level managers and front-line workers.

Managers learn to communicate the "big picture" to their work groups—what and how FedEx is doing company-wide and how the work groups' activities relate and contribute to overall company goals. Equally important, FedEx managers learn to communicate individual work-group goals, roles, and information about project progress.

Assessment Every spring FedEx Express conducts a company-wide survey, the SFA (Survey, Feedback, Action), to gather employee feedback about individual managers and working conditions.

About one-third of the survey questions contribute to a "leadership index," which measures employees' perceptions of their managers' leadership skills. Most of the remaining survey questions evaluate managers' communication skills.

The SFA is the main mechanism for improving working conditions throughout the company and for strengthening employee-management relations. This formal process is the main upward communication link between employees and management. Communication initiated by the SFA builds trust and confidence between managers and employees.

Development and Training The Global Organizational Learning and Development department provides training workshops on such topics as communication skills and group dynamics, which are tailored to address the needs of particular groups of managers. As a backup to their training, all managers also receive a copy of the *Manager's Guide*, which features an entire chapter on communication and has sections covering management theory and leadership theory.

Support Corporate policy reinforces managers' communication efforts, for example, by allowing employees credit for attending official work-group meetings on company time.

Measurement and Reward Each manager receives a communication profile generated from employee SFA

surveys during the SFA assessment phase. Top management uses annual SFA survey results to gather feedback from employees on the work environment and to review and, when needed, to change corporate policy. Managers use the information in their own profiles to work on skills that need improvement.

Communication and Corporate Culture

The focus on communication is apparent in the company's use of internal media ranging from online communications via the intranet to FXTV, the FedEx television network. These media keep employees up-to-date on issues, policy changes, company activities, and benefit plans.

Managers act as opinion leaders, opening dialogues with employees, keeping communication lines between employees and upper management open, and generally helping their employees perform their jobs better. At FedEx Express communication has gained a cultural dimension that helps managers develop as aware, able, face-to-face communicators who reinforce the company's commitment to maintaining satisfied employees, satisfied customers, and financial corporate health: People—Service—Profit.

You can visit FedEx online at www.fedex.com.

WRITING PROMPT

FedEx depends on managers to relay information upward and downward in its organizational structure. What does this arrangement tell you about its organizational culture? What leadership/management style do you think works best at FedEx? Why?

▶
```
The response entered here will appear in
the performance dashboard and can be viewed
by your instructor.
```

Submit

2.3.1: Goal-Setting Process

Once you have recognized its importance, goal setting in business communication is not much different from setting goals for other aspects of performance. You can achieve effective goal setting by using six steps,[35] shown in Figure 2.3:

⊗ Step 1: Identify the Problem

Specify as exactly as possible what is to be accomplished from the communication event: the job, assignment, or responsibility to be completed. Whether you are giving a persuasive presentation, being interviewed for employment, or just talking with your boss, specific goals ensure that your performance will be effective.

Figure 2.3 Goal-Setting Process
Effective goal setting is achieved by using these six steps.

Based on Locke et al., "Goal Setting and Task Performance: 1969–1980." *Psychological Bulletin* (90), 1981; pp. 125–152. Copyright © 1981 by The American Psychological Association and Edwin A. Locke. Adapted with permission from The American Psychological Association and Edwin A. Locke.

6	Obtain feedback.
5	Recognize contingencies.
4	Identify resources.
3	Set a performance goal.
2	Map out a strategy.
1	Identify the problem.

⊗ Step 2: Map Out a Strategy

Determine the level of performance necessary to achieve the desired goal, and create an evaluation measure that will tell you
if you have reached that level. This measure may be as simple as an informal checklist that points out specific items necessary for success, or it may be a complex and sophisticated formal evaluation form that measures your level of performance in a variety of categories.

⊗ Step 3: Set a Performance Goal

High goals are preferable to low goals because low goals may keep you from realizing your full communication potential. But in setting your goals, you must realize your limitations. You may not be able to "give the best public speech in the world," so stating that as a goal is not productive. But it is a good idea to push yourself beyond what you honestly feel would be your best performance. You will reach that goal more often than you think!

⊗ Step 4: Identify the Resources Necessary to Achieve Goal

Time, equipment, money, favors, encouragement, and moral support are just a few of the resources you may need to achieve your goals. Anticipating your resource needs will strengthen the plans and actions you take later, and planning how you will use resources can make your goals more real and concrete.

⊗ Step 5: Recognize Contingencies That May Arise

Contingencies are events, obstacles, or circumstances that may arise and prevent you from reaching your goal. If you keep in mind the adage "If communication can fail, it will," you will anticipate potential problems such as equipment failure (for example, overhead and slide projector failures), hostile people, cramped spaces, time constraints, and even illness.

⊗ Step 6: Obtain Feedback

Feedback clarifies messages and verifies shared meaning. Feedback also makes goal setting more effective because it indicates when and where you may need to adjust your direction or methods so that you are achieving your best. Feedback can also provide encouragement. If you receive feedback messages that support your goals and your progress toward them, you are more likely to reach those goals and set higher ones in the future.[36]

36 Locke et al., "Separating the Effects of Goal Specificity"; Locke et al., "Goal Setting and Task Performance."

The following example illustrates the goal-setting process:

Kevin Burd was elected chairperson of the program committee of the chapter of the Preprofessionals Club at the local junior college. His responsibility was lining up speakers for each month's meeting. He immediately identified his duties as getting speakers committed well in advance of the meeting (Step 1). He knew that he had to contact a variety of people to suit the varied interests of the club membership, that the speakers had to be well respected in their fields, and that they had to be willing to participate on an assigned date (Step 2). He set the following as performance goals (Step 3): speakers must be known to the members, have ten years' relevant experience in their field, possess effective speaking skills, and be willing to answer questions and socialize with the members after the presentation. Kevin then developed a game plan for attracting the best speakers (Step 4).

First, he listed all the people he personally knew who fit his speaker profile. Next, for names of qualified speakers, he contacted the local chamber of commerce, the speakers' bureau on campus, all the professional associations in town, and his relatives who were businesspeople in the community. Then he submitted the names to other committee members for their advice and feedback. Finally, he contracted with the campus media center to provide all the visual aids needed by the speakers.

Kevin then listed all the things he thought might go wrong (Step 5). He made sure that he called the speakers one week before and then one day before the presentation to ensure that they were still committed. He made sure to contact in advance the proper person regarding audiovisual support and double-checked that all equipment was in working order on the day of the presentation. He also arrived early for each presentation to ensure that the room temperature was appropriate, that the refreshments had arrived, that the chairs were set up, and that ample lighting was available.

Finally, Kevin devised an evaluation sheet that he submitted to each club member after the speaker left to determine how he or she felt about the speaker, topic, visual aids, and other details that were relevant to his job as program chair (Step 6). In this way, he was able to gauge his performance through feedback and improve on each month's meeting.

2.3.2: Benefits of Goal Setting

The primary benefit of effective goal setting is higher performance level, but that is not the only benefit.[37] Goals help to direct attention and action during communication because they give you a target to shoot for. During communication you can become easily confused or distracted if you do not have a specific goal toward which to direct yourself.

Goals are useful in mobilizing the effort you need to perform at peak levels. Setting goals makes you aware of the mental, emotional, and physical energy you will need for the communication task and encourages you to conserve and mobilize energy carefully.

Goals can help you persist in your efforts over time. If you lack desirable goals, you may feel the temptation to reduce your effort when you meet with an obstacle or other interference, and you may be easily distracted from your mission. Goals hold you to specific results within specific time periods. Goals also aid you in developing relevant and innovative strategies. When you have set important goals, you will be surprised at how ingenious and innovative you can be in devising communication strategies to reach those goals.

2.4: Communication Competence

2.4 **Express guidelines to achieving communication competence**

Communication competence, the third component of our model, is the ability to communicate both appropriately and effectively with other people. Communication strategies can be effective without being appropriate. Consider the following example:

> Trudy Berstein knew months in advance that her budget would be exhausted before the end of the fiscal year. She thought that if she asked the district manager, Joe Chang, for more money ahead of time, he would simply ask her to wait until she had run out of money. So she waited, calling Joe on the phone just before the end of the year with the message that she needed him to transfer funds to meet her budget obligations. Not happy with the request because he was virtually out of money himself, Joe told Trudy that he would go along with her request this time, but he stressed that he did not appreciate her phoning him at the last minute: "Next time, put your request in writing, well in advance of the end of the budget year!"

Trudy's communication may have been effective because she accomplished her goal, but it was inappropriate. Trudy did not handle the situation properly and may have hurt her chances to gain Joe's cooperation in the future. To ensure effective and appropriate communication, you must consider four factors: messages, internal communication, external communication, and channels.

2.4.1: Messages

Messages are the ideas you wish to communicate. Whether instructive, informative, persuasive, humorous, complimentary, or critical, a message must be effective and appropriate to be competent. You will not be able to achieve communication competence if your message does not meet that standard.

Relaying Competent Messages

Strategic Skills

Follow these general suggestions to ensure that your messages are competent:

1. **BE SPECIFIC.** Include as many details and definite facts as necessary to prevent vagueness.

2. **BE ACCURATE.** Ensure that what you are communicating is as authentic and reliable as possible.

3. **BE HONEST.** Don't give in to the temptation to use data, facts, and relationships in ways that are less than forthright just to strengthen your case.

4. **BE LOGICAL.** Keep in mind that messages are most easily understood when they follow a logical, rational, and sequential path that others can readily follow.

5. **BE COMPLETE.** Check your potential message to ensure that you have provided all the information the receiver requires.

6. **BE SUCCINCT.** While being complete, be as brief or concise as possible. No one in the professional world has time for unnecessarily long messages.

7. **INCLUDE TIME FRAMES.** All receivers need to know the time frames you have in mind for acting on your message. When you need action, give a specific indication in your message.

8. **BE RELEVANT.** Make sure that the only people getting your message are those who need or want it. Sending messages to just anyone wastes your time and theirs.

9. **BE TIMELY.** Be sure to send messages in a timely fashion. Messages should not arrive too early or too late.

10. **ASK FOR FEEDBACK.** Ask receivers for feedback to elicit information about their feelings and reactions to your message.

2.4.2: Internal Communication

Messages that are sent and received within the organizational boundaries of the company are called **internal communication or intra-organizational communication.** Formal types of internal communication include policy statements from the president, notices of changes in operating procedures, and instructions from superiors. Less formal types include conversations in the hallway, phone calls at home, and any number of forms of electronic communication. Of course, not every organization communicates in the same way.

Messages can be exchanged in three directions: downward, upward, and horizontally. In tall organizations, communication tends to be vertical, from the top down or the bottom up. Vertical communication typically focuses on work-related issues. In flat organizations, communication tends to be horizontal. Of course, communication in all three directions occurs in both tall and flat organizations. There are specific reasons for communicating in each direction, and how you use these strategies depends on your needs.[38]

DOWNWARD COMMUNICATION   Downward communication consists of messages from superiors to subordinates. Examine the following five types of downward communication in organizations:[39]

1. **JOB INSTRUCTION:** Messages that specify how to conduct tasks on the job: "Always submit budget requests two months in advance."

2. **JOB RATIONALE**: Messages that explain why tasks must be performed and how these tasks relate to other activities of the organization: "We require advance notice so that we can plan ahead."

3. **PROCEDURE AND PRACTICE:** Messages that inform organizational members about responsibilities, obligations, and privileges of the organization: "According to the procedures manual, we follow affirmative action guidelines to the letter."

4. **FEEDBACK:** Messages that inform employees of their performance in the organization: "I am happy to note that your last project was a real success."

5. **INDOCTRINATION OF GOALS:** Messages that teach employees the mission, goals, and objectives of the organization: "As you can see from our shared-values list, we feel that customer service is our number-one job."

Though very common and often necessary to ensure that employees can do their jobs, downward communication generates its share of trouble. One problem results from the chain of command. Typically, a message originates near or at the top of an organization (for example, in the president's office) and is sent down the chain person by person. This serial communication negatively affects the accuracy of the message.

Think of the "gossip" game, in which one person whispers a message to another, who in turn whispers it to the next person. By the time the message reaches the last person in the chain, it is usually quite different from the original message. The same effect can occur in a message that must travel down a long chain of command, especially if the message is circulated through more than one channel. Figure 2.4 shows the percentage of information lost in each transfer.

When practicing downward communication, imagine yourself as the receiver. Does the message make sense to you? Is it effective without being disrespectful? Asking these questions of all your messages can help prevent miscommunication. A carefully considered message can forestall many of the most common communication failures.

UPWARD COMMUNICATION   Upward communication consists of messages from subordinates to superiors. Upward communication usually consists of information relating to performance, peers, confirmation of understanding, and reporting tasks.

Four Types of Upward Communication

Remove card   1 of 4   Reset Deck

Upward communication offers several advantages.[40] It shows superiors whether subordinates are accepting their ideas, plans, and policies. Upward communication also gives subordinates an opportunity to participate actively in the decision-making process and thus satisfies their need to feel valued. Talking to superiors can release tension or stress that subordinates feel as they cope with their jobs. Often, people simply need someone to listen to them in order to feel good about what they are doing. Finally, upward communication can alert superiors to impending problems from which they may be isolated. Be aware, however, that upward communication tends to be rosy because organization members rarely want to send bad news to their supervisors.

HORIZONTAL COMMUNICATION   Horizontal communication consists of messages exchanged at the same hierarchical level in an organization that is typically focused on

Figure 2.4 Effect of Serial Communication

Information is lost as a message travels down the organizational chain of command.

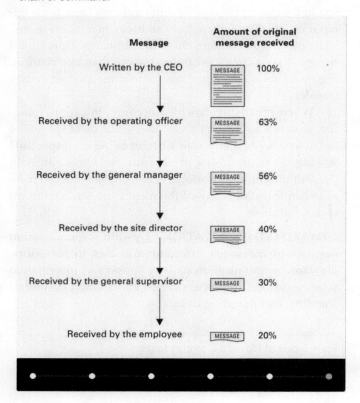

Message		Amount of original message received
Written by the CEO	MESSAGE	100%
Received by the operating officer	MESSAGE	63%
Received by the general manager	MESSAGE	56%
Received by the site director	MESSAGE	40%
Received by the general supervisor	MESSAGE	30%
Received by the employee	MESSAGE	20%

relationships.[41] Take a look at the several functions of horizontal communication that follow:[42]

1. **FACILITATES PROBLEM SOLVING:** "Why don't we get together over lunch to hammer out the details?"

2. **ALLOWS INFORMATION SHARING ACROSS DIFFERENT WORK GROUPS:** "Send that information over the computer network to the Dayton office."

3. **PROMOTES TASK COORDINATION BETWEEN DEPARTMENTS OR TEAMS:** "I am glad that the public relations and advertising departments are exchanging information on the Donavon project."

4. **ENHANCES MORALE:** "It helps to know that other units experience similar frustration."

5. **AFFORDS A MEANS FOR RESOLVING CONFLICTS:** "When we are able to get together, it makes it easier to see the respective points of view."

The frequency and effectiveness of horizontal communication depend on the structure of the organization. Some organizations, particularly tall ones or those in traditionally conservative fields such as banking, may rely primarily on vertical (especially downward) communication. Flat organizations frequently use horizontal communication because it is appropriate to their structures. Companies in highly innovative or creative fields—for example, software

development companies or toy manufacturers—use horizontal communication because they need flexibility.

Despite its benefits, horizontal communication does have drawbacks. There are at least three conditions for problems: territoriality, specialization, and lack of motivation.[43]

⊗ Territoriality

Individuals or departments may feel that communicating with others will reveal ideas and plans prematurely and thus reduce their overall impact. In other cases, jealousy or envy may prevent effective horizontal communication.

⊗ Specialization

As members of departments work together on projects, they develop certain frames of reference, mind-sets, and jargon specific to their responsibilities. Lacking this knowledge, people outside the departments (even if they are at the same level in the organization) have a difficult time understanding or appreciating such specialized communication.

⊗ Lack of Motivation

Some employees may not understand the importance of horizontal communication and simply avoid it because it is too much trouble. Attitudes such as "If you want something done right, do it yourself" and "Why cooperate with the other departments if they get all the credit?" demonstrate cynicism about horizontal communication.

Another way that companies are encouraging horizontal communication is through work teams. Management will take employees from different work areas and ask them to solve problems that affect the entire organization. Usually the team will manage itself without much oversight from upper management. Although each team decides its own decision-making rules and operating procedures, these small entrepreneurial units work best in an informal structure where horizontal communication is free-flowing and unrestricted. Companies such as Colgate-Palmolive, Hallmark Cards, and Johnson & Johnson are jumping on the "team approach" bandwagon in an effort to involve more workers in decisions that affect them. The Boeing Company, for example, designed work teams made up of engineers, pilots, mechanics, marketing specialists, and a customer (United Airlines) for developing the Boeing 777.[44]

Teams perform well for the following reasons:[45]

1. The synergy created by bringing together complementary skills and experiences exceeds what any individual on the team can provide.

2. Teams establish communication methods to support problem solving and provide initiative by jointly developing goals and methods.

3. Teams provide a social communication dimension that enhances economic and administrative aspects of work.

4. Teams have more fun.

INFORMAL NETWORKS Informal networks frequently open up outside of official paths of communication. Often called the grapevine, informal networks are a substitute for formal downward, upward, or horizontal communication. Messages exchanged in the hallway, in the coffee room, at parties, or in restaurants are examples of informal communication. Informal networks develop more rapidly in flat organizations that emphasize team building than in formal, tall organizations. Figure 2.5 shows the path of informal communication along a grapevine.

Figure 2.5 Path of Information Through the Grapevine
Communication in the grapevine tends to be informal yet efficient, diffuse yet effective.

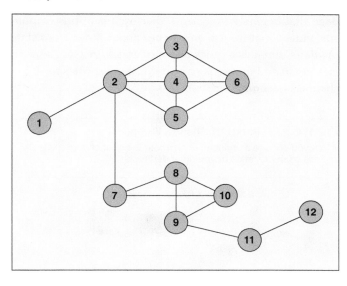

Much of the research in the area suggests the following:[46]

- The grapevine is fast.
- The grapevine is generally accurate.
- The grapevine carries much information.
- The grapevine gives an indication of employee attitudes and sentiment.
- The grapevine is a common channel for rumors.
- The grapevine travels by clusters.

Experts sometimes argue that informal communication occurs because there are not enough opportunities for formal communication. Although some people believe that informal communication must be minimized or controlled, the grapevine is generally highly effective, especially if formal paths of communication are overburdened. For example, one manager in a paper-manufacturing firm became so frustrated with the delay in getting information to his fellow workers via formal paths that he used Friday afternoon socials to provide them with the needed information.

2.4.3: External Communication

Messages that are exchanged between the organization and its environment are called **external communication.** Although many of the messages that are sent to, and received from, the environment are perfunctory—for example, newsletters, annual reports, advertising, goodwill speeches, or notices of corporate sponsorship of nonprofit events—many of these messages are exchanged in an effort to improve communication. They can also enable workers to understand how the environment affects the internal efficiency of the organization.

An excellent method of learning about the external environment is through the Internet. Literally millions of businesses now advertise their services and products on Web pages. Browsing these Web sites can provide useful information about the organizations' customers, competitors, and current conditions. Search engines—such as google.com, yahoo.com, or bing.com—will direct you to places on the Internet that interest you. One such place is brint.com, a search engine or index of Web sites that are specific to business. This resource can help you find the information you need when you type in keywords such as "economic trends," "profitable companies," or "business technology."

Listening carefully to customers' needs, being receptive to new ideas or to information from competitors, learning new techniques from new employees, employing expert consultants, and searching the Internet are some of the ways that organizations can "listen" to their environments in order to reduce uncertainty. To a large extent such activity is compatible with our discussion of situational knowledge: as you gain additional information about the environment, you build on your knowledge of the overall situation.

Communicating in organizations today is a truly global experience, using all forms of technology and occurring at all times of the day.

SOURCE: Amana images inc/Alamy

Organizations have much at stake in communicating a positive image to external stakeholders. Web pages have served this purpose for some years and continue to provide "front porch" information about what the organization does as well as to serve other functions of communication. More recently blogs (or Web logs) have become a communication option for organizations interested in getting the message out. A recent study examined the effectiveness of blogs and Web pages for this purpose and found that respondents felt that blogs offered a more "conversational voice" than regular Web pages.[47] Blogs also seemed superior in communicating relational characteristics about the organization, increasing perceptions of trust, satisfaction, and commitment. Have your own experiences with blogs made you feel more relationally connected with the host organization?

2.4.4: Channels

Choosing the appropriate channel for your messages is critical to communication competence. **Channels** are the media that carry messages to receivers. Channels include conversations, speeches, interviews, memos, letters, phone calls, and computer and satellite networks. A channel's characteristics, especially its richness, determine its usefulness.

CHANNEL RICHNESS   **Channel richness** is the ability of a communication channel (such as a telephone call) to handle information or convey the meaning contained in a message.[48] Some channels are best for certain types of messages, whereas other channels may be inappropriate for those same messages. Whether a channel is high or low in richness depends on four conditions:

1. The capacity for obtaining immediate feedback from the receiver

2. The ability to transmit multiple communication cues such as facial expressions, body language, appearance, and dress

3. The shaping or tailoring of messages for the specific situation

4. Language variety, or the ability to use a wide range of word choices

If you think about those criteria, it becomes clear that the richest channels are face-to-face meetings with few language restrictions. The least rich channels are undirected written memos (such as flyers addressed to "Occupant"). Figure 2.6 shows the range of channel richness. As you

move through, from highest to lowest, each successive channel is less able to satisfy the four criteria of channel richness.

Channel richness is also dependent upon familiarity.[49] For example, the first time a manager uses Skype (a free online phone/videoconferencing service) to hold a conference call she may feel nervous and frustrated due to lack of familiarity with the software. However, with practice and repeated use, the manager may find that she actually prefers Skype to other channels of communication. The more familiar you are with a channel the richer it will be perceived.[50]

Organizations differ about which channels are most effective for sending messages. In "memo happy" organizations, communication is defined as an 8.5-by-11-inch page that begins with "To." Other organizations emphasize videos that inform employees about the current state of affairs. Email is a quick and moderately rich channel. In fact, email and intranets have become substitutes for other channels of communication.

Figure 2.6 Range of Channel Richness
When you choose a channel, think about the goal of your message and the characteristics of your intended receiver.

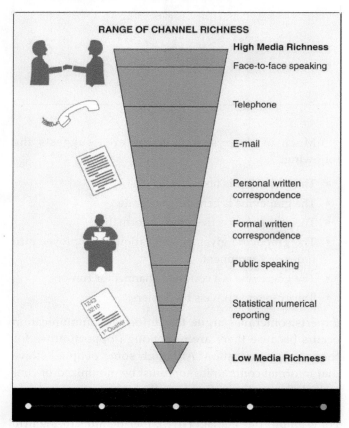

RANGE OF CHANNEL RICHNESS

High Media Richness

Face-to-face speaking

Telephone

E-mail

Personal written correspondence

Formal written correspondence

Public speaking

Statistical numerical reporting

Low Media Richness

SELECTING THE PROPER CHANNELS   Competent communication involves choosing the appropriate channel for the message.[51] Think about the effort you have put into the message so far—setting a goal, collecting situational knowledge, and formulating an effective message. Your work will be wasted if you send the message through an ineffective channel—for example, if you send an important report on a competitor's product through interoffice mail rather than hand-delivering it to your supervisor. Research has shown that managers prefer the richest types of media or channel: face-to-face meetings and telephone calls.[52] Increasingly, however, they are choosing email as a channel for conducting business because using email at home or on the road can be convenient and time-saving.

The rule of thumb is that rich channels are best when messages are designed for specific people, when time is important, when immediate feedback is necessary, when the situation is stressful, when the message is vague or difficult to understand, and when personal information is to be conveyed. Less rich channels are most useful for communicating routine information, for giving orders or conveying policy, for communicating to large numbers of people at once, and when immediate feedback is unnecessary or formal communication is appropriate (such as public presentations at an awards banquet).[53]

Choosing the proper channel for communication is not easy, but consideration of these factors can help you evaluate your options:[54]

- **SPEED:** Oral and electronic channels provide the fastest means of communicating.

- **ACCURACY:** When accuracy is at a premium, written and, to a lesser extent, electronic means are the preferred channels.

- **FEEDBACK:** Feedback can be obtained from any of the three channels. Oral communication, especially when conducted face-to-face, provides a great deal of immediate feedback, not only about the content of the message but also—from nonverbal behavior—about the state of mind of the communicator. Written channels are less likely to encourage spontaneous feedback. Even email may not yield an immediate response.

- **SELECTIVITY:** Some messages are not appropriate for or effective with everyone in an organization or even in a work group. Highly sensitive or confidential messages may need to be directed to only some people. Therefore, oral communication channels are often used for sensitive messages, although private memos may be used as well.

- **APPROPRIATENESS:** Some communication channels are not appropriate for some messages. Communicating company-wide policy changes through an oral channel exclusively is not appropriate, nor is communicating the termination of an employee on a bulletin board. Some issues are sticky and require a special channel.

- **COST:** A number of cost issues may affect the selection of a communication channel. While it may be ideally effective to have a telephone conversation with someone, if that person is on another continent, the cost may be prohibitive. Low cost is one reason companies encourage employees to use email. The ability to attach documents, photos, and other files to email messages has greatly reduced the need for surface or interoffice mail. Fax machines, once the cutting edge in electronic communication, are now used primarily to fill in gaps, as when a document requires a signature or isn't available in electronic format. Employee expenses must also be kept in mind and that includes time. It could take someone an hour to craft a well-written memo. If the telephone were used instead, forty-five minutes of company time could be saved.

- **ACCOUNTABILITY:** Accountability is the responsibility that a receiver has for responding to a message—not only providing feedback to the sender but also responding to the instruction, information, directive, request, or other purpose of the message. Message senders also have accountability for what they communicate. Consider, for example, the recent lawsuit against stockbrokers who made fraudulent buy/sell recommendations to clients over the Internet. Written channels are the most obvious form of message accountability since there is some form of documentation involved such as a memo, letter, or email post.

- **ACCEPTABILITY:** Some forms of communication are more acceptable to some people than to others. Some people despise memos; others believe oral channels are too informal. If you are concerned about the impact of your message, you should try to choose a communication channel that your receiver will find acceptable.

Surveys of businesspeople suggest that these are the most effective modes of communication (in descending order):[55]

1. Presenting information through both oral and written channels

2. Presenting information to a group orally

3. Presenting information to each member of a group in written form

4. Posting information on a bulletin board

5. Making no presentation of information in either oral or written form but instead allowing informal channels to pick up the slack

Because humans tend to be attracted to multimedia stimuli, it stands to reason that information presented through oral and written channels will be most effective. Consider the following example:

> A small southwestern bank was acquired by a large northeastern bank. The president of the small bank sent a memo to the vice presidents informing them of a meeting to provide the details of the takeover. News of the takeover spread rapidly through the grapevine. Some key employees changed jobs, morale was low, and customers began to complain about ineffective treatment by bank employees. Many customers and employees changed banks after news of the takeover became generally known.

This outcome indicates that the channel to convey sensitive and confidential material needs to be carefully chosen.

WRITING PROMPT

How do you use communication media in a typical day? For which situations do you prefer to use one channel over another? What do you think your media preferences say about you?

▶ The response entered here will appear in the performance dashboard and can be viewed by your instructor.

Submit

2.5: Anxiety Management

2.5 Recount different causes for anxiety and the importance of managing anxiety in communication

Anxiety management is the ability to control nervousness, fears, stress, and worries associated with a communication event. Some people are most anxious prior to the act of communicating. Some are most anxious while they are communicating. Others worry and fret about their communication performance after it is over. In any case, one thing is certain: each person handles the anxiety associated with communication episodes differently.

Because stress or anxiety can prevent you from doing your best, the ability to manage communication anxiety is an essential ingredient of an effective communication strategy. Such management requires knowing the causes and effects of your anxiety and knowing how to treat it.

2.5.1: Causes of Communication Anxiety

For many years, researchers have tried to identify the causes of communication anxiety. The best conclusion that can be drawn from their studies is that multiple factors are responsible for the fears and worries that people have

about communicating. Some of the causes are based in a person's culture. Common factors include the following:[56]

- **NOVELTY:** People are especially anxious in new communication situations.
- **FORMALITY:** Communication situations that require prescribed actions and behaviors and allow little deviation from those norms frequently cause anxiety.
- **SUBORDINATE STATUS:** Being in a subordinate position often causes people to feel intimidated and ill at ease.
- **CONSPICUOUSNESS:** Communication situations that put people at the center of others' attention (such as public speaking) can be uncomfortable.
- **LARGE GROUPS:** Some people, while comfortable in small groups, struggle when speaking in front of large groups.
- **LACK OF SKILL:** A communicator who knows that he or she does not have the communication skills necessary to be effective in some situations is likely to feel anxious.
- **PAST EXPERIENCES:** Failure in certain communication situations (such as job interviews) may cause anxiety about future encounters.
- **EVALUATION:** Knowing that communication skills are being assessed can cause anxiety, especially if there is a lot at stake.

Another cause of anxiety stems from the channel preference of the sender. Sometimes communicators experience nervousness when using a highly rich channel. For example, someone delivering bad news may experience anxiety because of the likely uncomfortableness of a face-to-face encounter and so may try to reduce the anxiety by choosing a less rich channel, such as a memo.

Because the choice of a channel can create problems for both the sender and the receiver, anxiety management is a crucial component of strategic communication. Knowing the causes of communication anxiety is a first step toward managing the stress and fears associated with communication. Take out a piece of paper and rank-order the causes of communication anxiety that most affect you. Think about them as we continue our discussion.

2.5.2: Effects of Communication Anxiety

Communication anxiety takes a toll on the occupational, professional, and vocational interests of some individuals. Research has demonstrated a number of negative effects resulting from the uncontrolled anxiety associated with communication.[57] People who are afraid to communicate may be viewed negatively by others. Coworkers and bosses will see those who refuse to communicate as uncooperative and may not trust them with important tasks. In others cases, communication anxiety may cause people to pause, stutter, fail to maintain eye contact, and appear incompetent. People who suffer from a high degree of communication anxiety may be less assertive and more shy than people who do not experience such anxiety.

These negative perceptions result in many unfavorable outcomes for anxious communicators. They have fewer leadership opportunities, they are less likely to be chosen for leadership positions, and they take less initiative in attempting to gain leadership roles. Anxious communicators are also perceived as less attractive because communication skills are considered socially important in occupational settings. Because of these factors, anxious communicators are granted fewer job interviews, receive lower pay and fewer promotions, enjoy less job satisfaction, and do not retain their jobs as long as communicators who are less anxious do. It is no wonder that people who experience high degrees of communication anxiety seek out occupations with relatively low communication demands (accountants, forest rangers, telecommuters, computer programmers, construction workers).

Use the Strategic Skills self-evaluation survey here to rate your own stress in certain situations, then read on.

Identifying Stressful Situations

Strategic Skills

On a scale of 1 to 10 (with 10 being the highest level of stress and 1 being the lowest), rate your degree of stress for the following communication situations.

1. Interviewing for a job
2. Leading a group
3. Arguing with your boss
4. Asking friends for a charitable donation
5. Disagreeing with a coworker
6. Speaking up in a hostile group
7. Telling jokes or funny stories at a bull session
8. Making an excuse for a mistake
9. Giving a media interview
10. Challenging someone's point of view
11. Presenting a report to your boss's boss
12. Giving a brief report to coworkers
13. Conversing with a new acquaintance
14. Persuading a coworker
15. Giving a formal presentation to strangers
16. Answering questions
17. Explaining your actions
18. Demonstrating leadership skills
19. Denying responsibility for a misunderstanding

2.5.3: Manage Communication Anxiety

You may think that we have painted a very dreary picture for those who experience some degree of communication anxiety. Actually, most people are anxious in at least some situations. As you look back at the causes of communication anxiety, you may feel that only one or two of them apply to you, or you may identify with many of them. Controlling anxiety requires understanding where you stand and how you feel about the stressfulness of a communication situation. When you listed the causes of anxiety, you learned what may be producing nervousness in certain situations. Another way of identifying anxiety is by recognizing which specific communication situations are most stressful for you.

As you look over the ratings you gave yourself in the self-evaluation survey, Identifying Stressful Situations (section 2.5.2), you will probably notice that some situations elicit a greater degree of stress than do others. It is perfectly natural to be *situationally anxious*. In certain circumstances, each of us has to work especially hard to be an effective communicator. You can do so by learning to focus your nervous energy and thereby maximize your effectiveness.

Strategic Scenario Wrap-Up

The Model of Strategic Communication

⊗ Strategic Scenario:

Sam Klausner is one of four associate vice presidents for administration at Kempinik Industries in the Midwest. Sam was called into the executive suite to meet with CEO/president Joan Randall and Antonio Montegro, vice president for administration and his direct superior, to discuss a plan to reduce the work force. The company is in jeopardy of being bought by a fierce competitor if they do not quickly and substantially improve the bottom line. Since a large investment was made in automation earlier in the year, Ms. Randall and Mr. Montegro feel the time is right to reduce the enormous costs associated with employees. This means that 1,000 employees (about 25 percent of the company) will be let go.

The executives want Sam to develop a series of messages that clearly and accurately communicate their plans for the massive layoff and to devise the best ways for carrying these messages to the work force. They stressed to Sam that the plans must be kept secret, because they do not want the best employees to be alarmed and quit, nor do they want the public (competitors, media) to know about the layoffs until the time is right. Sam is concerned about this responsibility, since he has a lot of friends in the company who will likely be laid off, many of whom have debts and families. Ms. Randall and Mr. Montegro want Sam to take a week to prepare his plan and report back to them on how he will implement this plan successfully.

Sam does not have an easy assignment. However as an associate vice-president, he has a stake in the company and understands the need for the layoffs at this time. Sam does not care for secrecy, but understands that a leak would be damaging. A firm believer in ethical communication, Sam set his main goal to speak to the workforce exactly as he would have liked to be spoken to: as soon as possible, and with openness, honesty, and complete information. Sam proposes the following to the vice-presidents:

1. He will write a concise summary of the economic situation the company is in, providing background for the need for the layoffs. Upper management should meet to clarify the facts and decide on supporting material that would be appropriate to share with employees.

2. Sam suggests the information go out to all employees in a personalized letter. Soon after, employees who lose

their jobs should be told personally by their division managers and offered employment counseling.

3. The company's use of automation and other important plans for its future should be clarified and shared with the employees who will be staying.

Sam wouldn't have been honest if he denied that he felt anxious about this difficult task. It helps him to know that he paved the way for the company to share as much information as quickly as possible, and in a well-organized way.

Summary

The Model of Strategic Communication

- The **model of strategic communication** presents a practical perspective on communicating in organizations. It also offers tools for dealing with the effects of globalization on business and the dependence on information.

- **Situational knowledge**, the first element, allows for greater flexibility in assessing, selecting, and evaluating the messages that are exchanged within the organization and with the external environment. Such knowledge also reduces uncertainty and helps the communicator to know when strategic ambiguity is appropriate.

- **Goal setting**, the second element of the model, enables you to plan the most effective campaign or tactics.

- **Communication competence**, the third aspect, enhances your ability to achieve goals in the context of differing communication networks, allowing greater opportunity for improved productivity.

- **Anxiety management**, the fourth element, focuses on maintaining the elements of organizational

communication that are essential for establishing and maintaining the highest level of performance.

Chapter 2 Quiz: The Model of Strategic Communication

Chapter 3
Diversity in Business and the Professions

Learning Objectives

3.1 Define diversity

3.2 Explain how conflicts in diversity stem from negative or inaccurate stereotyping

3.3 Analyze the discrimination that occurs due to factors like age, ethnicity, gender

3.4 Explain how conflict occurs because of differences in cultural expectations

3.5 Examine how differences in personality traits influence competence in communication

3.6 Analyze how understanding one's own perspectives and appreciating those of others is important to successful cross-cultural communication

Strategic Scenario: Cultural Dilemma

James Sixkiller is a Cherokee student who has a large extended family. He has lived all of his life in Tahlequah, Oklahoma, a town with a high number of American Indians in the general population. Growing up he attended the local Cherokee schools, then went to a nearby, mid-sized state university. For his junior year, James has transferred to a very large university in a much larger Eastern city. The city and the university's students are primarily White. The populations of the town and university are primarily mainstream with little diversity.

Until this move, James had friends who were Indian and a few who were White. He is bilingual, a fluent English and Cherokee speaker. At the university, some of his courses are in very large lecture halls with over 200 students. This term, James is taking a public speaking class. In addition to learning about the various types of speeches and how to organize them, students are required to make five individual presentations to the class and work with others in an assigned group. James's professor will evaluate his work in front of the other students, and then James's fellow students will critique his speech. Of course, James will then have to publicly critique his peers. The assignment—being critiqued and critiquing others—is culturally appropriate for mainstream U.S. students, but it is contrary to his Cherokee culture. James has become more and more reluctant to participate. He has begun to miss classes. Without intervention of some sort, he will probably drop out of that class.

Think about James's dilemma as you read this chapter. What should he do? What should his professor do? What should his group partners and class peers do? At the end of the chapter, we will revisit this scenario and discuss some solutions.

3.1: Overview
Diversity in Business and the Professions

3.1 Define diversity

Researchers in communication, business, sociology, psychology, and other areas of study have consistently found that diversity is a positive factor in business and the professions. People who are different from one another can provide interesting and rich experiences that enhance the working climate and the possibilities for innovative thinking. Yet when you are different from people around you, you will probably communicate differently than the others. Verbal and nonverbal language may create breakdowns in communication. Your taken-for-granted ways of communicating and your expectations for other people's behaviors are usually not the same. During interactions with diverse people, the dissimilar communication patterns and expectations of behaviors can result in cultural conflict. The conflict is often inevitable, but it can be positive rather than negative.

Diversity is the state of differences among people. These differences can be due to gender, age, ethnicity, physical abilities or differences, religious and spiritual beliefs, sexual orientation, nationality, life experiences, and other societal factors.

Business and professional people face daily challenges in management and work relationships in a diverse workplace. You face the same challenges in your social, educational, and work worlds. In this chapter, we define and characterize diversity in the United States so that you will be able to

1. Understand your own cultural perspectives by being self-reflexive

2. Develop tolerance and appreciation for the cultural perspectives of others

3. Achieve positive outcomes from conflict caused by diversity

Self-Assessment

Strategic Skills

Please briefly answer a few questions about yourself.

(x) **Question 1**

Many lucky people have immediate family members (e.g., parent or guardian by birth or law, siblings, or perhaps a grandparent) whom they trust with many areas of their life: finances, romantic advice, personal admonitions about behavior, and so forth. However, the question is how far down your family tree do you go and still allow those second and third cousins and great-great uncles and aunts the same privileges as your closest family members?

(x) **Question 2**

If you have a death in your immediate family, what are your obligations as a student (at your current age and family circumstances)? What are your obligations to your family?

(x) **Question 3**

As a student or an employee, you will probably need to miss work or classes. Other than travel time, how much time will you need to be absent and still meet family expectations?

Read the story of one woman's responses to these questions in section 3.6.2.

In order to have the tools to manage your conflicts, please try to analyze your communication and your behavior in a self-reflexive way. We use the term *self-reflexive* to encourage you to become more aware of the reasons why you speak and behave as you do. In intercultural studies, self-reflexivity implies self-awareness in the present; seeing your words and actions as they occur, rather than reflecting upon them later.[1] With the insights into your own culture and more understanding of others' cultural perspectives, you will have the beginning of tools to help you in your social, educational, and work contexts. Using the strategic communication model, we discuss the importance of goals, situational knowledge, communication competence, and anxiety management in interactions with culturally different people. We also present the federal definitions and guidelines that help keep the workplace and educational settings relatively free from discriminatory behavior and interaction.

3.2: The Issues of Diversity

3.2 **Explain how conflicts in diversity stem from negative or inaccurate stereotyping**

The word *diversity* is one of many terms used to explain how people differ by gender, age, ethnicity, physical abilities or differences, religious and spiritual beliefs, sexual orientation, nationality, life experiences, and other societal factors.

Discrimination due to negative stereotyping is often based on these differences. Terms such as *ethnicity* and *culture* are used by people in everyday language and by researchers to explain those elements of diversity. **Culture** is a broad term that explains why people from various nations and co-cultures (groups different from mainstream populations within those nations) act and speak as they do. While there are hundreds of academic researchers who have defined culture, we define culture as the attitudes, beliefs, and values of a people in a particular group.

- **ATTITUDES:** a person's learned likes and dislikes. (Advertisers of products attempt to change your preferences so that you will buy their product; it is possible to change people's attitudes.)

- **BELIEFS:** a person's judgments about right and wrong. (Although your belief in what is good or bad may change some through life experiences, most people do not give up easily their beliefs about right and wrong.)

- **VALUES:** a person's deep cultural assumptions that affect all areas of life. (Changing your values is possible, but rarely can people be persuaded to change values without a threat of some kind.)

Your university newspaper has printed a letter to the editor that argues that words or phrases that are considered racist or sexist are really not important. The writer insists that such terms are not meant to be demeaning. For instance, the letter says that diva (referring to a woman) could be just humorous or that chief (referring to a Native American) could be used in fun. Do you agree or disagree, and why?

▶ The response entered here will appear in the performance dashboard and can be viewed by your instructor.

Submit

Media channels and other pathways report conflicts based on bias and discrimination in many settings, including private lives, the courts, and even public acts of violence.

Perhaps the simplest way to explain your own culture is "it just feels right." Although individuals in any group may have some differences, culture consists of generally acceptable language and behavior by people in that group. Culture includes these issues and more:

Choosing life partners

Architecture

Treatment of children, elders, people with mental or physical illness, and the indigent

Judgments about beauty and ugliness, useful or not useful actions or choices

Clothes

Speech and behavior

Cultural ways-of-doing affect all parts of society. Because U.S. society is heterogeneous, successful organizations cultivate diverse cultural perspectives, which in turn are likely to result in positive, productive climates in business and the professions.

TECHNOLOGY TOOLS

Diversity Resources Online

The waters of diversity can be tricky to navigate as both a citizen and a businessperson. Your ability to interact and communicate effectively with diverse people is vital to building relationships with employees, managers, coworkers, vendors, and customers. One Web site that is dedicated to helping people enhance their competencies in diversity and cross-cultural management is Diversity Central. The site offers information and programs for executives, managers, employees, educators, students, and consumers, providing a wide array of resources to help readers gain a stronger understanding of diversity and its function within business and the professions. In the past, this information required a membership, but the originators of this site are working to provide open access to students and many others.

3.2.1: Diversity in the Workplace

In the 1960s, demographers began making some startling predictions: that European American males soon would be the smallest population group in the work force and that more women would work outside the home than not. Researchers predicted that business and professional organizations would be transformed into transnational companies that would hire more part-time than full-time employees and would adopt an employment philosophy that would induce employees to work at many companies and change careers several times. In retrospect, these predictions were cautious when compared to today's statistics for the United States.

Our country and many other countries have transnational and global professions and businesses. Most employee groups are culturally diverse, as represented by local co-cultures (those outside the mainstream), internationals, gay and transgender workers, people who are physically different by abilities and stature, those who are religiously diverse, and so on. However, while diversity has been noticeably more prevalent, inequities in representation by women and people of some co-cultures remain. Today, as old and new financial and ideological crises come and go, businesses and the professions actively need employees who have the skills to work with others who are culturally different.

To better understand diversity in the workplace, note Table 3.1, where a scale of 1–6 denotes the highest and lowest numbers of employees in a particular group (1 is the highest number of employees, and 6 is the lowest number).

Table 3.1 Distribution of Diversity in the U.S. Workplace

American Indian and Alaska Native	5
Asian	3
Black/African American	2
Native Hawaiian/Pacific Islander	6
Hispanic or Latino (of any culture), mixed	4
White/non-Hispanic/Caucasian	1

SOURCE: www.bls.gov/cps/cpsrace2013.pdf

3.2.2: How We Are Affected by Diversity

As a student or employee, you are a product of your own culture just as others around you represent their culture. The same elements that create diversity can become sources of conflict in the workplace because of prejudices against unfamiliar language or different behaviors, or disagreements about understanding a task or how to do it.

Ethnocentrism is belief in the superiority of one's own culture. Our levels of ethnocentrism can be on a continuum from low to high.

Continuum of Ethnocentrism

Ethnocentrism refers to the very human tendency to evaluate other cultures based on preconceptions we have developed in our own cultures. It is a term commonly associated with "the dark side."

People who have extremely low levels of satisfaction with their own culture can suffer consequences by becoming discontented and disassociated. People with very high levels of satisfaction with their own culture may become so proud and perhaps isolated that they become alienated against another culture or cultures resulting in acts of bias or prejudice. Those in the extremes on this continuum may experience conflicts in work and society, disharmony, loss of work time, and damage to the people involved.

Those with high levels of attachment to their culture *may* have the following issues: anger at groups who seem to take more than their share of the assets or resources available in the community; fear of those who are different for unexplained but real (to them) reasons; inability to compromise with those who are different personally or socially; and intolerance of ambiguity or changes. Extremely high levels of ethnocentrism are likely to result in repeated and unproductive conflicts in diverse business and professional settings.

People who have moderate levels of ethnocentrism have fewer problems dealing with ambiguity and those who have different language and behavior.

Comparing and contrasting your culture with the culture of someone else is natural and can be enlightening. You can use this activity as a self-evaluation tool, rather than as an opportunity to disparage the cultural activities of others.

How would you describe yourself?

Most people rush to say "I'm not prejudiced." Within every cultural group in the United States, the members have particular opinions about what is good or bad, acceptable or unacceptable. Children and young adults often mirror their culture's attitudes toward others, positively and negatively. As you age, you have choices about your attitudes, beliefs, and values and opinions about groups who are different from you. What is prejudice? **Prejudice** is a negative preconception about people, activities, places, ideas, and other parts of our lives. The use of stereotypes can lead to prejudice; however, the mental practice of stereotyping is needed for common, everyday navigation through life to handle ever-increasing amounts of data. We process the information through stereotyping or drawing conclusions about things based on knowledge that we have gained. However, when your opinions are based on limited personal experiences, hearsay, or other incomplete data, your stereotypes can become negative.

Diversity conflicts arise primarily from negative and inaccurate stereotyping. Some real-life examples of such conflict are shown here.

ⓧ **Gender**

A professor at a small community college objected to the inclusion of evaluations by students in her promotion dossier. The students wrote that she was not a good professor because women should not be as "pushy" and "bossy" as she was.

ⓧ **Age**

A biochemist who was one of fifteen employees fired from his job of twenty-five years at an international corporation discovered that, like him, the others fired were all over forty-five years of age.

ⓧ **Ethnicity**

In preparation for the Thanksgiving program at a local elementary school, the teacher of the third-grade class called the parents of an Apache child in her class and asked that the child and her parents come to the program in their "Indian" clothes.

ⓧ **Physical Ability**

An employee requested that the annual picnic not be held at a park because the attractions at the site were not accessible to people with disabilities.

ⓧ **Religion**

A new employee complained because the only company-paid dinner was held with a Christmas holiday theme—a holiday that the employee did not observe according to his religion.

ⓧ **Sexual Orientation**

A woman petitioned her employer to provide domestic partner benefits for her same-sex partner equal to those available for heterosexual spouses.

In the examples above, the conflict occurs because one group's perspective differs from another's. Some of the people involved may not have communicated their needs or preferences, and others may not have had self-knowledge and information about the other person's needs. It is management's responsibility to make decisions that avoid or remedy damaging conflicts at work. Examining the source of conflict (was it culturally based, even in part?) can help the manager and employees understand what the conflict was about so that it does not continue.

Our perspectives arise from our cultural beliefs and attitudes that this is the "way things are" and that certain things can be "taken for granted" in our lives. We tend to assume that our work partner, supervisor, or employee lives in a house like ours, worships as we do, or has a family like our own. Often these assumptions are not accurate. The ultimate goal of a diverse society and workplace should not be to make everyone alike but to ensure that people have the self-knowledge, knowledge about others, and skills necessary to manage conflict arising from diverse perspectives. The experiences and the talents of people who are different from you can assist you in your effort to succeed. Understanding that your assumptions about others are sometimes inaccurate is the beginning of a positive approach to cultural conflict.

3.2.3: Cultural Descriptions of the United States

U.S. history includes stories of many visitors and their failed or successful attempts at colonization (taking land and resources by physical conflict with disregard for the indigenous residents). European explorers from the early Middle Ages through 1767 included Vikings (in approximately 1000 A.D.), Italians, Spaniards, French, English, Dutch, and many more. From the time of permanent colonies, immigrants included Germans, Irish, English, Scots, French, Italians, Scandinavians, Scottish, Portuguese, Welsh, Eastern Europeans, and others.[2]

Members of the media and researchers often describe the United States as having one of the most diverse populations in the world. According to the last census and projections for the future from the U.S. Census Bureau Web site www.census.gov, the United States has over 500 federally recognized American Indian/Native American groups (including people who are indigenous to Alaska and Hawaii) and thirty-one ethnic groups with more than one million members each, including individuals from Mexico, Puerto Rico, the Virgin Islands, Central and South America, and many Asian countries. Latino/a groups (Chicano/a or Hispanic) from Mexico, South and Central America, and Spain are the largest minority group and the fastest-growing population. African Americans (Blacks) and Asian Americans—including Native Hawaiians and Pacific Islanders—are a third significant minority, along with other groups from the Philippines, China, India, Vietnam, South Korea, and Japan.[3] In addition, people continue to immigrate to the United States from many other countries. The U.S. population is not only diverse but also constantly changing.

People come to the United States for many reasons. Many Africans were brought here as part of the slave trade to work primarily in the South. Some English and European groups were also relocated here against their will because of England's policy of emptying prisons by loading individuals (men, women, babies, and children) onto ships that took them across the Atlantic Ocean to serve as indentured workers for the colonists. Other individuals,

then and later, came to escape political oppression, to seek religious freedom, or to seek a better life. American Indians, Alaskan natives, and Native People of Hawaii, who already lived in regions that we call the United States, were forced to leave their lands and move to other inhospitable regions of the country.

Because the United States has more diversity than any other country, many attempts have been made to describe it. A common metaphor, the country as a *melting pot*, discredits the importance of individual cultures. This description assumes that everyone should be just "American." In fact, many immigrants or Native Americans choose not to teach their children their native language and ancestral ways to protect them from discrimination. Of course, people who try to explain what American culture is soon realize that no matter how long a person's family has been in the United States (or even if the person's family was native to this land), the person's culture is unique to the part of the country he or she lives in and his or her family ancestry, economics, religion, and many other influences. You are part of a country in which each person needs to examine the different cultures of others and have tolerance for them.

WRITING PROMPT

Cultural conflicts can arise due to negative or inaccurate stereotyping of gender, age, ethnicity, physical ability, religion, and sexual orientation. Do you think any of these is more damaging than another? Why or why not? Is there another form of stereotyping you would add to this list?

▶ The response entered here will appear in the performance dashboard and can be viewed by your instructor.

Submit

3.3: Communication Among Diverse People

3.3 **Analyze the discrimination that occurs due to factors like age, ethnicity, gender**

Cultural groups have preferred names for themselves; however, because group members are individuals, they do not always agree with one another. Cultural groups name and rename themselves to solidify their own group identity and to keep nonmembers at a distance. As a nonmember of a cultural group, you should be aware of the names that group members prefer to be called. You can become familiar with the group's preferred names by listening to news reports and people around you.

During the last few decades, the U.S. Census Bureau and the thousands of unnamed writers of surveys and applications that ask for ethnic/racial/national identity have made assumptions that have not always been in sync with the groups themselves. The primary choice for people who were not members of minority groups was *Caucasian.* This term emerged during early anthropology research. The classifications of race based on those physiological criteria have since been found to be erroneous. For some the term has connotations of racism because the criteria showed the superiority of those who had light skin and features of Europeans and English. Recently the labels *White non-Hispanic* or *Euro-American* have become part of the choices in self-report documents.

The words that cultural groups use to describe themselves are important. Not using the preferred name is insensitive. Name-calling and racial slurs encourage discrimination, perpetuate negative stereotypes, and lead to verbal and sometimes physical conflict. Sensitivity to currently accepted group names promotes positive communication and provides insights into others' perspectives.

Among some indigenous people in the far U.S. West, *Native American* is the preferred name. Ironically, the term originated in the U.S. Census Bureau. Native American people in the South and East and in the near West prefer *American Indian.* Different names that are more inclusive on the census include Native People of Hawaii and Alaskan Natives, and those in U.S. non-state possessions. The indigenous people object to the use of the word *tribe* and prefer *nation.* The use of the name of the nation (e.g., Creek, Osage, Apache, Sioux, and others) is always correct for any Native Person.

No single name can refer to people who are from Mexico, Spain, Latin America, Central America, or South America. In the early 1990s, as the population of this group of people began to grow, and research was revealing the influence that they would have on the United States, a strong movement began calling for all in this umbrella group to use one term—*Latino/a.* One of the leaders of the movement went to the University of New Mexico at Albuquerque. He spoke to over 400 students. As he made his argument that one term should be used by all, the Hispanics as a group got up and left. They were highly insulted by his proposal.

Things have changed. And, although most populations formerly called Hispanic are now known as Latino (male) and Latina (female), there are many variations and subtleties based on specific histories and preferences:

- The Hispanics of New Mexico, who trace their ancestry to the Spanish explorers of the 1500s and 1600s, do call themselves *Hispanic* because their roots are in Spain.
- A large group of Latinos/Latinas in California is determined not to be called *Chicano* (male) or *Chicana* (female), although some Mexican Americans in the West use those terms.

- From time to time, Hispanics in the East have identified themselves as *Hispanic Euro-Americans.*
- Migrant workers who have lived in some Midwest areas for generations use the term *Latino/a.*

More recently researchers and the media have been referring to diversity with more encompassing phrases, such as *people of color* or *minorities.* The word *minorities* has become inappropriate for some people because it seems to imply that members of minority groups are less worthy or capable than people with European ancestry. *Black* took the place of *Negro* and *Colored* during the civil rights movement in the 1960s, although some older Blacks continued to use those last two terms. By the late spring of 1991, however, *African American* as a term was being used more than *Black.* On May 13, 1994, the *Chicago Tribune* reported that in a speech the Black poet Gwendolyn Brooks urged her fellow Black people not to use *African American.* She exhorted them to emphasize their Blackness by using the word *Black;* she held that opinion throughout her life. Today, both terms are used; the differences in use appear to be more regional, revealing the preferences of urban and rural communities.

Four terms used to describe **cultural communication** are based on specific interactions.

Cultural Communication Interactions

Remove card   1 of 4   Reset Deck

Please note that some people do not prefer the term *race*[4] and others do.[5] We use many criteria to identify ourselves or others as members of a cultural group—for example, gender, age, and ethnicity. What are the meanings of these labels, and what are some of the critical issues that they raise among group members and with others?

3.3.1: Gender

Each society—indeed, individuals within every society— view and value the roles of men and women in different ways. *Gender* usually refers to social roles; *sex* generally refers to physicality that distinguishes between men and women. Conflict occurs when cultural groups' interactions collide with other perceptions.

For centuries in Western European societies, women were considered to be chattel or property. Immigrants from these countries brought their ideas to the United States. Even after laws changed their roles, both in England and in the United States, women were not permitted to own property, to vote, to sell property, or to retain custody of children if they sought a divorce. The women's male relatives—father, brother, husband, or nearest male relative—became the owners of their possessions and had the right by law to beat them and physically force them to do the will of the males. Until the late 1980s, the state of Oklahoma still required that the "head of the household" be a male. Women were not allowed to serve on juries, and so on. By contrast, among some Native American nations prior to White contact, women were honored to the extent that the colonizers were incensed and outraged by the unacceptable role of women. The colonists were angry and threatened by women who served on Indian councils, rode to war, and were honored as a source of the continuation of the Nation and the culture.

In recent times, U.S. researchers have found that gender influenced the success of women in business and education. In education, gender is one of the primary factors in students' preferences for faculty appearance, behavior, and personality in the classroom. As a result of such differences in role expectations, women are often perceived as poor managers or teachers if they do not display expected female role behavior, which includes smiling, friendliness, hospitality, and nurturing.

Laube, Massoni, Sprague, and Ferber (2007) researched the role of gender in student evaluations in universities. Student evaluations are anonymous; professors do not

People can experience discrimination due to many factors (age, ethnicity, gender, physical differences), but your success in business and professional communication depends on your being able to recognize each person for his or her individual capabilities and not for external differences.

know the identity of students who complete them. These evaluations carry a great deal of weight in university decisions on merit raises, retention, promotion, and tenure for a professor who is on a tenure track. Research revealed gender bias that the quantitative portion of the student evaluations did not capture. Qualitative analysis of responses to open-ended questions revealed bias against women professors.[6]

An outcome of these perceptions is the phenomenon described as the **glass ceiling**—a barrier that is not visible but is real enough to keep women from top-management positions in many businesses, professions, and education. Some have suggested that the glass ceiling was broken by the House Speaker Pelosi and Secretary of State Hillary Clinton; we suggest that the ceiling may be cracked, but it has not disappeared.

Prejudicial language conveys negative cultural assumptions about people, which can then lead to other types of discrimination. For example, in older books the words *mankind* or *man* were used to mean all persons. Examine this sentence: "A person is entitled to a second opinion; he should see another doctor." If the person in question is a woman, the speaker or writer is excluding her.

Sexual harassment is an issue that women and men face daily. **Sexual harassment** in the workplace includes (1) inappropriate demands made on an employee by a fellow worker or supervisor and (2) the development of uncomfortable and unprofessional work environments. Behaviors that make a work environment uncomfortable include but are not limited to name-calling, touching, making rude remarks, joking, making overt sexual requests, and using innuendo. Name-calling is a prejudicial use of language. It maintains stereotypes that are hurtful to men and women. Offices of the U.S. Equal Employment Opportunity Commission (EEOC) have federal guidelines that clarify issues that include topics ranging from inappropriate behavior to types of posters in the workplace.

Another issue is differences in communication styles between men and women. The two main arguments supporting the theory are (1) women/men are socialized to communicate and behave differently and (2) women/men communicate and behave differently from one another not just because of socialization but also because of hormonal and other physiological reasons. In the 1960s and early 1970s, this theory was fiercely denied by some members of the Feminist Movement. However, as the debate has continued, new research in medicine and the social sciences has fueled new arguments. Regardless of causation, many men and women believe that the other gender has problems communicating, and many are quite vocal about communication conflicts between genders.

WRITING PROMPT

Daria is a new mother of a child who has special needs. To help meet her demands at home, Daria asked her supervisor, who is the owner of the accounting firm, if she could cut back to an 80 percent schedule. The firm agreed to the schedule change with prorated salary and benefits. The arrangement seemed like the perfect solution, until Daria's coworkers began making remarks about her shorter work hours; a male manager of strategic planning did not include her on the yearly planning retreat; and she was not listed in rotation for presentations to new clients. Others began to complain that the quality of her work had slipped.

Think about this conflict from the points of view of the parties involved: the business owner, Daria, and her coworkers. In what ways might this situation be problematic for each, and what solutions would you suggest?

 The response entered here will appear in the performance dashboard and can be viewed by your instructor.

Submit

3.3.2: Age

During the economic crisis of 2009, competition for jobs became even more acute. Older men and women were willing to work any job, even ones paying minimum wage. This in turn affected college-age and high school students working to pay for education expenses because they had to compete for the same jobs as older workers.

Many schools limit the number of older applicants who are allowed to enter, although the age requirement has been changed to accommodate older students applying for medical school. Airline companies and certain food-service companies have used age and body size and shape as criteria for firing. Some court cases were decided in favor of people who were discriminated against due to age, and they were able to keep their jobs. However, our society's general bias toward youth is side by side with continuing negative beliefs about older workers; and all of this contributes to the real problem of ageism in the workplace.

People of any age can experience age discrimination (ageism). Organizations may think that an employee is too old, too young, or unsuitable because he or she is middle-aged. Certain national accounting firms have shown a bias against married middle-aged men or women for jobs that require travel, anticipating that the employee will not focus on the job. All branches of the military have maximum-age ceilings, although since the military conflicts in Afghanistan and Iraq, the age limits have been raised to allow older men and women to serve. The chances for middle-aged Americans of any ethnic group to find new jobs decrease with every year of age.

What is EEO? What is Affirmative Action?

Anyone born after 1964 has grown up with governmental protection from discrimination in educational, governmental, and private work sites. The 50th anniversary of the game-changing 1964 Civil Rights Act was celebrated in 2014.

In 1961, then-President John F. Kennedy made an executive order that created the Committee on Equal Employment Opportunity (EEO), an agency that used federal funds to make sure hiring and employment practices were free of racial bias. After the assassination of President Kennedy in November 1963, the newly sworn-in President Lyndon Johnson made civil rights, including Kennedy's plan for equity in the workplace, his primary goal. In the traumatic aftermath of the assassination, the Office of the President and the legislative branches of the U.S. government worked together to pass the Civil Rights Bill. Since that time, the courts have been adjudicating details, refinements, and changes.

Equal Employment Opportunity is defined by the U.S. Department of Labor as follows:

ⓧ **Definition**

Equal Employment Opportunity laws prohibit specific types of job discrimination in certain workplaces. The Department of Labor has two agencies which deal with EEO monitoring and enforcement, the Civil Rights Center and the Office of Federal Contract Compliance Programs.

- Civil Rights Center, part of the Office of Assistant Secretary for Administration and Management, oversees EEO in programs and activities receiving federal financial assistance. CRC also assures equal opportunity for all applicants to and employees of DOL.
- The Office of Federal Contract Compliance Programs oversees employers holding federal contracts and subcontracts.

Affirmative Action is defined by the U.S. Department of Labor as follows:

ⓧ **Definition**

For federal contractors and subcontractors, affirmative action must be taken by covered employers to recruit and advance qualified minorities, women, persons with disabilities, and covered veterans. Affirmative actions include training programs, outreach efforts, and other positive steps. These procedures should be incorporated into the company's written personnel policies. Employers with written affirmative action programs must implement them, keep them on file and update them annually.

Federal Legislation Supporting Fair Employment Practices ❭

Title VII of the Civil Act 1964	The Philadelp President Ric Nixon guaran
President Johnson's Executive Order Enforcing Affirmative Action 1965	
Equal Pay Act	Age Discrimination ir Employment Act (AD 1967

1960   1970

Most of you have lived under the protection of federal legislation that protects your employment. However, there were protests in 1964 against the first rulings and subsequent additions to the laws. Challenges to limit the scope and practices of Affirmative Action and the efficacy of the U.S. EEO Commission (EEOC), which is responsible for enforcing the laws in education, business, and industry, began in 1969 and continue through the present. Many of these challenges are based on individual perspectives about the role of government.

http://www.dol.gov/dol/topic/discrimination/index.html
http://www.eeoc.gov/policy/compliance.html
http://www.civilrights.org/resources/civilrights101/affirmaction.html
http://www.infoplease.com/spot/affirmative1.html

WRITING PROMPT

Your boss has asked you to interview a prospective new hire for a job you know requires a lot of evening overtime. During the interview, the applicant reveals that she has five young children. You know your boss is not aware of this information. Do you tell your boss what you learned? Why or why not?

 `The response entered here will appear in the performance dashboard and can be viewed by your instructor.`

Submit

3.3.3: Ethnicity

Ethnic issues are broad and pervasive because they are dynamic, multilayered, and affected by social changes. Ethnicity arises from a variety of sources that include but are not limited to the following:

• People were born in a country other than the one in which they are living (for example, political refugees from Cuba).

• They are living in another country temporarily (a Nigerian living in Sweden for two years while working as a consultant).

• They identify themselves with the region from which their ancestors originally came (African Americans).

• They have physical abilities or characteristics different from those of many of the people with whom they work (color of skin or body type).

In some states with large Native American populations, the history of conflict between European Americans and Indians is such that people who identify themselves as Native Americans are perceived as incompetent and unreliable. However, in states with few Indians and without a recent history of conflict, American Indians may be treated no differently than any other group. Ironically, when a member of the Osage Nation visited a state with a low Indian population to consult with another professor on a research study, a stranger approached him in a restaurant and (we assume because he had long hair and dark skin) asked, "Are you an Indian?" He replied, "Yes, Ma'am." Her response in a louder, incredulous tone was, "A *REAL* Indian?" Without laughing or looking shocked, he again answered, "Yes, Ma'am." Beyond the almost humorous telling of this encounter, we see a stranger who seemed to think that because another stranger was different from her she had the right to speak to him and ask intrusive personal questions.

Prejudice against certain ethnic groups also increases and decreases in response to public events. People of Arab heritage have been treated with considerable suspicion in the United States since the 9/11 attacks, in which nineteen terrorists—all Middle Eastern men—hijacked planes and crashed them into the World Trade Center, the Pentagon, and a field in rural Pennsylvania in 2001. The resulting wars in Afghanistan and Iraq have led to increased security measures. Some fear the new restrictions violate the civil liberties of U.S. citizens and visitors from other countries. Others believe that the new rules are necessary for our safety.

At other times in our history, U.S. citizens who had roots in other countries were treated with suspicion. The first Chinese men were brought to the United States to build railroads and were later deported; Chinese women were not allowed to come to avoid a new generation of Chinese people born in the United States. Discrimination continued against the Chinese then and continues in more subtle fashion today. The word *Oriental* was used indiscriminately for all Asian people (Chinese, Japanese, Korean, etc.), but none of these groups wants to be called *Oriental*.

During World War I, the large German American population suffered from association with Germany. Soon after the 1942 Japanese attack on Pearl Harbor in Hawaii, which touched off U.S. participation in World War II, Japanese American families on the West Coast were forced into internment camps and not released until after the war, some immediately and some more than two years later because the families had nowhere to go. German and Italian Americans were also treated with distrust, but they were not imprisoned. The Korean War in the early 1950s and the extended U.S. military involvement in Vietnam in the 1960s and 1970s increased ethnic bias against Vietnamese and Korean Americans during and after the wars.

Ethnicity is a fact of life in the workplace today because business is global. Some U.S. companies have plants in other countries; some businesses from other countries have plants in the United States. Since the Fair Trade Act of 2011, the amount of imported goods has increased greatly. The controversy over products that are made in the United States has created more conflict based in ethnicity or nationality. During the recession that began in 2009, for example, the automobile industry experienced thousands of layoffs, and many jobs were eliminated. The industry received various financial stimuli from the government, money that will be repaid in taxes. The millions of lost jobs became an ideological and pragmatic problem, as jobs were exported to foreign plants owned by the U.S. automakers to take advantage of lower labor costs. Consumer and legislative demands for fuel-efficient cars was a contributing factor.

WRITING PROMPT

In the first years of President Obama's presidency, polls and media (and possibly your family and friends) discussed this topic: Did some attitudes expressed by politicians and others in the public eye appear to be tinged by racism? What do you think? Was some of the opposition in to Obama's initiatives (health care as the prime example) racially motivated in some, all, or no cases? Why or why not?

▶ The response entered here will appear in the performance dashboard and can be viewed by your instructor.

Submit

3.3.4: Physical Abilities and Appearance

Humans have many different physical characteristics. Cultural groups show their preference for particular physical features through rewards and punishments (sanctions). They decide (1) what an acceptable body type is for men and women, (2) what facial features are attractive or unattractive, and (3) what physical skills are essential for a person to be considered a productive member of society. People learn to accept individuals who are able to work or play with the same physical skills that the society honors and to shun those who are not.

Depending on the society and an individual's social status, people may discriminate against those who do not have the physical attributes of the more powerful culture: height, weight, health, hair color, skin color, facial features, and so on. Some societies may consider people less capable in all ways if they have physical limitations or different physical appearances.

While some societies consider thinness to be a sign of low status and poverty, U.S. culture imposes the image of thinness as the ideal body type for women and men. It is also the trigger for many young men and women to develop eating disorders that can threaten their lives. Older men and women have the potential to hurt their bodies through yo-yo diets and poor nutrition in general. Standards of beauty based on fitness are a good example of the shifting perspective of acceptable body types.

The American with Disabilities Act of 1991 and many court cases have provided help for those whose disabilities could potentially keep them out of the job market. Some of the many court cases were about perceived barriers to career advancement rather than complaints about work sites. The researchers found that most complaints were from White men. People with mental limitations were most often discriminated against in seeking a job, advancing, and retaining a job.[7]

Each person at this conference table shares in organizational goals, but because of diversity, they will have different ways of presenting ideas, revealing their contributions, and working cooperatively. Difference can mean richer communication.

SOURCE: Dean Drobot/Shutterstock

WRITING PROMPT

In a doctor's office, the medical files from previous years are on the top shelf, which the former employee (who was six feet tall) could reach with ease. You are a new employee who is four feet eleven inches tall. What will you do if your first request for changing the location of the files is not answered? How would you best make your case?

▶ The response entered here will appear in the performance dashboard and can be viewed by your instructor.

Submit

3.3.5: Religious Affiliation

Although the Constitution guarantees the right of Americans to worship as they choose, work weeks and holidays in business, government, and educational organizations in the United States reflect the assumption that the mainstream population is Christian. In business, the professions, and educational organizations, the calendar following the Christian beliefs can have unfortunate consequences for employees who have other faiths.

Muslims, whose religious practices require several times of prayer a day, often find that organizations are not sympathetic to their needs. Only recently have concessions been made to accommodate people whose holy days, days of worship, and dietary requirements are different from those of Christians. Planners of a cultural seminar for new international teaching assistants at a major university provided food vouchers at the university cafeteria. The planners were chagrined to discover that neither vegetarian nor kosher meals could be obtained with the vouchers. Universities have begun to send reminders to faculty about the holy days of Muslims and Jews and other religious organizations.

Honoring Religious Practices

Ethical Issues

Many religions have holy days or practices that can conflict with a person's duties at his or her place of work. Many Christians observe Lent, a forty-day period that may consist of fasting and other penitential practices that can affect daily life.

(x) Read more

Among Muslims (or people who practice Islam), it is customary to recite the *salat* prayer five times a day while facing Mecca, the site of the sacred Ka`aba shrine. Prayers are said at dawn, noon, mid-afternoon, sunset, and nightfall, thus determining the rhythm of the entire day. Although it is preferable to worship together in a mosque, Muslims may pray almost anywhere, such as in fields, offices, factories, and universities. Similarly, for many Jews, keeping the Sabbath (or *Shabbat*) holy is a central tenet of faith. The Sabbath is the seventh day of the week, beginning around sunset Friday night and ending around nightfall Saturday night. It is a time to rest the soul and spirit, a time to rejuvenate, and a time to study the Torah. Since activities such as cooking and driving a car are forbidden on the Sabbath, observant Jews must arrive home and finish preparations before sunset. In the winter sunset comes early, so Sabbath observers have to leave work early. They arrange with their management to make up the time by working extra hours other days or by coming in early on Friday to make up for leaving early.

Now, consider the following scenario:

The Independent Student Senate (ISS) meets on Friday afternoons at Ocean State University. The campus has a history of uninterested students and of faculty who rarely meet with their students. After several months of negotiation, both students and faculty are determined to solve this problem. Because of busy schedules, the only time that both groups are willing and able to meet is after the senate meetings on Fridays. For four Fridays, they plan to meet from 5:00 P.M. to 9:00 P.M. Joseph Stein, student president of the ISS, has led the way toward this important breakthrough between students and faculty, but he has listened to the discussion of meeting times with growing dismay. His Sabbath begins at sunset on Fridays, and he is not permitted to work.
What should Joseph do?

3.3.6: Sexual Orientation

A frequently debated topic in local, state, and the federal government is the right of individuals to live and work openly in accordance with their sexual orientation. An outcome of this debate is a challenge to mainstream traditions and definitions of family, spouses, work benefits, and living styles. States and cities are considering the rights of same-sex marriage or life partners who choose not to marry. The implications for changes in health and retirement benefits are multiple. Since 1996, some states have presented bills for approval of same-sex marriage, and some have discussed bills that have excluded gay marriage. In 2008, California approved same-sex marriages. In 2009, the law was repealed but the courts ruled that those who married under the protection of the law were legally married and would remain so until the participants decided to dissolve the marriage. People in business and professions may choose not to disclose their sexual identity, while others choose to live openly. Still others in certain organizations have been compelled to not reveal their orientation. The "Don't Ask, Don't Tell" policy of the U.S. military, which required members to be silent about the sexual orientation, was repealed in 2011. In June 2015, the Supreme Court ruled that marriage equality was a right guaranteed by the U.S. Constitution.

In the workplace, people who are gay, lesbian, bisexual, or transgender may keep their sexual orientation private either because of direct risk or simply because they do not want to deal with both subtle and the openly expressed negative remarks and behaviors of others. At this time, the federal government does not consider sexual orientation to fall under Affirmative Action protection. However, many companies now do offer benefits to same-sex partners of employees.

Your new personnel manager has petitioned for health benefits for her same-sex life partner. As the company owner, specifically how do you go about addressing her request?

▶ The response entered here will appear in the performance dashboard and can be viewed by your instructor.

Submit

3.4: Understand Your Perspectives

3.4 Explain how conflict occurs because of differences in cultural expectations

The three steps mentioned at the beginning of this chapter to improve cultural communication are to (1) understand your own cultural perspectives by being self-reflexive; (2) develop tolerance and appreciation for the cultural perspectives of others; and (3) achieve positive outcomes from conflict caused by diversity. How can you reach the first goal of understanding your own cultural perspectives?

You are who you are because of where you were born, to whom you were born, and the attitudes, beliefs, and values with which you were raised. You are unique. You could find a person your age who practices the same religion, is of the same gender, and so on, who would be very much like you in many ways but would still have different behaviors and attitudes.

Your perspectives about life are based on your culture, but those perspectives are affected by the thousands of experiences of your daily life. Your **attitudes** (learned likes and dislikes), **beliefs** (judgments about right and wrong), and **values** (deep cultural assumptions that affect all areas of life) form your perspectives, patterns of language, and behavior. These communication patterns constitute language culture and are both verbal and nonverbal.

Language culture is the means by which we represent ourselves and the means by which we interpret others. Language culture includes the spoken word, written word, and body movements. At home you reveal your culture through architectural styles, furniture placement, signs on walls, and color schemes.[8] Language culture can foster positive feelings, but it can promote negativity or conflict as well. For instance, handwritten signs in the lobby of a free public health clinic for American Indians warned that patients who miss their appointment times will not be allowed to receive health care. Through language culture, the signs promoted an adversarial climate that is not usually found in private health-care clinics.[9]

Your language culture and that of others are the means by which culture comes into being and changes. Language

culture reveals what you think about yourself and your world. Analysis of your language and the language of others can give you insight into your own perspectives and the perspectives of others.

Analysis reveals that certain issues between culturally different people become "sites of conflict."[10] These sites are cultural dilemmas that occur again and again. The reasons for continued, repeated, and negative conflict can often be related to the societal role that a person believes he or she plays in an organization. For instance, an African American woman who is a middle-level manager may see herself as a productive and professional member in the workplace, but another person may perceive her as an example of a successful placement through affirmative action efforts. The two perspectives can lead to conflict.

In business and professional settings, your work standards, expectations of the use of time, relationships, status, and verbal and nonverbal behaviors reflect your cultural training. Conflicts occur because your colleagues have different cultural expectations.

3.5: Personality Traits and Competence

3.5 Examine how differences in personality traits influence competence in communication

When you experience cultural conflict because others do not share your perspectives, certain personality traits can help you be an effective intercultural communicator.[11] We all have traits such as flexibility and tolerance for ambiguity in varying degrees. These traits help us deal with cultural differences, and if we cultivate them, we can improve our communication competence.

3.5.1: Flexibility

The ability to tolerate change and the willingness to compromise are necessary when you are working with someone who is culturally different. Even if differences outnumber similarities, your goal should be to find specific areas in which you can "give" without endangering your primary goals. While it is not appropriate for you to always adopt the other's point of view or culture, you may be able to create a positive climate through your self-knowledge and your increased flexibility.

3.5.2: Ability to Tolerate Ambiguity

Most people feel more comfortable knowing what to expect from a supervisor, a parent, a friend, or a social situation. When you are not in your own social group—when you will be interacting with persons from Brazil, for example—you may not know how familiar your companions' accents will be or how different their nonverbal communication will be from yours. Ambiguity in such instances makes some people uncomfortable.

In traditional U.S. bureaucracies, employees are accustomed to having a list of job duties. If a new supervisor from another country uses an ambiguous management strategy, what should employees do? They might give themselves time to get used to the new style of management. Or, if they find the new level of ambiguity intolerable, they might choose to discuss the issue with the supervisor. In either case, they will be handling intercultural conflict in a positive fashion.

WRITING PROMPT

Having spent your career working in a manufacturing company, you join a state bureaucracy and receive your first assignment. You will be working with a group to change the organizational structure to improve productivity and communication. You acquired some knowledge about this not-for-profit organization and its history before you took the job, but you are by no means an expert, and your peers and subordinates are resentful of the many changes taking place. Your supervisor has yet to provide information on the project's timetable, funding, or criteria for evaluating the final results. At this point, how do you handle this level of ambiguity? Where do you start?

> ```
> The response entered here will appear in the
> performance dashboard and can be viewed by
> your instructor.
> ```

Submit

3.5.3: Nonjudgmental Attitudes

One of the difficulties in communication is the tendency to pass judgment on the behavior of others. That which is familiar and taken-for-granted is perceived as "good," and the unfamiliar is deemed "bad." Withholding, delaying, and tempering judgmental responses are ways to deal with this often involuntary negative reflex. While it may not be possible to avoid having an emotional response to a given cultural conflict, in order to be professional in the workplace, you must be able to control your behavior and language.

3.5.4: Respect for Self and Others

At the foundation of any work environment and work relationship is the respect for individuals that the organizational culture fosters and that you bring as part of your personal culture. Respect is embodied in the belief that others have the right (1) to opinions that differ from yours, (2) to behave in ways that you may find confusing or wrong, (3) to not to be ridiculed, and (4) to feel confident that they will be treated fairly.

Sometimes it is simply a matter of learning a bit more about cultures and differences and not assuming that what works for you will work for them.

Cultural Facts

Strategic Skills

The following facts about various cultures suggest that knowledge of facts about others can help in international communication. First, discuss the impact on your communication if you knew this fact before you communicated with a member of that culture; second, discuss the impact if you did not know this fact before you communicated.

 Japanese Culture:

Japanese businesspeople rarely invite foreign business colleagues to their home to meet their family. Business and private life remain separate in Japan.

 American Indian Cultures:

Some traditional Plains Indians, such as the Kiowas and Apaches, do not touch each other casually. They are offended if people, particularly non-Indians, touch them during conversation.

 Arab Cultures:

Members of many Arab cultures have a different sense of personal space than do people in the United States. Arabs stand very close to the person to whom they are talking. Americans require a greater distance between themselves and others.

 Physical Differences:

People who are physically different do not wish to have people help them without asking. Although you might perceive that a person in a wheelchair needs help, do not touch that person or his or her chair or possessions. Ask whether your help is needed, and then do what is requested.

 Elder Population:

Age does not necessarily make people incompetent or out of touch. Automatically speaking louder, using a condescending tone, and assuming that elders will be incompetent in a social gathering are inappropriate behaviors. Do not make assumptions about a person's abilities or interests based on his or her age.

 Religious Affiliation:

Unsolicited inquiries about coworkers' religious practices ("Where do you eat after church on Sunday?") reveal ethnocentric perspectives. You risk making inaccurate assumptions that the person goes to church, goes to a religious service that is held on Sunday morning, and follows the custom of eating out afterward.

(✗) **Sexual Orientation:**

Assuming that all people have the same sexual orientation can result in embarrassing situations. Don't automatically ask a new employee if his wife or her husband likes the new town. Don't assume that workers in a specific career field have a particular sexual orientation.

3.5.5: Ability to Analyze

Often your own ways of behaving and speaking are unconscious. Unless you are working on becoming self-reflexive—that is, unless you try to examine your own behavior and language culture as it unfolds—you may find it difficult to be flexible during intercultural interactions.

The first of the three steps to succeed in a diverse workplace is to analyze your own cultural perspectives. Write brief descriptions of the items listed in the Cultural Analysis Inventory (CAI) in the Strategic Skills journal.[12] This activity will give you insights into your "taken-for-granted" ways of thinking or "everyone-knows-to-do-this" ways of behaving.

Cultural Analysis Inventory

Strategic Skills

For each topic, there are two or more questions. Write brief responses to each. After you are finished, your instructor may wish to discuss your responses as a class, or you may decide to share them in small groups.

1. **Weddings**
   a. Of what importance are weddings in your world?
   b. What does your family do for weddings?
2. **Meals**
   a. Are family meals a part of celebrations in your world? If "yes," go to b. If "no," go to c.
   b. If so, who cooks? Cleans? Acts as the person in charge?
   c. If family meals are not a part of your family life, what role does food play in your family?
3. **Death**
   a. Describe your family practices when a death occurs in the immediate family.
   b. What is your role in these practices?
4. **Ethnicity**
   a. How would your family describe itself ethnically?
   b. What practices, beliefs, food, activities, etc., define your family's ethnicity?
   c. Do you identify your ethnicity in the same way as your family?
5. **Family**
   a. When you describe your family, who is included?
   b. If a relative asks to borrow money, how close does the relative have to be for you to consider granting the request?

The Social Perspectives Explanation Form (SPEF)[13] in the Strategic Skills journal may help you discuss the "why" for your interpretations of how people are, what they are, and who they should be. Most people tend to find either logical and reasonable justifications for their individual behaviors or blame someone else for unreasonable, biased behavior. Your explanations for the events described in the SPEF can give you clues about your perspectives.

WRITING PROMPT

Imagine this scenario: You have never traveled more than 200 miles from your Midwestern home. You attended a local state university, and your work experience has been at one locally owned firm. Your excellent work came to the attention of a recruiter. Within a month, you are living outside Madrid, Spain, making a large salary, battling traffic for two hours each day, working with people from all over the world, and learning how to live in a large urban setting. Ethnocentrism, or experiencing other cultures through a lens colored by one's own cultural experiences, is not uncommon, and you find yourself struggling with feelings of loss despite the fact that you really want this career opportunity. What strategies or actions can help you handle these conflicting feelings constructively?

▶ The response entered here will appear in the performance dashboard and can be viewed by your instructor.

Submit

Social Perspectives Explanation Forms

Strategic Skills

Each statement is followed by a question or an instruction. Write your response. There are no right or wrong answers, but you can interpret your answers when you are done.

1. The surgeon was not able to save the little boy. Make up a name—including first and last names—for the doctor.

   (✗) **Interpretation**

   The name given the surgeon reveals the gender of the physician.

2. Benjamin was waiting for a bus with several others in a large, unfriendly city. Two strangers spoke to Benjamin and offered to help him, and one person actually put

hands on Benjamin and on his possessions without his permission. Why did this happen?

⊗ Interpretation

Benjamin could have any type of physical difference that was visible to others.

3. Lou Jane is a quiet person with long black hair and dark skin. She is an environmentalist; she respects the land and its people. She protested against the celebration of Columbus's supposed discovery of America. She protested with her whole family against the use of the word *Braves* for the Atlanta baseball team. Identify her ethnicity.

⊗ Interpretation

Lou Jane is probably Native American, but she could belong to any ethnic group.

4. The Jones family has three teenage children—one girl (Mindy) and two boys (Joe and George). They are required to do the family chores. List the basic household chores, and assign them to each child.

⊗ Interpretation

The assigning of tasks reveals expectations of gender behavior.

5. Mary had a severe asthma attack. She took a public bus to the hospital—one that she had been to many times for the same problem. The attending physician was friendly and helpful. Mary was a partner in her health care because she was knowledgeable about her own health. The physician was eager to get Mary's medical file. When it came, the physician read it and immediately started speaking to Mary in a louder and higher-pitched voice, using simple words as if speaking to a child. The physician started over explaining the decisions that were being made, refusing to continue treatment until Mary's husband or parents were in the hospital. What information in the file prompted the physician to change the way in which Mary was treated?

⊗ Interpretation

Mary (in real life) was legally blind, but the physician could have had the same response to any physical or mental difference that was noted in Mary's file.

Interpretation: The key to processing the SPEF is that the answers are somewhat predictable. Discuss the predictable responses, and understand why they are predictable. Discuss different responses, and attempt to understand their implications: (1) The name given the surgeon reveals the gender of the physician. (2) Benjamin could have any type of physical difference that was visible to others.

(3) Lou Jane is probably Native American, but she could belong to any ethnic group. (4) The assigning of tasks reveals expectations of gender behavior. (5) Mary (in real life) was legally blind, but the physician could have had the same response to any physical or mental difference that was noted in Mary's file.

Your working environment and working relationships are both created and maintained by communication. Gaining insights into your cultural perspectives will help you to understand others and to communicate more effectively.

The second step to working successfully with different people or managing a diverse workplace is to know that the perspectives of others may be different from your own. The importance of knowing about other cultures cannot be overstated. Culture is not static but is an ever-changing, dynamic reflection of human interaction. Total knowledge and complete understanding of another culture are impossible, but you can begin by realizing that your colleagues may not see the world exactly as you do. Knowing facts about people who are different can also prepare you for some of their reactions to you or for their behavior toward you.

Cultural facts can be helpful, but they neither guarantee harmony nor prevent conflict. Although you are part of a cultural group, you are also an individual. None of us are cultural clones. Be prepared for the individual differences among, for instance, fellow workers in Japan. Many research studies and books provide specific information on various cultures. Some of them focus on specific business and professional settings, such as *Cross-Cultural Business Behavior: Negotiating, Selling, Sourcing and Managing across Cultures*[14] or *Cases in the Environment of Business: International Perspectives*.[15] Research articles, intercultural communication texts, general-information books, and media reports on cultural facts are readily available at libraries, in bookstores, on television, on DVDs, and in movies. Guard against taking these or other data on specific cultures as absolute; do not allow the information to turn into stereotypes.

3.6: Cultural Conflict

3.6 **Analyze how understanding one's own perspectives and appreciating those of others is important to successful cross-cultural communication**

Just as it is not possible to understand everything about another culture, it is also not possible to eliminate all conflict—even with people who are very similar to you. The third step to working in or managing a diverse workplace is to realize that conflict resulting from diversity can be positive.

3.6.1: Positive Cultural Conflict

Negative effects from diversity occur because participants do not analyze their own language culture or the language culture of others to identify the source of conflict. People select sites of conflict as a result of cultural experiences, expectations, prioritized life decisions, and communication contexts. Certain topics or issues give rise to conflict because they revolve around differing values that are important to one or more communicators, who insist on either discussing the controversial topic or retreating until it is discussed. Unaddressed, sites of conflict create tension that can stop work or hinder relational activity. Furthermore, if both parties fail to identify and discuss the sites, the conflicts often increase in number and intensity.

As conflict continues or new incidents occur, we might mistakenly decide that all interactions with people who are different will be unproductive. We might also conclude that we must solve all cultural differences in order to work well with others. That, however, is not a realistic goal. Specific conflicts can be managed, even if many differences remain unresolved. To manage anxiety successfully, one should have an understanding of oneself and others while using competent communication skills.

The first two steps, understanding your perspectives and appreciating the perspectives of others, are prerequisites for managing the third step, which is acting in ways that render cultural conflict positive. If you are informed about your own perspectives and sensitive to the perspectives of others, you may find these assumptions helpful:

1. Language and behavior may vary among different U.S. cultures; people from other countries may have different language and behavior.

2. Complete knowledge about diverse cultures is not possible.

3. Conflict is likely to result from interaction between unlike people.

4. Workers and managers are generally not willing to change their own behavior, language, attitudes, beliefs, and values just to avoid conflict.

5. Managing conflict is necessary for organizations to continue to function.

If there is agreement on those assumptions, the question is, "Can conflict between culturally diverse people be productive rather than destructive in business and the professions?" The answer is "yes." However, passive communication and less interaction will not result in positive conflict. Sites of conflict must be identified. They are important because they reveal people's pressure points or high-priority agenda items. For conflict to be productive, participants must analyze themselves, events, contexts, and their language cultures in order to identify the sites and what they and others believe about the issues.

For example, when some Native Americans workers complained that they could so the jobs of other construction workers at a project on a reservation, the site of conflict was revealed to be the workers' pride in their professional behavior, their safety record, and their camaraderie, which had developed over time. The men resented the assumption that untrained workers could do their job as well as they did it. The conflict was not with the Native Americans because they were Indians. The conflict was with the Indians' assumption that the workers were not professionals who could do the difficult and dangerous work.[16]

Diversity training is used in many organizations. Some training is effective; other training is less so. In your workplace, you can serve as your own consultant. The following steps are suggestions to help you analyze conflict and potentially turn it into a productive discourse:

1. Examine the topic of the conflict, which has great importance in understanding the perspectives of the other person or group. The topic may be the primary point of the conflict, or it may suggest another, more value-centered problem.

2. Analyze your own contributions. Did you initiate the confrontation, enable (or encourage) others in their conflict, or react to someone else's agenda? Knowing who initiates certain types of encounters can help determine both the "whys" and the sites of conflict.

3. Make notes in a permanent file about the encounter so that over time you can identify patterns of behavior, timing, and relational activity. Use dates, names, and specific references. You may be able to compare this information with other activities, issues, or recurring topics. This file will help you to analyze conflict and language culture in cultural conflict. The analysis can help you to understand others' perspectives. You can adapt your behavior and language culture to mediate the most critical points of controversy. These notes are also invaluable if conflicts go from productive to destructive and lead to court cases or intra-organizational disciplinary hearings about issues such as firing with or without cause, sexual harassment, and unfair work conditions.

4. In some cases you may decide to discuss the conflict with a trusted supervisor, an affirmative action officer, or an employee advocate who attempts to handle

conflict in a non-biased way. Be careful about this step. Confidentiality about interactions is important to ethical behavior.

You are a manager at a manufacturing plant in Alabama. You have lived in Alabama all your life; you are a friendly, non-drinking, church-going person. A group of employees from Italy are working on a term-of-project basis. Before you can invite a junior account-ant to your home, he invites you to his. There you see him giving wine to his ten-year-old son, and you can't say you approve. At the next evaluation meeting, you have the final vote on whether this accountant will be offered a permanent position. What factors should you consider in your decision? Why?

▶ ⌜ **The response entered here will appear in the performance dashboard and can be viewed by your instructor.** ⌟

Submit

3.6.2: The Cultural Communication Conflict Triangle

One way to think of the process of conflict analysis is to compare it to a dynamic triangle in which communication is constantly in flux but reaches intersections of (1) cultural self-knowledge, (2) knowledge about the organizational context, and (3) discourse from the conflict (see Figure 3.1). At one intersection of the triangle are your perspectives and, if you've analyzed your own perspective, some cultural self-knowledge. A valuable tool in productive cultural communication is what you know about your own culture and your assumptions about the ways things should be.

Figure 3.1 The Cultural Communication Conflict Triangle

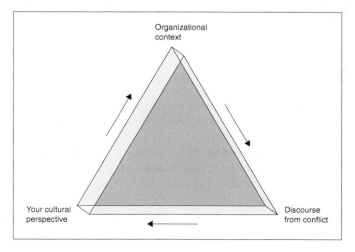

At another intersection of the triangle is the organizational context (for example, the school, the corporation, the accounting firm, the manufacturing plant) in which communication between culturally different people occurs. Types of clothing, modes of behavior, social rules, appropriate language style, nonverbal communication, and topics of conversation are all affected by where and under what circumstances they occur.

At the last intersection is the discourse from the conflict. Your language culture and that of the other person give clues to the perspectives of each. Your ability to communicate effectively is based on your ongoing analysis of yourself and the other person.

The discourse—the talk—that emerges during conflicts should be carefully examined. First, use the triangle by examining the elements in the conflict that are products of your own cultural perspectives. If the conflict is about the timeliness of meetings, consider your attitude toward punctuality. For example, being ten minutes late for the weekly sales meeting may be acceptable if people always just eat doughnuts and drink coffee during the first ten minutes of the meeting.

Second, analyze the organizational context to determine its effects on you, on the other person, and on the conflict. For example, conflict in an insurance company that prides itself on a formal, high-status climate results in low voices, euphemisms instead of plain talk, and an understated description of conflict.

Third, the discourse between people during conflict reveals cultural perspectives and points to the sites of conflict. As an example, a company's Chinese representatives said that they were offended by the lack of respect shown to their company by the joking manner of the U.S. representatives during business meetings. The site of conflict is respect. The fact that the Chinese representatives feel that their organization has been dishonored by less-than-serious behavior provides deep cultural information. Unlike their Chinese counterparts, few U.S. workers would assume that disrespect to their company was more important than disrespect to them personally.

The dynamic qualities of the Cultural Communication Conflict Triangle show that the same conflict can occur over and over. With attention to the language culture, the U.S. representatives may discover that the Chinese are not without humor but are careful to segregate humor from business. Their personal agenda and need for relational activity may not be the focus in a business setting, as they often are for American workers. Chinese culture requires honor to be shown to the organization and attention to be given to the primary task.

In this model, each person is allowed to retain his or her own cultural identity and manage conflict positively by learning from the process. Representatives of the

United States are not required to become Chinese, but their positive response to their Chinese counterparts will promote productive business interactions.

The following example of two women from different cultural backgrounds in the workplace further demonstrates the Cultural Communication Conflict Triangle:

> Yasuko, from Japan, is a manager for a Japanese computer chip company in South Carolina. Margo, her supervisor, is from the South and believes in Southern hospitality. The organizational context is a Japanese computer chip company that hires both American and Japanese employees, who work together in teams. Margo tells Yasuko that she will bring a welcome basket to Yasuko's home on Saturday so that she can see her employee's new apartment. It is obvious that Margo expects to be invited into Yasuko's home.
>
> Yasuko analyzes her cultural reaction—horror and dismay—at the rudeness of the American woman who expects to invade the privacy of her home. Yasuko responds to Margo's offer in a noncommittal way that appears to Margo to be a rejection of her goodwill.
>
> As Yasuko reflects overnight on the embarrassing encounter and recalls hearing other American employees discussing their social gatherings at one another's homes, she realizes that she has offended her supervisor. This example of American informal behavior is confusing to Yasuko, but as she reflects on it, she comes to understand that Margo is not trying to be offensive. Margo is simply applying her "taken-for-granted" cultural perspectives in an inappropriate manner.
>
> Margo may or may not be aware of the reasons behind Yasuko's rejection, especially at first. But if she, too, is analyzing her perspectives, she will come to understand that her manifestation of goodwill is not accepted by all cultural groups.
>
> As both people analyze the discourse from the conflict, they may realize that their individual expectations were based on their different definitions of friendliness, courtesy, and hospitality. When Yasuko examines Margo's language culture, she becomes aware that Margo equates friendliness with personal activity in individual homes. Margo may not understand fully that many Japanese people keep their homes isolated from business acquaintances, but she may conclude that Yasuko doesn't see friendliness in the same way that she does.
>
> This conflict can help both understand that they have different perspectives. Coping and managing this one site of conflict does not mean that either Yasuko or Margo must give up her unique cultural identity. Rather, they may find a neutral way to define friendliness—to share the welcome basket in a park or have a meal together in a restaurant. Such a solution allows for Southern hospitality and maintains Japanese standards of privacy.

The differences between Japanese and American ways are not solved by one positive conflict outcome. Rather, the continual interaction will provide other opportunities to use the Cultural Communication Conflict Triangle as a model to evoke positive outcomes from conflict.

Responses to the Self-Assessment

Strategic Skills

At the beginning of this chapter (section 3.1), we asked you three self-assessment questions about family, work, and cultural practices. Here is a response from someone who is probably very different from you.

She is a woman of the Diné Nation, also known as the Navajo People. She is 48, college-educated, mother to three grown children, and faithful to her culture. She has spent parts of the last four years off the reservation on which she was born and where she stayed until she went to college.

1. In our culture, we define family beyond blood relations. We include people who have in any way lived with us or with whom we have lived as family. We trust anyone who is a family member in this sense, except in very special circumstances.

2. As a woman, I will participate in ceremonies that assure that the spirit of the deceased is no longer tied to the Earth. In order to protect the spirit, traditionally the deceased Diné are burned inside the hogan (a dome-shaped dwelling made up of mud/clay and sometimes twigs, if available). The burning is necessary so that witches do not take the spirit of the person or have power over any of the family. As family members come from many places to grieve, I will help cook and clean for all family members and other Nation's citizens as long as elders or children need me. There are many rituals to cleanse the family and the land.

3. My family always comes first. Regardless of work obligations, I will be with my family for as long as I am needed. Naturally, I would let my boss know that I will be gone an indefinite time. I would not say the name of the person who died nor refer to the family connection. To say the name of the deceased is to call the spirit from peace to, possibly, perpetual disassociation with those living and who have passed.

Strategic Scenario Wrap-Up

Diversity in Business and the Professions

 Strategic Scenario

James Sixkiller is a Cherokee student who has a large extended family. He has lived all of his life in Tahlequah, Oklahoma, a town with a high number of American Indians in the general population. Growing up he attended the local Cherokee schools, then went to a nearby, mid-sized state university. For his junior year, James has transferred to a very large university in a much larger Eastern city. The city and the university's students are primarily White. The populations of the town and university are primarily mainstream with little diversity.

Until this move, James had friends who were Indian and a few who were White. He is bilingual, a fluent English and Cherokee speaker. At the university, some of his courses are in very large lecture halls with over 200 students. This term, James is taking a public speaking class. In addition to learning about the various types of speeches and how to organize them, students are required to make five individual presentations to the class and work with others in an assigned group. James's professor will evaluate his work in front of the other students, and then James's fellow students will critique his speech. Of course, James will then have to publicly critique his peers. The assignment—being critiqued and critiquing others—is culturally appropriate for mainstream U.S. students, but it is contrary to his Cherokee culture. James has become more and more reluctant to participate. He has begun to miss classes. Without intervention of some sort, he will probably drop out of that class.

James Sixkiller is reluctant to participate in the non-Cherokee classroom activities because of his cultural allegiance. Many traditional Indians prefer to maintain a greater amount of personal space between themselves and others. Group work, which is based on close physical proximity and interpersonal skills that aim for positive relational activity, would seem intrusive to many Indians. Yet at college James is experiencing a new cultural situation where expectations are different, and he values the education and degree he will receive.

James, his professor, and his classmates all have obligations in their situation. James may be able to handle his dilemma by talking to his parents and getting their advice. He should, if possible, approach his professor and ask for an appointment to talk about this problem. Eventually, James might be able to talk to an approachable peer who has some understanding of his perspective. Through this work, rather than seeing the class's demands as unreasonable, he may be able to see that they are the mainstream ways of conducting education, and he may be able to survive and thrive in a very different educational context.

WRITING PROMPT

As a peer, what elements of James's predicament resonate with you, and why? Would it make sense for the professor to create alternative assignments for James? Why or why not?

▶ The response entered here will appear in the performance dashboard and can be viewed by your instructor.

Submit

Summary

Diversity in Business and the Professions

- **Diversity** is the state of differences among people.
- **Differences** can be due to gender, age, ethnicity, physical abilities and appearance, religious affiliation, and sexual orientation.
- **Cultural perspectives** are the result of the society in which people are reared and reflect their differences from others.
- Business and the professions should be **representative of the society in which they exist**. As such, they should mirror that society and gain from the strengths that each cultural group brings to the workplace.
- We suggest that you have **three personal goals**:
  - Understand your own perspectives that make you unique
  - Appreciate the perspectives of others
  - Work toward achieving positive outcomes from diversity conflict
- **Personality traits** and associated behaviors that can help you be a successful business communicator

include (1) flexibility, (2) tolerance of ambiguity, (3) nonjudgmental attitudes, and (4) respect for yourself and others.

- **Analysis of language culture** and facts about cultures can help you analyze your own and others' cultural perspectives.

- **Manage conflict** with these steps (1) examine the topics of conflict, (2) analyze your own contributions to the conflict, (3) make notes, and (4) ethically choose an unbiased person with whom you can discuss the conflict with guarantees of confidentiality.

- **The Cultural Communication Conflict Triangle** is a tool that can help you analyze conflict by visualizing the context in which the conflict occurs, the organizational perspective, and the discourse that emerges from the conflict.

- **Analyze discourse associated** with conflict to gain information about the culture of others and to reveal more about your own culture. Insights into the discourse of conflict will give you the tools to produce positive outcomes.

- **To improve intercultural communication competencies** further, remember that no member of one culture has complete knowledge of another culture, but knowledge and analysis can inform people as they move in a positive direction.

- A **successful conflict outcome**, however, does not mean that all differences are or need to be fully understood.

- The **sites of conflict** are likely to recur as they are deemed important to each person.

- **Your strategic goal for positive intercultural interactions in business** can be achieved by utilizing situational knowledge about yourself and others, improving your communication competency, and managing anxiety by your knowledge of diversity and the realization that conflict can be productive.

SHARED WRITING: DIVERSITY IN BUSINESS AND THE PROFESSIONS

Imagine this scenario: It is 1955, and you are an engineer working in a country very different from your own. The people's diet bothers you; you suspect the food is not good for them. One weekday you walk by the local school and see all the children lined up. Officials in special ceremonial outfits are doing something to each child. The children are screaming in pain and are in distress. Others tell you that the children will be disfigured, and that they will be subjected to this pain and disfigurement twice before they are twenty years old. What culture might you, the observer, be visiting? What culture might you be from? What information would help you as an outsider understand this activity?

▶ A minimum number of characters is required to post and earn points. After posting, your response can be viewed by your class and instructor, and you can participate in the class discussion.

| Post | 0 characters | 140 minimum |

Chapter 3 Quiz: Diversity in Business and the Professions

Chapter 4
Listening Skills

∨ Learning Objectives

4.1 Recognize the importance of active listening

4.2 Explain how excellence at work can be demonstrated through effective listening

4.3 Express the importance of active listening

4.4 Analyze how perception determines the level of the listener's attention

4.5 Examine the role of goal setting in active listening in accomplishing your business objective

4.6 Describe the factors that affect a listener's listening capabilities

4.7 Analyze how interactive listening makes a competent communicator

4.8 Express the need to control anxiety for effective communication

4.9 Show how to evaluate success in the strategic interactive listening process

4.10 Review the necessity of being an expert in managing the received information

---

Strategic Scenario: The Intern Observes

Randy is a summer intern working as a nurse's aide at a leading cancer center and hospital. The person to whom Randy reports is the vice president for human resources. Typically, nurse's aides' duties are to answer patients' calls, observe patients' vital signs, clean rooms, and change linens. Randy's assignment, however, is different. Because of his outstanding grades, previous work experience in a physician's office, and strong recommendations, Randy is participating in a unique program that rotates the nurse's aides among senior staff nurses in different departments.

At the end of the internship, he is expected to write an essay about the specific career path he has chosen. Randy must rely on his observations and one-on-one interactions with the hospital staff to help him learn more about his environment.

As you read this chapter, think about the listening challenges that will confront Randy during his internship, and how listening can help him write his essay. At the end of the chapter, we will return to this scenario and discuss some of the best choices.

4.1: Overview

Listening Skills

4.1 **Recognize the importance of active listening**

Listening is the most frequently used communication skill. Researchers have estimated that employees typically spend much of their workday communicating, and a large portion of this time is spent listening to auditory channels.

Because reading email, texts, and online content is visual rather than auditory, yet can fulfill the same function, which is real-time interpersonal transfer of information, people must also develop skills and strategies to "listen to" and respond to written communication.

Most people take auditory listening for granted.[1] Effective listening in interpersonal communication is challenging, in part, because people often are more focused on what they are planning to say next. Effective listening is particularly important if you are attending a presentation or in a meeting. As your time and your employer's time is valuable, the goal is retention of information. You need to learn how to handle internal noise as well as external noise.

Today, our listening ability is particularly susceptible to information overload. We are constantly exposed to sounds—from televisions, radios, peers, professors, supervisors, and others. It is more difficult to filter out and analyze important information than ever before and easier to get distracted and lose concentration.

This chapter incorporates the strategic communication model from the receiver's perspective. Goal setting, situational knowledge, communication competence, and anxiety management are important elements of effective listening. Listening ability, as well as speaking ability, creates a competent communicator.

4.2: Listening in Your Career

4.2 Explain how excellence at work can be demonstrated through effective listening

Many people assume that competence and excellence in a career must be demonstrated through speaking—showing others what the speaker knows and how well she or he can articulate it. In many cases, however, excellence can be demonstrated through effective listening as well. In organizational settings, the managers who are perceived as most competent are those who know their employees well and are sensitive to their ideas and concerns. These managers are also rated as the best listeners in the organization.

Many theories of communication emphasize effective listening. According to research, workers respond to encouragement and are motivated when coworkers and managers carefully listen to their ideas and thoughts. As a future manager or employee, and as a student, developing the ability to listen well will be a vital part of your accomplishments.

4.2.1: Benefits of Good Listening

You may be a full-time student; you may work and carry a full or a reduced load of classes. You may or may not know exactly what field you want to pursue after graduation, but you will find that effective listening is a critical skill in becoming successful. For a student, listening is crucial during presentations such as a professor's lecture or a public speech. For a prospective employee, listening is critical during a job interview. It is also essential to develop listening skills in order to work in the teams that are integral to many companies in diverse career areas.

Many people earn a great deal of their income by listening. Physicians, therapists, and attorneys must listen carefully to patients and clients to provide desired services effectively. Listening can save lives in other jobs: emergency health care, law enforcement, and many others. For example, police officers assigned to work on emergency 911 hotlines use their listening skills to identify and respond to emergencies as they occur. According to an officer in the division of training and education in the Boston Police Department, 911 officers are required to take a forty-hour training course that emphasizes skills such as listening for key information (for example, specific descriptions of people or locations), using silence to calm upset callers, and focusing listening concentration to make up for the lack of visual cues inherent in phone communication. This training yields more and better information—even from highly disturbed callers—and enables officers to use new technology, such as computerized response programs, to supplement their listening skills.[2]

WRITING PROMPT

What situations have you experienced in which a breakdown in listening occurred? Write about an instance in which poor listening may have created major problems for you or someone else. Why and how you think better listening would have helped?

▶ The response entered here will appear in the performance dashboard and can be viewed by your instructor.

Submit

4.2.2: Problems with Ineffective Listening

Trouble arises when a person does not listen carefully to others. Comments such as "You need to pay closer attention to directions," "Concentrate on what you are doing," and "I don't think you understand what I'm saying" are good indications that a person's listening skills can use improvement. Failing to listen effectively can produce some embarrassing moments, such as the time a business traveler sleepily boarded the red-eye flight to Oakland, California (she thought), and landed hours later in Auckland, New Zealand. Faking attention, or **pseudolistening**, can be just as harmful and embarrassing as failing to listen altogether! There are three areas in which poor listening can cause trouble in your career.

POOR LISTENERS ARE PERCEIVED AS LESS INTELLIGENT When other people perceive that someone is not listening carefully, their first reaction is that this person is unable to handle what is being said. This is especially true when poor listening becomes a habit. Others become wary of a poor listener's ability to handle even the simplest amount of information, and the results can be quite negative, as the following example illustrates.

FLORENCE: Why don't we get Zack to join our work group?

FERNANDO: Oh, I don't know. He doesn't seem all that bright. He has to have stuff repeated all the time, and sometimes he doesn't seem plugged in at all.

BUD: I know. He is either slow, or he is uninterested in what other people say. Either way, I would prefer to think of someone else for our team.

FLORENCE: I guess you're right.

POOR LISTENING IS COSTLY One of the greatest costs of ineffective listening is wasted time. For example, if everyone in a five-person shop made one listening-related error per day that cost the shop only $5 in time or material, how costly might this be per week? Five people times $5, times five days, would equal $125 per week. If the labor rate was $10/hour, this would result in 12.5 extra hours of work needed to recover the money lost to poor listening!

POOR LISTENING LIMITS YOUR CHANCES FOR SUCCESS Most people's careers are characterized by steps toward a particular goal. Effective listening is necessary in the journey toward this goal. Promotions, recognition, salary increases, and awards are possible only after employees have demonstrated their competence in critical areas, and performance appraisals are often based on criteria directly related to effective listening abilities. Even now, while you are in school, you can achieve more success by improving your listening skills. Concentrating on what others are saying before you ask a question can prevent you from repeating a question that someone has already asked. Being open to new information allows you to make creative connections while learning.

Many books, professional articles (both online and in print), and in-house training programs provide evidence that emphasis on improved listening leads to success at all levels of a company or organization.

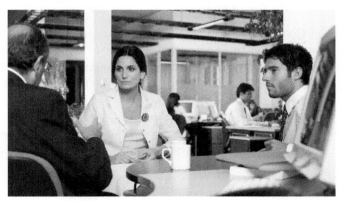

Attentive listening indicates interest in what others communicate.

SOURCE: Image Source Plus/Alamy

4.3: Hearing Versus Listening

4.3 **Express the importance of active listening**

You have been using your sense of hearing longer than you are able to remember. Even before you were born, you heard sounds generated outside your mother's body. Of course, there is a critical difference between the sensory process of hearing and the skill of listening, which we will address in this chapter. **Hearing** is a physiological activity and involuntary process in which sound waves stimulate nerve impulses to the brain. **Listening** is a psychological and voluntary process that goes beyond simply reacting to sounds and includes understanding, analyzing, evaluating, and responding. Listening is also more than just part of "spoken communication." Messages are both verbal and nonverbal. An effective listener must use more than just her or his sense of hearing to understand, analyze, evaluate, and respond, as Table 4.1 shows.

Table 4.1 Hearing Versus Listening

Involuntary	Voluntary
Passive	Active
Physiological	Psychological
Requires no conscious effort	Requires effort and concentration

SOURCE: From *Communication Works*, 8th ed. by Teri Gamble et al., p. 193. © 2005 by The McGraw-Hill Companies, Inc. Reprinted with permission.

Listening requires concentration, which means holding a key idea in your mind while you consider alternative or conflicting concepts. Effective listening entails synthesizing new information with what you already know.[3] You may have heard people refer to others' "short attention span," "lack of consideration," or "weak concentration." All these remarks boil down to the same message: "that person does not listen well."

Both now and after graduation, you will need strong listening skills, and others will expect you to use them. By reading this chapter, you can learn why effective listening is indispensable in organizations. You can also understand how listening fits into the total human communication process—that is, you can comprehend the interactive nature of communication. You can acquire skills and techniques to help you become a more effective listener.

We cannot guarantee that this chapter will solve all your interpersonal problems, make the rest of your college years a smashing success, and get you the job of your dreams. We cannot even guarantee that it will make you a perfect listener. But we can assure you that skillful listening will improve your chances for personal and professional success.

4.4: The Role of Perception

4.4 Analyze how perception determines the level of the listener's attention

You may have heard the adage "You have to know where you are before you can go anywhere." To improve listening skills, you need an idea of your listening framework—your perceptions. **Perception** is the process of creating meaning based on experience. In other words, your understanding of events depends on your accumulation of sensory knowledge about people, objects, and events.

Think about the Department of Homeland Security's Terrorism Advisory System. Different people may perceive the various color levels differently. Which seems like a more threatening color to you: blue or green? Does a blue level of terrorism alert seem "safer"? Blue is generally a "cooler" color than green. Green, however, is often associated with "go," as in traffic lights. In the case of the Terrorism Advisory System, green is the lowest level of threat, while blue is a "guarded" level of alert. But then what does that mean? Some might interpret "guarded" as meaning that we are guarded and protected. Others might see "guarded" as signifying the presence of threats of terrorism from which we need to be guarded. Because of this variation in perception, different people often interpret a given message in different ways. Such dissimilar perspectives often lead people to respond to messages in unpredicted ways.

Take a moment to look at Figure 4.1. What do you see in these four images? Your perceptual framework determines what you initially see in the figure.

Figure 4.1 Perceptual Tricks

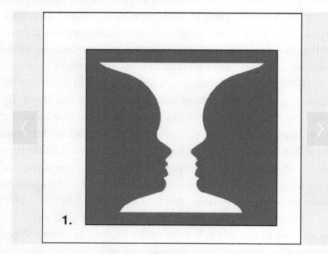

1.

● ● ● ●

What do you see in the image?
Depending upon your own perceptions, your first impression of the image might be of a vase. However, look again, and the image becomes two faces staring at each other.

If every person who receives a message perceives it somewhat differently, consider what happens when a message is sent in a business environment. The message is likely to be received by a large number of people from a wide range of backgrounds and with very different organizational experiences. A message such as "Because of a drop in business, some personnel cuts in some key areas may occur in the near future" can become a source of controversy and insecurity among employees because it is vague and thus likely to be interpreted in myriad ways. Therefore, it is extremely important to assess your perceptual framework and the possible perceptions of others when communicating. The first step is understanding the factors that influence perception.

4.4.1: Factors Influencing Perception

Reception and attention are important factors in perception. **Reception** is the physical process of hearing aural and seeing visual stimuli (including nonverbal cues). Although it may seem obvious, the condition of your hearing and sight determines to some degree the amount and type of information you receive. If your hearing is impaired or your prescription eyeglasses need updating, you are likely to miss information and thus have inaccurate perceptions of messages.

Even if reception is perfect, so much information reaches the brain that only some of it can actually be processed meaningfully. **Attention** is the cognitive ability that allows us to select certain types of information for processing and ignore others. Selective and focused attention to the message is crucial for accurate perception and therefore good listening.[4] Blaine Goss has suggested three principles that describe the listener's attention process:[5]

1. The *number of stimuli* to which a person can attend at one time is very limited.

2. Some *stimuli go unnoticed* or are attended to only in an *unconscious* way.

3. The *amount of attention* a person gives to a stimulus varies according to the difficulty of the task at hand.

Goss's three principles highlight what you probably already know from everyday experience: there's only so much you can do, or pay attention to, at one time. Being a good listener requires paying attention. The greater the number of distractions—from either external factors (such as an uncomfortable seat or a pressing time constraint) or internal ones (such as fatigue or emotional state)—the more difficult it will be to concentrate on what a speaker is saying, and the poorer a job of listening you will do.

LISTENING IN GROUPS In the group context, listening is important because we spend far more time listening than talking. Group interactions are more complex than dyadic interactions because group conversations frequently include competing side conversations or multiple speakers striving to gain other group members' attention. But the basic principles of listening identified by Goss can help you become a better listener in groups.

Why is listening so important in groups?

 Audience Reach

First, speakers don't often realize that other group members are not listening, so they continue to talk, assuming that group members are listening. As a result, listening errors go undetected. This is particularly problematic because several group members are in the listening role. Some members even fake listening, believing that the presence of other group members will cover for their lack of attention. In comparison to dyadic interaction, there is less social pressure to listen in groups, and as a result, ineffective listening goes unnoticed.

 Group Setting

Second, group settings can lend themselves to extraneous interaction, which gives some group members the license to take a break from listening (called social loafing). Some group members might even try to work on other activities when they should be listening.

 Interpretation

Third, listening errors can occur when listeners interpret the message differently from the sender of the message. The problem is compounded in groups—three listeners can mean that three different interpretations exist, four listeners can result in four different interpretations, and so on.

 Focus

Fourth, listeners have a more difficult job in group interactions because it is difficult to attend to the many points of view being presented. It is easier to concentrate on one person speaking or one idea at a time.

WRITING PROMPT

Imagine that you are with a group of people and several people are talking at once. Could you listen to more than one person at a time and make sense of what they are saying? Or would you have to concentrate on just one person? Explain why or why not.

▶ The response entered here will appear in the performance dashboard and can be viewed by your instructor.

Submit

4.4.2: Assess Your Own Perceptions

Although perception is often blamed for communication problems, it is a necessary element in making sense of the world. Your perceptions act as a category system that helps you to understand messages. If you were unable to categorize messages according to your supply of knowledge and experience, every message would be difficult to understand.

It would be like having to learn how to read every time you open a book.

Problems with perception occur when erroneous impressions or category systems distort your interpretation of people or events. Such impressions can distort perception in either a positive or negative way. Even a positive bias toward someone—imagine interviewing someone whom you happily discover went to the same school as you—can result in unfair treatment for someone else if that erroneous factor is weighted too heavily. In extreme cases, perception is clouded by prejudice—preconceived negative judgments or opinions formed without a basis in reality.

Prejudices and biases inhibit effective listening. These biases are not limited to cultural differences; they can also arise from differences in gender, age, sexual preference, religious affiliation, and ethnic background. Instead of facilitating communication, prejudice acts as a barrier to effective and open exchange. Separating the message from the speaker and concentrating on the message can aid in overcoming prejudice. In addition, good listeners take care to hear what is actually said, not merely what they wish to hear. One's own desires or expectations can bias the perception of a message, resulting in hearing nothing but confirmation of your existing beliefs. Therefore, it is essential to be aware of your expectations and try to separate those from the message itself.

The first skill necessary for interactive listening is the ability to diagnose your own listening behavior. The personal listening profile in the Strategic Skills box shows you "where you are" and can help you to plan specific improvement strategies. Think carefully about each statement before responding. Only honest and well-considered answers will allow you to learn about yourself. The personal listening profile helps you to understand your own listening preferences in specific circumstances. For example, if you rated statements 4 and 7 with a five, you may be uncomfortable with nonpersonal communication—that is, communication mediated by technology. You can then cultivate awareness of this perception and make a conscious effort to overcome your hesitation so that you can benefit more from communication such as email or videoconferencing.

Personal Listening Profile
Strategic Skills

Rate each statement according to the following scale: (5) Always true for me; (4) Frequently true for me; (3) Sometimes true for me; (2) Rarely true for me; (1) Never true for me.

1. _____ Listening to public speeches is boring.

2. _____ Listening to someone talk on the radio is very entertaining.

3. _____ It is easy to concentrate when others talk about their problems.

4. _____ Listening to my supervisor over the telephone is more difficult than talking to him or her in person.

5. _____ Listening to several people talk at once in a group discussion is very distracting.

6. _____ Listening to small talk is an enjoyable activity.

7. _____ Listening to online instructional or training materials bothers me.

8. _____ Listening to critically important information makes me nervous.

9. _____ Listening to people in authority is exciting.

10. _____ I avoid listening to people I do not like.

11. _____ I am often distracted if I must listen for a long time.

12. _____ It is easy to concentrate on what others are saying if they gesture with their hands.

13. _____ I enjoy listening to others talk about themselves.

14. _____ I feel uncomfortable when listening to technical information.

15. _____ I look forward to the opportunity to listen to people argue skillfully about a controversial topic.

Look back over the responses you gave. Add your score for numbers 1, 4, 5, 7, 8, 10, 11, and 14. Call the total "Score A." Add your score for numbers 2, 3, 6, 9, 12, 13, and 15. Call the total "Score B." Subtract Score A from Score B. If the resulting total is between 20 and 27, you see yourself as a very competent listener. If you scored between 12 and 19, you see yourself as an average listener. If you scored between 11 and –15, you see yourself as a below-average listener. If you scored –16 or below, you perceive yourself as a poor listener.

Of course, the listening profile is not comprehensive. People often mistake their ability levels, and you may find that particular situations that influence your perceptions have not been included. But thinking about these issues is a good way to identify others and can be the first step toward improving your listening.

A second step in understanding your perceptions is discovering your listening priorities. Listening priorities can vary quite a bit among people and situations. Some people set their listening priorities highest for situations involving close interpersonal relationships (family, relatives, close friends, coworkers). Others reserve listening priorities for social situations (socializing at the office, talking to neighbors and acquaintances). Still others focus their listening priorities on occupational or professional matters (listening to reports, superiors, subordinates, peers, briefings). If you perceive a listening situation as important, you are likely to be open and willing to engage in interactive listening.

Finally, it's a good idea to consider how emotionally charged words affect your perceptions of people and ideas. You may hold very strong opinions about certain words or subjects, such as conservative, liberal, AIDS, climate change, or taxes. Your opinions are likely to be accompanied by strong emotional energy that derives from your experiences

or knowledge of those issues, the way you have been brought up, or the environment you are living in.

Emotion is a positive quality because it reflects the strength of your beliefs. However, it can also be a barrier to listening if you focus on the charged words, instead of on the message, and fail to process information objectively. You may stop listening to the speaker entirely to prepare a defense of your position on the issue. To listen effectively, you are wise to recognize others' points of view and actively control your emotions.

4.4.3: Assess Others' Perceptions

Sympathy is identification with others' feelings. **Empathy**, on the other hand, is the act of sharing the feelings of another person. For example, while a sympathetic friend could tell you what he or she would do in your situation, an empathetic friend would know what you would do. Sympathy and empathy are important elements of perception. By attempting to feel the same way as a speaker does (to empathize with her or him), you can better understand the message.

Nevertheless, it is important to remember that total empathy is impossible because individuals perceive things differently. No one can share the exact feelings of another. In fact, trouble often begins when you think "I know just how you feel." You can, however, try to assimilate what you perceive another to be feeling. Furthermore, by demonstrating that you understand a speaker's feelings (sympathize with him or her), you can enhance the shared meaning of the communicated message.

Keep in mind, however, that it may not be appropriate in all situations to use these techniques, for some speakers do not wish to share their feelings. Lastly, be careful not to misinterpret cues, particularly an emotional display or tone. Don't assume that because you observe someone being happy, sad, angry, and so on, you know the reason. The boss who snaps at you when you knock on the door may be angry that your report is overdue, but she may also simply be bothered by something else. Avoid taking such emotional cues personally. The most important part of empathy is true concern for others and respect for what they have to say.

4.5: Goal Setting for Interactive Listening

4.5 **Examine the role of goal setting in active listening in accomplishing your business objective**

As with all important communication activities, such as speaking up in meetings, talking to coworkers, or interviewing, preparation for listening allows you to do the best job you can. You can prepare for listening situations by accomplishing several tasks. These include identifying objectives, knowing your listening style, building motivation, and generating energy. For example, attending a meeting or presentation can be more profitable if you identify specific objectives ("I will learn at least five new things at this meeting"), build motivation for the event ("I know that the things I learn will benefit me later"), and generate sufficient energy to be alert ("I will conserve my physical and mental energy for the meeting"). Let's examine each of these steps individually.

4.5.1: Identify Objectives

Three questions are worthy of consideration in goal setting:

1. What must I get out of this listening situation?
2. What would I like to get out of this situation?

3. What should the other persons get out of my listening to them?

As you answer these questions, keep in mind that goals should identify basic objectives, such as getting background information needed to perform at an adequate level.

Comprehensive goals also identify additional rewards that might be reaped from the listening situation, such as learning about how you and your actions affect larger processes in the organization or how the speaker feels about the subject of the conversation. Goals for listening situations, like all communication goals, must be specific, appropriate, and realistically obtainable given the resources and abilities available.

PRACTICING BUSINESS COMMUNICATION

Ball Corporation

More than 125 years ago, when the five Ball brothers decided to go into business together, they began with only a modest plan to produce wooden-jacketed tin cans. Today Ball Corporation is an international manufacturing company employing over 15,600 people in more than ninety locations worldwide. The high quality of its metal and plastic food and beverage and household containers is recognized around the world. In 2013 it reported net income of over $400 million. However, part of that income derives not from containers but from a somewhat different product: aerospace engineering.

(X) Read More

Ball Aerospace & Technologies Corp.—a wholly owned subsidiary of Ball Corporation that is based in Boulder, Colorado—produces space systems engineering products; telecommunications technology; and electro-optics and cryogenics materials for government and commercial customers. In this arena, Ball's business plan has involved the creation of remote sensing systems and other solutions for the aerospace and defense markets; Ball develops products and services that are used to collect and interpret information needed to support national defense and scientific discovery. Among its contributions to all four of NASA's great observatories, Ball Aerospace provided seven instruments for the Hubble Space Telescope—including the corrective optics that space shuttle astronauts delivered to fix the telescope's originally flawed vision.

Ball's ability to meet the complex and difficult technology challenges of space exploration was dramatically demonstrated in 2005. On July 4, 2005, the Deep Impact space probe—of which Ball was a primary developer—successfully intercepted a comet in the first-ever attempt to obtain core sampling data from such a celestial body. The encounter with the comet, Tempel 1, occurred nearly 83 million miles from Earth and at speeds approaching 23,000 miles per hour. After imaging the encounter and sailing through the tail of the departing comet in a protected-shield mode, the flyby spacecraft performed flawlessly. In the decade since, there have been five encounters with comets through the program, known as deep Impact.

You can visit Ball Aerospace online at www.ballaerospace.com.

The James Webb Space Telescope

The James Webb Space Telescope (JWST), designed to observe extremely faint objects, is in development. Scientists hope JWST will provide information to answer questions about the formation of galaxies and stars, as well as about the early history of our solar system. Named after NASA's second administrator, James Webb, JWST will journey approximately three months to reach its destination: an orbit 940,000 miles (1.5 million kilometers) from Earth. The JWST program is led by NASA's Goddard Space Flight Center and consists of an international team involving the European Space Agency, the Canadian Space Agency, industry, and academia. Northrop Grumman, the primary contractor, leads the design and development effort.

(X) Read more

Ball Aerospace was selected to lead a consortium of subcontractors that will produce the sophisticated optics for the project. The company is now responsible for the entire optical subsystem that will act as the "eyes" for JWST. But the project involves considerable engineering expertise in other areas besides optics, such as mechanical and electrical engineering. For example, in order to launch the large optical system that the telescope requires, engineers on the JWST team created a special design for the telescope's primary mirror: they divided it into three sections. The sides of the mirror will be folded back to fit into the launch vehicle, then deployed while in orbit.

No Room for Error

With such a large group of contractors involved in the project, effective communication is essential. Written specifications developed from NASA's mission objectives are conveyed to the contractors, who then create even more detailed specifications for the electrical, optical, mechanical, and aerospace engineers who are actually designing the various parts. Radiation and thermal engineering specialists must also be brought in at every stage to make sure all components are able to operate within the extreme environmental conditions of space.

⊗ Read more

Perfection may often be the goal of business operations, but for Ball Aerospace on the JWST, it is an imperative. Unlike the Hubble telescope, which can be serviced using the space shuttle, JWST's orbit will be unreachable by astronauts for the foreseeable future. That means the project has virtually zero margin for error.

Given these constraints, development is rigorously monitored with major evaluations at three checkpoints: the requirements stage, the preliminary design stage, and the critical (or detailed) design stage. Each component system passes through each of these phases, and at each checkpoint, project managers and

engineers must meet to ensure that specifications are being met, that proper testing protocols are in place, and that programs are meeting schedule and budget targets.

Communication strategies include one- to two-hour-long conference calls every week, to keep teams in various locations in touch, and one- to two-day-long technology interchange meetings (TIMs) every couple of months, where the teams meet to evaluate progress on all component systems of JWST. These face-to-face TIMs provide an important opportunity to discuss design options and the potentials of different technologies. Listening at these meetings is an essential skill as project managers and engineers convey ideas about the capabilities of a particular design and listen to their colleagues' critiques and alternative ideas.

This part of the listening process is not without challenges. "Sometimes obstacles to good listening can occur when people get emotionally invested in an outcome," says one project manager at Ball Aerospace. "Accepting someone else's point in a discussion may mean your own design does not get accepted. In that kind of situation, I try to encourage an engineer to just 'sit' with the [new] idea for a couple of days. That almost always works to refocus the person on the overall goals of the project and make the right decision."

When identifying your objectives, it is also important to determine the setting in which the communication will occur. With certain technologies, you might need to modify your listening skills. For example, participating in your first videoconference changes the way you speak and listen. It can seem peculiar to speak to a television set or computer monitor and even stranger to realize the person you are listening to can watch you listening.

Consideration for the other person or people in the listening situation is another important goal. Remind yourself to keep an open mind, respond honestly, and concentrate fully on what is being said. It is a great advantage for those who are speaking or talking to know whether you are comprehending the communication.

4.5.2: Know Your Listening Style

Try to get a sense of what type of listening is called for. There are four types: for information, for enjoyment, for evaluation, and for feelings. Some people make more of an effort to listen in situations where information is exchanged

than in situations that speak to feelings. Others are more interested in being effective listeners when evaluation comes into play than when enjoyment is the point.

Knowing more about your listening style helps to improve your motivation. Several listening styles have been identified: appreciative, empathic, discriminative, analytical, passive, and negative.

Listening Styles

Remove card   1 of 6   Reset Deck

Characteristics of Good and Bad Listeners

Strategic Skills

⊗ **Good Listeners:**

- Maintain steady eye contact
- Devote full attention to the speaker
- Keep posture and demeanor alert
- Give verbal cues
- Paraphrase to clarify

- Demonstrate empathy
- Are patient
- Share the limelight
- Indicate an open mind
- Leave the answer for the speaker
- Listen for intent as well as content

 Bad Listeners:

- Interrupt
- Are inattentive and easily distracted
- Use negative body language
- Change the subject
- Give no short verbal prompts
- Are very critical
- Are impatient
- Take over the conversation
- Are discouraging
- Play "Mr. Fix-it"
- Think what they will say next

B. Lampton, "What Good Listeners Do: Becoming the Company Others Love to Keep!" *Expert Magazine* (2003) [online]. Available: http://www. expertmagazine.com/artman/publish/article_309.shtml.

C. Reid, "How to Promote OSH," *OSH Promotion in the Workplace* (1998) [online]. Available: http://www.safetyline.wa.gov.au/institute/level1/course7/lecture26/126_02.asp.

Appreciative listening is used to judge the aesthetic value of what is heard, such as a public speech, play, or comedian's routine, and is used mostly for enjoyment. **Empathic listening** concentrates on the feelings or attitudes of the speaker, rather than on the message, and is employed to discover the feelings of the speaker, such as during a therapy session or when listening to a friend's problem. **Discriminative listening** involves drawing inferences from auditory cues and evaluating reasons for the message. This is "reading between the lines" listening. **Analytical listening** encompasses a concentration on the content and includes understanding, interpreting, and analyzing a message. This style is useful in an exchange of information or ideas, such as at a staff meeting.

The appropriateness of appreciative, discriminative, empathic, and analytical listening styles depends on the situation. In any case, passive and negative listening are undesirable styles. **Passive listening** means that the receiver is not concentrating on the message and consequently loses much of its meaning. **Negative listening** is defensive in nature: the receiver is listening to find fault with the sender or is listening to attack what is being said. At times styles overlap. A business presentation, for example, can require both discriminative and analytical listening. Recognizing the listening situation will help you identify objectives, build motivation, and adopt an effective listening style.

WRITING PROMPT

Think of an event, activity, or meeting coming up in the near future where it will important for you to listen well. What type of listening situation will it be (for information, enjoyment, evaluation, feelings)? What goals do you want to achieve in this listening situation? After the event, look back at your goals and assess how well you accomplished them.

▶ The response entered here will appear in the performance dashboard and can be viewed by your instructor.

Submit

4.5.3: Generate Energy

Effective listening takes effort. Interviews with business professionals reveal that success comes more easily when listeners are engaged and energetic.[6] Some communication situations demand more energy than others. Consider the difference between listening to a fellow student talk about the success of a project that the two of you worked on together and listening to a group of people you do not know very well talk about their plans for the summer. You may be surprised to realize that the hidden benefits of the second situation far outweigh those of the first. Whereas you already know about the successful project (after all, you worked on it), you have the opportunity to learn quite a bit about the possibilities for summer jobs from listening to the group conversation. The key is to energize yourself and make the most of the situation. Listening requires two types of energy: physical and mental. Physical energy is required to listen effectively. Fatigue can also have a surprisingly strong effect on listening ability, yet many people do not take this factor into account, particularly students for whom late nights and inadequate sleep are facts of life. Fatigue dulls the senses and can lower your ability to process information. If you are tired, sick, stressed, or otherwise incapacitated, the following advice can help you to make the most of the situation:

1. Indicate to the source of the message your physical condition and ask for consideration.

2. Muster stored energy for the listening situation (deep breathing, muscle tension/relaxation, avoidance of physically stressful activities ahead of time).

3. Avoid listening situations for which you simply cannot build any energy. Postponing such situations is preferable to not listening well.

The level of a person's mental energy also shapes the listening process. Many people put less mental energy into activities at the end of the day, either because they are tired or because they are beginning to think of other things—what to do after work or after class. Worries, anxiety, and apprehension over work-related or personal matters are other common causes of low mental energy.

Fatigue, disappointment, frustration, and even hunger can take their toll on maintaining concentration. How effective do you think this employee's concentration will be when a coworker drops by to offer suggestions on a project they are working on? What can he do to generate enough energy to listen productively?

SOURCE: Naka/Fotolia

Of course, putting such concerns aside to prepare for a listening situation is difficult (and sometimes impossible), but putting your worries in perspective nevertheless helps. If there is nothing you can do about a worrisome situation at the moment, accept that fact, resolve to tackle the matter at another time, and stop worrying about it.

4.6: Situational Knowledge and Interactive Listening

4.6 **Describe the factors that affect a listener's listening capabilities**

Situational knowledge is information that is useful for recognizing and understanding the variables operating in communication situations. Taking situational details into account as much as possible enables you as a listener to prepare effectively for the communication encounter. Such external factors include the speaker's communication style, various environmental distractions, emotions, and even the message itself. The communication style of a speaker is one of a number of situational factors that can affect your listening effectiveness.

4.6.1: Speaker's Communication Style

The speaker's communication style may call for the application of special listening considerations. Some people tend to talk rapidly, gesture broadly, or otherwise distract you from the message. Others show no expressiveness or talk slowly; this style may leave you second-guessing the meaning of the message because you have insufficient cues to guide your interpretation and a lot of time to question the meaning of the words.

Unusual dialects or accents may also cause listening difficulties. One of the best ways to overcome this obstacle is to familiarize yourself with new speech patterns. You can do this by listening especially carefully, talking little, and concentrating hard when communicating with someone who uses a dialect or has an accent that sounds strange to you. Do not focus on your own comprehension difficulties; listen instead for the speaker's ideas, the content of the message. Identify common speech patterns (for example, many native Spanish-speakers pronounce *bit* as "beet," and many people from the northern United States pronounce *hair* as "here") and become comfortable with them.

Do not hesitate to ask a speaker to repeat what she or he said or to slow down. You will both benefit from such requests, particularly if they are phrased in a polite, confident voice. The worst response is to decide that you simply cannot comprehend a speaker and to stop trying.

4.6.2: Environmental Distractions

The communication setting may contain a variety of distractions. Noise, the presence of others, or even listening on someone else's "turf" can lessen your capacity for listening. If possible, try to move the communication event to a setting with less noise or fewer distractions. If this is not possible, make the best of the setting. If you are in a crowded room, see whether you can find a relatively quiet corner. If you are in an unfamiliar office, visualize a more comfortable setting. Although setting is a situational parameter that is often difficult to adjust, both you and the speaker will benefit from making the setting as comfortable as possible.

The act of listening and communicating demands more attention than you might realize. Consider having a conversation on a cell phone while driving. We don't think about how much of our brain power is devoted to carrying on a conversation. However, research shows that driving while talking on a cell phone actually impairs your abilities more than being legally drunk.[7]

Is the weakening of your driving ability due simply to having too much of your finite attention drawn to the conversation or to trying to juggle the phone itself? Not really. After all, most people are easily able to both drive a car and have a conversation with someone else in the car with them. Rather, the problem arises with cell phone usage (even with headsets) because the other talker, who is not in the car, cannot view the driving environment and is unable to see the driver's nonverbal cues. Inside the car, however, most talkers recognize when the driver needs to give more attention to the road—and they will pause to allow him or her to do so. A prime example of interactivity in communication!

4.6.3: Emotional Distractions

The emotions of the communicators are a determining factor in any listening situation. Emotionally aroused people often react to communication situations differently from people who are calm. If you are negatively aroused, you may not listen effectively and thus compound the problems you already have. Speakers who are emotionally charged may mislead you into thinking that they are passionate about the topic when something else is actually bothering them.

When you listen to a highly emotional speaker, focus on the content of the message rather than on the delivery. Control your impulse to argue until you have heard the complete message. As you listen, evaluate the strengths and weaknesses of the speaker's position by summarizing the main points of the argument in your head. Doing so will help you to remain calm (much like forcing yourself to count to ten before losing your temper) and will also help you to respond effectively when the time comes.

WRITING PROMPT

Think of a news or entertainment program that you dislike because it is emotional in its presentation. While you watch or listen to the show, consciously fight the distractions that you normally may experience. Did you catch the speaker's position and main points? How you were able to put aside emotional distractions? If you were successful, you have gained some of your own personal strategies for listening when emotion is involved.

▶ The response entered here will appear in the performance dashboard and can be viewed by your instructor.

Submit

4.6.4: Message Content

The message itself plays an important role in listening. Most people are motivated to listen effectively if the consequences of the communication are important. Formal situations, such as presentations, lectures, or interviews, usually require systematic listening and precise comprehension of the speaker's language.[8] If the situation is informal, or if the topic is not particularly meaningful to you (for example, a colleague tells you about a report unrelated to your area), you may be tempted to minimize your listening effort. Keep in mind, however, that it is impossible to predict all the outcomes of a listening situation, so it is a good idea to make the most of every listening opportunity.

That colleague's report may contain information you will find useful at a future date.

Small talk, social conversation, and personal self-disclosures usually do not require the same type of listening skills as does content that is highly technical, vague, controversial, or innovative. By considering the content of the message, listeners can anticipate the conditions of the listening situation.

Ethical Listening Situations

Ethical Issues

When most people consider ethical issues, they usually think of situations in which a person is acting, speaking, or behaving in a way that is unethical. There are also many situations in which listening or receiving information can have ethical consequences. Consider the following listening/receiving situations and determine which you feel generate the least or most ethical implications.

- Not replying to an email message and saying that you never received it.
- Intentionally overhearing a conversation that is none of your business.
- Ignoring an urgent voice mail to which you do not want to respond.
- Failing to record information you gained in an interview with job candidate because you do not like her personally.
- Telling a fellow employee that you "heard" information when in fact it is only your suspicion.
- Acting bored in a meeting in order to distract the speaker with a competing idea or proposal.
- Monopolizing conversations because you feel you are the only person worth hearing.

4.7: Competence in Interactive Listening

4.7 Analyze how interactive listening makes a competent communicator

Research from the workplace reports that listening is the number one reason given for believing that another person is a competent communicator.[9] Interactive listening is an ongoing, complex, and dynamic process. The maximum rewards from listening result from strategic planning, assessments of self and others, and feedback and verbal encouragement. Interactive listening is not only an auditory skill. You listen best if you listen with all your senses. Elements of verbal and nonverbal behavior can help you process maximum amounts of information in a listening context.

To become more interactive as a listener, reduce the amount of time you spend talking, use questions to become more aware as a listener and to help others, and use the strategic aspects of nonverbal behavior. These skills, along with the listening competence skills you learned earlier in the chapter, will be invaluable in improving your listening.

4.7.1: Talk Less

It is difficult to listen when you are talking. People who believe that what they have to say is the critical component of any conversation feel compelled to provide a play-by-play commentary on every event and idea that occurs to them. People with reputations as good listeners are admired—and their primary skill is the ability to keep quiet!

As a strategy, silence works in many communication situations. Speakers frequently elaborate or provide additional information if their conversational partner is silent. Consider the following situation:

> Clarissa knew that José recently had an important meeting with the district manager of the software division in which they both worked. She overheard two coworkers, Joan and Peter, pestering José with questions about the meeting. José's responses were evasive; he seemed uncomfortable with their aggressive questioning and gave them very little information. Clarissa and José were not particularly good friends, but she decided that if she approached him in a nonthreatening way and allowed him to talk, she might find out what had gone on at the meeting. When José referred to the meeting in a later conversation with Clarissa, she was strategically silent and did not prompt him for information. This behavior seemed to put him at ease, and soon they were discussing the goings-on of the meeting. José had wanted to talk to someone about the meeting, but he was uneasy and distrustful of people who seemed to care more about their questions than about his answers. He wanted to talk to someone who would really listen.

4.7.2: Ask Questions

Interactive listening entails more than simply receiving a message. It requires listeners to respond at critical points in the communication process. Questioning techniques are one type of response that can improve listening by making speakers more efficient. When listeners and speakers agree on the topic, consequences, and language use, listening effectiveness improves immensely.

Closed, open, probing, and leading questions improve the speaking/listening process. Each type is used for different purposes, depending on the listening situation. Table 4.2 summarizes the differences among these types of questions.

Table 4.2 Techniques for Questioning

Type of Question	Purpose	Example
Closed	Obtain a short, specific response	"Do you mean this fiscal year or last fiscal year?"
Open	Allow freedom and choice in the response	"What is your attitude toward cost accounting?"
Probing	Encourage the speaker to elaborate on the topic (by using why-type questions)	"Why do you feel that way?"
Leading	Imply expected response in question	"Are you saying that our computer system needs to be upgraded?"
Reflective	Show empathy with speaker	"Are you excited because we get more time off or because we get overtime pay?"

Hide All Cells   Show All Cells

Questioning techniques are especially useful in guiding a speaker toward a conversational point that is necessary to accomplish a goal. Speakers can get off the track, mislead, provide aimless and useless information, or even deceive listeners. In the following situation, notice how one communicator uses questions to keep the discussion on track:

> VINCENT: I'm really glad that Phyllis joined the office staff.
> TANYA: So am I. Aren't we going to finish our discussion about the new alarm system?
> VINCENT: I guess. I think Joanne ought to replace the old copier. It's worn out.
> TANYA: That's her choice. Vincent, should the new alarm system have both heat and smoke sensors? It would be more expensive if it does.
> VINCENT: Both. I found a system that operates less expensively when both sensors work in tandem.

4.7.3: Use Nonverbal Behavior

To receive the optimum amount of information in the message, it is important to interpret a speaker's nonverbal cues correctly. It is just as important to give the speaker nonverbal cues to show that you are comprehending (or not comprehending) the message.

Of course, it is important to listen when someone speaks to you, but it is perhaps even more important for the other person to perceive that you are listening. Head nods, leaning forward, gestures, "uh-huhs," smiles, and so forth, are vital cues that let the speaker know that you are interested in what is being said.

Understanding, agreement, empathy, and emotional responses can be displayed effectively by means of nonverbal cues. For example, frowning generally indicates disagreement or misunderstanding. Nodding connotes agreement or comprehension. Shrugs communicate lack of interest or ambiguity. No response at all can convey a lack of awareness. To get a sense of how nonverbal behavior facilitates interactive involvement, take a look at Table 4.3.

Other behaviors—such as using time, taking turns, and avoiding racist and sexist language—also function to regulate the interactive nature of listening. Because nonverbal communication is crucial to speakers, you are wise to recognize how your nonverbal behavior affects communication in particular situations.

Table 4.3 Nonverbal Behavior and Interactive Listening

Behavior	Function
Eye gaze, eye contact	Facilitates others conversation
Gestures (open palm, motioning)	Encourages additional information
Paralanguage (increase volume, pitch)	Encourages clarification
Proxemics (giving people more space)	Makes people more comfortable
Tactile (pats on the back or shoulder)	Provides confidence builder
Body orientation (face person directly)	Provides sense of importance
Nodding, shaking head	Gives information about feelings
Posture (slouching, head down)	Indicates attentiveness
Facial expressions (smiling or frowning)	Demonstrates interest

Hide All Cells	Show All Cells

4.7.4: Dismantle the Three D's

Competent listening involves dismantling the barriers to your own reception of the message. The most common listening problems are the three D's: distraction, disorientation, and defensiveness. Several strategies, such as listening for ideas, "planning to report," and taking notes, can help you both combat the three D's and make your listening pay great dividends.

Distraction, disorientation, and defensiveness severely inhibit listening. Distraction moves the focus of attention away from the message. Disorientation is a breakdown in the mental and emotional processes that assign meaning to the message. Defensiveness produces biased judgment

about messages because of overly emotional feelings about certain issues or people. Table 4.4 gives a more complete picture of the three D's.

Table 4.4 The Three D's

Problem	Components	Consequences	Actions
Distraction	Mental Environmental	Missing needed information Appearing uninterested	Place greater emphasis on the speaker. Withhold attention to distraction until you can deal with it. Take notes to stay on track.
Disorientation	Confusion Boredom Self-reflection	Appearing dazed, flustered Seeming apathetic Appearing self-centered	Simplify information to its basic level. Focus on main points. Relate what speaker is saying to personal interests.
Defensiveness	Disliking the speaker Resenting the situation	Making biased judgments Reducing alternatives	Understand that it's not about "you" personally. Ask self-objective questions about content.

One way to avoid the three D's is to listen for ideas by asking yourself questions while you listen. Ask yourself whether the speaker's points are logical, whether you agree or disagree, and whether what is being said corresponds with or contradicts your own experience. In this way, you can keep yourself focused on the content of the message and at the same time put the message in the context of what you already know.

Another method for dismantling the three D's is taking notes. You can take notes in two ways: writing down the highlights of what is being said or identifying the organizational pattern that the speaker is using. For example, many people organize their ideas into lists, arrange events in chronological order, identify a problem and then a solution, or present one point of view and then an opposing position.[10]

Listen for cues such as "The three causes of increased productivity are," "Since 1987, several important events have occurred," or "Absenteeism is increasing; we can survey the employees to find out why." If you hear a cue, get ready to take down that important information. Remember that other people are impressed by the care and effort demonstrated when a listener takes notes.[11]

4.7.5: Fight Boredom

Fighting boredom is another important skill for competent listening. Because the human brain processes information very efficiently, it is easy for listeners to become uninterested. The human brain can process from 400 to 800 words a minute, but the average rate of speech is only 150 words per minute.[12] This efficiency leaves people with a great deal of extra brain time to think about other things than what a speaker is saying. Because of this, listeners must sometimes force themselves to concentrate on a speaker's message.[13] Inevitably, there are going to be instances when you are acutely aware of this difference—you are bored. In many other listening situations, without realizing it, you are tuning in and out of effective listening simply because the information is coming in much more slowly than you are processing it. In many business situations—particularly for managers and customer service environments—you may be required to listen to similar problems over and over again. These situations are probably the most dangerous kinds because what has become routine—and perhaps less interesting—for you is likely a matter of concern and urgency to the other party. To be a good listener in these situations, it is essential that you cultivate a genuine concern for the other person. To reduce your boredom, make the situation a contest in which you challenge yourself to retain the important information. Here are some suggestions for minimizing boredom in listening situations:

- Set goals for obtaining information in a listening situation.
- Remember the costs associated with missed information.
- Focus on the content of the message.
- Relate this information to your current knowledge base.
- Identify the main points of the message and memorize them.

4.7.6: Make the Most of Listening Opportunities

Experts believe that most of us listen only at 25 percent capacity. We can put a lot more into it if we try.[14] When we talk about making the most of a listening opportunity, we are referring to improving both the situation and your own skills. You can improve the setting of a communication by moving office furniture so you can listen better, ensuring that your seat at a luncheon faces the speaker, or getting a central seat in a group or committee meeting.

Controlling your listening is an important skill. If you hold strong opinions about a point that others are discussing, you may feel the urge to jump into the conversation prematurely, without invitation or planning. Patiently waiting until a speaker finishes allows you to know the other side of the issue better and gives you time to formulate just the right rebuttal. Table 4.5 gives you

additional clues for maximizing the benefits of communication encounters.

Table 4.5 Making the Most of Listening Situations

Area of Improvement	Factors	Techniques
Situation control	Setting	Improve seating arrangements
		Enhance privacy
		Adjust room temperature to comfortable level
		Reduce competing messages
		Ensure ready access to necessary data
		Establish adequate and appropriate lighting
	Time/timing	Do not over-schedule appointments
		Ensure enough time to avoid being rushed
		Prepare necessary materials in advance
		Avoid situations that are poorly timed
Personal control	Emotions	Avoid hasty generalizations
		Control emotions by objectifying the situation (this is not about you)
	Patience	Wait until all the facts are on the table
		While you wait to speak, analyze the speaker's points

Can You Tell When a Listener Is Bored?

Strategic Skills

While it may not always be possible to keep a listener closely attuned to your every word, good communicators remain aware of listener reaction—whether it is positive or negative—and take steps, if possible, to increase the interest level. How to tell if a listener is bored? Look for any of the following signs:

- Being easily distracted
- Needing to have information repeated
- Watching the clock
- Grooming or preening himself or herself
- Reducing eye contact
- Fiddling with objects or clothing

And remember, others can identify these signs of boredom if you display them, as well! So even if you are bored in a meeting, try not to show it.

4.8: Manage Listening Anxiety

4.8 **Express the need to control anxiety for effective communication**

You may be wondering why anyone is anxious in listening situations. But if you think carefully about it, you will recognize that some situations evoke anxiety. Listening to a boss's reprimand, listening to highly technical information, listening to criticism, and listening to bad news are just a few of the circumstances that can cause anxiety. Other difficult situations can also evoke anxiety. Listening to jargon or other hard-to-understand material and listening to someone brag are also anxiety-producing situations. A small amount of anxiety or apprehension may actually stimulate and motivate your listening, but too much anxiety is harmful.

The problems associated with listening anxiety are numerous. Anxiety during the listening process can be distracting and can lead to forgetfulness, disorganization of information, distortions of data, and other cognitive shortcomings. Anxiety hampers your ability to process information and ideas in an efficient manner.[15] In addition, listening anxiety lowers your ability to pursue effective arguments.[16]

It is up to you to identify listening situations that may elicit anxiety. Then, prepare for the situation—gather necessary information so that your background knowledge is at the level expected by the source. If you are not able to do this, tell the source of the message if possible. If you are able to control anxiety, you will be better prepared to move successfully through the subsequent stages of the interactive listening process.

Listener Anxiety Checklist

Strategic Skills

This scale is similar to the personal listening profile, but it focuses on listening anxieties rather than on listening preferences and habits. As a result, your score will have a different meaning from your personal listening profile score.

Use the following checklist to determine your level of listener anxiety. Determine whether you strongly agree (1), agree (2), are undecided (3), disagree (4), or strongly disagree (5).

(×) Checklist

1. _____ I have no fear of being a listener as a member of an audience.
2. _____ I feel relaxed listening to new ideas.
3. _____ I am generally overexcited and rattled when others are speaking to me.
4. _____ I often feel uncomfortable when listening to others.
5. _____ I often have difficulty concentrating on what is being said.
6. _____ I seek out the opportunity to listen to new ideas.
7. _____ Receiving new information makes me nervous.
8. _____ I have no difficulty concentrating on instructions given to me.
9. _____ People who attempt to change my mind make me anxious.
10. _____ I am generally relaxed when listening to others.

Add up your scores for items 1, 2, 6, 8, and 10 (Score A). Now add up your scores for items 3, 4, 5, 7, and 9 (Score B). Subtract the Score A total from the Score B total, to get a composite score. If this score is positive (between 15 and 20), you have a strong tendency toward anxiety across a range of situations. If your score is between 5 and 15, you have an average level of anxiety. If your score is between −20 and 5, you have a low base level of listener anxiety.

Understanding your own level of listener anxiety is the first step toward managing anxiety. Obviously, this test is limited; it does not ask about many listening situations. Nevertheless, this test should give you a rough estimate of what your general feelings are toward the emotional component in the listening process.

SOURCE: Reprinted with permission from the National Communication Association: www.natcom.org

4.9: Evaluate Your Interactive Listening

4.9 **Show how to evaluate success in the strategic interactive listening process**

The final step in the strategic interactive listening process is evaluating your success. Although we discuss evaluation at the end of this chapter, you can use these skills to make evaluations at each stage of communication. It is important to conduct ongoing evaluations to determine how best to proceed as a listener even as the listening situation evolves. But it is critical for you to get into the habit of evaluating listening situations immediately after they occur.

The first step in evaluation is to assess whether you were able to achieve the goals you set for yourself. Assessing yourself can be difficult if you do not take an objective approach. You can achieve objectivity by answering these questions honestly:

1. To what extent did you fulfill your goal? If you had more than one goal, how many of them did you achieve?
2. Did you adapt your listening behavior during the course of the situation to better achieve your goals?
3. Were the goals that you set for this listening situation realistic?
4. What elements prevented you from achieving part or all of your goals?
5. What can you do in the future to achieve the same goals?

Answering these questions gives you a good picture of how to assess your current listening behavior and how to plan to become an even better listener.

TECHNOLOGY TOOLS

Listening Skills Online

It is easy to understand the importance of listening skills in business and the professions when you become aware of the large number of online resources for services for developing listening skills. We selected five resources from many others for two reasons. First, these seemed highly relevant to listening skills in business and professional settings. Second, it was our feeling that these Web sites (and their respective organizations) would be in operation for some time to come. Visit these Web sites and others that emphasize the skill of listening!

www.toastmasters.org This is the most recognized organization for developing communications skills. It emphasizes listening skills as well as speaking skills. It is a nonprofit organization with local chapters in just about every major city.

www.listen.org This is another nonprofit, professional organization that promotes the "study, development, and teaching of listening." It offers a wide range of services for its members.

www.highgain.com This corporation offers individuals and companies a number of programs for developing listening skills.

www.esl-lab.com Focusing their services on Web-based instruction, this company can administer audio listening tests to determine your listening skills. A great deal of their focus is on people trying to master English as a Second Language.

www.thepargroup.com The Par Group is a comprehensive business consulting organization, although it has an extensive program for listening improvement.

4.10: Information Literacy

4.10 Review the necessity of being an expert in managing the received information

A great deal of our professional lives is spent dealing with information that is received via display screens (phones, computer monitors, digital tools, etc.). Listening with our eyes for essential information is becoming increasingly important. Keeping up with an ever-exploding amount of information is a skill in itself. Not unlike the process of interactive listening, becoming adept at managing information you receive, or what is referred to as "information literacy," commands front-and-center attention. Many people feel that information literacy is accomplished when they have conducted a search for information on the Web or in databases and feel like they found what they were looking for. That is only part of the process of effective information management.

The rest of the story unfolds when the information makes sense and can accomplish the purpose behind the search in the first place. The information has to be evaluated for its credibility to determine if it is worth dealing with. It has to be broken down into a form that makes sense for you and others, it has to be summarized so that it does not waste your time or the time of those you are preparing the information for, and it has to be stored properly so that you can retrieve it when you need to.

The Association of College and Research Libraries has identified basic standards for information literacy. The standards listed below are essential components of a skill set that can put you in more control of the information that you receive:

- Identify the extent of the information that you will need.
- Evaluate the information you need efficiently.
- Integrate the new information into your own knowledge and experience.
- Leverage the information to accomplish your specific goals.
- Ensure that the manner in which you use the information is legal and ethical.[17]

Strategic Scenario Wrap-Up

Listening Skills

(X) Strategic Scenario

Randy is a summer intern working as a nurse's aide at a leading cancer center and hospital. The person to whom Randy reports is the vice president for human resources. Typically, nurse's aides duties are answer patients' calls, observe patients' vital signs, and to clean rooms and change linens. Randy's assignment, however, is different. Because of his outstanding grades, previous work experience in a physician's office, and strong recommendations, Randy is participating in a unique program that rotates the nurse's aides among senior staff nurses in different departments. At the end of the internship, he is expected to write an essay about the specific career path he has chosen. Randy must rely on his observations and one-on-one interaction with the hospital staff to help him learn more about his environment.

Randy, who just finished a summer internship in nursing at an urban medical center, has an important report to write. He has worked a busy hospital floor for three lightening-fast months, following a staff of 45 nursing professionals. Although he was not supposed to be performing his regular duties as well as observing, he was not surprised when asked to pitch in often. Double duty!

In this situation, a busy hospital with so much happening at once, managing environmental distractions was a major listening priority for Randy. Analytical listening was important, as Randy found it necessary to concentrate closely on the content of what the nurses were telling him regarding patient care. They were unable to slow down or repeat themselves for him. There were emotional distractions as well.

Randy tried hard to understand, interpret, and analyze the messages he heard. Two aspects of communication competence, *talk less* and *ask questions*, were key to Randy's success.

Do you think there is a place for discriminative listening in Randy's experience? Remember that this involves "reading between the lines." Why or why not?

> The response entered here will appear in the performance dashboard and can be viewed by your instructor.

Submit

Summary

Listening Skills

- **Interactive listening** is a complex but invaluable method of communicating.
- Although many people take listening for granted, listening is a **crucial component** of personal and professional activity.
- Much of people's **financial compensation** on the job is earned by listening, and as a person rises in her or his profession, the percentage of salary earned as a result of listening also rises.
- **Skilled listening avoids problems** for the listener, such as being perceived by others as less intelligent, costing time and money, and limiting chances for success.
- Listening is difficult to conceptualize unless it is viewed as part of the **whole communication picture**, which includes the elements of perception and capacity to understand others' points of view.
- The communication process is **interactive**; it depends on at least two people exchanging verbal and nonverbal messages.
- Successful listening derives from **setting appropriate goals** for the communication, knowing your listening style, building motivation, and generating energy to make the most of the encounter.
- With specific goals as a basis, the masterful listener obtains the necessary **situational knowledge** about

the speaker's communication style, environmental distractions that may be present, and any emotional distractions or physical conditions that may be relevant for participants.
- Once engaged in communication, the effective listener **cultivates silence**, speaks to ask **clarifying questions**, and uses **nonverbal behavior** to communicate empathy and sympathy.
- Even the most accomplished listener encounters **anxiety-producing situations**.
- To manage them, the listener can use his or her analytical skills to identify and deal with **causes of anxiety** and then **evaluate what is successful** in the communication.

List three behaviors that you need to concentrate on to improve your own skills in listening. Next to each behavior, devise an action plan that you can implement to improve your skills.

> A minimum number of characters is required to post and earn points. After posting, your response can be viewed by your class and instructor, and you can participate in the class discussion.

     0 characters | 140 minimum

Chapter 4 Quiz: Listening Skills

Chapter 5
Verbal and Nonverbal Skills

 ## Learning Objectives

5.1 Scrutinize how strong verbal and nonverbal communication is necessary for personal success and the success of an organization

5.2 Examine how goal setting in verbal and nonverbal communication is important for success in business settings

5.3 Inspect how personal and environmental parameters influence situational knowledge

5.4 Review guidelines about how to increase the effectiveness of verbal and nonverbal skills for communication effectiveness

5.5 Use different ways to manage anxiety for effective communication

5.6 Analyze the three different message strategies

Strategic Scenario: Space and Meaning

You go to an interview for your first job. The office is very large. You have to walk across the entire room to get to the interviewer, whose desk is against the far back wall with just enough space for her desk chair. She remains seated and gestures with her hand toward two chairs that are at right angles to the oversized desk. If you sit in either one of the chairs, you will not be facing the interviewer. You begin to wonder if this is some kind of test she devised. Is this deliberate or inadvertent? This scene contains nonverbal spacial information and tells you something about the interviewer, but it may or may not call for action on your part. For assistance, you look for other nonverbal clues from the interviewer, and you realize you must now choose how to best reveal information about yourself, both verbally and nonverbally.

As you read this chapter, think about what if anything you would do in this situation. At the end of the chapter, we will revisit this scenario and discuss some solutions.

5.1: Overview
Verbal and Nonverbal Skills

5.1 **Scrutinize how strong verbal and nonverbal communication is necessary for personal success and the success of an organization**

Imagine you are talking to an acquaintance (not a close friend) or someone with whom you work named Sean. Sean asks your opinion about a problem that he has because he says he respects your opinion. As you talk to Sean, you notice that he rarely makes eye contact, he looks at his watch several times, and he asks you to repeat something that you just said. How would you evaluate the sincerity of his words? Does his nonverbal communication fit his words? Which would you believe—the verbal or nonverbal communication?

Clearly, along with listening skills, verbal and nonverbal skills are the foundation of successful communication in social and business communication. Researchers tell us that most people find nonverbal communication more believable than verbal communication.[1]

When you consider how much time a professional spends communicating with others during a normal workday, it is easy to understand the importance of this activity. The ability to send clear and coherent messages to supervisors, coworkers, outside vendors, the media, and the public is critical to maintaining productivity and a positive image regardless of the industry. Furthermore, as a person rises in the organization to higher levels of management, the need for communication increases. Strong verbal and nonverbal skills are essential for personal success and for the success of an organization. A part of success as a communicator is your understanding that all verbal and nonverbal messages are sent and received in cultural codes.

Verbal communication includes all messages composed of words, either spoken or written. Many of us take verbal communication for granted. Our lifelong familiarity with words and speaking makes it easy to neglect the importance of planning the oral messages we send to others, particularly in professional settings. Thoughtful preparation can help you avoid communication failures. Current technologies require even more preparation for your words, physical presentation, and skill in using them. Landlines, answering machines, and older cell phones have been replaced by smartphones and Web communications that display PowerPoints, Prezi, and other presentations through streaming, along with the many other channels mediated through technology. Business and professional people have had to learn new communication skills.

Effective communication via technology started with telephone etiquette, which set the rules on how to communicate when the speaker and listener were not face to face in real time. Through the decades, written communication, formerly not a real-time media, has changed as well, as the Internet expanded through email, Twitter, and social Web sites (such as YouTube, Facebook, and so on). With each additional choice of technology, communicators must adapt their written and oral skills to fit that technology. Understanding the limitations and possible barriers to communication is an ongoing process, and the technology creates new possibilities and the potential for new problems.[2]

Nonverbal communication is any message—other than spoken or written words—that conveys meaning. These include innumerable combinations. Some of these are:

- Pitch, quality, and volume of your voice
- Face, expressions (smiles, frowns, intensity of gaze, and many others), muscles in your face, the set of your mouth and teeth
- Body, posture, size, where you place yourself in relationship to others in public and private conversation
- Clothing choices, style, the fit of the clothing, the condition and care of garments, appropriateness of clothing and footwear for the context or the weather (athletes wearing flip flops to meet the President of the United States after the 2008 Olympic Games in China created an international buzz), and the overall impression of your garments as they relate to you
- Use of hands and arms in gestures, habitual actions (cracking your knuckles, wiping your palms against your sides, touching your hair), and other actions (scratching your nose, holding your hands or wringing them), gestures that seem to reveal your nervousness or unease.

5.1.1: Architectural Nonverbal Communication

The interior and exterior of an office communicate nonverbal messages to the employees and visitors. The specific nonverbal messages sent by fixed and nonfixed architectural features may be planned by the organization; the employees and customers may or may not understand the organization's purpose in architectural decisions. Although you are not responsible for the overall architectural features of the building where you work, you may be able to customize your fixed space and moveable features to reveal your personality or your talents. Be aware that your choices send messages to all who come in the office.

FIXED SPACE Generally, fixed space includes your office walls, any windows, the room's width, the height of ceilings, and the size of the office. You will rarely have the opportunity to change these characteristics, although you may be allowed to decorate the office walls. It's possible you may have a workstation instead of an office. The station may be in an open bay with many other stations, without any barriers for sound or sight. The stations may have moveable walls five to six feet high and offer little privacy. Through the years, you will have the opportunity to be in many offices. You will find that some are productive to your work and others impede it. Some arrangements and choices are not effective for your personality, just as some job duties are not those that you do well or enjoy.

Some companies control and dictate what decorations, paintings, or posters can be on the walls; these may be historical pictures of the early history of the company or other archival prints. Management may insist that pictures of the company's products or owners/innovators be on the walls. Some companies use "soothing" pictures, similar to those in medical buildings or hotel rooms. If you are free to decorate your walls, you may choose to display your diploma, family pictures, and drawings by your child or a niece or nephew.

MOVEABLE ARCHITECTURAL FEATURES Moveable features are those that traditionally have been controlled by the person who is using the office or workstation. Among these features are the desk or computer stand, desk chair, other chairs, and possibly a small table. In good economic times, employees, depending on their status in the company, may be asked to pick out new furniture. In small companies, new employees probably will inherit the office furniture from a previous occupant.

Many companies have policies that dictate what you can put on your desk. Some companies have very strict rules, such as only two personal items on your desk, no papers left on your desk at the end of the day, and so forth. Other business cultures say "no" to plants, excessive pictures of family, children's drawings, mementos from vacations, and other personal items. Each place that you work will have a company culture that will encourage or discourage personal displays. Use your observation powers to evaluate and read the hidden messages that lie in the decorations and rules.

If you are free to use items that define you as a person, you might be tempted to choose a cup that repeats the commercial "What happens in Vegas, stays in Vegas," family pictures, your dog's diploma from obedience school, and the Niagara Falls salt and pepper shakers you received from your second cousin twice removed on your father's side of the family. Are your choices sending messages that will enhance your role within the company? Will visitors have more faith in you because of your decorations or will they worry about you as a person?

The placement of your desk and other furniture is also important. If your desk faces the back wall of your office and leaves your back to the door, does this say that you do not wish to interact with peers or with outsiders? Or does it suggest that you are a very hard worker who does not waste time chatting? Does your desk against a sidewall give you access to people walking by or people who stop to see you? If your desk allows you to face your open door, does the free access to you interfere with your job activities or does it say that you are available as needed? If you do confidential work, does the placement of your computer give access to confidential materials if someone walks to your desk? In the last few years, in many academic, professional, and business settings, office managers or other administrators have encouraged employees to use a small table with chairs in an effort to remove the barriers of desks so that people feel that you are meeting them on an equal basis. However, a higher status person may use this method because it calls for the guests to remain standing as the boss or another person greets the visitor, usually with handshakes, and then the higher status person invites the visitor to sit. If an employee is meeting with his or her boss or interviewer, the supervisor will usually be the one to invite the visitor to sit, indicating where.

5.2: Goal Setting for Effective Messages

5.2 **Examine how goal setting in verbal and nonverbal communication is important for success in business settings**

Successful verbal and nonverbal communication requires careful planning. Analysis of the encounter should follow with evaluation from the perspective of the visitor and/or the employer. In this chapter, we will apply the components of strategic communication to verbal and nonverbal interaction. Then, we will cover verbal and nonverbal strategies that you are likely to encounter in business and professional contexts. You will undoubtedly recognize some of these strategies. You may already know the ones at which you excel and can identify others that you would like to improve. We will start by discussing goal setting for effective messages.

Achieving success in business settings requires that you know the purpose of your verbal communication. You can anticipate the response or reaction to your message by knowing your purpose and preparing yourself for either negative or positive results. Social conversation, discussions in common areas, and organizational messages serve three purposes or functions: task, maintenance, and human relations.

⊗ Task Messages

Task messages accomplish specific goals. Task messages include orders, questions, and even confrontations (as long as they promote the primary goals of the organization). Task messages direct a specific project, activity, or behavior. They address performance of tasks. Here are some examples of task messages: "Do you have that order ready today?" "When will that shipment of microchips arrive next week?" "Put those graphs at the end of the report."

⊗ Maintenance Messages

Maintenance messages keep the organization in working order so that tasks can be performed. Maintenance messages provide support for people who perform tasks. These messages indicate policy or procedure that directs the organization as a whole. For example, additional information about process serves maintenance functions. Here are some examples: "Be sure to fill out the departure form in triplicate." "Elias should contact Margaret about safety procedures."

⊗ Human Relations Messages

Human relations messages help employees fully realize their potential in the organization. Examples include statements such as "Sylvia, I appreciate the way you always give us more than we ask for on special projects; you're a valuable employee," and "I really think you have potential in the area of accounting. Why not consider getting a degree?" Human relations messages promote workers' personal development and occur frequently in organizations that emphasize open communication.

When setting goals for oral communication, consider the purpose. Identify the purpose of each of the following, and consider possible results.

1. "In the next quarter of the fiscal year, our efforts should be a combination of success in external and internal communication."

2. "George, I need extra security tonight because one of the members of the visiting representatives of Australia's Aboriginal Council will be joining with the representatives of U.S. Native American National Council and Canada's First Nation Council."

3. "Karen, thank you for staying late to help with the visitors and their transportation. I can always count on you to give more than you have to."

Human relations messages generally encourage employees or verbally reward them for their extra effort. Often, a manager may not see a direct result of human relations messages, but as time goes on, an improved working climate and work success of individuals may result from such messages. Task messages are specific to a particular person, and the speaker expects to get a concrete and definite response to such messages. Maintenance messages keep the organization on target and usually apply to process rather than new activities.

5.3: Personal and Environmental Factors

5.3 Inspect how personal and environmental parameters influence situational knowledge

To set effective goals in communication, you must consider the persons who will receive the message as well as the work environment in which the communication takes place. Additionally, research has been done that illustrates the differences between the communication of men and women.[3] Characteristics that determine how receivers respond to the message include perceptual differences between you and the receiver and the number of people who will ultimately need to receive the message.

Employees, supervisors, directors, and owners use many electronic devices, but all employees should consider which channel is most appropriate for the receiver, the purpose, and documentation. If several people need the information that you plan to send, a group presentation may be the most appropriate means of communication. If large numbers of people need to hear your message, you may be most effective if you deliver a public speech or stream your presentation. Human relations messages can take place over the phone or through other technological means, but they should be given face to face if possible. While many task messages are given face to face, they are often sent via email, which creates an instantaneous electronic record (easily turned into a private or public paper trail).

5.3.1: Structure of Messages

Many communication specialists have argued that messages have two parts: a **content element** (what you are trying to communicate) and a **relational element** (your work connection and/or personal links to the receiver). The relational element creates anticipation of the consequence. Considering the **relational consequences**—that is, how the message will influence future communication with the receiver—requires careful reflection on the structure and the channel.

The content element is important because words are symbols that the receiver may or may not understand. Misunderstandings may occur because our society is internationally diverse and different cultures coexist within the United States. You may speak U.S. English, but your culture will be the foundation of what you say. Often, you will unconsciously send messages with embedded cultural perceptions and expectations that hinder mutual understanding.

We often do not take into consideration the life experiences of our audience members. Graduation ceremonies for large universities often include speakers who are well known across the state or country. Speakers from out of town should work with locals so that they can refer to local politics, events at the university, and favorite gripes from the students. The resource providers may give good material, but there could be resistance to the speaker if he or she has perceptions and biases that do not match with the university's students. Attempts at inside humor do not ensure success with the audience.

You should not underestimate the importance of anticipating the relational consequences of your message. If you tell a coworker to "get that report in by 5 P.M.," you are not only asking for a task to be performed but also asserting that you have the power to make such a demand and expect others to acknowledge your power. You could have said, "Would it be possible for you to have that report to me by the end of the day?" The relational consequences of such a query would be quite different because you addressed the coworker as an equal engaged in a cooperative endeavor. Misuse of task messages can antagonize coworkers. A think-before-you-speak pattern of communication encourages a positive climate.

The content and relational connection between speaker and listener can have unexpected consequences. If one of your friends says, "I need to see you after this meeting," you will possibly take it in stride. However, if your professor says, "I need to see you after class," your reaction could be quite different. The relational consequences of your friend's message may be pleasant or mildly uncomfortable, but you probably will not worry. When a professor or boss says the very same words, you might become anxious and fearful. Relational consequences have the potential to make a simple request a matter of concern.

5.3.2: Status

In verbal and nonverbal communication, perceptions of power and status influence both higher and lower status persons. When we discuss status, we must put the emphasis on power. Status is a broad topic, but the sources it is identified with include legitimate power, position titles, wealth, education, and family influence.

Bases for Status

Remove card   1 of 5   Reset Deck

Table 5.1 Nonverbal Indicators of Power and Status

Power and High Status	Lack of Power and Low Status
Relaxed posture and body position	Erect and rigid posture and body position
Less attentive to others	More attentive to others
More expansiveness	More restrictiveness
Seated position	Standing position
Dark conservative clothes	Light or unusual clothing
More access to space	Less access to space
Finger pointing	Recipient of finger pointing
Less direct body orientation	More direct orientation toward superiors
Closed arm position (akimbo)	Open body orientation
Give less/receive more eye gaze	Receive less/give more eye gaze
Sarcastic smiling/laughing	Respectful smiling/laughing
Touch others more/touched less by others	Touch others less/touched more by others
Making others wait for you	Waiting for others (superiors)
Determine meeting time and length	Told of meeting time and length
More flexible time schedule	Rigorous and strict time schedule
Expensive office furniture	Economical office furniture
Larger office in nicest and most private location	Office location dependent on job duties

Within everyday interactions, ordinary, acceptable touching such as a handshake can be subject to unethical power plays. For example, a man with high status or who perhaps flaunts physical size and strength might shake hands with one hand and use the other to grab the other person's forearm or arm just above the elbow. A lower status person is conflicted whether to move his or her hand and arm just enough so that the other person must let go, or appear to be in a physical struggle. Neither person wins in this situation. When the situation involves a woman, either of the same status or lower, the situation and action can appear to be inappropriate beyond a status level. Has this happened to you? What did you do?

All of us have certain status with related powers in different contexts. Our nonverbal communication conveys that status. Each of the various cultures in the United States recognizes power from different categories of status. The higher status individuals assume nonverbal behavior either consciously or unconsciously. Those who aspire to status and power may try to influence others by using high-status and high-power nonverbal communication. You may anger higher and lower status colleagues if you use high-status nonverbal cues when you do not have the power. It is important for you to know which nonverbal cues are generally associated with status and power so that you can use or respond to these forms of communication in appropriate ways. In Table 5.1, we summarize much of the research on nonverbal indicators of status and power.

Although it is important to recognize the nonverbal cues that reveal status or power, there is evidence that traditional positions of power are changing. Some of the changes relate to societal developments and some to economic prosperity or hardship.[4] Many organizations are breaking down layers of power in favor of establishing teams. Teamwork and concessions from union and nonunion workers now characterize the work force of the future.

The economic crisis of 2008–2012 revealed public outrage about business leaders' salaries and their bonuses; these were post-contract benefits that were in the millions for some presidents and chairs of boards of directors. Restrictions on conspicuous consumption came during a time of high unemployment, failure of banks, bankruptcy of car companies, and high rates of foreclosure. As the economy improved through 2013–2015, the relationships of employees, managers, and owners improved as well, and people have a more positive opinion of business leaders. It is important to remember, however, that nonverbal power cues may, at another time, inhibit the perception of managers. (In other words, it can happen again.)

5.3.3: Perceptions

Although perception is most commonly associated with the receiver of a message, it also influences how messages are sent. **Perception** is the process of creating meaning based on experiences. These meanings affect verbal communication in several ways.

Your attitudes toward other communicators influence your perceptions. When you speak to someone you like and respect, your verbal and nonverbal messages are likely to reflect those positive attitudes—smiling, using a friendly tone, and offering an unthreatening pat on the shoulder. You may say, "Jim, could you present a progress report on the XYZ project tomorrow?" If you have negative attitudes about the receiver—if you believe that he or she is lazy, untrustworthy, or careless—your message may reflect that perception; for example (frowning and using a stern tone), "Tom, regardless of your attitude about the XYZ project, I expect you to make a five-minute report on it tomorrow; make sure you have all the facts straight."

Another factor that influences perception is emotion. When you are highly aroused by emotions such as anger, surprise, joy, or even fear, you are less likely to perceive a situation accurately, and you may confuse others by using excessive or contradictory nonverbal cues. You are influenced by the emotions of the situation itself and by memories of emotions you previously experienced in similar instances. For example, if you have ever experienced an embarrassing lapse of memory in a group presentation, your perceptions during later presentations are likely to be tainted by that memory.

In communication that involves emotions, attitudes, or the possibility of prejudice, ask yourself whether your message is based on accurate and objective perceptions or whether you are letting misperceptions limit your oral communication skills.

5.3.4: Proxemics

Proxemics is the study of personal space. Space plays an important role in communication. Personal space, or the distance between communicators, has two aspects: actual distance, which can be measured in feet and inches, and perceived distance, which varies among speakers. People differ in their need for personal space. Some prefer very close communicating distances; others require greater separation. Cultures within the United States and throughout the world view the use of space differently. One researcher, Hall, developed zones of personal space commonly used in business communication.[5] Hall was an anthropologist, and his research in the 1950s analyzed how businessmen in the northeastern United States in the 1950s communicated through proxemics. Although his research did not include women, the concept of culturally driven use of space has become an important part of the study of nonverbal communication. Subsequent contributions by other communication, psychology, and anthropological researchers in the United States and in other countries has verified the importance of personal distance in culture. The following sections discuss categories of typical "people space" as explained by Hall.

INTIMATE ZONE The zone where people interact at the closest distance is the **intimate zone,** which ranges from skin contact to eighteen inches. Business associates rarely interact at this distance with the exception of special needs: to give and receive congratulatory nonthreatening hugs, to speak quietly during a meeting to another, to help someone with a coat, and so forth.

PERSONAL ZONE Ranging from eighteen inches to four feet, the **personal zone** is usually reserved for interactions that are personal or private, although some business interaction does occur in this zone. Shaking hands; talking semiprivately; illustrating something to someone on paper; sharing a handout, chart, or other visual aid in a meeting; and other legitimate types of communication all occur in the personal zone. Often people use the personal zone when attending a reception or a conference that includes dozens or hundreds of people in a meeting room. In order to talk to several colleagues at once, people move into close casual groupings that break the zone, a movement that is usually considered appropriate. However, even if the activity requires the personal zone, you should be aware that you should ask permission.

SOCIAL ZONE The **social zone**, with a slightly larger distance of four to twelve feet, is used a great deal in business settings. Interviews, small meetings, conversations among several people, and chance encounters usually occur in this zone. At this distance, people communicate in a normal voice and generally feel comfortable both verbally and nonverbally.

Our physical proximity to coworkers and clients influences the effectiveness of our communication.

SOURCE: Rawpixel/Shutterstock

PUBLIC ZONE Used for speeches and other high-attendance events, the **public zone** ranges from twelve feet and beyond. It is used for events such as speeches and presentations, large-group meetings, and demonstrations. The public zone reduces the chances for immediate feedback among the participants and the ability to read facial expressions and eye movements. Vocal pitch and volume are usually at high levels, and gesturing may be exaggerated so that everyone within the zone can see. Often portable public announcement units, a podium, and a microphone (e.g., fixed, remote, on a tether) are used when it is difficult for all to hear adequately. Be sure to check out the system and your voice for each venue.

In private life, if you are on your own property and a stranger approaches, you will probably make verbal inquiry to the person. A polite question is sometimes used, "May I help you?" Alternatively, a more stern response might be, "Do I know you?" Touching is not a part of this zone. It is important to recognize the social and cultural norms reflected by the four zones. When you violate the rules of proxemics, you may be perceived as rude or ignorant of common courtesy.

These zones and the explanations are for U.S. cultures in general. Some cultural groups in the United States have different rules, and people from various national cultures will have perceptions of proxemics that are very different. In some European and Latin American countries, for example, hugging is equivalent to shaking hands. Some of the natives may also use the social kiss. The social kiss is generally a kiss on both cheeks, with some cultures kissing both cheeks with a last kiss (the third) on the first cheek. Some parts of the United States also use the social kiss. Most U.S. cultures use a handshake. By your observations, you can get a good idea of the norms in each context. During the 2008–2009 H1N1 pandemic (commonly known as the "swine flu"), many people temporally stopped or reduced shaking hands, hugging, and kissing out of fear of contagion.

WRITING PROMPT

You are a work-study student in a department of communication. Your friend Carol has been looking for a job. You know that the office manager, Ryan, needs another worker. However, Ryan has a habit of physically touching people; you are not sure whether he does it as a friendly gesture, as a power move, or as a prelude to sexual harassment. Carol really needs a job, but you are conflicted about whether to suggest the job. What should you do?

▶ `The response entered here will appear in the performance dashboard and can be viewed by your instructor.`

Submit

PERSONAL, CULTURAL, AND ORGANIZATIONAL NORMS ON TOUCHING Many ethical issues are involved with accidental and deliberate touching in the workplace. Our gestures, body movements, and touching are culturally acceptable by personal preference, ethnicity, and the organization in which contact takes place.[6]

While it is possible to generalize about national cultures and their citizens' ideas on touching, these may not accurately describe the actions and personal preferences of every individual from that culture. A further complication is that the culture of a specific organization may reflect the category of business (e.g., car manufacturing, nonprofit charity organization); the specific organization; and a transfer of culture from the local community, city, geographical setting, or nation in which the home office is located.

- Americans need more private space in professional settings than members of other cultures do. However, informal observations indicate that Southerners, particularly women, touch each other more than women from other parts of the country. Men and women professionals who prefer distance are often from New England, the West, and the northern Midwest. Generally, American men rarely stand as close to other men as some men in cultures such as France, Spain, Saudi Arabia, Iraq, Iran, and other countries. Interacting with women from some Muslim countries is forbidden unless the man is a family member.

- Japanese business people working in the United States appear to need more personal space than Americans. Casual touching is rarely seen among the Japanese or between Japanese business people and individuals from other cultures. Japanese women are very conscious of space between them and men and women from other cultures. Although many Chinese and Japanese are well trained in the U.S. custom of shaking hands, the practice is not preferred.

- Latino/a and Hispanic professionals touch members of their community more than they do strangers, but as they become comfortable with others, they often touch more than mainstream Americans. Depending on the country, women adapt well to the specific culture of their country or society.

When personal preferences, organizational demands, and cultural constraints influence physical interactions, each person needs to be both skilled at observing the other person's behaviors and mindful of his or her own touching habits. Inappropriate touching—to make sexual advances, assert physical dominance over another person, or humiliate someone—is damaging and in many cases illegal. This is true for men and women in many countries. You should also become aware of your own touching patterns with different people. We often touch others—both strangers and people we know—without conscious thought. Unfortunately, your unconscious touching may be highly offensive to many people, including those of your own culture.

Interesting tidbits on proxemics are popular in the news. U.S. President George W. Bush once unexpectedly stepped behind German Chancellor Angela Merkel and rubbed her shoulders for a few seconds. This breach of protocol was captured on cameras, resulting in a short-lived but sensational media event. On another occasion First Lady Michelle Obama met Queen Elizabeth II of Great Britain during when she and President Obama made their first trip to England after his election. As the two women met, talked, and began to move toward another place in the room, Mrs. Obama lightly put her arm around the Queen. This, too, was a rule-breaking event: Queen Elizabeth II may touch, but others may not touch her. In this case, sensational media coverage ensued but quieted after the spokesperson for the English royal family made a statement about the appropriateness of the unusual event. Younger British royals followed less restrictive protocols in public interactions during later meetings. And a seemingly major breach of religious protocol occurred when President Obama and First Lady Michelle Obama attended a funeral in Saudi Arabia because she did not have her hair covered. News releases later reported that because it was a funeral and not a political meeting, the absence of a scarf in Saudi Arabia was not a problem.

5.3.5: Territoriality

Another aspect of personal space is **territoriality**, which is the behaviors or actions associated with the use, maintenance, or defense of physical space to indicate ownership.[7] Territories are readily recognized in organizational settings, and many people go to great lengths to preserve and protect theirs. Examples include people's choices of chairs in a conference room with the same people frequently meeting there. This again is played out with status. In general, employees do not rush to sit at the head of a meeting table if the supervisor always chooses that spot.

Why is territory important? Territories provide a space for people to take comfort and refuge. Just as you may claim the same seat in a classroom lecture after lecture, members of organizations look for places that they can call their own. Offices are probably the best examples of territories. Some people strongly identify with their office, cubicle, or desk. Many feel personally threatened or violated if others enter without asking or rifle through items on their desk. Because confidential information is often on people's computers, visitors should not stand where they can see the screen unless invited to do so. If for some reason employees must share a computer, both employees should work out an agreement on what to keep and change in the settings. Close friends or acquaintances who have worked together for a long time may use a friend's pen, notepad, or other supplies and then make a casual comment or tell the friend about it later. However, to do this with a work acquaintance's desk is not appropriate. Some employees will go to the receptionist's desk and think that they are permitted to use her or his supplies because the person is "only" the receptionist. That is not ethical. Personal space and territory should be respected.

Use of technology has become a territoriality issue, along with an ethical one. Many employees bring private mobile devices to their workplaces and subsequently

questions about appropriate use of the technology. Most people recognize that personal use of a work telephone that inhibits customers or vendors from reaching the company is unethical, yet access to a personal phone is another story. The issue now is workers' ethical use of any technology, including a company-owned computer, for private reasons during working hours. The hours for which a person is paid belong to the employer. If employees shop online, surf the net, go onto their YouTube page, Tweet, or chat with friends and family, they are effectively cheating their employer. Businesses have sued to legally access the email and phone records of employees to verify their negligence or their noncompliance with rules. Many disputes have resulted in companies winning the right to examine emails and other records when they believe that an employee is abusing the right to technology. In addition, in some organizations or businesses, disgruntled or unreliable employees have posted pictures and messages online, sending communications that proved harmful to the organization. Some of these were fraudulent, and others were based in truth. One example was online pictures of employees in a pizza restaurant contaminating the food—not good for business. Mentors and researchers urge employees never to write an email or leave a voice mail message that cannot be given comfortably to all employees, including their supervisor. Even if you delete an email or voice mail, experts can retrieve the data. All communication stored electronically belongs to the company.

The use of territory can also be a function of habit or routine. For example, a certain table in the cafeteria may be informally reserved by a group of people who sit there day after day and who may become annoyed or angry if another group *takes* the table. Informal observations by a professor and graduate teaching assistant in a large communication class at a university in the Southwest focused on how students marked their territories in a large lecture class of 300. Two female students would often sit side by side, while two male students usually kept an empty seat between them, marked with their belongings—but three or more males would sit side by side. People who chose to sit by themselves would place personal belongings on the two seats on either side of them, thereby signaling their preference to be alone. Although the room was very crowded, the last seats to be taken were, of course, the seats at the very front.

A fairly extreme case of seizing territory is a true story about a woman and her adult daughter. After driving around a mall for thirty minutes looking for parking, the mother let her daughter out with the instructions, "Find an empty spot and save it; I will go around one more time and look for an opening." The daughter found an empty parking place. She stood in the middle of the spot and waited for her mother to return. During the few minutes that she waited, she turned away several cars. The result was, obviously, some very angry drivers who honked their horns and yelled unkind remarks. Nevertheless, the mother and daughter had a great parking place. This is not a recommended action. Perhaps you have seen people at social gatherings, such as receptions or buffet dinners, lay possessions on certain seats to guarantee their place. This too is considered discourteous behavior.

By being observant, you gain information about others' habits, territories, and preferences regarding personal space and your own preferences. You can then demonstrate your competence as a communicator by your knowledge.

WRITING PROMPT

Have you ever been in a cafeteria or restaurant standing, holding a tray, and looking for a seat, only to discover that people have used their possessions to block the only available seats? How did it make you feel? Did you think their actions were personal? If this behavior happened at your university, would it make a difference if the offenders were faculty or administrators rather than fellow students?

The response entered here will appear in the performance dashboard and can be viewed by your instructor.

Submit

5.3.6: Clothing and Personal Appearance

Clothing and personal appearance communicate a great deal about the wearer, especially in the workplace. You may have what you refer to as "interview clothes," clothes that you wear only to interviews or formal presentations. Some men have a particular (or only) suit with traditional tie and dress shoes as opposed to athletic shoes. Women often take their cues from previous decades and wear a suit that is made for a woman, but without the neck scarf that marked the 1970s through the 1980s. Special clothes show that you are aware of the importance of an event, whether professional, social, religious, or political.

Interviewers often judge hopeful applicants within the first few minutes of an interview. Interpersonal relationships are established, reconfirmed, or denied at the beginning of the contact. The most important cues that can be analyzed are your appearance and nonverbal communication.

Today no one set of rules is available. Each industry, organization, and area of the country may have different cultural expectations for clothing as well as behavior. In the past few decades, casual Friday became a perk. However, as employees began to enjoy the freedom, casual sometimes became sloppy and inappropriate. Some companies made new rules, but in general, clothing choices are more loosely and casually defined now than at any other time.

Do not make assumptions about the clothing choices for any company until you look at the Web site, ask someone who works there, or talk to the human resources manager. In business and professional settings, dressing

appropriately is a decision that may be conscious or unconscious. Strong impressions of others are formed in the first few minutes.[8]

When you are trying to decide what to wear to work, observe what others are wearing and consider the climate of the organization. Is it formal, friendly, or trendy? The organizational context may suggest that variations can be made in standard dress. The term *business casual* is not universally defined, but it generally refers to dress that is more casual than a business suit, for both men and women.

Context can allow a modification in company dress codes. For example, in some companies where employees are expected to wear suits, people hang their suit jackets on their doors as soon as they arrive at work and do not put them on again until they leave the office. Because everyone does it, the dress code is contextual. President Obama was criticized early on for not wearing a suit coat in the Oval Office during meetings. Do you think his preferences have since changed the dress code context in the West Wing? On-camera male news readers and interviewers have begun to report without a tie or without a coat, while women newscasters choose dresses that reflect innovative fashions or layered clothes. Interestingly, high-heeled shoes continue to be worn by media personalities, campus women, and other public figures.

For an idea of how dress codes have changed over the years, look at old yearbooks or old family pictures for the casual shots of people on campus or with family. Compare the styles in these candid shots to your own dress habits. Be prepared for continued change in the workplace, and make your own decisions about any changes that you choose to make.

5.3.7: Environmental Factors

You should take into account the influence of the business environment. Office arrangements, reception areas, and even furniture, lighting, fixtures, color schemes, floor coverings, music, and plants are carefully chosen in professional settings. Visitors cannot help but form impressions of an organization based on how the building or individual offices appear.

The physical temperature of the building and the offices has a profound effect on employees, vendors, customers, and so forth. In the early 1980s, the energy crisis was severe; prices for heating oil and other sources of fuel were devastating to people on fixed incomes and government organizations. A community college in Kentucky had a very large shortfall. They turned all of the heating thermostats down to 58 Fahrenheit degrees. Professors and students spent the day in heavy coats, gloves, scarves, and hats. The most annoying problem for many of us (yes, the author was there) was when our ballpoint pens were too cold to write well.

Think of any visits you have made to a building for an interview, a tour, or a meeting. What impressions did you have of the company before you even entered the front door? Several factors probably colored your impression. Was the organization located at the epicenter of business and financial affairs? Was the building's architecture traditional or contemporary? Was the building old or new? Did it look cold and forbidding or warm and inviting? Just as you should find a career that you enjoy, the type of setting is also important if you have choices. In many businesses, the public areas are considered the primary public relations message.

In both of these pictures, the participants are at a table, but the long table scene with a rug, and with the informality of movement and dress, gives a sense of individuals talking with each other in a comfortable and positive environment. In contrast, the two men in suits at a table with others appear to be involved in unshared communication in a more formal climate without the friendliness of the other group.

SOURCES: *top*: Ryan McVay/Getty Images; *bottom*: Cardinal/Corbis

5.4: Verbal and Nonverbal Competence

5.4 **Review guidelines about how to increase the effectiveness of verbal and nonverbal skills for communication effectiveness**

It is important to think about the setting in which your message will be sent and received. The reaction elicited by a message that is received in the privacy of an office is likely to be different from the reaction elicited by a message received in the company cafeteria or in the presence of casual bystanders. Messages sent and received in formal settings, such as a class or a meeting, sound different from messages communicated in informal settings, such as a hallway.

5.4.1: Choose the Setting for Communication

Consider the following situation:

> Peyton was anxious because her boss Allie had not informed her of the raise she expected for next year. Peyton had spent a lot of time thinking about how much she needed and deserved a raise and how to phrase her request to Allie. The issue was so important to Peyton that when she saw Allie talking to some other employees in the hallway, she immediately approached her and asked whether she had made a decision about her raise. Peyton did not pause to think about the appropriate setting for the request. Allie wheeled around and in a hostile tone said, "I can't talk about that right now!"

Three variables are worth considering when you are choosing a setting: (1) the likelihood that bystanders will receive the message unintentionally; (2) the physical characteristics of the setting—high ceilings, sources of noise, and so on; and (3) the formality of the situation as dictated by social or company norms. You can increase the effectiveness of spoken communication by thinking about these variables beforehand. If Peyton had done so, she would have realized that the hallway was an inappropriate setting for a discussion of her raise for several reasons.

First, money and salary issues are generally sensitive and private and should not be discussed in front of others unless the organizational culture promotes such discussions. Second, the hallway is generally not an appropriate setting for lengthy discussions because such talk can distract others or interfere with their work. Third, most companies have specific procedures for giving raises. Peyton should have familiarized herself with the company's formal procedures before confronting Allie.

Have you given much thought to an ideal office or workspace? Would it be functional, stylish, or both? Where would you sit? Would you have windows? What inferences can your classmates make about you from your office design, and why?

```
The response entered here will appear in the
performance dashboard and can be viewed by
your instructor.
```

Submit

5.4.2: Chronemics

Chronemics is the use of time as each culture determines it to be appropriate. The use of time can affect verbal and nonverbal communication. At business meetings, U.S. businesspeople spend relatively little time on interpersonal relationships as they rush to the main purpose of the meeting. In some countries, such as Japan and Spain, some business people consider multitasking activities and the intense pressure to keep to a schedule as rude behavior.

Just as the use of time is important, so is the timing of messages. The story about Peyton's asking about a raise in the hallway shows not only that the place was inappropriate but also that the timing was poor. Additionally, the length of the message becomes an important factor. Even if a person chooses the right place and time, it is better to make an appointment with the topic of the meeting clearly expressed.

Most people do not consider how long a specific message actually needs to be. You have undoubtedly suffered through long and wordy messages. To keep a message concise, you can write it out on a piece of paper and then circle the key words, crossing out all unnecessary words. Communicators in professional settings often provide extra details and elaboration to impress the receiver when in fact most receivers are busy and want the quickest and most efficient message possible.

Another way to check the length of a message is to see whether you can break it into two or more separate messages. Frequently, people try to communicate too many ideas at once. Your communication will be much more successful if you send several short, self-contained messages instead of one long message that wanders from point to point. Of course, your message must be long enough to contain the necessary information.

It is important that messages arrive at their destinations at the appropriate time. The timing of messages is something of an art—it is often difficult to gauge when receivers can best handle the message you wish to send. In deciding when to send a message, consider these three elements of timing: when messages are likely to pile up, what the receiver's schedule is, and whether all aspects of your message are in sync.

⊗ Know the Organization

Know the organization well enough to understand when messages are likely to pile up all at once. In a university, for example, messages are most numerous at the beginning and end of the semester, and telephone calls are likely to be most numerous during mid-morning and mid-afternoon.

⊗ Know the Receiver's Schedule

Know the schedule of the receiver. Find out if the receiver's duties and responsibilities are seasonal or cyclical. You can obtain some of this information from the receiver or from an assistant.

⊗ Sync Your Messages

Be sure your messages are in sync. We often use email or voice mail as an alternative to actually speaking to a person. The person can get back to you when it is convenient for him or her, especially if you leave a choice of times for the person to call when you will be in your office. However, if you send more than one email, remember that some people start with the last message and others with the first message from the previous day. The receiver may be confused about the messages. If you find it necessary to leave a message both in voice mail and email, make reference to the second message but have the same information in both.

Think of yourself, the receiver, and your message as a coordinated strategy. All three must be in sync before you send the message. The more receivers agree with the timing of the message, the more likely you are to get an appropriate response. Receivers, in other words, need to believe that now is the best time to receive your message.

5.4.3: Use Language Effectively

Using language effectively, particularly in business and professional settings, is not always easy. The relationship between a word and what it represents is not always based on real or concrete shared characteristics that can be analyzed or predicted. You can increase your skill in using language by continually learning new ways to say what you mean.

⊗ Learn the Language

One way to familiarize yourself with the language of the field you plan to enter is by reading journals, technical magazines, newspaper articles, and perusing Web sites and blogs. Another way is by writing down new words and their definitions when you come across them. The act of writing helps you to remember the word and how it was used. It is in your best interest to be familiar with as many words related to your field as you can.

Language varies in its preciseness. Legal, medical, academic, and technical languages are very specific and not open to a wide range of interpretation. Other types of language are vague, abstract, or open to multiple meanings. For example, *toast* can be used as both a noun and a verb. As a noun, it can mean a slice of heated and browned bread or a clinking of glasses in celebration. As a verb, it can mean the act of clinking glasses or a method of cooking (such as toasting marshmallows). As a slang noun, *toast* means that a person or an idea is finished or has lost significance.

When you formulate a spoken message, choose words that are neither too specialized nor too general. Be accessible without being ambiguous. For example, "I will try to accommodate you" sounds cooperative and flexible, unlike "Well, I don't know if I will be able to help you." Also, be aware of the difficulties that you are likely to encounter if you use jargon, euphemisms, or tag questions.

JARGON Jargon is the specialized language that professionals use to communicate efficiently with one another. Jargon is also confusing and ineffective in communication with a person not familiar with the words. The contrast between these two meanings vividly shows the potential and the limits of jargon. At its best, jargon makes communication among members of a group more efficient and precise and provides definite advantages for shared meaning. Medical-care personnel, for example, cannot live without specialized vocabulary ("Myocardial infarction in the later stages of pulmonary edema suggests a code four procedure."). But the use of jargon in inappropriate situations, such as around people who are unfamiliar with it, tends to result in an undesirable image—silly, inconsiderate, out of touch—for the communicator and a failure to achieve shared meaning.

EUPHEMISMS Euphemisms are agreeable, neutral, or indirect phrases used to describe unpleasant events. A vice president who says, "Because of declining sales, we have to implement a retrenchment program that might temporarily displace some people or make them redundant" is using euphemisms. What she or he really means is "The drop in sales means that we have to cut costs and fire people."

Some euphemisms become mainstream terminology and, therefore, require euphemisms of their own. An example of this is the succession of terms for the act of firing. Prior to the 1960s, people were fired. In the 1970s, people were not fired but laid off. In the 1980s, they were given the opportunity for new career experiences. The expression *laid off* was so widely adopted that it was no longer effective as a euphemism. New euphemisms were coined to replace it: temporary displacement, voluntary retirement, and redundancy. Terms such as *right-sizing* or the military's *build-down* also appear in managerial texts.

Euphemisms are often used to soften the blow of communicating bad news, but they are also used in less positive ways. Some speakers use euphemisms to build ambiguity or vagueness into their messages. Stressful or difficult circumstances promote making something that is bad sound not as bad or distorting explanations that forestall confrontations or criticism. These communicative acts call into question the communicator's integrity. Euphemisms are also used to avoid realities of life when people attempt to talk around emotional pain or experiences, death, addiction, divorce, and so forth. Use euphemisms with care, and employ them only when you are making an honest effort to help or to spare the feelings of others.

TAG QUESTIONS "These cost overruns are killing us, don't you think?" "I'm really feeling the heat from the accounting department, know what I mean?" "It's disgraceful that we have to attend this meeting, isn't it?" "You'll finish the report, OK?" Tag questions tacked onto the end of a statement undercut the effectiveness of your message. They soften the original statement to the point of feebleness. The use of tag questions by women or men does nothing to advance important points and makes the speaker seem overly dependent on the opinions of the receiver. Another self-denigrating choice of words is to precede a part of a conversation with phrases such as, "I am not sure, but the problem may be in the concept." Or "I am new but it seems to me that the answer is in the customer's methods of asking." Every time you begin your contribution with a "tempering phrase that dilutes your idea" you create a negative impression about yourself.

WRITING PROMPT

Do you belong to any groups that use jargon? Do certain situations cause you to use tag questions? What about euphemisms? Think for a moment about your personal relationship to these three language patterns. Choose one and describe it briefly. What alternative phrasing would help you communicate more effectively, and why?

▶ The response entered here will appear in the performance dashboard and can be viewed by your instructor.

Submit

5.4.4: Avoid Racist and Sexist Language

Phrases that had negative ethnic or gender connotations have in times past been used with impunity because of the passive responses of a large part of the population. With changes in society, the words became unacceptable in public but were still used within the confines of extreme organizations who vilify anyone who is not just like themselves. For example, it is insulting to refer to a female employee as a "girl" or to a male African American as a "boy." Many other words and phrases are equally objectionable. For example, the term *stewardess* has been replaced with *flight attendant*, and the use of "man" and masculine pronouns to refer to both women and men is avoided by savvy communicators using plural forms of words.

Here are some examples of sexist language and language that is gender-neutral:

 Sexist

A human seeks **his** physical comforts.

Man needs language to create reality.

The **chairman** is ready to begin.

ⓧ Gender Neutral

Humans seek **their** physical comforts.

People need language to create reality.

The **chair** is ready to begin.

Regardless of your position, you need to cultivate respect for the people with whom you work and communicate. You need to avoid sexist, insulting, and racist language. The guidelines for nondiscriminatory communication are easy to understand and remember. Respect and be considerate of others, and commit yourself to thoughtful language choice. Do not immediately say the first words that come to mind; instead, consider the connotations (the imbedded emotional meanings of words) of your words and the values and assumptions that they imply. A quick mental check before speaking will prevent you from promoting stereotypes and making damaging generalizations.

If you assume that the people with whom you are speaking do not care about such issues, and if you make no effort to avoid offensive language, you will not be prepared to communicate effectively with people who care very strongly about this issue. Racist, sexist, and insulting language is likely to cause many receivers to refuse your message and to perceive you as incompetent and insensitive.

Table 5.2 provides a list of terms that reflect gender stereotypes and suggestions for neutral alternatives.[9]

Table 5.2 Examples of Gender-Neutral Language

Sexist	Gender Neutral
actress	actor (to refer to male or female)
airman	flier, pilot
anchorman	anchor
businessman	businessperson
chairman	chair, chairperson, moderator
cleaning lady	cleaner, maintenance worker, custodian
congressman	congressperson, congressional representative, member of Congress
fireman	firefighter
foreman	foreperson, supervisor
gentleman's agreement	honorable agreement
mailman, postman	mail carrier, letter carrier, postal worker
male nurse	nurse
man and wife	husband and wife or man and woman
manpower	staff, labor, personnel
poetess	poet
salesman	salesperson, sales representative
secretary	assistant, associate, clerk
waitress/waiter	waitperson, wait staff
woman doctor	doctor

5.4.5: Paralanguage

Paralanguage refers to voice qualities, or characteristics of speech, such as pitch (how high or low the voice is), tempo (rate of speaking), volume (loudness of voice), rhythm (timing and emphasis on words), and articulation (how clearly words are pronounced).[10] You can get a good idea of the personality and mood of a speaker by paying attention to his or her voice qualities. Rapid, high-pitched speech often signals that the speaker is excited or distressed. Poor articulation may suggest fatigue, lack of interest in the topic, physical handicaps, or other problems.

Paralanguage has significant effects on communication. You often inadvertently communicate certain ideas to others through the sound of your voice rather than the words you use. It is important to monitor whether your vocal cues are signaling what you are thinking and feeling. Changes in vocal tone and rate, for example, can help you to manage a conversation. When you want to signal that you are ready to give up the floor of conversation, you can use a rising vocal inflection to indicate a question or a falling inflection to show the end of your message.

Frequent and loud sighs are often unconscious examples of boredom, inattention, or extreme fatigue. When a speaker is face to face or making a speech to a small group, head nods and "mmm" or "uh huh" are generally supportive counterpoints to the speaker's message. We also make many sounds to show contempt, disbelief, or rejection of an idea or concept.

You can also use paralanguage to communicate your feelings. When you greet someone in a pleasant tone of voice, you reinforce the verbal message that you are glad to see that person. An expressionless greeting gives a person the impression that she or he is unwanted. Either way, paralanguage gives people an idea about your feelings toward them.

5.4.6: Interpret Nonverbal Cues Accurately

Nonverbal communication accompanies verbal communication. Nonverbal behavior can reinforce what is said verbally (smiling while saying that you are satisfied with a business report). It can help to regulate verbal behavior (breaking eye contact to signal that a conversation is about over). It can complement oral communication (talking very slowly and deliberately to make an important point). It can take the place of words (nodding, winking, or gesturing your approval). It can even contradict what you say verbally (avoiding eye contact when you say that you are really glad to meet someone). Those types of nonverbal expression require accurate interpretation: facial and eye expressions and kinesics.

FACIAL AND EYE EXPRESSIONS The face is the most expressive outlet for nonverbal communication; it can display more than a thousand different expressions. The expression *poker face* refers to people who keep their expressions neutral. Not many people are effective at this. That the face serves as a conspicuous mode of communication is both advantageous and problematic. Facial expression can be a powerful reinforcement of a verbal message, whether the message is positive or negative. However, facial expressions and phenomena, such as blushing, may be difficult to control—and many people often are unaware that their emotions are clearly visible on their face. For the message recipient, interpreting facial expressions is often challenging.

Our discussion here is about the facial and eye expressions of members of mainstream U.S. culture. It is impossible to generalize about all groups in the United States. Many Native Americans and some Asian cultures, for example, are taught that direct eye contact with elders and strangers is a sign of disrespect. An effective communicator appreciates cultural diversity. Understanding how the meanings of facial and eye expressions differ in various cultures may prevent misinterpretations and promote the acquisition of shared meaning. Our discussion, however, is only an overview of commonly practiced facial and eye expressions in the U.S. work force.

Understanding the facial expressions of coworkers can give you an opportunity to determine the real motivations and intentions behind their actions (for example, are smiles real, or do frowns mean suspicion or contemplation?). However, simply observing another person's face for emotional cues is probably not enough to establish a high degree of accuracy. Rather, you must act like a detective and put together a number of cues that help to paint a complete picture of the person's emotional state.

Eyes are an important source of information. Because humans are visually oriented, **oculesics,** or **eye behavior**— the movement of the eyes and how they are focused on other people and objects—reveals a great deal of information. It is only natural to search the eyes of others in an effort to understand their feelings, intentions, and motives. The cliché "the eyes are the windows to your soul" may or may not be accurate, but how often have you heard people refer to the eyes: illness ("She does not look good around her eyes."), dislike or fear ("I didn't like the way his eyes looked."), and credibility ("You could just tell he was a good person by his eyes.").

The eyes are also an important tool for regulating the flow of communication. With a direct look, you can notify another person that you are ready to communicate. Eye contact is also useful when you wish to influence others. Why does a salesperson who is trying to convince a buyer to make a purchase seldom resort to letters or phone calls, especially to close a sale? The salesperson needs to read the buyer for signs of support, anxiety, or hesitancy. Lack of direct eye contact, a shifting gaze, or a fixed stare can signal that the buyer has doubts about the seller or the product or has lost interest.

Whenever you are trying to influence someone, communicate in person so that you can use the other's eye behavior as a source of information to strengthen your case. Keep in mind that U.S. standards for eye contact are not the same for some cultures in the United States and throughout the world.[11]

ⓧ Eye behavior and the regulation of communication:

- People have a tendency to "match" the gaze duration of their conversational partners.

- Speech rate is higher when the speaker looks at the listener.

- Eye gaze increases when the information being communicated is positive and decreases when it is negative.

- Smiling causes a decrease in direct eye contact.

- People in groups tend to look more while speaking and less while listening (the opposite effect occurs when only two people are talking).

- People who gaze longer are better liked.

- Increased gazing causes favorable impressions when positive information is communicated and unfavorable impressions when negative information is revealed.

- People with lower status (less power) look more when listening than when speaking compared to high-status people.

KINESICS **Kinesics** is the study of gestures and body movement that can be intentional or unintentional. Although it is difficult to monitor what you are doing with your hands and body at all times, familiarizing yourself with a few nonverbal cues can enable you to be more aware of the nonverbal messages you are sending to others. If you use your hands as a counterpoint to your speech, check with friends to determine if it is helpful or annoying. Again, culture dictates our types and amounts of gestures and body movements.

Emblems are body movements that substitute for words. A thumbs-up signal indicates "Go ahead," "Good job," or "Keep up the good work." A thumbs-down signal indicates disapproval or disagreement. Making a circle with the thumb and index finger signals "OK" or "I understand." Emblems are intentional nonverbal acts and are usually reserved for people who know their meaning. If you try to use emblems with people who are unaware of their meanings—particularly with people from another culture—you risk miscommunicating with or even insulting them. In the Korean War after North Korea and the Chinese attacked South Korea in the early 1950s, U.S. troops sent to help South Korea were in many deadly battles, and some were captured. Because North Korea had a foreign policy of isolationism, their knowledge of popular culture in the United States was limited. The North Koreans endeavored to make propaganda film clips and take still pictures with the first soldiers who were captured. They forced them to participate by threatening not just their lives but also the lives of their fellow soldiers. The U.S. soldiers discovered that the rather common U.S. insult toward others, the middle finger, was unknown in Korea. For a short time, the soldiers were able to send the cultural message to those at home that their conditions were terrible and that others were dying from inhumane treatment.

Illustrators are body movements that amplify, accent, or supplement what is being said orally. Illustrators generally are less intentional than emblems and are often used without conscious thought. For example, someone who has a habit of waving her or his arms wildly when trying to make a point may have no idea how flamboyant she or he appears to others.

In business and professional settings, illustrators can help make verbal communication more meaningful as long as they clearly correspond to the message. Some illustrators, however, contradict the verbal message. Consider the following situation:

> Kaitlyn always smiled when she presented material to her coworkers. Several years previously, at a company communication seminar, she had been encouraged to smile while speaking publicly; she continued to do so. One afternoon some time later, she was asked to tell her coworkers about an impending plant closing. As she spoke about the closing, her coworkers looked at each other, wondering why Kaitlyn was smiling. Kaitlyn's nonverbal cues did not change with the message.

⊕ **How do our illustrators give us away?**

Consider your own use of illustrators. How often do you illustrate with your hands, arms, and body without really thinking about it? Do people readily recognize and understand your illustrators? You can improve your illustrating behavior by observing others who are good at illustrating and modeling what they do. By analyzing the gestures of effective illustrators, you may be able to enhance your overall communication ability.

Some people use their fingers in a very detailed manner; others use their hands and arms to depict their thoughts.

By analyzing the gestures of effective illustrators, you may be able to enhance your overall communication ability.

Some people telegraph their ideas through the use of hands and face. One particular professor was grading a make-up test while Blake waited in the same office. After a few minutes, Blake moaned and said, "Oh, no." The professor responded quickly with "What's the matter?" Blake said, "Whenever you have bad news to tell a class or a student, you always lean forward and put your first and second finger across your mouth." The professor was amazed at the student's ability to put meaning to her unconscious signals.

Regulators are nonverbal, usually automatic acts that help to maintain the flow of a conversation. Communicators are often unaware of how these nonverbal behaviors control conversation. Regulators function in a number of ways. You can signal to others that you are ready to give up the floor of conversation, for example, by opening your palms, reducing your gestures, or even motioning toward another person to encourage him or her to take a turn. If there is a moderator, you can use your eyes or hands to discreetly point out a person attempting to speak. You can signal to others that you would like to keep talking by increasing your gesturing, holding up your hands, or leaning toward your conversational partner. You can request a turn by raising your index finger or hand or by rapidly nodding your head. You can even deny someone else the chance to speak by holding up your hand or shifting your posture away from that person. By moving back in your chair, you can signal that you have said all that you plan to say or that you are not willing to continue to talk.[12]

Adaptors are actions that reveal psychological or physical needs. Head-scratching, ear-pulling, or hair-fussing, as well as pointing, shrugging, or nodding, can be interpreted as positive or negative by the other person. You may have a new haircut and may keep trying to nervously tuck the hair behind your ear. The listener, however, may misinterpret the action to mean that you are distracted and not really listening. Adaptors are not conscious behaviors, but they can be very distracting to the other person.

Affect displays are also unintentional movements that reflect the sender's true emotions. Slumping or showing a sad facial expression could reflect problems in your own life or could indicate empathic responses to the other person's words. People can "tear up," involuntarily revealing their emotional state. They can grind their teeth, bite their lips, and show the movement of muscles in their jaws/cheeks as they attempt to restrain an outburst.

Monitoring gestures, body movements, and other nonverbal cues will help you to respond appropriately to the needs of friends and coworkers. If you work to become aware of the various nonverbal cues with which people communicate, you will develop skills that will improve your strategic communication.

5.5: Minimize Communication Stress

5.5 **Use different ways to manage anxiety for effective communication**

Do you associate anxiety primarily with formal speaking presentations and speaking in front of large groups? Alternatively, are you aware of how nervousness affects your everyday speech? For example, if you are speaking to someone who outranks you in an organization, or if you are discussing an important subject or a topic that makes you uncomfortable, your voice may rise to a high pitch, you may stammer, or you may speak very softly.

Everyday situations such as meeting someone new, presenting ideas for a group project, or disagreeing with a friend may cause communication anxiety. This anxiety can give rise to verbal and nonverbal communication problems and cause the receiver to perceive you negatively. Verbal symptoms of nervousness include a shaky voice, dry mouth, mispronunciations, and incoherent sentences or phrases. Nonverbal symptoms include a change of voice pitch, fidgeting, and shaking. There are several skills that can help you manage these symptoms of nervousness.

One tactic for managing anxiety is to identify particular weaknesses in your spoken communication. The best way to do this is to record yourself by video or audio. Choose a topic that is important to you, such as asking for a raise. Record your reasons for requesting the raise; then play back the tape. Did your voice sound convincing? Were there mispronunciations or attempts to use the right word? Did your phrases form complete thoughts? Even if your reasons are valid, you can undermine their effectiveness by speaking softly, stammering, or choosing inappropriate language (such as tag questions added to your statements).

An effective way to control anxiety is to breathe deeply and regularly. Indeed, if you breathe too shallowly and rapidly (hyperventilate), the build-up of carbon dioxide in your bloodstream may cause you to feel dizzy and disoriented in addition to feeling nervous. Hyperventilation can cause tingling in your arms and legs, a "lump" in your throat, or tightness in your chest. Breathing deeply and regularly will relieve these physical symptoms and help you relax.

Another way to relieve the anxiety is to take a brisk walk. Walking will help dissipate some of the adrenaline that your body produces in stressful situations. The decrease of adrenaline has a calming effect.

An additional tactic is to slow down your communication and consciously focus on one idea at a time. As you well know from your school experiences, a workload sometimes seems so overwhelming that you do not want to begin or you cannot understand where to begin. The same can be true in communicating—you have much to say but do not know where to begin. If you say nothing, your anxiety will only increase. Just as you prioritize your schoolwork and tackle one project at a time, you can sort out which ideas are most important and concentrate on communicating them first.

Finally, do not be too hard on yourself. If you create unrealistic scenarios ("I'll instantly win my coworkers' respect by telling them about my dedication to the organization.") rather than appropriate goals ("I'll speak to others with respect and plan my messages so that they are clear and effective."), you are likely to be anxious when you communicate. Give yourself a break.

Be aware that others in the communication situation may be nervous as well. Most people have experienced communication anxiety, so you are not alone in feeling nervous.

5.6: Message Strategies

5.6 Analyze the three different message strategies

Message strategies are combinations of skills designed to communicate specific ideas to achieve a goal. A vast array of message strategies is used in business and professional settings. In this section, we analyze three: conversation, making requests, and giving directives.

5.6.1: Conversation

Many people believe that they are good conversationalists— that they have the ability to talk with ease about a wide range of topics. Even such gifted individuals, in professional settings, should handle conversation carefully. Conversation is an important message strategy because the business and professional environment provides so many opportunities for it to occur.

CONVERSATIONAL TURNS Turn-taking is one of the most important elements of conversation. Turns may vary in length and intensity but are necessary to maintain a conversation. You come to understand the "rules" of conversational turn-taking by watching others engaged in conversation.

An interruption occurs when a challenging speaker is successful in taking an unsolicited turn. Interruptions are useful for correcting inaccurate information or verifying what has been said. Other reasons for interruptions include disagreement ("Wait a minute; I think that there are four, not three, departure points for that supply order."), agreement ("Yes, you're absolutely right in hiring her!"), and changing the subject ("Excuse me, but aren't we late for that meeting with Lou Jane?").[13]

Although interruptions can serve important functions, most people do not appreciate being interrupted. If you have a tendency to interrupt without thinking, ask yourself whether the interruption is worth the risk it entails. Many times you will realize that it is best to wait for your turn in the conversation to get your point across. When your strong enthusiasm prompts you to interrupt, your actions send the message that the conversation cannot proceed or be successful without your input right at that moment. You can try to prevent yourself from being interrupted by using stronger and more active language and by leaning forward. You can also assert yourself in conversations simply by speaking up more often.

CONVERSATIONS BETWEEN WOMEN AND MEN
Researchers have observed several differences in the ways

women and men participate in conversation. Men interrupt more often than women do; thus, men control conversations more often than women do. Men also talk more than women do, both by taking more conversational turns and by taking longer turns. Women are generally more informative, more receptive to ideas, and more concerned about others in their conversations than men are. Stop for a moment and consider what this means for communication between coworkers.

Another difference in men's and women's conversational patterns is in giving orders.[14] Many women are often less comfortable with hierarchy than men are, and some prefer to achieve goals through consensus. Men are more likely to give orders without options. This difference causes confusion. Men may feel confused or manipulated if a woman does not give a direct order but nevertheless expects results. Women may be put off by a man's use of rank, authority, or power in giving orders.

INTERCULTURAL CONVERSATIONS Culture influences communication and can therefore lead to communication differences.[15] Strategies for improving conversations among a diverse work force include open-mindedness, recognizing equality, restraint or avoidance, interaction management, and other orientation.

Strategies for Intercultural Conversations

Restraint or avoidance

Remove card   1 of 5   Reset Deck

Participants in successful intercultural conversations show concern for others as individuals and do not expect an individual to speak for an entire group. They avoid lazy and thoughtless communication based on broad stereotypes—for example, not all British citizens are stuffy, not all Hispanics enjoy Mexican food, and many Italians are not overly expressive.[16] Treating others with respect and acknowledging their professional status can also help to bring about shared meaning.

CONVERSATIONAL ETHICS Each time you speak, you should provide enough background information to give listeners a frame of reference. In most organizations, manipulating listeners by giving them only partial information is unacceptable. It is generally unproductive as well; receivers who discover that they were treated unethically in conversation may refuse to work with the person who misled them or may tell coworkers that the person cannot be fully trusted.

Conversational messages should be truthful. Speakers should not provide false information or exaggerate knowledge to accomplish some goal or make claims for which they lack evidence. In both instances, the conversationalist is violating ethical principles. Unfortunately, deceiving others and lying are common in professional settings, even though they rarely produce the desired results over the long term. Most lies are discovered and do more harm than telling the truth would have done.

The final rule of conversational ethics involves clarity. When you converse with others, articulate your thoughts and ideas in ways that reduce the uncertainty the listeners may have about you and your messages. Avoid obscure language, make points logically, and eliminate extraneous information that may distract receivers from your primary message.

UNDERSTANDING AND AGREEMENT Conversationalists do not always understand or agree with one another. Consider the following four combinations of understanding and agreement.[17]

ⓧ **Mutual Understanding with Agreement**

Communicators understand each other's point of view and agree with it. This type of casual and nonconfrontational conversation is very common.

ⓧ **Mutual Understanding with Disagreement**

Conversationalists understand each other's viewpoint but disagree with it. This is a case of honest disagreement between parties.

ⓧ **Mutual Misunderstanding with Agreement**

As a polite way of carrying on conversation, participants may act as if they understand each other's viewpoint (agreement) even though they actually do not. On the other hand, each conversationalist may agree with what the other is saying but may not understand the purpose or deeper meaning of the topic. This is why it is often necessary to revisit a topic or phrase it in a different way in order to find out if the other person has understood the message.

ⓧ **Mutual Misunderstanding with Disagreement**

Participants in a conversation often have no understanding of each other's viewpoints and demonstrate no agreement about the issues. This is a stalemate situation until each party agrees to respect and sympathize with the other's position.

Keep those four possible outcomes in mind when you are speaking to others. Do not assume that a person who agrees with you necessarily understands what you have said or that someone who disagrees with you did not understand your point. Also, do not jump to the conclusion that people who disagree with you have nothing relevant to say. The best way to achieve shared meaning is to make sure you have answered the basic questions about the *what*, *where*, *who*, *when*, *why*, and *how* of the subject and that you and the receiver agree on the answers to those questions, even if you do not agree on the best action to take.

5.6.2: How to Make Requests and Give Directives

Making requests is a crucial activity on the job, particularly when you are a new employee. Consider your past working experiences. During your first few weeks at a job, you undoubtedly needed to ask a large number of questions to learn the basic requirements of your position.

Many people are reluctant to request information or help for fear of appearing unintelligent or helpless. However, you can phrase requests so that they benefit you in two ways: by providing you with necessary information and resources and by fostering a positive image of you because of your curiosity and enthusiasm for your job.

How can you be sure your requests are effective? First, be specific. Second, be sure you are asking the right person for the information. If you are not sure, ask an exploratory question first, such as "Are you in charge of accounts?" If the answer is affirmative, make your request—for example, "How do I allocate the money for next month's regional meeting?" Third, be confident when making your requests. If you have tried without success to find the information or to complete the job yourself, you are justified in asking for help. Others are usually willing to cooperate, particularly if you know exactly what you are asking for and phrase your request in clear and friendly language. Do not keep asking the same person for information or help. Doing so can give you a narrow view of the organization, and the person may come to resent the time necessary to help you.

Giving directives is another important message strategy, particularly when it complements a positive request-making style. Regardless of your position in the organization, you are likely to need both of these strategies to achieve your goals. Table 5.3 shows the difference between requests and directives.

Making requests can create a supportive climate and gives people a sense of control in carrying out their responsibilities. Those who carry out requests are likely to have a better attitude and to perform their duties in a more effective manner than those who are expected to obey directives. Nevertheless, in situations that call for specific action, directives may be more appropriate than requests.

It is possible to give directives in a positive way that does not assume a power imbalance. You can do this by explaining the reason for the directive. Do not simply make a demand without telling coworkers why they should do what you say. Indeed, if you give a directive, you should have an important reason for doing so and be willing to explain it to others. They are much more likely to cooperate when they see the need for such action. Table 5.4 gives ways to rephrase the directives listed in Table 5.3.

Table 5.3 Difference Between Requests and Directives

Requests	Directives
"Can you help me solve this project problem today?"	"Be sure you finish this project today."
"Can we meet some time today?"	"See me at 10:30."
"In which file should this go?"	"File this."
"Is there any way we can finish this project today?"	"I am expecting the report today."
"Can you help me find the XYZ file?"	"Find the XYZ file now."

Hide All Cells	Show All Cells

Table 5.4 Turning Directives to Requests

Original Version	Rephrased Version
"Be sure you finish this project today."	"Please finish this project today. Lisa needs the results tomorrow morning."
"See me at 10:30."	"See me at 10:30. We need to discuss the plans for the sales meeting."
"File this."	"File this. I am expecting an important call."
"I am expecting the report today."	"I need the report today because it is important that we stay on schedule."
"Find the XYZ file now."	"Please find the XYZ file. I have my hands full looking for the Logan file."

Hide All Cells	Show All Cells

Strategic Scenario Wrap-Up

Verbal and Nonverbal Skills

 Strategic Scenario

You go to an interview for your first job. The office is very large. You have to walk across the entire room to get to the interviewer, whose desk is against the far back wall with just enough space for her desk chair. She remains seated and gestures with her hand toward two chairs that are at right angles to the oversized desk. If you sit in either one of the chairs, you will not be facing the interviewer. You begin to wonder if this is some kind of test devised by the interviewer.

The interviewer may have chosen to place her office furniture near the far back wall so that interviewees and others have to walk to her. This may give her a sense of power and give others a feeling of inadequacy—the sense that they are on display and must show respect to her by walking to her power position. Or she may have chosen the position in order to feel secure by having a wall to her back. If other clues indicate that she is insecure, your conscious nonverbal behavior should be nonthreatening.

- Don't offer to shake hands unless or until the interviewer does so.
- Don't cross your legs with the ankle on the knee or slump in the chair.
- Do smile and use a moderate volume in speaking.

The chairs placed at right angles to the desk could be a test for the interviewee. By just sitting at the odd angle, you might give the impression that you do not have initiative or that you do not want to look at your interviewer. This is problematic, however, because it is inappropriate to move someone else's furniture, especially when you are the lower status interviewee. One alternative is to ask the interviewer if she minds if you move the chair. Her response should indicate whether this is a test or whether the chairs have just accidentally been left at the odd angle.

WRITING PROMPT

If roles were reversed and you were the interviewer, how would you arrange your office furniture to interview a job candidate in a way that is effective for both of you? Would you rise to greet your interviewee, extend your hand, and indicate where they should sit? Why or why not?

► `The response entered here will appear in the performance dashboard and can be viewed by your instructor.`

Submit

Summary

Verbal and Nonverbal Skills

- A great deal of care must be taken when anticipating, preparing for, delivering, and evaluating **verbal messages**.
- **Problems with communication** can usually be traced back to people who take this important process for granted.
- The **oral communication skills** you can develop to avoid these problems can be categorized by their relation to the model of strategic communication.
- Skills related to **goal setting** include identifying your purpose, analyzing your target, and understanding the influence of perception.
- **Situational knowledge skills** relate your communication to the organizational culture as a whole.
- **Communication competence** includes choosing the appropriate setting, deciding on the length and timing of the message, using language effectively, and avoiding racist, sexist, and insulting language.

- **Anxiety management** can, and should, be accomplished in your daily communication with others.

SHARED WRITING: VERBAL AND NONVERBAL SKILLS

Below are four communication zones. For each, describe in detail a typical setting in a business or organization that matches that zone. Explain your reasoning, and discuss how your nonverbal communication would fit each situation. 1. Intimate 2. Personal 3. Social 4. Public

► `A minimum number of characters is required to post and earn points. After posting, your response can be viewed by your class and instructor, and you can participate in the class discussion.`

Post   `0 characters | 140 minimum`

Chapter 5 Quiz: Verbal and Nonverbal Skills

Chapter 6
Leadership and Management Skills

Learning Objectives

6.1 Report ways to develop leadership skills

6.2 Examine the relationship between leadership and management

6.3 Describe different theories of management

6.4 Describe different theories of leadership

6.5 Examine how leadership differs from management

6.6 Analyze three considering factors while setting personal and organizational goals

6.7 Examine how learning and knowledge enhance strategic communication

6.8 Analyze how trust, understanding, and empowerment enhance effectiveness of leadership

6.9 Identify four ways of controlling anxiety

Strategic Scenario: Four Must Be One

The Melanae Group is a B2B (business-to-business) company that delivers information and data management services to other businesses. It is a company constructed from four smaller businesses that have either been bought or merged into the larger business. The four groups comprising Melanae are (1) the information storage/encryption/security (ISES) division, (2) the data entry/management (DEM) division, (3) the Web page design (WEB) division, and (4) the management consulting (MC) division, specializing in entrepreneurship. The business plan of the Melanae Group is to offer a wide range of information and data services and thus to position itself as a "knowledge company" that helps other businesses—such as insurance companies, banks, financial institutions, and government agencies—with their information and data needs.

Jacquere Shubar has been made regional manager for Melanae, with responsibility for all four operations in his geographic region. Jacquere came from the management group (MC), which is open minded, energetic, and optimistic about the merger. His employees, scattered in four offices within his region, include some telecommuters working from home. Employees from the ISES division are distrustful and disillusioned, and they are unhappy that they must now report to someone outside of their group. DEM employees are friendly but set in their ways. The WEB division employees are young and on the edge, stressing creativity over typical management practices. In essence, Jacquere is considered to be one of "the suits" who has been made boss. He prefers to work with other consultants but his performance as regional manager is based on his ability to get his region thinking and working as one organization, not four. Jacquere will have to draw upon his very best leadership and management skills to pull this off.

Think about the challenges facing Jacquere as you read through this chapter. At the end of the chapter, we will revisit this scenario and discuss some solutions.

6.1: Overview

Leadership and Management Skills

6.1 **Report ways to develop leadership skills**

When you graduate and acquire a new job position, you will be expected to assume a variety of complex roles. If you are in management, you may be expected to act as a generalist who coordinates the technical, human resources, operational, and creative functions of your organization. If you are in research, design, or other production-related jobs, you may be expected to master specific technologies and communicate effectively with a diverse set of coworkers. Added to these responsibilities may be a need to increase competitiveness of your products and efficiency of production. To meet challenges at work, you will want to apply the skills you are learning now in new and creative ways. In this chapter, we provide you with the means to incorporate your knowledge of strategic communication and your communication skills into leadership development. Regardless of your position in the organization, this chapter will help you to know and apply leadership skills in the performance of your duties.

One way to develop leadership skills is to adopt an *outside-in* perspective on your organization. This means focusing on the technological forces outside the organization and assessing its strengths and weaknesses from the perspective of external stakeholders, such as customers, suppliers, and even the government. It means adopting a wider view of your organization's role in the environment.

Leadership can be learned, and it can be adapted to solve problems. That is what this chapter is all about: understanding and developing leadership skills. We review the skills and functions traditionally associated with management and leadership. We give a brief overview of management theory, which will help you understand and cope with different management styles. We introduce an approach to leadership based on the strategic communication model. Our approach includes skills, attitudes, and techniques to help you succeed professionally, academically, and personally.

6.2: What Does a Leader Do?

6.2 **Examine the relationship between leadership and management**

The terms *leadership* and *management* are often used interchangeably. The result sometimes is confusion about the actual delegation of responsibilities in organizations. Leadership and management are complementary concepts that emphasize slightly different mind-sets and courses of action. **Managers** coordinate and organize activities. **Leaders** influence people and their behaviors and motivate the organization toward constructive change.[1] For example, when you work on a classroom group project, your professor acts as a manager when he or she makes assignments and organizes the groups. Leaders, in contrast, are the individuals in each group who motivate other members to excel in the assignment. Management and leadership, despite their differences, are based on the same fundamental skills. We begin with some of the behaviors, skills, and functions generally associated with both management and leadership.

6.2.1: Managerial Functions and Leadership Skills

Management generally has four functions: planning, organizing, motivating, and controlling.[2] **Planning** comprises setting goals and outlining steps to achieve those goals. **Organizing** is the process of accumulating and coordinating the human and capital resources necessary to undertake a plan. **Motivating** is generating commitment and support for a plan. **Controlling** means using authority and power to ensure that a plan succeeds. All of these functions are important to organizational success, but the degree to which each is emphasized depends on the circumstances. The planning function may be most important in industries that experience a great deal of change or innovation. Controlling may be used least in businesses where creativity is at a premium. Organizing may not be particularly important in routine labor operations such as assembly lines, where motivating may be the most important function.

While management always seeks to accomplish planned goals, it rarely succeeds without solid leadership—whether that leadership comes from managers themselves or from someone else involved. Good leadership means that worthy, achievable goals are set in the first place. Leaders also excel at the motivation aspect of management. And while managers are often the ones who *have* control, leaders are the ones who effectively put control (theirs or someone else's) to its best use in achieving team goals. Good managers, on the other hand, typically excel at organizing.

To some extent, these management functions and leadership skills are also important to you as a student. You are already developing the ability to plan your time, organize study or research materials, and motivate yourself to finish your work. You may or may not now be in a position to control others. But consider your experiences on sports teams, in previous jobs, or at other activities in which you were in a position to direct a group of people toward a goal. You may be surprised at how many potential leadership situations you have already encountered. You can prepare yourself for leadership responsibilities now by identifying those opportunities and actively seeking to incorporate leadership functions in your daily routines.

Technical, human, and conceptual abilities are important to managers' work.[3]

⊗ Technical Skills

Technical skills include the ability to use data, information, innovations, and techniques. As a new employee, you may be given special training in technical areas, such as seminars in using the company's computer software. Often you may be expected to learn technical skills on your own. One of the best ways to do this is to observe an expert or someone with a lot of experience. Asking questions is another way to gain technical information and at the same time show your enthusiasm for learning. Online training is also a good option.

⊗ Human Skills

Human skills include the ability to work with people to accomplish goals. Regardless of your position in an organization, you will be called on to understand your coworkers' needs and motivations and to recognize their strengths and weaknesses. With what types of people did you work best? Developing leadership ability starts with being able to figure out which people will work well together. To make these decisions, you must know how to gauge others' abilities objectively and to draw on your past experience. Get to know your coworkers and pick up on their attitudes and perspectives.

⊗ Conceptual Skills

Conceptual skills include the ability to see your job in its relationship to the entire organization and to recognize how the organization interacts with its environment. A good way to begin developing conceptual skills is to think critically about how organizations in which you are currently a member interact with the environment. For example, think about the relationship your school has with the town or city in which it is located. How could the relationship be improved? In particular, what could students do to encourage the improvement? Students at several college campuses hold a biannual "Neighborhood Day," when they help to clean up the campus and surrounding neighborhood, volunteer to make minor repairs to neighbors' houses, or run errands for neighbors who are elderly or incapacitated. Be the one who starts the ball rolling. Such activities can promote leadership skills.

6.2.2: Future-Oriented Skills

The ability to handle information is a vital leadership skill and an important management function. Gareth Morgan suggested that as information becomes the most important product in the global and national economy, the ability to obtain, assimilate, analyze, and communicate information will be critical to organizational success.

As a new employee, you may be faced with unexpected technological demands. If you are a recent graduate, you may be expected to know more than longtime employees about new communication and information technology. If you have been out of school or the work force for some time, you may find that you are still expected to know about the latest in technology, regardless of your experience.

Be sure to do your best to prepare for the technological demands of the workplace. Keep up-to-date and well-practiced in using writing, reviewing, database, and presentation software as well as online resources. This is an invaluable way of making yourself effective. If, despite your best efforts to prepare, you find yourself in need of additional skills training, consider taking workshops or classes that will benefit you and others in the company as well. In this way, you can demonstrate forward-thinking leadership skills.

6.2.3: Listening Skills for Leaders

In addition to future-oriented skills, managers must acquire excellent communication skills. While communication entails giving and acknowledging feedback about actions or decisions made in the workplace, probably the most important communication skill is listening. Listening skills are necessary for understanding and responding to employees, motivations, and intentions. On a broader scale, upper-level managers must listen constantly to information in the environment as well. To improve business, managers must keep an "ear to the ground" in terms of monitoring market conditions, managing relationships with suppliers and other business partners, and keeping abreast of government regulations.

Although most leaders and managers practice the skills and functions described here, the ways in which they do so vary widely. Just as organizations develop different structures and patterns of communication to achieve goals, leaders and managers use a variety of techniques to motivate and reward employees. In the next section, we will introduce you to some important theories of management that describe these techniques.

6.3: Management Theory

6.3 Describe different theories of management

A number of researchers have proposed theories about how management is accomplished in organizations. Organizations are structured differently, and organizational structure indicates the flow of communication within an organization. Researchers have developed theories to account for the specific styles of communication within organizations. Rensis Likert and the team of Robert Blake and Jane Mouton based their work on the ideas of Douglas McGregor, who presented explanations, known as Theory X and Theory Y, of what motivates workers. Other ideas have been suggested in response to changes in the structure and goals of business organizations and in employees. We will introduce you to some of them.

6.3.1: Likert's Systems of Management

Rensis Likert described management in terms of whether managers focused on tasks or on relationships with their employees; he assumed that more emphasis on one meant less emphasis on the other.[4] Likert's thinking can be illustrated by a continuum bounded by task orientation at one end and relationship orientation at the other (see Figure 6.1). He proposed four systems that characterize common management styles.

Figure 6.1 Likert's Management Continuum

In Likert's theory, as a management system becomes more nurturing, it becomes less authoritarian.

⊗ System 1: Authoritarian

A system 1 style of management is task oriented and has a highly structured, authoritarian focus. Interpersonal relationships do not seem important. System 1 managers trust subordinates very little and do not involve them in decision making. Subordinates work in a climate of intimidation and fear. Communication takes place from the top down, following the chain of command. *Example*—meatpacking plants. Overlord work managers trample upon workers, legal and illegal alike. The turnover rate is high, and managers make no attempt to involve themselves in the lives of their subordinates. Suggestions, if ever made, are cast aside, and employee progressions toward improvement stagnate.

⊗ System 2: Controlling

A system 2 style of management is task oriented, but control of the organization or unit is less authoritarian. Managers are condescending to subordinates and, though not as strict, continue to demonstrate distrust of subordinates. Some decision making is allowed at lower levels, but organizational problems are resolved at the top of the organization. Although most of the communication from managers follows the chain of command, some interaction is carried out directly between upper management and lower-level subordinates. *Example*—fast-food industry. Frazzled managers scurry around spewing orders to low-level cashiers and fry cooks. Hapless attempts at employee outreach come in the form of monthly team meetings, dusty suggestions boxes, and "empowering" posters. Employees may have a say in small day-to-day problems, such as duration of smoke breaks, but the opportunity for anything larger is virtually nonexistent.

⊗ System 3: Collaborative

System 3 managers openly place confidence and trust in subordinates. Managers control subordinates through negotiation and collaboration. Decision making is allowed at lower levels, especially in matters that directly affect workers. Communication flows relatively freely both up and down the organizational hierarchy. *Example*—low-level office park sales department. Turnover is significantly lower when compared to the aforementioned fields. Managers develop more in-depth interpersonal relationships with their employees after directly interacting with them on a daily basis. Meetings are held frequently that allow team members to input their feelings and ideas. Employees are encouraged to work, act, and think independently, while at the

same time remembering not to step outside certain boundaries. By incorporating activities such as employee picnics, ropes courses, and casual Fridays, bosses may make an attempt to foster cohesion.

⊗ System 4: Nurturing

System 4 managers concentrate on the relationships between superiors and subordinates. They nurture confidence and trust in workers and encourage decision making at all levels of the organization. System 4 managers do not use fear, threats, and intimidation. Workers' motivation results from their participation in goal setting. Free and open message exchange occurs among superiors, subordinates, and peers. *Example*—family-owned, tightly knit business. The owner still works directly with his or her employees and takes pride in his or her entrepreneurial endeavor. That being said, the owner strives for improvement and encourages a sound work ethic, while at the same time maintaining continual contact with all of his or her workers. This contact allows workers to communicate with and bare grievances to the top of the hierarchical system without traipsing through miles of managerial mire.

These systems are quite similar to the classical and humanistic schools of organizational theory. Classical theory emphasizes structure, rules, and control (e.g., Taylor's scientific management, Weber's theory of bureaucracy), whereas humanistic theory focuses on the needs of labor rather than on the structure of management. Systems 1 and 2 correspond to the assumptions of classical theory. Systems 3 and 4 reflect more concern for the worker's personal growth and satisfaction, a tenet of the human relations and human resources schools of thought.

6.3.2: Blake and Mouton's Research

In a theoretical model such as Likert's—that is, a single continuum with two opposite ends—an increase in (or movement toward) one end *requires* a decrease in (or movement away from) the other end. But what if the so-called opposites can actually exist together at the same time? In other words, what if they're *not* mutually exclusive opposites? In the case of management, is it possible for managers to focus on *both* relationships and tasks? Robert Blake and Jane Mouton thought so. They considered each potential focus—concern for people and concern for production—as having its own amount of variability. Blake and Mouton created a managerial model in which concern for people and concern for production goals are separate variables, but they combine to create a wide variety of management styles.[5]

Concern for people can be seen in a manager's regard for employees, particularly the concern that subordinates are treated well by the organization. Concern for production refers to a manager's emphasis on achieving the goals and objectives of the organization. A leader can explore how the two concerns, for people and for production goals, interact to form his or her distinct style of relating to others in the workplace.

6.4: Leadership Theories

6.4 Describe different theories of leadership

There are many theories on leadership, but we have selected three to focus on. According to the first theory, employees can be encouraged to participate in decision making. This theory values flexibility in decision-making styles and recognizes that people can better accept decisions when they participate in making them. The second theory says that leadership can be facilitated by appeals to the deep-seated values that organizational members hold. The third theory describes relationships between superiors and subordinates that are based on exchanges for mutual gain.

6.4.1: Vroom and Yetton's Leader-Participation Model

How difficult is it to get people to do things when they had no part to play in reaching the decision? Victor Vroom and Philip Yetton's research focused on followers' participation in decision making.[6] According to their model of leader participation, five options describe how subordinates can be involved in decision making. The options range from no participation at all to full participation. Table 6.1 indicates how the five levels of leader participation differ. As the table shows, decision making can range from authoritarian (levels 1 and 2) to democratic (levels 4 and 5). Level 3 represents moderate follower involvement.

The leader-participation model is important for two reasons. It can describe leaders who choose one level of participation consistently and whose subordinates have come to expect that level of participation in decision making. It also shows that flexibility exists among decision-making styles. Sometimes more participation by employees is appropriate; at other times, less participation is needed. Some situations may not involve employees directly, so no participation is necessary. In emergency conditions, because of time constraints, decisions may be made without participation by employees. People are most likely to accept decisions when they have had a hand in making them.

6.4.2: Kuhnert and Lewis's Transactional Leadership Theory

Transactional leadership, a theory proposed by Karl Kuhnert and Philip Lewis, describes relationships between superiors and subordinates that are based on exchanges for mutual gain. According to this theory, leaders offer subordinates things they want—such as higher salaries, time off, or benefits—to obtain certain things in return—such as their extra work on special projects, working overtime, and loyalty. A **transaction** occurs when each party gives up something in exchange for something else. In extreme cases, such as the economic crisis starting in 2008, some organizations took drastic steps outside the give-a-little/get-a-little circle by slashing employee benefits to stay afloat financially. Loss of perks, mandated furloughs, salary slices, and ultimately layoffs put significant strain on companies focusing on the ethos of the transactional leadership theory.

Transactional leadership works only if each party has something the other wants. What happens, however, if leaders cannot offer anything that followers value? In times of financial hardship, for example, leaders may be unable to provide bonuses for extra work, yet the work still has to be done. In such a situation, a leader must find alternatives to offer workers, such as promises of raises when times improve or public approval or recognition. For this leadership style to be effective, both parties have to realize their mutual dependence.

6.4.3: Kuhnert and Lewis's Transformational Leadership Theory

Kuhnert and Lewis identified a type of leadership known as transformational leadership.[7] In contrast to transactional leadership, transformational leadership focuses on reaching goals through appeals to deep-seated values among organizational members.[8] The transformation begins when the manager communicates her or his values to employees. As employees reach agreement on a set of organizational values, they elevate one another to new heights of inspiration, motivation, and morality.

Transformational leaders do more than just communicate their values to followers; their behavior reinforces the values they represent. According to Kuhnert and Lewis, successful transformational leaders possess self-confidence, a dynamic personality, strong convictions, the ability to communicate goals, a facility for image building, and a talent for motivating others. Notice that those qualities are not used in an exchange process—transformational leaders do not view the needs and desires of followers as bargaining chips, as is the case in some forms of transactional

Table 6.1 Vroom-Yetton Leader-Participation Model

Level	Follower Participation	Decision Process
1	None	Leader only
2	Leader gathers information from followers	Leader only
3	Leader obtains ideas and suggestions from selected followers	Leader only
4	Leader shares problem with followers as a group and collectively obtains ideas and suggestions from them	Leader only
5	Leader shares problem with the group	Joint decision making of leader and group of followers

management. Transformational leaders communicate well and thus inspire others by their own example to achieve excellence in the workplace. Their goal is to emphasize workers' growth and development.

Transformational leadership is important because it is value based. The identification and promotion of values are keys to organizational success. Transformational leaders view workers as willing participants in a value-conversion process that strengthens the entire organization.

6.5: Leadership Versus Management

6.5   Examine how leadership differs from management

The famous leadership scholar Peter Drucker said that "Management is doing things right; leadership is doing the right things."[9] Knowing what is the right thing to do requires a different skill than getting it done. This kind of leadership skill may or may not be part of a person's management style. Many mid-level managers, in particular, can function very well without tremendous vision. Most management positions, however, offer the opportunity to demonstrate leadership. Consider the following example:

> Manuel and Ahmad are managers in a video production company. Manuel is in charge of accounts receivable, and Ahmad is a marketing manager. The company has recently created a new job, director of human resources, and plans to promote a current employee to the position soon. Manuel and Ahmad are top candidates. Upper management wants the chosen candidate to demonstrate exceptional leadership skills because the job is an important and highly visible component of the company's new program to recruit more women and minorities to management positions.
>
> Manuel is a superb technician. His department has a flawless record, and he has been very loyal to the company, even turning down competing job offers. But Manuel tends to do things the way they have always been done; his personal motto is "Why fix what isn't broken?" Ahmad, in contrast, is quite vocal in his recommendations for change in his unit and focuses more on "what should be instead of what is." He has an effective track record in his department, although he is not overly concerned about the day-to-day details of the job. Upper management selects Ahmad for the new position, and Manuel is outraged that someone like Ahmad has been chosen.

⊕ What would you tell Manuel if you were in the upper management?

In this situation, upper management chose Ahmad's creativity over Manuel's dependability. The high profile of the job, as well as the program's newness and forward-thinking focus, made Ahmad the better choice. Manuel's skills, though recognized and valued, were not as appropriate for the job.

In your career, you will find that some promotions are made on the basis of creativity, personality, or other intangible qualities, and other promotions are based on demonstrated talent and dedication—however, some are based on nepotism and connections. The job, not the candidates themselves, often determines whether a leader or a manager is needed.

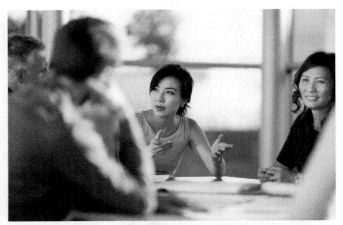

Organizations are shaped by effective managers and leaders, but the terms *manager* and *leader* are not interchangeable. As a manager, the woman pictured here might oversee the workload and budget, among other tasks. As a leader, she will move her team and her company in new directions by taking measured risks and implementing plans for the organization to change and grow.

SOURCE: John Wildgoose/Getty Images

There is no shortage of definitions for leadership. Table 6.2 compares several views of leadership.[10] These definitions agree that leadership is a process and that leaders are influential in achieving important goals. After considering these definitions and our own leadership experiences, we define leadership as the process of influencing subordinates, superiors, and peers toward the attainment of goals by using strategic communication methods. Strategic communication methods encompass values, vision, goal identification, future-oriented thinking, and other important behaviors that enable adaptation to the challenges of the information age.

With determination and practice, you can develop the communication skills vital to becoming an effective leader. Keep in mind that leadership is not reserved for the wealthy or the well connected, nor are people necessarily born with leadership skills.

The model of strategic communication provides the direction for our discussion of leadership skills. The skills are divided into four major components: goal setting, situational knowledge, communication competence, and anxiety management. Attending to each of these areas can ensure that you cover all the bases necessary for developing leadership ability.

Table 6.2 Views of Leadership

Theorist	Leadership Definitions
Terry	Leadership is the activity of influencing people to strive willingly for group objectives.
Tannenbaum, Weschler, and Massarik	Leadership is the interpersonal influence exercised in a situation and directed, through the communication process, toward the attainment of a specialized goal.
Koontz and O'Donnell	Leadership is influencing people to follow in the achievement of a common goal.
Kotter	Leadership refers to the process of moving a group of people in some direction through noncoercive means; it also refers to people who are in roles where leadership is expected.

For a more thorough comparison of leadership theories from a communication perspective, we highly recommend Gail Fairhurst's chapter in *The New Handbook of Organizational Communication*. G. Fairhurst, "Dualisms in Leadership Research," in F. Jablin and L. Putnam (eds.), *The New Handbook of Organizational Communication* (Thousand Oaks, CA: Sage, 2001), pp. 379–439.

6.6: Goal Setting for the Present and Future

6.6 **Analyze three considering factors while setting personal and organizational goals**

We know that goal setting is needed in any communication situation. Leadership is no different. Leaders must be forward thinkers and doers. To set goals for yourself, as well as for an organization, consider three factors: shared values, vision, and management of change.

6.6.1: Shared Values

A widely discussed aspect of leadership is the values that leaders hold (recall transformational theory). A leader's identification and promotion of values are critical to organizational success because values provide all members of the organization with a sense of guidance as they perform their daily tasks. Without shared values, a leader is unlikely to be successful. The following example is helpful in beginning our discussion of shared values:

Chita, Ming, and Sallie are entry-level unit management trainees at HighTech, Inc. During their orientation sessions, the personnel director stressed the shared values of the organization. Chita was impressed with these values but was impressed even more by the fact that the company believed in them enough to actively promote them to new employees.

Chita decided to follow the personnel director's example. She made up a laminated handout identifying the values to distribute to each of her subordinates. She held three meetings to discuss the values, and her subordinates were eager to embrace them as their own, especially after suggesting two more that were specific to their unit.

Ming and Sallie were also impressed with the values of the company, but they made no obvious attempt to instill the values in the members of their units. Indeed, Sallie's and Ming's behavior sometimes contradicted those values. After a while, other managers began to notice that Chita's unit was showing impressive increases in customer satisfaction and operating efficiency and decreases in absenteeism.

At HighTech's annual awards luncheon, Chita was asked why her unit had been so successful. She distributed copies of the laminated handout of values to everyone in the room and stated, "The single best action I took last year was believing in this company's values and having my people believe in them, too. Once people know, understand, and believe in the company's values, you really don't have to do much more. They will know what to do." Chita's understanding of the importance of shared values paid off.

How do leaders ensure that values are shared by organizational members? Two approaches can help leaders promote shared values among their coworkers: clarity and consensus.[11]

CLARITY Good leaders try to ensure that values are clear to all. Asking people how they feel about the organization's stated values is one way to evaluate how clear they are. Workers' impressions of, and reactions to, stated values reveal the depth of their understanding of those values. As an effective leader, you will often act as a cheerleader for the organization's values, articulating them frequently in clear and concise language. Once values are clear, workers can internalize them and even adapt them to specific work situations.

CONSENSUS When there is consensus about values, people not only understand the stated values but also share them. Leaders and those who aspire to leadership can do a great deal to achieve consensus by setting an example. When followers see a leader acting on the stated values of an organization, they are assured that those values really are important to the organization.

Leaders can also use values to assess the work of others. If employees excel on a project, the leader can point out ways in which their work promotes the values of the organization. Consider work experiences you have had. Did managers consistently relate the importance of organizational values? Did they respond to suggestions from subordinates, but only after lengthy complaints? If you were in a management position, how would you treat your coworkers?

THE SIGNIFICANCE OF SHARED VALUES Barry Posner, James Kouzes, and W. H. Schmidt studied the merits of shared values.[12] They surveyed more than 2,300 employees in a number of different organizations across the United States. An organization with strong shared values has these benefits.

• High levels of company loyalty
• Strong norms about working hard and caring
• Strong feelings of personal effectiveness
• Consensus about key organizational goals
• Reduced levels of job stress and tension

Shared values also promote ethical behavior at work. The ethical differences of a culturally diverse work force can be transcended by a coherent set of ethics for the organization as a whole. Indeed, the organization's ethical standards may be better suited to resolve differences than members' specific codes of ethics are.

6.6.2: Vision

The visions that leaders have for their departments, units, or organizations are based on shared values and play an important role in goal setting. According to Warren Bennis and Bert Nanus:

> A leader must first have developed a mental image of a possible and desirable future state of the organization. This image, which we call a vision, may be as vague as a dream or as precise as a goal or mission statement. The critical point is that the vision articulates a view of a realistic, credible, attractive future for the organization, a condition that is better in some important ways than what now exists.[13]

DEVELOPING VISION   A key aspect of vision is originality—the ability to see new goals and new ways to reach those goals. Developing original ideas is not easy. It helps to be always looking for alternatives as well as getting inspiration from your own experiences. Leaders should also conduct "environmental scanning" to see what other organizations do right and do wrong.

Jeff Bezos had a rather ridiculous-sounding idea for a business. He wanted a bookstore, only he didn't want his bookstore to have a store at all. In fact, the bookstore he envisioned wouldn't even have any books! The idea was to have an automatically run Web site that could connect customers with book distributors. Customers could order books online. The order would then automatically be sent to publishers and distributors. In this way, he would need almost no real estate, capital, or workers. In 1994, Amazon. com "opened its doors." A year later, the price of his stock had doubled, and within two years, the price was seven times higher than its initial offering. Bezos's vision, Amazon.com, was one of the few "dotcom-boom" companies to survive the "dotcom-crash." This idea was a truly new, original, and very successful vision of how to do business.[14]

Managers practice creativity in a specific context and with a specific focus. For example, Joyce, a marketing manager, believed that her department could increase its profits by offering its market research service to outside clients for a subscription fee. She knew demand for the service existed because her department had received many requests from outsiders to use the marketing statistics it had gathered. Although Joyce was not sure how to approach potential subscribers or how to bill for the service, she knew that Randy, an administrative executive, would be able to give her some suggestions. His experience plus her own interest in developing new ideas helped Joyce to create a realistic and worthwhile vision for her department.

CLARIFYING VISION   Just as values must have clarity, so too must visions be readily understood by those who are expected to act on them (recall Vroom and Yetton's theory). According to Edwin H. Friedman, "Leadership can be thought of as a capacity to define oneself to others in a way that clarifies and expands a vision of the future." A vision must be presented so that others can see the potential benefits of acting on it. Followers of a vision know that they are contributing to its fulfillment in a large or small way. Employees often need to feel that the tangible results of a vision will benefit not only themselves but also the organization in which they work.

The most effective visions are described in language that others can understand. Choosing the right words may be one of the hardest things a leader has to do, not only because of the inherent difficulty of the task but also because articulating a vision makes it less of a personal dream.

ADJUSTING VISION   Developing a vision can pose a major challenge, but leadership does not stop there. Leaders must make a conscious effort to behave in ways that consistently reflect the vision.

The vision may require occasional adjustment. When problems occur, workers and leaders are wise to remain flexible and strive to modify and improve the original vision. A vision need not be scrapped the moment an obstacle appears. Visions are general images of the future that can be achieved with the understanding that different approaches often lead to the same destination. A vision that produces a rigid pattern of behavior instead of presenting an inspirational challenge may do more harm than good.

THE BENEFITS OF VISION   Many people face an ongoing problem of keeping up with the various maintenance activities their jobs require. Routine phone calls and visitors, meetings, and paperwork take time. So, too, do unexpected crises that must be taken care of immediately. One manager taped an eloquent summary of her company's goals to her desktop but then found that she usually could not read the list because she had so much paperwork on her desk.

The organization as a whole can benefit from a clearly articulated vision. Vision can be used to prioritize daily activities, guide decisions about what project to handle first, and remind managers to delegate some activities to others who are dedicated to the same vision.

6.6.3: Management of Change

Articulating a vision almost always entails changing the status quo for an as-yet-untested alternative. Consider Nintendo. Did you know that this videogame company was founded in 1889? One of Japan's most successful makers of playing cards, Nintendo had been profitably producing cards for close to a century when it produced its first piece of electronics (toy Beam Guns) in 1970. The success of this new direction for Nintendo was quickly apparent. Within twenty years, Nintendo went from a highly successful Japanese playing card manufacturer to the global giant in home videogames. In 1989, exactly one hundred years after Nintendo was founded, the "Nintendo Entertainment System" videogame console was the best-selling toy in the United States.

Think about how hard it must have been to initiate such a drastic change—from printing cards on paper to producing consoles, microchips, and programs. Nintendo had been producing cards for eighty years and was very successful at it! Why change anything? Changing meant hiring new employees such as electrical engineers and computer programmers. It was a huge and very risky investment. Many people within the Nintendo company must have felt uneasy about the change in corporate direction.[15]

To set goals, astute leaders anticipate and manage change effectively. There is always resistance to change. Some people like the status quo. Others fear that change will affect them adversely. Still others resist change because the effects of change are unpredictable. For example, an update of technology within an organization, such as a new computer system, might cause employees to become apprehensive about learning new procedures, become resistant to the time required to install the new system, or become defensive about the old system because the new computer is unfamiliar to them. Leaders become agents of change by making and publicizing decisions that support the plan for change.

Managing change in an organization requires a four-step strategy that centers on anticipation, vision, results, and network building.[16]

ⓧ Anticipate the Problems

Anticipate the problems that are likely to occur when a vision is implemented. A back-up plan can help avoid potential problems. For example, confusion can result when people perceive a vision differently. This difficulty can be avoided when employees have written details for reference.

ⓧ Focus on the Vision

Focus the organization on the vision. Day-to-day obstacles frequently discourage dedication to the original vision. After evaluating the obstacles, the leader can either modify the vision or solve the problems.

ⓧ Focus on the Results

Leaders and employees alike look at results rather than at processes. This step enables everyone to consider alternative approaches to tasks.

ⓧ Build a Strong Network

Build a strong, supportive network of people committed to change. Several members of this network must be in key positions of power, maintain strong working relationships with one another, and be highly motivated to accomplish tasks related to the change.

Once leaders have made change agents out of influential people in the organization, they can motivate others to recognize the value of change and embrace it with enthusiasm. Leaders cannot manage change alone. They must empower others to advocate productive change at all levels of the organization. Think of this process as a spider-web of change (see Figure 6.2).[14]

Figure 6.2 Spider Web of Managing Change

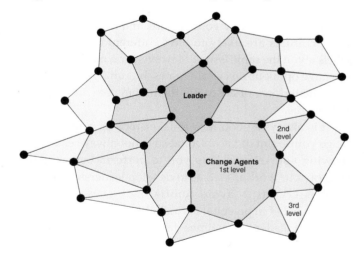

6.7: Situational Knowledge and Strategic Leadership

6.7 **Examine how learning and knowledge enhance strategic communication**

John F. Kennedy once observed that "leadership and learning are indispensable to each other." Within our model of strategic communication, learning involves gaining as much situational knowledge as possible. The ability of leaders to set goals is enhanced by situational knowledge—the information a leader needs to manage a situation effectively. This knowledge includes information about the organization and its employees as well as knowledge about one's self. The more leaders discover about their own abilities, weaknesses, and personal style, the better prepared they are to take charge.

6.7.1: Knowledge About Self

How well defined is your self-concept? Most people think they have very accurate self-awareness. Like everyone else, leaders are not perfect. They have shortcomings and weaknesses that challenge their ability to lead. Effective leaders inventory their imperfections and minimize them to gain others' support.

Your opinion of yourself—your self-concept—is important to the development of leadership skills. Leaders need to have a healthy view of themselves. This does not mean that leaders should be self-righteous, self-promoting egotists. It does mean that they should know their own strengths and weaknesses. As you think about your own strengths and weaknesses, recognize that your perception of yourself is culturally specific. This perception is further complicated by organizational culture, which has its own perception of what a leader should be.

Another method of self-evaluation is to assess your views on current issues that affect you. Your views have been formed in part by your culture, and people from different cultures are likely to have different attitudes and beliefs about the same issues. However, you may think that you have opinions on certain issues, but until you actually write them down or articulate them, they may be surprisingly vague.

It is always a good idea to take stock of yourself and gauge your point of view. Doing so is not always easy, but knowing yourself can help you to perform better in all areas of your work as well as to develop leadership ability.

It is crucial to avoid hubris. Hubris is excessive pride—a belief in personal invincibility and omnipotence. Successful leaders sometimes develop hubris and tend to believe that they are able (and permitted) to do anything, including illegal or unethical actions. Success does build self-confidence. But when you are successful, you are smart to consider the organization, its vision, and others' contributions to your success so as to avoid developing hubris.

In school and in your career, consider keeping a journal of your achievements, and in that journal mention others who also received or deserved credit for these accomplishments. You can refer back to these cooperative accomplishments when you are tempted to give yourself all the credit for whatever success you achieve. Chances are that if you give others the credit they deserve, they will do the same for you.

6.7.2: Organizational Knowledge

Astute leaders recognize all the tasks involved in the organization's operation, although they are unlikely to know the specifics of every single job description. Only by recognizing both the big picture and the fine print are leaders able to coordinate all the factors required for achieving goals.

Thomas Peters and Robert Waterman suggested that managers learn about the business by "wandering around."[17] Others have talked about "hands-on management." Such phrases suggest that effective leadership is both active and interactive and depends in part on leaders taking an interest in others' contributions to the organization. Such phrases also suggest that the best leaders may be people who began modestly and worked their way up from the lowest levels of the organization. Such people bring years of real and practical experience to leadership decisions.

Organizational knowledge extends beyond the internal structure and functions of the company. Leaders and workers must also be receptive to the environment in order to know what the competition is doing, what the customers want, what the national economy is doing, and how the global market is performing. This type of knowledge is acquired only by continual learning.

An important source of continual learning is failure. Most people view failure as something to avoid. Leadership experts, however, stress the importance of taking risks and learning from failure. Effective leaders experience failure but are able to learn from it and use what they learn to strengthen their leadership. It is often said that employees who do not fail every now and then are not trying hard enough.

You can become more comfortable with risk (and demonstrate your leadership potential) by developing a response plan to turn failures into learning experiences. Formulating such a plan entails performing four tasks in response to failure:

Review → Assess → Predict → Resolve

Immediately after a failure has occurred, *review* the chain of events leading to the failure, either by yourself or with those involved. Determine the point at which reality deviated from the ideal. Next, *assess* the deviation. Was the problem minor or major? Were there several problems? Did the problem result from lack of preparation, incorrect information, conflicts between workers, or some other factor? Use the assessment to *predict* the likelihood of such a problem occurring again. Was it a one-in-a-million situation? Or is the problem likely to recur next week? Finally, using your analysis of the first three factors, *resolve* how to handle such a situation in the future. Consider the following example:

> David Wildon is responsible for supplying data charts to an account manager whose projects are generally behind schedule. David noticed that the spreadsheet program for preparing the charts had recently caused some errors in the account figures but assumed that taking care of the problem was not his responsibility. One month, the data provided by the manager did not match the results produced by the spreadsheet, so David decided to use estimates to save time and get the project finished. The manager, running late as usual, did not check the finished chart before sending it to his boss for the annual planning meeting. The next day, the manager stormed into David's office demanding to know how the mistakes got into the chart and warning that David would get both of them fired.

In this situation, David and his boss can make several resolutions to avoid the recurrence of such a failure. The boss can resolve to keep his projects on schedule. David can resolve to alert those responsible for maintaining the software if he notices a problem with it. David and his boss can resolve to go over the completed charts together to make sure that they are free of error. Such resolutions can reduce the likelihood of failure as well as the stress resulting from fear of failure. Implementing plans for learning from failure can be an important step in developing leadership ability.

6.8: Competent Leadership

6.8 Analyze how trust, understanding, and empowerment enhance effectiveness of leadership

What communication skills are necessary for leadership, and how can you begin to develop them now? In addition to effective listening and verbal and nonverbal skills, the critical elements of communication are building trust, promoting understanding, and empowering others. **Trust** results from a strong commitment to ethical behavior within the organization's system of values. **Understanding** comes from listening to others, using clear and respectful language, and relying on appropriate techniques for behavior control. **Empowerment** means giving people the opportunity to think and act for themselves within the guidelines of the shared values and vision of the organization. The benefits yielded by trust, understanding, and empowerment include enhanced creativity and increased productivity as workers take initiative to succeed without the direct control or coercion of managers or leaders.

6.8.1: Trust

Trust, the first of the critical leadership skills, is the faith and confidence that workers place in the organization's leaders. Leaders do not receive trust automatically; they must earn and re-earn it.

Trust is a two-way street. Followers will not trust leaders who do not trust them, and vice versa. Mutual trust is important. Managers or supervisors who trust employees with additional or important responsibilities often win respect for their insight into the employees' abilities. Followers then begin to trust managers in other areas ("Well, if she trusted me with the ABC project, she must know what she's doing; I trust her judgment"). Over time, leaders and workers can build a mutual store of trust that can be tapped to achieve important goals.

Another characteristic of trust is its fragility. Building trust can be a long and slow process, but often only one or two betrayals are all it takes for many followers to lose faith in a leader they have trusted for years. What if you found out someone you trusted did not write his or her own blog? Consider the fact that 83 percent of organizational executives admit their blogs were written by someone else.[18] Blog services provide content, writing, and research and can even help with scheduling blog posts. One such service is Ghost Blog Writers. Many professionals in the blogsphere express a wide range of opinions about the ethics of ghost blogs. Do you think it ethical to send out information through a blog that you did not write?

THE RELATIONSHIP BETWEEN TRUST AND ETHICAL BEHAVIOR Trust in organizations begins with leaders serving as role models of ethical behavior. Employees may refrain from ethical behavior if they see their leaders performing unethical acts.

Ethical behavior reflects the values espoused by the organization. Values can be directly stated. A code may state: "We value honesty and integrity as a way of doing business." Ethical standards can also be communicated indirectly. Leaders may choose to uphold standards of honesty and equality instead of pursuing questionable courses of action that may be more profitable.

DEFINING ETHICAL BEHAVIOR Employees constantly watch managers and executives for cues to guide their actions. It is imperative that managers demonstrate ethical behavior for employees to emulate. According to Kenneth

Andrews, "The personal values and ethical aspirations of the company's leaders, though probably not specifically stated, are implicit in all strategic decisions. They show through the choices management makes and reveal themselves as the company goes about its business. That is why this communication should be deliberate and purposeful rather than random."[19]

Defining a code of ethics is one of the most difficult aspects of leadership. All employees have personal systems of ethics that they have cultivated over the years, and these codes are their first reference in a questionable situation. Although a grand set of rules by which to communicate in the business world would be helpful, such a code would ultimately fall short in specific circumstances.

Managers may ask, "If ethical behavior means different things in different situations, how do I know for sure that my own actions are proper?" This question is best answered by consulting experts in business ethics.[20] Their experience and research have generated a number of guidelines that can help individuals determine whether their behaviors are in line with ethical principles.

SUSTAINING TRUST   Once leaders and employees have achieved a state of mutual trust, they have to work at maintaining that trust. You should be aware of four keys for sustaining trust: constancy, congruity, reliability, and integrity.[21]

Constancy is the ability to stay on course, to remain focused on the vision and goals regardless of setbacks. Followers respect and trust leaders who stay calm and undistracted in the face of adversity. **Congruity** is the parallel between what a leader says and what a leader does. Leaders' actions and behavior should match their statements, goals, and views. **Reliability** means that leaders support employees and coworkers in times of need, whether personal, organizational, or professional. **Integrity** is the keeping of promises and commitments, coupled with the refusal to make promises that compromise the well-being of coworkers and the organization. Employees may not like all of a leader's decisions, but they will trust a leader who clearly upholds their interests and keeps her or his word.

PROBLEMS WITH MISTRUST   As you can imagine, a number of complications are associated with mistrust. People generally do not give their best effort to someone they do not trust. Furthermore, when leaders are mistrusted, the whole organizational climate may deteriorate. The outcome may be the withholding of information, the distortion of facts, rampant suspiciousness, low levels of information exchange, deception, closed-mindedness, low morale, and poor interpersonal relations.[22]

Trust is an essential component of leadership. Without it, leaders fail. With it, leaders have a chance to make a real impact on how the organization prospers. Most of the characteristics, elements, and qualities of strategic leadership discussed in this chapter can only be actualized if trust is established between leaders and followers.

6.8.2: Understanding

Understanding, the second critical leadership skill, begins with attending to what employees are saying. Listening promotes understanding because it shows that leaders think highly of employees' input and take their comments seriously. Asking for advice, gathering opinions, and soliciting suggestions from followers are ways in which leaders can demonstrate their openness to listening. Consider these helpful suggestions to leaders for asking advice from followers:[23]

- Include coworkers in discussions of problems and issues.
- Encourage individual thinking.
- Make it easy for subordinates to communicate their ideas to you.
- Follow through on these ideas.
- Reward those who give advice.

When employees see that their advice is valued, they are more likely to give it. This is just one example of how effective listening helps to accomplish the goals of the organization.

Understanding also requires that leaders sidestep the trap of "framing." Framing refers to the tendency to frame problems in ways that are familiar, comfortable, or easy to deal with instead of identifying and developing problems as they are actually presented.[24] If a leader is prone or biased to seeing problems, say, from a sales perspective, he or she is framing problems in a narrow way. The problem may very well be in marketing, finance, or public relations.

LANGUAGE   The capacity for understanding includes a conscious and respectful relationship with language. The language of effective leaders has been studied, and the conclusions are quite interesting. In his study of U.S. presidents' language, Rod Hart identified four categories of commonly used words or phrases: words that are realistic, optimistic, active, and certain.[25]

Presidential language

Remove card   1 of 4   Reset Deck

The use of words from these four categories produces successful communication. Think about the language choices of your professors, elected officials, fellow students, or coworkers. What types of words do they use most?

6.8.3: Empowerment

Empowerment, the third critical leadership skill, means entrusting people with the authority to act independently. Empowerment can promote creativity, cooperation, and inspiration among employees. Warren Bennis writes, "Good leaders make people feel that they're at the very heart of things, not at the periphery. Everyone feels that he or she makes a difference to the success of the organization. When that happens people feel centered and that gives their work meaning." Although managers may resist the idea because they fear losing control of their employees, allowing employees to be independent increases managers' effectiveness. Employee empowerment can be realized only through effective leadership skills, such as reduction of status differences and team building.

REDUCTION OF STATUS DIFFERENCES Effective leaders are generally perceived to be of higher status than followers. Their status allows them to assume responsibility for making important decisions. Large status differences between leaders and followers, however, can have a debilitating effect on morale, efficiency, and productivity. Leaders who concentrate on creating status differences are likely to encounter those problems. A workable balance occurs when employees view leaders as senior partners working with employees to achieve goals.

Leaders can reduce status differences by being considerate. Consideration for employees includes showing warmth, asking for opinions, showing concern for employees' welfare, giving credit where credit is due, and being open to suggestions. An example of considerate leadership can be found at RLI Insurance in Peoria, Illinois. RLI avoids giving away big prizes for suggestions and instead rewards every idea, whether it is used or not, with a $2 bill. When an idea is used, the responsible employee is entered into a quarterly drawing for prizes ranging from $50 to $100. RLI reports a dramatic increase in the total number of suggestions made as well as an increase in the quality of suggestions received.[26]

Leaders can also reduce status differences by being less directive in their communication. Getting cooperation and productivity through positive communication reduces the perception of a leader "cracking the whip" over employees and results in a more enthusiastic climate. Cultural difficulties, however, can be related to status differences. Leaders who are less directive and ask for employees' opinions may find that a response is not forthcoming or comes slowly or tentatively from employees whose culture views such inaction as inappropriate. These cultural differences must be considered in the empowerment strategies of a leader.

TEAM BUILDING Team building empowers people because it enables work to be accomplished with less direction from management. Team building contains two related elements: involvement and integration.[27]

(x) Involvement

Involvement, or getting people working on activities other than their daily tasks, gives employees a sense of importance in the organization. Participating in special activities such as self-directed teams, goal-setting sessions, professional development workshops, and organizational surveys can give employees a sense of involvement and enhance their feelings of empowerment.

(x) Integration

Integration, or bringing people together so that their varied talents and skills can be complementary and mutually supportive, gives employees a sense of cooperation. Just as sports teams integrate members' talents to win contests, employees can appreciate one another's skills when they successfully complete a project together. Teamwork can be especially gratifying because working with others can make each employee perform better than she or he would perform alone.

6.9: Confident Leadership

6.9 **Identify four ways of controlling anxiety**

Managing anxiety is an important part of leadership. You may have heard people make remarks such as "He could really be a successful person, but he is afraid of failing" or "She has all the skills, but she is afraid of success." Leaders experience anxiety just as everyone else does. The nature of the fear may be different for each person, but it is present for all leaders at some time or other. Effective managers and leaders control their anxieties and do not let them become overwhelming. Optimism, persistence, passion, and accepting responsibility for failure enable leaders to overcome the anxieties of their jobs.

WRITING PROMPT

George is a dynamic, 30-year-old sales manager. Recently, his organization has acquired a new company. He has been assigned with the task of inducting the employees of this company. He is getting anxious about this task since the employees of this company come from a diverse culture and geography. If you were in George's position, what steps would you take to manage your anxiety? Your goal is the smooth completion of the induction process.

▶ | The response entered here will appear in the performance dashboard and can be viewed by your instructor.

Submit

6.9.1: Optimism

Effective leaders remain optimistic even in the face of adversity. Those with an optimistic attitude consider setbacks a challenge. They try to justify their optimism by overcoming setbacks and proving pessimists wrong. Strong self-confidence and self-awareness form the basis for an optimistic attitude. Notice the different outlooks revealed in this dialogue:

> NEW ATHLETIC DIRECTOR: This program has potential because of dedicated team members, strong alumni support, and a new leader who is willing to do what it takes to produce a winning attitude and a winning season.
>
> BOARD MEMBER: I wish I could say the same. Our head coach was caught paying players, and we were put on probation for a year. The following year we were unable to recruit top players and ended the season with one win and eleven losses. Team morale is low, and the stands are empty.
>
> NEW ATHLETIC DIRECTOR: Once the program's reputation is restored [trust is reestablished] the team will realize that only by coming together as a team [empowering others] can we all earn the right to enjoy a winning season.

6.9.2: Persistence

Leaders overcome anxieties by being persistent in their actions and behavior in spite of the pessimism of others and short-term setbacks. Persistence reflects dedication to the vision of the organization in spite of tense situations, ominous events, or failures. All these have the potential to cause great anxiety among employees and managers alike, but persistence can diminish fear of them. Where would Sam Walton's family be today if he had given up on his small local drugstore in Arkansas in the 1960s? Persistence, or "hardiness," helps people to "take the stress of life in stride. When they encounter a stressful event—whether positive or negative—(1) they consider it interesting, (2) they feel that they can influence the outcome, and (3) they see it as an opportunity for development."[28]

6.9.3: Passion

Passion reduces the anxiety that leaders face. Enthusiastic commitment helps managers to set aside their doubts and worries and concentrate on the important issues. Employees have confidence in managers who demonstrate commitment to the shared values of the organization, and their support helps to lessen the anxieties that leaders may have. Do you know of people with the passion that will make them successful leaders?

6.9.4: Accept Responsibility for Failure

To accomplish goals, leaders must take risks. Some risks result in mistakes and failure. Leaders have an obligation to own up to their mistakes and accept blame for failure. People under supervision know that management is fallible, and their trust in the organization's leadership will waver if they observe managers blaming subordinates for their own mistakes.[29] Consider this example:

> Ms. LeFann, a junior high school band director, loved to challenge her symphonic band students. A spring concert was coming up, and Ms. LeFann decided at the last moment to include a difficult but popular piece of music as the last number on the program. Her students rose to the challenge and practiced the piece to perfection. But when the selection was performed at the concert, the timing was off. The woodwinds lagged behind, and the brass section rushed ahead. After the concert, Ms. LeFann apologized to the audience and to her students and took full responsibility for the poor performance of the last number.

Once you have decided that you will admit your mistakes, you will be less anxious about what you do. Think about it. One of the most stressful activities is speculating on the possible outcomes of your actions. You can decrease your anxiety, if only a little, by resolving to accept whatever happens and to be honest about it. You can believe in your integrity no matter what else happens. You will have more respect for yourself if you admit mistakes instead of trying to blame them on someone or something else.

Figure 6.3 illustrates the major aspects of personal leadership development.

Figure 6.3 Strategic Model of Leadership

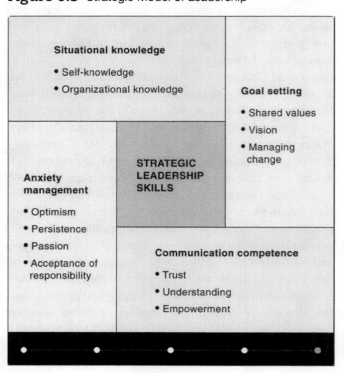

Consider an activity you have recently engaged in and enjoyed—giving advice to a friend, working on a group project for a class, or organizing a social event. Which strategic leadership skills (goal setting, situational knowledge, communication competence, and anxiety management) did you apply to this effort? Which skills will be the most important to your career plans? Should you try to develop these skills now, or will they evolve naturally on their own? Why or why not?

> The response entered here will appear in the performance dashboard and can be viewed by your instructor.

Submit

Strategic Scenario Wrap-Up
Leadership and Management Skills

ⓧ Strategic Scenario:

The Melanae Group is a B2B (business-to-business) company that delivers information and data management services to other businesses. It is a company constructed from four smaller businesses that have either been bought or merged into the larger business. The four groups comprising Melanae are:

1. the information storage/encryption/security (ISES) division,
2. the data entry/management (DEM) division,
3. the Web page design (WEB) division, and
4. the management consulting (MC) division, specializing in entrepreneurship.

The business plan of the Melanae Group is to offer a wide range of information and data services and thus to position itself as a "knowledge company" that helps other businesses—such as insurance companies, banks, financial institutions, and government agencies—with their information and data needs.

Jacquere Shubar has been made regional manager for Melanae, with responsibility for all four operations in his geographic region. Jacquere came from the management group (MC), which is open-minded, energetic, and optimistic about the merger. His employees, scattered in four offices within his region, include some telecommuters working from home. Employees from the ISES division are distrustful and disillusioned, unhappy that they must now report to anyone outside of their group. DEM employees are friendly but set in their ways. The WEB division employees are young and on-the-edge, stressing creativity over typical management practices. In essence, Jacquere is considered to be one of "the suits" who has been made boss. He much prefers to work with his own kind—consultants—but his performance as regional manager is based on his ability to get his region thinking and working like one organization, not four. Jacquere will have to draw upon his very best leadership and management skills to pull this off.

Jacquere realizes he must start by setting goals as a leader as well as a manager. To define his goals, he revisits the business plan of the company: *as a knowledge company, to offer a wide range of information and data services that helps other businesses with their information and data needs.* The plan is based on the organization's vision. Each division plays an essential role. He understands that his real task is managing change.

However, that's a tall order, so he breaks it down. If the entire company is going through this challenge of change, his region can certainly handle it. He decides to treat the region as a unified force, building a strong network of communication between the four divisions while understanding they can never be expected to be alike—and that is good. They are all specialists in their own fields and this wide range was what clients are looking for. Jacquere's ultimate focus is on results and shared values, not differences and problems.

Which elements of Jacquere's strategic leadership will be most difficult, and why? Please elaborate if you can relate this scenario to similar experiences of your own.

> The response entered here will appear in the performance dashboard and can be viewed by your instructor.

Submit

Summary

Leadership and Management Skills

- **Management and leadership**, though not the same conceptually, do share several functions—planning, organizing, motivating, and controlling—and do require similar technical, human, cognitive, and future-oriented skills. These functions and skills are made more effective by astute and practiced communication.

- How management is conducted and what makes for good management are subjects of **research and debate**. Likert's systems of management, Blake and Mouton's research, Vroom and Yetton's leader-participation model, and Kuhnert and Lewis's transactional and transformational leadership theories provide a broad perspective on the varieties of management found in organizations.

- **Strategic leadership skills** can benefit anyone who needs to communicate with a group or win support for an idea. These skills are not the exclusive property of executives; they can benefit everyday communications.

- The four components of the model of strategic communication can show any communicator how to address the major aspects of **personal leadership development**.

- **Goal setting** includes developing and promoting shared values and visions and managing change. **Situational knowledge** encompasses obtaining information about the organization and oneself.

- **Communication competence** means demonstrating organizational ethics, promoting understanding in decision making, and learning effective communication strategies for the purpose of empowering others.

- Anxiety often accompanies the risks of leadership communication, but a leader can manage it and **build confidence** through optimism, persistence, passion, and acceptance of responsibility for mistakes.

SHARED WRITING: LEADERSHIP AND MANAGEMENT SKILLS

What can managers and employees do to learn from communication failure? Discuss the four-step process of continual learning, and explain its role in the development of organizational knowledge. Give examples to prove your points.

▶ A minimum number of characters is required to post and earn points. After posting, your response can be viewed by your class and instructor, and you can participate in the class discussion.

Post   0 characters | 140 minimum

Chapter 6 Quiz: Leadership and Management Skills

Chapter 7
Work Relationships

Strategic Scenario: Needs Assessment

Tomás Chavez was hired recently by Vangard Equipment Corporation as its director of training. Vangard manufactures heavy earth-moving equipment. Although it is one of the youngest and smallest companies in its industry, Vangard has a solid track record for earnings and profits. Tomás found out on the first day of his job that his position had gone unfilled for almost a year. During that time, training had been conducted by the various departments in the corporation. He knew he had a lot of catching up to do. His first task was to conduct a needs assessment to determine where the corporation had the greatest training needs. He sent out surveys, conducted interviews, reviewed policy manuals, read memos exchanged among employees, and even conducted some focus groups.

He rapidly learned that several training needs were apparent. First, customers of Vangard were having a great deal of difficulty getting their questions answered about new equipment purchases. Some customers became so disgusted that they switched their business to a competitor. Second, dozens of employees expressed a great deal of resentment toward upper-middle and upper

management for its lack of sensitivity to their needs. Salary wasn't so much the issue as respect and recognition for their performance on the job. Third, many younger employees were leaving Vangard after only a year or two. Although a lot of reasons were given for their exodus, Tomás got the distinct impression that these less-experienced employees were not given enough guidance, direction, and encouragement for their efforts. Fourth, Tomás learned that Vangard, much like the industry itself, was male-dominated. Two recent sexual harassment suits (settled out of court) were testament to the fact that many employees lacked the knowledge and/or sensitivity to deal with gender and sexual issues in the workplace. Finally, Tomás learned that a general lack of respect and civility was the norm among coworkers in the organization. He couldn't put his finger on why, but it was apparent that few of the employees or managers enjoyed positive professional relationships.

As you read this chapter, think about the issues that Tomás uncovered during his needs assessment. At the end of the chapter, we will revisit this scenario and discuss some solutions.

7.1: Overview

Work Relationships

7.1 **Examine the common traits in relationships in business and the professions**

Interpersonal relationships are critical to achieving organizational goals. In your work experience you have probably encountered many of the relationships we discuss in this chapter, but you may have been unaware of their importance to you and to the organization itself. The following cases are just two examples of how relationships can promote organizational goals and values:

> Ben, an employee at Delen Corp., was strongly committed to Delen's mission statement, which emphasized providing service to customers and promoting good relations with the local community. He frequently thought about how business practices and community relationships might be improved. Nevertheless, he usually felt a little nervous about suggesting changes. Angela, Ben's supervisor, was an experienced employee who knew the organization well. Her opinions and decisions were generally well respected, and she had achieved a reputation for supportiveness and honesty. Ben approached her with some ideas, and the two of them worked out a plan for starting an educational partnership with the local high school and providing internships for college students. In doing so, they increased Delen's visibility in the community and ensured that young, well-educated people would be interested in working for the organization.

> Cheryl, a sales manager in a large department store, noticed that customers frequently became annoyed when approached by clerks. She knew the clerks were trying to provide prompt and courteous service, yet she also understood the customers' desire to be undisturbed. She resolved the situation by suggesting that the clerks remain alert, attentive, and visible to customers but refrain from approaching unless invited by a customer. She emphasized that when clerks did interact with customers, they should strive to be friendly and responsive at all times. In the weeks after her suggestions were implemented, several customers commented to Cheryl on the wonderful service in her department. Cheryl had succeeded in identifying and providing the level of service that customers wanted and needed.

Strong, positive work relationships can be difficult to achieve, despite their importance. Developing positive relationships is an area frequently neglected among coworkers in the quest for increased productivity. Increasing dependence on technology-mediated communication creates an environment that may discourage relational development. Office politics and striving to get ahead may create friction among coworkers. The organizational culture may discourage dynamic relationships, or it simply may not suit individuals' communication styles. Strong interpersonal skills can help you to overcome these obstacles and develop relationships that benefit both you and the organization in which you work.

Most work relationships, such as the relationship between a salesperson and a customer, follow norms, standards, and rules. All work relationships, in addition, rely on ethical communication.

⊕ Guidelines for ethical communication

- Refrain from comments intended as personal attacks, from gossip, and from careless communication that reveals sensitive information

- Be straightforward and honest with coworkers, customers, and supervisors

- Avoid delays and distortions, do not hide information, and do not manipulate a relationship for personal gain

- Recognize that work relationships exist for the primary purpose of achieving organizational goals and act on this principle when and if a conflict of interest arises

These guidelines are applicable regardless of the type of relationship in which you are involved.

In this chapter, we examine the basic elements of several relationships common in business and the professions: relationships between managers and employees and between coworkers, mentoring relationships, romantic relationships, and relationships between employees and customers.

7.2: Manager-Employee Relationships

7.2 **Report the manager-employee relationship to be the most important of all work relationships**

One of the most important of all work relationships is the one between managers and employees. These relationships are so important for the simple reason that everyone (except perhaps the chief executive officer in some cases!) has a boss.

Research continues to confirm the high importance of the manager-employee relationship. In a survey of over 2 million people at 700 organizations, the top reason employees reported for either staying with the organization or leaving was the relationship they had with their immediate supervisor.[1] Table 7.1 presents an activity[2] that will help you identify the characteristics of your "ideal boss."

7.2.1: Set Goals for an Important Relationship

Here we examine the manner in which communication is used by managers and employers to establish and maintain effective interpersonal relationships. **Goal setting** is an important feature of manager-employee relationships in ensuring coordination. Situational knowledge is also a

Table 7.1 Who Is Your Ideal Boss?

Rate the importance of the following characteristics that make up an ideal boss (5 = most important; 1 = least important).

Allows you to show initiative and responsibility	1	2	3	4	5
Communicates clear goals and objectives	1	2	3	4	5
Listens well	1	2	3	4	5
Is reliable	1	2	3	4	5
Gives credit and praise where it is due	1	2	3	4	5
Is not moody	1	2	3	4	5
Is fair and understanding	1	2	3	4	5
Is not afraid to reprimand employees for improper behavior	1	2	3	4	5
Is talented	1	2	3	4	5
Is persuasive with her or his boss	1	2	3	4	5

Figure 7.1 Manager-Employee Relationships

Characteristics of strong manager-employee relationships include good communication, mutual influence, and power sharing.

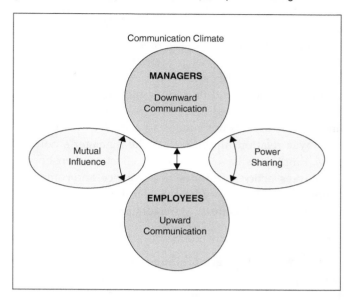

key element in this type of communication relationship, especially in determining the climate in which managers and employees work. Communicating competently is most effectively accomplished between managers and employees when power is shared and diversity is carefully managed. Since the manager–employee relationship is one of the most important relationships you will form on the job, it is essential that you learn how to communicate effectively with both managers and employees.

Managers and employees have not only personal and organizational goals but also goals for the manager-employee relationship. Setting goals for a work relationship requires an analysis of the organization, its communication flow, and its political atmosphere. The goals set for a manager-employee relationship should be consistent with the values of the organization. Typical goals are openness, cooperation, honesty, and friendliness.

7.2.2: Communication Climate

As Figure 7.1 shows, the manager-employee relationship develops within a communication climate that is produced by the behaviors and attitudes of all managers and employees. Important contributors to the climate are patterns of communication (upward and downward) and the personal characteristics of managers and employees. The outcomes of the relationship are mutual influence and power sharing.[3]

The organizational climate is affected by how decision-making power is shared and how supportive supervisors and workers are toward each other. Climate is changeable because organizational members' behaviors and their attitudes toward the organization can change.[4]

⊕ What effect does climate have on manager-employee relationships?

It may encourage or discourage employees' communicating in the organization, exerting control over matters that affect them, and obtaining satisfaction from carrying out their responsibilities. In a healthy climate, managers and employees communicate effectively and support each other.

Effective managers have a number of characteristics that make their communication successful. They are approachable, sensitive, credible, supportive, confident, and honest. Their communication demonstrates frankness, respect, empathy, and calm. Effective managers are quick to explain decisions, are articulate and clear in their messages, and encourage information and input from employees. Strong managers are also those who are effective with their own supervisors.

Managers are most pleased with employees who display:

- Good job performance
- Ability to handle pressure
- Help in promoting the boss's success
- Cooperativeness
- Supportiveness

Subordinates who enjoy good relationships with their bosses:

- Provide feedback about how superiors perform their jobs
- Demonstrate appropriate forms of persuasion
- Disagree in a constructive manner
- Confirm the messages that are sent downward

In an effective climate, employees are encouraged to give their opinions about a new advertising slogan, and employees willingly provide constructive feedback about improvements or changes for the ads. Managers then consider the feedback and explain why the decisions to incorporate or ignore suggestions were made. In an ineffective climate, managers would not welcome suggestions or comments about the new ad campaign, employees would not give suggestions or constructive criticism, and managers would not offer any explanations for decisions made about the campaign.

Managers and employees rely on each other to get their jobs done. When they possess the characteristics that we mentioned earlier, and when they display open and appropriate communication styles, they do more than simply work together: frequently they positively influence one another.[5] Thus, it is not enough to consider the manager-employee relationship only from the manager's point of view. Employees have a significant effect on their bosses. Employees' actions, attitudes, performance, and communication styles play a very large role in how managers conduct their own business. Managers cannot do the job of their unit or department without the cooperation of employees.

A popular approach to understanding how managers and employees mutually influence one another is through Leader–Member Exchange Theory, or LMX. Employees get a sense of trust and respect with their boss when she or he offers or exchanges resources, support, and influence. This can be particularly effective when these exchanges occur outside normal business hours or the business context. Likewise, members or employees reciprocate with support, resources, effort, and influence.[6]

Mutual influence is an informal negotiation process between managers and employees. Each party affects the attitudes and work performance of the other. When managers are approachable, sensitive to employees' needs, and supportive, employees are responsive with feedback about their concerns, dedicated to improving on-the-job performance, and cooperative. In a healthy communication climate, the two parties can recognize and understand each other's needs and work to accomplish mutual goals.

7.2.3: Manage Power and Diversity Competently

Communicating effectively in a manager-employee relationship means understanding the power structure and diversity of a work force. Understanding power sharing will enable you to adapt your communication in a manner that demonstrates a sensitivity to the power structure of an organization. Recognizing diversity will enable you to communicate effectively and appropriately with all sorts of people.

POWER SHARING At first glance, an organizational chart may imply that people in management hold all the power and those they supervise possess none. Signs of power in an organization include decision-making ability and the authority to distribute rewards (such as pay

raises) and punishments (such as firing people). Power, however, can be distributed in four ways: (1) managers hold all the power, and workers hold none; (2) neither supervisors nor workers have much power; (3) workers hold most of the power, and supervisors hold little; and (4) managers and workers share power.[7] Let us briefly consider each arrangement.

Organizations in which *management holds all the power* are rare now, but they were common in the early part of the twentieth century and were described by Frederick Taylor, Max Weber, and Henri Fayol, among others. Such organizations are characterized by rigidity, strict adherence to process, and communication from the top down.

When *neither managers nor employees have much power*, organizations suffer numerous problems. Small or family-owned businesses often have figurehead managers who possess little power. According to James Kouzes and Barry Posner, "People who feel powerless, be they managers or subordinates, tend to hoard whatever shreds of power they have. Powerless managers also tend to adopt petty dictatorial management styles. Powerlessness creates organizational systems where political skills become essential and 'covering' yourself and 'passing the buck' become the preferred style for handling interdepartmental differences."[8]

Organizations in which *subordinates hold most of the power* are also rare, but they are becoming somewhat more common as the demands on business for innovation and competitiveness increase. For example, companies such as Ben & Jerry's Homemade Ice Cream and Honda put most of the power in the hands of the employees. These companies de-emphasize differences in status between managers and employees and encourage employee input through lateral communication. However, such a structure may be too loose or decentralized for some companies.

When *managers and subordinates share power*, workers enjoy satisfaction and commitment without losing direction. When people feel they have some control and influence over the ways decisions are made and actions are carried out, they are more energetic in accomplishing the goals of the unit and the organization. Managers, in turn, have enough power to effectively manage the unit.

Like mutual influence, power sharing between supervisor and worker has to be negotiated. Management expert Rosabeth Moss Kanter identified four methods for sharing power:[9]

1. Give people important work to do on critical issues.
2. Give people discretion and autonomy over their tasks and resources.
3. Give visibility to others, and provide recognition for their efforts.
4. Build relationships for others, connecting them with powerful people and finding them sponsors and mentors.

In return, employees actually increase their productivity and strengthen their relationships with managers.

Remember that power and power sharing occur on a unit or department level as well. Power that is earned or bestowed on any member of a unit, whether manager or subordinate, is essentially the unit's power. Conversely, when a worker is denied power, the entire unit will suffer.

WEALTH OF DIVERSITY Manager-employee relationships are affected by issues of gender and ethnicity. Since 1972, the number of female managers in the United States has nearly doubled. According to the U.S. Bureau of Labor Statistics, women, members of minority groups, and older workers are expected to increase as a percentage of the work force through the year 2020. Percentages of the Latino/a population and Asian Americans in the work force continue increasing at a high rate, with Latino/a people maintaining their status as the largest group.[10] The prospect of a great influx of managers and workers from a wide variety of backgrounds has focused attention on the relationships between male and female managers, on the relationships between male and female subordinates, and on how people of different cultural backgrounds can make the most of their work relationships—a concept known as managing diversity or valuing diversity.

Diversity of gender, culture, and managerial preference illuminates two key issues: stereotypes and competence. Different experiences, opportunities, and educational preparation may account for varying levels of managerial skills in people, but these differences are not specific either to gender or to culture.

What are specific to groups are the stereotypes associated with them. Stereotypes associated with male and female managers are fueled by societal stereotypes about males and females in general. Men have traditionally been stereotyped as competitive, ambitious, assertive, risk taking, and power seeking. Women have traditionally been stereotyped as soft-spoken, passive, emotional, understanding, and sensitive. Whether or not typically masculine or feminine behavior is most effective for a given task, problems can arise when women and men do not behave as traditional gender stereotypes suggest they will. Consider the following example:

Amber and Kelly were recently hired as manager trainees for a fast-food company. Most of the employees they supervise have never had a female manager before. Amber decided that the best way to advance in the company would be to emulate the management style of her two bosses, Fred and Juan. Fred and Juan are very task-oriented; they rarely socialize or show their emotions when on the job.

Modeling the behavior of these men, Amber maintained her distance from her line employees. She answered their questions but never volunteered additional information, and she tried not to get involved in her workers' personal problems. She figured that her efficient demeanor would ensure that her shift performed professionally.

Kelly, however, treated her line workers in a warm and informal manner. She asked about their personal lives and attempted to establish close relationships. She figured that her obvious care for her workers would ensure their doing a good job for her.

At their semiannual evaluations, both Amber and Kelly were informed by upper management that their relationships with employees needed improvement. Line workers had complained about how they were treated. Amber and Kelly were stunned by these comments. What were the causes of the line workers' complaints?

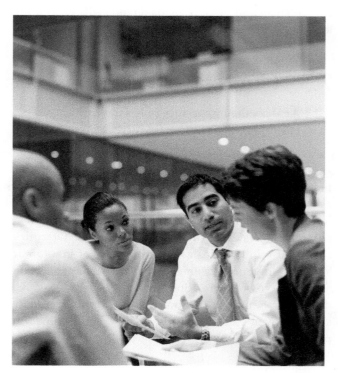

Effective communication is a great equalizer in diverse work relationship situations.

SOURCE: Digital Vision/Getty Images

It is difficult for members of the majority to recognize subconscious stereotyping, yet it is nearly always present. The most destructive approach to managing diversity is to claim lack of prejudice. That claim usually masks a failure to acknowledge biases that are apparent to others or a tendency to dismiss others' perceptions of bias as misguided.

The double bind that minority and female managers experience is diminishing. As more minorities and women enter the work force and become managers, stereotypic behaviors will become more widespread and are likely to be perceived as positive. The most effective managers and leaders are sensitive to employees' needs, take a personal interest in their subordinates and nurture them, and are passionate about the goals and values of the organization. Most subordinates appreciate such positive traits. Moreover, research has revealed that, increasingly, the gender of a boss is no longer that important of an issue. A Gallup Poll reports that about half of those surveyed said that gender would play no role in their preference for a boss.[11] As women make up a larger percentage of the work force, support from subordinates will make a big difference in the overall success of female managers.

The best approach for managing people effectively is to capitalize on their individual strengths to get the most from them. Most managerial jobs require a certain level of competitiveness, risk taking, and power seeking as well as sensitivity, empathy, and emotional involvement. Good managers have always recognized this fact. An approach that stresses goals, situational knowledge, communication competence, and anxiety management will yield a high level of excellence for any manager.

7.3: Coworker Relationships

7.3 **Analyze the importance of having cordial coworker relationships for increased productivity**

Coworker relationships are the glue that holds an organization together. Positive and constructive coworker relationships enhance productivity, creativity, and teamwork as well as make work an agreeable place to be. Coworker relationships are based on proximity, shared interests, common tasks, and satisfaction of needs. Of course, coworker relationships can be voluntary or involuntary. You will do yourself a considerable service if you understand how coworker relationships develop so that you can devise a method for dealing with involuntary relationships or even technologies that could undermine your productivity.

7.3.1: Proximity

The closer you are to people physically, the more likely you are to develop relationships with them. Officemates form friendships and alliances simply because of their **proximity,** or physical closeness, to one another. (Of course, common lounges, meeting areas, restrooms, and hallways are places where you can meet people who do not work in your area.) Think about the classes you are taking. You have probably become friends with the people who usually sit near you in the classroom.

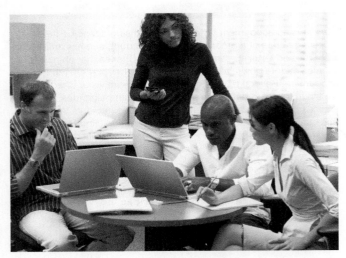

Collaborating on projects brings into play a number of critical relationship skills.

SOURCE: Lwa/Getty Images

7.3.2: Shared Interests and Common Tasks

People like to be with others who share their interests. Working in an organization automatically provides a number of common interests on which to build work relationships. Coworkers share a corporate identity, a work location, and possibly even the same bosses at times. Relationships often develop naturally around these common interests. The grapevine is one expression of shared-interest relationships among coworkers.

More and more jobs require the joint effort of two or more people. Work groups, task forces, and team projects show that cooperation is an increasingly popular way to solve problems and address complex issues. People are usually assigned to particular work groups because of their talents and expertise and regardless of whether they like the other group members.

Working with people on common tasks can provide both a great deal of satisfaction with the resulting relationship and professional enrichment. The more often you communicate with coworkers, the more likely you are to understand them on a personal level and form friendships with them. Unfortunately, the opposite is also sometimes true: the more you work with someone, the more you may dislike that individual's personal qualities.

Regardless of your personal feelings about your coworkers, several guidelines can help you to form positive shared-task relationships. These guidelines will help you to establish strong organizational relationships and overcome difficult or uncooperative coworkers. You may discover that it is actually very rewarding to work with someone you initially disliked for personality reasons.

7.3.3: Satisfaction of Needs

One of the most common reasons why relationships develop at work is to satisfy basic needs. In addition to basic subsistence needs such as food, clothing, and shelter, you have emotional and intellectual needs at every point in your life. As a student, for example, you are fulfilling your need for knowledge and skills.

Needs do not go away when you join an organization. Your needs for affiliation, social exchange, and the sharing of ideas with others are just as strong at work as they are in your personal life. Many people spend half or more of their waking hours at work, so it is only natural to satisfy these needs through their jobs. Most of the needs that can be fulfilled at work can be grouped into four areas: *support, power, expertise,* and *social exchange.*

SUPPORT The need for support can take various forms. People need professional support to ensure that they are performing correctly at work. They need friends at work who can provide professional support by serving as a sounding board for new ideas, giving suggestions, and acting as cheerleaders. On-the-job friends can also provide personal support. A friend can give you a lift after you have had a disagreement with your boss or have found out that you did not get the promotion or raise you were counting on.

POWER When people leave their jobs, it is often because they feel powerless. To accomplish professional goals, workers need power, and sometimes relationships are the best source of power and control. Although power relationships can be abused, there is nothing inherently wrong with them.

Coworkers who have attained a certain level of power can serve as resources for learning how the organization's power structure operates. You can learn from those who have power by observing their actions and deciding whether their methods are acceptable to you. Some powerful people may use unethical means, and we encourage you to avoid mirroring them. You may want to observe unethical behavior, however, if only to protect yourself from it.

EXPERTISE You have probably found that you sometimes need the expertise of others to achieve a goal. It is worthwhile to keep track of your coworkers' areas of expertise so that you know whom to call when you need

help. For example, some people may be mathematical or statistical whizzes who can help you interpret quantitative trends, others may be experts in budgeting matters, and still others may possess computer skills.

Remember that asking for expert advice is a reciprocal process, a two-way street. Some people are eager to share their expertise without any strings attached. Others may agree to help but are interested in getting something tangible in return. When asking someone for expert advice, think of some way you can offer some specialized help in return. A commitment to helping others increases your chances of receiving their expertise when you need it.

SOCIAL EXCHANGE Humans have a basic need for social interaction; the need does not go away when they enter the work environment. Some socializing occurs at coffee breaks, at lunch, or in the lounges of the organization. Socializing also occurs during work, often to the chagrin of corporate leaders.

Socializing reflects the desire for self-expression and for knowledge of coworkers. Many people feel comfortable telling coworkers their thoughts, feelings, and opinions on any number of topics—politics, company policies, marriage, children, economics, finances, and even religion. Socializing helps people to handle the stress of a hectic, fast-paced work environment.

WRITING PROMPT

Assume that you are assigned to a team project with three other employees. All members of the team work equally hard on the project. One of the team members, Jay, happens to be a personal friend of your supervisor's husband. After the completion of the successful project, Jay receives a commendation and pay raise from your supervisor. In response, the other two team members plan to meet with your supervisor's boss to complain about her action. You are not sure who, if anyone, has behaved unethically, nor if the planned action of the other team members is ethical or wise. What strategies would you use to remedy the situation?

 The response entered here will appear in the performance dashboard and can be viewed by your instructor.

Submit

7.3.4: Technology and Work Relationships

It is easy to underestimate the importance of your work relationships. Technology has become so integrated that "a third of chief information officers and information-technology managers said a week without a working corporate email system would be more traumatic than a car accident or getting a divorce."[12] Because of this influx of technology into the modern workplace, face-to-face communication has been giving way to a strictly electronic communication network. In some organizations, nearly all communication takes place digitally. Think about the digital communication you have with people at work. While productivity and efficiency have been increased by technology, it also has its downside. Tim Sanders, the chief solutions officer at Yahoo!, has described a problem that is caused by the information overload: constant interruption by technology and increasing personal isolation. He calls this state of work-related stress "New Economy Depression Syndrome." Some of his coworkers would instant-message him when they were only a few feet away. Sanders himself began to suffer from emotional detachment and problems with work relationships because of his almost exclusive use of technology to communicate.

According to research conducted about technology and the workplace, information overload at work costs businesses $900 billion a year.[13] This issue of information overload can affect employees' creativity, productivity, and interpersonal relationships. Many people do not even know that they are over-connected to technology and thus experience the symptoms overload but not the cause. Many experts suggest that time be prioritized each day for when we should disconnect.

7.3.5: Relationships with Difficult Coworkers

Just about every organization has employees who are difficult to deal with. Some people cannot get along with anyone, others get along with only a few people, and still others have good relations with everyone but you. The chances are very good that at some time you will have to work and associate with someone whom you consider difficult. The maintenance of appropriate work relationships with difficult people can be accomplished in several ways if at least one of the parties is willing to work out the problems. Below is a summary of helpful steps to take when you deal with difficult people.[14]

Steps for Improving Relationships with Others

Strategic Skills

1. Make sure you are not the difficult person.
   a. Listen open-mindedly to others' suggestions.
   b. Don't be dogmatic.
   c. Be open, friendly, and approachable.
2. Ensure that you are doing your job.
3. Ascertain the goals of the "difficult" person.
4. Assess perception levels.
   a. Consider the different backgrounds of yourself and the other person.
   b. Ask the other person to explain the situation as he or she views it.
5. Accept the difficult person for what he or she is, not for what you want that person to be.
   a. Forget the past, and focus on the future.
   b. Do not sweat the little things.
6. Confront the person.
   a. Take the initiative toward establishing good relations.
   b. Ask questions.
   c. Ask for input/suggestions.
   d. Listen carefully.
   e. Focus on job-related issues as much as possible.
7. State how you feel.
   a. Express your goals.
   b. Do not apologize if you are certain you are right.
   c. Demonstrate political sensitivity. (Recognize the power dimensions of the organization.)
8. Give recognition when the other person deserves it.
9. Maintain a professional demeanor during interactions.
10. Seek mediation if all else fails.

You may find yourself in situations that require all of the steps in the outline. Less complicated situations might require only two or three steps for resolution. In the following scenario, Della is able to use steps 1 through 8 to resolve a conflict with Victor:

Della and Victor are coworkers who share a large office suite with four other employees. Although they usually work on different projects, their work often overlaps, and they depend on each other's commitment to doing a good job. Lately, Della has perceived Victor's behavior to be increasingly unfriendly and aloof. Della has also heard rumors (apparently spread by Victor) that she is not doing her share of the work on their joint projects. Even Della's boss remarked that Della and Victor should work things out.

Della did not see that she had done anything to upset Victor, and after evaluating her performance on their joint projects, she decided she was certainly pulling her weight. She thought about her goals and wondered whether she and Victor were striving for different results. She also suspected that they did not perceive the value of their work projects in the same way. Although Della had other independent projects that concerned her, she knew that Victor placed the highest priority on their joint projects.

Della decided to approach Victor with an open mind and to listen sincerely to his complaints. At first Victor refused even to talk about the matter, but after a while he told Della that he was upset because she appeared to give their projects low priority and sometimes was not available when he wanted to work with her on them. Della acknowledged Victor's complaints. Although she did not feel that an apology was required, she did agree to be more cooperative with Victor.

Later, when one of their joint projects enjoyed great success, Della openly and generously credited Victor for his role in the achievement. Although Victor and Della never became personal friends, their professional relationship grew stronger as they understood each other better.

Of course, not all difficult relationships can be untangled in a productive manner. When you are dealing with people who are simply impossible and who refuse to work at resolving the difficulties, maintain a professional demeanor. Be patient, and do not lose your temper. Remain task-oriented: focus on the goals you are trying to achieve. And seek third-party mediation from a boss, coworker, or counselor. There is no reason to allow others to affect your performance when they are unwilling to reason things out. You have a right to be productive without the distraction of an unfriendly coworker.

WRITING PROMPT

Imagine, you are a second-year employee with your company and you are facing some tough choices about a work relationship. You would like to go to your boss to seek her advice. However, you have noticed that when others went to her with concerns, it never ended well for them. You don't feel that you can go to your boss with any problem, lest you be viewed as incompetent. What would you do in this situation? Would you seek the advice of your boss? If you do seek the advice of your boss, what steps will you try to take to ensure your meeting is successful? If you do not seek her advice, explain why not.

▶ | The response entered here will appear in the performance dashboard and can be viewed by your instructor.

Submit

7.4: Mentoring Relationships

7.4 **Analyze how mentoring relationships can be enriching for new employees**

One of the most valuable relationships that you can establish early in your career is with a mentor. **Mentors** are experienced, mature, and successful employees who give help and guidance to newer employees (**protégés**) in many areas, including knowledge, skills, and appropriate attitudes and behavior.[15] The mentor acts as a role model who demonstrates how the new employee can develop and become successful.

In the places where you have worked, you may have already experienced the benefits of having a mentor. If so, you can compare this information to your experience and learn more about the workings of mentor relationships. For those of you who have not enjoyed a mentoring relationship, we provide suggestions for becoming involved with a mentor when you take a job after graduation.

7.4.1: Importance of Mentoring Relationships

Successful mentoring relationships usually benefit everyone involved—the protégé, the mentor, and the organization.

An organization that wants to be more successful should encourage mentor-protégé relationships.[16] Young employees can develop faster when they have the help of a mentor. John Kotter, the noted author and management consultant, championed these relationships when he stated, "Virtually all of the successful and effective executives I have known have had two or more of these kinds of relationships early in their careers. Some have had upward of a dozen people they were able to rely on for different needs—some provided important contacts, others gave key information in specific areas, and still others taught them certain valued skills."[17]

BENEFITS TO THE PROTÉGÉ   Once a mentoring relationship has been established, the protégé has access to opportunities that may otherwise be unavailable. Benefits from mentoring relationships include the following:[18]

- Receiving support from the mentor
- Having the mentor influence others on behalf of the protégé
- Getting public recognition from the mentor
- Having the mentor as a friend and role model
- Obtaining greater knowledge of the politics of the organization
- Being promoted by the mentor

The results of these benefits include rapid promotions, salary increases, challenging work assignments, career mobility, and work satisfaction. Although mentoring relationships usually require extra dedication to a job and possibly longer work hours, if you are serious about the "fast track," they can be extremely valuable.

Finding a Mentor
Strategic Skills

If you are new to an organization and want to benefit from a mentor, what do you do? The following steps may be useful for securing an appropriate mentor in your first job:

1. Ask the personnel or human resources department about formal mentoring programs in the organization.
2. Identify people who have the same specialization and interests as you do. Try to determine whether they possess the "mentor characteristics" listed earlier.
3. Approach some of the people whom you have identified, and take an interest in what they do. Ask questions that reveal your enthusiasm for their jobs. If appropriate, volunteer for tasks that would facilitate their jobs and careers.
4. Let them know that you are upwardly mobile and interested in learning as much as you can about the profession and the organization.

5. Ask for advice on matters where their expertise would improve your productivity.

6. Ask them whether they would be interested in sponsoring you. Explain why you might be a good choice. Indicate your confidence in yourself, your admiration for their work, and the appeal their career track has for you.

SOURCE: R. A. Noe, "Women and Mentoring: A Review and Research Agenda," *Academy of Management Review* 13 (1988): 65–78.

TECHNOLOGY TOOLS

Virtual Mentoring

For several reasons, finding the right mentor can be a difficult task. The Internet and the Web can help. Numerous Internet sites offer professional guidance, coaching, and mentoring. Some are free services; others charge a fee or membership dues. Regardless of their approach, visiting Internet sites for mentoring opportunities can offer a number of possibilities that would otherwise be unavailable. Listed below are a few of the more prominent sites that specialize in mentoring services. Visit these sites and see for yourself how important mentoring relationships can be.

- International Telementor Center—This is a nonprofit organization (COLORADO State University) that connects mentors and protégés electronically.
- Center for Coaching & Mentoring—This site provides services for those interested in being a mentor or protégé.
- The Mentoring Group—This site offers several services and products for mentors and "mentees."

7.4.2: Characteristics of Mentor and Protégé Roles

While age and prestige are sometimes factors in selecting a mentor (who is usually eight to fifteen years older than the protégé), the mentor may be a person who has prestige and the communication skills to effectively help a new employee. The protégé is usually new to the organization or unit and is interested in career advancement.[19] Although assigned mentoring relationships exist in some organizations, prevailing opinion suggests that voluntary relationships are best, for required relationships may be viewed as a burden by one person or the other.[20]

Mentoring relationships require both partners to agree on their relative roles and understand each other

well. Mentors must possess the knowledge and skills necessary to benefit protégés, and protégés must be willing and skillful learners. For a relationship to be successful and productive, mentors must also be confident, approachable, successful, skillful in communication, able to make decisions, secure, and possessed of strong interpersonal skills; protégés must be ambitious, eager to learn, open-minded, loyal, talented, energetic, and communicative.[21]

Nicole's Protégé

Ethical Issues

Accuum Enterprises, a wholesale and distributing company, started a new mentoring program. All senior employees were expected to develop mentoring relationships with a younger, inexperienced employee. Nicole looked through the company directory and spotted Brian Fitzgerald's name. She knew him from when she was on the interview team that hired him, and she had seen him at several social functions sponsored by the company. He seemed bright and eager to learn. When asked, Brian jumped at the chance to be mentored by Nicole, given her strong reputation in the company. They began to meet frequently, and things were going very well. In fact, they began to see each other outside of work, and eventually they began a romantic relationship. They agreed that the relationship should be kept private, since the company was not keen on such relationships among its employees. The relationship deteriorated after a while, when Brian insisted on seeing other people. Nicole was very unhappy with this turn of events. Brian asked that the mentoring part of the relationship continue, but Nicole refused. She told Brian that continuing a mentoring relationship would be very awkward. After a couple of weeks, Brian told Nicole that if she would continue the mentoring arrangement, he would be willing to conform to her romantic relationship requirements.

Was it unethical for Nicole to terminate the mentoring relationship? If Nicole goes along with Brian's new plan, does this constitute sexual harassment on her part? What other ethical issues do you see in this situation?

BENEFITS TO THE MENTOR AND ORGANIZATION
Mentors can obtain a great deal of satisfaction from helping a less experienced employee. They may learn from the protégé. They may also increase their own value to the organization by demonstrating an ability to help new employees to develop.

The organization benefits from mentoring because protégés tend to develop faster than employees without mentors, have stronger leadership skills, demonstrate teamwork and shared values, and be less likely to leave the organization for other opportunities.[22] The following example shows how mentoring can benefit everyone involved:

> Connie worked part-time as an inventory clerk at Brooks, Inc., while attending City College. Brooks had a good reputation, and Connie hoped that if she proved herself as a part-time employee, she might land a job with the company after graduation.
>
> She noticed that Roger, an inventory manager, was competent, well liked by others, and friendly. Connie took on some paid overtime tasks in inventory control (a new area for her) and asked Roger for some advice on how best to do the work. Roger really appreciated having help from an enthusiastic worker and took time to teach Connie what she needed to know to handle inventory control. Soon, they were taking their breaks together to discuss various company and professional issues.
>
> Connie learned a lot about Brooks from Roger, and after graduation she started work full-time, bringing to the job the experience, knowledge, and contacts that had made her a valuable employee from the start.

7.4.3: Gender and Cultural Issues

Minorities and women can particularly benefit from mentoring relationships. Even if an organization's corporate culture is geared toward white male norms and attitudes, a personal relationship with a successful person of the same gender or ethnic group can help women and minorities to adapt successfully. Unfortunately, it may be difficult for women and minorities to find such mentors because of the relatively low numbers of women and minorities in middle and upper management.

Although there is nothing inherently problematic about male-female or cross-cultural mentoring relationships, the potential for controversy can restrict opportunities for the protégé. Suggestions of romantic involvement, fraternization, and sexual intimacy may scare off male mentors. In mentoring relationships between white mentors and black protégés, whites are sometimes afraid to correct their protégés out of fear of appearing racist. Members of minority groups may also resent special attention if it appears to be presented as remedial help.[23]

The lack of mentors for female and minority employees is especially unfortunate because the absence of such relationships may significantly reduce job effectiveness.[24] Research on cross-gender mentoring relationships suggests that a large share of successful female executives benefited from mentoring by male role models.[25] Professional organizations such as the National Consortium for Black Professional Development, the American Society of Professional and Executive Women, the Hispanic Organization of Professionals and Executives, and the National Association of Asian-American Professionals can provide support and networking opportunities for women and members of minority groups.

7.5: Romantic Relationships in the Workplace

7.5   Scrutinize the pros and cons of organizational romance

Have you ever been romantically attracted to someone you worked with? Have you ever dated someone from work? If you answered "yes" to either of these questions, you are not alone. Romantic relationships in the workplace have become relatively commonplace. And yet, although only limited research has been done in this area, it is clear that romantic relationships in the workplace have the potential for creating widespread controversy if handled in inappropriate ways. Romantic relationships between superiors and subordinates might result in resentment from other coworkers, charges of discrimination or sexual harassment, or job termination. Romantic relationships with coworkers might result in diminished work performance or a hostile work environment. It is therefore important for you to be aware of the issues involved in organizational romance—whether or not you are a participant.

7.5.1: Pervasiveness

You may be wondering whether organizational romances are really all that prevalent. Organizational romance has been defined as an intimate interpersonal relationship between employees of the same organization—a relationship that is characterized by a substantial degree of mutual sexual attraction.[26] According to research, two-thirds of the workers surveyed observed romantic relationships where they worked, and one-third of those surveyed claimed to have been involved in such a relationship.[27]

This latter number is probably an under-estimation. If you think about the workplace as a dynamic environment where people are interacting with one another for extended amounts of time, it is little wonder that close personal relationships form. As we mentioned earlier, work may offer the best opportunity for meeting and socializing with people. Romance often springs from close interaction.

Suppose you have worked for three months in an organization. As a beginner in public relations, you are eager to learn as much as possible as quickly as possible. You have often volunteered to work nights and weekends to help the vice president in charge of public relations meet important deadlines. During this time, the two of you have established a mutual appreciation, and he has agreed to be your mentor. As his protégé, you are often included in important projects. Lately, your coworkers are cool and aloof when you approach them. What situational knowledge can help you assess your coworkers' attitudes? What communication is necessary to maintain both your mentor-protégé relationship and your positive relationships with your coworkers?

▶ The response entered here will appear in the performance dashboard and can be viewed by your instructor.

Submit

7.5.2: Consequences

Negative and positive consequences can result from romantic work relationships.[28] Problems resulting from organizational romance can appear in task and relational areas and can include tardiness, absenteeism, poor work quality, and absent-mindedness. In addition, when people become involved in romance, their goals and emphasis in the workplace may become personal instead of organizational. According to an extensive survey conducted by the

Organizational romance occurs because people naturally develop relationships after frequent interactions. Organizations and their members face many challenges when organizational romances spring forth, including office gossip, charges of sexual harassment, and even termination of employment.

SOURCE: Image Source/Alamy

Society for Human Resource Management, many employees see the dangers in workplace romance and claim that they personally avoid such relationships. However, they also report that they do not completely agree that these romances always end in disaster.[29]

Relational problems may also emerge. If the romance hits a snag, relational partners may become distracted by their personal problems and neglect their other responsibilities. If the relationship is severed, the former romantic partners may be reluctant to work together.

Coworkers may also have problems with the romantically involved couple. Coworkers may feel envy, jealousy, or even disgust toward the romance. In extreme cases, disapproving coworkers may shun or ignore the couple.

Nevertheless, several positive consequences are associated with organizational romance. In a number of studies, organizational romance either did not affect the work performance or attitudes of participants or actually improved their behavior at work.[30] Participants in these relationships were easier to get along with, worked better in teams, improved their work flow, and were generally more productive. From the best available evidence, it appears that the nature of the consequences stemming from romantic relationships depends on the particular couple.

7.6: Sexual Harassment

7.6 Review sexual harassment in the workplace

In 1991, the world looked on as Clarence Thomas's Supreme Court confirmation hearings by the Senate became a public forum for the discussion of sexual harassment. Although the Equal Employment Opportunity Commission had set forth definitions and guidelines regulating sexual harassment in the workplace a decade earlier, it was the Thomas hearings that brought this issue into the living rooms, break rooms, and offices of everyone in America. Since then, numerous scandals involving high-ranking officials, corporations, the military, and various colleges and universities have made and continue to make headlines. Over 90 percent of Fortune 500 companies have reported cases of sexual harassment, and many instances go unreported.[31]

The Equal Employment Opportunity Commission describes sexual harassment as unwelcome sexual advances, requests for sexual favors, and other verbal or physical conduct of a sexual nature if:

- Submission to the conduct is made a condition of employment
- Submission to or rejection of the conduct is made the basis for an employment decision *or*
- The conduct seriously affects an employee's work performance or creates an intimidating, hostile, or offensive working environment[32]

Simply put, sexual harassment is unwelcome, unsolicited, repeated behavior of a sexual nature.

Two different, although sometimes overlapping, types of sexual harassment have been identified. The first type, termed **quid pro quo,** involves a situation in which an employee is offered a reward or is threatened with punishment based upon his or her participation in sexual activity. For example, a supervisor might tell his employee, "I will give you Friday off if you will meet me at my place tonight." The second type of sexual harassment creates a **hostile environment**—conditions in the workplace that are sexually offensive, intimidating, or hostile and that affect an individual's ability to perform his or her job. For example, if two males talk explicitly about the physical features of a fellow female employee in her presence, she asks them to stop, and they repeat the offense, sexual harassment has occurred.

Why does sexual harassment occur with such frequency in the workplace? The most obvious answer is attraction. One person can become so attracted to another that status and authority are used to convey sexual requests and suggestions. A second reason for harassment is power. The harasser attempts to exert power and authority by controlling the behavior of the victim. The perpetrator believes that obtaining sexual favors from another conveys ultimate power. A harasser may think that he or she can wield power over another until sexual favors are delivered. Whether real or not, it is a perception of an imbalance of power that allows sexual harassment to occur. When that perception is changed to one of balanced power, sexual harassment is harder to perpetrate.[33]

A third reason for harassment is communication styles. Women are more likely than men to disclose personal issues to men. Some men perceive this communication as flirting or sexual interest. In fact, most women have no thoughts of sexual intimacy when mentioning personal matters. In addition, many women have been conditioned to act less assertively and aggressively than men. Consequently, when a man signals sexual interest in a woman, her unassertive behavior may be interpreted as game playing or as an invitation to express more sexual interest. Even nonverbal communication plays an important role in how men and women interpret their counterparts' communication. Women often use smiles and eye contact and touch innocently to indicate interest in a topic or person, whereas men may use these signals as openings for sexual intimacy.[34]

Reports summarized by Hal Witteman indicate that most targets for harassment are females under the age of thirty-five who have some college education and work in areas that are predominantly male. The woman is usually younger than the man and is either single or divorced. Men can also be targets of sexual harassment. Any unwanted sexual activity directed at either males or females is sexual harassment.

A major obstacle to ending sexual harassment is the tendency of the target to avoid confronting the harasser. Most instances of sexual harassment are not confronted, exposed, or reported. Instead, the victim usually avoids the situation by taking time off, transferring to another area, or changing jobs. One of the primary reasons for avoidance is that the perpetrator is usually someone in the organization with authority and status, and the victim feels that exposure or confrontation will backfire.

What are the signals of sexual harassment? Most come in the form of verbal and nonverbal communication. Verbal forms of sexual harassment include the following:

- Unwelcome remarks
- Embarrassing jokes
- Taunting
- Sexist remarks
- Displays of pornographic or offensive materials and photographs

Victims of sexual harassment report that perpetrators use pinching, patting, hugging, leering, touching, and kissing as means of nonverbal harassment.

TECHNOLOGY TOOLS

Preventing Sexual Harassment

Businesses are always in need of advice that can help them prevent instances of sexual harassment in the workplace. Although a large number of profit and nonprofit organizations offer such services, they can be costly and a bit awkward to put in place. The World Wide Web is a place that can respond to the need of business for rapid, reliable, and credible information on sexual harassment. The Richardson Company–Training Media Group www.richardson.com provides a comprehensive online program called "Preventing Sexual Harassment" at www.richardson.com. Visit the site and compare their offerings with other types that you are familiar with.

Addressing Sexual Harassment

Strategic Skills

Sexual harassment is a degrading and dehumanizing act. *It is wrong!* A number of local, state, and federal agencies protect employees against sexual harassment, and these powers should be used whenever possible. If you believe that you are being subjected to sexual harassment in the workplace, you do not have to tolerate it. There are several things you can do to address the problem:

⊗ Corrective Measures

1. If you believe that certain conduct is wrong, say so. Tell the perpetrator in very clear terms that his or her conduct is not appreciated or welcome.
2. Immediately report the incident to your boss or to someone in the personnel office.
3. Document each incident in written form.
4. If witnesses were present, have them verify the details of the incident.

If you are a supervisor who hears of sexual harassment in your area, you must take the following steps:

⊗ Corrective Measures

1. Take the complaint seriously. Listen carefully to the complainant.
2. Conduct your own investigation. Gather as much information as possible about the situation. Find out who was involved, who could serve as witnesses, how often this has happened, where the incident occurred, what the accused perpetrator did, and so on.
3. Maintain objectivity throughout the investigation. Do not become caught up in the emotions of the situation. Remember, making a sexual harassment complaint is a difficult act, and complainants will need your professional support.
4. Suspend judgment. Not all sexual harassment complaints are valid. The alleged perpetrator has rights, too. Your job is to gather facts. A professional group such as the personnel department has expertise in evaluating the situation.

Summarized by H. Witteman, "The Interface between Sexual Harassment and Organizational Romance," in *Sexual Harassment: Communication Implications*, ed. G. Kreps (Cresskill, NJ: Hampton Press, 1994).

Is This Sexual Harassment?

Strategic Skills

Read each description. If this happened to you, would you consider it sexual harassment?

Yes	Maybe	No	1. Your supervisor often uses a suggestive and domineering tone of voice when speaking to you.
Yes	Maybe	No	2. Your coworker grasps your hand or arm to the point that you notice it lingering too long.
Yes	Maybe	No	3. Your coworker engages you in a conversation with implicit or explicit sexual tones.
Yes	Maybe	No	4. Your supervisor requests sexual favors.
Yes	Maybe	No	5. Your supervisor stands close to you, invading your personal space and making you feel uncomfortable.
Yes	Maybe	No	6. Your coworker speaks indirectly about things of a sexual nature.
Yes	Maybe	No	7. Your supervisor offers to help you with a project or promotion in exchange for "something in return." You perceive this to be a sexual favor.
Yes	Maybe	No	8. Your supervisor discusses his or her sexual activity with you.
Yes	Maybe	No	9. Conversations between you and a coworker frequently turn to personal, usually sexual, topics.
Yes	Maybe	No	10. Your coworker seeks or offers advice of a sexual nature.
Yes	Maybe	No	11. Your supervisor gazes at your body while you talk to him or her and there is little or no eye contact.
Yes	Maybe	No	12. Your coworker's sexually suggestive conduct has made you uncomfortable.
Yes	Maybe	No	13. Your supervisor constantly and unnecessarily brushes up against you.
Yes	Maybe	No	14. Your coworker makes private sexual remarks in a common gathering area, such as a break room.
Yes	Maybe	No	15. Your supervisor suggests changing your appearance to make you look more attractive in the workplace.

SOURCE: Reprinted with permission from Joann Keyton, North Carolina State University, 2009.

7.7: Employee-Customer Relationships

7.7 Analyze the importance of customer relations in the current business environment

The twenty-first century [offers] the greatest opportunity for planned success ever seen. It won't be necessary to discover oil, . . . develop the telephone, or create the electric light bulb in order to gain wealth and influence. The only absolutely essential management characteristic will be to acquire the ability to run an organization that deliberately gives its customers what they have been led to expect and does it with pleasant efficiency.[35]

Those words by Phil Crosby illustrate the importance of customer relationships. Knowing who the customers are, what they want, and how they will react to products or services is a basic goal of businesses, especially now, when the economy has shifted from a manufacturing to a service orientation. More than three-quarters of all jobs created in the United States in the last ten years are in service industries; thus, customer relations are a high priority for organizations and are likely to be part of your work experience.[36] Customers often base their opinion about a business and its ability to meet their needs on their communication with a business representative. Interpersonal communication is at the heart of customer relations. Customers must feel that the people they give their business to can listen carefully to and understand their needs. Five basic rules of conduct can ensure successful customer relationships, each corresponding to elements of the strategic model: know the customer; take responsibility for customer satisfaction;

avoid unresponsive behavior; employ effective communication skills; and treat difficult customers with respect.

7.7.1: Know the Customer

It is difficult to please customers if you are ignorant of their needs. All too often, excellent products fail because customers are not convinced that they need them. Successful organizations work to find out what customers want and to provide it.[37] You can work toward the same goal in your relationships with customers. The Internet and social marketing strategies are seen as some of the most viable options for addressing customer needs. If nothing else, examining and adapting to the data provided from would-be customers who visit the company Web site provides information about what people are looking for.

Customer service can include solving problems to help customers obtain goods and services that are right for them. Often, this problem-solving process means planning for the customer's future needs and desires (changes in taste, technology, and economic outlook are constants in the business environment). Customer relations can also include mutual goal setting by employees and clients. Employees and clients together can set business goals for the client. If you understand customers' present and future needs, you will be able to plan for the services you will have to deliver. Knowing the customer well enough to set effective goals requires understanding and cooperation.

7.7.2: Communicate with the Customer Competently

Communicating effectively with customers means taking responsibility for customers' needs, addressing those needs enthusiastically, employing appropriate communication skills, and dealing sensitively with customer complaints.

TAKE RESPONSIBILITY FOR CUSTOMER SATISFACTION Customers enjoy doing business with organizations that personalize their service. Personalized service at its best means ongoing attention from a specific person. When customers call to place an order, make a complaint, specify a correction, or even give a compliment, they want to deal with someone who they know takes a personal interest in them, not an automated voice that gives them numerical options.

Customer satisfaction can be monitored in a variety of ways. Many organizations provide comment cards as a means of gauging customer satisfaction. Surveys, studies by market research firms, and analyses of sales data can also give clues. The most effective way to learn about customers' level of satisfaction is to ask them in phone calls, face to face, or through your Web site. Questions such as "How do you like our new product line compared to the last?" "What would work better for you?" and "What are your most important concerns about the services that you use?" show the customer that you care about his or her satisfaction.

Taking responsibility for customer satisfaction also means taking follow-up actions. Attention to details, such as keeping customers notified about work-in-progress (even misplaced orders or other setbacks), sending holiday greetings, giving advance notice of specials, and taking interest in their personal lives, gives customers a feeling that someone is looking out for them. Customer loyalty is usually the result.

Working with Difficult Customers

Strategic Skills

These guidelines can help you work through difficult situations with customers:

⊗ List of Guidelines:

1. Let customers talk. Listen carefully and with an open mind to their complaints, making note of instances in which your company may be at fault.
2. Reassure customers that their concerns will be heard and addressed.
3. Do not personalize the issue. Recognize that customer anger is not directed personally at you. People who go to the trouble of making a complaint are usually concerned with getting satisfaction rather than with making employees feel bad.
4. Acknowledge instances in which the customer is correct. Customers like to be told that they are right when they are.
5. Apologize and provide immediate satisfaction if you determine that the company was wrong. If blame cannot be determined immediately, promise the customer you will respond at a specific time, and be sure you follow up.
6. Ask the customer to suggest how problems could be avoided in the future.

This list is adapted from D. Finkelman and T. Goland, "The Case of the Complaining Customer," *Harvard Business Review* (May–June 1990): 9–21.

AVOID UNRESPONSIVE BEHAVIOR Customer relations can be enhanced significantly if you make the effort to avoid unresponsive behavior.[38] You may have seen problems caused by apathy, coldness, and inflexibility in the organizations with which you do business.

⊗ Apathy

Apathy—lack of emotional involvement in the job—usually results in employees failing to treat customers with care and concern. The best way to avoid customer neglect caused by apathy is to learn about each customer. By remembering customers' names and expressing interest in their jobs or families, you can show that you view customers as more than simply a source of income for the organization.

⊗ Coldness

Coldness also damages customer relations. Coldness is displayed in several ways. Condescending answers to legitimate questions or concerns, negative facial expressions, or demeaning comments indicate to customers that their satisfaction is not your highest priority. Sometimes you may give an impression of coldness unintentionally, especially if you are tired, under stress, or nervous about the customer relationship. Although keeping personal frustrations and concerns hidden is difficult, revealing them to customers is likely to hurt relations with them.

⊗ Robotism

Robotism—rigid and inflexible behavior—is another form of unresponsive behavior. An organization's rules and procedures may encourage robotism among employees, but customers are likely to hold you personally accountable for any rigidity they encounter in their dealings with you. You may have experienced robotism if you have been systematically put on hold or transferred from department to department when calling a firm with a question, or if you continued to receive junk mail or solicitations long after you canceled a subscription to a publication. Another example of robotism is to be given the same answer at a service desk that everyone else gets.

Avoiding robotism means keeping an open mind about how to handle customer desires within the context of your organization's current policies and regulations. Some flexibility is nearly always possible, and recognizing occasions when customers deserve special consideration will keep them satisfied.

COMMUNICATION SKILLS FOR THE CUSTOMER RELATIONSHIP Customers prefer to deal with company representatives who display effective communication skills. Successful employee-customer relationships are based on assertive, open, and friendly communication. Customers expect to be treated well by someone who knows what he or she is talking about, can explain problems, and does not make the customer feel ignorant or pushy for asking questions. You can communicate effectively by smiling, making eye contact, asking pertinent questions, answering questions promptly and accurately, and using encouraging nonverbal communication.

TREAT DIFFICULT CUSTOMERS WITH RESPECT Handling difficult or hostile customers is often a thankless job. Nevertheless, few job duties are more satisfying than turning an angry customer into a happy one. Handling difficult customers is vital to maintaining successful customer relationships in general, for even the best customer relationships sometimes hit snags, and you are wise to be prepared for them.

You may think that appeasing difficult customers is not worth your time and energy. Statistics show, however, that hostile customers, through word of mouth, can reduce a company's business by 2 percent—certainly an amount worth considering.[39] The key to improving your relationship with a troublesome customer is maintaining a conscientious communication style. By giving an unhappy customer the attention he or she is seeking, you may be able to turn an enemy into a friend. In the following situation,

the clerk successfully resolves a customer's anger about a damaged product:

CLERK: Can I help you?

CUSTOMER: I want a refund. The cell (phone) I bought here is junk.

CLERK: I'm sorry you're not happy. What exactly is the problem?

CUSTOMER: Quite a few things. The keyboard doesn't light up every time and the speaker fades in and out. I want my money back!

CLERK: Sometimes keyboard illumination can be easily fixed by going to the "options" area, but just in case it's a more serious problem, I'll be happy to get you a new phone and send this one back to the manufacturer to be checked out.

CUSTOMER: Well, OK. Thanks. I need a few other items while I'm here, too.

CLERK: I'm sorry about this inconvenience. Always let us know when you're not completely satisfied.

CUSTOMER: Yes, I will.

Learning to communicate effectively with hostile customers can bring success to your organization through repeat business and can help you to achieve your career goals.

7.7.3: Manage Anxiety in the Customer Relationship

Building relationships with customers, setting goals for customers, and communicating with difficult customers can produce anxiety. Nervousness may prevent you from effectively communicating with a new customer, or tension may limit your ability to deal with a difficult customer.

To reduce anxiety, concentrate on your goals. Remember that you are the representative for your organization and that your goal is to provide satisfaction for customer needs. Listen open-mindedly to the customer's suggestion or complaint. Rephrase the statement or problem so that you are sure you understand it. If you have questions, don't be afraid to ask. The customer will appreciate your desire to fully understand his or her needs.

Do not interpret complaints or hostility from a customer as a personal attack. When people become frustrated or angry, they often blurt out verbal attacks. Remain calm, and try to empathize with the customer's situation. Take a few deep breaths, and address the complaint without resorting to verbal attack. The calmer you appear, the more likely it is that the customer will soon run out of steam.

To control nervousness when establishing relationships with new customers, begin a conversation with small talk, and let the customer talk as much as he or she wants. Ask specific questions. Be enthusiastic and energetic. Once you realize that customers are ordinary people, your nervousness will disappear.

Strategic Scenario Wrap-Up

Work Relationships

Strategic Scenario

Tomás Chavez was hired recently by Vangard Equipment Corporation as its director of training. Vangard manufactures heavy earth-moving equipment. Although it is one of the youngest and smallest companies in its industry, Vangard has a solid track record for earnings and profits. Tomás found out on the first day of his job that his position had gone unfilled for almost a year. During that time, training had been conducted by the various departments in the corporation. He knew he had a lot of catching up to do. His first task was to conduct a needs assessment to determine where the corporation had the greatest training needs. He sent out surveys, conducted interviews, reviewed policy manuals, read memos exchanged among employees, and even conducted some focus groups. He rapidly learned that several training needs were apparent. First, customers of Vangard were having a great deal of difficulty getting their questions answered about new equipment purchases. Some customers became so disgusted that they switched their business to a competitor. Second, dozens of employees expressed a great deal of resentment toward upper-middle and upper management for its lack of sensitivity to their needs. Salary wasn't so much the issue as respect and recognition for their performance on the job. Third, many younger employees were leaving Vangard after only a year or two. Although a lot of reasons were given for their exodus, Tomás got the distinct impression that these less-experienced employees were not given enough guidance, direction, and encouragement for their efforts. Fourth, Tomás learned that Vangard, much like the industry itself, was male-dominated and somewhat chauvinistic. Two recent sexual harassment suits (settled out of court) were testament to the fact that many employees lacked the knowledge and/or sensitivity to deal with gender and sexual issues in the workplace. Finally, Tomás learned that a general lack of respect and civility was the norm among coworkers in the organization. He couldn't put his finger on it, but it was apparent that few of the employees or managers enjoyed positive professional relationships.

Because the company hired him a director of training, Tomás's superiors know they have some problems. Gratefully, he doesn't have to convince them that a plan is needed, rather he has to come up with the right plan. His research was a good start.

- Tomás decided to recommend that upper management start at the top and bring in an executive counselor to discuss the issue of sharing power.
- Training in gender discrimination is top of the list for the entire company, along with training in understanding and appreciating diversity.
- Employees need support to do their jobs, and training in customer relations is next.
- Over time, Tomás's plans to develop workshops on managing conflict in the workplace, tailored specifically to each working group. In the meantime, he is optimistic that civility will improve as employees begin to absorb the benefits of the fundamental trainings.

Despite its problems, the company has been financially successful, and Tomás has set his overarching goal to helping it stay that way.

WRITING PROMPT

Are some of the problems uncovered by Tomas related to one another? Could he design one training program that would address related needs? Why or why not?

 The response entered here will appear in the performance dashboard and can be viewed by your instructor.

Submit

Summary

Work Relationships

- **Developing and maintaining relationships** in the workplace is no simple task. Relationships require planning and effort to be desirable and productive. Ethical communication is vital to all forms of work relationships.
- The workplace **promotes a variety of relationships**, including those between managers and employees, coworkers, mentors and protégés, friends and lovers, and employees and customers.

- **Manager-employee relationships** are affected by the communication climate of the organization, the communication patterns and personal characteristics of the two parties involved, and the degree of mutual influence and power sharing in the relationship.
- **Coworker relationships** develop through proximity, shared tasks, shared interests, and satisfaction of needs.
- Some coworker relationships are involuntary and may involve **working with difficult people**. Getting

along with these people requires that you keep focused on the job at hand and maintain a professional demeanor.

- **Mentoring relationships** provide valuable benefits for new employees, such as support, influence, recognition, friendship, role models, organizational knowledge, and even promotions.
- The **drawback to mentoring** relationships is the difficulty of finding a willing mentor, especially in organizations that do not have structured mentoring programs in place.
- **Romantic relationships** are a potential source of controversy in the workplace. Positive and negative consequences of romantic relationships in the workplace have been noted.
- **Sexual harassment** is unwelcome sexual advances or comments by someone. It is a degrading and dehumanizing act that should be confronted when it occurs.
- Action can be taken by the complainant and the supervisor to **prevent sexual harassment** in the workplace and **ensure a safe environment** in which to work.

- **Employee-customer relationships** benefit from the employee's knowing the customer as well as possible, taking responsibility for customer satisfaction, avoiding unresponsive behavior, using effective communication skills, and treating difficult customers with respect.

SHARED WRITING: WORK RELATIONSHIPS

What do you usually do when you encounter a difficult person? How would you react differently with a difficult person in a work setting versus a non-work setting? List and explain ways to improve relations with difficult coworkers. What factors (personal or organizational) may stand in the way of improvement?

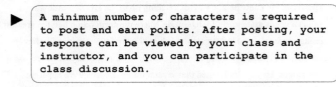

> A minimum number of characters is required to post and earn points. After posting, your response can be viewed by your class and instructor, and you can participate in the class discussion.

Post   0 characters | 140 minimum

Chapter 7 Quiz: Work Relationships

Chapter 8
Interviewing Skills

Learning Objectives

8.1 Review the importance of proper communication and interpersonal skills in an interview	**8.6** Enumerate the five broad response types of an interview
8.2 Discuss the features of an interview	**8.7** Report an overview of business interviews
8.3 Review the role of goal setting in an interview	**8.8** Describe the four ways to make an employment interview successful
8.4 Examine the role of situational knowledge in strategic communication during an interview process	**8.9** Analyze the importance of a successful appraisal interview
8.5 Report the importance of asking effective questions for a smooth interview process	**8.10** Analyze the three main aspects of disciplinary interviews

Strategic Scenario: Practice and Training

Marci Cohen is a junior in college, majoring in public relations. As a graded assignment for her business communication class, Marci has to set up an interview with a person who (1) does a considerable amount of interviewing and (2) is engaged in professional work related to her major. Marci has made an appointment to interview William (Bill) Walker, executive director of university relations at her university, at his office. Her task is to learn about Mr. Walker's interviewing practices (the techniques and methods he uses when interviewing) and interviewing training (things he has done to help him become a better interviewer). Marci is anxious about this assignment; interviewing the interviewer seems like a daunting task.

As you read through this chapter, think about the skills that Marci will need to conduct a successful interview with Mr. Walker. At the end of the chapter, we will revisit this scenario and discuss some solutions.

8.1: Overview
Interviewing Skills

8.1 Review the importance of proper communication and interpersonal skills in an interview

In the world of business, "as soon as you move one step up from the bottom, your effectiveness depends on your ability to reach others through the spoken word."[1] So said management consultant Peter F. Drucker. Although Drucker was not talking specifically about the communication skills involved in interviewing, he might well have been. Indeed, John Galassi and Merna Galassi, summarizing sixty years of research on the most important factors in employment interviews, conclude, "Researchers consider communication and interpersonal skills as the single most important set of factors in the interview."[2]

Not only are interviewing skills crucial for obtaining a job; they are equally important for success and promotion once you have a position. In a research report, Dan Curtis, Jerry Winsor, and Ronald Stephens identified more than thirty studies of employers' needs that agreed that the skills most valued in today's job market are the ability to communicate and to work effectively with other people.[3] Leaders in business and industry not only voice this view but also support their beliefs financially. Anthony Carnevale, Leila Gainer, and Janice Villet report that "employers spend $30 billion on formal training and approximately $180 billion on informal on-the-job training each year"—about the same amount spent for education at the primary, secondary, and college levels.[4] By far the most common type of business training is focused on interpersonal communication skills: more than 90 percent of business organizations provide communication training for their employees.[5] Many of these efforts and much of the money spent by business and industry are to improve employees' interviewing skills.[6]

8.2: The Interview

8.2 **Discuss the features of an interview**

So what is an interview? It's communication that is planned, dyadic, and interactive. Let's explore each of these features briefly.

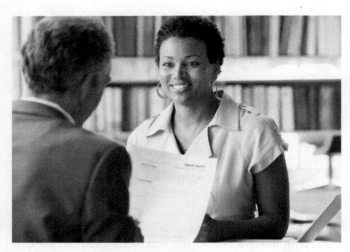

An interview allows two people to discuss a job opening using face-to-face communication. You will learn that, whether you are the interviewer or the interviewee, the first few minutes of your time together will set the stage for the entire interview process.

SOURCE: Ariel Skelley/Getty Images

8.2.1: Planned Discourse

The interview has a purpose beyond initiating and developing a relationship between the two parties involved. Even though the interpersonal relationship is important to the interview, at least one of the two parties (sometimes both) has a predetermined goal—for example, to share information, to persuade, or to solve problems. That goal exists before the start of the interview, so you can plan in advance how best to initiate and conduct the interview.

8.2.2: Dyadic Discourse

A dyad is two units that are considered to be a pair. In an interview there are two parties; there is no third party to act as a mediator or arbiter if the two parties do not agree. Although each party in **dyadic discourse** is typically one person, there can be more than one person in each party. Thus, for example, in an employment interview, a number of representatives of a firm may interview a job applicant in a group interview; or, less commonly, one or more representatives of a firm may interview a number of applicants at the same time.

8.2.3: Interactive Discourse

An interview is a dialogue rather than a monologue. It involves the two-way interaction of two parties—both speak and listen. As a result, an interview requires that both parties adapt to the verbal and nonverbal messages being exchanged. Although an interview normally occurs face-to-face, it also can and does take place over the phone or by means of a computer. In fact, many larger organizations are now using online interviewing tools to ensure optimal selection of job candidates.[7] Such tools allow organizations to maintain accurate records, decrease geographical barriers, reduce costs, and expedite the interviewing process.[8]

Since we know that an interview is planned, two-party, interactive discourse, it should be easy to see why it is important to use strategic communication when participating in an interview. To illustrate, let's look in on Communication Design, a small advertising studio with multiple clients, and identify a small number of interview possibilities. Table 8.1 defines each type of interview by providing a situational view.

Table 8.1 Interviews at Communication Design: An Example

Interview Type	Description
Employment interview	A recent college graduate participating in a job interview with the owner
Orientation interview	The personnel manager explaining insurance benefits to a new employee
Research interview	An account executive gathering information from a potential client
Appraisal interview	The office manager conducting an evaluation interview with a graphic artist
Grievance interview	The art director talking with a client who is very unhappy with the design of a brochure
Problem-Solving interview	Two copywriters meeting to discuss potential copy for a new advertisement
Persuasive interview	An account executive attempting to convince a client that it is time to redo the company's full-page advertisement

Hide All Cells   Show All Cells

In each of these examples, the two parties in the interview are striving to achieve goals. They bring information to the interview and increase their knowledge as the interview progresses. They must employ appropriate questioning, responding, and listening skills, and they must regulate their levels of anxiety. These are general principles that apply across all types of interviews, as we illustrate in the latter part of the chapter. We begin our discussion of these basic principles with the first component of the *model of strategic communication:* setting goals.

8.3: Goal Setting: Dyadic Communication

8.3 **Review the role of goal setting in an interview**

In most interviews, we can say that the interviewer carries the major responsibility for the success of the interview (the therapist in a counseling interview, the pollster in a public opinion survey, the persuader in a sales pitch). In some situations, however, we can't assign this responsibility as easily. To illustrate, in a problem-solving interview, the responsibilities for the interview's success may be equally shared. Even in an employment interview, it may not always be clear who should have the major responsibility: the employer, the applicant, or either one—depending on who has a greater stake in the outcome.

Whoever is primarily responsible for the interview's success (the interviewer, the interviewee, or both) is also primarily responsible for clarifying the goal of the interview. Is the goal, for example, to gather information, give information, counsel, or persuade? Goal setting brings the purpose into focus, and the purpose then shapes the relationship between the interviewer and interviewee.

If you decide that the goal of a particular interview is to gather information, you must then consider what type of relationship between the interviewer and interviewee will make that goal easier to reach. Without goal setting, you are likely to focus too much attention on interpersonal concerns. For example, because you want to be friends with the other person, you may hesitate to ask provocative but necessary questions. Or, without goal setting, you might not focus enough attention on interpersonal concerns. For example, you might ignore nonverbal feedback telling you that the other person doesn't understand your questions. In either case, your decision of whether or not to emphasize the interpersonal relationship can interfere with achieving your goal: gathering information.

Once you determine your reasons for engaging in an interview, you can move on to the next task: identifying potential barriers to achieving the goals of the interview. Such obstacles can include an interviewer who isn't well prepared or who may have biases, misperceptions, and preconceived notions about the interviewee that can interfere with the interview. On the interviewee's side, obstacles can include his or her inability or unwillingness to help achieve the interviewer's goals; demographic, social, or psychological factors that detract from the interview; or a negative response to the interviewer.

The setting can also be a problem. The time of day or week, location of the interview, and seating arrangement can affect the success of an interview. Of course, careful preparation by the interviewer (and often by the interviewee as well) usually pinpoints these potential problems and remedies them. The following list shows possible barriers to effective communication in interviews. One goal common to both the interviewer and the interviewee is to expect and minimize these obstacles as much as possible:

- Competing demands
- Ego threats
- Lack of courtesy
- Trauma
- Forgetfulness
- Confusion
- Jumping to conclusions
- Distracting subconscious behaviors

WRITING PROMPT

Compared to a face-to-face interview, how do you think you would perform in a Skype interview or in another type of online interview, such as a live chat? What are some tips you might give yourself? Can you imagine that you might feel at an advantage or a disadvantage? Why or why not?

 The response entered here will appear in the performance dashboard and can be viewed by your instructor.

Submit

8.4: Structuring the Interview

8.4 **Examine the role of situational knowledge in strategic communication during an interview process**

Because an interview involves two parties—each of whom will have an idea of how he or she wants it to proceed—its structure is seldom known ahead of time. Although each party may prepare in advance, each must be ready to use the second component of strategic communication—situational knowledge—to make the exchange of messages as smooth as possible during the interview. Nevertheless, it is useful to think of an interview in terms of three identifiable parts: the opening moments, the body of the interview, and the closing moments. Each part gives the interviewer and the interviewee a chance to get to know more about each other, the purpose of the interview, and the direction it takes. Although there are no hard-and-fast rules—or time limits—for any of these parts, consider the functions they potentially serve.

8.4.1: The Opening

The **opening** moments of an interview are useful for addressing three issues that may concern the interviewee: credibility (Will I like and can I trust this person?), orientation (What will this interview be about?), and motivation (What will I gain from participating in this interview?). The context of the interview may provide answers to these questions, but that is not always the case. Thus, the interviewee can use these three questions to determine if it is necessary to address one or more of the issues specifically.

If, for example, the interviewer and interviewee are getting together for the first time, issues of credibility will be important. When this is the case, the interviewer and interviewee are wise to consider and adapt to one another. Both must be sensitive to anything they learn about each other that is based on nonverbal assets and liabilities. The astute interviewee asks herself or himself these types of questions: What is an interviewer likely to conclude from my physical appearance, body motion, vocal cues, use of space, and so on? Can I modify any of these characteristics? Do I want to do so? Is there anything I can do to tone down the effect of possibly unfavorable characteristics that I can't change?

An interviewer is smart to ask herself or himself similar questions about orientation and motivation. Will the interviewee know what the interview is about? If not, how can I provide orientation to the interview? Will the interviewee want to participate in the interview? If he or she doesn't really want to participate, what sources of motivation (for example, humanitarian appeals, promises of rewards, fulfillment of expectations, recognition, sympathy, or understanding) can I use to get him or her more involved?

Credibility, orientation, and motivation are, of course, not independent; ways to achieve one may work to achieve the others as well. As you consider the unique requirements of your situation, you may find that one or more common opening techniques apply. Table 8.2 outlines ten of the most common interview opening techniques.

Table 8.2 Common Opening Techniques for Interviewing

Technique	Comments
Make a brief statement or rapid summary of the problem, issue, or need.	This strategy is appropriate when the interviewee is vaguely aware of a problem but not well informed on details.
Explain briefly how you happened to learn about the problem and suggest that the interviewee might want to discuss it.	This strategy avoids the appearance of lecturing or talking down to the interviewee and encourages a spirit of cooperative, objective discussion of a mutual problem.
State an incentive (goal or outcome) that the interviewee wants that he or she may reasonably expect if the proposal is accepted.	This is potentially the most powerful opening of all but is easily abused—it is frequently too obvious or exaggerated. Avoid sounding like someone giving a high-pressure sales pitch, and instead emphasize honesty and sincerity.
Request the interviewee's advice or help with a problem.	This approach is good when the request is sincere. Do not use this technique as a slick gimmick.
State a striking, dramatic fact.	This too is a potentially powerful opening, but it can be corny. This opening must be sincere, logically justified, and related to the interviewee's motivations; it can easily be tied in with incentives. This technique is particularly appropriate when a real emergency exists and when the interviewee is apathetic and must be aroused.
Refer to the interviewee's known position on a given problem situation.	This is the "common-ground" approach. It is excellent to use when the interviewee has taken a public position or the interviewer has already asked the interviewee to bring in proposals.
Refer to the background (causes, origins, and so on) leading up to the problem without stating the problem itself.	When the interviewee is fairly familiar with this background, the application of the common-ground approach may be useful when you expect the interviewee to react in a hostile manner when you reveal the purpose of your proposal.
Identify the person who sent you to see the interviewee.	This approach is appropriate when the interviewee is a stranger and when the interviewee respects the third party.
State the name of the company, organization, or group you represent.	This strategy is appropriate when added prestige is needed or when you have to explain why you are there.
Request a specified, brief period of time.	This opening can be too apologetic; use it only when necessary—for example, when dealing with an impatient, irritable, or very busy interviewee.

| Hide All Cells | Show All Cells |

SOURCE: Adapted from R. S. Goyer, W. C. Redding, and J. T. Rickey, *Interviewing Principles & Techniques.* Published by Wm. C. Brown Group, 1968.

8.4.2: The Body

While the opening sets the stage for the interview by establishing credibility, orientation, and motivation, it is in the body of the interview that the participants' goals are (or are not) achieved. When developing the body of an interview, the interviewer can choose from a spectrum between two contrasting approaches: directive and nondirective.

In a **directive interview,** the interviewer controls the purpose, structure, and pacing of the interview. Interviews that lend themselves to a directive approach include public opinion polls, employment interviews, and sales interviews. As an interviewer plans for a directive interview, the choices range from "nonscheduled" to "highly scheduled, standardized."

In a nonscheduled interview, the interviewer prepares an interview guide that lists potential topics and subtopics. These topics may or may not be covered in the actual interview and may or may not be covered in the listed order. What actually happens in the interview depends more on the interviewee's responses than on the interviewer's guide.

In a moderately scheduled interview, the interviewer prepares an interview guide that includes all major questions, with possible probe questions under each major question. The questions are asked in the order in which they are listed, but the probes may or may not be used.

In a highly scheduled interview, the interviewer prepares an interview schedule that contains all the questions that will be asked (including all probe questions) and the exact wording that will be used with each interviewee. Every interviewee receives exactly the same questions in exactly the same order.

In a highly scheduled, standardized interview, the interviewer prepares an interview schedule that includes not only all questions but also all answer options. The answer options normally ask the interviewee to select one of a number of alternatives (for example, "Do you intend to vote in the student government election?"—"Yes," "No," "Undecided").

In contrast to a directive interview, in a **nondirective interview** the interviewer chooses to cede control of the purpose, structure, and pacing of the interview to the interviewee. This option is typically chosen for problem-solving interviews and counseling. In such situations, the interviewer either does not have enough knowledge to structure the interview or feels that more reliable and valid responses will be gained by allowing the interviewee more of a chance to participate in structuring the interview. In a counseling interview, for example, the interviewee may be asked to describe the problem to be confronted and possible solutions to be considered. The interviewer, instead of planning a structure before the interview, may instead react to the needs and thoughts developed by the interviewee during the interview, incorporating situational knowledge gained by interacting with the interviewee.

The choice of a directive or nondirective approach depends in large part on the interviewer's situational knowledge (which has increased during the opening of the interview). Once the decision has been made, it greatly affects the amount and kind of situational knowledge that may be discovered and employed during the rest of the interview.

8.4.3: The Closing

Effectively **closing** an interview requires as much careful thought as does opening an interview. Even though it may be tempting to move the process quickly to a close once you have achieved the purpose of the interview, an abrupt, awkward ending can do long-term damage to the relationship between the two parties. Thus, it is important to think through the functions of a closing and the nonverbal and verbal strategies that can fulfill these functions.

Communication researchers have studied the functions and norms involved when people take leave of each other. Within the interviewing context, these functions can be described as concluding (signaling the end of the interview), summarizing (reviewing the main portion of the interaction), and supporting (expressing pleasure with the interaction and projecting what will happen next). These functions can be accomplished nonverbally as well as verbally—for example, by breaking eye contact, straightening up in your seat, leaning toward the exit, smiling, rapidly nodding, or looking at the clock. The following closing techniques capitalize on both verbal and nonverbal strategies.[9]

1. *Offer to answer questions.* Be sincere in the desire to answer questions, and give the interviewee adequate time to ask. Do not give a quick answer to one question and then end the interview.

2. *Ask whether the candidate has anything more to add to the interview.*

3. *Explain the next stage in the interview process, including whether there will be further interviews, when you will make your decision, and how the candidate will be communicated with going forward.*

4. *Leave a good impression.* Interviewees will tell others about the interview and in essence become a public relations tool for you.

5. *State that the interview is completed.*

6. *Express appreciation or satisfaction.* A note of thanks or pleasure is a common closing because interviewers

usually have received something—information, help, a sale, a story, and so on.

7. *Plan for the next meeting.* It is often appropriate to arrange the next interview or reveal what will happen next, including date, time, place, topic, content, and purpose.

8. *Ensure that all information is accurate and that you are satisfied with the level of information you obtained.*

9. *Summarize the interview.* A summary is a common closing for all types of interviews. Summaries may repeat important information, stages, and agreements or verify accuracy or agreement.

8.5: Ask Effective Questions

8.5 **Report the importance of asking effective questions for a smooth interview process**

In addition to setting interview goals and gathering situational knowledge before and during the interview, both the interviewer and the interviewee need to be able to think of effective and appropriate questions and responses. The ability to do so—and to use verbal, nonverbal, and listening skills to make the information flow smoothly—is the third part of the model of strategic communication.

In *The Art of Asking Questions*, Stanley Payne makes the important point that asking the right question in the right way is central to the success of the interview process.[10] Doing so requires that everyone participating in the interview masters three important characteristics of questioning: the question's meaning, form, and sequence.

8.5.1: Question Meaning

A well-known saying is "Garbage in, garbage out"—that is, what you get out of a computer can be no better than what you put in. Because this principle applies just as strongly to questions and answers in an interview, consider the clarity and possible bias of each question you will ask.

CLARITY The questioner's first concern should be whether the respondent will understand the words used in the question. To get the most valid response to a question, Payne suggests a number of strategies:[11]

1. Start by making sure you clearly understand the issue yourself. This means defining the issue precisely even if your words are hard to understand. To achieve this goal, ask yourself the stock journalistic questions: who, what, when, where, and how?

2. Once you have stated the issue precisely, turn to the dictionary to determine whether you can restate the question more directly or more simply. Look up each word and ask four questions about it: Does it mean what you intend? Does it have other meanings? If so, does the context make the intended meaning clear? Is a simpler word or phrase suggested (either in the dictionary or in a thesaurus)?

3. Try to keep questions somewhere in the neighborhood of twenty words or fewer. A study that compared "tight" questions with "loose" questions found that, on average, loose questions were one and one-half times as long as tight ones—thirty-one words to twenty-two words.[12]

4. Phrase questions positively. For example, "Do you agree with the statement 'School should be mandatory until age 16'?" is better than something like "Do you disagree with the statement 'School should not be mandatory until age 16'?" Research indicates that questions can be highly confusing when stated negatively; always phrase questions in a clear, positive manner.

BIAS Once you have phrased a clear and relevant question, be sure to locate unintended potential bias. The issue here is whether the wording of a question will lead some respondents to give different answers than they would give to a different wording of the same question. When a question doesn't give the respondent hints about the expected response, it is labeled *neutral*. When a question either subtly or blatantly clues the respondent to the expected response, it is labeled *directed*. **Directed questions** can be either leading or loaded. When the cue is subtle ("You like ice cream, don't you?"), the question is labeled *leading*. When the cue is blatant ("Are you a women's libber?" or "When was the last time you got drunk?"), the question is called *loaded*. Loaded questions typically use emotionally charged words or name-calling ("women's libber") or ask one question that is really two questions ("Have you ever been drunk?" "When was the last time you were drunk?").

There are many ways in which questions can produce unintended bias. One of the most commonly recognized forms of bias appeals to the desire for prestige. Probably the strongest and most common prestige influence in interviews is respondents who feel that they should have an opinion on an issue. The prestige influence often operates in a subtle fashion, and its effects are sometimes unexpected. A straightforward question such as "Do you own a laptop computer?" can, for example, be loaded with prestige.

As another form of influence, the words used to state alternatives affect the proportion of middle-ground and undecided replies. The less extreme the choices are, the more willing people are to report a commitment. For example, people who are asked whether they prefer or do not prefer an idea are more likely to express a commitment than are people who are asked whether they would vote for or against the same idea.

Given a list of ideas or statements, respondents tend to select the statements at the extreme position rather than those near the middle, and they favor the top of the list more than the bottom. When you ask respondents to select from a list of ideas, therefore, rotate the order of the ideas for different respondents.

Questions that emphasize the existing situation take advantage of people's strong tendency to accept things as they are. Thus, when people read or hear such phrases as "as it is now" and "as you know" with a question, they are likely to give it higher approval than they would if the idea were presented without the leading phrase.

When there are two alternatives, it is safer to state both choices rather than just one. For example, the following versions of the "same" question are likely to produce different results:

- Do you think the United States should allow instant press coverage of wars?
- Do you think the United States should forbid instant press coverage of wars?
- Do you think the United States should allow or forbid instant press coverage of wars?

In addition, the list of alternatives should be exhaustive if you intend to cover the range of possibilities. Otherwise, an idea may be underplayed not because it ranks low in the respondent's thinking but because the questioner either overlooked it or considered it insignificant.

It is normally best to avoid all-inclusive or all-exhaustive words such as *all*, *always*, *never*, and *none*. Such words usually produce an overstatement. Many people will go along with the general idea, accepting the overstatement as a form of literary license, but purists may refuse to give an opinion or choose the other side in protest when they see words that imply an absolute position.

Our discussion of bias in question wording up to this point could easily be taken as a blanket prohibition against directed questions (either leading or loaded). This is not the case. Although they should never be used unintentionally, there are circumstances in which directed questions can be put to good use. The interviewer may, for example, be dealing with an ego-threatening topic and may wish to let the respondent know that her or his response will not shock the interviewer. A direct question may, under certain circumstances, produce a more truthful answer than a neutral stating of the same question. This is why Alfred Kinsey used directed questions in his well-known study of sexual practices (e.g., "When was the last time you did X?"). He felt he would get more honest answers this way. There are also circumstances in which the interviewer may wish to use directed questions to see how the respondent reacts to stress. The key point, then, is to recognize the difference between neutral and directed questions and to use directed questions only when they help you get an unbiased answer from the respondent.

8.5.2: Question Form

In addition to considering the meaning of a question, the questioner must also consider the form. It is possible to identify many characteristics of questions, but we will examine only two dimensions: open/closed and primary/secondary.[13] Each and every question in an interview can be characterized in terms of both dimensions.

OPEN/CLOSED QUESTIONS The distinction between **open** and **closed questions** can be drawn by the form of response. Open questions ask respondents to answer in their own words from alternatives that they construct—for example, "If you could create your ideal job, what would it be?" Closed questions ask respondents to select from a list of offered alternatives—for example, "Answer 'yes,' 'no,' or 'no opinion' to the following question: 'Do you believe that women should be in combat roles in the military?'"

There are advantages and disadvantages to questions that fall at each end of the open/closed continuum. Open questions allow respondents the greatest amount of freedom and are thus useful when the questioner is initiating a topic, knows less than the respondents do about the topic, or wants to get an uninfluenced view of the respondents' thinking. Because there are normally no incorrect responses to an open question, respondents are also less likely to be threatened by it. Such advantages are, of course, gained at the cost of increased time per interview and answers that are difficult to summarize and compare. Thus, when the situation requires greater control by the questioner or when the questioner plans to compare the responses of numerous respondents, closed questions are normally the better choice.

PRIMARY/SECONDARY QUESTIONS **Primary questions** introduce new topics or areas of questioning. **Secondary questions** develop topics or areas that have already been introduced by primary questions. You can start an area of questioning by asking, for example, "If you could create the ideal job for yourself, what would it be?" and then follow up or probe with a number of secondary questions (such as "Where would the job be located?" "Do you think, then, that it is important to work with like-minded individuals?" "Can you tell me more?"). While there are many different secondary questions, a number of the most useful are summarized in Table 8.3.

Table 8.3 Secondary Questions and Examples

Secondary Questions	Examples
Clarification:	Directly requesting more information about a response: "Could you tell me a little more about the kind of person you would like to work for?"
Elaboration:	Directly requesting an extension of a response: "Are there any other features of the location that you would consider important?"
Paraphrase:	Putting the response in the questioner's wording in an attempt to establish understanding: "Let's see whether I've understood what you're saying: you consider the type of people you work with more important than salary and benefits?"
Silence:	Not speaking while waiting for the respondent to begin or to resume speaking.
Encouragement:	Using brief sounds and phrases to indicate your attention to and interest in what the respondent is saying: "Uh-huh," "I see," "That's interesting," "Good," and "Yes, I understand."
Mirror:	Repeating the response while using the respondent's language: "You say, then, that it is important to you to be located near a university."
Summary:	Summarizing several previous responses and asking the respondent if your summary of his or her responses is correct: "Let's see whether I've got it: Your ideal job involves a boss who appreciates you, supportive colleagues, interesting work, and a chance to live in a large metropolitan area."
Clearing-house:	Asking if you have received all the important or available information: "Have I asked everything that I should have asked?"

Hide All Cells   **Show All Cells**

8.5.3: Question Sequence

Once the interviewer is sure that the questions are clear, relevant, and unbiased for the respondent (meaning) and has resolved choices between open/closed and primary/secondary questions (form), he or she then considers the best order to ask questions to develop the topics of the interview (sequence). Three organizational patterns for sequencing questions are funnel, inverted funnel, and tunnel.

FUNNEL In a **funnel sequence**, depicted in Figure 8.1, the questioner starts with broad, open questions and moves toward narrower, closed questions—hence the label *funnel* (an object that is broad at the top and narrow at the bottom). In Figure 8.1, the interviewer is interested in exploring a personnel manager's advice on the best way to conduct a job interview.

As this example illustrates, the funnel sequence is an excellent choice for situations in which the interviewee knows more about a topic than the interviewer does. In such situations, a funnel sequence lets the interviewee begin talking about a subject in an unbiased, nonthreatening way—

thus opening up areas that the interviewer can explore later with narrower secondary questions that require clarification and elaboration.

Figure 8.1 Funnel Sequence

In this technique, the questioner starts with broad, open questions and moves toward narrower, closed questions.

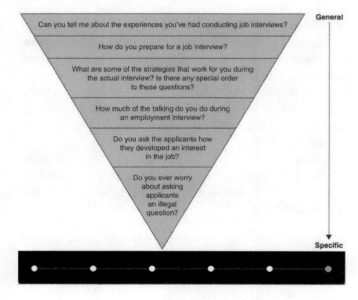

INVERTED FUNNEL The **inverted-funnel sequence,** depicted in Figure 8.2, turns the funnel sequence upside down. It begins the questioning process with a closed question that seems to require a "yes" or "no" answer and gradually moves toward broad, open questions. The example in the figure assumes that you are exploring the

Figure 8.2 Inverted-Funnel Sequence

This questioning technique begins with a closed question and gradually moves toward broad, open questions.

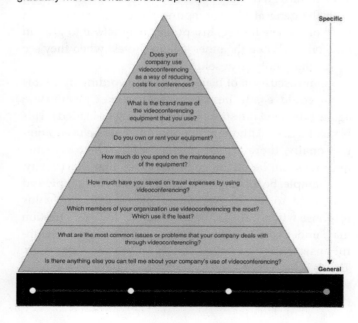

use of videoconferencing in a small business organization with the owner.

The inverted-funnel sequence assumes that the interviewer has enough information about the topic and about the interviewee to frame specific, narrow questions. It is useful when the interviewee's memory requires focusing. A series of closed questions can jog the interviewee's memory on the topic and motivate her or him to respond to more open questions. This can be especially true when the topic involves an unpleasant event or when the interviewee may otherwise feel threatened or inadequate to comment on the topic.

TUNNEL The **tunnel sequence** consists of a series of questions at a similar level of openness or closedness. Most frequently, the questions are closed, and the form of response is restricted: the interviewer asks a number of people a series of yes/no and multiple-choice questions. Because responses to open questions are difficult to replicate, code, tabulate, and analyze, interviewers who ask questions of more than one person and then summarize the results typically ask closed rather than open questions. Table 8.4 provides an example of a tunnel sequence.

Table 8.4 Tunnel Sequence Example

Use the following scale (VF = very frequently, F = frequently, O = occasionally, R = rarely, and N = never) to indicate how often you have participated in the following types of interviews:

Employment	VF	F	O	R	N
Information-giving	VF	F	O	R	N
Information-gathering	VF	F	O	R	N
Disciplinary	VF	F	O	R	N
Appraisal	VF	F	O	R	N
Problem-solving	VF	F	O	R	N
Persuasive	VF	F	O	R	N

SPECIAL PURPOSE SEQUENCES The three sequences (funnel, inverted funnel, and tunnel) can be put together in various combinations within a single interview. Thus, an interviewer may start with a funnel sequence, develop the next two topics with a tunnel, and conclude with an inverted funnel.

There are also sequences that cannot be described by any of the three labels. Perhaps the best known of these is one that George Gallup developed for use in public opinion polls aimed at determining the intensity of opinions and attitudes. Labeled the **quintamensional plan,** it has five steps:[14]

(×) Step 1

Awareness of the topic is first gained through a free-answer, knowledge question (sometimes labeled a filter question): "What, if anything, do you know about the use of computer conferences for problem solving in business?"

(×) Step 2

Uninfluenced attitudes on the subject are next developed in a free-answer question: "What do you perceive to be the advantages and disadvantages of using computer conferences for business problem solving?"

(×) Step 3

Specific attitudes are then elicited through a two-way or a multiple-choice question: "Do you approve or disapprove of the use of computer conferences for problem solving in business?"

(×) Step 4

The reasoning behind the attitudes is elicited in a free-answer question about the reasoning: "Why do you feel this way?"

(×) Step 5

Intensity of feeling comes last in the form of an intensity question: "How strongly do you feel about this: strongly, very strongly, or 100 percent committed?"

TECHNOLOGY TOOLS
Consult Interviewing Experts on the Web

You can learn a great deal about the nature of questions and their sequencing by examining a professional public opinion poll. Use an online search engine (Google, Yahoo!, Infoseek, Excite) to locate a current public opinion poll. Enter a simple query (public opinion polling) to identify or link to specific sites or organizations. You can also visit Princeton University's Survey Research Center Web site:

http://www.princeton.edu/~psrc/

Use the terminology of this chapter (e.g., open/closed questions, primary/secondary questions, funnel/inverted-funnel/tunnel sequence) to label the questions and their sequence. See if you can discover helpful devices that will aid Marci Cohen (from the Strategic Scenario) in her preparation for her interview with Bill Walker.

8.6: Respond and Provide Feedback

8.6 **Enumerate the five broad response types of an interview**

In the reaction phases of the interview, the interviewer can benefit from the information gleaned by Carl Rogers in a series of research studies examining how people communicate with each other in face-to-face situations.[15] Rogers found that when one person reacts to what another has said, 80 percent of all responses can be classified into five response categories: evaluative, interpretative, supportive, probing, and understanding.[16]

⊗ Evaluative Responses

Evaluative responses indicate that the interviewer has judged the relative goodness, appropriateness, effectiveness, or rightness of the interviewee's response. The interviewer in some way implies what the interviewee might or ought to do.

⊗ Interpretative Responses

Interpretative responses indicate that the interviewer's intent is to teach or tell the interviewee what the response means, how the interviewee really feels. The interviewer either obviously or subtly implies what the interviewee might or ought to think.

⊗ Supportive Responses

Supportive responses indicate that the interviewer's intent is to reassure, pacify, or reduce the interviewee's intensity of feeling. The interviewer implies that it is either appropriate or not necessary for the interviewee to feel as she or he does.

⊗ Probing Responses

Probing responses indicate that the interviewer's intent is to seek further information or to provoke further discussion.

⊗ Understanding Responses

Understanding responses indicate that the interviewer's intent is only to find out whether he or she correctly understands what the interviewee is saying.

To illustrate Rogers's categories, consider the following situation, and compare the five responses that the interviewer might offer:

INTERVIEWER: How do you go about motivating employees?

INTERVIEWEE: Well, that varies with the employee. For some, rewards are intrinsic to the job itself—things like the satisfaction of knowing they are doing a good job. For others, motivators are more extrinsic—things like pay, benefits, and vacation.

- **Evaluative response:** "That doesn't seem like a very practical way of thinking to me. How can you get any work out of employees if you spoil them?"
- **Interpretative response:** "I guess that means that you think you need to be fair but firm with your employees. You find out what motivates them but make sure they understand your expectations for job performance."
- **Supportive response:** "I've noticed the same things where I work. Some people are intrinsically motivated; others, extrinsically."

- **Probing response:** "What are some of the best ways to motivate employees who are motivated extrinsically?"
- **Understanding response:** "So the first step is to find out whether the employee is intrinsically or extrinsically motivated."

Carl Rogers discovered that people in a wide variety of settings use the five alternatives in the following order of frequency (from most frequent to least): evaluative, interpretative, supportive, probing, and understanding. He also discovered that if a person uses one category of response as much as 40 percent of the time, others will see that person as always responding in that way. The message of Rogers's research is not that a person should prefer (or avoid) one type of response more than another. All five types of response are useful to an interviewer. Overuse or underuse of a category, however, or a failure to think about the importance of a category for a specific situation may well be dysfunctional. Thus, an interviewer should know how to produce all five types of responses and know when each is appropriate. In many situations it may be best to start with probing and understanding responses before moving to evaluative and interpretative responses.

WRITING PROMPT

Recall any recent conversation you've had. Think of a statement in that conversation and respond to it using each of Rogers's five response styles: evaluative, interpretative, supportive, probing, and understanding.

▶ The response entered here will appear in the performance dashboard and can be viewed by your instructor.

Submit

8.7: Interviews in Business Settings

8.7 Report an overview of business interviews

The first part of this chapter introduced you to the principles and procedures of interviewing. In the second part of the chapter we apply the techniques and skills discussed there to interviews in a variety of business and professional situations. Our first focus is on employment interviews. They are likely to be of immediate importance to you, whether you are actively job hunting, considering the possibilities for summer or part-time employment, or anticipating your next move after graduation. And once you are established in your career, you will probably conduct such interviews to hire employees for your own organization. We also cover appraisal interviews, which are vital to maintaining strong and positive manager-employee relations, and disciplinary interviews, which prevent work problems from getting out of hand.

8.8: Employment Interviews

8.8 **Describe the four ways to make an employment interview successful**

Employment interviewing is probably the one work experience that everyone in the work force has in common. If you have gone through a job interview and have felt it was the most stressful event of your life, you are not alone. Most people are particularly anxious in this communication setting because the stakes are so high. Your future and career may seem to hinge on a successful job interview. Even interviewers are likely to be nervous. The success of their organization or department depends on their choosing correctly from among a number of candidates, many of whom appear to be equally qualified.[17] Recall that *strategic communication* in an interview situation, however, can reduce anxiety. Goal setting, situational knowledge, communication competence, and anxiety management can aid you in making an employment interview successful.

Handling Tricky Questions

Ethical Issues

Malore Brown, a single mother of an eight-year-old son, is interviewing for a position as a pharmaceutical sales representative. During her interview, she is asked, "Do you have children? If so, who will take care of them while you are at work?" Malore knows these and other such questions are illegal according to the guidelines set forth by the Equal Employment Opportunity Commission. How should she respond? If you found yourself in a similar position, how would you respond?

Such questions are asked—sometimes out of malice, but more often out of ignorance on the part of the interviewer. One strategy for handling tricky interview questions is to identify and consider the concern behind the interviewer's question. Ask yourself, "What concerns this interviewer so that he or she would ask me this question? How can I address that concern ethically?" In Malore's case, the interviewer is concerned that her status as a single mother will interfere with her abilities to perform her job competently. By addressing and responding to the concern behind the question rather than to the substance of the question, an interviewee can successfully manage a tricky or outright illegal interview question while still maintaining his or her own code of ethics.

Malore might respond to her interviewer by saying, "My son is a very important part of my life, but so is my career. I've had eight successful years of practice managing both at the same time. My previous employers can tell you that I am punctual, responsible, and well focused."

If you've ever been in a situation such as this one, in which you are asked a shocking or even offensive question but still must maintain your composure and continue the conversation, you know how difficult it can be to think on your feet and come up with a response that is at the same time polite, ethical, and personally advantageous. You can avoid this dilemma by thinking about these issues long before you arrive at the interview site. Spend some time thinking about how you might ethically and respectfully respond to the concerns behind any illegal, embarrassing, or otherwise tricky questions that may be asked of you without looking foolish or destroying the interview. Ask yourself: "Would a man who is a single father have been asked the same question?"

8.8.1: Goal Setting in Employment Interviews

INTERVIEWER Although employment interviews vary in their sophistication, comprehensiveness, and formality, *interviewers* all have at least one goal in common: to select the best person from the pool of applicants.

INTERVIEWEE As an *interviewee,* you may have numerous goals in a job interview, such as acquiring a decent salary, but your primary goal is to be offered a position with the organization. Achieving this goal requires situational knowledge of what to do before the interview and how to communicate effectively during the interview.

8.8.2: Situational Knowledge in Employment Interviews

HOLDING AN EMPLOYMENT INTERVIEW Conducting an interview means knowing your responsibilities as an *interviewer* and understanding how to acquire information about the person you are interviewing. Your situational knowledge as an interviewer will prove to be a valuable asset.

Businesses always face the challenge of attracting, recruiting, and hiring the best people. On the one hand, tight labor markets contain fewer qualified workers with highly developed job skills.[18] On the other hand, selecting from among dozens of solid applications per available position in a softer economy is not the simplest matter, either—although most personnel departments would rather have the latter problem. Whatever the economy, the challenge of getting the right person into the right job can be made much easier through effective preparation and interviewing techniques.[19]

DEVELOPING JOB SPECIFICATIONS When a position needs to be filled, the person (interviewer) responsible for filling it must first develop job specifications, which are commonly referred to as bona fide occupational qualifications, or **BFOQs.** These include the necessary experience, educational background, and skills—the *concrete* requirements—for performing the job. Some BFOQs are highly specific because of the technical nature of the position—for example, an auditing accountant position that requires applicants to be certified and have from three to five years of experience in tax law in the state of Illinois, or a quantitative marketing position that requires applicants to possess strong communication skills, two years of experience in computer systems sales, a degree in applied mathematics, and superior analytic ability.

It is helpful for the interviewer to define the minimum qualifications necessary for the job as well—for example, a sales representative position that requires a B.A. in business or communications and one year of sales experience in any industry. Candidates with additional experience and demonstrated management ability might be welcome to apply, but it is important that the hiree be able to grow in the job. Interviewers who select overqualified candidates are likely to end up with bored and frustrated employees. When describing a position for a specialized area, the interviewer is wise to review past and current job descriptions similar to the one in question. Such a review is also an opportunity to redefine jobs that have become outdated.

Regardless of the industry, organizations want to hire people who are honest, self-motivated, conscientious, and intelligent. In a survey, respondents reported that the personal characteristics most important for supervisory positions are general competence, leadership abilities, oral communication skills, and human relations skills.[20] It is important to think of the job qualifications in terms of these personal qualities, which will make the difference between a successful employee and another turnover statistic. For example, if one duty of a position is "to review sales reports and make regular presentations to management on profits and losses," the best candidates will have strong analytic and oral presentation skills. This notion of finding a candidate who is the best "fit" for the position has come to the forefront of Human Resource departments as they are taking longer to find the right person with the right skills for the right job.[21]

Many people use social-networking sites to stay in touch with family and friends as well as network for business opportunities. Users personalize their pages and sites with endless combinations of text, pictures, video, and music. However, what some think is personal space potential employers see as a source of character information.

TECHNOLOGY TOOLS

Improving Your Résumé

Visit a job-search website such as www.monster.com and research jobs in your field. Look at the minimum qualifications. What can you do before graduation to help improve your résumé? Could you find an internship to gain the experience needed to give you an edge over the competition? Could you volunteer to do research with a professor in your field? Are there nonrequired classes in which you could enroll? Are you even in the correct major for the type of job you want? What qualifications will set you apart from the other applicants?

Brad Karsh, president of a small consulting firm in Chicago, uses social-networking sites as a way to find out more about potential employees before an interview. When he views sites that have questionable material posted for public viewing, he thinks, "What kind of judgment does this person have?"[22] Mr. Karsh is not alone. Many potential employers are using these sites to eliminate the candidates that they feel would not represent their company in a socially acceptable light.

It is not just Facebook and other sites that are aiding potential employers in their quest for the best employee. It is now common practice to Google a potential employee's name to see what information is revealed.[23] Tien Nguyen, a senior at the University of California, Los Angeles, signed up for interviews on campus with corporate recruiters, but he was seldom invited. When he searched for his own name on Google, he found a link to an essay he had published as a student. The title of the satirical essay, "Lying Your Way to the Top," may have been responsible for his lack of interviews. He contacted the site and eventually had it removed. Since then, he has begun to receive invitations to job interviews. "I never really considered that employers would do something like that," he said. "I thought they would just look at your résumé and grades."[24]

Whether you agree or disagree with these practices is not the issue. The important point is that potential employers are trying to find out personal information about you long before you come in for an interview. "In fact, a recent survey found 77 percent of employers use search engines to uncover information about candidates and 35 percent have eliminated a candidate based on information they found online."[25] As graduation draws near, it may behoove you to search for your own name and remove any potentially defamatory or embarrassing information that you or someone else has posted about you. If you are unwilling to remove your personal information from a social networking site, then protect yourself by setting your profile to private.

ADVERTISING THE POSITION   Most midsize and large organizations have full-time personnel departments whose main concern is to advertise job openings, hold recruitment sessions on college campuses, screen and interview applicants, and make formal offers of employment. In countless other organizations, especially small businesses and highly specialized firms, employee recruiting and hiring are more problematic. Interviewers in small or specialized organizations may not be well trained in employment interviewing techniques, or they may be distracted by numerous other responsibilities in addition to interviewing. Regardless of organizational size, more and more organizations are relying on online avenues for cheap, widespread advertising.[26] For example, 90 percent of Fortune 500 companies advertise job openings on their corporate Web sites.[27]

Although advertising in newspapers, magazines, and professional journals is an acceptable approach to finding employees, professional recruiters generally agree that it is not the best way. How can organizations avoid the expense and hassle of over-response while still reaching a good number of qualified people? Several popular methods include networking (both online and in person), providing internships, and using employee referrals.

The prevalence of networking, or finding a job through personal contacts, highlights the fact that many, possibly most, people get their jobs because they "know someone." The familiar saying, "It's not *what* you know, but *who* you know" is often times very true. Social networking sites such as Facebook and LinkedIn provide job seekers the ability to expand their contacts and opportunities.[28] It is estimated that blue-collar workers find out about jobs through friends, family, and coworkers about 80 percent of the time. About 60 percent of white-collar workers initially use networks for job finding, and the number increases as they advance in their careers.[29] Employers can build their own networks by cooperating with college career centers, attending job fairs or community career days, or working with government employment agencies.

REVIEWING RÉSUMÉS   Once applicants have responded to the job opening, you as the interviewer must review the materials that these applicants provide. Your primary goal is to reduce the applicant pool to a manageable size and to invite only top candidates in for interviews. Many companies interview only eight to ten candidates from a pool of 200, and of those perhaps three to five may be offered the callback interview on which the selection will be based. Résumés actually screen out 90 percent of all job candidates.[30]

What should a well-prepared interviewer look for on an applicant's résumé? First, consider the applicant's work experience. Does the progression of positions show increasing levels of skill and responsibility? If not, what might be

the reason? Are there any periods when the applicant did not work? What were the reasons? Has the applicant switched careers? Why?[31]

Next, look at educational background. Is the level of education adequate? For example, does the applicant possess a B.A. or B.S. degree if it is required? Is the applicant certified to practice in a particular field if certification is required to do so? Does the candidate's educational background indicate that the person has the knowledge and skills necessary for the job? Look for instances in which the candidate had to demonstrate mastery of basic skills.

For an entry-level marketing position, for example, look beyond each candidate's college major and consider the basic skills that anyone occupying the position will need to succeed. Someone with a major in English literature might possess valuable skills in analysis, writing, and organization. Automatically considering only applicants who majored in marketing could deprive your organization of the opportunity to hire a person with unusual insights. It is best to assess educational background in light of the demonstrated skills and abilities that are implied by the applicant's description of her or his work experience.

References provide a second opinion for the interviewer. Are any of the names familiar to you? What are the professional backgrounds of the references? What is each reference's relationship to the applicant? If you are seriously considering a candidate, it is a good idea to contact several of the references to get additional information on the candidate's skills, experience, and career goals. Be aware, however, that it is standard policy at many companies to refuse to give any information other than dates of employment, and this should not be viewed negatively.

WRITING PROMPT

Visit a job-search website such as www.monster.com. With a partner, see how your résumé meets job criteria listed in your field. Look at the questions in the Reviewing Résumés section. Where do you see potential red flags in your résumé? How can you strengthen any weak spots?

 The response entered here will appear in the performance dashboard and can be viewed by your instructor.

Submit

HAVING AN EMPLOYMENT INTERVIEW   Understanding your responsibilities as an *interviewee* is the first step to a successful interview. Merely responding to job board ads is not enough for today's career-oriented candidate to get noticed.[32] The work you do prior to an interview can be as important as the interview itself. This type of preparation requires your obtaining situational knowledge about yourself and the organization and written documentation.

A number of steps, procedures, rules, and behaviors are associated with the interviewee role. Indeed, much of your work in performing this role occurs before you ever shake hands with an interviewer. If you want to impress wary, experienced, and professional interviewers, you have to do your homework. Much of this initial work can be conducted online. In fact, online sites are an increasing source of information about local jobs.[33]

RESEARCHING THE COMPANY Once you have identified the organizations that interest you, learn as much about them as possible so that you have a sense of whether your values are compatible with theirs and can tailor your résumé to the positions available. In addition, researching a company will give you detailed knowledge that you can demonstrate in the employment interview. A job seeker who wanted to land a job at a major fundraising organization checked through business journals to find out which organizations had made large contributions recently and complimented his interviewer on those successes. There is nothing so impressive as a job candidate who cares enough about the job or organization to become familiar with it before the interview. And knowing about the company can increase your self-confidence about your ability to fit its needs.

⊗ Multiple Resources Available for Research:

- School placement offices
- The company's Web site
- On-campus recruiter presentations
- Brokerage offices
- The company's public relations department
- Present or past employees
- *Macmillan's Directory of Leading Private Companies*
- *Career Guide to Professional Organizations*
- *American Society of Training and Development Directory*
- *Dun & Bradstreet's Million Dollar Directory*
- *Standard & Poor's Directory*
- Issues of *Forbes, Fortune, Business Week, Money, Inc.*, and the *Wall Street Journal*
- Various online sources, such as "Step-by-Step Guide to Researching Companies" (http://www.quintcareers.com/researching_companies_guide.html) or BusinessWeek Online's Company Research (http://www.businessweek.com/bschools/)

PREPARING A RÉSUMÉ AND COVER LETTER It is best to prepare the résumé and cover letter after you have done your research on a company. In this way, you can design these documents to reveal relevant personal strengths and genuine interest in the company. All too often, job candidates prepare only one résumé and cover letter, save them on a computer, find some jobs to apply for, change the company name and address on the cover letter, and send the same documents to every company to which they apply. This type of generic job search deprives you of the opportunity to demonstrate your uniqueness. Base your résumé and cover letter on your personal biography and on specific information about each company that you have researched.

Résumés should generally be one page long and never longer than two pages. For individuals with more money than time, there are literally hundreds of résumé services that can provide advice about preparing résumés, but we want to discourage you from using them. Doing your résumé yourself can give you the self-knowledge and self-confidence necessary to make a difference in an interview.

Most résumés include basic and essential information such as your career objectives, educational background, and work experience. Although this information will not change from one job application to the next, the manner in which it is presented may vary. For example, if an organization emphasizes teamwork, you will want to relate your experiences to team efforts; if a company values creativity, you will want to present your information as creative innovations or ideas. Often, information can be worded in such a way as to highlight its relevance to a specific organization.

Although the information is likely to be presented differently to different organizations, the résumé must be readable at a glance. Cluttered, confusing, and disorganized résumés probably will not make it past the first reader. Résumés should be concise, well organized, neat, and error-free. Some organizations will not consider a candidate whose résumé has even one typographical, grammatical, or printing error. Here are some résumé basics based on research from hiring professionals.[34]

⊗ Identify Your Job Objective

At the top of the résumé, state your goal and the skills that directly demonstrate your qualifications for the job. In short, energetic phrases, spell out the area in which you wish to work.

⊗ Specify Education

Give names of institutions, major fields of study, and dates of attendance. Begin with your most recent educational experiences. Include continuing education classes or training classes if they are relevant. Mention academic awards or honors, such as membership in an honor society.

⊗ State Work Experience

Along with your educational background, employers find work experience to be the most valuable piece of information about you. Most employers want to see your previous jobs listed in reverse chronological order (most recent first). They will be most interested in full-time positions, especially those with supervisory or leadership roles.

⊗ Include School Projects or Volunteer Achievements

Especially for new graduates, the skills and responsibilities used in these contexts can substitute for a lack of formal work experience.

ⓧ Do Not Cite Personal Characteristics

Your experience and achievements will imply relevant personal qualities such as leadership, ability to work with others, and resourcefulness. There is no need to repeat them in a separate section. Listing other personal characteristics such as your age, race, height, weight, or marital status is also unnecessary.

ⓧ References:

Simply state, "Available on request." An employer who is interested will be sure to ask for names. Applicants should be able to produce a list of references —including name, company and position, contact information, relationship, and years known—immediately when asked. Therefore, one should bring this list, prepared in presentable format, to the interview. Lastly, be sure to contact each person beforehand to ask if he or she is comfortable giving you a positive reference.

Here are samples of two résumé formats attractive to organizations.[35] Figure 8.3a shows a résumé organized according to specific jobs and activities. Figure 8.3b shows a functional résumé, which highlights general skills and

Figure 8.3a Basic Résumé Format
This format organizes "experience" using a chronological listing of jobs and responsibilities.

Barbara Dominco

Present Address		Permanent Address	
1100 Woodbury Road		35 Marshall Avenue	
Philadelphia, PA 19235		Eau Claire, WI 12345	
Phone: (215) 936-1744		Phone: (423) 671-5783	
Email: bdominco@eagle.com			

OBJECTIVE	Public relations or marketing position requiring strong communication skills, creativity, and computer experience
EDUCATION	Temple University, Philadelphia, Pennsylvania Bachelor of Arts degree 2011 Major in business with emphasis on marketing, public relations, and organizational communication GPA: 3.5 cumulative; 3.7 in major Elected to Alpha Chi student honor society
EXPERIENCE September 2011 to present	**Public Relations Assistant,** Temple University, Philadelphia, Pennsylvania Assisted director of Public Relations in development campaign. Researched potential donors and wrote direct-mail correspondence. Participated in annual fundraising telethon.
May 2010 to August 2011	**Customer Service Representative,** Mellon Bank, Philadelphia, Pennsylvania Wrote a series of 15 "Answers to Common Questions" brochures for customers' questions about banking services. Used computer database to analyze customer needs and concerns.
Oct. 2009 to May 2010	**Manager/Sales Clerk,** Strawbridge's, Philadelphia, Pennsylvania Scheduled cashiers and other personnel and worked on merchandise inventories. Provided customer service and set up displays.
ACTIVITIES 2008 to 2009	**Classified Editor,** *The Temple Times,* Temple University Layout staff Used desktop publishing techniques to design and produce classified pages. Supervised five staff members.
2009 to 2010	**Chair,** United Way Student Volunteer Committee Member. Organized campus-wide Volunteer Day. Participated in community rehabilitation projects.
SKILLS	WordPerfect and Microsoft Excel on PC and Macintosh computers Desktop publishing Typing (approximately 60 wpm) Fluent in Spanish
REFERENCES	Available on request

Figure 8.3b Functional Résumé Format
This format contains a chronological listing of jobs/responsibilities, but also highlights general skills and areas of strength.

Gervase Jackson
34 Waverly Street
Houston, Texas 77592
(806) 862-9913
jacksong@waverly.com

CAREER GOAL	To obtain a sales position leading to management that utilizes strong communication and marketing skills.
SALES AND MARKETING	Managed over twenty accounts for large music club. Developed promotional campaigns for new product lines. Increased sales by $240,000 in nine-month period.
ADMINISTRATION	Implemented and supervised office records. Coordinated purchase orders and prepared contracts. Handled customer service training program for telemarketing employees.
WORK HISTORY 2009–2011	Account Manager, SuperDisc Compact Disc Club, Houston, Texas
2008–2009	Telemarketing Coordinator, SuperDisc Compact Disc Club, Houston, Texas
2006–2008	Telemarketer, SuperDisc Compact Disc Club, Houston, Texas
EDUCATION 2011	Certified by International Association of Business Communications
2009	Colorado State University, Fort Collins, Colorado, B.A. in English
REFERENCES	Available on request

areas of strength. Functional résumés are generally used by people who have extensive experience in numerous jobs or by people who are applying for a job in a new field and need to call attention to their relevant skills.

Cover letters should begin with a specific, impressive paragraph. It is essential to grab the reader's attention, get him or her excited about looking at your résumé, and create the impression that you will be a valuable asset to his or her organization without actually using those words. Here is an example of a successful opening paragraph: "My experience in volunteer community work has provided me with the communication, management, and organizational skills required for the position of assistant to the public relations manager. During the past four years, I have designed and organized three fundraising campaigns for local hospitals that have brought in more than $450,000."

The body of the letter should specifically tell the reader what position you are applying for and briefly mention one or two accomplishments that demonstrate your qualifications. Indicate how you learned about the position and whom you know as a contact at the company. Close with specific language, such as "I will be in Houston on November 8 and would like to arrange an appointment" or "I will call on Thursday, May 22, to set up a time for an interview."

Figure 8.4 shows an effective cover letter for the résumé presented in Figure 8.3a.

Figure 8.4 Sample Cover Letter

A strong cover letter is an important complement to the résumé.

1100 Woodbury Road
Philadelphia, PA 19235
March 24, 2007

Mr. Harold Britten
Personnel Manager
Phillips-Margolis Company
195 Hennepin Ave.
Minneapolis, MN 55213

Dear Mr. Britten:

Please accept this letter and the enclosed résumé as application for the position of assistant marketing manager at Phillips-Margolis. The Director of Public Relations at Temple University, George Holton, suggested that I contact you about the position as it is appropriate for someone with my background, experience, and interest in the area.

While at Temple University, I have balanced academic success in marketing and communication with real world experience. As a public relations assistant, I produced a direct mail campaign that raised over $238,000 with a response rate of 7 percent—compared with the previous year's 3 percent. As a customer service representative, I used computers for writing and producing brochures, news releases, and promotional materials as well as for research. As a sales clerk in a major department store, I shared rotating management and scheduling duties with a staff of three in my department.

My immediate goal is to apply this experience to the needs of Phillips-Margolis upon my graduation this May. I would like to meet with you to discuss my qualifications for the position. I will call you the week of April 2 to arrange an appointment. If you wish to contact me before that time, please call me at (215) 936-1744.

Thank you for your consideration.

Sincerely,

Barbara Dominco

Barbara Dominco

enc: résumé

Résumés and cover letters must be neat and contain no spelling or grammatical errors. Such mistakes lead to a negative first impression, which is difficult if not impossible to remedy.[36] Give your current address, email, and phone number on the cover letter just in case the résumé is lost.

Given today's economy, successful job candidates go beyond merely submitting generic résumés via large employment search engines. Today's job seekers should have a visible online presence, or "brand," with the use of professional career-based Web pages that are easily found by recruiters through Web searches. To create a personal brand you can create separate profiles on Facebook or other social media that focus solely on your career (save the personal anecdotes for your nonprofessional Web pages). In addition, show you are active in your career field by using Twitter to openly converse with others regarding field-related topics (i.e., using Twitter handle "@MarketingQueen" to indicate your line of work).[37]

8.8.3: Communication Competence

BEST PRACTICES AS AN INTERVIEWER After you, as an *interviewer,* have acquired situational knowledge, you must be prepared to communicate appropriately with the interviewees.[38] Contact the interviewees in writing via email, and follow up with a phone call. Be sure the candidates know the exact location of your office and the times of their interviews. When scheduling interviews, keep in mind the nature of the position. For example, if the job requires alertness early in the morning, try to schedule the interviews for early in the morning so that you can assess the candidates' energy levels at that time of day.

Preparing a List of Questions Before the candidates arrive for their interviews, prepare a list of questions to guide and to organize the interview. The list will help you maintain control of the interview, and it will ensure that you question candidates consistently and focus on areas that you have identified as important to the job. Remember to craft your questions carefully and strategically (using the techniques described earlier) so that you can find out as much information about the candidate as possible in the most effective and ethical manner.

The Dilemma of Knowing Too Much

Ethical Issues

Assume that the personnel director has given you the responsibility for interviewing job applicants to eliminate all but the top three candidates. Several times during casual conversation, the personnel director has commented that the worst candidates are young, newly married women, because they are the most likely to become pregnant and take maternity leave. Although you do not ask candidates if they are married or if they have or intend to have children (because you know that the question is illegal), you establish a good rapport with a highly qualified candidate, who voluntarily tells you that her new husband is very eager to "start their family." Laughing, she says that she has given too much personal information about herself and returns to her qualifications for the job. After conducting all the interviews, you decide that she is one of the top three candidates. Are you going to include her in your recommendations to the personnel director? Why or why not? Are you going to tell the personnel director what you learned about this woman's personal life? How can you handle this situation legally without betraying the trust of the personnel director?

Legal Issues The process of obtaining information from job candidates is regulated by laws, and it is critical that these regulations be followed in both letter and spirit. The responsibility for conducting an interview legally rests with the employer, not the interviewee.

Title VII of the 1964 Civil Rights Act prohibits discrimination in employment on the basis of color, race, religion, sex, or national origin. This law has been supplemented by the Americans with Disabilities Act, which bans discrimination against individuals with disabilities.[39] In addition, an Employee Non-Discrimination Act (ENDA), which would prohibit employment discrimination on the basis of sexual orientation, has been proposed. Although a federal ENDA has not been passed, a number of state and city governments have enacted this legislation—adding to the large number of corporations that now include sexual orientation in their employee nondiscrimination policies. When asking questions of a candidate, interviewers have to be particularly careful to maintain a legal profile conforming to the spirit of the law.

The official source for legal guidance in hiring is the Equal Employment Opportunity Commission's Uniform Guidelines on Employee Selection Procedures.[40] This guide provides prescriptive advice for avoiding potentially discriminatory practices during the interview process. It is a good idea to become familiar with its guidelines and to be aware of changes (which occur frequently).

As an interviewer, you must adhere to two general legal requirements: the same basic questions must be posed to all candidates, and all questions (even those touching on personal qualities, goals, hobbies, affiliations) must be job related. Technically, questions that touch on personal or non–work-related issues are not illegal in themselves; it is the interviewer's action on the information that constitutes discriminatory hiring practice.

An additional aspect of employment interviewing and of the law has significant implications for anyone responsible for conducting employment interviews. A flurry of lawsuits by customers, clients, and coworkers accusing companies of negligent hiring practices have been introduced in court. A plaintiff in Texas, for example, won a $4.5 million suit against a taxi company when she was abducted and raped by one of the company's drivers.[41] The court found that the company was negligent in hiring this driver because he had a criminal record prior to his employment with the company. In other words, the company should have known about his past and should not have hired him in the first place.

A situation like that is difficult for employers, especially if they are committed to protecting the rights of interviewees. But employers who base a hiring decision on incomplete information are leaving themselves open to litigation. Again, the best course of action is to be an effective interviewer: ask legal questions that elicit valuable information from a job candidate, and check references.

Legal and Discriminatory Questions

Strategic Skills

The following list gives examples of legal and discriminatory questions.

(X) Legal and Discriminatory Questions:

- Have you been convicted of a felony?
- Would you mind working overtime?
- What three adjectives best describe you?
- Where do you see yourself in five years?
- Are you a U.S. citizen?
- Do you speak any languages fluently?
- Are you willing to relocate?
- Why do you feel qualified for this position?
- What do you like and dislike about your current (or previous) job?
- Why should we hire you?
- Can you give me some indication of your communication skills?
- Have you ever been arrested?
- Would your husband mind if you worked late?
- Do you consider yourself to be happily married?
- Will you need to arrange for child care?
- Where were you born?
- Where did you learn to speak Spanish?
- Could your family relocate with you?
- How old are you?
- Do you get along well with members of the opposite sex?
- Do you qualify for minority status?
- Will you continue to dress like that once you are hired?

Evaluating Candidates As an interviewer, you are required by law to keep an accurate record of each interview. One way to do this is to complete a standardized evaluation of each interviewee (see Figure 8.5). Once the interviews are over, list areas of expertise and personal characteristics that are most important for the position. Although your review of the job in an earlier step accomplished this, the interviewing process may have modified your expectations. Rank each candidate either quantitatively (on a scale of 1 to 10) or qualitatively (poor to excellent) in each area.

Complete the evaluation immediately after concluding the interview[42]—your memory is subject to unintentional

Figure 8.5 Standard Employment Interviewee Evaluation Form

Completing a standard evaluation form after each candidate's interview allows the interviewer to more fairly compare and rank a number of candidates.

Poor (P), Fair (F), Average (A), Good (G), Outstanding (O)

INTERVIEW WORK SHEET

Applicant's name _____ Interviewer _____

Last name

Internal _____ External _____ Other _____

Identify

Position(s) best 1. _____   Type of Interview
qualified for: 2. _____   ❑ Screening
                                     ❑ For a specific job
                                     ❑ Other

Salary discussed? Yes ____ No ____ If so, range quoted: _____
Earliest starting date _____ Interview availability _____
Special instructions for contacting applicant (if any) _____
Was the employment application completed? Yes ____ No ____

	P	F	A	G	O	Interviewer's specific comments (use back if necessary)
Communication skills						
Motivation						
Analytical skills						
Personal qualities						
Experience						
Reference and/or performance evaluation						
Other skills or impressions						

Overall evaluation of applicant: ____ Outstanding (we should make extra effort to remember and place)

____ Above average (probably able to do a good job)

____ Below average

Referrals: (Use back if necessary)

Unit   Supervisor   Date

distortions or revisions over time. Finally, check to see that information gained in the interview supports information on the résumé or cover letter. For example, a candidate may have listed programming skills on her résumé, but when she was asked about them in the interview, she was vague and displayed only rudimentary knowledge.

WRITING PROMPT

Many supervisors Google potential employees to find out more about them prior to an interview. As an interviewer performing a Web search on someone, what kind of weight would you be tempted to place on certain social details you discovered on Facebook? Might there be a "make or break" fact-finding moment for a particular job? Why or why not? Add any necessary examples.

▶ The response entered here will appear in the performance dashboard and can be viewed by your instructor.

Submit

BEST PRACTICES AS AN INTERVIEWEE As the *interviewee,* once you have been invited for an interview, you will need to present yourself as a competent communicator and potential asset to the organization. Doing so requires effective and appropriate communication—both verbal and nonverbal.[43]

Listening and Using Nonverbal Communication Skills
Although you may be tempted to focus on responding to questions as the central interviewing skill, listening and nonverbal behavior can strengthen and improve your responses. During the interview, listen carefully to the entire question before responding. Pause briefly before answering questions. Doing so gives you a chance to formulate your response and indicates to the interviewer that you are developing a considered response. Focus on the content of the response, and speak with confidence. Always look the interviewer in the eye when responding. If you are asked a question that you cannot answer, simply say so and do not act embarrassed. An interviewer has more respect for an interviewee who admits to ignorance than for one who tries to fake an answer.

Just as your résumé should have a competent, neat, professional image, so should you. One of the first and most obvious ways in which you will make an impression is by the way you dress. The general rule is that you should match the style of dress of the interviewer. If you have a chance to visit the company before your interview, take note of the general style of dress of the employees. If you cannot visit before your interview but know someone who works for the company, ask what the standard attire is. If visiting or making inquiries is impossible, use these general guidelines: for professional positions, dress conservatively (dark suits, white shirts/blouses, standard ties/ribbon ties, dark socks/neutral hose, dark shoes). You really cannot go wrong with that attire. Wear clothes that fit and are comfortable but not casual.[44] Bottom line: most interviewers decide in the first 30 seconds of meeting you if they are going to make you an offer.[45]

Establishing Trust One of the most important aspects of a successful interview is establishing trust between you and the interviewer. Trust is a mutual process and begins in the initial encounter.[46]

The level of trust established between you and the interviewer is based on:

• Predispositions (i.e., Do you have a "trusting impulse"?)
• Appearance (i.e., Facial expressions, cleanliness, appropriate dress)
• Personality characteristics (i.e., Friendliness, positive outlook)
• Points of reference (i.e., What is your reputation prior to the interview?)
• Your behavior during the interview (i.e., Are you fidgety? Do you look the interviewer in the eye when you shake hands?)

Interviewers perceive interviewees to be trustworthy if they are honest regarding the references provided, offer explanations for any gaps in employment, and demonstrate that they are flexible in the responsibilities in which they are willing to take on.[47]

Preparing to Ask and Answer Questions   After you have been invited for an interview, you must prepare for your performance. The first step is devising questions that elicit information about the company that you were unable to obtain through your research. Arrange your questions so that the most important ones come first because you may not get a chance to ask all your questions during the interview. If some questions are answered spontaneously during the course of the interview, mentally move down your list to a question that has not yet been answered. Preparing and asking questions provides you with insight into the company, shows your interest in the job, and demonstrates communication skills. Inquisitive interviewees seem competent to interviewers. Table 8.5 shows five categories of common interview questions.

Table 8.5 Employment Interview Questions

Type	Example
Closed questions	Would you describe yourself as a people person or an individualist? Are you more interested in a career in marketing or in corporate communications? Did you know the salary for this job is $40,000?
Open questions	Why did you major in _____? How did college prepare you for the real world? What are your immediate and long-term career goals?
Hypothetical questions	How would you handle a hostile coworker? What would you do if a customer demanded a refund and you were not authorized to give one? How would you resolve conflicting demands on your time by department managers?
Probing questions	Why? Could you elaborate on your decision? What happened next? Who else was involved in the project?
Mirror questions	So, you're saying that salary is less important than flexible work arrangements? Did I hear you correctly in that you would be willing to travel four to five times a month? Let me be sure I understand you; you can't begin work until January?

Hide All Cells	Show All Cells

Your responses during the interview (regardless of how the specific questions are phrased) should be candid, well organized, incisive, relevant, to the point, and positive. It is fine to volunteer some negatives, especially in the context of challenges you have met or problems you have resolved. Ralston, Kirkwood, and Burant describe effective interviewees are those who tell their story well.[48] Stories provide a vehicle for constructing attractive images through descriptions of past behaviors and events.[49] In addition, a well-told story can serve as a reminder to interviewers: be unique, you won't get the job if you don't make an impression. When responding, avoid making disorganized or irrelevant statements, evading or rationalizing, being overly critical of others, changing the subject or giving many

unimportant details, talking only of favorable points, or making bad jokes. The following dialogues show weak and strong responses to basic questions, beginning with weak responses.

QUESTION: Describe a typical day in your current job. What are your major responsibilities?

ANSWER: Well, every day is different, so it sort of depends on the whim of my supervisor. You know, I really think that my skill in word processing would fit your company's needs. That's something I do a lot. Most of the time, I hardly make any errors, except for spelling, but I can always use a spell-checker. In fact, I think people who can't take advantage of computer technology are out of place in today's business environment.

QUESTION: I see. What other computer skills do you use in your job?

ANSWER: We use a database and spreadsheet to prepare budget reports, and the publications department produces a newsletter through desktop publishing.

QUESTION: How often do you prepare budget reports?

ANSWER: Ummm . . . That isn't exactly part of my job, although I am responsible for requesting funds for my department. It's a very important responsibility.

The interviewee has (intentionally or unintentionally) changed the subject, given a disorganized response, implied criticism of her or his current supervisor, given irrelevant details, and implied possession of skills not actually acquired.

Starting from the same question, the following exchange illustrates strong interviewee responses:

QUESTION: Describe a typical day in your current job. What are your major responsibilities?

ANSWER: Well, I am responsible for scheduling meetings in my department, so the first thing I do every morning is check the schedule to review upcoming meetings. I then prepare and distribute agendas for the meetings.

QUESTION: How do you do that?

ANSWER: These agendas are based on notes given to me by the department supervisor, who generally does a good job of getting me the necessary information early enough so that I can contact everyone who will attend the meeting. Recently, I have been doing a lot of the background research and preparation myself.

QUESTION: What do you find most challenging about this responsibility?

ANSWER: It is difficult to get people together, and I am sometimes frustrated when others don't seem to care about meetings that I have spent a lot of time trying to organize. Overall, though, I feel that this responsibility has taught me a lot about communicating with a variety of people, following up on messages, and working out conflicting interests and goals in order to find convenient times for people to meet.

The interviewee answers the questions asked, giving relevant, detailed responses. She or he volunteers some negative information in a candid way but in general speaks well of coworkers. The responses are well organized, describing a task and the skills necessary to accomplish it.

Handling Discriminatory Questions   An interviewer may ask a question such as "What would your spouse think about relocating to the Southwest?" In an attempt to get a "complete" profile of a candidate, interviewers may purposely or unknowingly pose questions that are illegal. What do you do when asked an illegal question? You have several choices. You can answer it and hope to get the job. You can refuse to answer it on the grounds that it is illegal and risk losing out on a job offer. You can respond, "I'm sorry, but my spouse's opinion about relocating is not a bona fide occupation qualification, so I'm not going to answer that question." Such a reply, however, is not likely to promote good relations between you and the interviewer, especially if she or he was merely trying to be friendly.

The best way to handle marginal or illegal questions is to politely put the ball back in the interviewer's court. For example, if you are asked, "Do you have any small children at home?" you can respond, "I understand your concern about identifying possible obstacles to my commitment to the job, but be assured that I am fully prepared and qualified for the tasks and responsibilities involved and have the ability to manage my time effectively." In this case, you are answering an unasked question that reflects the interviewer's real concern.

If a job applicant thinks she or he has been discriminated against during the hiring process and can provide evidence of such discrimination, the law requires the employer to prove that no discrimination took place.[50] It is often difficult for the employer to do this. If you feel that you have legitimate cause for complaint and were unsuccessful in alerting the employer to illegal interviewing or hiring practices, the courts provide a last resort.

Following Up the Interview   The employment interview does not end when you, the interviewee, walk out of the interviewer's office. If you are sincerely interested in the company and the job, take the time to follow up the interview with a letter of thanks to the interviewer.

Such a letter accomplishes several purposes. It demonstrates your enthusiasm for the job and the company. It also reflects excellent communication skills, provides the interviewer with additional feedback about you and your interview, and can serve as a reminder of your interview and set you apart from the crowd. Although the letter is short, it is important because it creates a favorable impression of you and demonstrates communication competence. Leaders in today's organizations claim that thank-you letters can come in the form of the traditional handwritten note or as an email. Regardless, the letter must follow proper business etiquette (i.e., error proof, sent within 48 hours of interview).[51]

8.8.4: Manage Anxiety in the Interview

INTERVIEWER   Although the interviewee feels most of the anxiety in an interview situation, as the *interviewer* it is likely that you will also experience anxiety and pressure. Finding the best candidate for a job is an enormous responsibility. The candidate hired will reflect the decision-making ability of the interviewer. Being prepared with a list of questions and researching the interviewee can relieve anxiety for the interviewer. Providing a comfortable environment to relax the prospective employee can also reduce the interviewer's nervousness.

Creating a Comfortable Atmosphere   Nervous candidates are less likely to open up and fully disclose the information you need to accurately assess them for a job. An atmosphere in which candidates feel comfortable talking about themselves and their career goals is therefore essential. How do you establish one? Begin by looking at the setting where the interview will take place. Is the office drab, sterile, or uninviting? If so, you may get responses to match. One interviewer we know has a very small, poorly lit, and crowded office, so when he interviews someone for a job, he reserves a conference room that is wood-paneled, well lit, and comfortable.

Positive communication can also decrease a candidate's nervousness and put him or her at ease. When a candidate first comes in, smile, introduce yourself by name and title, engage in direct eye contact, shake hands, and express sincere interest and attention. Once seated, provide a succinct orientation to the interview. Include a brief recap of the job description and expected responsibilities, an overview of the questions that you will be asking, and some indication of approximately how long the interview will last. This information puts candidates at ease by letting them know what is ahead.

INTERVIEWEE   As an *interviewee*, anxiety is produced primarily by the interview. After all, the result of the interview will affect your future. However, there are some things you can do to manage your anxiety.

One of the best ways to reduce anxiety is to be prepared. Although you cannot be prepared for all possible questions, you can be prepared with answers for questions that are likely to be asked. Rehearse your answers to probable questions, but remember to be flexible during the interview and adapt to the interviewer's questions. It is also wise to think of real life examples you can provide to support your qualifications and work experiences. You can also prepare a set of questions to ask about the company. Doing so can relieve the tension associated with fear of the unknown.

Another way to manage anxiety is to practice self-confidence. Reread your résumé, and concentrate on the positive qualities you possess. Think of your background and experiences as assets that you can bring to the company. Be confident about your ability to do the job for which you are applying.

During the interview, concentrate on putting the interviewer at ease. Once you see the interviewer becoming comfortable with talking, your nervousness will diminish. Managing anxiety is also easier if you appear friendly and open. Nonverbal cues, such as smiling and head nods, will help relax the tension you may feel.

8.9: Appraisal Interviews

8.9 Analyze the importance of a successful appraisal interview

The purpose of **appraisal interviews** is to evaluate employees' performances over a certain period of time, generally specified by company policy. A successful appraisal interview depends on two components: (1) efficiency—when there is a "concern for behavioral expediency" that leads to direct, immediate, and to-the-point conversation tactics;[52] and (2) effectiveness—meaningful information that promotes mutual understanding.[53] Some companies schedule an appraisal interview once a year to determine pay raises. Others hold appraisal interviews to address complaints or evaluate the work of new employees. Well-conducted appraisal interviews provide feedback to employees about their performance. Supervisors who conduct such interviews also obtain feedback from employees who prefer a confidential atmosphere in which to discuss their concerns. In some organizations, the appraisal interview may be the only time that managers and employees sit down face-to-face to talk about job performance and responsibilities. Although technology allows communication to occur from diverse geographic locations, appraisal interviews are perceived as more positive and effective by employees if conducted face to face.[54]

8.9.1: Purposes and Goals of Appraisal Interviews

Appraisal interviews are often used to motivate workers. By reviewing performance standards and comparing standards to the employee's performance, managers can motivate employees to increase the quantity and improve the quality of their work. Appraisal interviews can also build morale. Workers who know how they are doing and who are encouraged to continue their progress are likely to feel good about the organization and develop positive attitudes about the workplace.[55]

8.9.2: Performance Reviews

As a first step in the appraisal process, the manager reviews the performance of each employee. In many organizations, frequent appraisal interviews allow managers and employees to work consistently toward mutually understood goals. Files should document every noteworthy incident or behavior.

Before the evaluation, a thorough analysis of all pertinent information for each employee is conducted, and the employee is given a chance to provide personal input about the job objectives and his or her success at achieving them. During the evaluation, superiors may use preestablished criteria presented in a standardized format to judge the performance of each employee. Most evaluators rate performance factors that are elements of an employee's job description and that can be evaluated objectively according to some baseline measure. In advance of the evaluation period, the employee should be told on what factors she or he will be rated. Performance factors likely to be rated include the following:[56]

Punctuality	Responsibility
Initiative	Dependability
Job knowledge	Neatness
Creativity	Communication skills
Planning	Versatility
Cost control	Cooperation
Accuracy	Delegation skills
Leadership skills	Productivity
Organizational skills	Consistency

When managers use a qualitative rating system, they simply discuss each performance factor in a descriptive and evaluative manner. They may write paragraphs using adjectives to describe how they judge the employee's performance on each factor. More frequently, rating systems are quantitative, and the manager rates performance according to some numerical system. Some organizations use scales that range from 1 to 5 or 1 to 10. Other companies rank-order employees according to each relevant performance factor. Quantitative and qualitative ratings can be combined, and this approach is quite common in organizations. Employees receive a quantitative rating for each performance factor and a written explanation of the evaluation. Figure 8.6 is an example of an appraisal interview form.

Figure 8.6 Sample Appraisal Interview Form

Merryhill Enterprises, Inc.

Performance Evaluation Form

This form is to be used to evaluate all employees biannually. The immediate supervisor will consider all relevant factors associated with an employee's job description and render an objective evaluation along two dimensions. A quantitative score will be given for each area covered as well as a written description stating particular details. Employees will have an opportunity to discuss their evaluations with the evaluating supervisor before the evaluation is forwarded to the personnel office for disposition.

Scoring: 1 = very poor performance; 5 = average performance; 10 = perfect performance.

Motivation Comments:	1 2 3 4 5 6 7 8 9 10
Job knowledge Comments:	1 2 3 4 5 6 7 8 9 10
Executive potential Comments:	1 2 3 4 5 6 7 8 9 10
Communication skills Comments:	1 2 3 4 5 6 7 8 9 10
Leadership skills Comments:	1 2 3 4 5 6 7 8 9 10
Delegation skills Comments:	1 2 3 4 5 6 7 8 9 10
Overall evaluation Comments:	1 2 3 4 5 6 7 8 9 10

8.9.3: How to Conduct the Interview

When the interviewee arrives, quickly establish rapport, and then move directly into the interview.[57] Briefly discuss the purpose of the performance appraisal and give an overview of what will be covered. After this orientation, present your evaluation. Go over each major area of performance, explaining how you arrived at your rating and detailing the evidence used in the evaluation. As you discuss each issue, use specific language and provide examples, such as "One of your job responsibilities is to schedule quarterly meetings of the accounting staff and to distribute each meeting's minutes to the branch offices, ensuring that the data are accurate, readable, and timely. You have provided comprehensive minutes with clarity and speed, and it is my opinion that you are ready to take on some additional responsibilities in analyzing the data. I understand that the data are complex, and we have to discuss methods for setting new goals in this area."

During the interview, be sure to encourage participation, feedback, and explanation. Some interviewees may not provide verbal input because of the anxiety or stress associated with evaluation, yet it is important for you to know how they feel about your evaluations. Ask for their self-evaluation for each performance factor. Ask them to rate themselves objectively but from their own points of view. You will be surprised at how often employees overrate and underrate themselves. Such information can serve as a discussion starter for communicating about how they view their jobs.

Feedback is a critical element in an appraisal interview, and the responsibility for giving and receiving it rests with both the supervisor and the employee. The aim of feedback is not to pass judgment but to report specific events or behavior, their effects, and what to do about them. Subjective interpretations by the supervisor or the employee should be minimized during the interview.

Two types of feedback are given during an appraisal interview: corrective feedback and supportive feedback.

Corrective feedback attempts to alter negative or inappropriate behavior. To be effective, corrective feedback should be expressed in specific terms as much as possible. For example, "You did not prepare charts for the presentation yesterday as you were supposed to do" highlights a specific problem that must be addressed.

Supportive feedback encourages desirable behavior. Supportive feedback lets the employee know what he or she is doing right, and such knowledge is as important to performance as being told about areas that need improvement. When an appraisal interviewer concentrates not only on correcting problems or identifying new responsibilities but also on good work—especially behavior that goes beyond the employee's personal and work goals and contributes to overall organizational goals—the employee is likely to strive for outstanding rather than merely acceptable performance. For example, "I'm pleased that you have learned to work on the new computer system and have helped other people to use it too" shows the employee that the supervisor noticed and appreciates his or her willingness to go beyond what is expected. Providing supportive feedback is an opportunity for the supervisor to thank the employee for good work. Supervisors are wise to use both supportive and corrective feedback to achieve maximum benefits from a performance review.[58]

The appraisal interview is an opportunity for employees to learn about what is expected and valued in their work and to let their supervisors know how the employees are doing as well. The employee listens carefully as the supervisor discusses and gives feedback on each performance factor, noting areas of strength (supportive feedback), weakness (a combination of supportive and corrective feedback), or special problems (corrective feedback).

Assume you are the branch manager of a national retail chain. Company policy dictates that appraisal interviews be conducted every six months. As you schedule appointments with employees, you notice that one employee seems exceptionally reluctant to establish a meeting time. When he arrives for the interview, he is anxious and hesitant. What nonverbal cues alert you to his nervousness? How can you build rapport with this employee without minimizing corrective feedback?

 The response entered here will appear in the performance dashboard and can be viewed by your instructor.

Submit

8.9.4: How to Receive Bad News

If you are being evaluated and you disagree with the supervisor's assessment, discuss your reaction in a calm and objective manner and offer to provide evidence to support your position if necessary. If the supervisor has made general statements about your performance, ask for specifics—both of you may learn from them. Be familiar with your organization's policies on appraisal interviews. Knowing these guidelines ensures responsible communication by both parties.

8.9.5: Setting Revised Goals

Once both parties have discussed each performance factor, set mutually derived goals for the next evaluation. Both interviewer and interviewee should identify elements of the job that are critical to employee and organizational productivity and should specify realistic goals. Mutual goal setting during the appraisal interview encourages employee participation in a significant decision-making process.

Finally, end the interview on a positive note. Summarize the interview and ask for additional comments, questions, and explanations from the interviewee. Reemphasize the importance of the performance appraisal process and encourage the employee to think positively about the next evaluation period. Appraisal interviews are meant to help employees and supervisors work well together.

When receiving an evaluation, make a sincere effort to understand the supervisor's viewpoint and plan to act on the mutually agreed-to goals. When employees and managers seriously and conscientiously participate in the appraisal process, it provides a valuable source of feedback that can lead to improvements in their work relationship.

8.10: Disciplinary Interviews

8.10 Analyze the three main aspects of disciplinary interviews

One of the most sensitive areas of business and professional communication is discipline. Given the more than a million terminations that take place each year, it is unlikely that the need for disciplinary action is going to disappear anytime soon, so it is in your best interests to learn how to handle the need for discipline effectively.[59] Most people do not relish the idea of disciplining others. Punishing those who are rebellious, unproductive, or lazy is not a pleasant activity.

When problems with employees occur, the skillful manager or supervisor must be ready to administer a disciplinary response that will improve the problematic condition. The administering of discipline can lead to productive outcomes if it is handled properly. Other employees take note and recognize the goals, boundaries, protocol, and procedures that are appropriate in that particular organization. Effective discipline can prevent problems from occurring in the future.

Disciplinary interviews must be handled with care. The federal government and labor unions have spelled out procedures for conducting such interviews, and ignoring those procedures can get a manager into a lot of legal trouble. In addition, clumsy or mishandled disciplinary interviews can provoke controversy in the workplace and stir employee resentment of supervisors. The most critical aspects of disciplinary interviews include notifying the employee of the problem, reviewing the employee's side of the story, and instituting disciplinary action.[60]

8.10.1: Notify the Employee

Once misconduct has been noticed, the next step is to notify the employee so that corrective action can be taken. Some offenses result from problems associated with the system, structure, or technology of a job rather than from misjudgment, bad faith, or carelessness on the employee's part. If you decide that the cause of an offense is technical difficulties, you can simply inform the employee that you are aware of the problem and will work with him or her to correct it. Technical difficulties include lapses in mail service, computer problems, and equipment failure.

If the employee is at fault, however, it is best to inform her or him of the problem calmly, directly, and quickly. Do not wait for a few weeks for the situation to cool down. Smooth and decisive disciplinary action will deter other employees from similar behavior. Schedule a disciplinary interview for a time when you will not be disturbed and when the office is relatively uncrowded.

8.10.2: Review the Employee's Side of the Story

Interview the employee before conducting other investigations. If the particular situation requires you to interview others who may be involved in the misconduct or who know about the facts of the incident, be extremely careful to maintain the confidentiality of all employees.

Immediately get down to business, but maintain a nonhostile attitude.[61] Ask for the employee's explanation of his or her behavior. Facts and explanations do not always coincide, so be sure to clarify any apparent contradictions between the employee's account and your understanding of the occurrence. Appropriate questioning techniques include open, mirror, and reflective questions, such as "Why do you think the equipment malfunctioned?" or "When James noticed the malfunction, you told him everything was under control. Were you distrustful of James's involvement in your project?" Such questions are appropriate because they allow the employee latitude to respond and facilitate understanding between interview parties.

An accused employee may concede or accept responsibility for an act of misconduct, make an excuse, or justify his or her actions. It is your responsibility to listen carefully to the employee.

8.10.3: Institute Disciplinary Action

Base all decisions on company policy, and provide written documentation to the employee if necessary. Be specific in your evaluation, and apply disciplinary measures consistently.

If, for example, you have recorded several occurrences of tardiness and absenteeism, you will give a stricter punishment to this employee than to a first-time offender. Your organization is likely to have a standard policy for warnings and repeated transgressions. Be sure that your employees are aware of the rules. If an employee has given a reasonable explanation of what occurred during the offense, that explanation may lessen the punishment as well.

EXPLAIN THE PURPOSE OF THE DISCIPLINE Base discipline on objective facts and common goals. Stress the productive aspects of discipline. Discuss the disciplinary action in terms of the employee's past record and future with the organization. Once you have informed the employee of the disciplinary action to be taken, discuss ways in which the situation can be improved. For example, if an employee is being disciplined for alcohol-related absenteeism, the supervisor might suggest counseling or referral to an employee assistance program to give the person the best chance of returning to full productivity. Be reasonable in your judgment of employee behavior, and ensure appropriate disciplinary action in the case of misconduct.

DOCUMENT THE INCIDENT AND THE INTERVIEW Write an objective and detailed report of the incident, and file it with the appropriate offices (such as personnel and administration). Include in the report the steps that were taken with the employee, and note all aspects of the employee's defense. Doing so ensures that the case will be reviewed accurately if disagreements or additional problems arise later.

Strategic Scenario Wrap-Up

Interviewing Skills

Ⓧ Strategic Scenario

Marci Cohen is a junior in college, majoring in public relations. As a graded assignment for her business communication class, Marci has to set up an interview with a person who (1) does a considerable amount of interviewing and (2) is engaged in professional work related to her major. Marci has made an appointment to interview William (Bill) Walker, executive director of university relations at her university, at his office. Her task is to learn about Mr. Walker's interviewing practices (the techniques and methods he uses when interviewing) and interviewing training (things he has done to help him become a better interviewer). Marci is anxious about this assignment; interviewing the interviewer seems like a daunting task.

Marci Cohen, a college junior, is preparing to interview Bill Walker, executive director of university relations, concerning his interviewing practices and training. Marci is nervous,

so she plans well. Her goal is to gather information. She organizes the interview as non-directive—she is not an expert, and will be happy to sit back and hear what Bill has to say. Although her structure will not be tight, she has definitely prepared questions.

When she meets Bill, even though she has told him on the phone that she is a student and the purpose of the interview was to fulfill a requirement, she clearly reiterates her purpose and adds how interested she is in learning. Marci has familiarized herself with Bill's published work and establishes credibility by commenting on a recent interview of his that she has read. She cites a few examples of interactive communication that she has noted in that interview (she has a highlighted copy with her) and uses these as a spring board to encourage Bill to tell her more about how he works. As the interview progresses she finds opportunities to ask him about specific techniques and gather some great tips. Marci closes on time (she was allowed 30 minutes), thanking Bill and promising, at his request, to send him her essay and keep in touch.

Summary

Interviewing Skills

- This chapter covered basic **principles of interviewing** that apply generally to all dyadic (two-party) communication.

- The interview is a process of planned, dyadic, interactive discourse. **Goals for interviewers** may include gathering information, solving problems, persuading, counseling, or giving information. Preparation and cooperation by the interviewer as well as by the interviewee are essential to the achievement of any of these goals.

- Most interviews consist of three parts: **the opening, the body, and the closing**. In each part, the interviewer and the interviewee use verbal cues and nonverbal impressions to increase their knowledge of the situation and to respond to each other.

- Communication competence in interviews consists of the ability to ask **meaningful questions phrased appropriately and in an effective sequence**. Questions should be clear and unbiased. They may take either an open form (respondents answer in their own words) or a closed form (respondents choose from a set of offered alternatives), and they may be classified as primary or secondary.

- **Primary questions** introduce new topics; **secondary questions** develop topics introduced by primary questions.

- Questions can be **sequenced** in funnel, inverted-funnel, or tunnel patterns.

- A **funnel sequence** moves from broad questions to specific, closed questions.

- An **inverted-funnel sequence** begins with a closed question and moves toward open questions.

- A **tunnel sequence** consists of a set of questions at the same level of openness or closedness.

- The **interviewer's responses** can indicate a range of intentions and implications. People tend to use evaluative and interpretative responses most frequently. Overuse or underuse of one type of response can skew the interviewee's perception of the interviewer in a negative direction.

- **Anxiety is a common element** in interview situations. It can affect the interviewer, the interviewee, and the success of the interaction.

- Anxiety can be controlled through **conscious effort** by both the interviewer and the interviewee to be prepared, to listen well, and to communicate clearly and considerately.

- You are likely to encounter various interview situations in your career. The most prevalent type is the **employment interview**. You can be most effective as an interviewee by researching the company, preparing a résumé and a cover letter tailored to the specific job for which you are applying, dressing appropriately, and preparing to ask and answer questions.

- You must also know how to respond to **illegal questions** diplomatically but precisely.

- As you move up in your career, you will probably assume the **role of interviewer** at some time. The skills required in this role include developing job specifications, reviewing applicant materials, scheduling and conducting interviews, and choosing the best candidate for the job.

- **Appraisal interviews** can help to motivate workers, build morale, and allow an exchange of feedback between supervisors and workers. The appraisal is usually an evaluation of specific performance factors. The rating system can be quantitative, qualitative, or both.

- A **straightforward but considerate appraisal** interview yields the greatest benefit; it is non-hostile, encouraging, and specific.

- **Disciplinary interviews,** the hardest type of interview to conduct, must be handled with care. The interviewer identifies the problem, notifies the employee, reviews the employee's story, evaluates all the evidence, and institutes appropriate disciplinary action. The process must be documented carefully, and the interviewer must maintain objectivity.

SHARED WRITING: INTERVIEWING SKILLS

Think about the employment interview. List and rank-order ten factors that you feel can make or break the opportunity to produce favorable outcomes. In a second column next to each factor, state why you find each more or less important. Share your list with your classmates.

▶ A minimum number of characters is required to post and earn points. After posting, your response can be viewed by your class and instructor, and you can participate in the class discussion.

Post   0 characters | 140 minimum

Chapter 8 Quiz: Interviewing Skills

Chapter 9
Fundamentals of Group Communication

Learning Objectives

9.1 Describe the advantages of effective group communication

9.2 Analyze different ways of defining a group

9.3 Analyze the seven factors that affect group communication

9.4 Analyze the factors that affect group participation

9.5 Compare teleconferences with videoconferences

9.6 Scrutinize the role of special groups in business

Strategic Scenario: Break from the Past

Felipe Papageorgio arrived home from his first day of work sick at heart. He discovered first hand how his new employer, Stylist, Inc., is a firm believer in making work more productive by emphasizing teamwork, frequent group meetings, and team-based projects. Felipe was elated when he landed this job, since it paid 30 percent more than any other offer. Stylist is a rapidly rising company, and he was able to remain in his hometown. However, his consternation stemmed from the negative experiences he has had with groups in the past:

- In high school, the fundraising group he was assigned to in the Junior Achievement Club was a disaster. The group never set any realistic goals, individuals never jelled as a team, and everyone seemed to want to go their separate ways. As a result, the group never raised much money and was considered a failure by other club members.

- In college, Felipe joined a mock investment group that was suggested by his academic advisor. In no time, Felipe knew he was in the wrong group. The group elected a leader whom Felipe detested. This leader was arrogant, condescending, and wouldn't listen to other people's ideas—especially, it seemed, to Felipe's ideas. Secretly, Felipe knew he was a much better leader. The group quickly became embroiled in constant bickering, with several factions fighting for control.

- More recently, Felipe was assigned to a quality-control team during his senior-year internship at a large, local nonprofit organization. This group was especially frustrating because its members, employees and interns alike, all seemed to be more interested in generating ideas that they thought the bosses wanted than in taking risks and being creative. No one wanted to rock the boat.

Felipe shook his head as he reflected on his memories of group work. He was convinced that he was in for more of the same with his new organization. Think about Felipe's concerns as you read this chapter. At the end of the chapter we will return to this scenario and discuss some solutions.

9.1: Overview

Fundamentals of Group Communication

9.1 **Describe the advantages of effective group communication**

Take just a moment to think about all the groups in which you participate. If you are a fraternity or sorority member, belong to an athletic team, or attend meetings of some student society on campus, you are involved in a formal group. Indeed, your enrollment in this course makes you a member of the group that meets in this classroom! You probably also participate in a good number of informal groups. You have regular friends with whom you eat daily, others with whom you study, others with whom you go to movies or games, and still others with whom you interact as you travel to campus.

In the 1950s, social psychologist Kurt Lewin suggested that group dynamics are pervasive.[1] He argued that all people exist in a life space in which groups are an important part. Lewin based his theory on the notion that a person cannot be separated from the groups with which he or she identifies. This theory has several premises: people are members of many groups at one time; groups are an important part of a person's life space; groups create tensions in the life space; and groups therefore influence the movement of the person within the life space.

Groups are as prevalent in business and professional organizations as Lewin described them in humans' personal lives. As you enter the work force, you will be asked to become a member of work groups, and your participation will increase as you move up in the organization. (Research shows that managers spend between 25 and 80 percent of their time in meetings.[2]) You will become a member of formal departments—such as accounting, personnel, production, or computer services—which are likely to be subdivided into work groups. The human resources department, for example, may include groups that focus on employee benefits, training, recruitment, building maintenance, salary administration, and security. You will also serve as a member of formal committees within the organization, such as safety, credit union review, or security. In addition, you will participate in lunch groups, after-work "happy hour" groups, car pools, or break-room groups.

The communication between and within groups is vital to the organization. We cannot stress too much how differently businesses and professional organizations would operate without group communication. We offer the following propositions about communication in groups, all of which have a substantial research base:[3]

- Organizations that employ groups effectively have enjoyed substantial improvements in productivity, cost savings, and profits and have observed critical enhancements to employee commitment and satisfaction.
- Decisions made by groups are of higher quality than decisions made by individuals working alone.
- People who participate in group decision making are more committed to the group's decisions than to decisions given them by a manager or supervisor.
- Pitfalls and hazards that a person working alone may ignore are regularly uncovered by groups through debate and questioning.
- Employee morale is higher when people are teamed with coworkers on projects and tasks.
- People who regularly communicate with others in the organization are more satisfied on the job than are employees who are isolated from others.
- Employees who network with others in organizational groups are more committed to the goals and missions of their organizations than are those who do not so participate.
- People who are teamed together in work groups take greater responsibility for the task, and the blame for and fixing of errors is shared by all.

Can there be any wonder, then, why organizations devote a great amount of time and energy to the maintenance and perpetuation of groups? The positive outcomes can make the difference between a profitable company and a loser. People who develop strong communication skills and use them effectively in group situations regularly exhibit the best performance.

In this chapter, we introduce you to the basics of groups—what they are, how they function, and what types there are. We start with questions: What do all groups have in common? What makes a group different from a collection of people?

9.2: What Is a Group?

9.2 **Analyze different ways of defining a group**

Most of our communication in groups takes place in five types of groups: the family; adolescent friendship groups; work groups; committees, problem-solving groups, and creative groups; and therapy groups.[4] We concentrate on work groups and problem-solving groups in the organizational context.

For years, one of the great debates among scholars of group communication centered on what constitutes a "group" and, specifically, in what circumstances a "small" group is no longer small. Definitions of small groups ranged from three persons all the way to fifteen or twenty.

Clearly, the interaction that takes place between two persons—a dyad—is different from what takes place among three or more—a group. As the size of a group increases, the interaction among the members becomes more formal, there is less chance for each member to participate, topics become less intimate, and tasks take longer to accomplish. Unlike a dyad, which has one relationship, groups have many relationships. The larger a group is, the more relationships there are to maintain (see Figure 9.1).

Figure 9.1 Communication in Small Groups Versus Large Groups

Size, location, and frequency of interaction are important factors in group communication. Members of small groups have more consistent interactions than do members of large groups.

SOURCE: From Moorhead/Griffin. Organizational Behavior, 2E. © 1989 South-Western, a part of Cengage Learning, Inc. Reproduced by permission. www.cengage.com/permissions.

The best way to define a group is to look at the behavior of the people within the group. When a group is functioning, you can observe several important behaviors.

⊗ Participants Know Each Other

In public speaking situations, the speaker knows the audience en masse—for example, the Los Angeles Lions Club, the University of Michigan Business School faculty, the Dallas Masonic Lodge, the 11 a.m. M-W-F general accounting class. In group situations, however, the members know each other as individuals. In each group to which you belong, you know the participants' personal names, their roles (for example, boss, vice president, discussion leader), or both.

⊗ Participants Interact

Communication plays an important role in every productive group. During group meetings, some members request information, and others provide it; there are disagreements among members; and members clarify their positions and statements. Communication seldom occurs in a uniform or consistent pattern. In some groups, dominant participants "hog the floor" while isolated members contribute little, if anything. Sometimes participants are encouraged to interact with each of the other members. Sometimes the group leader controls who speaks, when, and for how long.

⊗ Participants Influence Each Other

When group members get together, each person influences and is influenced by the others to some degree. Participants who express forceful arguments that are backed by powerful documentation may strongly influence others in the group. Influence can be nonverbal as well as verbal. A group member who scowls at another may influence the way that person reacts, speaks, or even votes.

⊗ Participants Bond as a Group

Over a period of time, as a group continues to meet and its members interact, the participants bond together. They take pride in their work. They are proud to be members of the group and express these feelings to people who are not members. Outsiders identify them as members of the group. A sense of membership is a key characteristic of an effective group.

⊗ Participants Share Commonality

In almost all cases, common goals are the glue that holds a group together. They may be the reason why a person chooses to be part of a group. A person who does not see that working with others is a means to achieve a common goal, advance a common interest, or help facilitate a common benefit should withdraw and complete the task individually.

⊗ There Is Leadership

Within every functioning group, leadership is evident. External sources formally designate the leader of some groups. The manager at a restaurant, for example, was likely assigned that position by the restaurant owner. A leader can also emerge from the interaction of group members. Sometimes group members formally vote and select a person to lead. At other times, a person is simply considered the group leader because of the quality of her or his contributions to the group. In many groups, it is difficult to pinpoint any one person as group leader. Nevertheless, leadership is certainly present as group members interact. In these cases, we say that the group has shared leadership—all of the functions of leadership are present, but they are provided by several members, not just one.

9.3: Factors Influencing Group Communication

9.3 Analyze the seven factors that affect group communication

Achieving effective communication is not easy. Group communication, because of the variety of people who participate, requires special effort. Among the several factors that affect the quality and quantity of group communication are cohesiveness, norms, roles, conformity, groupthink, advocacy, and conflict. Some have a positive effect on group communication; others are barriers that must be overcome. We examine each of these, highlighting methods for achieving successful group communication. However, before launching into a discussion of each of these factors, it is important to stress the interlocking relationships among all of them. Each factor affects and is affected by all of the other factors, constituting a systems effect. Keep this in mind as you examine each of these factors separately in the following sections.

9.3.1: Cohesiveness

One major goal for any group is to remain intact no matter how difficult the situation or challenging the environment. **Cohesiveness** is the degree to which a group hangs together. There are two ways to talk about cohesiveness. A group is cohesive when each of its participants retains her or his membership. Reasons why group membership is desirable include attraction to other members, perceived benefits that an individual alone cannot obtain, and financial and social investments that cannot be abandoned. A group is also cohesive if members strongly identify with the group. The more participants identify with the group's purposes and goals, tell outsiders about the group's activities, and take pride in their membership, the more cohesive that group is. Rosabeth Moss Kanter suggests, in her book, *Evolve!*, that effective teams distinguish themselves from ineffectual ones through a feeling and commitment to the greater good.[5] Effective teams are those that take on a sense of ownership for the things they do, the decisions they make, and the ways that they feel.

Highly cohesive groups are much more likely to meet challenges successfully and overcome obstacles than are groups that have low cohesiveness. Consider the following propositions:[6]

- The quantity and quality of communication in highly cohesive groups are much more extensive than in less cohesive groups.
- Highly cohesive groups exert greater influence over their members than do less cohesive groups.
- Highly cohesive groups achieve their goals more effectively than do less cohesive groups.
- Member satisfaction is greater in highly cohesive groups than in less cohesive groups.

Maintaining cohesiveness in a group is a challenge, but strong and effective communication can help. Taking time to encourage participants to take pride in their membership, to reinforce accomplishments both inside and outside of formal meetings, and to allow others to express themselves freely are ways that you can promote cohesiveness

in your group interactions. The following case illustrates these principles.

Akeme and Carol are members of a professional group that meets once a week to decide on fundraising activities for local charities. Because so many different types of people are members, the group lacks cohesiveness. Akeme and Carol realized that nothing substantive would be accomplished unless they helped to build a sense of belonging among participants. During group meetings they began to make comments such as these: "Jim, you know this area of town—what is your opinion of our efforts there?" "Elena, you always know where the big donors are in your own business—whom do you think we should target for donations to our group?" "I'm so proud of how we have pulled together in the last two meetings!" "People around town are saying so many nice things about our group's accomplishments." "It is wonderful that anyone here can freely give his or her opinion without criticism." After three meetings, group members were making similar statements, and cohesiveness rose to a productive level.

9.3.2: Norms

Group **norms** are "recurring patterns of behavior or thinking that come to be accepted in a group as the 'usual' way of doing things."[7] Norms are determined by the group and are used to regulate communication within the group. Norms can range from the mundane ("no private conversations while someone is speaking") to serious rules ("voting is required on every issue"). It is usually during the first few sessions of a group's life that norms are developed and refined. When new members join a group, they learn about existing norms through observations and trial and error. Norms help to facilitate the behavior of the group and affect the conduct of individual members. Consider the following norms:

Negative criticism of another person is unacceptable.

Meetings are "strictly business."

First names are allowed during meetings.

The discussion of a single topic should be limited to ten minutes.

As you can see, norms reflect group members' preferences and can influence the operation of the group. A member who fails to follow group norms may be isolated from other members, ignored, and, in some cases, not notified of group meetings. In other cases, norms protect group members and lead them to greater levels of productivity. This is especially true when the norms are directed toward creativity and the self-esteem of group members and the group itself. Consider the following:

There is no such thing as a stupid comment.

Taking risks with ideas is encouraged.

We stand up for our group members.

It's all right to have fun while we work.

Electronic meetings are an acceptable form of participation from time to time.

Groups must carefully monitor their norms to prevent members from becoming disenchanted with petty rules or policies and to facilitate interaction among different members. That is why it is always a good idea to periodically review norms to ensure that they are serving the purposes of the group.

9.3.3: Roles

Every member of a group has a **role**. In many groups, members play several roles. Taking on a role leads others to have certain expectations about your behavior in the group. You have certain expectations about your teacher, for example. You expect your teacher to prepare for class, take attendance, lecture, facilitate discussion, meet with students outside of class, prepare examinations, and turn in final grades. You expect a work-group supervisor to regulate the work of employees, call staff meetings when necessary, give performance appraisal interviews, review complaints or grievances, and so on.

Group members can have clearly identifiable roles. A person's role is the function that the member performs in the group. Words like *leader, dominator, gatekeeper, joker,* and *analyzer* express some of the roles in a group.[8] Many roles are possible, but we will confine our discussion to three types: task roles, personal roles, and problem roles.

TASK ROLES Task roles are performed to achieve the goals of the group and to facilitate participation and decision making. They almost always focus on what the group is trying to accomplish. Here are some examples:

ⓧ Examples:

• **INFORMATION AGENT:** Offers facts, beliefs, personal experience, or other input; also asks for additional input or clarification of ideas or opinions that have been presented

• **ELABORATOR:** Offers further clarification of points, often providing information about what others have said

• **INITIATOR:** Helps the group get moving by proposing a solution, giving new ideas, or providing new definitions of an issue

• **ADMINISTRATOR:** Keeps people on track and aware of the time

PERSONAL ROLES Personal roles are enacted for the purpose of initiating, developing, or managing interpersonal relationships among group members. Sometimes these roles are described as socioemotional because they focus on the feelings, emotions, and personal needs of members. People filling these roles help the group operate during slack or difficult times. The following are a few examples of this type of role:

ⓧ Examples:

• **HARMONIZER:** Seeks to smooth over tension in the group by settling differences among members

• **GATEKEEPER:** Works to keep each member involved in a discussion by keeping communication channels open; may restrict information during periods of overload

• **SENSOR:** Expresses group feelings, moods, or relationships in an effort to recognize the climate and capitalize on it

PROBLEM ROLES Sometimes roles are dysfunctional or distracting for the group. These roles consist of behaviors that attempt to satisfy individual rather than group needs, which are often irrelevant to the task at hand. Sometimes they are played by individuals who do not have enough commitment to the group or are simply not competent. How many times have you seen evidence of these roles in the groups you belong to?

- **BLOCKER:** Indulges in negative and stubbornly resistant behavior, including disagreements and groundless opposition to ideas; reintroduces an issue after the group has rejected or bypassed it
- **AVOIDER:** Displays noninvolvement in the group's proceedings by such behaviors as pouting, cynicism, nonchalance, or "horseplay"
- **RECOGNITION SEEKER:** Calls attention to himself or herself by boasting, providing information about his or her qualifications, or reporting personal achievements
- **ISOLATOR:** Sits and fails to participate
- **DOMINATOR:** Speaks too often and too long
- **FREE RIDER:** Does not do her or his share of the work
- **DETRACTOR:** Constantly criticizes and gripes
- **DIGRESSER:** Takes the group on wild-goose chases
- **SOCIALIZER:** Is a member of the group only for social and personal reasons

A group of students are working on plans to renovate a dilapidated city park. Jaime (**information agent**) starts the meeting by illuminating the budget as the most sensitive aspect of the project's success. Next, María (**elaborator**) points out that the city has designated a mere $5,000 for the park's renovation, so the team should strive for frugality. Following María's input, Albert (**blocker**) displays his dissatisfaction with financial boundaries by claiming that the group should disregard strict budgetary guidelines so they can create an extravagant park. Megan (**digresser**) goes on a wild tangent about turning the public park into a zoo and charging admission. While Megan's mind takes a detour from the group, María tries to instill the concrete dollar number offered by the city to Albert, but he just shakes his head and looks out the window. Alice (**avoider**) chastises the group members for putting a monetary amount on an area of childhood joy. Sensing that the group is spiraling out of control, Akira (**administrator**) attempts to harness control by reminding the team of the task at hand. Robert (**harmonizer**) assures the group that a happy medium can be attained and not to let emotion cloud the common goal. Miguel (**gatekeeper**) suggests that speaking rights should go one-by-one around the table to include everyone. While Carl (**dominator**) takes his turn, the group members collectively roll their eyes as he prattles on endlessly without letting others get a word in edgewise. As the others began to discuss, Tasha (**isolator**) sits by idly and fails to add input of any sort, let alone open her mouth at all. As the proceedings continue, Kim (**free rider**), knowing the others will pick up her slack, silently slips out the door and heads home. Heather (**detractor/socializer**) turns from the group and begins to complain with Janine (**detractor/socializer**) about the "measly" budget provided to the group and the proximity of the parking lot to the office. Rudy (**initiator**) tells the group that they could expand the budget by transforming the project into a charity event and collecting donations. Upon hearing this, Steven (**recognition seeker**) goes into raptures about his extensive volunteer endeavors. Noticing that the meeting is unraveling, Jessica (**sensor**) suggests the group disperse and regroup later.

As you can see, one group member can embody multiple roles. Due to lack of care, there is a good chance a free rider will also be an isolator.

Do you excel at any of these roles? Which of them really irritate you? Which are incompatible with one another? Do you think that digressors and free riders get along well? What about isolators and socializers? Recognition of these roles provides the group with a means of maximizing the positive ones and minimizing the others.

9.3.4: Conformity

Conformity is agreement with or correspondence to a set of ideas, rules, or principles. In a group, the ideas are often the opinion of one or more dominant members. Participants who value conformity give in, compromise, or abandon their individual positions to align with others in the group. In a way, conformity can be seen as negative consensus. Although a unanimous decision is arrived on, group members were influenced by peer pressure or domineering attitudes.

REASONS FOR CONFORMITY People conform to group ideas and opinions for many reasons, not the least of which is that no one can act with complete independence of all other group members. Inevitably, simply interacting with others will influence how you think about the issues being discussed. An example of this is group polarization. When groups of like-minded people deliberate, the group as a whole tends to develop more extreme views. In an experiment organized by Cass Sunstein, a University of Chicago law professor, and sponsored by ABC News, citizens from Boulder and Colorado Springs were placed into groups with others who generally held similar beliefs. Each individual was asked to rate their agreement or disagreement on a few divisive issues. Then the group was asked to come to consensus on agreement or disagreement. Consistently, the consensus response was substantially more extreme than the individual responses. By the end of the experiment, they showed how "deliberation tends to move groups, and the individuals who compose them, toward a more extreme point in the direction indicated by their own predeliberation judgments."[9]

Another force for conformity is time. If a group is about to conclude its work, you may receive hostile or uncooperative treatment if you bring up another idea or try to spark debate on an issue that has already been resolved ("C'mon, Bob, we agreed a week ago that we would hire the new candidate"). Highly directive or authoritarian leadership, which suppresses individual contributions to a group, also encourages conformity. Social pressure or the need to "belong" may also discourage disagreement with other group members. In highly cohesive groups, the desire to maintain the group as a unified body can limit a person's freedom to disagree with others.

CONFORMITY AND GROUP FUNCTIONING Conformity may be necessary for group effectiveness. Groups eventually must reach decisions, and conformity among group members provides a basis for consensus. Conformity to various rules, to standards, and especially to group goals is necessary under all conditions of group decision making. Members may be encouraged to disagree about the definition of the problem, the alternatives generated, and the criteria by which to evaluate alternatives. But certain fundamental issues—such as why the group exists and how it should operate—must be agreed on by everyone.

Emergency situations, which require quick decisions, seldom offer the luxury of conflict or disagreement. Even in less tense situations, there are moments in group discussion when any additional advocacy or dissension among group members deteriorates into useless discussion. At that point, the group should strive for conformity to avoid wasting time.[10]

Groups that are naturally contentious and argumentative may benefit from promoting conformity. Getting group members to view a problem from others' perspective and to consent to a mutually agreed-on decision is a monumental task for some groups. In situations in which group conflict is common, failure to promote conformity can lower morale and undermine working relationships.[11]

9.3.5: Groupthink

Conformity, carried to its extreme, leads to groupthink. Figure 9.2 illustrates the relationship between conformity and groupthink.

Figure 9.2 The Relationship Between Conformity and Groupthink

Although some amount of conformity is positive for group interaction, after a certain point, conformity becomes a disadvantage rather than an advantage to the group's communication and productivity.

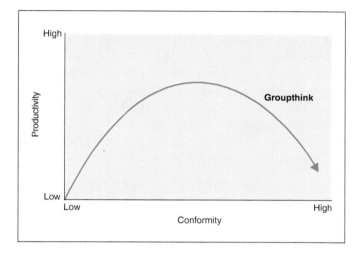

Groupthink is the tendency of group members to seek agreement solely for agreement's sake. A group gripped by groupthink fails to explore alternative solutions, problems, or concerns in an effort to present a united or cohesive front to outsiders. For example, imagine an impatient jury not giving enough thought into the outcome of the defendant's trial. Four conditions give rise to groupthink:[12]

⊗ **Being Out of Touch**

When a group meets for long periods of time away from its regular routines, members forget the big picture and do whatever is necessary to make the group succeed, regardless of how those actions may harm others.

⊗ **Being Out of Order**

Informal and non-standardized decision-making procedures let a group venture into unproductive areas with no way to get back on course.

⊗ **Being Overruled**

When group members feel that criteria and decision-making procedures are thrust on them by a leader, they are likely to follow along without much advocacy or dissension.

⊗ **Being Out of Resources**

When faced with a critical problem, a short time frame for deciding, and no reasonable alternative other than the one favored by the leader, the group falls back on groupthink.

A tragic example of the effects of groupthink was the space shuttle Columbia disaster in February 2003. During its launch, a piece of insulating foam about the size of a suitcase fell off the shuttle's heat-resistant underbelly and collided with the left wing of the space vehicle. NASA flight managers knew about the impact within a day of the launch but decided not to pursue repair options or even to use satellite images to evaluate the damage. Pieces of foam had dislodged from the space shuttle in the past without causing any problems. Higher-level NASA officials decided that the missing foam presented little danger, but lower-level engineers were concerned that the falling piece of foam might have punctured Columbia. In actuality, the foam had indeed torn a fatal hole in the heat shielding of the left wing. Upon reentry, the damage let superheated gases inside the wing, where it melted the wing's frame. The shuttle broke up fifteen minutes before it was scheduled to land, forty miles over Texas, killing all seven astronauts.

In retrospect, a fundamental breakdown in communication contributed significantly to the disaster. "NASA's organizational culture had as much to do with this accident as foam did," described the Columbia Accident Investigation Board. Plans for rescue and repair missions had been considered, and with better communication they might have been implemented. However, we will never know if the tragedy could have been prevented because no attempts were ever made. In its review and recommendations the board concluded that the space agency suffered from all four of the conditions just mentioned: *being out of touch*—"organizational barriers that prevented effective communication of critical safety information and stifled professional differences of opinion"; *being out of order*—"the evolution of an informal chain of command of decision-making processes that operated outside the organization's rules"; *being overruled*—"engineers initially presented concerns as well as possible solutions," but "management did not listen to what their engineers were telling them"; and *being out of resources*—"NASA's budget was inadequate for all the programs the agency was executing."[13]

SYMPTOMS OF GROUPTHINK How can groups determine whether they are victims of groupthink? Three major symptoms can be observed: group members tend to see the group as all-powerful, and there is closed-mindedness and pressure toward uniformity.[14]

⊗ **The Group's Tendency to View Itself as Omnipotent**

Prior success, self-indulgence, and feelings of superiority can produce this attitude. Group members may share illusions of invulnerability that encourage excessive risk taking. Furthermore, as a whole the group may feel that its behavior is beyond scrutiny and may therefore enact decisions without regard to moral consequences.

⊗ Closed Mindedness

A group experiencing groupthink tends to shut out information that does not conform to prevailing group opinion. Group members rationalize this avoidance by claiming that the contradictory information is insignificant or irrelevant to the group task or that the source of the information is ill advised or inconsequential.

⊗ Pressure Towards Uniformity

Uniformity in members' opinions, values, and ideas usually leads to one-sided decisions. Pressure toward uniformity comes from two sources: self and group. Self-imposed uniformity minimizes personal doubts or counterarguments about prevailing group opinion. It may occur because individuals value the opinion of the group more than their own opinion ("We know they must be right; they always are"). Groups press for uniformity by exerting direct pressure on deviant members to compel them to conform to group desires. Such pressure may range from subtle tactics, such as expressing disapproval nonverbally (frowning) and ignoring nonconforming members, to attacking deviant members verbally and questioning their motives and loyalty ("So, Betsy, you want to make us look as if we don't get along just because you're nervous about the decision?").

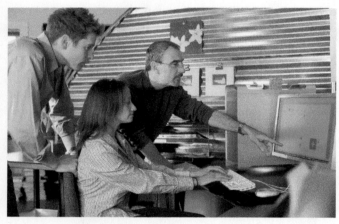

Technology makes it possible to collaborate in ways that control groupthink.

SOURCE: Marc Romanelli/Getty Images

MINIMIZING GROUPTHINK There are several ways to lessen the tendency toward groupthink.[15] Group members must question themselves and their actions to ensure high-quality decision making. One technique that encourages open discussion is to have the group leader ask each member to assume the role of critical evaluator. It should be stressed that the role is that of constructive rather than destructive questioner. Another technique is to have the group from time to time divide into subgroups with similar tasks to determine whether group composition and size affect the ability of group members to remain adversarial and objective. Sometimes splitting a group into subgroups leads to fresh perspectives.

A third technique conducive to warding off groupthink is to have each group member discuss the group's communications and actions with trusted outsiders to obtain an untainted and objective viewpoint. Even friends or spouses can serve in this role. A fourth way to avoid groupthink is to have the group hold a special meeting where all misgivings, second-guessing, and objections are aired. At such a meeting, each member is encouraged to express any doubts she or he may have about any phase of the group deliberation.

A very special method of minimizing groupthink is to have a measure of cultural diversity within a group. When groups are composed of males and females, Whites, Blacks, Hispanics, and Asians, as well as young and old group members, the opportunity for diverse thinking increases, and the emergence of diverse ideas, opinions, and arguments can counteract the effects of groupthink. When group members from various cultural backgrounds feel free to express their feelings and thoughts on all of the issues being discussed, one-track thinking is likely to be avoided and groupthink minimized.

9.3.6: Advocacy

Another factor that can help minimize groupthink is advocacy. **Advocacy**, or presenting competing views on a controversial issue, greatly increases a group's insight into that issue. Advocacy improves group problem solving by identifying alternative positions and promoting awareness of the important issues that must be resolved. Advocacy also forces group members to consider the strengths and weaknesses, pros and cons, and advantages and disadvantages of various viewpoints.

Without advocacy, groups tend to become closed-minded, likely to choose solutions that are personal favorites or are easy to implement or sell to upper management. Advocacy in group problem solving can take two forms: devil's advocacy or dialectical inquiry. Both are attempts to encourage groups to compare the relative values of competing viewpoints.

DEVIL'S ADVOCACY You are probably familiar with the term *devil's advocate*. You may even have been accused of playing this role. Devil's advocacy is described as "structured conflict in business decisions. . . . The **devil's advocate** role should involve the formal introduction of dissent into decision-making processes in which premature consensus inhibits the challenging of assumptions and the consideration of a range of alternatives."[16] In other words, devil's advocacy is a good way to fight groupthink or excessive conformity.

Some group members may enjoy playing devil's advocate and challenging the assumptions and ideas of other group members. Although sometimes called detractors because of their apparently negative attitude, "volunteer" devil's advocates provide the group with a valuable service if their arguments are constructive. You may recall the scene in the film *Big* in which twelve-year-old Josh (in adult form) responds to a slickly packaged, jargon-filled marketing report about a less-than-exciting new toy with "I don't get it." His remark broke the group's conformist attitude and sparked inquiry and brainstorming.

Devil's advocacy is a sequential process beginning with formal or informal commitment from the group.[17] Group members must recognize the value of devil's advocacy during problem solving and commit themselves to an objective and open-minded attitude toward the arguments presented against prevailing opinion.

If a devil's advocate does not emerge naturally from a group, the role may be assigned to a group member. Assuming the role can be both fun and challenging if the advocate is prepared. By playing this role properly, you can command the attention of important decision makers and enhance your stature within the group and the organization.

Selection of the devil's advocate (in the absence of volunteers) must involve group members who are competent and credible. Group members must feel that the advocate knows what she or he is talking about and has a track record of effectiveness. In other words, the advocate must be credible enough to be taken seriously.

The devil's advocate has to decide which part of the problem-solving process to focus on. Advocacy can be advanced in the problem identification phase through challenges to the assumptions on which the problem is based. It can also be employed in the problem definition and analysis phase through questioning of the evidence or data presented in support of particular arguments. And it is often used during the phase of problem solving when group members are evaluating and promoting possible solutions. The devil's advocate may even decide to engage in all these phases, although strategic selection is advised to avoid being labeled a detractor.

The next step is preparation. The devil's advocate must do her or his homework so that the case presented against differing viewpoints is solid and persuasive. Although other group members may focus their attention on information and ideas that lead to solutions, the job of the devil's advocate is to present information and opinions that contradict these viewpoints. When you as devil's advocate conduct research in preparation for group meetings, concentrate on information that weakens, denies, or threatens positions that are likely to be taken by group members.

The final step in this process is issuing the challenge. Challenging others' viewpoints, opinions, ideas, or information can be accomplished in different ways. A devil's advocate can point out inconsistencies, irrelevancies, or inaccuracies in the data or the logic being used to present arguments. In addition, a devil's advocate can use previously established criteria to undermine positions being taken by group members. Of course, the most competent

method of refutation or advocacy relies on critical thinking skills and effective techniques of argument. By way of example, consider the following group meeting, in which John has decided to assume a devil's advocate role during the problem identification phase.

The group was formed to determine what could be done about poor customer service. The group has concluded that the fault lies with customers' not being informed about services that the company offers. It thinks that customers' expectations about what the company can deliver are too high. John remarks, "It seems that if we want to increase our share of the market, we should not be blaming customers for their lack of knowledge of our services. Rather, we should be responding to their needs by providing new services that they want. Let me give some evidence that proves my point. Research and development has mentioned on several occasions that they can develop new products if they know the market is there." Notice how John moves the discussion into a new light by playing devil's advocate.

DIALECTICAL INQUIRY   Dialectical inquiry is similar to devil's advocacy in that the advocate opposes prevailing opinion but then goes one step further by proposing another opinion or plan of action.[18] Consider the four stages to this process:[19]

1. A prevailing or recommended strategic plan and the data used to derive it are identified.

2. An attempt is made to identify the assumptions underlying the plan.

3. A counterplan is identified that is feasible, politically viable, and generally credible but that rests on assumptions opposite those supporting the first plan.

4. A structured debate is conducted. Those responsible for formulating strategy hear arguments in support of both the plan and the counterplan. The debate, in contrast to a traditional management briefing, is a forceful presentation of two opposing plans that rest on different interpretations of the same data.

The following example illustrates key elements of this process:

During the testing of a new hypertension drug, a pharmaceutical company learns that the drug induces hair to grow in places where none existed before. A meeting of researchers and marketers is held to discuss the problem. One team of researchers is concerned that this side effect may prevent the introduction of the drug into the hypertension market ("People will search for something else that doesn't grow hair on their necks and backs. We should just shelve the product until we can eliminate this side effect"). Marketing people argue that the drug should be refined to capture the market of people going bald who are trying to grow their hair back. The research team retorts that the idea is impossible—there is no way to stop unwanted hair growth on other parts of the body. After a pause, one person responds, "Why can't you formulate the drug as a topical treatment that grows hair only where it is applied?" Research members look at one another and agree that that may just be possible.

This new interpretation of the problem and its potential solution opened the way for a different product to be developed and marketed—and it prevented the loss of time, effort, and resources that had gone into developing the original drug.

Advocacy in the form of dialectical inquiry must attack and defend, whereas a devil's advocate only has to attack. Some researchers rate dialectical inquiry as superior to devil's advocacy because advancing a counterplan leads to the generation of constructive alternative positions.[20] In addition, some people may not appreciate someone who attacks their position without offering one of her or his own ("If you're so sure this won't work, what can you suggest that's better?").

When group members are faced with competing plans, however, they may tend to focus myopically on the relative advantages and ignore the underlying assumptions supporting their positions.[21] Devil's advocacy can prevent this myopia. Groups may decide to employ both techniques, enacting them strategically. Regardless of which approach is taken, advocacy is an essential part of the problem-solving process.

9.3.7: Conflict in Groups

Conflict is a greatly misunderstood facet of group communication. Many group leaders avoid conflict because they think it detracts from a group's purpose and goals. Their attitude is that a group experiencing conflict is not running smoothly. In fact, avoiding conflict can lead to conformity and groupthink since there is a lack of lively discussion. We believe, however, that conflict is what group meetings are all about. Leaders can use conflict productively to test group-generated ideas or propositions before they are implemented.

Conflict does not signal that a meeting is disorderly, raucous, or rude. It is a sign that people are actively discussing issues. We believe that if a group does not exhibit conflict by debating ideas or questioning others, there is very little reason for it to exist. The members might as well be working by themselves. Conflict, then, is part of the essence of group interaction. Leaders can use conflict as a means to determine what is and what is not an acceptable idea, solution, or problem. In a very real sense, conflict and advocacy are kindred spirits.

There is one word of caution, however. The conflict we are talking about is debate about issues, not about personalities. A group will not be productive if arguments are centered on the participants rather than on what the participants are talking about. A contribution such as "You've never known what you're talking about before, and you don't know what you're talking about now" is not the type of conflict we advocate. When conflicts arise, group members and especially leaders must be diligent in refocusing members' attention on the issues, not on personalities.

9.3.8: Groups as Systems

As we mentioned at the beginning of this section, the various components of group communication processes can be thought of in an integrated manner as producing a systems effect.[22] Systems theory refers to interdependency, or how various parts are related to each other; if one part changes, the other parts are also affected. Likewise, synergy describes how the various parts of a system work together to produce something greater than the sum of the individual parts.

Both interdependence and synergy characterize group communication. Take, for example, the relationships among norms, roles, and conflict. Because of a certain norm ("do not interrupt someone who is speaking"), a frustrated group member assumes the role of "distractor," which inflames other group members, leading to conflict. Or, the same norm may allow members to instill greater cohesiveness in the group. For example, groups with an overemphasis on conformity tend to slide into a groupthink mentality. Effective leaders avoid this pitfall by utilizing certain norms and roles to manage productive conflict. In this case, a "don't interrupt" norm helps group members air their doubts, frustrations, or new ideas. As you consider the dynamics of group communication, keep these issues in mind.

9.3.9: Group Leadership

Participation and leadership in groups are likely to be interrelated. The degree to which group members make their own decisions affects the leadership style with which they will be most comfortable. There are many different descriptions of leadership. Some emphasize that a **leader** is a person who influences the actions of others. A communication-specific definition is that a leader is the member of a group who speaks the most, speaks the most to the group as a whole, is spoken to the most, and directs communication in the group to productive levels.

A manager or supervisor is not necessarily a group leader. A person can be in charge of a group without exhibiting any leadership qualities. A member who leads a group may be its *least* experienced, *lowest*-ranking participant. If you have played organized team sports, you probably remember teams in which the captain did not exhibit true leadership and the person who fired up the team, gave it direction, and assisted others when needed was just one of the gang, not the designated leader. Many training and development programs today attempt to teach managers or supervisors how to be leaders. The focus of these programs is on transforming managers from people with titles into people who exhibit true influence, direction, and motivation.

Leaders in business organizations and the professions can be viewed in four ways.[23] Each defines leadership differently and provides insight into how a person can become a leader. These four approaches are traits, style, situational leadership, and functional leadership.

TRAITS Think of some people you believe are leaders. Now contrast them with some people you definitely know are not leaders. In what ways do the personalities, physical appearances, or behaviors of people in these two groups differ?

The **trait** approach is the oldest method by which people have attempted to measure leadership. In general, leaders seem to be higher than nonleaders in intelligence, scholarship, dependability and responsibility, activity and social participation, and socioeconomic status.[24] Leaders also outdo nonleaders in presenting a compelling vision, exhibiting power, exemplifying organizational values, taking risks, and displaying entrepreneurial imagination and transformation.[25] Negative traits that prevent a person from assuming a leadership role include lack of knowledge, nonparticipation, extreme rigidity, authoritarian behavior, and offensive verbalization.[26]

STYLE One way to conceptualize leadership is to focus on **leadership style**—the behaviors that leaders use when interacting with group members. A discussion of leadership style assumes that there is one style that works best in most situations.

The most popular classification of leadership styles divides them into authoritarian, participative, and laissez-faire styles. Notice that when you classify a leader into one of these three categories, you necessarily focus on behavior. Actions—what leaders say or do—determine whether a leader exhibits one style or another.

Another way to conceptualize leadership style is by determining how a leader emphasizes tasks (the problem at hand) and relationships in the group through communication with the participants. According to Robert Blake and Jane Mouton, an emphasis on both people and production (tasks and relationships) yields the best results in most situations.[27]

SITUATIONAL LEADERSHIP Another view of leadership suggests that there is no one best style, but rather that the best style is the one adapted to the situation at hand.

Situational leadership can manifest itself in two ways (see Figure 9.3). In one, the leader is flexible and adapts his or her behavior to the demands of the situation. The leader reads a situation and selects behaviors appropriate for that circumstance. An effective situational leader of this type does not always place equal emphasis on tasks and relationships because a given situation might call for the emphasizing of one over the other.

One of the best examples of this view of situational leadership is the work of Paul Hersey and Ken Blanchard, whose situational leadership theory is based on a leader's ability to *adapt* to a group's maturity level.[28] According to the theory, **maturity** is a combination of a group's willingness and ability to perform a task. The more willing and able a group is, the more mature it is. As a group progresses in maturity, it requires less direction and less socioemotional support.

Hersey and Blanchard suggested that a group begins in a **directing phase**; here the leader must provide a great deal of guidance. As the group matures, it moves to a **coaching phase**, which allows the leader to instruct, act as a role model, and nurture group members. In the **supporting phase**, the leader is in the role of peer and gives compliments, reassures, minimizes doubts, and encourages productivity. In the most mature phase, the **delegating phase**, the leader directly or indirectly moves responsibility for group tasks, creativity, solutions, and decisions to group members. In this phase, members shoulder much of the group's work.

Figure 9.3 Situational Versus Functional Leadership Styles

Situational leadership theory suggests that the best style of leadership is adapted to the situation at hand. If a group's ability to handle problems on its own increases, the situational leader is flexible and decreases his or her direct involvement appropriately. If a leader's style is inflexible, the best situation is one whose style matches the needs of the project. With functional leadership, a group's members take turns leading the group to meet various needs, such as task orientation or social relations.

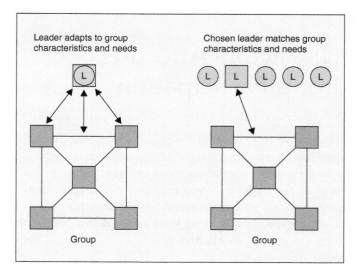

In the second type of situational leadership, the leader's style is inflexible, and the goal is to match the leader to situations that are appropriate for his or her style. It is assumed that leaders cannot with any degree of effectiveness act one way with some groups and another way with other groups.[29] This approach calls for leaders who are competent in particular tasks and with particular types of people to be placed with groups that are similar in their task and relational orientations. For example, a communication department composed of young faculty members who were bright and energetic and demanded complete participation in the decision-making process chafed under the leadership of a department head who was very experienced and somewhat dogmatic and preferred to make decisions first and then inform the faculty. She was replaced by a person who was young, energetic, less experienced, and certainly less set in her ways. The new department head sought input from department members to assure herself that decisions were correct. This appropriate match between group and leader was very successful.

FUNCTIONAL LEADERSHIP Sometimes groups contain several members who can perform many of the duties and responsibilities of a leader. When various group members rise to an occasion and perform needed leadership functions, the group is demonstrating **functional leadership**. Some group members may be very task oriented and push the group toward solving the problem. These members supply the group with a task function. Other members may be adept at maintaining harmony and social relations within the group.

Think about the last time you were in a group situation. Did you notice that several people were fulfilling the roles and functions of leadership? Perhaps you were successful at persuading group members to adopt a particular viewpoint or were able to reduce conflict. If so, you were providing the group with functional leadership.

9.4: Factors Affecting Group Participation

9.4 Analyze the factors that affect group participation

Now that we have covered the basic factors (size, norms, cohesiveness, and so on) that influence group dynamics, we turn to factors that affect members' participation in a group. In the workplace, you may be assigned to formal task groups, or you may choose to volunteer for special project groups. In any case, your level of involvement affects the group process and your attitudes toward the group.

9.4.1: Approachability

Approachability gives group members the impression that you are open to their ideas and opinions. Effective listening is one way to demonstrate approachability, such as displaying an accessible nonverbal demeanor (smiling, eye contact, open body orientation, and so on).[30] Approachability can also be established by asking for opinions, commenting on ideas, and expressing positive regard for the groups or team members.

9.4.2: Commitment

Commitment to the group and its mission must also be present. Commitment reflects group members' willingness to care personally for the group and its members and to maintain a dogged determination to help the group succeed. This type of commitment is developed primarily through explicit clarification of the goals entrusted to the group. Facilitation skills must also include convincing members of the importance of the group's mission and providing feedback about how their efforts are making a difference within the larger organization. Commitment can be demonstrated by the following:[31]

- Caring personally about the group and its success
- Being loyal to the group, its members, and its mission
- Remaining focused on the group's mission and goals
- Maintaining high-intensity levels for the group's work
- Demonstrating to others your positive attitude about the group's mission and vision
- Ethical Qualities of Leaders
- Asking for commitment from others
- Taking pride in being part of the group effort

Ethics in Leadership

Ethical Issues

Leaders who adhere to ethical principles of leadership are open and honest, selfless, fair, consistent, and willing to give credit where it is due. How could unethical leadership affect the following?

- Norms
- Conformity
- Cohesiveness
- Groupthink
- Roles
- Conflict

9.4.3: Participation Styles

An important factor affecting group involvement is the style of participation possible in the groups. Authoritarian, laissez-faire, and participative styles of decision making allow varying degrees of participation by members, with very different results.

An **authoritarian** style of decision making is one in which a leader hands down a decision to the group. The participants are not involved in making the decision; they simply do what the leader tells them to do. Two situations call for authoritarian decision making: crises and lack of knowledge. When a group faces a crisis, decisions must be made swiftly, and there is little time for discussion. When members are asked to give opinions, provide evidence, or supply details on material about which they have no knowledge or information, valuable time and effort are wasted, and other participants may be embarrassed or offended. Consider decision making in the armed forces. Clearly, there will be occasions when involving those potentially affected by the decision is not practical or not possible. Decisions must be made that negatively affect an individual, yet are for the greater good. In such cases, the most efficient decision-making style is authoritarian.

Apart from those circumstances, authoritative decision making has major disadvantages. It lowers morale among participants who want to contribute but cannot. It reduces the members' confidence in their leader and stirs feelings of suspicion about the leader's intentions. The chance for a poor decision is high because some valuable input may never surface and ideas may remain untested. John Dean III, Richard Nixon's legal counsel, a man deeply involved in the Watergate scandal, would later explain that authoritarian thinking "was the principal force behind almost everything that went wrong with Nixon's presidency."[32]

A **laissez-faire** style of decision making is one in which there is minimal involvement by the group leader. Members of a group operating with this type of decision making in essence make decisions without guidance or direction from a leader. The group is on its own. This type of group is difficult to deal with because some people may see themselves as fulfilling the leadership function without actually demonstrating the necessary skills. Laissez-faire groups are likely to grope around for ways to identify problems or establish decision criteria unless various group members make a concerted effort to do so. Some people probably enjoy group work without a directive leader, but research indicates that valuable time and resources can be wasted in a directionless group.

Managing Participation Styles

Strategic Skills

Some group members have problem styles that interfere with group functioning. These styles can be managed through effective facilitation skills.

Style	Description	Facilitation
Rambling	Much discussion except on the subject; gets lost.	Raise hand slightly, get the floor, and refocus attention on the issue. Glance at watch.
Verbose	Excessive talkativeness, anxious to show off; very wordy.	Ask difficult questions to slow them down. Ask others to interpret their meaning. Ask for additional input.
Inarticulate	Can't put thoughts into a coherent form. Can't express themselves.	Paraphrase their comments. Ask others if they feel the same way.
Prone to sidebar	Two people talk privately during group discussion.	Call one by name and ask for his or her feelings on the discussion.
Avoiding	Noninvolvement; little participation.	Call on them by name. Ask for opinions.
Blocking	Indulge in negative or disagreeable comments.	Ask why they feel that way. Have them compare their view to others'.

Adapted from D. O'Hair, M. Wiemann D. Mullin, and J. Tevon, *Real Communication*, 3rd ed. (New York: Bedford/St. Martin's Press, 2015); "Dealing with Different Types of Participants," http://www.wi-scd.org (accessed June 19, 2001); R. Schwartz, *The Skilled Facilitator* (San Francisco: Jossey-Bass, 1994); D. O'Hair, R. Stewart, H. Rubenstein, *A Speaker's Guidebook*, 4th ed. (Boston: Bedford/St. Martins, 2007).

One illustration of the possible problems associated with laissez-faire style of decision making is FEMA's response to Hurricane Katrina. Following hearings for the House Select Bipartisan Committee to Investigate the Preparation for and Response to Hurricane Katrina, there was evidence that then FEMA director Michael Brown's decision-making style could be classified as laissez-faire. The email evidence provided to the committee revealed that Brown "made few decisions" and provided "few emails that show Mr. Brown taking charge or issuing tasking orders." This demonstrates a minimal involvement by the leader, characteristic of laissez-faire decision making.[33]

According to Gary Yukl, participation "usually refers to a management style or type of decision procedure through which subordinates are allowed to influence some of the manager's decisions."[34] When decision making is authoritarian, the leader makes decisions for the group. When decision making is laissez-faire, the leader turns decisions over to the group. But when decision making is **participative**, the leader makes decisions with the group.

Research indicates that participative decision making offers a number of benefits. Group members who participate in decision making are more committed to the outcome or result than are group members who have no say about what happens. Participation also yields an interesting and satisfying experience for group members. In addition, the quality of decisions improves when group members who have skills or knowledge not possessed by the leader are willing to cooperate with the leader.

For participative decision making to work, several conditions must be met. A leader must have sufficient authority to delegate and share decision making with the group. Within the group there must be members who are knowledgeable about the subject matter and willing to participate in discussions about it. There must also be enough time for the group to complete discussion and reach consensus. And the leader must be competent in such participative methods as questioning, delegating, defining, gatekeeping, and agenda setting.

However, there is a downside to participative decision making. Participative decision making not only takes more time than other forms of leadership but also can create expectations among members that they will be influential in all group affairs. Some participants may perceive their leader as deficient in confidence and expertise. Furthermore, when a decision belongs to a group as a unit rather than to individuals, assigning responsibility for failures and shortcomings is difficult. On balance, however, participative decision making seems to be highly valued in organizations that practice it.

WRITING PROMPT

How would you classify the leadership styles of these famous leaders? Are their leadership styles authoritarian, laissez-faire, or participative?

- Sonia Sotomayor
- Bill Gates
- Hillary Clinton
- Pope Francis

▶ The response entered here will appear in the performance dashboard and can be viewed by your instructor.

Submit

9.5: Teleconferences and Videoconferences

9.5 Compare teleconferences with videoconferences

In business today, time pressures, financial limitations, and the need for interconnectivity across geographical distance all dictate that various electronic methods of conducting group meetings are essential. More than other types of meetings, discussions that are conducted electronically require precise and well-defined rules of interaction because nonverbal communication is restricted or unavailable.

In teleconferencing, participants are limited to the voice. There is no way to judge the reactions that can usually be discerned from facial expressions. These reactions—confusion, anger, hesitancy, surprise, dismay, displeasure, pain—are evident to participants in face-to-face meetings.

In videoconferencing, nonverbal reactions are available to participants but on a limited basis. Members may not feel that the group is "in a meeting." And there is a great loss of control over who takes the floor when. As a result, there is no naturally identified way of deciding "who speaks when on what."

In an ordinary meeting, a change of speakers is signaled by behavior such as pointing, leaning forward, and sitting back. These signals are not available in teleconferencing or videoconferencing. Thus, the group must establish rules and procedures for changing speakers. Without them, there may be offensive interruptions, "floor hogging," several people speaking at once, and shouting, among other possibilities.

The group leader can control the flow of communication by stating, "To obtain the floor, you must be recognized by me." Another may say, "No one may speak longer than three minutes at a time." Controlling the flow of communication through these or other means is a major challenge in teleconferencing and videoconferencing. Furthermore, there is no bona fide way to make sure group members are paying attention during electronic conferencing. As far as the speaker knows, the audience is in rapt attention, but they could just as easily be surfing the Web.

Yet electronic conferencing is here to stay, as corporate travel budgets tighten, deadlines shorten, and the global political climate and weather present their ongoing challenges. Electronic conferencing technology has become better and cheaper as well. Equipment that started out at $40,000 to $100,000 years ago now costs as little as $10,000. Thus, videoconferencing is not only easier in many ways than traveling, but it is also more economical and reduces the organization's carbon footprint. With the latest hardware and bandwidth, video and audio streaming can be of excellent quality. Given all of these factors, many firms have decided that even in a brighter economic climate, they will not increase their travel budgets, preferring instead to invest in videoconferencing equipment.

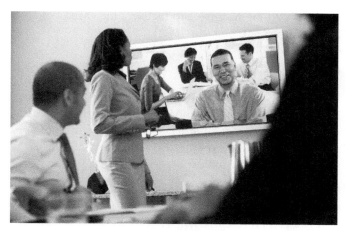

Videoconferencing allows group communication over geographical distance.

SOURCE: Blend Images/Shutterstock

9.6: Special Groups

9.6   Scrutinize the role of special groups in business

While video- and teleconferencing represent forums that increase efficiency in group meetings, other efforts to increase productivity have resulted in new kinds of groups altogether. Quality circles, self-managing teams, and affinity groups are a few examples of groups that bring together people with different experiences and perspectives to encourage mutual learning. All these special group formats have significant impacts on group communication.

9.6.1: Quality Circles

Quality circles are groups of employees who meet on a regular basis during work time to improve quality control and job methods. These groups have increased in prominence in many kinds of organizations and saved countless numbers of businesses thousands of dollars. Quality circles were extremely popular in the 1970s and 1980s, and their impact and presence are still felt today.[35]

The benefits of quality circles have been reported by a number of organizations, and we will only summarize their findings here.[36] Quality circles produce high-quality solutions to work-related problems. Enhanced work productivity results from the implementation of these solutions. Substantial improvement in horizontal and vertical communication

within the organization occurs after quality-circle work. This benefit seems to derive from the increased diversity of communication among participants who would otherwise not interact. Participants in quality circles demonstrate an increased commitment to the organization and its goals. A related advantage is enhanced job satisfaction and lower absenteeism among employees involved with quality circles. Finally, members of quality circles claim that their participation in these groups provides both information and emotional support for dealing with the complexities and uncertainties of the organization. Although considered by some as a passing fad, quality circles as a form of group communication yield benefits that are difficult to deny. Perhaps that is why many organizations continue to enjoy their advantages.

Quality circles are based on the belief that the people who know the work the best are those who do it. In today's exceedingly specialized working world, many managers or supervisors are not as skilled or as knowledgeable about tasks as subordinates are. Quality circles invite these workers to attend meetings and actively participate in making their work better and more productive. They are commonly employed throughout the company. A quality circle whose focus is improved customer relations may include a vice president, a receptionist, a public relations manager, an accountant, and a dock worker. The diversity of the group creates a climate of uniqueness and unfamiliarity that leads to creative solutions.

9.6.2: Self-Managing Teams

Self-managing teams, which are similar to quality circles, are small groups of employees who share the responsibility for a significant task. These employees work together to solve day-to-day problems and are involved in planning and coordinating activities. Because these teams manage themselves, they do not need to report directly to a supervisor. This is the primary difference between quality circles and self-managing teams, as quality circles still have an authority figure (manager or supervisor), whereas self-managing teams have autonomy. Self-managing teams also speak to a trend in the marketplace to lower the vertical hierarchy by eliminating or thinning the ranks of middle management and chunking the system into small, lateral units. In addition, organizations are increasingly relying on employees to be heavily involved in decision making and problem solving. Table 9.1 provides an overview of the benefits of self-managing teams.

Table 9.1 Benefits of Self-Managing Teams

Employee Benefits	Organization Benefits
• Higher job satisfaction	• Increased flexibility
• Increased self-esteem	• Increased productivity
• Greater employee development	• Leaner staffs
• Increased job security	• Less bureaucracy
	• Lower turnover
	• Decreased absenteeism

Major companies in the United States—such as Xerox, Procter & Gamble, Volvo, and General Electric—have introduced self-managing teams and have reported a 25 to 40 percent gain in productivity and a lowering of production costs by as much as 25 percent.[37] At Federal Express, for example, a team of clerks spotted and solved a billing problem and thereby saved the company more than $2.1 million a year. Self-managing teams at Federal Express reduced billing problems and lost package problems by as much as 13 percent.[38]

Self-managing teams have demonstrated that it can be a major mistake to underestimate the value of involving lower-level workers. When given the opportunity, these workers manage themselves quite well and accept high levels of responsibility. Workers who have participated in self-managing teams have discovered a sense of ownership in their jobs that they otherwise would not have experienced.

Teams perform four major activities. They uncover and analyze problems, complete tasks, establish and maintain personal relationships, and facilitate group and organizational processes. In accomplishing these tasks, each member of the group is considered a credible resource, and the team is committed to making maximum use of individual contributions. Thus, team members tend to be committed and motivated to implement team decisions. Team building entails attention to both tasks and relationships. When a team is charged with the responsibility of performing tasks, it must identify and diagnose problems, implement action to provide a workable solution, and follow up with a strong and thorough evaluation of any action that has been taken.

The relationship dimension shapes the climate in which the team operates. Teams operating in a favorable climate exhibit a strong degree of participation in group decision making, demonstrate productive and managed conflict, and use feedback effectively. There are substantial advantages for a group that can work as a team. Participants are motivated to pull together, decisions are made with high levels of commitment and motivation, and a spirit of camaraderie develops within the group.

Texas Instruments (TI) provides a good example of the team concept working well. In the past, at a TI factory in Dallas, workers put in their forty hours and went home. They had little commitment to the job or to the product they were helping to produce. Pressured by defense contract cutbacks and intense competition, TI developed self-managing teams. The teams operate according to their own schedules and responsibilities and monitor their own attendance and productivity. Communication within the team is much more frequent than in the old assembly-line style of production, and as a result, team members discover potential problems before they ever happen. TI was

pleased with the results—productivity increased between 20 and 50 percent.[39]

9.6.3: Affinity Groups

WHAT IS AN AFFINITY GROUP?   An **affinity group** consists of eight to twelve members in a sponsoring organization that meet on a regular basis to exchange information, ideas, opinions, and experiences on a variety of issues in a safe and supportive atmosphere, resulting in personal and professional growth.

WHAT IS THE PURPOSE OF AFFINITY GROUPS IN ORGANIZATIONS?   Participants in affinity groups do not hold membership in the same or in any single business unit or division within an organization. Indeed, one of the landmark characteristics of an affinity group is that it meets in a safe, confidential atmosphere, where members may freely and openly share information, opinions, and recommendations in order to discuss issues, solve problems, and harness emerging opportunities.

Participation in affinity groups has a positive impact for the individual and the sponsoring organization. For example, it provides the following:

- A sounding board of peers to discuss personal and professional issues and to solve problems
- A nonthreatening environment in which to explore options; to receive impartial and objective, yet caring, feedback; and to contribute to the success of others
- Knowledge that there are others who share similar experiences and a source to find new ways to approach life and work opportunities and challenges
- The opportunity to associate with peers who are committed to personal and professional growth
- Development of friendships and an experience of community within the organization

Organizations, whether businesses or associations, have reported the following benefits after implementing affinity groups:

- Increased relevance to their employees and members, brought about by providing a uniquely differentiated benefit of high value
- Closer relationships with their employees and members, resulting in their serving the organization more effectively
- Heightened loyalty and increased employee or member retention

Table 9.2 compares and contrasts affinity groups with other types of groups in which employees may participate.

Table 9.2 Affinity Groups Compared with Other Types of Groups

Characteristic	Therapy Group	Recovery Group	Religious Study Group	Professional Group	Networking Group	Affinity Group
Membership makeup	Emotional issues, history	Addiction history	Shared theological belief	Similar work focus	Entrepreneurial	Diverse peer group
Objective	Improved mental health	Addiction cessation	Expertise, insight	Idea exchange or development	Personal advancement	Personal and professional growth
Meeting length	1 hour	1 hour	1–2 hours	1–2 hours	1–2 hours	3–4 hours
Meeting frequency	Varies	Varies	Varies	Varies	Varies	Varies
Retreats	No	No	Sometimes	Sometimes	No	Yes
Leadership	Certified professional	Member	Professional clergy or certified volunteer	Member	Professional	Member
Confidentiality	Yes	Yes	No	No	No	Yes
Conflicts of interest	N/A	N/A	N/A	Yes	Yes	Non-competitive
Member behavior protocol	No	No	No	No	No	Yes
Specific attendance requirements	No	No	No	No	No	Yes

Strategic Scenario Wrap-Up

Fundamentals of Group Communication

ⓧ Strategic Scenario

Felipe Papageorgio arrived home from his first day of work sick at heart. His new employer, Stylist, Inc., is a firm believer in making work more productive by emphasizing teamwork, frequent group meetings, and team-based projects. Felipe was elated when he landed this job, since it paid 30 percent more than any other offer, Stylist is a rapidly rising company, and he was able to remain in his hometown. However, his consternation stems from the negative experiences he has had with groups in the past. In high school, the fundraising group he was assigned to in the Junior Achievement Club was a disaster. The group never set any realistic goals, they never jelled as a team, and everyone seemed to want to go their separate ways. As a result, the group never raised much money and was considered a failure by other club members. In college, Felipe joined a mock investment group that was suggested by his academic advisor. In no time, Felipe knew he was in the wrong group. The group elected a leader whom Felipe detested. This leader was arrogant, condescending, and wouldn't listen to other people's ideas—especially, it seemed, to Felipe's ideas. Secretly, Felipe knew he was a much better leader. The group quickly became embroiled in constant bickering, with several factions fighting for control. More recently, Felipe was assigned to a quality-control team during his senior-year internship at a large, local nonprofit organization. This group was especially frustrating because its members, employees and interns alike, all seemed to be more interested in generating ideas that they thought the bosses wanted than in taking risks and being creative. No one wanted to rock the boat. Felipe shook his head as he reflected on his memories of group work. He was convinced that he was in for more of the same with his new organization.

Felipe Papageorgio was a member of three unsuccessful groups in the past and is not optimistic about group work.

To be successful in an organization that relies on group work, Felipe needs to promote the positive factors that influence communication in groups. A successful group:

- Has a clear common purpose
- Defines its preferences for ways of working
- Sets expectations for individual members
- Problem solves through advocacy of positions
- Recognizes civil conflict as positive

Felipe also must recognize barriers to successful group communication, specifically:

- Too much conformity
- Groupthink

Felipe won't always be group leader, nor does he want to be. However, by understanding the dynamics of groups in business, he can ask questions and make clear requests to fellow group members to influence positive outcomes.

WRITING PROMPT

Analyze the three groups Felipe participated in prior to starting his new job. What were the factors that created or contributed to their failure? Why are individuals negatively affected by working with unsuccessful groups, as Felipe was?

▶ | The response entered here will appear in the performance dashboard and can be viewed by your instructor.

Submit

Summary

Fundamentals of Group Communication

- The focus in this chapter is on **fundamental issues** associated with group communication in business and professional settings.
- Groups are necessary because **decisions reached by groups** are usually superior to decisions generated by individuals.
- The **nature of group communication** grows out of what groups do, what purposes they serve, and what constitutes a group.
- The various **elements of group behavior** include roles, interaction, influence, membership, common goals, and leadership.
- A number of factors influence group communication.
- Cohesiveness refers to how connected group members are with one another; research demonstrates that **cohesive groups are more successful** than noncohesive groups.
- **Norms**, the standards or limits for defining acceptable behavior, also shape groups in obvious and not-so-obvious ways.
- Group members who do not conform to norms may be **sanctioned** by others.
- Another factor influencing groups is the **roles** that group members play.
- Roles can be positive or negative, and **recognizing the differences** among them is important.
- **Conformity and groupthink** are critical factors in group work.
- Groups must be able to conform to various procedures and methods of discussion to reach **consensus on issues**.
- Groups must be wary of groupthink, or **failing to discuss critical issues** so as to maintain agreement and positive group relations; groupthink can lead to poor decision making.
- **Advocacy**, including use of the devil's advocate role and dialectical inquiry, also reduces groupthink.
- **Conflict**, on one hand the most problematic aspect of group communication, can be the essence of group vitality and creativity.
- Another important dimension of group communication is **leadership**. Leaders can be classified according to the traits they exhibit, their behavioral styles, their adaptability to the situation at hand, or their ability to perform the duties and responsibilities of a leader.
- The extent of a group member's involvement depends on the nature of the group's **participation style**—is it authoritarian, laissez-faire, or participative?—and on how much team building occurs.
- **Teleconferencing and videoconferencing**, which reduce costs and increase convenience, can rob participants of the benefits of face-to-face interaction, so appropriate adjustments have to be made to keep communication flowing.
- **Quality circles**, self-managing teams, and affinity groups can enhance productivity and increase communicative effectiveness.

SHARED WRITING: FUNDAMENTALS OF GROUP COMMUNICATION

Have you been a member of any group that had the group characteristics listed here? For any (or all) of the group types you were in that matched these criteria, explain how effective and efficient each group was. Provide details that support your conclusions: 1. High degree of cohesion; 2. Participative group leader; 3. One dominant member; 4. Interpersonal conflict during discussion; 5. Unprepared, uninformed members.

> ▶ A minimum number of characters is required to post and earn points. After posting, your response can be viewed by your class and instructor, and you can participate in the class discussion.

Post   0 characters | 140 minimum

Chapter 9 Quiz: Fundamentals of Group Communication

Chapter 10

Meetings as Forums for Problem Solving

Learning Objectives

10.1 Express the utility of meetings in business settings

10.2 Describe the role of the agenda in business meetings

10.3 Scrutinize some of the matters to attend to before holding a meeting

10.4 Exhibit how to incorporate the four critical thinking skills in communication

10.5 Describe the three basic qualities necessary for effective problem solving

10.6 Identify some of the causes of anxiety in a meeting

10.7 Evaluate group effectiveness as preparation for the future

Strategic Scenario: Plan for Success

Chelsea Moreno is a regional sales manager for Inspirion Corporation, an organization that sells and distributes seasonal gift items such as decorative artificial plants, caps, T-shirts, blankets, jewelry, and some perishable items. Inspirion advertises and markets its products in the United States to the public through catalog and Internet sales and to organizations through direct-sales representatives who call on business managers in need of gifts for their clients.

Chelsea has been assigned to organize a meeting for all district and regional sales managers in a mountain resort in Colorado. The purpose of the meeting is to create a strategic plan for developing the Spanish-speaking market—something they know very little about. Chelsea knows that many of the "old guard" sales managers are resistant to the idea of moving into an entirely new, and potentially very large, market at this time. She also knows

that she has been selected for this task because she has been actively supporting the idea of developing new markets, particularly this one, and that her chances of being promoted to vice president depend on the success of the venture.

Chelsea has many tasks facing her. How will she organize the meeting? How can she keep the group sharp and focused on the mission of developing an appropriate marketing strategy for the Spanish-speaking community? How can she promote the exchange of well-reasoned ideas? How will the groups eventually make a decision? It is imperative that the group members buy into the decision before they leave for their own regions and districts. How will Chelsea know if she has been successful?

Think about the issues facing Chelsea as you read this chapter. We will return to this scenario at the end of the chapter and discuss some solutions.

10.1: Overview

Meetings as Forums for Problem Solving

10.1 Express the utility of meetings in business settings

We focus on the group process—the meeting—to show how groups use meetings to identify and achieve goals, share information, make decisions, and solve problems. As a functioning member of a business or professional organization, sooner or later you will have the opportunity to plan, participate in, or lead a meeting. An understanding of the basic process of communication in this context can improve your ability to contribute to meetings.

Your familiarity with meetings precedes this course. You may already participate in planning meetings, staff meetings, creative meetings, and annual meetings, which bring together groups of employees or stakeholders to share information and update them on the direction the group and your organization as a whole are taking. Typically, these meetings are scheduled regularly and have set agendas—that is, the same basic issues are discussed in every meeting. For example, production schedules and budget control might be discussed at every weekly editorial staff meeting at a publishing company, but each week the group will have new developments and information to share and learn. Annual meetings present a similar situation. The basic activities—election of officers, a state-of-the-company address, voting on various referenda, and so on—take place every year, but each year the nominees are different, the company's performance varies to some degree, and new referenda are proposed.

We focus on problem-solving meetings that have the potential to affect the organization's performance. Whether problem-solving groups are called task forces, troubleshooting teams, or strategic communication committees, their basic function is to identify and resolve specific problems by applying strong communication skills and problem-solving techniques. We structure our discussion of this process around the four components of strategic communication (situational knowledge, goal setting, communication competence, and anxiety management) to show you how to maximize your effectiveness in problem-solving meetings.

10.2: Goals Set the Agenda

10.2 Describe the role of the agenda in business meetings

An agenda is like a road map. Have you ever decided to go on a vacation and just taken off with no prior planning? If you did, you probably missed seeing a lot along the way because you did not think in advance about what you wanted to experience. You also probably wasted a lot of time. The same principle applies to meetings. A meeting that is not well planned can neglect issues that need to be resolved, waste time, and produce frustration among members. An **agenda** is a guide that specifies what is to be discussed, when, in what order, and for how long. The degree to which each of those considerations is detailed and the format in which they are presented vary widely because of differences in organizational policy and the nature of the meeting itself.

We begin by presenting a formal agenda that contains the basic components that can be adapted to suit other types of meetings. Figures 10.1A and 10.1B show two formats for agendas. A formal agenda for a meeting may contain these items:

- Roll call of participants
- Reading and approval of minutes from previous meetings
- Presentation of topics
- Requests for additional topics
- Communications to be read
- Reports of special committees
- Reports of standing committees
- Unfinished business
- New business
- Closing concerns
- Adjournment

Figure 10.1 Variations on the Formal Agenda

You may be familiar with the format of the formal agenda, but let us take a moment to clarify the purpose of each item. **Roll call** is simply an attendance check—is everyone present and ready to begin? For many groups, a certain percentage of members must be present and without this **quorum** (such as 50 percent, two-thirds, or three-fourths of the members), the meeting cannot proceed. **Reading the minutes** summarizes what took place in previous meetings of the group. If this is the first (or only) meeting, this step is omitted. Often, the leader of a group will dispense with a reading of the minutes and simply ask if anyone has additions or corrections. In cases where formal approval of minutes is required, some member must "move" that the minutes be accepted and someone else must "second the motion." After the minutes, the leader reviews the topics on the agenda to be discussed. If a group member wishes to add a topic to the list, it is done at this point, not later. Communications to be read include messages from people not present at the meeting that have to be considered during discussions. Many agendas present this information as an "overview" given at the start of a meeting.

Committee reports often form the bulk of formal meetings. **Special committees** are temporary subgroups created to look into short-term or specific problems. **Standing committees** are permanent subgroups that concentrate on long-term developments in broad areas such as budgeting, personnel, and purchasing. These committees meet on their own time and regularly report back to the complete group. In less formal meetings, individual members may report on findings or update the group on developments in a particular area.

Unfinished business and **new business** include topics that were not agreed on at earlier meetings and new issues that have to be addressed. Committees may be formed to look into these areas. In problem-solving meetings, addressing such issues takes the bulk of the meeting time. The agenda may include a "working lunch," periods of time set aside for small-group work on subparts of a problem, for training sessions, or for brainstorming possible solutions.

Closing concerns and adjournment round out the meeting, giving a summation of what has been accomplished and where the group may go next. Informal agendas may simply include a "wrap-up" or "summary" to provide closure to the meeting.

The Managers' Meeting Agenda (Figure 10.1A) shows an excerpt from a multiday conference held to plan the sales campaign of a small regional company. The Agenda for Training Session (Figure 10.1B) shows the framework for a meeting in which employees from branch offices of a large national organization meet at company headquarters to participate in training activities.

The group leader takes the agenda and fills in any details about the business that are known in advance. One section of an agenda might look like this:

> ***Reports of Standing Committees***
> Finance (M. Jackson—5 minutes)
> Suspensions and reinstatements (D. Holloway—
> 10 minutes)
> Unfinished business
> Permanent meeting location (10 minutes)

Why are time limits included on the agenda? Time limits are not always rigid boundaries that cut off discussion. Rather, they provide the group with a guide to the importance and depth of the discussion intended for specific topics.

If possible, all participants should receive a copy of the agenda before the meeting. The agenda can be mailed, emailed, or hand-delivered, or participants can pick up a copy. In this way, everyone has an opportunity to prepare for the meeting and bring whatever materials may be necessary to have a productive discussion.

The agenda serves as the framework within which the group leader organizes time and topics. But leaders are not the only contributors to a group's direction. Effective group members must consider organizational, group, and individual goals.

10.2.1: Organizational Goals

Organizational goals are set at upper levels of the organization's hierarchy and describe pathways to excellence. Groups are directly and indirectly affected by organizational goals because the ultimate purpose of groups is to solve problems that may prevent the attainment of organizational goals. To work effectively, serve the purpose of the organization, and avoid conflicts between group agendas and organizational goals, groups are wise to keep in mind the overarching goals of the organization.

10.2.2: Group Goals

Group goals serve the mission and purpose of the group itself. Often a higher authority forms a group and specifies a "charge." The charge serves as the fundamental goal of the group. For example, a chief executive officer may appoint a group to recommend a change in the distribution of wholesale products. The group's fundamental charge may be "to develop a new and more effective wholesale distribution system." Specific subgoals can then be established, such as "to develop a computerized tracking system for wholesale customers" or "to establish a new method for routing trucks to final destinations." Each of these goals may require a series of meetings in which strategies for achieving it are devised.

Groups that meet periodically without a specific charge from a higher authority develop their own goals. These goals depend on the nature of the group's tasks and the reason for its existence. For instance, ongoing groups devoted to improving on-the-job productivity may designate the general goal of "determining methods of increasing productivity." Specific subgoals such as "monitoring productivity in the social marketing task force" and "evaluating quality-control techniques" can then be set for individual meetings.

Groups may also set process goals. **Process goals** attempt to improve the working of the group itself. If, after a series of meetings, group members feel they are not working together as well as they could, they may set goals to improve their internal harmony, research skills, decision-making methods, or ability to deal with time pressures.

Because group goals may change as groups mature or as new information becomes available that affects original plans, a group must continually monitor its goals to ensure that its actions are serving the best interests of both the group and the organization.

WRITING PROMPT

Think about a group project that you worked on in one of your classes. Visualize the group members, the group meetings, and the finished project. In your opinion, what process goals could have been established to improve group harmony? What goals could have been defined to improve creativity? On the whole, do you think that having these specific goals could have helped accomplish the groups' primary goal? Why or why not?

▶
> The response entered here will appear in the performance dashboard and can be viewed by your instructor.

Submit

10.2.3: Individual Goals or Needs

Individual goals are goals or needs that group members have in addition to the group's stated goals. Your motives for joining a group may reflect an individual goal such as to meet new people at work. Some people join groups to satisfy their need for achievement. Others set goals to gain recognition, knowledge, power, information, or skills. You probably belong to some groups now for personal reasons, and it is very likely that you will be involved in some work groups for personal reasons.

The setting and maintaining of individual goals are key ingredients in group effectiveness. Group members who are unable to accomplish their personal goals are likely to be unhappy and therefore less effective. All three types of goals—organizational, group, and individual—should be considered by participants in a meeting. As Figure 10.2 shows, they can reinforce one another. Groups function most effectively when members set effective and appropriate goals of each type.

Figure 10.2 Individual, Group, and Organizational Goals
The relationship among individual, group, and organizational goals affects group performance.

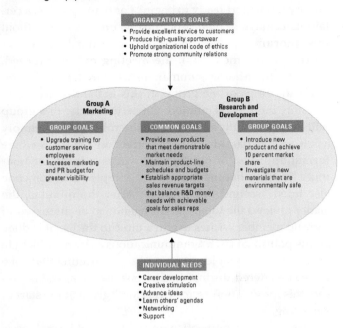

10.3: Prepare for the Meeting

10.3 Scrutinize some of the matters to attend to before holding a meeting

Proper advance planning is important for the success of a meeting. Location, participants, scheduling, and other environmental issues can affect the outcome of a meeting. Think about a meeting that took place in a very cold room. Were you eager to participate or pay attention to the discussion? More than likely your mind was on the temperature of the room, the sweater you left at your apartment, or the weather forecast for the next day. Or consider a meeting in an auditorium-style arrangement in which the leader wants full group participation. How frequently will people need to turn around to see who behind them is talking? Finally, consider meetings in which you were thirsty but there were no refreshments. All you could think about was the soft drink you were going to get afterward. Knowing the conditions of the meeting beforehand will allow you to be a much more effective planner and participant.

10.3.1: Meeting Facilities

There are several issues to consider when you are deciding where to hold a meeting. The primary concern is that the physical characteristics of the room meet the needs of the people planning to attend. Visit the facility before scheduling your first meeting there. Does the room you are considering have enough space for everyone in your group? Does the room have plenty of electrical outlets, proper storage space, adjustable lighting switches, and adjustable temperature controls? Does it have a projection system for your PowerPoint presentation? Will you need to bring your own laptop (if for no other reason than as a backup)? Are other meetings booked into the facility at the same time that yours is planned? If so, is the room soundproof so that noise from an adjacent room does not "bleed" through the walls? How far away from the room are restrooms, soft-drink machines, water fountains, and telephones? Is the room large enough to provide for whatever seating arrangement you think is best?

There are several ways to arrange a room for a meeting, and it is important that the arrangement you choose be appropriate for the type of meeting to be held (see Figure 10.3). For example, an auditorium-style arrangement is not conducive to full-room participation, and a conference setup can isolate participants from the leader.

Figure 10.3 Typical Meeting Setups

U-shaped setup

● ○ ○

An **auditorium setup** includes chairs but no tables. The chairs are lined up in straight rows with a center aisle between them. All eyes are to the front, where the leader conducts the meeting. A **classroom arrangement** uses tables and chairs. Tables are typically lined up in straight rows with a center aisle separating them. Two or three participants sit at a table. As in the auditorium setup, everyone looks straight ahead. The **U-shaped setup** is designed for full-room interaction. Tables and chairs are arranged so that participants sit adjacent to or directly across from one another. This arrangement is good for meetings that require discussion as well as presentation. The **conference arrangement** seats all members around the same table. The leader typically occupies the seat at the end. **Satellite tables** are an innovative arrangement that gives considerable room

for the leader to roam around the room while conducting a discussion. Participants sit around individual tables, and each table occupies its own independent space in the room. This setup is excellent for subgroup meetings or breakouts when participants separate into teams to work on specific problems.

If you are responsible for renting a meeting area outside your company, do not overlook the need for a clear, signed contract specifying exactly what you expect to be furnished and how much you expect to pay for meeting items. Do not assume that a projector is always available or that pitchers of water are furnished free of charge. Find out in advance, and save yourself much grief later.

AUDIOVISUAL REQUIREMENTS   If you are meeting on-site or are bringing portable equipment to an off-site meeting, your primary concern is to ensure that the audiovisual equipment you plan to use works. Testing light bulbs in slide projectors, checking for adequate paper in a flip chart, and making sure that marking pens have not dried up are routine activities.

Often you will find it most convenient to use or rent equipment provided by the facility where you will hold the meeting. Many hotels and convention centers have slide projectors, microphones, projection screens, and lighting that can be controlled from a podium. Ask yourself, "Given the requirements of this meeting, what equipment is necessary for the meeting to be effective and productive?" Items you may consider include the following:

Display easels	LCD projector
Document camera	Microphone and speakers
Extension cords and electrical adapters	Notepads and pencils
Overhead projector	Laptop computer
Flip charts and marking pens	Podium
Internet connection	Projection screen

10.3.2: Setting Rules of Order

Meetings run most smoothly when conducted according to an orderly procedure and established rules. The best-known set of rules is *Robert's Rules of Order*, which gives precise standards of parliamentary procedure to follow in specific situations.[1] For a quick primer on parliamentary procedure, consult the National Association of Parliamentarians at http://www.parliamentarians.org/procedure.php. How much you depend on rules of order for your meetings is determined by how formal the interaction is and the nature of past participation. If you have a group that is boisterous and disorderly, falling back on formal rules can be very effective for proceeding through an agenda. If, however, your group has always worked well informally, using strict rules for voting and points of order can have a chilling effect.

One major advantage of using established rules of order is that the group leader is less likely to be accused of personal bias in decision making. The leader's credibility increases when she or he states that "according to the rules, we must have a two-thirds majority to pass the amendment; because we do not, the motion fails." It is essential that rules be developed and communicated before the group begins deliberating. Everyone should know from the start what the rules are.

10.3.3: Knowing the Group

Group roles and norms, as well as tendencies toward conformity, cohesiveness, or conflict all may be at play in a meeting. When preparing for a meeting or group activity, find out who the other members of the group are and how they are likely to interact. For example, you may find that the group consists of several dominators but also includes a person known as an excellent facilitator. You can thus hope that any problems of groupthink caused by the dominators will be lessened. Collect as much information as possible about how the meeting will be conducted, what topics will be discussed, and who will be present. The more prepared you are, the greater your opportunity will be to contribute to the group.

10.3.4: Nonverbal Communication

The importance of nonverbal communication in business and professional settings also holds true for the group context. Nonverbal communication—including such concepts as proxemics, territoriality, and chronemics—plays a key role in members' levels of participation, decision-making procedures, and ability to get along. You perhaps can imagine the effects of status in the group situation ("Oh well, since she has been a member longer than me and is older and more experienced, I'd better agree with her"). Territoriality certainly affects how groups operate ("Hey, he is sitting in my spot; I really resent that and now I won't even acknowledge his comments"). Chronemics are important in group functioning as well ("At least this group always ends on time. That's one reason why I always attend").

Research has demonstrated other critical aspects of nonverbal communication during group interaction.[2] Proxemics, or more specifically, seating positions, play a powerful role in group communication. The more central the seating position in a group, the more likely the potential for influence, dominance, and participation. So, if you are looking to be more involved and to exert more influence on the group's outcome, try finding a place to sit that is in the center of things. If the table is long or rectangular, you will be perceived more as a leader if you choose one of the end seats. If you know where certain people are going to sit or notice this as you walk into the room, and you

want them to have a better chance of directing their comments to you, sit across from them. Termed the "Steinzor effect," this is the tendency of people to talk more to people directly across from them instead of to the people adjacent to or beside them.[3]

Group size has an effect on group communication as well. Larger groups have a tendency to disrupt equal participation rates among members. This "large-group" effect produces participation among only one or a few members, who are often thought of as leaders. Groups that communicate via technology (computer-mediated communication systems) are more likely to produce higher-quality ideas when they are large (nine to eighteen members) than when they are small (fewer than nine members).

10.4: Develop Critical Thinking Skills

10.4 Exhibit how to incorporate the four critical thinking skills in communication

Many skills are necessary for effective communication, participation, and problem solving in meetings. The foundation of these skills is the ability to think critically about the subject or issue under discussion. Doing so allows group members to formulate and express ideas that move the group toward achieving its goals. In this section, we discuss the basic skills of critical thinking—analysis, reasoning, interpretation, and evaluation—and how to incorporate them into your communication.

10.4.1: Analysis

Analysis is the process of tearing apart an issue and examining its component parts to see how they relate to the whole. This skill is particularly important when group members are exploring the characteristics of a problem. To develop strong analytic skills for use in a group meeting, participants must exhibit the following:

- Patience with alternative viewpoints and methods
- Ability to define terms clearly and willingness to demand that other participants do the same
- A broad, open-minded approach to the problem
- A search for commonalities and differences
- A comparison and contrast of the problem under discussion with other problems that have been previously discussed
- A summary of what the group has discussed up to a certain point

As you can see from this list, group members must demonstrate a wide range of competencies for effective group communication, including the ability to hear a number of competing viewpoints. This is healthy for decision making. Furthermore, it is essential that group members stay on track with a focused purpose so as to reduce inefficiency. Comparing and contrasting viewpoints are two of the most important communication behaviors in a group context. And when group members summarize previous statements, they have an easier time recognizing where they have been and where they hope to go.

10.4.2: Reasoning

Reasoning is the ability to pull various data together and draw sound conclusions from them. There are two broad categories of reasoning: deductive and inductive. **Deductive reasoning** moves from general truths to specific conclusions. The most popular form of deductive reasoning is the **syllogism,** a three-part argument containing a general truth, a related claim, and a conclusion. A famous example is "All men are mortal; Socrates is a man; therefore, Socrates is mortal."

You can use deductive reasoning when others make general statements in a meeting. By relating general truths to specific experiences, you can draw valid conclusions. For instance, consider the following dialogue in a meeting of corporate managers:

> DAVE: Our company reputation is built on keeping our regular customers happy.
>
> AMANDA: The last reports showed customer complaints are rising. They're displeased with our service, from what I hear.
>
> CHRIS: (drawing conclusion) I think we should put new product development on the back burner until we address current customer complaints with better service.

Chris listened to two general premises, then drew a convincing conclusion based on what had been presented in the first two premises.

Inductive reasoning moves from specific statements to general conclusions. There are four forms of inductive reasoning that you can use in a group meeting: example, sign, comparative, and causal.

EXAMPLE REASONING   Reasoning by example is the most popular form of inductive reasoning. You will probably notice instances of it during most people's communication, whether in group, interpersonal, or public speaking situations. **Example reasoning** involves collecting specific cases and then making a generalization based on them. For example, if a staff member concludes that a temporary employee is needed because several employees are home sick with the flu, the conclusion is based on example. Effective group communication frequently depends on the ability to persuade group members to adopt a common point of view. Because it is based on true, observable situations, the conclusion is very persuasive.

The best way to argue *against* this kind of reasoning (if you *disagree* with the conclusion being expressed) is to show that the examples cited are not typical, representative, or timely. If a flaw can be found in the examples, the resulting generalization will also be flawed. For example, in response to the conclusion that a temporary employee is needed because of excessive employee absences, you could point out that the flu epidemic is an unusual circumstance and that no temporary employee has been needed in similar circumstances in the past. As this response shows, reasoning from examples is not the only way of looking at a problem.

SIGN REASONING   **Sign reasoning** involves drawing conclusions from simple observations. Consider how often you use sign reasoning. You wake up in the morning, pull up the window shades, see heavy clouds, and assume that it will rain. You hear the bell clanging from the fire station and suppose that there is a fire somewhere. You pass a government building with the flag at half-mast and conclude that an important person has died. These are signs that lead to conclusions.

Those examples point out the drawback of sign reasoning: it encourages **hasty generalizations**—conclusions based on small or nonrepresentative samples of data. Basing your conclusions on a single observation, you have no way of knowing whether the bell is a false alarm or the worker who raises and lowers the flag was called inside to take a telephone call in mid-job. You cannot safely assume that a sign has only one meaning (the one you are thinking of) that applies in all cases. Your perceptions have a strong influence on how you use sign reasoning in communication. It is important to remember that your view of the world may be different from the views of others and that the assumptions underlying sign reasoning can easily communicate misunderstanding, bias, or stereotypes detrimental to effective group interaction.

COMPARATIVE REASONING   **Comparative reasoning** occurs when a participant in a meeting pulls together two examples and reasons that what is true in the first case must be true in the second. Consider the following example. Rosa, a plant safety supervisor at Delmore Co., remarks, "Over at Bennzoil, a six-week course in new safety techniques cut work accidents more than 17 percent in just one year. We really need a program like that here. We could probably cut our accident rate 25 percent."

Rosa is reasoning by comparison. After comparing safety measures at Bennzoil and Delmore, she concludes that what worked at Bennzoil can work at her firm as well. She assumes that the two firms are similar enough to make the comparison valid. If, however, the two firms are not similar, or if Rosa's conclusion is based on inaccurate information, the comparison is *fallacious*, or unsound.

If you think that fallacious reasoning is being introduced in a group discussion, you will have to disconnect the two cases being compared and demonstrate the major differences that invalidate the comparison. For example, in response to Rosa's position, Loretta, an engineer, says, "I know someone at Bennzoil. He told me their original accident rate was so high that even with a 17 percent reduction, they still have more accidents than we do. We don't need a program like that because we don't have a problem like theirs."

Comparative reasoning is important to communication because it works to clarify the issue under discussion. Clear understanding by all group members is essential for sound decision making.

CAUSAL REASONING Causal reasoning tries to answer the question "Why did that happen?" When using causal reasoning, you assert that one factor is strong enough to produce an effect in another factor. If you have had several unsuccessful job interviews, for example, you may purchase a conservative or professional-looking outfit to improve your appearance when you interview for jobs.

During group meetings in businesses and professional organizations, the search for causes takes up a considerable amount of time and communication effort. Consider the following meeting in which several military officers are discussing low levels of morale in their division:

> LT. COFFEY: The enlistees hardly ever get a chance to get out of here. They need some time away from the same old routine.
>
> CAPT. JOHNSON: Maybe. But I think that what's really bothering them is the poor quality of food they get here.

Both Johnson and Coffey assert causes for low morale. But because the officers are engaged in a discussion, their ideas are open for rebuttal, which comes quickly from two others.

> LT. BETTS: That's rubbish. You spend the money to make elaborate meals for them, and they might feel better for about five minutes. They won't work one bit harder, and you know it.
>
> CAPT. GONZALEZ: Yeah, and we're really talking about the wrong stuff here anyway. Lack of off-base activity and bad food may hurt morale, but the real cause of the problem includes lack of recognition, lack of pride, and lack of motivation.

The example shows two ways to counter causal reasoning. Lieutenant Betts claims that Captain Johnson has identified the wrong cause of low morale—food could not possibly have that much effect. Captain Gonzalez argues that there are multiple causes, not just one cause, of the problem. Strong communicators can evaluate and discuss multiple causes without losing sight of the need for a solution. A group that becomes enmeshed in a search for causes may lose sight of its original goals. For this reason, group members need the ability to interpret causes.

10.4.3: Interpretation

Interpretation is an extension of causal reasoning in which you ask not only "Why did that happen?" but also "What does it mean?" Simply listening to facts, arguments, data, or opinions in a group meeting will not improve your decision-making ability. You must be able to take all this information, interpret it, and use it to draw valid conclusions.

What do you do when you interpret information? In essence, you are saying, "What this means is. . . ." When you interpret, you apply your own knowledge and experience to the data to figure out what they mean, especially for other group members. Persuasive and effective interpretations typically stress the relevance, importance, or impact of data on the group and clarify information for the group. The key to interpreting information for others is to have a clear understanding of why the data look as they do. This understanding allows you to communicate a strategy for change.

In a group sales meeting, Maria, a manager, wants to make sure that all the sales representatives understand what three consecutive months of downward numbers mean to them and to the business:

> MARIA: Bill, please put the graph of our three-month sales plan and results up on the board. [He does.] As you see, we were down 3 percent in June, 4 percent in July, and 6 percent in August.
>
> TIM: Doesn't look too good.
>
> MARIA: No, it doesn't. These figures mean that we have fallen short of our goals for three consecutive months. I believe the shortfalls result from slow sales in our new mall outlets. We need to improve our relationships with the mall vendors.

How many of the salespeople would have been able to draw that conclusion without Mary's interpretation? Furthermore, would the numbers have meant much to them without this input? Probably not. Interpretations are very important because they tie information and ideas together, helping to create shared meaning for group members.

10.4.4: Evaluation

Evaluation means making judgments about information or data. In most cases, judgments are made in categories such as positive/negative, favorable/unfavorable, valuable/worthless, workable/unworkable, expensive/cheap, or good/bad. Of course, evaluations are rarely clear-cut. People usually make evaluations in degrees, using qualifiers such as *fairly, moderately, basically, ordinarily,* and *partially*.

Some scholars advocate avoiding evaluation in group situations whenever possible. They believe that placing a value label on another person's contribution to a group produces hurt feelings and disharmony in the group and undermines the group's ability to communicate freely and openly. We believe, however, that before casting a vote or conforming to a group consensus, a group member must evaluate the information that has been presented.

Even if you try to avoid evaluation, you are likely to be asked for your opinions on ideas or proposals during meetings. Participants in a group expect you to assess information you have heard. If evaluation is an inevitable part of individual involvement in group decision making, then why not share your evaluation with all the participants? Evaluations are an important part of feedback in meetings, and feedback is essential to the group's success.

10.5: Competence in Problem Solving

10.5 Describe the three basic qualities necessary for effective problem solving

In addition to improving communication, critical thinking allows problem-solving and decision-making meetings to succeed. **Problem solving** involves defining a problem and generating solutions. Problem-solving groups are very common in organizations; they exist in more than 90 percent of the Fortune 500 companies.[4] Entire volumes have discussed the advantages and disadvantages of various problem-solving techniques. These techniques have much to offer groups that meet to make decisions in response to organizational and group goals. Decision-making meetings allow group members to decide on a course of action to incorporate the proposed solution.

Three qualities are necessary for competent problem solving:[5]

⊗ **Variety**

When group members' perspectives differ, many aspects of the problem can be suggested and discussed.

⊗ **Simplicity**

Ideas generated during group deliberations should be arranged logically and checked for repetition and relevance.

⊗ **Usefulness**

Because ideas have varying degrees of usefulness to the group, members must be able to focus their energies on ideas that are most likely to result in the right decision.

Communication competence is vital to ensure that group members are able to understand the problem and share their ideas with one another appropriately and effectively.

Selecting the most appropriate problem-solving technique and then adhering to its format enable groups to recommend effective decisions. Popular and proven problem-solving methods include reflective thinking, the nominal group technique, and the Delphi technique. After surveying each of them, we present options for decision making.

10.5.1: Reflective Thinking

Reflective thinking is a five-step process whose success depends on each group member's willingness to participate. A major advantage of the reflective thinking technique is its efficiency. Reflective thinking provides a clear and concise road map that can save both time and energy; it prevents a group from rambling and floundering about with a problem.

STEP 1: INTRODUCE THE PROBLEM Group members state their perceptions of the problem and list the general goals the group is striving to achieve. The statements should be brief. At this point, no discussion, questions, or debate should be allowed. At the conclusion of step 1, the group knows the dimensions of the problem as perceived by the members. A variety of perspectives are essential in this stage.

STEP 2: DEFINE AND ANALYZE THE PROBLEM Members try to agree on the problem and objectives. In this step, the group discusses qualities, characteristics, and elements of the problem. The leader quashes any attempt to talk about solutions. Members may present personal philosophies, evidence, opinions, statistics, or other relevant information, and they may compare and contrast the present problem with any related problems. Group members probe and challenge one another's perceptions of the problem.

The following substeps can increase the group's ability to define the problem:[6]

⊗ **Problem Recognition**

Problem recognition involves clarifying the extent of the problem, presenting evidence supporting the claims, and even challenging the problem's existence.

⊗ **Development of the Problem Statement**

Development of the problem statement identifies those who have a stake in the problem, specifies values or goals associated with the problem, elicits various viewpoints on and attitudes toward the problem, and proposes a workable definition of the problem.

Exploration

Exploration illuminates possible directions for the solution phase by breaking the problem into small parts for subsequent analysis, identifying related or associated problems, and suggesting possible causes for the problem's existence.

ⓧ **Internal Summary**

Internal summary builds consensus before moving to the next step. The leader may say, "We have decided what the problem is and what are related issues and probable causes."

As you can see, critical thinking skills play a vital role in defining the problem. When the problem has been identified, defined, and analyzed, it is time to move to step 3.

STEP 3: ESTABLISH CRITERIA   The group decides what elements the solution to the problem should include. These criteria will be used later in the discussion to evaluate potential solutions. For example, if you and your friends are deciding how to spend a Saturday night, and there are several activities to choose from, establishing criteria can help you to decide which activity is best for the group. One person may suggest that money is a factor, thereby establishing the criterion "Whatever we do, it can't cost more than $10 per person." Another may have to get up early the next morning, thereby establishing the criterion "We have to be back at my place by 12:30 A.M. at the latest." Still another may request that the activity be something new—for example, "Let's not go to a movie; we always do that." These criteria can help your group narrow the options and make the best decision for all concerned.

The criteria must be relevant to the problem at hand. The following guidelines can ensure the choice of relevant criteria:

ⓧ **Overall Strength**

The criteria address the effectiveness and efficiency of proposed solutions, including the extent of the solution, possible future consequences, and realistic chances of carrying out the plan.

ⓧ **Resources**

The criteria assess the time, money, effort, or employee morale necessary to implement each possible solution.

ⓧ **Ethics**

Ethical criteria prevent possible infringements on the rights of other people or organizations. These criteria should address the legality, morality, honesty, and decency of each possible solution. Ethical criteria may focus on the employees of the organization ("Eliminating all vacation time for employees is simply not acceptable"), on other organizations ("We can't tell our competition we are going out of business when we are not"), on the environment ("Dumping waste into the river is cheap but will have serious consequences for the river ecosystem"), or on the community ("Building an adjacent plant would displace a lot of residents"). Ethical criteria should address each of the groups affected by the solution.

The best solutions are those that suit the criteria established in step 3. Keep in mind that criteria must be established before the group tries to come up with solutions. Doing so keeps group members from changing their minds about what they are trying to accomplish during the course of the meeting.

Establishing and adhering to criteria are essential for effective decision making and save the group countless hours of directionless deliberation. In sum, group members should probe and challenge one another to ensure they have worthy criteria against which to judge a solution. Selecting a solution will then be much easier.

STEP 4: GENERATE POSSIBLE SOLUTIONS   In this step, often referred to as brainstorming, group members present logical and workable solutions to the problem. The goal is to generate a list of creative solutions but not to evaluate their worth. No solution is dismissed or even criticized at this stage. Although some ideas may seem bizarre when first presented, they can be modified to be effective and ingenious. Before moving to the next step, the leader reviews the list of possible solutions to make sure that all have been recorded correctly and to ensure that they do not repeat each other.

STEP 5: EVALUATE POSSIBLE SOLUTIONS   Using the criteria established in step 3, group members discuss the worth of each of the solutions generated in step 4. The leader introduces each proposed solution and asks the group to evaluate it by the criteria agreed on in step 3. The goal of this step is for the group to make a final decision by selecting the most viable solution—the one that best satisfies the criteria.

What if more than one proposed solution meets all the criteria, or what if no solution can meet all the criteria? In the first instance, the group must decide whether the two solutions are mutually exclusive. If they are not, then the group may implement both. In the second instance, the group selects the solution that fulfills the most criteria. Before adjourning the meeting, moving on to another problem, or continuing to another point on the agenda, the leader restates the problem and the solution so that all group members understand them.

Reflective thinking is a powerful tool for finding solutions to particular problems. The Strategic Skills example on the next page shows how reflective thinking works. The dialogue presented is typical of the discussion in problem-solving meetings. Although real-world discussions don't always progress to a mutually agreeable conclusion so easily, the example shows how reflective thinking can be effective. After working through the example, you can understand the importance of taking each step in its proper order and systematically working through all five steps.

Problem Solving on the Job

Strategic Skills

The scene is a meeting to discuss how restaurant owners can be persuaded to increase the size of the soft drinks they offer in their restaurants. The group includes some of the top sales managers in the division, and the meeting is led by a vice president (VP). To understand this example, you need to know that the term *cup* refers to the size of the soft drinks sold in fast-food restaurants. The profits for a restaurant increase when large cup sizes are sold. Follow how, as the meeting progresses, group members bring up specific aspects of the problem as they move toward possible solutions, and how the VP/group leader summarizes succinctly so that an overall solution is reached.

GOAL: *To convince food-service operators to increase the size of their fountain drinks.*

PROBLEM: *Operators do not want to sell large drinks.*

⊗ Introduce the Problem

VP: Let's start off by having each of you give a brief summary of the problem as you see it. Why are restaurants reluctant to increase their drink sizes?

Linda: Operators don't understand that larger sizes are more profitable.

Robert: Operators are afraid consumers won't buy the larger drinks.

Ingrid: Large drinks jeopardize our other promotions.

Jack: We just don't have the marketing materials we need to sell large drinks.

⊗ Define and Analyze the Problem

VP: Now that we've seen everyone's perception of the problem, let's dig into these ideas and find out exactly what we're trying to solve here. I want you to elaborate on what you've just said. Everyone should feel free to disagree, ask questions, add comments or experiences, or say whatever. I want to make sure we really know what we're dealing with, so let's analyze it in detail. Just as a springboard for discussion, Linda, let's start with your observation that the operators don't understand our strategy very well.

Linda: Operators don't really understand why selling large sizes helps their business. We need to educate them about what kind of a gold mine they're sitting on.

Robert: I think they're just scared to put a large cup in front of the consumer. They're afraid it won't sell.

Ingrid: I think we've made our free refill promotion so successful that we can't sell the big cup idea. No one will want to offer refills on forty-four-ounce cups. If they can't offer the large-size cup and the refill, they're going to stick with what's worked in the past—the refill.

Jack: Our promotional materials are really good on the forty-four-ounce cup, but they don't show the benefits of increasing the other drink sizes as well. Our salespeople don't have prepackaged information that they can use to push the larger drink sizes.

VP: So, if I could try to summarize what we've said here the last few minutes, it seems that although our sales force has been very effective in selling the forty-four-ounce cup, we have not been pushing the complete set of large cup sizes. We do not have promotional brochures outlining the advantages of the larger cup sizes, and restaurant owners need to be told about them. We've also said that many operators see refill promotions and large cup sizes as a contradiction.

⊗ Establish Criteria

VP: OK, we've got a handle on the problem! Before we start to look for specific solutions, let's try to figure out what we want the solution to do. Remember, we will judge our suggested solutions by these criteria, so make sure you consider effectiveness, resources, and ethical questions when devising them! I'll be listing them on a flip chart as we go.

Linda: I think the solution has to include a written explanation of why the large sizes are better. Operators will trust us if we put it in writing.

Robert: We need to have the solution ready as soon as possible.

Ingrid: The solution must consider the customers. We can't expect operators to sell large drinks if customers end up getting less for their money.

Jack: The solution has to include some kind of financial bonus that equals the selling power of free refills.

VP: So, we've decided on criteria that our solution has to meet: the solution has to include written material that the field sales force can use with the trade; it has to be efficiently implemented; it has to include some sort of financial incentive for the food-service operator; and it has to be acceptable to consumers.

⊗ Generate Possible Solutions

VP: Now, let's think of as many possible solutions as we can. We are not going to evaluate any of these right now; I'll just make a list as you call them out. Now, it's OK to ask a question for clarification or to get more information, but we won't challenge or debate any of these solutions while they are being given. I'll list these for us.

Linda: Let's talk to marketing about putting together a brochure for our field sales force that begins with information about the profitability of soft drinks, moves to our brand, and then shows the value of increasing the drink cup sizes for the operator.

Jack: I think we should offer a free tank of syrup to any operator who goes to the large cup sizes and stays with them for three months.

Robert: We could just work with our bottlers in phasing out small cups. If the small cups weren't made, the restaurants couldn't sell them!

Ingrid: We can use a coupon incentive to get operators to try the large cup sizes.

VP: So, these are the solutions we've come up with. Anything else? OK, let's move on to evaluating these solutions.

⊗ Evaluate Possible Solutions

VP: Now we'll take the solutions in this chart one by one and match them against our criteria. We'll rule out or modify any solution that doesn't match up and see what happens. OK, our first solution was to have a brochure made focused on upgraded cup sizes. Now, does this satisfy our requirement for written material? Yes! Does it touch on some kind of financial incentive for the operator? No, but we might be able to modify it. [Matching of solutions to criteria continues.]

VP: So, as a result of this discussion, we've decided to produce a marketing brochure that our sales force can use to show operators why they should increase their cup sizes. The brochure will include an incentive coupon for a free tank of syrup if operators increase their cup sizes for a minimum of three months. The solution meets our criteria of providing written information and financial incentive to operators, and because consumers can still purchase a twenty-four-ounce drink at the same price they have always paid for it, we are not proposing anything unacceptable to them.

10.5.2: Nominal Group Technique

The **nominal group technique (NGT)** allows groups to discuss problems and solutions in a relatively structured setting. This technique is especially useful in newly formed groups and in groups with large differences in status and communication dominance among members. NGT has five steps: preparation, silent generation of ideas, round-robin recording of ideas, discussion, and voting.

PREPARATION The group leader or facilitator prepares a question for discussion. The question must be succinct and simple to understand and cover only one topic. Here is an example of a poor question: "What are our safety problems and objectives, and what specific projects and programs can we undertake to ensure greater safety and efficiency in our plant?" The question is vague and wordy and contains at least three different topics. A far better question clearly addresses one issue: "What objectives must our plant safety program accomplish?"

Before the meeting starts, the facilitator gathers flip charts on which to record members' responses, tape to attach the charts to the wall, and index cards on which participants can write ideas. At the outset of the meeting, the facilitator explains the subsequent four-step process and emphasizes the meeting's importance for the group and organization.

SILENT GENERATION OF IDEAS After the question is posed and understood by all participants, the leader announces a specific period of time in which the group members may write down ideas related to the question. These ideas are best stated as phrases or brief sentences. The time period should be restricted to four to eight minutes.[7] A short time period limits the number of items that the participants produce so that the group will be able to manage all or most of them. During this time, participants work independently and silently. Group members should be encouraged by their leaders to write down and expand upon their thoughts to the question posed. They should keep this process individualistic and quiet, rather than trying to gauge other opinions or promote a dialogue, which will come later.[8]

ROUND-ROBIN RECORDING The leader calls on each participant and asks for one idea. The leader writes each contribution on a flip chart as it is given. No discussion or elaboration is allowed. The leader then moves to another member and takes an idea, moves to another, moves to another, and so on until all ideas written by the participants have been recorded. As a page of the flip chart is filled, the leader tapes it to the wall, where it is visible to all participants. To save time, the leader asks participants not to contribute any ideas that have already been recorded. Each idea is numbered to simplify voting on the ideas.

DISCUSSION This step clarifies any confusion among group members about ideas. The leader reads each idea and invites comments and questions. The leader encourages members to discuss any items they wish, not simply those they contributed to the group. No voting, expression of opinion, or other type of debate takes place at this point.

VOTING In the final step, group members make decisions about the ideas that have been generated. The leader distributes five index cards to each participant. Each participant reviews the list, selects what he or she thinks are the five best ideas, and writes those numbers in the center of the cards (one number per card). The participant then ranks the five ideas by placing a number from one to five in the upper right-hand corner of the card, with five being the highest rating and one the lowest. When the participants have finished, the leader collects the cards and assembles a tally in front of the group. Figure 10.4 shows the results of applying the nominal group technique to the fountain-drink problem presented in section 10.5.1.

Figure 10.4 NGT in Progress

A flip chart shows the nominal group technique in progress. Each group member has considered the list of ideas on the left and ranked each one on a separate card. The completed tally for each idea is shown on the right. Idea 2 emerges as the highest-ranked idea.

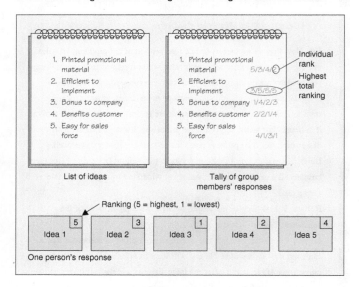

In many cases, a clear winning idea emerges. In others, a dead heat between ideas requires the group to rank the tied alternatives.

10.5.3: Delphi Technique

The **Delphi technique** uses questionnaires to collect opinions and judgments from experts, who usually remain anonymous. Typically, questionnaires are sent by mail, although they can be distributed via the Internet by means of teleconferences. The Delphi technique is not a survey or a one-time poll. The questionnaire is repeated over several rounds to collect progressively more specific information. The results from one round of questions dictate the questions for the next round. You would select this method of decision making in circumstances in which subjective judgments are desirable, face-to-face exchange is not possible because of time or cost restraints, or participants disagree to the extent that anonymity must be ensured to achieve results.

The Delphi technique includes four steps:

1. Deciding to administer a questionnaire and selecting a group to respond
2. Formulating the questions and producing the questionnaire
3. Noting a deadline date for return of the questionnaires
4. Receiving and analyzing the questionnaires.

When using this technique, you must take into consideration several matters. The people to whom you address the questionnaire must be experts. To maximize response rates, you should include a personalized cover letter (or, in the case of a teleconference, personalized instructions), guarantee anonymity, and promise to provide all respondents with a copy of the results.

Keep the questionnaire brief and to the point. It is far better to increase the number of Delphi rounds than to complicate the questionnaire. The questionnaire will be easier to respond to if it includes closed questions (such as true/false and multiple choice) rather than open questions that require the respondents to write answers. Anticipate approximately a ten-week time frame for the process to be completed.

Here is an example of the Delphi technique in action.

⊗ Example:

The personnel department of a large company wanted to improve its minority recruiting, so it surveyed personnel directors from similar-sized corporations throughout a three-state region for ideas. The first-round question posed by the Delphi technique was "What problems inhibit recruitment in large corporations?" Based on the results of the first questionnaire, the second-round questionnaire asked respondents to rank the top five problems and invited them to list others. Finally, based on those results, the third round solicited solutions for the problems. The outcome of the study allowed the firm to see which problems it had in common with other firms and to devise means to correct those problems. The results of the study were sent to all personnel directors who participated.

10.5.4: Decision-Making Options

There are many ways in which groups can engage in decision making. The entire reason they engage in that process,

however, is to produce a result or a final decision. Two techniques that leaders can use to bring about effective decisions are consensus and voting.

CONSENSUS **Consensus** is unanimous agreement among group members concerning a particular decision. Reaching consensus is the goal of many decision-making groups. Most reach consensus through the correct application of issue-specific conflict. Proper conflict management permits participants to debate, test ideas, question evidence, and so on. In groups in which conflict is used properly, consensus can be reached because all participants are testing ideas in a systematic manner. Conflict as a means for discussion allows members to resolve their differences by identifying the single best solution to a given problem.

The major advantage of achieving consensus is that all group members leave the meeting committed to the same outcome. This is not true of decision-making methods that rely primarily on voting. In many cases in which voting is employed, members remain committed to the positions that they supported in the discussion but that the group voted down. As a result, they are uncommitted to the decision that was made, and they are resentful toward the group and the solution.

How do you achieve consensus in a group discussion? Several rules are useful:

1. Drop your personal position when it is shown to be unworkable or illogical.
2. Maintain an open mind concerning conflict and differences of opinion. Remember that conflict is a means by which the group can achieve its goals. If the group does not argue and exhibit conflict, why does it need to meet in the first place?
3. Unless pressed for time, do not substitute majority votes, trading, compromising, or averaging for reaching a consensus decision. Continue to work through the problem until all members agree with and are committed to a solution.
4. When discussion reaches a stalemate, try to identify issues that are agreeable to all members present so as to isolate issues about which there is disagreement. This is the *most-common-denominator rule*. Participants have to know on what issues opinions are divided; otherwise, arguments occur on several different issues at once.

VOTING One of the most frequently used methods of resolving problems is voting. In most cases, voting imposes the will of the majority. Unlike consensus, voting forces a decision on some of the participants. The risk of having group members uncommitted to a decision and holding a negative attitude toward the group and the

Voting in meetings is one of the oldest forms of democracy. Decision making by voting still remains the most common forms of participation in organizations who entrust power in its members.

SOURCE: Andrey Popov/Shutterstock

decision is, in our opinion, not desirable, and we urge that this method be avoided if at all possible. Nevertheless, there are two circumstances in which voting is useful: (1) if the group is under time constraints that do not allow the group to proceed through a normal discussion and reach consensus and (2) if the group is too large to hold a consensus discussion.

If at all possible, use voting to narrow options on which a consensus decision can be reached. For example, suppose that a group has five mutually exclusive solutions that all seem reasonable and workable and that the size of the group and time constraints prevent the group from working through the proposed solution in a consensus-building fashion. The group can take a vote on each option and determine which two of the five the majority of the members seems to favor. Having narrowed the solutions down to two, the group can then hold a consensus discussion and work through to a single desired option. Notice that when the members finish this type of discussion, they have actively participated in the decision-making process and will be committed to the decision reached.

Each of the different problem-solving methods discussed here has its own merits, depending on the situation. Table 10.1 summarizes the techniques and suggests when to use them.

Table 10.1 Choosing a Problem-Solving Method

Problem-Solving Method	Essential Characteristics	Reasons to Use
Reflective thinking	• Group members not necessarily experts • Face-to-face interaction valued and encouraged • Opportunity to clarify issues in person	• Straightforward process for complex problems • Develops cohesion and productive advocacy • Gives members a sense of ownership of solution
Nominal group technique	• Ideas generated silently • Repetitive, round-robin development of ideas • Potential solutions rank-ordered	• Effective with new groups • Useful if members have ample time to prepare for group problem • Useful if members perceive excessive risk or feel threatened
Delphi technique	• Progressive, repetitive process • Anonymous respondents/members • Participants experts in subject matter	• Opinionated, subjective judgments desired • Face-to-face interaction not possible (distance) • Useful if participants hold strong, disagreeable viewpoints that may lead to unproductive conflict

Hide All Cells   Show All Cells

Ethics When Working Alone

Ethical Issues

It can be difficult to maintain ethical behavior in businesses and the professions when individuals work alone on projects. At times their thinking can become focused on issues such as getting results or solving problems. Sometimes this single-minded purpose can lead to less-than-ethical decisions. When people work together in teams, there is a greater opportunity to challenge assumptions that are formed by individuals. Issues that border on unethical thinking and behavior can be brought out into the open through reflective thinking, reasoning, and devil's advocacy. Individuals working alone should strive to get feedback from others. Meetings provide excellent opportunities to ensure ethical communication during the problem-solving process.

WRITING PROMPT

Assume you work for the bursar's office at your school. You are a member of a group that was formed to address complaints made by students who were billed twice for the same semester. What are the organizational goals and the group goals? Which problem-solving technique would you suggest? Why?

 The response entered here will appear in the performance dashboard and can be viewed by your instructor.

Submit

10.6: Manage Anxiety in Meetings

10.6 Identify some of the causes of anxiety in a meeting

There are several causes of anxiety in meeting situations. In some instances, the meeting is not an opportunity for open discussion but rather a closed forum in which powerful members monopolize communication or coerce others into agreement on issues. If you have low status in the group or simply are uncomfortable with an authoritarian style, such a meeting may upset you and result in communication anxiety. To address your nervousness, you can suggest that the group take a break from the discussion and allow everyone a turn to summarize the group's progress up to that point. In this way, others who may also be apprehensive will gain mutual support.

Another cause of anxiety is not knowing the other participants. If you are a newcomer and all the other participants know one another, you may feel shy, anxious, and nervous about speaking up or stating a position, and it may be difficult to become friendly with group members before the initial meeting of the group. Once you know people's names and positions in the organization, however, you will have some basic information with which to work. By approaching the relationship with the goal of improving group communication as well as lessening your own anxiety, you will be able to shift the focus from yourself and your nervousness and concentrate on becoming comfortable with group members.

In companies that have diverse work forces—people of many different educational or cultural backgrounds or varied ages—differences in communication styles may cause apprehension in a group meeting. Many companies, for example, cite instances in which men ignored a woman's input but accepted the same suggestion for discussion when it was made by a man. Conflicting cultural norms pertaining to boastfulness, dominance, or even use of nonverbal gestures such as touching, eye contact, or facial expressions may make group meetings anxiety-producing events if you fail to prepare for such differences by becoming familiar with different norms and styles.

Finally, meetings held to resolve a group conflict or to mediate serious arguments can cause apprehension because of the sensitivity of issues involved.

10.7: Evaluate Group Effectiveness

10.7 Evaluate group effectiveness as preparation for the future

No matter how successful, productive, or effective modern business and professional organizations are, they are rarely satisfied. Unless there is a strong and clearly articulated vision for the future, today's successes are tomorrow's busts. One key method that organizations use to prepare for the future is evaluating the present. To define what we mean by evaluation, we must contrast it with description. Description focuses on what a group or person is doing; evaluation focuses on how well the group or person is performing the task. Evaluation requires a judgment or an assessment.

As John Brilhart noted, "Unless practice is constantly evaluated, it may result in bad habits. The means to learning is practice with analysis and evaluation leading to change in future discussions."[9] Therefore, you must monitor and evaluate the effectiveness of the groups in which you participate if you intend to join the future.

Many students of group communication have devised categories, rating forms, evaluation instruments, and questionnaires to assess the strengths of different units. In this section, we discuss the dimensions of group evaluations and techniques for conducting them successfully.

PRACTICING BUSINESS COMMUNICATION

Creative Communication Network

Creative Communication Network (CCN) is a business-consulting company based in Dallas, Texas, that provides informative, dynamic, and entertaining presentations and workshops. Although they create customized performance solutions for small businesses seeking to increase productivity and profitability, CCN specializes in working with large corporations and associations to assess and improve competency, teamwork, and communication.

CCN helps organizations by facilitating problem-solving meetings and improving group processes and procedures for departments and divisions. Here we describe three types of CCN meetings: two types that it facilitates for other organizations and one type that it conducts for its own organization.

⊗ Process Mapping

In one client organization, CCN facilitated a meeting for human resources managers to design a procedure for placing an employee on a leave of absence. The CCN facilitators used a method called **process mapping**. In process mapping, facilitators work with participants to design a linear, step-by-step, start-to-finish procedure. During such a meeting, the facilitators draw the design on flip charts posted on the walls around the room. These posters are then used to create the final product, which is typically a flowchart outlining the process discussed.

In general, a facilitator's role in a meeting is to establish ground rules, obtain agreement on the agenda, regulate interaction among the participants, ensure that the process moves forward on schedule, challenge participants with probing questions, provide summaries at key points, and encourage participants to explore differences of opinion.

The facilitators began the human resource managers' meeting by obtaining agreement on the final box: "the employee is on leave of absence." They then moved back to the beginning, eliciting each step in the process from the participants. Not all the steps followed a linear sequence: some occurred simultaneously, and the facilitators used special symbols to indicate them.

In such meetings, the facilitators often divide participants into small breakout groups so they can work on issues in depth. These groups then return to the general session to report and receive feedback from everyone. Before the process is complete, all participants go through the steps outlined in the charts. On an individual basis they (1) place sticky notes where they have questions; (2) play devil's advocate to test the process by asking, "Why would this work?" and "What are we missing?"; and (3) work through a recent actual case to see if the procedure they have designed works.

⊗ Visioning

CCN also facilitates strategic planning for organizations. In these situations, it leads meeting participants through the process of establishing their mission, vision, goals, and objectives. In one session for the officials of a suburban city council, CCN facilitated a "rocks-in-the-road" session to explore potential barriers to their objectives and to design preventive action and contingency plans.

⊗ Corporate Strategizing

The officers of CCN hold an annual meeting to plan their own business for the upcoming year. At that meeting, they discuss issues such as budgets, marketing plans to attract clients, maintenance plans for existing clients, attendance at professional development conferences, capital expenditures, and plans to develop and revise new training and development materials for the business. During the meeting, the participants brainstorm ideas, explore options, and resolve differences in viewpoints about how to allocate resources. They conduct this meeting at an off-site location in a retreat format and then print the finished product in a booklet.

Process mapping, visioning, and corporate strategizing are basic meeting types that are integral to the business of CCN. Not only do they allow CCN to help its clients create workable performance solutions, but they also enhance the corporate environment of the organization itself.

You can visit Creative Communication Network online at http://www.creativecommnet.com.

WRITING PROMPT

What characteristics might a CCN facilitator need to successfully consult with a range of clients or audiences? It's clear that specific techniques such as process mapping and breakout group discussions help the facilitators do their jobs. Would you modify the techniques for a smaller group with a specific goal as opposed to a company with broader strategic planning needs and, if so, how?

 The response entered here will appear in the performance dashboard and can be viewed by your instructor.

Submit

10.7.1: Dimensions of Group Evaluation

Albert Kowitz and Thomas Knutson divided group evaluation into three dimensions: informational, procedural, and interpersonal.[10]

INFORMATIONAL According to Kowitz and Knutson, the **informational** dimension is concerned with the task that the group is working on. Evaluation of that task can be broken down into several components. One is whether the task before the group lends itself to discussion. If it does not, the group may have to expand the scope and nature of its topic. If the task is suitable for discussion, a second component presents itself: How prepared is the group for discussion? Was needed research or necessary advance planning done by the members before the meeting? Is there a need to get more information before the group can make an adequate decision?

A third component is how well the group "tears apart" the problem. Analysis depends on successfully reducing an issue to its component parts. Is there evidence of high-quality information giving, opinion giving, evaluation and criticism, elaboration and integration? Note that evaluation and criticism are extremely important to the success of the group. The group meets to test ideas. If there is early agreement and signs that certain participants are reluctant to express reservations, the meeting is headed toward groupthink. Does anyone say, "Let me play devil's advocate for a moment"? In evaluating a group, you should see evidence of productive conflict—debate, questioning, and exploration of alternatives.

PROCEDURAL Evaluation of **procedural** functions looks at how well the group's activities and communication are coordinated. We said earlier in this chapter that the leader performs most of these functions. Yet in groups where leadership is a shared function, each participant has a responsibility to exhibit some essential leadership behaviors.

The key functions to be evaluated include eliciting communication, delegating and directing action, summarizing group activity, managing conflict, evaluating process, and releasing tension. Let us highlight a few problems that you may see in these areas.

One behavior that occurs with regularity in groups is some members talking too much and others talking too little. To counteract this behavior, an astute leader and others attempt to keep the lines of communication open among all group members. This function is known as *gatekeeping*. A remark such as "Tim, I think you've covered that issue pretty well. Bob, do you have anything to add?" is a tactful way to suppress and elicit contributions simultaneously.

Another recurring behavior is a return to issues that have seemingly been resolved or worked through. When this happens, many members get frustrated and tense. You will hear, "We never get anything done in here" or "We're just spinning our wheels." There are two possibilities for corrective action. One is the use of summaries. Does the leader or do other members continually keep the group posted on its progress with remarks such as "What we've been talking about is . . ." or "So, what we seem to be saying is . . ."? A second possibility is to determine whether the group has lost sight of its objectives. What is the group trying to accomplish, and how well does the present discussion help to accomplish these objectives?

Finally, there is a need for members to release tension at certain points of interaction. This can be done through a joke, a sharing of feelings, and so on. Kowitz and Knutson stressed that participants may need to be reminded of their individual responsibilities and importance in the overall group function. Once members are aware of what is expected of them, tension can decrease and the group can resume making progress.

INTERPERSONAL In the **interpersonal** portion of the evaluation, the emphasis is on how well the members of the group work with each other. Of interest is the climate or atmosphere in which the task is accomplished. There can be little doubt that when the circumstances under which a group operates are uncomfortable or unpleasant, productivity and results are affected in negative ways. Interpersonal assessment can focus on four areas: positive reinforcement, solidarity, cooperativeness, and respect toward others.

One of the most dangerous things that can happen in a meeting is conflict shifting from tasks to individuals. Personality conflicts can distract the group from its primary task and responsibility. Whenever an outburst occurs—such as "You've never known anything about this before, and who are you to talk about it now?"—the group leader and the other members should attempt to reiterate that the group should "stick to the facts" or "get back to the problem."

If the atmosphere is negative or unpleasant, the leader or any other group member can use rewards to emphasize the positive aspects of the meeting. There may, however, be underlying reasons for the negative statements being made, such as an objection to the person's proposed solution or resentment over a stolen idea. If this is the case, the reason for the derogatory comments should be explored because it may provide information helpful for achieving the group's goals.[10]

10.7.2: Individual Evaluation

Apart from the group as a whole, each individual participant can be assessed. The focus of such an evaluation is how well members helped the group accomplish its task and how well they performed functions during the process.

Larry Samovar and Steven King created two excellent instruments for evaluating individual participants and leaders.[11] Eleven factors make up the individual member evaluation form we have created, shown in Figure 10.5. The form may be completed by the group leader or by another group member. There are also eleven factors on the leadership evaluation form (see Figure 10.6). This form operates best when the group has an assigned or designated leader. The evaluator can focus on one individual and how well he or she performs the leadership role. Assessments can be made about the relative strengths and weaknesses of each group member. Evaluating these areas contributes to improvement in group work.

Figure 10.5 Participant Evaluation Form

SOURCE: Evaluation form developed by the authors based on their own work and the work from the following sources: L. A. Samovar and S. W. King, *Communication and Discussion in Small Groups* (Scottsdale, AZ: Gorsuch-Scarisbrick, 1981).

http://www.sampleforms.org/group-evaluation-form.html

http://www.readwritethink.org/classroom-resources/printouts/group-self-evaluation-31049.html

---

NAME OF GROUP MEMBER: _____

NAME OF RATER: _____

DATE: _____

For each characteristic, fill in a rating from 1 (excellent) to 7 (poor). Write any comments in the space below the rating list.

Participant Characteristics

1. _____ Preparation
2. _____ Speaking
3. _____ Listening
4. _____ Open-mindedness
5. _____ Sensitivity to others
6. _____ Worth of information
7. _____ Critical thinking skills
8. _____ Group orientation
9. _____ Procedural contribution
10. _____ Assistance in leadership
11. _____ Overall evaluation

Comments:

Figure 10.6 Leader Evaluation Form

SOURCE: Evaluation form developed by the authors based on their own work and the work from the following sources: L. A. Samovar and S. W. King, *Communication and Discussion in Small Groups* (Scottsdale, AZ: Gorsuch-Scarisbrick, 1981).

http://www.sampleforms.org/group-evaluation-form.html
http://www.readwritethink.org/classroom-resources/printouts/group-self-evaluation-31049.html

NAME OF LEADER: _____
NAME OF RATER: _____
DATE: _____

For each characteristic, fill in a rating from 1 (excellent) to 7 (poor). Write any comments in the space below the rating list.

Leadership Functions

1. _____ Opened discussion
2. _____ Asked appropriate questions
3. _____ Offered reviews
4. _____ Clarified ideas
5. _____ Encouraged critical thinking
6. _____ Limited irrelevancies
7. _____ Protected minority viewpoints
8. _____ Remained impartial
9. _____ Kept accurate records
10. _____ Concluded discussion
11. _____ Overall leadership

Comments:

WRITING PROMPT

Suppose you are working in a group with three other members. Two of the members are adversaries, and you have heard each gossiping about the other to employees outside the group. The group facilitator has asked for suggestions for advertising budget reductions. One of the members begins his suggestion but is interrupted by his adversary, who snaps, "I don't like that idea!" The first member retorts, "That's because you don't like me!" A verbal brawl begins between the two. As a member of this group, what would you do? Is it your place to intervene and attempt to reestablish a more rational, critical-thinking type of atmosphere? Why or why not?

> The response entered here will appear in the performance dashboard and can be viewed by your instructor.

Submit

Strategic Scenario Wrap-Up

Meetings as Forums for Problem Solving

(×) Strategic Scenario

Chelsea Moreno is a regional sales manager for Inspirion Corporation, an organization that sells and distributes seasonal gift items such as decorative artificial plants, caps, T-shirts, blankets, jewelry, and some perishable items. Traditionally, Inspirion has advertised and marketed its products to the public through catalog sales and to organizations through direct-sales representatives who call on business managers in need of gifts for their clients.

Chelsea has been assigned to organize a meeting for all district and regional sales managers in a mountain resort in Colorado. The purpose of the meeting is to develop a strategic plan for implementing a new Web-based strategy for online sales—something they know very little about. Chelsea knows that many of the "old guard" sales managers are resistant to the idea of e-business and online sales. She also knows that she has been selected for this task because she has been actively supporting the idea of online sales and that her chances of being promoted to vice president depend on the success of the venture. Chelsea has many tasks facing her.

Chelsea Moreno's challenge is achieving buy-in for a new idea from fellow employees who are different from her in age, experience, and attitudes. From an organizational standpoint, goal setting is vital. If Chelsea can clearly explain, with documentation, how important the Spanish-speaking market is for the success of the company as a whole, she has a much greater chance for buy-in. The commonality of the group works in Chelsea's favor; most of the company's sales managers have been strongly supporting the success of the organization for many years. Chelsea knows her idea will require more work for them for a period of time, respects this fact, and will convey her understanding to the attendees at the meeting.

Analysis will be the best method of critical thinking to encourage at the meeting, and she will use reflective thinking techniques to encourage participation. Despite her preparation, if Chelsea finds that detractors try to divert the meeting's purpose, she can suggest a break. When the group returns, she can ask for a summary from everyone's point of view so that she can address issues and misunderstandings.

WRITING PROMPT

If serious issues brought up at the meeting indicated that a change of direction was needed, could the meeting have been successful? Why or why not?

> The response entered here will appear in the performance dashboard and can be viewed by your instructor.

Submit

Summary

Meetings as Forums for Problem Solving

- This chapter discussed how to **conduct effective meetings**—how to set the agenda, keep the focus on goals, and evaluate meeting effectiveness.

- To solve problems effectively, groups must develop strong and realistic **organizational, group, and individual goals.**

- The **situational aspects of meetings** include obtaining proper meeting facilities, setting up audiovisual equipment, maintaining rules of order, and getting to know the other participants in the group.

- The **communication competencies** for strategic problem solving in groups rest on the ability to think critically.

- This skill is made up of **analysis, reasoning, interpretation, and evaluation.**

- Groups must select the problem-solving technique that best suits their needs. **Three problem-solving techniques** available to them are reflective thinking, the nominal group technique, and the Delphi technique.

- To make **effective decisions**, groups can either vote or reach a consensus (the preferred method).

- Meetings are **not without anxiety-provoking circumstances**, particularly when meetings are closed forums, when they are composed of people with diverse backgrounds, or when they are called to mediate serious arguments.

- Managing anxiety takes skill and inventiveness but is **neither complicated nor impossible.**

- No matter how successful a group's communication is, it cannot be maintained without evaluations. **Group evaluations** can be informational, procedural, or interpersonal. Evaluation can also be made of the specific individuals involved in the group.

- The **Group Behavior Inventory** can be adapted and used for the group to which you belong.

SHARED WRITING: MEETINGS AS FORUMS FOR PROBLEM SOLVING

If you were group leader of a decision-making body and consensus was difficult to achieve, what steps would you take to reach a decision? Review the techniques for group decision making and apply one of them to your plan for reaching consensus.

▶
```
A minimum number of characters is required
to post and earn points. After posting, your
response can be viewed by your class and
instructor, and you can participate in the
class discussion.
```

[Post]   0 characters | 140 minimum

Chapter 10 Quiz: Meetings as Forums for Problem Solving

Chapter 11
Negotiation and Conflict Management

Learning Objectives

11.1 Report how negotiation and conflict are important for the growth of a company and its employees

11.2 Contrast argumentativeness with verbal aggressiveness

11.3 Explain how negotiation can be used to one's advantage in the workplace

11.4a Define conflict

11.4b Review the sources of conflict

11.5 Describe the factors that can lead to successful conflict management

Strategic Scenario: Benefits and Concessions

Lynn Shaefer, director of operations, has just returned from an emergency meeting in the senior vice president's office. He learned that he is to leave in two days to negotiate a contract with a local labor union over health benefits, maternity/paternity leave, and on-site day care at one of the company's manufacturing plants. The person who was going to handle the negotiation, the general manager of the plant, suddenly passed away, and Lynn seemed like the ideal choice, since he is somewhat familiar with the situation. The plant was in his territory when he was a sales representative four years ago. Union support for the contract is very important to the company, although negotiations will not be easy since the company is losing money and must find ways to reduce costs. The biggest sticking points will be maternity/paternity leave and the day-care center. Lynn's company knows that giving in on these benefits to this local union will set a precedent and create the same demands among other local unions. The people who Lynn will be negotiating with run the gamut from older workers who have long had benefits to young workers who want to start families to workers with established families. Lynn has heard from the grapevine that even his negotiating counterparts cannot completely agree on their highest priorities. They are simply saying that the company must produce a contract granting all their demands, in spite of how unrealistic this would be. Lynn also knows that the negotiating sessions could become very heated, even volatile.

As you read this chapter, think about the situation that Lynn faces. We will return to this scenario at the end of the chapter and discuss some solutions.

11.1: Overview

Negotiation and Conflict Management

11.1 **Report how negotiation and conflict are important for the growth of a company and its employees**

Groups serve a number of vital functions in organizations. Groups are also a source of competitive communication in organizations. Competitive communication is characterized by interdependent yet conflicting goals, and it can occur at all levels of an organization. Commitment to organizational values and ethical standards, strong verbal and listening skills, interpersonal communication ability, and understanding of group roles, norms, and dynamics are all essential to the successful handling of competitive communication.

Sometimes people choose to avoid negotiation and conflict because of their difficulty and the stress they produce. People may also choose to avoid negotiation and conflict because they dislike arguing or have been the targets of attacks by verbally aggressive communicators. Certainly, failing to reach a resolution in either situation can produce negative results for individuals and for the organization. Nevertheless, negotiation and conflict are vital to the long-term growth and health of a company and its employees. Tension resulting from conflicts that have not been addressed can undermine employees' morale, motivation, and trust in the organization. By learning productive methods of negotiation and conflict management, you can contribute a great deal to the groups, organizations, and people with whom you work.

That is the true focus of this chapter—helping you apply the skills necessary to communicate successfully and effectively in difficult, even competitive, circumstances. We begin with a brief summary of the difference between argumentativeness and verbal aggressiveness. Then we address the unique skills and demands of negotiation and conclude with one of the most complex situations in communication: conflict management.

11.2: Argumentativeness and Verbal Aggressiveness

11.2 **Contrast argumentativeness with verbal aggressiveness**

Are you more prone to become embroiled in one controversial issue and not do so in another? What makes one person more likely than another to engage in argument? What happens when people who are arguing about issues refocus their attention on each other? Here we show you how to evaluate your own tendencies toward verbal aggressiveness, and we explore the implications of verbal aggressiveness for communication in your career.

An inclination to argue or a fondness for arguing is called **argumentativeness**. "Argumentativeness includes the ability to recognize controversial issues in communication situations, to present and defend positions on the issues, and to attack the positions which other people take."[1] Generally speaking, argumentativeness in the workplace is a positive and constructive strategy. Arguing for causes, positions, and ideas within organizations is often viewed favorably because people who are effective arguers are likely to achieve their goals. Research has shown that subordinates prefer superiors who are high in argumentativeness because they feel that their bosses will be more successful with their superiors and therefore the entire unit or department will benefit from effective argumentation skills.[2]

The tendency to attack other people instead of other points of view is termed **verbal aggressiveness**. "Verbal aggressiveness . . . denotes attacking the self-concept of another person instead of, or in addition to, the person's position on a topic of communication."[3,4]

ⓧ Difference between argumentativeness and verbal aggressiveness

The difference between verbal aggressiveness and argumentativeness is the focus of the attack. Argumentative people concentrate on positions, issues, reasoning, and evidence. Verbally aggressive people attack others personally. The difference affects others' view of the arguer/aggressor, career relationships, productivity in groups, and ability to achieve organizational goals. People can possess both traits, but people with a high degree of argumentativeness are less likely to use verbally aggressive strategies.

11.2.1: Controlling Verbal Aggressiveness

Are you inclined to be verbally aggressive? One way to find out is to score yourself on a scale designed to measure verbal aggressiveness.[5] The Strategic Skills feature below measures this quality. It reveals how you usually try to get people to comply with your wishes. To ensure honest and accurate results, when responding to each statement, think of specific examples that confirm your assessment.

Whether or not you yourself feel prone to such behavior, verbal aggressiveness exists in the workplace, which means you will likely encounter it at some point in your career. Uncontrolled verbal aggressiveness can lead to interpersonal difficulties. Attacking the personalities or self-concepts of others demonstrates lack of sensitivity to feelings and usually hurts those who are targets of this aggression. Controlling verbal aggressiveness is a multistage process that begins with identification of the various forms of such aggressiveness. Types of verbal aggressiveness include the following:[6]

character attacks	nonverbal signs
threats	ridicule
teasing	insults
physical appearance attacks	ethnic or gender slurs
competence attacks	profanity

When you notice yourself using any of these tactics, change your strategy to focus on the issues instead.

The next step in reducing verbal aggressiveness is to understand how and why it occurs. There are at least four reasons for this behavior.[7] Psychopathy, or mental disorder, can stimulate attacks on people (clinical counseling is recommended in this case). Dislike of others can cause verbal aggressiveness, especially if you are put off by the appearance or personality of the person with whom you are communicating. Social learning—or observing and imitating parents, siblings, peers, and significant others who use verbal aggressiveness with you or in your presence—can encourage verbal aggressiveness. Desperation can lead to verbal aggressiveness in a final effort to win an argument. Desperation as a motive is particularly common if the aggressor possesses deficient critical thinking skills. She or he may be unable to express clear and objective dissenting opinions and may feel there is no alternative to attacking the self-concept of others. Understanding and being aware of these causes of verbal aggressiveness can help you to control the urge to attack people personally, as well as be more understanding of those who attack you.

The best way to control verbal aggressiveness is to become a better communicator. Use critical thinking skills to formulate and express your ideas, including:

- Conduct a thorough *analysis* of the situation.
- Provide logical *reasoning* for your position.
- Develop a careful *interpretation* of the conflict issues, both yours and theirs.
- *Evaluate* your position and that of your partner.

Learn and practice these skills on a regular basis. You will find that engaging in constructive argumentation decreases the urge to attack others personally.

Verbal Aggressiveness Scale

Strategic Skills

If the statement is almost never true for you, place a 1 in the blank. If the statement is rarely true for you, place a 2 in the blank. If the statement is occasionally true for you, place a 3 in the blank. If the statement is often true for you, place a 4 in the blank. If the statement is almost always true for you, place a 5 in the blank.

⊗ Statements about Verbal Aggressiveness

1. _____ I am extremely careful to avoid attacking a person's intelligence when I attack her or his ideas.
2. _____ I use insults to "soften" stubborn people.
3. _____ I try very hard to avoid influencing people by making them feel bad about themselves.
4. _____ If someone refuses to do a task I know is important for a reason that does not seem valid to me, I accuse him or her of being unreasonable.
5. _____ When others do things I think are misguided, I try to be extremely gentle with them.
6. _____ If someone I am trying to influence really deserves it, I attack her or his character.
7. _____ When people demonstrate poor taste, I insult them to shock them into proper behavior.
8. _____ I try to make people feel good about themselves even when I think their ideas are useless.
9. _____ When people simply will not budge on a matter of great importance, I lose my temper and make strong emotional outbursts.
10. _____ When people criticize my shortcomings, I take it in good humor and do not try to get back at them.
11. _____ When people insult me, I get a lot of pleasure out of overreacting.
12. _____ When I dislike someone strongly, I try not to show it in what I say or how I say it.
13. _____ I like poking fun at people who do or say careless things to "wake them up."
14. _____ When I attack a person's ideas, I try not to damage his or her self-concept.
15. _____ When I try to influence people, I make an effort not to offend them.
16. _____ If I see someone act cruelly, I tell everyone else how terrible he or she is in hopes of changing his or her behavior.
17. _____ I refuse to participate in arguments when they involve personal attacks.
18. _____ When I am unable to influence others through conventional tactics, I resort to yelling or screaming at them.
19. _____ When I am not able to refute others' positions, I try to make them feel defensive to weaken their positions.
20. _____ When an argument shifts to personal attacks, I try very hard to change the subject.

Add your scores on numbers 1, 3, 5, 8, 10, 12, 14, 15, 17, and 20. Call this Total A. Add your scores on numbers 2, 4, 6, 7, 9, 11, 13, 16, 18, and 19. Call this Total B. Subtract Total B from Total A. If the result is between twenty and forty, you have a low tendency toward verbal aggressiveness. If your score is between zero and nineteen, you have a moderate tendency toward verbal aggressiveness. If your score is a negative number, you probably use verbal aggression frequently.

SOURCE: Reprinted with permission from the National Communication Association: http://www.natcom.org.

11.3: Negotiation

11.3 Explain how negotiation can be used to one's advantage in the workplace

Negotiation, or bargaining, frequently involves argumentation and verbal aggressiveness.[8] It generally occurs when communicators—for example, buyer and seller, union leader and company representative, supervisor and employee—are not in agreement. Since managers spend more than one-fifth of their time dealing with conflict, they need to learn how to negotiate effectively.[9]

11.3.1: Goal Setting for Negotiation

Because of differences in affiliation, the goals, needs, and communication styles of negotiators are likely to be very different from those of problem-solving groups that work toward one goal. Or participants in a negotiation session may have a common goal but disagree on the means and methods to achieve it.

Negotiation is usually a planned and structured process of communication. Although arguments may arise spontaneously from something said in the course of discussion, negotiators frequently plan tactics to be used and topics to be covered before an encounter. In a negotiating session, two or more people with different goals exchange communication to produce a mutually desirable outcome.[10] The parties involved must recognize that they are mutually dependent—seldom can an acceptable outcome occur unless all parties to negotiation recognize this fact.[11] Most bargaining scenarios require give-and-take in the form of concessions or acknowledgments of an opponent's truth, right, or privilege in a specific instance. Communicators must bargain forcefully and strategically, using effective argumentation skills while at the same time remaining aware that some concessions must be made so that all parties feel satisfied with the outcome. It is vital to remember that there are two sides to any negotiation, and keeping multiple perspectives in mind during this process will lead to greater satisfaction and more long-term benefits.

11.3.2: Formal Versus Informal Bargaining

The bargaining process can be observed in both formal and informal situations. **Formal bargaining** situations develop when recurring issues require deliberation and confrontation over time. One of the most important examples of formal bargaining is labor-management negotiations. Labor contracts usually run for a specified length of time, so bargaining sessions are needed when the contract expires. Formal bargaining is recurring, anticipated, planned, and structured. Other examples of formal bargaining include negotiation between representatives of government and industry over laws or policies, bargaining with subcontractors or law firms over services to be rendered, bargaining with financial institutions over credit or credit ratings, and negotiation with suppliers over prices.

Informal bargaining, also quite prevalent in the workplace, usually involves spontaneous situations that are seldom repeated. Informal bargaining may occur any time two or more parties must depend on one another to resolve divergent goals. For example, managers and employees often bargain over job descriptions, salary, roles, and performance standards. Each is interested in having the other accommodate her or his goals. Peers bargain with each other to resolve issues such as turf or territory disputes, recognition for accomplishments, work schedules, and even personality differences. Informal bargaining may even occur across organizational boundaries. Asking for discounts from vendors, negotiating with airlines about how frequent-flier miles are counted, and bargaining with hotels about corporate rates constitute informal bargaining situations. Regardless of whether a situation is informal or formal, similar negotiation strategies are used.

11.3.3: Present Your Position Competently

The first step in negotiation is advancing an offer within limits acceptable to the other bargaining party—making sure, of course, that the offer is also within limits acceptable to your own organization! Many bargaining positions are first expressed as broad statements that lay out a general goal. An offer that appears to be unreasonable on first hearing may in fact become persuasive as the negotiator takes it through the subsequent steps in the bargaining process.

Of course, it is better for the negotiator to begin with an offer that is obviously reasonable. Reasonable offers, which seem to make sense and correspond to known facts and standard beliefs, show that the negotiator is bargaining in good faith. Regardless of the quality of your initial offer, you will usually need to persuade others that your position is worthy of their support. Strong use of evidence gives credibility to your position more effectively than does any other tactic. Evidence usually consists of some form of information—published documentation, statistics, expert opinion, examples and illustrations, or testimony. Summarizing is another persuasive element because it demonstrates consistency and steadfastness during negotiation. Summarizing your argument may clear up confusion about the position you have taken and your reasons for taking it. Negotiation is most effective when all participants understand one another's positions on the issue and when there is no equivocation or inconsistency.

Finally, look at the position taken by the other side. In what ways is the position realistic or unrealistic? If any elements of the opposing position are weak or irrelevant, identify them as such and try to avoid having them become the focus of the negotiation. In the long run, it is best for you to address the major strengths of the opposing position, mindful of opportunities to use such arguments to support your own position. Throughout the negotiation, use critical thinking skills to analyze, evaluate, and interpret the opposing position. Doing so allows you to formulate effective counterarguments.

PRACTICING BUSINESS COMMUNICATION

Tootsie Roll Industries, Inc.

America's original penny candy, the Tootsie Roll, celebrated its 110th birthday in 2006. Despite its long history, the famous Tootsie Roll (named for company founder Leo Hirschfield's five-year-old daughter) still looks today very much like it did when it first appeared in candy stores, and the cost is still just a penny a piece. At that price, Chicago-based Tootsie Roll Industries (TRI) must surely sell a lot of candy to generate annual sales of over $487 million—and they do. TRI, also the world's largest lollipop producer, makes more than 60 million Tootsie Rolls and 20 million Tootsie Pops per day.

(X) Read more

TRI management encourages an open organization where employees confront and resolve conflicts, and a culture where business thrives on skilled negotiating with business partners, competitors, and even the government.

In the 1990s, TRI president Ellen Gordon negotiated with city officials in Chicago to secure an urban enterprise zone around the company's headquarters on the city's South Side. The agreement offers area businesses tax incentives. Chicago also offered TRI a low-interest loan to buy the plant it was leasing and $200,000 in job-training funds.

Since TRI employs union workers, its hundreds of middle-income jobs were valuable to Chicago's economy. For its part, TRI agreed to open a loan fund for employees who wanted to buy homes in Chicago and to add about 200 more jobs by the end of the decade.

Communication Top-Down and Across the Organization

Even with operations in Massachusetts, Tennessee, Wisconsin, Mexico, and Canada, TRI employs fewer than 2,000 workers. The basic corporate structure is traditional. Departmental staff report to department directors who report to TRI vice presidents. Corporate VPs report to president and COO Ellen Gordon and to chairman and CEO Melvin Gordon.

(X) Read more

TRI complements its top-down structure by encouraging accessibility and teamwork as keys to successful communication. Employees are invited to learn more about how other departments work by sitting in on their meetings, offering their viewpoints, or simply observing. Employees initiate frequent, impromptu meetings in the workplace, a function of TRI's "open-door policy."

Employees from different departments work in cross-functional teams to solve problems and to come up with business ideas. For example, employees from research and development, finance, marketing, manufacturing, and purchasing team up to analyze the feasibility of introducing a new product.

By cross-training, TRI workers learn different aspects of the business, broaden the range of creative solutions to business problems, and increase team members' sensitivity to the implications a proposed action might have on other business functions. The go/no-go decisions made on proposed new products or business ventures at TRI are thoroughly informed and well thought out.

Building Negotiating Skill

The flexibility reflected in TRI's internal communication is equally important—but more strategic—in its negotiations with suppliers. The company requests bids from suppliers, indicating exact specifications for ingredients and for quality. TRI negotiates with potential suppliers to obtain the best balance between high quality and low price within these specifications. Even after suppliers are chosen, negotiation continues as part of the business relationship.

(X) Read more

More than fifty years ago, TRI began to explore foreign markets. It opened a subsidiary in Mexico in the late 1960s. Encouraged by Mexico's warm reception to "Tutsi," TRI opened a branch in Canada in the early 1970s.

Negotiating skills have proven pivotal to the growth of TRI. It has expanded its sales revenue not only by expanding its own product line, but also by acquiring established candy companies. In 1972, TRI purchased the Mason Division of Candy Corporation of America, adding well-known brands such as Mason Mints to the product line. In 1985, TRI bought Cella's Confections, makers of chocolate-covered cherries. In 1988, TRI acquired the Charms

Company, thereby becoming the world's largest lollipop producer. TRI's purchase of the chocolate and caramel brands of Warner-Lambert Company in 1993 increased TRI's business by 20 percent and added such well-known brands as Junior Mints, Sugar Daddy, Sugar Babies, and Charleston Chew to the product line. Concord Confections of Toronto, which in 2004 became its latest acquisition, has now given TRI market leadership in the bubble-gum category with the popular Dubble Bubble brand. When looking at an acquisition, TRI management meets over time with the other company's management or parent company. At successive meetings, opportunities and risks for both parties are debated and discussed. The ability of TRI and the representatives of the potential acquisition to resolve their conflicts and to negotiate to their mutual satisfaction makes or breaks the deal.

You can visit Tootsie Roll Industries, Inc., online at http://www.tootsie.com

WRITING PROMPT

How do cross-functional teams benefit TRI internally? Explain how and why effective negotiating skills have been vital to TRI's external expansion. Also, why does TRI discuss the benefits and problems entailed by the deal during acquisition negotiations, and how does this tie in with corporate culture?

> The response entered here will appear in the performance dashboard and can be viewed by your instructor.

Submit

DIMENSIONS OF NEGOTIATING According to the experts, there are three dimensions to negotiation: information management, concessions, and positioning.[12] Each of them represents a category of strategies, tactics, and behaviors that are used by negotiators to advance their goals.

INFORMATION MANAGEMENT When engaging in bargaining with others, have at hand as much research and information as possible, but manage the information effectively. Use it to promote your goals for the negotiation session. Information can be managed in a number of ways that strengthen a bargaining position. You can seek explanations from your opponents in an effort to clarify the issues, realign their position according to prevailing evidence, or reduce ambiguity that can be used against you. Sometimes bargainers enter a negotiation session with a grocery list of objectives they hope to achieve, knowing they will have to compromise on some. You can manage information in a bargaining session by requesting that your adversaries assign priorities to their goals and objectives. Ask the opposing party to rank its objectives in order of importance.

You can also refocus the discussion on your own agenda. In bargaining sessions, abundant information favoring the opposition's position may be introduced. If one negotiating party has access to greater resources—time, money, special research, legal services—than the other, that party may attempt to overwhelm the negotiation with excess data. Such information, however, does not decrease the importance of your evidence and your group's position. If you feel you are being overwhelmed by the quantity of your opponents' information (regardless of its relevance), redirect the focus of the discussion toward your own objectives so that you can move the negotiation toward a settlement that supports your position. For example, saying, "I can see your point, but if you look at our data, you will see that the statistical trends point to a strategy more in line with what we are offering" can prevent sheer quantity of information from overriding a fair negotiation.

POSITIONING Positioning is moving the focus of the negotiation to issues that are important to you. You must use this technique carefully to remain ethical. Ask yourself whether the issues that interest you are the central issues in the discussion. If they are not, refrain from emphasizing them at the expense of more important organizational goals. Many negotiators use positioning to show their side in its most favorable light. Be careful that when you highlight the positive aspects of your group's agenda, you do not distort or misrepresent your actual position.

Positioning can result from preestablished rules and procedures. Many formal bargaining situations prescribe certain methods of discussion, procedures for decision making, or an agenda of topics to be discussed. Here is a list of preestablished rules.

ⓧ List of Preestablished Rules:

1. Each side must allow the other to take a turn talking.
2. All parties must agree on each major issue.
3. We will determine relevant topics before beginning the negotiation.

If during a negotiation session the other group's representatives prevent your side from having a turn to speak, you can remind them that the negotiation is to follow a pattern of alternating turns, and you can request an opportunity to speak. In this way, you will be able to bring up your side's concerns within the agreed-on rules. You can then go on to discuss your side of the issues under negotiation.

Positioning can also be accomplished by asserting your side's right to a balanced negotiation. If you sense that the discussion has concentrated on the other side's goals and objectives, call the imbalance to the attention of the entire group in an effort to bring the discussion back into balance. Negotiators have ethical obligations to bargain in good faith, respect the rights of other negotiators, and encourage fair and open discussion of issues.

CONCESSIONS Negotiators come to the bargaining table expecting to give up, or concede, some of their goals to obtain something in return. **Concession** is useful in several ways. Making concessions demonstrates cooperativeness, which usually makes a positive impression on others and may encourage them to reciprocate.

Making concessions is also a good way to maintain interest in the negotiation. Lags or lapses in the bargaining process can occur as participants become bogged down by old issues and stale ideas. Providing a minor concession from time to time can open new windows of opportunity, stimulate fresh approaches to the negotiation, and revitalize communication among the bargaining parties. Concessions early in the bargaining process communicate a conciliatory tone. You can avoid accusations of rigidity and closed-mindedness by making concessions that demonstrate a belief in cooperative discussion.

When you decide to make a concession, objectively evaluate the opposing argument's strengths to identify a concession that will be appropriate. Concessions can take the form of time, money, resources, responsibilities, autonomy, and even changes in job descriptions. After you make a concession, show how it serves both your own and your opponent's needs and goals, and clearly redefine your position so the negotiation can continue. Consider the North American Free Trade Agreement (NAFTA). Theoretically, a agreement to free trade between countries needs only one sentence. There will be no tariffs or subsidies inhibiting free trade between our countries. However, due to concessions demanded by negotiators for all three countries, the NAFTA document requires 1,700 pages of a preamble, eight parts, twenty-two chapters, and ten annexes.

STRATEGIC BARGAINING The bulk of research literature on negotiation points to two types of communication strategy: cooperative and competitive. **Cooperative strategies** are open, honest, and upfront attempts at objective and productive problem solving.[13] They are often termed integrative because they frame the bargaining session with the potential for mutual gain and multiple goals. Bargainers using cooperative strategies are interested in fully understanding the respective positions of all parties.

Information is exchanged in a frank and open manner so that everyone has a clear picture of all the issues. Effective listening and responding skills aid in minimizing misunderstandings. The primary objective of cooperative strategies is to use communication in a way that maximizes the goals of the bargaining participants. Cooperative tactics include the following:

⊗ List of Cooperative Tactics

- Expressing agreement with or approval of the opponent's position
- Offering information or assistance
- Offering concessions
- Offering promises/commitments
- Summarizing arguments
- Indicating conciliation
- Providing clarification
- Seeking a problem-solving approach
- Facilitating discussion through adherence to proper procedure

Cooperative strategies can be used to achieve a win-win outcome, in which both sides benefit from the bargaining session.

Competitive strategies, often referred to as distributive, seek to maximize one's own position at the expense of the adversary. The term **distributive** refers to the bargainer's assumption that a gain for her or his side equals a loss for the other side—that is, limited benefits are redistributed through bargaining. Competitive bargaining strategies do not consider problem solving and cooperation to be valid tactics. Rather, the goal of these strategies is to win at all costs. In fact, these strategies tend to result in a lose-lose outcome—neither party leaves the negotiation satisfied.

Competitive strategies use information in self-serving ways, giving only enough information to create the impression of disclosure while eliciting maximum information from the opponent. Competitive bargainers see each other as combatants whose side must either prevail or perish. These tactics may even involve deception or diversionary maneuvers to gain a competitive edge. Competitive tactics such as the following rarely involve concessions or compromise:

- Challenging, disagreeing with, or rejecting the opponent's position
- Changing the topic to refocus the discussion to one's advantage
- Asking for concessions
- Accusing an opponent of incompetence, negligence, or bad faith

- Making threats or demands
- Issuing ultimatums
- Making personal attacks against an opponent
- Advancing arguments against an opponent (rather than the opponent's position)

Notice that none of these tactics would occur if critical thinking were used.

You should be aware of one caveat at this point. In professional situations, it is seldom a good idea to become involved in bargaining and negotiation at the level of personal values and beliefs. Multiple reasons exist for this cautionary note, but we will discuss the two most salient ones. First, values and beliefs stir up emotions like no other bargaining topic. When emotions come into play, negotiation processes take on a different form and can easily lead to verbal aggressiveness. Second, many people are not equipped for a discussion focusing on values.

For example, imagine a situation in which your job requires you to negotiate for the best multimedia equipment among prospective suppliers on a project. Imagine further that the supplier who ultimately offers the best deal recently laid off your best friend. Would that affect your decision?

Understanding the deep-seated thoughts and feelings of another person's values takes time, sensitivity, and commitment. These are not elements that come naturally to negotiation contexts. When values come into play (as they naturally can), you are better off acknowledging that these issues are important but are best left for discussion at another time, while at the same time asking that the discussion focus as much as possible on the issues, facts, and merits of the opposing sides.

USING BARGAINING TACTICS EFFECTIVELY As you look at the lists of competitive and cooperative bargaining tactics, you will quickly notice that the cooperative tactics appear positive and the competitive tactics seem negative. This is true in a general sense, but remember that bargaining situations are demanding, complex, and argumentative and that a combination of tactics is usually required for effective negotiation. Cooperative tactics promote rationality and reasonableness; only in extreme cases should competitive tactics be used to ensure that your side is not taken advantage of.

How are bargaining tactics to be used? That depends on the situation, although there are some general guidelines to follow:[14]

1. Initial strategies should include firm but cooperative messages. Adversaries should get the idea that you are serious about the negotiation but are not so inflexible that you will refuse to yield on any issues. ("I don't think my salary compensates me fully for the work I do.")

2. Opening bids (such as offers or proposals) should be high because you value your proposals. By asking for more than you really expect to get, you allow concessions to be made later while at the same time communicating your desire to obtain your highest goals. ("I would like a salary increase of 25 percent.")

3. Cooperative tactics (such as promises and concessions) can be used to clear roadblocks in negotiations. When you sense that the discussion is going nowhere, it is often helpful to give in a little to get the bargaining back on track. ("A 25 percent increase may be too much. How about 20 percent?")

4. Competitive tactics may be introduced (although they are not encouraged) if you perceive that the opposition is taking advantage of the situation. ("That offer is not acceptable.")

5. A high level of enthusiasm should be maintained during bargaining. An upbeat and energetic attitude communicates commitment and perseverance to achieve goals. ("I'm sure we can work this out.")

6. A variety of information should be relied on in order to maintain a strong position. Remembering what has been said and approved in previous sessions as well as keeping track of information during the current session ensures a high degree of bargaining competence. ("In my appraisal interview, you said I was doing an 'excellent' job.")

7. Issuing threats, ultimatums, or demands against adversaries is rarely useful. Negative tactics such as these usually lead to resentment and conflict. ("If I don't get that raise immediately, I'll quit today.")

8. A professional demeanor should be maintained throughout the bargaining sessions. Avoid resorting to underhanded or unethical tactics during bargaining. Be sure your conduct is beyond reproach. ("You just don't like me, do you?")

9. The equality of bargaining parties should be acknowledged. ("What is your counteroffer?")

10. Effective critical thinking skills should be used. Strong use of evidence, reasoning, and analysis can improve your position in the bargaining situation. ("I've been a productive employee, I have good rapport with customers, and others in my career field have higher salaries.")

11.3.4: Manage Anxiety in Negotiation

Negotiations can often produce anxiety, but there are some strategies you can use to reduce nervousness.

First, remember that bargaining is a normal, accepted business practice; you are not a troublemaker for entering into a bargaining situation. Second, set a specific date and time for the bargaining session. Although negotiations can take place informally, scheduling a bargaining session will give you time to gather the evidence and data needed to support your position. This will build your confidence and reduce anxiety. It may also be helpful to practice your negotiating skills with a friend. Ask a friend to listen to your position and to help you practice the bargaining session. Third, keep in mind that bargaining is not a do-or-die situation. Be open and flexible during negotiations. Sometimes making the first concession to demonstrate your willingness to bargain cooperatively will create a less hostile bargaining environment.

Negotiation is a common communication strategy in business and professional settings. The more effectively you can bargain, the more likely you are to attain positions of enhanced responsibility and authority because you can be trusted to get the best deal for your group. In the first scenario in the Strategic Skills example on successful and unsuccessful bargaining (section 11.4.3), identify the positive and negative actions taken by each group.

11.4: Conflict Management

11.4a Define conflict

11.4b Review the sources of conflict

When bargainers come to the table with serious purposes, strong negotiation skills, and mutual dependency, they can attain productive outcomes. But there are many examples of bargaining sessions that lead to serious conflict among parties. The second scenario in the Strategic Skills box in section 11.4.3 shows a breakdown in the bargaining process. The bargaining session escalated into a full-blown conflict that was unproductive and out of control. How did this happen? What is the role of conflict in negotiation? We first need an understanding of competing goals and conflict styles and tactics.

11.4.1: What Is Conflict?

Conflict can take many shapes in the workplace. It can occur between people representing different organizational units, it can occur between organizational levels such as labor and management, and it can occur between people who work together. Conflict is a dynamic process that is precipitated, developed, and governed by the joint communication strategies of the parties involved.

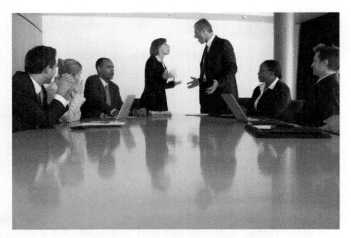

Conflict is a necessary part of organizational life but must be managed in constructive ways.
SOURCE: Nick White/Getty Images

Conflict is "an expressed struggle between at least two interdependent parties who perceive incompatible goals, scarce rewards, and interference from the other party in achieving their goals."[15] The parties must be interdependent. Conflict results when people view other people—people on whom they depend—as the reason they cannot attain their goals.

⊗ How do interdependency and conflict complement each other?

Interdependency forces the conflict. If a person could accomplish goals without the interference of others, conflict would not arise. The same dynamic properties that make group and organizational communication valuable are also the spark for potential conflict.

Interdependency forces the conflict: If a person could accomplish goals without the interference of others, conflict would not arise. The same dynamic properties that make group and organizational communication valuable are also the spark for potential conflict.

The ability to recognize, engage in, and manage conflict is an important skill for everyone but especially for those who aspire to succeed in organizations. Conflict is widespread in organizational life. It is not overstating the case to say that dealing with conflict is one of the most troublesome communication activities in organizations. Conflict in organizations may range from disputes over territorial encroachment to personal disharmony. A major source of conflict is misunderstanding and communication failure. Conflict may also erupt from differences in goals or values, diverse economic or financial interests, role conflict, environmental changes, or even contradictory group loyalties.[16] Even technology can be blamed, since computer-mediated communication creates a more de-socialized work atmosphere, with a resulting decrease in interpersonal skills. Any time people perceive that a person, group, or difficult situation is preventing them from accomplishing a goal, conflict is possible.

11.4.2: Competing Goals and Conflict

The primary cause of conflict is competing goals. Even though people usually enter into a conflict situation with established goals, the goals may change as the situation develops and understanding of the opponent increases.[17] As goals shift, so does the communication of the conflict. Essentially, there are two types of goals in most conflict situations: content and relational.

CONTENT GOALS **Content goals** involve the apparent issues or obvious reasons for a dispute. They are characterized by such issues as competition for finite resources (computers versus offices), decision making (participation in decisions), and rights (maintaining fairness). Here are three examples of competing content goals.

(X) **Three examples:**

1. Jim: If Joe gets the new service vehicle, I'll have to wait.
   Joe: Jim's new service route lets him get home earlier.
2. Mary: Tanika is taking over this project without much input from me.
   Tanika: Mary hasn't shown much initiative with special projects in the last six months.
3. Roberto: Cicely never consults me on the important decisions made around here.
   Cicely: Roberto always seems too busy to ask about the new emerging issues in the company.

In each example, the conflicting parties believe they understand the real content goals in the situation, yet each has a perspective that is different and unknown to the other. Each party understands his or her own goals but has few ideas about the goals of his or her conflict partner.

Failure to communicate differing goals usually leads to conflict. Understanding the respective goals of conflict partners is one of the keys to conflict management.

RELATIONAL GOALS In every conflict situation, the conflicting parties pursue goals that are likely to be less obvious than the content goals. **Relational goals** "define each party's importance to the other, the emotional distance they wish to maintain, the influence each is willing to grant the other, the degree to which the parties are seen as a unit, or the rights each party is willing to grant to the others."[18] Relational goals are not openly discussed as often as content goals because doing so draws attention to personal differences. They are, however, no less important than content goals. Indeed, conflict may not be managed until relational goals are managed. In the Strategic Skills feature in the next section (11.4.3), the relationship between the two bargainers emerges as a clear cause of additional conflict, despite the focus on content goals (new computers and offices) expressed by the communicators. Many people are willing to acknowledge only content goals when involved in a conflict, but it is rarely the case that relational goals do not also exist.

Now look back to the three examples of conflicting content goals. If you were to manage those conflict situations, it would help you to know that Jim and Joe have been competing for a promotion for the past few months, that Tanika and Mary have different personalities and work styles that do not mesh, and that Roberto and Cicely formerly were dating but recently had a traumatic breakup. Relational goals are always present in conflict and have to be brought out for effective management to occur. Submerging or denying their existence can postpone a resolution.

11.4.3: Managing Conflicting Goals

To be manageable, goals must be clarified so that parties can accurately understand the respective positions of their counterparts. Both content and relational goals must be brought out into the open and honestly discussed to prevent confusion and misunderstanding. The only way that people in a conflict can share the perspective of their adversaries is by understanding their goals. The following steps can help you to clarify goals:

(X) **Steps to Clarify Goals:**

1. State your goals in clear, unambiguous language. Use language that the other party will understand.
2. Elicit clearly stated goals from the other party.
3. Openly discuss the difference between your content and relational goals.
4. Make sure that you and your opponent have a shared understanding of each other's goals.
5. Show that upholding your goals will not prevent productive management of the conflict.

The next step is to assemble collaborative goals. The key to managing any conflict is working toward an interdependent solution. If you consider only your own goals, without regard for the other party's interests, you will delay the productive resolution of differences. Adversaries probably will not want to work toward achieving your goals unless you show a willingness to do the same for them.

Collaboration begins by clarifying each party's goals. Then conflicting parties strive to promote collaboration by actively rejecting selfish or incompatible goals. Here are some ways to encourage goal collaboration.

1. Search for commonalities among the competing goals.
2. Recognize that some of your opponents' goals may not have long-term implications and you may be able to live with them.
3. Give some concessions while asking for some.
4. Develop new goals that incorporate and complement the competing goals of all parties.

Successful and Unsuccessful Bargaining

Strategic Skills

Treecorp, a paper-manufacturing company in the Northwest, is expanding its corporate headquarters by moving into a new multi-story complex in a large downtown area. The executive vice president (VP) for planning and facilities has told the public relations (PR) and training and development (TD) departments that they are to be housed on the same floor because their departments report to the same vice president and have some functional overlap. She tells the departments together that the furnishings equipment budget is limited and they will have to compromise and work out an arrangement for spending the $2 million allocated for office space and computer support. She concludes by saying that the $2 million is theirs to spend as they wish as long as there is agreement between the departments. She gives the departments one month to reach their decision and report back to her.

The department members gather in their respective areas to formulate strategy for the upcoming bargaining sessions. Members of training and development are strongly in favor of fully enclosed, standard offices for private counseling sessions with clients and trainees. Equipment and computer support are important to them but not as important as private offices. The public relations people believe they must have new computers, tablets, smartphones, and an upgraded network to better communicate, enjoy graphics support, and print high-quality documents at high speed. Although the PR people really want standard offices, they are willing to live with cubicle offices if they can get the technology upgrade. Both PR and TD plan to bargain for maximum benefits—that is, for both computers and offices.

Some other issues are likely to be discussed but are not directly relevant to the office/technology problem. Some members of the PR department are jealous of the attention focused on TD at this time. The previous vice president in charge of the departments was originally from PR and favored the PR department. The new vice president, however, is from TD and seems to favor it. Some members of PR used to be in TD and vice versa. There is considerable gossip between departments, and some personal feuds have developed between employees. The departments compete with each other for new positions, salaries, travel budgets, and operating expenses.

The following two scenarios are excerpts from the final bargaining session to decide on the new office setup. The first shows an effective use of information management, concessions, and positioning that leads to a mutually acceptable win-win outcome. Note where the negotiators use each strategy effectively.

Winning a Bargain at Treetop

TD: Now let's see. You want the technology upgrade as well as fully enclosed offices, and you think we should make do with a less sophisticated system. Right?

PR: Well, in principle that may sound like an unfair exchange. But if you look at the last three annual budgets, you will notice that your operating expenses and travel budget have exceeded ours by 28 percent. Don't you think it is unfair for us to have to split the $2 million down the middle when we have been getting fewer funds all along?

TD: I thought we had already resolved that issue. In a paper company, training costs more money than public relations

does. Besides, we must have private offices to do our job; it's a separate issue from new technology that will make us more efficient.

PR: Now wait a minute! You can't be serious that you want more than 50 percent of the construction budget.

TD: Our department has increased productivity in every quarter over the last four years, whereas your department has only done so in three quarters. Your department has also expanded by three employees, while we have not been allowed to expand.

PR: Hold on now. You know that it is difficult to gauge the actual productivity of a public relations department. Nevertheless, those new positions are critical to maintaining our public awareness campaign.

TD: All I am saying is that from a bottom-line perspective, we are one of the most productive departments in the company, yet we receive little reward in return.

PR: What if we were to give up one position now and one new position in the next budget? In return you would allow us to get the hardware and network.

TD: We still want the regular offices, but we might be willing to share some of our operating expenses with you.

PR: Would it be possible for you to give up some travel money so we can expand our public awareness campaign into the Southwest?

TD: Perhaps, if the positions that you are giving up are people with a training background.

PR: I think we have a deal.

TD: Fine.

Negotiation Breakdown

TD: Now let's see. You want the technology upgrade as well as fully enclosed offices, and you think we should make do with a less sophisticated system. Right?

PR: Now hold on a minute! You people in TD always seem to be in a rush to get things settled. Let's clarify some issues first.

TD: What issues? You get either offices or new toys. PR is always trying to distract us from the real issues. Our deadline for making the decision on the budget is approaching quickly, and we don't seem to be making much progress.

PR: Of course, wait until the last minute to make important decisions. I can't believe you people! What about travel budgets and operating expenses? Those are issues that ought to come into play here.

TD: Why? Those are fixed costs. If the CEO thought you needed more funds, he would give them to you. You have to prove yourself worthy first.

PR: Give me a break! When you were in PR, we were really unproductive but had a bigger budget. Now that you're in TD, you think you own the company.

TD: How dare you attack me personally! Why, I ought to. . . .

PR: Forget it. You're no negotiator. Send someone in next time who can at least pretend to be objective.

TD: Right. And next time why don't you bring your babysitter with you?

11.4.4: Conflict Styles and Tactics

Whether you are an employee, group leader, or manager, you will have both content goals (achieving the specific task at hand) and relational goals (preserving a dynamic with others) in a conflict situation. Because every conflict includes some level of concern for content goals and some level of concern for relational goals, we can characterize a particular conflict style by the relative importance it places on each of these goals. In conflict, as in all communication situations, the cultures of the people involved (and context) have a strong influence. Members of some cultures need to feel that the outcome does not affect them as individuals, and others need to release tension with volume and gestures in order to feel that they have been allowed to express their passion about the topic.

COMPETING   A competing style represents a high concern for content goals and a low concern for the relationship. Tactics related to a competing strategy reflect more concern for content goal achievement than for relational stability. For example, a group member may be more concerned with wanting to get her solution accepted to win recognition from the boss rather than with listening open-mindedly to other possible solutions. Competitive messages include denial, hostility, confrontation, and verbal aggressiveness. Here are some examples of competitive messages.

(×) Competitive Messages:

- "That is simply not the case."
- "It's obvious that you do not pull your weight around here."
- "How can you argue for a position as groundless as this?"
- "If you ever bothered to look at the data, you might be able to see a trend in the direction I'm describing."

ACCOMMODATING   At the opposite side of the grid is the accommodating style, which represents low concern for content goals and high concern for relational goals. The style is known as accommodating because the person using it places a high priority on the relationship with the conflict partner and in all likelihood will give in to his or her wishes to preserve it. Accommodating tactics reveal eagerness to satisfy the goals of the other party even if doing so means giving up content goals. Someone pursuing this strategy is unassertive, cooperative, yielding, and obliging. For example, an employee who believes that disagreeing with an idea expressed by another employee will create hostility or hurt feelings will accommodate her or him to prevent this situation. Here are some examples of accommodating messages.

(×) Accommodating Messages:

- "If it's important to you, then let's do it."
- "I see your point of view."
- "Let's do it your way this time."

AVOIDING   The avoiding style represents low concern for both content goals and relationships. This is the preferred style of people who simply do not care whether a job gets done or whether they have satisfactory relationships with those with whom they compete. Avoidance tactics include passive and uncooperative messages, postponements of conflict, complete apathy, and denial that a conflict situation exists. For example, a group member may not care whether the group reaches a solution to a problem and thus is not concerned with any conflict that arises within the group. Here are some examples of avoidance messages.

(×) Avoidance Messages:

- "I don't really care if we work this out."
- "Why don't we wait until there is a real problem before we argue over this?"
- "This is really a nonissue for me."
- "I don't know what you are talking about; I feel fine about our relationship."

COMPROMISING   Moderate concern for both content and relational goals results in a compromising style. For example, Paul and Wendy both want the newly vacated office with a window, but Paul wants to upgrade the furniture in his office, whereas Wendy wants a new computer. Even though they are not friends or colleagues, they respect each other. Their conflict over the vacated office is likely to be one of compromise. Compromising usually indicates only moderate concern for the goals and the relationship. Tactics of compromise include vagueness, conciliation, and concessions. Here are some examples of compromise messages.

(×) Compromising Messages:

- "I am not certain that we should be discussing this."
- "Perhaps I ought to reconsider my initial position."
- "Maybe we both ought to give a little."

COLLABORATING   Extreme concern for both content and relationships promotes a collaborating style. Recall our explanation of how collaborative goals can help parties realize their goals in a conflict and at the same time maintain their relationship. An ideal strategy that promotes both content and relational goal attainment, collaborating emphasizes problem solving, qualified support, and integration. For example, employees assigned to a research and development department would examine all relevant evidence and data before reaching a decision. If conflict arose about the best possible solution, a reexamination of the data might occur. Here are some examples of collaborative messages.

(×) Collaborative Messages:

- "Let's take a look at our respective positions and identify their strengths and weaknesses."
- "If the data are correct, I can back your plan."
- "If you combine our two requests, the end results will actually resemble our initial plans."

11.5: A Strategic Approach to Conflict

11.5 Describe the factors that can lead to successful conflict management

What happens in real conflict? It is quite unlikely that there is one best style for any particular conflict situation.

When approaching conflict situations, communicators must remain flexible so that the strategy they select is suitable for the people concerned, the goals to be achieved, and the situational constraints involved. Multiple strategies may be necessary, especially when the conflict changes course and reveals new patterns of communication, goals, or motives for participants. Communicators must be able to respond to the changing conditions of a conflict situation. A number of factors can influence the selection of a conflict strategy.

Goal setting, situational knowledge, communication competence, and anxiety management are no less important to productive conflict management than to any other communication situation. Let us discuss each of these factors in turn to determine how it can lead to successful conflict resolution.

WRITING PROMPT

Consider the expression, "In business, you don't get what you deserve; you get what you negotiate." Do you agree or disagree with this statement? Why or why not?

▶ The response entered here will appear in the performance dashboard and can be viewed by your instructor.

Submit

11.5.1: Set Goals for Conflict Resolution

An important consideration in any conflict situation is that the goals of communicators can change over the course of a conflict. Acknowledging valid arguments from opposition members, recognizing the importance of their goals to them, and understanding how they communicate can lead you to modify your initial content goals. If the goals of the conflict appear to be changing, you should be ready to respond with an alternative conflict style.

A second consideration for selecting a conflict style is the likelihood of multiple goals.[19] You choose a particular style (such as competing or accommodating) because of your main goal and your perception of your opponent's primary goal. But be flexible enough to shift to a more compromising style if it shows promise of promoting additional goals for both parties. If you boil down discussion to just one issue, there will be little room for negotiation.

Relational goals also influence the choice of a conflict style. The degree of cohesiveness you feel with your conflict partner can affect your choice. If you feel connected to him or her in some personal way, you are less likely to use competing or avoiding strategies and more likely to use positive strategies.

Also consider the professional relationship you have with your conflict partner. Her or his status, influence, and organizational position will probably influence your choice of style. Research has shown, for example, that managers tend to be accommodating with superiors, collaborative with subordinates, and compromising with peers.[20]

When you decide on a conflict style, consider the long-term relational consequences of your actions. If your adversary is someone with whom you hope to carry on a long-term relationship, employing avoiding or competitive tactics throughout the conflict may destroy your relationship. The destruction of a long-term relationship may not be worth the short-term gains you make by using such tactics.

When workers go on strike, communication has broken down in negotiation between workers and management. Repairing broken relationships is a very difficult process, so it is important to avoid negotiation breakdowns whenever possible.

SOURCE: Robert Galbraith/Reuters/Corbis

TECHNOLOGY TOOLS

Conflict and Email

Email has a tendency to create a false sense of security in the minds of its users. Many employees have acknowledged that they have sent pointed, even aggressive, messages to colleagues that they would never have communicated in person—often with dire consequences. Because it is asynchronous and buffered by a computer screen, email seems to encourage negative messages. Sometimes this is a good thing, allowing reticent or apprehensive people an opportunity to vent and speak their mind, which they would normally refrain from doing in public. In other instances, the vile and vicious barbs flying from the fingers of disgruntled or hurt employees are ill advised and have even led to reprimands and termination. There are three tactics you can use to help ensure that the "flaming" email messages you send are appropriate and won't get you in trouble.

⊗ **Don't send a regrettable email**

1. *Think before you type.* Wait an hour, an afternoon, or even a weekend before typing the email. Time has a way of tempering your emotions.

2. Type the email but don't send it right away. Put it in your drafts folder and read it over after waiting a period of time. Sometimes just drafting the email could be therapeutic and might even calm your emotions. However, after a waiting period you may find that the only audience it's appropriate for is you.

3. Send it to a trusted friend and ask for that person's honest advice. Hearing a different perspective may change your mind about sending that "email from hell."

11.5.2: Use Situational Knowledge to Understand Conflicts

Situational factors are elements in the conflict that affect the nature of conflict and the styles you select to deal with them. For example, the physical environment (where the conflict takes place, such as in a private office, in the cafeteria, or in a meeting) will affect how you communicate during a conflict. Aggressive tactics are particularly risky when the conflict occurs in public view.

Time constraints can also affect how you use conflict tactics. For example, if you are expected to settle your differences with someone in a limited time period, you may feel unable to develop a successful, positive style and may resort to tactics such as avoiding or competing. If you have a lot of time in which to work out the conflict, more elaborate styles such as collaborating and compromising may be possible.

11.5.3: Communicate Competently in Conflict Situations

In conflict situations be aware of your strengths and weaknesses—your **communication competence.** Competencies include argumentation skills, control of verbal aggressiveness, listening skills, and verbal and nonverbal skills. The ability to analyze, evaluate, and communicate ideas is vital to the management of conflict. The better you understand the situation, the better chance you have of achieving your goals.

Conflicts escalate because of many factors, not the least of which is taking a competitive, rather than cooperative, posture during deliberations. **Conflict escalation** is particularly troublesome because, once it starts, it can perpetuate itself.[21] People in the conflict begin to feel trapped in a process of unproductive communication. For

instance, Deutsch's research discovered that conflict escalation can result in the following:

⊗ **Autistic Hostility**

You break off contact with the conflict partner, thereby increasing chances of misunderstanding and misperceptions.

⊗ **Self-fulfilling Prophecies**

You make a false assumption about a partner that then leads to communication behavior that causes the very assumption you anticipated.

⊗ **Unwitting Commitments**

You overcommit to rigid positions and unwittingly commit to negative positions because of poor perceptions and unskillful communication.

One of the keys to reversing the escalation of conflict is to focus on issues and pursue cooperative and collaborative communication messages. If all else fails, parties may need to seek the help of a third party or a mediator to help them move back to positions of normalcy and objectivity.

Controlling verbal aggressiveness is important in conflict situations as well. Allowing (or encouraging) the discussion to drop to the level of personal attacks accomplishes nothing in the way of conflict management. It only escalates the conflict.

Listening skills are essential to the choice of a conflict style. Knowing what your opponents are saying and why they are saying it can tell you a lot about what style will work best in resolving conflict with them. Poor listening is a frequent cause of conflict and a large obstacle to conflict resolution.

A sincere effort to remain flexible also aids in resolving disputes. Flexibility allows you to adapt to the changing dynamics of a conflict. For example, you may decide that an accommodating strategy is effective in the initial stages of a conflict, but as the conflict progresses, the opponent's stubbornness or hostility may make competitive tactics more useful. By remaining flexible, you will be able to make a change in your conflict style to counter the shift. In general, successful conflict managers are highly sensitive to shifts in conflict strategies by their opponents.

11.5.4: Manage Anxiety in Conflict Situations

Many people will do just about anything to avoid a contentious situation. Conflict can be a major cause of anxiety in the workplace. You may dread or avoid particular situations, such as an argument with a superior, hostility in a group meeting, or even a sensitive bargaining session, if the possibility of conflict makes you uneasy. Conflict, however, can have productive outcomes, and on most occasions it is better to engage in conflict than to avoid it. The following example illustrates a common form of conflict in the workplace:

> Katrina and George have never liked one another, primarily because of contrasting personalities and competition for company resources. Their usual method of handling disagreement or competition has been to work behind the scenes to achieve their goals (gossip, grapevine, coalitions, and so on). One day their manager invited the two of them to a private meeting to discuss the problems that were arising from their conflict—tension, lowered morale and productivity, and less attention to their work, to name just a few. After controlling their anxiety at being confronted with the fact of their difficulties, both opened up and related why they did not appreciate the way the other operated. Each was surprised at how honest the other was and at how serious the conflict had grown simply because they had never faced it.

To Tell, or Not to Tell?

Ethical Issues

Assume you work in a department with two other employees. One of them is an older person nearing retirement; the other is a new college graduate. Although you are friendly with both, they often use verbal aggressiveness toward each other. Your supervisor told them to work out their differences, but neither has made an effort to do so. A coworker in another department has confided to you that one of them is planning to delete an important message from the other's email to create an impression of incompetence about the other. However, the coworker will not tell you which employee is planning this action and says that she will not get involved in their dispute. This rumor is the only evidence you have of potential foul play. Would you communicate your knowledge of the unethical behavior, and if so, to whom? Do you think it is ethical or unethical for you to become involved in a conflict between your coworkers?

To lessen your anxiety in a conflict, focus on goals and outcomes. Consider the relief you will feel after working through a conflict situation rather than avoiding the conflict and allowing distrust, resentment, or other negative feelings to simmer. You can also manage conflict-related anxiety by viewing your conflict partner in positive, human terms rather than as an enemy who means to undermine you or your career.

Seeking the support of others who share your goals and position in a conflict can be reassuring. If you dread conflict because you feel isolated by it, discovering that others support your side can lessen your anxiety considerably.

Taking a break to collect your thoughts and clear your head is also an effective way to manage anxiety in conflict situations. Often the tension of a conflict continues to build as the conflict progresses, and you may find that you are becoming too anxious to use your communication skills effectively. If it is possible to call a time-out to take a deep breath and relax, doing so can help you to calm your nerves and regain your composure. All these tactics for managing anxiety can increase your chances of resolving the conflict in a successful and positive manner.

Strategic Scenario Wrap-Up
Negotiation and Conflict Management

(×) Strategic Scenario

Lynn Shaefer, director of operations, has just returned from an emergency meeting in the senior vice president's office. He learned that he is to leave in two days to negotiate a contract with one of the local unions over health benefits, maternity/paternity leave, and on-site day-care centers. The person who was going to handle the negotiation, the local general manager of the manufacturing plant, suddenly died and Lynn seemed like the ideal choice since he is somewhat familiar with the local situation. This plant was in his territory when he was a sales representative four years ago. Union support for the contract is very important to the company, although it will not be easy since the company is losing money and must find ways to reduce costs. The biggest sticking points will be maternity/paternity leave and the day-care centers.

Lynn's company knows that giving in on these benefits to this local union will set a precedent and create the same demands among all the union's locals in the company. The people that Lynn will be negotiating with run the gamut of older, traditional workers; young workers wanting to start families; and workers with established families. Lynn has heard from the grapevine that even his negotiating counterparts cannot completely agree on their highest priorities. They are simply saying that the company must produce a contract granting all their demands, in spite of how unrealistic this would be. Lynn also knows that the negotiating sessions could become very heated, even volatile.

Lynn must rely on formal bargaining in this situation. This is an ongoing situation with recurring issues requiring serious deliberation. Channeling conflict in as positive a way as possible is Lynn's main challenge. He must know before he sets foot in the door exactly what his company is prepared to offer to start and where it can compromise. Bargaining involves flexibility, however, and he knows he will go back to his company once he has more information from the union. As an individual he cannot make promises but instead must consult with management during each step of the negotiations. However, he must listen carefully so that he can properly reflect the employees concerns back to management.

After seeing first hand that union leaders disagree among themselves, he emphasizes that they must clarify exactly what they need so that the company can respond. Above all, Lynn keeps listening, even when the dialog gets repetitious, and at no point does he take any emotional displays in a personal manner.

WRITING PROMPT

If serious issues brought up at the meeting indicated that a change of direction was needed, could the meeting have been successful? Why or why not?

> The response entered here will appear in the performance dashboard and can be viewed by your instructor.

[Submit]

Summary

Negotiation and Conflict Management

- The **nature of any conflict situation** derives from how inclined the adversaries are to use argumentativeness and verbal aggressiveness.

- **Argumentativeness** is a willingness to stand up for and promote ideas despite opposition.

- **Verbal aggressiveness** is the tendency to attack the personal characteristics or self-concept of an opponent instead of the issues under discussion. Verbal aggressiveness is a negative trait that often results from poor critical thinking skills and that prevents conflict resolution.

- Most competitive communication situations can be addressed through **negotiation**, which can occur formally or informally.

- Three dimensions of negotiation are **information management** (being able to acquire, retrieve, and use information in a bargaining session), **positioning** (refocusing attention on issues of concern or advantage to you), and **concessions** (knowing when, where, and how much to give to opponents).

- Strategic bargaining consists of **cooperative tactics** (problem solving) and **competitive tactics** (maximizing one's own position at the expense of the other side's position).

- The selection of the most appropriate **bargaining strategy** depends on the situation, although general guidelines can be applied.

- Conflict, the struggle between **interdependent parties who perceive incompatible goals**, may exist in all levels, situations, and relationships in an organization.

- The primary cause of conflict is **competing goals**, which can be managed through clarification of opposing or conflicting goals so that collaborative goals can be worked out.

- **Content goals and relational goals** have to be specified so that a comprehensive resolution can be achieved.

- **Successfully resolving conflict** requires strategic communication—goal setting, situational knowledge, communication competence, and anxiety management.

SHARED WRITING: NEGOTIATION AND CONFLICT MANAGEMENT

Consider the last time you received a grade on a term paper or essay exam that you thought should have been higher. Assume you are going to approach your professor about raising your grade to a level that you think is fair. What positioning will you use? What data will you need to support your position?

> A minimum number of characters is required to post and earn points. After posting, your response can be viewed by your class and instructor, and you can participate in the class discussion.

[Post]   0 characters | 140 minimum

Chapter 11 Quiz: Negotiation and Conflict Management

Chapter 12
Develop and Deliver Effective Presentations

Learning Objectives

12.1 Report the importance and effect of the right presentation

12.2 Describe communication apprehension and its different forms

12.3 Enumerate ways of selecting an appropriate topic for presentation

12.4 Examine the general and the specific purposes of a presentation

12.5 Express the importance of doing a background analysis of the audience for an effective presentation

12.6 Examine the need of identifying and researching the main points to be covered in a presentation

12.7 Explain how supporting materials facilitate learning

12.8 Report the importance of a proper introduction and conclusion in a presentation

12.9 Report the three basic types of outlines

12.10 Scrutinize the need to deliver an effective presentation appropriate for the message, audience, and occasion

12.11 Report the need to prepare for fielding audience questions

---

Strategic Scenario: Structure and Function

The B. J. Turock Art Museum Museum is a university museum founded in 1903. It occupies a 70,000-square foot facility on the university's main campus and houses over 90,000 works of art. Particular strengths exist in American 19th and 20th century art, Russian and Soviet Art, and glass art. The Museum's Director of Education, Danielle Bechta, trains and coordinates a group of approximately 40 docents who provide tours of the museum's collections and special exhibitions. In addition to educating the docents on the art itself, she works with them on how to best present the information to small groups of visitors. Danielle has decided to offer two trainings: 1) an all-day workshop on developing presentations skills, and 2) certification training on the permanent and temporary exhibitions. She must clarify her specific purposes and goals and structure each of her presentations accordingly.

As you read this chapter, think about Danielle's work in crafting two different presentations, each successful in its own right. At the end of the chapter, we will return to this scenario and discuss some solutions.

12.1: Overview

Develop and Deliver Effective Presentations

12.1 Report the importance and effect of the right presentation

Opportunities to speak publicly are multiplying rapidly in this age of information. Although people may think that information technologies and videoconferencing have replaced some of the functions of business presentations, this assumption isn't true. Actually, reliance on technology goes hand-in-hand with rapid decision making as the norm. Many business decisions are now made more quickly and more diverse groups of people are participating in decision making than ever before. Face-to-face presentation is still the most effective way to reach these audiences.

Successful presentations demonstrate that the speaker is confident and sincerely believes in the message being delivered. In a successful presentation, the speaker and the audience establish a mutual understanding of or commitment to goals that is not possible through written or electronic channels. Given the large number of people who can usually be touched by the message, under the right circumstances an effective presentation can be even more powerful than small-group communication.

In general, presentational speaking shares some similarities with other forms of oral communication. All depend on the components of strategic communication—goal setting, situational knowledge, communication competence, and anxiety management—which require adequate preparation and ensure effective performance. In addition, speaking to a group shares a common problem with all other forms of oral communication. Unlike visual or written communication, which can be reread or reviewed, any form of spoken communication must be clear and convincing the *first* time it is made.

Nevertheless, making a presentation is quite different from speaking with others in two-party or small-group contexts. Ensuring audience comprehension is more difficult because feedback is less direct and less spontaneous. During a presentation, the speaker must read the audience's nonverbal behavior to infer members' moods and reactions to the message being presented.

In the business world, public speaking takes the form of making presentations to fellow employees, managers, and supervisors or to an audience of people outside of the speaker's organization. The following scenarios illustrate two examples of such presentations.

Nancy is a communication major working as an intern in the human resources division of a local computer software firm. The firm is experiencing strained management–employee relationships and a high turnover rate in its staff. Mark, the vice president of human resources, believes that the company will be severely hurt by the current situation. He assigns Nancy the job of researching the employees to determine how their needs can be better met. Two weeks into her research, Mark asks her to make a preliminary report of her findings to a group composed of Mark, the chief executive officer, the chief financial officer, and the three members of the company's communications department. Nancy realizes that she may not get another chance to speak directly to these people, and she wants to give them a clear and comprehensive understanding of her findings, their importance, and what each of her listeners can do about the situation. She knows this will be the most significant presentation she has ever been asked to make.

Akbar is an entrepreneurial student who has been involved in a university-sponsored program to collect leftover or unused hotel food supplies and to distribute them to homeless shelters. He would like to initiate a similar program in his hometown. To do this, he must persuade a group of hotel managers and administrators that this project is an opportunity to benefit the community greatly and to reduce operating costs at the same time. He has already made contacts at a variety of hotels and has received replies from twelve interested managers. His final challenges are preparing the presentation (which includes targeting the hidden costs of wasted supplies), anticipating and overcoming legal or regulatory obstacles, and demonstrating how to get such a program started with minimum time and resources. He needs to have the managers agree with him and implement the program he believes in. He understands how crucial this presentation will be.

These scenarios show the potential range of presentations and audiences you will encounter in your career. For many people, speaking before a group is the most frightening activity imaginable. Yet some basic guidelines can help you understand the fundamentals of presentational speaking, thus lessening your anxiety.

This chapter focuses on preparing for a presentation by using the model of strategic communication. We begin by explaining the phenomenon of public speaking apprehension and methods of handling it. Second, we discuss how to select and narrow a topic. Then we discuss the significance of situational knowledge and the importance of performing an audience analysis to understand the relationship between the topic and the audience. Finally, building on that preparation, we discuss communication competence as demonstrated in the creation, structure, and delivery of a message.

We focus on basic principles of the presentation.

12.2: Communication Apprehension

12.2 Describe communication apprehension and its different forms

Anxiety management is particularly important in presentational speaking. Consider the following example:

> A popular Washington hostess, entering a room in one of the capital's finest hotels, recognized a well-known government official. Hands clasped behind his back, head bowed, he was pacing up and down the length of the room.
>
> "I'm going to deliver a speech," he told her.
>
> "Do you usually get this nervous before addressing a large gathering?" asked the woman.
>
> "Why no," he answered. "I never get nervous."
>
> "In that case," demanded the woman, "what are you doing in the women's room?"[1]

The experience of this government official is one with which many people can identify. Although there are many symptoms besides disorientation, the sense of panic that frequently accompanies speaking before a group is quite unlike any other fear. When Americans are asked to answer the question "What are you most afraid of?" they report that one of their worst fears is having to speak before a group.[2] Fear of public speaking ranks highly, along with fear of the dentist, heights, insects or bugs, snakes, death, and flying, as a widespread phenomenon.

Given this fear's widespread nature, you are likely to encounter **communication apprehension**—which can appear as *reticence, shyness,* and *unwillingness to communicate*—sooner, rather than later, in your career as a speaker. Based on our discussion of apprehension in other contexts, you know that many conditions can cause communication anxiety, even in informal situations, and that anxiety may be a trait that some people are more likely to have than others. There are also some additional causes of anxiety about public speaking and some remedies to deal with them effectively.

12.2.1: Why Is Public Speaking Frightening?

To understand why public speaking frightens people, let us review the origins of anxiety about communicating in public and discuss specific suggestions for countering them. Experts have proposed three ways of explaining how apprehension develops, is maintained, and can be treated: skills deficit, conditioned anxiety, and negative cognitive appraisal.

SKILLS DEFICIT One explanation for anxiety is that the speaker lacks the adequate skills for making a successful presentation, and so he or she fears or even avoids doing it.

A real lack of presentation skills results in the speaker's embarrassment, failure to reach the audience, and sense of frustration and helplessness. In a business setting, it may also result in loss of sales, fewer chances to participate in major projects that may lead to promotions, and a perception that the speaker is not a particularly talented or qualified employee. These are serious problems, so a speaker who feels she or he lacks adequate skills should do everything possible to bring them up to speed by targeting the points we will discuss in this chapter about choosing a topic, analyzing an audience, and so forth. Most important of all is *practice.* We cannot overemphasize the role of experience in calming anxiety—even if you are never completely comfortable speaking before a group, you can learn exactly what you are capable of and what to expect from yourself through experience. Once you have mastered the skills of public speaking, you no longer need to feel threatened by personal failure.

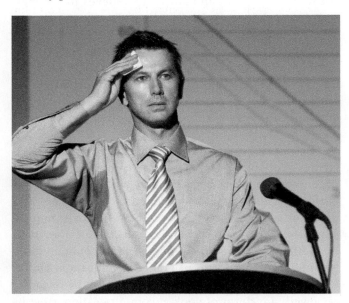

This chapter suggests several methods of preparing to deliver a speech that can assist you with anxiety management. What are your options when, despite using them, you still find yourself anxious during your presentation? What would be your advice to the speaker pictured here?

SOURCE: Image Source/Alamy

CONDITIONED ANXIETY Conditioned anxiety results when neutral communication situations collect negative connotations, images, and memories over time. The speaker is informally "taught" to be anxious about speaking through a succession of negative events, such as a teacher punishing her or him for speaking up in class or a parent telling her or him to be quiet around adults. Being punished for early attempts to communicate can lead to fear of communication situations, especially public speaking, later in life.

One method for reducing conditioned anxiety is *systematic desensitization (SD).*[3] SD is based on the theory that a person cannot be relaxed and anxious at the same time, and so the process attempts to overlay pleasant, relaxing images and experiences on the anxiety-causing situation. SD also uses deep muscle relaxation techniques that can help the speaker maintain a real physical sense of relaxation while speaking. The following list illustrates a typical step-by-step process for using SD:

1. Before you begin, make a list of situations that cause you varying degrees of anxiety, from lowest to highest. For example, one list may include lying in bed just before going to sleep, discussing the upcoming speech a week before it is scheduled, getting dressed on the morning of the speech, entering the room on the day of the speech, walking up to the podium, and giving the speech.

2. Then assume a relaxed position, take several deep breaths, and become as relaxed as possible.

3. Moving from your hands through to your feet, systematically tense muscle groups, hold the contraction for several seconds, relax the muscles, and then concentrate on the relaxed state you experience. For example, make a fist and tense the muscles of your right hand and forearm for five seconds; then relax and note how these muscles feel as relaxation flows through them.

4. After you relax all the muscle groups, envision a pleasant scene and associate the feeling of relaxation with the image.

5. Stay relaxed and think about the situation with the lowest anxiety level on your list.

6. Move down the list of progressively anxious situations. Stay relaxed and consciously link the physical feeling of relaxation with the scene you are thinking about. Breathe deeply as needed.

7. If you feel a twinge of anxiety at any point, leave the list of situations and envision the original pleasant scene. Then take deep breaths and tense and relax muscle groups to bring back the sensation of relaxation.

8. When you have gone through every item on the list, return to the original relaxed state by breathing deeply and imagining pleasant scenes.

Although SD may not work for every person, it is one of the most successful techniques for reducing conditioned anxiety. For those who find it effective, SD's conscious efforts to promote relaxation inhibit anxiety, thus weakening the link between communication and nervousness.

NEGATIVE COGNITIVE APPRAISAL Negative cognitive appraisal is a process of unrealistic, negative self-evaluations in which communicators assume that they are going to fail and then worry about failure and its consequences. Negative cognitive appraisal is best handled by reducing negative self-statements (such as "I know I'm going to lose my train of thought") so that you are able to concentrate on

your skills and the message and are able to speak more confidently and competently. This is done through the process of *cognitive restructuring (CR)*.

CR attempts to change or modify the thought process by identifying the impact of negative statements you have made about the speaking situation. Once you see how the negative statements result in your discomfort and negative behavior during a presentation, you can then focus on reducing negative thoughts by substituting more positive, coping statements.

Keeping a log is important for using CR successfully. In the log, you note the negative self-statements that you use frequently. When writing these statements, you also become aware of what these statements really are: irrational. For example, if you find yourself thinking, "I'm going to sound stupid," consider your skill and experience and the preparation that you have put into the presentation. In reality, you will undoubtedly be among the people most knowledgeable about the topic in the room. Write down these positive coping statements in your log.

There are two types of coping statements. *Context statements* emphasize the nonstressful aspects of the situation. *Task statements* emphasize what you can do to ensure a successful presentation. To be most effective, confront negative self-statements that occur before, during, and after the presentation. Table 12.1 shows a sample entry in a cognitive restructuring (CR) log.

Situation: I have been asked to give a thirty-minute presentation at a monthly breakfast meeting.

Description: My presentation will deal with financial projections and strategic planning; my audience consists of colleagues as well as upper management.

Table 12.1 Cognitive Restructuring Log

Negative Self-Statement	Coping Statement
Before: I will forget some of the data for my financial projections.	*Context:* I have not forgotten important information in previous speeches. *Task:* I will have all the important data on both my outline and my slides.
During: I'll sound like an amateur.	*Context:* I know everyone in the audience, and we respect each other's knowledge. *Task:* I am well prepared and have excellent visual aids.
After: Upper management won't find my projections credible.	*Context:* I have an established track record with upper management. *Task:* My charts are based on data provided by the company treasurer.
	Hide All Cells Show All Cells

These techniques for managing anxiety are not independent—they work best together. If you wish to manage anxiety, you will find it useful to practice all three. Learn and practice the skills of public speaking, use relaxation and deep breathing to achieve physical comfort when speaking, and learn to identify irrational negative statements that increase your anxiety and replace them with positive task and context coping statements.

12.3: Identify the Topic

12.3 Enumerate ways of selecting an appropriate topic for presentation

The starting point for developing a message is selecting a topic. Making this decision in a work setting is usually quite easy; topics emerge naturally from the interplay of your job, your audience, and the organization's needs. For example, as a business manager, you may be asked to talk to new employees about the benefits package provided by your organization.

Nevertheless, you are also likely to encounter occasions when the topic is relatively unclear, when you must choose among several possible topics, or when you have been assigned an inappropriate topic and need to suggest an alternative. In these situations, you can use several techniques to identify a topic. Although there are no fail-safe formulas, there a definitely a few good methods you can use.

ⓧ Four techniques for identifying a potential topic

1. Engage in personal brainstorming. Sit down and think about any special knowledge that you may already possess, things that you have done, experiences that you have had, or issues that are important to you.

2. Brainstorm with others. When you use this option, you not only gain additional ideas that result from group synergy, but you also get a preview of how relevant a topic is to others. Thus, it can be helpful to use classmates, coworkers, friends, or colleagues to assist you in generating potential topics.

3. Use the reference room of your library. If necessary, email the reference librarian for help in using general online databases.

4. Go online. Google (**www.google.com**) and Yahoo! (**www.yahoo.com**) are among the best ways to locate information on the Internet. Each site has instructions for making your searches effective and efficient.

After you have generated several potential topics, you will select the actual topic for your presentation. As you do so, consider three criteria for evaluating your potential topic in order to finalize it.

ⓧ Three criteria for selecting a final topic

1. Are you knowledgeable and/or interested in this topic? Because you will speak most authoritatively on topics you know best, choose a familiar topic whenever possible. When circumstances prevent making such a choice, look for topics that you have always wanted to know more about. An active interest in the subject will make your research more exciting.

2. Is the topic relevant to your audience? Consider what you know about the audience. Will this group of people find your topic informative, useful, or interesting? While most, if not all, topics can be made interesting, starting with a topic that your listeners need and want to hear about will make your task much easier.

3. Is the topic a good one for this assignment or situation? Presentations are given for many reasons, and an effective topic may be inappropriate if it does not support or correspond to the reason for the presentation. For example, a company seminar on health-care benefits would appropriately include presentations on employees' health insurance choices, on how the company's wellness and nutrition program has improved work quality, or on changes in the workers' compensation policy. All these topics relate directly to health care as it is mediated by the company. Good speech topics, then, are topics the speaker is knowledgeable about and/or interested in, are relevant for the audience, and meet the requirements of the assignment or situation.

When you are in doubt about either your assignment choice or the relevance of a particular topic, ask the person who is organizing the presentation (or the instructor supervising an in-class presentation). Be sure to have your questions answered far enough in advance so that you can change your topic if necessary.

12.4: Identify General and Specific Purposes

12.4 Examine the general and the specific purposes of a presentation

Once you have selected a topic, the process of refining it begins. The first filter, or question to ask yourself, is about the **general purpose:** why will you give a speech on this topic to this audience? This question identifies the basic goal of your presentation. The second filter for refining your topic is determining the specific purpose. The **specific purpose** of a presentation is derived from the general purpose and identifies what you as the presenter want the audience to think, believe, feel, or do as a result of listening to your presentation.

12.4.1: General Purpose

The goal is usually motivated by one of four general purposes: to *inform, persuade, motivate,* or *celebrate.* That is, you may want to enlighten your audience on a topic by providing new information or ideas (inform), change or reaffirm the audience's attitudes (persuade), urge audience action for your cause (motivate), or help your audience acknowledge an individual achievement or event (celebrate).

TO INFORM   Informative presentations provide ideas, alternatives, data, or even opinions, but most important, they provide credible, reliable information to back up your major points. When giving an informative presentation, you function as your audience's teacher. It is not always easy, however, to know the audience's level of background knowledge on the topic, nor is it easy to narrow the topic so that you are working with a manageable and teachable amount of information.

Expanded sources of information, such as online databases and chat groups, make the selection of material for informative presentations more important and challenging than ever before.

An informative presentation must be accurate, reliable, and credible. For example, if you are asked to give a report in your communication class on problems with financial aid disbursement at your school, check and double-check your statistical information, the conclusions you draw, and any other elements of the presentation that may contain inaccuracies. Cite your sources to increase both your credibility and the significance of the data. Remember that to teach your audience effectively, you are wise to act as an expert, not simply a layperson with a few statistics to present.

TO PERSUADE   Persuasive presentations can work at three levels: they can change or reaffirm existing attitudes about important topics, strive to gain audience commitment, and motivate action. For example, if you are concerned about the environment, you may decide to attend a presentation on your company's recycling program. As you listen to a manager speak about recycling and conservation, you suddenly realize the importance of these issues. You leave the session determined to recycle cans and avoid Styrofoam coffee cups. If you actually follow through with these intentions, the manager's presentation was effective at all three levels.

In persuasive presentations, you are asking the audience to make a commitment to your viewpoint and to act in ways that you advocate. As with informative speaking, persuasive presentations require conscientious research to uncover the best available data on the topic. In addition, persuaders must present a course of action that can be accepted by a group of people who might choose otherwise.

TO MOTIVATE   Presentations designed to motivate audience members are a special type of persuasive speech. **Motivational presentations** employ persuasion but rely more extensively on stimulating the emotions and feelings of listeners as a method of inducing action. Members of the clergy may use biblical images and the subconscious fears and hopes of their audiences to encourage spiritual action. Drill sergeants may use highly charged, emotional language to push "raw" recruits to new levels of physical exertion. Although drill sergeants and clerics employ different motivational strategies, the emotional intensity they can inspire is often very similar.

In the business world, managers are often called upon to motivate their employees. At a typical annual sales meeting, for example, during which sales representatives are brought together to learn about the latest company products and initiatives, sales managers and company executives are likely to take some time to "pump up" the sales force with tales of success in the past year and promises of good fortune to come.

TO CELEBRATE   Ceremonial presentations often share many of the elements found in informative, persuasive, and motivational speaking. At least six different types of presentations are considered ceremonial.

Ceremonial presentations

Remove card   1 of 6   Reset Deck

Ceremonial presentations demonstrate your commitment to organizational ideals or your organization's commitment to its valued ideals. For example, many organizations hold "roasts," or comic tributes, for retiring employees who have been vital members of the organization throughout the years. Ceremonial presentations require you to consider the common ties that bind participants together as a group.

While in this course you may be given a general purpose and asked to select a topic, in business you are frequently assigned a topic and must then choose the general purpose (approach) that will be most successful. As a result, general purpose normally takes a purer form within the classroom—an assignment for an informative presentation will largely avoid persuasive, motivational, or celebratory goals—whereas in the workplace it is not at all unusual for a manager to use one message to inform, persuade, motivate, and celebrate. We focus on each of these goals separately, an approach that introduces beginning speakers to the unique characteristics and demands of each purpose and better prepares them to combine or adapt goals for presentations later in their speaking careers.

WRITING PROMPT

List several topics that you think might make good speeches for this class. For one or two of them, consider how you might convert that topic into a speech to inform, to persuade, to motivate, or to celebrate. Which general purpose (inform, persuade, motivate, celebrate) would create the most difficulty for you? Why do you think so?

▶ The response entered here will appear in the performance dashboard and can be viewed by your instructor.

Submit

12.4.2: Specific Purpose

Specific goals are preferred for directing communication to achieve shared meaning and desired results. Public speaking requires deliberate and specific goals, just as interpersonal, group, and organizational communication do.

The specific purpose should contain a single idea. Some basic considerations for the specific purpose include the following: Is the idea manageable in the time allowed for the presentation? Is the idea challenging to the audience? Is the idea important to the organizational values and/or career goals of the audience? The specific purpose is then translated into a **thesis statement**—a single, declarative sentence that summarizes the main ideas to be presented to the audience.

The thesis statement may emerge as the speaker researches and develops the message. For example, a first specific purpose may be stated as "I want my audience to know about the role of electronic interconnectivity in an advertising agency." After the speaker researches the topic, he or she may devise a more specific (and useful) thesis statement: "Within an advertising agency, electronic interconnectivity serves the areas of business development, account management, research, creative development, graphic design, and internal communication." A well-considered thesis statement is crucial for delivering an effective message.

The above speaker has identified a specific purpose and translated that purpose into a thesis statement for an informative presentation. The process is the same for all four general purposes (to inform, persuade, motivate, and celebrate). Say, for example, the speaker has been assigned the task of coordinating the company's participation in the United Way campaign (general purpose: to persuade). After reflection, the speaker decides that the specific purpose of the presentation is to convince coworkers to make a donation. This specific purpose is then translated into a thesis statement: "I want my audience to pledge to make a financial contribution to the United Way."

Successful communication results from the achievement of a series of interrelated goals, each flowing from the one before it. This element of continuity means that you must set goals at every stage of the presentation process, from selecting a topic and doing research to practicing your delivery. Goals prompt you to monitor your work continually, thereby ensuring that you attend carefully to each phase of your presentation's development.

12.5: Analyze the Audience

12.5 Express the importance of doing a background analysis of the audience for an effective presentation

In presentational speaking, the process of finding out about those to whom you will be speaking is termed **audience analysis**, and it corresponds to the second component of strategic communication: gathering situational knowledge. When preparing for a presentation, you can research individual members of the audience, organizational factors that affect the audience, and even location, time, or other physical influences. Audience analysis helps you to understand the speaking situation as it unfolds as well as how best to prepare for the audience's needs and likely responses to your message. In other words, effective speakers continue to gather information and monitor the situation throughout the presentation.[4]

Demographic information—the audience's size, age, social class, educational level, gender, cultural background, and occupational status—is fundamental to any audience analysis. Demography (the collection and study of such information) is a necessary first step toward establishing more specific and complex analyses of a target audience. The target audience—the key decision makers who are members of the general audience—is an important focus for your analysis. You are more likely to succeed by tailoring your ideas, information, and appeals to these audience members.[5]

Audience attitudes toward many social and economic issues can be predicted through careful demographic analysis. For example, if you learn that your audience will be composed of employees in the manufacturing division of your company—mostly blue-collar males ages 40 to 60 who are union members—you can conclude that a presentation on why the company should deunionize to encourage new hiring policies will have to be approached with careful preparation and an understanding of possible negative audience response.

This is not to say that audience analysis encourages stereotyping or can be ignored if you think you already know, for example, what a typical clerical worker is like. It is vital to approach audience analysis with an open mind because you are likely to discover unexpected characteristics of audience members that may provide the key to connecting with them. By analyzing and understanding the implications of the audience analysis, you will have a good sense of how to aim your presentation and what language and imagery to employ.

Remember also that it is important to know whether you are speaking to accountants, engineers, marketers, janitors, or a combination of various employee groups. They may all work for your company, but each group has a different perspective on the organization, and it is also likely to differ from your own. Be sure to modify your presentation to accommodate each group because the most successful presentations are those that address every member of the audience and make each person feel involved and important.

Three categories of audience analysis can be considered when doing a profile. Each of the three categories provides a different starting point for thinking about your audience's needs.

1. *Audience type*—Why have these people decided to attend your presentation?
2. *Audience characteristics*—What are the religions, education levels, ages, ethnicities, and genders of typical audience members?
3. *Environmental characteristics*—How will the setting and surroundings affect the speaking situation?

Presentations made to familiar coworkers may require less investigative work than do presentations made to people you do not know; nevertheless, do not underestimate the importance of any category of demographic information just because it is easy to collect. For example, you will make presentations in this class, and you can simply look around the room to determine the gender ratio, ethnic makeup, approximate age bracket, and educational level of your audience members. Obtaining other demographic information may be more difficult, but not impossible. One excellent method is to ask questions of people who are knowledgeable about the audience—friends, supervisors, coworkers, or even people who have presented to the group before. Less obvious categories, such as sociopolitical status, religious affiliations, and economic status, can often be discovered through research, which can be done in the library with the assistance of a librarian. The environmental characteristics of the speaking situation, such as time limit, size of the audience, and location, can be learned by visiting the site ahead of time and by talking with the people who asked you to speak.

PRACTICING BUSINESS COMMUNICATION

American Red Cross

Well into its second century of existence, the American Red Cross continues its tradition of providing relief to victims of home fires, wildfires, hurricanes, floods, earthquakes, tornadoes, transportation accidents, explosions, and other natural and human-caused disasters. One hundred thirty-five years have passed since founder Clara Barton carried in her purse the funds to conduct Red Cross operations. The organization has greatly expanded from the small association she founded in 1881; today hundreds of thousands of relief workers, donors, and volunteers are still motivated by that same humanitarian concern to alleviate human suffering and help during times of crisis.

Proud as the Red Cross is of its achievements, the organization continuously tries to prepare itself to better respond to emergencies and to make both its communications and its service delivery more efficient and more effective for the recipients.

A Grassroots Culture

The focal point of Red Cross activity in the United States is its headquarters in Washington, D.C. But its organizational culture reflects a grassroots, volunteer base of more than 340,000 and nearly 500 local chapters nationwide. In fact, volunteers make up the vast majority of the organization's total work force. Characterized by dedication, loyalty, a strong sense of the organization's mission, and commitment to social ideals, many Red Cross employees and volunteers view the organization as an integral part of their lives and as a way to give something of themselves back to their communities and to society.

⊗ Read More

An appreciation of the bottom-up nature and community focus of the Red Cross guides the national headquarters staff in supporting a complex organizational structure that employs around 25,000 paid staff in addition to its volunteers in hundreds of regional offices, blood services facilities, and Red Cross stations on U.S. military installations.

National headquarters staff develop and guide the services available through the Red Cross; help people throughout America to understand the Geneva Conventions, which the U.S. government has agreed to; and participate, along with other national Red Cross and Red Crescent societies, in the mission of the International Red Cross and Red Crescent Movement to provide humanitarian relief worldwide.

Founded in 1881 and first chartered by Congress in 1900, the American Red Cross shoulders two major national responsibilities: (1) providing assistance to disaster victims, and (2) providing emergency communication between members of the U.S. armed forces and their families. Today, the Red Cross also operates the nation's largest blood service and helps more than 15 5.6 million people each year gain the skills they need to prepare for and respond to emergencies in their workplaces, homes, schools, and communities. Across the nation, the Red Cross offers educational programs in the areas of first aid, CPR and the use of AEDs (automated external defibrillators), swimming, lifeguarding, and water safety.

Targeted Communication

The Red Cross runs a multifaceted internal communication operation that targets an array of audiences, including the nearly 500 local Red Cross chapters, 36 blood regions, and more than 50 Red Cross stations on U.S. military bases at home and abroad.

Internal communication ranges from official memoranda from the organization's chair or president, to biweekly emails highlighting all pertinent organization-wide information and other announcements targeted to specific audiences. In addition, top Red Cross leaders participate in regular conference calls with employees nationwide to answer questions and support their roles as leaders of major initiatives.

In addition, the Exchange, the sophisticated Red Cross intranet, is updated throughout each day to ensure that volunteers and employees have access to the information they need, when they need it. Major organizational announcements are often linked to complex and detailed Exchange sections containing multimedia presentations, FAQs, talking points, and template materials for local Red Cross units to use. The Exchange complements the Red Cross public

The American Red Cross is also a nationally recognized leader in social media and social strategy. The social engagement team at national headquarters is focused on empowering social media communities to execute the mission of the American Red Cross online. In addition to managing social communities on Facebook and Twitter, the Red Cross has robust social listening and digital volunteer programs that broaden the reach of the organization.

The charity organization also maintains a proactive media relations and public affairs team focused on telling the Red Cross story. Trained public affairs representatives from the field and its national headquarters are dispatched to serve as spokespersons in the event of a major disaster relief operation. In this way, the organization is able to make use of its network of field units and its national headquarters to communicate its message.

You can visit the American Red Cross at http://www.redcross.org

WRITING PROMPT

What do you consider to be the organization's most significant internal communication challenges? Its most significant external communication challenges? Give the Red Cross your recommendation for using social media to advance its communication.

▶ The response entered here will appear in the performance dashboard and can be viewed by your instructor.

Submit

12.6: Identify and Research Main Ideas

12.6 Examine the need of identifying and researching the main points to be covered in a presentation

Once you have narrowed a topic to a specific purpose and thesis statement and identified the outstanding characteristics of your audience, the next step is to identify and research your main points. Ask yourself, "What does the audience need to know and accept if I am to accomplish the specific purpose I have selected for the presentation?" If, for example, you are an account executive for an advertising agency and your goal is to persuade a local restaurant owner to select your agency to handle the restaurant's advertising campaign, what are the main ideas you need to stress to show her or him the benefits of selecting your agency?

12.6.1: Generate Potential Main Ideas

A good method for locating main ideas is to think systematically about the topic. Doing so reminds you of what you already know about the topic and suggests areas that require additional research.

Although there are many ways to generate main ideas, we recommend a *topical* system based on the methods of such famous writers on public speaking as Aristotle, Cicero, and Francis Bacon. The **topical system** uses a small set of headings or topics to identify standard ways of thinking and talking about any subject. The basic premise of the approach is that the infinite number of possible topics contain a finite

number of themes—a result of our shared ways of thinking about human affairs. The following sixteen topics can be used to describe any subject on which a presenter might choose to speak. They are categorized according to *attributes* and *basic relationships*.[6]

Topical System: Sixteen Topics

 Attributes:

1. Existence or nonexistence of things

2. Degree or quantity of things or forces

3. Spatial attributes, including location, distribution, and position of things, especially in relation to other things

4. Time—when an event took place, how long it lasted, and so forth

5. Motion or activity—type, degree

6. Form—the physical or abstract shape of a thing

7. Substance—the physical or abstract content of a thing

8. Capacity to change—whether an event or situation is predictable or unpredictable

9. Potency—power or energy, including the ability to further or hinder something else

10. Desirability—whether the thing results in rewards or punishments

11. Feasibility—how well the thing works or how practical it is

ⓧ **Basic Relationships:**

1. Causality—the relation of causes to effects, effects to causes, and so forth

2. Correlation—correspondence between, coexistence of, or coordination of things or forces

3. Genus-species relationships—common characteristics or distinguishing characteristics of a thing or group of things

4. Similarity or dissimilarity in appearance, content, form, shape, and so forth

5. Possibility or impossibility of an event happening

Let us return to our hypothetical account executive preparing to make a pitch to the restaurant owner and managers for an account. How can she or he stress any of the sixteen themes? After some thought, the account executive comes up with the following points:

1. The ad agency has been serving the community for more than thirty years (existence).

2. The agency handles more than twenty restaurant accounts and gains more every year (degree of experience/expertise).

3. The agency is conveniently located in the downtown business district (spatial attribute).

4. The agency can put together a trial campaign in two weeks (time).

5. Restaurants that have used the ad agency have reported substantial increases in customers (activity).

6. The agency can provide several choices for the look of the campaign and specializes in the latest design and graphics (form).

7. The agency will work with the restaurant owner to articulate a precise message for the campaign (substance).

8. The agency will modify the campaign if it is not bringing the desired results (capacity to change).

9. The agency projects a 32 percent increase in the restaurant's business based on campaigns done for similar restaurants in the past (potency).

10. The agency can promote increased business that will allow the restaurant owner to open another restaurant and enjoy greater profits (desirability).

11. The agency is a practical choice because of its expertise in the area of restaurant advertising and its competitive rates (feasibility).

Of course, it would be an overwhelming task to stress all these themes in the course of one presentation. Nevertheless, the account executive now has a wealth of main ideas and can select the two or three most suited to the needs of this restaurant owner.

12.6.2: Perform Research

The topical system, although useful for generating potential main points, must be supplemented by additional research to find information to support your ideas, especially if the topic is in an area in which you are not an expert. A good starting point for such research is consultation with experts and specialists on your topic through the process of informational interviewing. Questions to be asked in such an interview include "What books and articles do you recommend I read?"; "What resources have proven especially useful to you?"; and "Do you know other people who might provide additional help?"

Following up leads provided by experts and filling in missing details often mean conducting an online search. A search of the library's card catalog or database, its reference room, and the periodicals section are all good starting points for research. If you don't know about the location of materials in the library, ask for help; reference librarians are trained to find relevant information quickly and efficiently. Not only will the reference librarian be familiar with special indexes and guides to materials; he or she will also be able to assist you with online computerized indexes, databases, and abstracts that provide the most up-to-date information. You can also use the general-purpose search engines identified earlier in this chapter to locate information on the Internet.

One of the most useful tools for organizing your research is taking notes on an index card or your laptop. You can use this information to create a bibliography and to take comprehensive notes. A **bibliography** is a detailed list of all the books, articles, interviews, and abstracts you have reviewed in the course of your research. For each publication, record the complete title and reference information in case you need to find it again later. Also, write a brief summary of the content.

Then, take specific notes on each of the sources. If you are writing a direct quote, be painstakingly careful to copy it exactly, including spelling and punctuation. Only include information related to one main idea per card or per page—that way, you can easily organize your finished research into main ideas. These notes will be the basis for developing supporting materials for your presentation.

You are likely to generate dozens of viable main ideas. Although you may believe that the more ideas and research you include, the stronger the resulting presentation will be, using a large number of main ideas can test the audience's attention span and tolerance for fatigue and require you to exceed the normal time limit for a presentation (from five to thirty minutes). No strict definition exists for the "correct" number of main points, but for most messages it is wise to keep the number within the range of three to five.

12.7: Provide Support for Ideas

12.7 Explain how supporting materials facilitate learning

Regardless of the purpose of your presentation, you will use some form of **supporting materials** to give credibility to your main ideas and to make the message more informative, interesting, relevant, clear, and acceptable—all the better to reach the audience. Supporting materials facilitate learning. Although teaching the audience is a fundamental goal of most presentations, for some people learning something new or unexpected can be an uncomfortable or frightening experience and can therefore be resisted. Indeed, people tend to resist a speaker's attempts to change them or to provoke some action. Supporting materials can greatly help the speaker to overcome these barriers to complete a successful presentation. These materials include explanations, examples, statistics, testimony, and visual aids.

12.7.1: Explanations

Explanation is the act or process of making a subject plain or comprehensible. This is often accomplished through a simple statement of the relationship of a whole and its parts—for example, "The Southwestern Region is composed of the sales areas in Arizona, Utah, New Mexico, and Nevada." Other methods include the following:

- Providing a definition: "The Southwestern Region contains sales representatives responsible for all product sales, new product leads, and recruitment in Arizona, Utah, New Mexico, and Nevada."
- Using synonyms (words with approximately the same meanings) or antonyms (words with opposite meanings): For a synonym thesaurus that also includes antonyms and definitions, go to http://www.synonym.com.
- Using comparisons (showing listeners the similarities between something familiar and something unfamiliar): "Like the North Central Region, the Southwestern Region will have four sales representatives, with approximately seventy-five accounts totaling over $4 million."
- Showing contrasts (supporting an idea by emphasizing differences between it and something else): "Unlike the California group, the Southwestern representatives will not be required to complete Spanish-language training."
- Giving a brief history.
- Providing an operational definition: "Intelligence is defined operationally as a score on the Wechsler Adult Intelligence Scale."
- Explanations should be framed within the experiences of audience members. The presenter must also be careful not to make such explanations too long or too abstract.

12.7.2: Examples

Examples connect the main ideas of a presentation with a real or an ideal state envisioned by the speaker. Examples take a variety of forms, including extended, detailed illustrations and brief, specific instances. Illustrations can be either hypothetical (a story that could happen) or factual (a story that did happen). A presenter may involve the listeners in a hypothetical illustration by suggesting, "Imagine yourself in an employment interview. You want this job, and for the first ten minutes or so everything has been going smoothly. Then, the interviewer starts to ask a series of personal and, in your view, illegal questions."

When using hypothetical or factual illustrations, the speaker is wise to consider whether the story is relevant and appropriate to the audience, whether it is typical rather than exceptional, and whether it is vivid and impressive in detail. If the illustration fails to fulfill any of these criteria, the speaker should find a more suitable alternative.

A specific instance is an undeveloped, very brief illustration—more a reference than an example. Using specific instances successfully requires that the audience recognize the names or events to which the speaker is referring. For example, a reference to "GATT" in a presentation on foreign trade will be ineffective if the audience is not familiar with the role of the General Agreement on Tariffs and Trade in the post–World War II international economy. Nevertheless, citing specific instances with which the audience is familiar can foster an audience's belief in and identification with the speaker as "one of us."

12.7.3: Statistics

As a form of supporting material, **statistics** represent the result of collecting, organizing, and interpreting numerical data. They are especially useful when you wish to accomplish the following objectives:

1. *Reduce* large masses of information to general categories ("According to the USDA's Center for Nutrition Policy and Promotion, the average monthly cost for a moderate meal plan for a family of four in the United States is $771.10.")

2. *Emphasize* the size of something ("Business and industry currently spend more than $200 billion annually for training and development—more than is spent for education at primary, secondary, and college levels.")

3. *Indicate trends* ("After adjusting for inflation, state general fund spending on prison-related expenses increased over 140 percent between 1986 and 2013. During the same period, state spending on K-12 education increased only 69 percent, while higher education saw an increase of less than six percent.")

When using statistics, you must concern yourself with their accuracy and bias as well as with their clarity and meaningfulness. Addressing the first issue involves answering such questions as these: Were correct data-collecting techniques used to obtain the statistics? Do the statistics cover sufficient cases and lengths of time? Are the statistics taken from competent sources? The second issue includes pragmatic considerations such as these: Can you translate these difficult-to-understand numbers into more immediately understandable terms? How can you provide adequate background for the data? Would a graph or visual aid clarify the data or statistical trends that you are presenting?

12.7.4: Testimony

Testimony is a statement by a credible person (source) that lends weight and authority to the speaker's presentation. Credibility is based on whether the source is an acknowledged expert on the specific subject and is free of bias and self-interest. The audience's perception of the source is important as well. Is the source well known to the audience? If not, the speaker must tell the audience why the source is a good authority. If the source is known, does the audience accept her or his opinion as knowledgeable and unbiased? To lend support to a message, the testimony of a source must *be credible* and *be perceived as credible* by the audience.

12.7.5: Visual Aids

Like all forms of supporting material, visual aids enhance the clarity and credibility of the message. And, by using multiple channels of communication, they appeal to multiple senses and so increase listeners' retention of significant points. They also help the presenter control his or her own apprehension by providing a point of familiarity in an uncertain situation.

These advantages are especially important for business and professional settings. As Tom Cothran points out in a review of the research literature, numerous studies (at the universities of Wisconsin, Harvard, Columbia, and Pennsylvania) demonstrate that visual aids reduce the time necessary to present content ("time required to present a concept can be reduced by up to 40 percent"), improve learning and retention ("audiovisuals improved retention by 14 to 38 percent over presentations where no visual were used"), while leading to a more positive perception of the speaker using them (presenters using visuals were "perceived as significantly better prepared, more professional, more persuasive, and more interesting" than those using no visual support).[7]

TYPES OF VISUAL AIDS   Obtaining these advantages requires skill in selecting appropriate aids and using them well. There are three basic categories of visual aids: the actual object or a model of it, pictorial reproductions, and pictorial symbols. In the first category, for example, an architectural model of a building may be used to present

information about a new building design. Also consider logistics when using a visual aid from this category. Actual objects should be used only if they can be easily handled during the presentation. Likewise, a model built in painstaking detail may lose its impact if the audience is too far away to see it clearly.

Seen here is an artist's rendition of the aerial view of the World Trade Center memorial (*Reflecting Absence*) as seen from the southeast looking north. Assume that you are the speaker and want your audience to learn about this memorial. What are the advantages and disadvantages of using this visual as part of your presentation? What alternatives might you consider? What are some important criteria to remember when using this visual during your presentation?

SOURCE: Dbox for the Lower Manhattan Development Corporation/Corbis

PICTORIAL VISUAL AIDS   Photographs, slides, sketches, videotapes, cartoons, and drawings are included in the category of pictorial reproductions. In keeping with the old saying "A picture is worth a thousand words," pictorial reproductions show the main ideas of a presentation in new, exciting, and interesting ways.

Abstract concepts and statistical data are often represented through pictorial symbols such as graphs, charts, and diagrams. These may be prepared on a variety of media, including PowerPoint presentations, flip charts, chalkboards, overhead projections, white boards, or handouts.

Using Audiovisual Aids Competently

Strategic Skills

Chalkboards and Flip Charts

Advantages: They are easily available and inexpensive.

Disadvantages: They are hard to "hide" from the audience and so can draw attention away from the speaker.

Advice for their use:

1. Face your audience as you write.
2. Before your presentation, practice using the writing surface.
3. Plan every written word, its placement, and its accuracy (content and grammar).
4. Collect and arrange materials ahead of time.

Audio and Audiovisual Equipment

Advantages: There are many ways of presenting high quality and vivid audio (sound only) and/or audiovisual (sound and image) examples to an audience.

Disadvantages: They require great effort to ensure that an audience can see and/or hear them. They also involve technologies that can fail.

Advice for their use:

1. Know where electrical outlets are and whether extension cords are needed.
2. Test the sound levels.
3. Test the quality of the recordings.
4. Check the sound volume and quality in all areas of the room.

Subject Objects

Advantages: They command attention and can enhance clarity.

Disadvantages: They can be overly complex and too large to easily manage.

Advice for their use:

1. Use only items that can be seen by everyone in the audience.
2. Use objects that are appropriate to the purpose and subject of your speech.
3. Plan the specific times in your presentation when you will use objects.

Pictorial Reproductions or Symbols

Advantages: They can simplify complex ideas and objects.

Disadvantages: They require artistic skill to create.

Advice for their use:

1. Make sure that all pictorials are visible to everyone.
2. Label graphics and charts clearly with various colors.
3. Explain the source of, the significance of, and the context of any pictorials.
4. If posters are not glued, taped, or speared to a firm surface, they will flop or fall over. This will interrupt your audience's concentration and damage your credibility.

Handouts

Advantages: They are inexpensive and do not depend on technology for their use.

Disadvantages: The audience can too easily focus on them rather than on the speaker.

Advice for their use:

1. Use an assistant to pass out the materials.
2. Have more than enough handouts available.
3. Choose carefully when and how you plan to use handouts, because members of your audience will often read, make noise with, and doodle on your handout during your speech (thus ignoring you, the speaker).

TECHNOLOGY TOOLS

Presentation Software

METHODS FOR COPING WITH STRESS

Cognitive Method
Thinking of stressors as challenges rather than threats; avoiding perfectionism

Emotional Method
Talking about one's problems to a friend

Behavioral Method
Implementing a time management plan; where possible, making life changes to eliminate stressors

Physical Method
Progressive relaxation training, exercise, meditation

Methods For Coping With Stress

Cognitive method
Thinking of stressors as challenges rather as threats; avoiding perfectionism

Emotional method
Talking about one's problems to a friend

Behavioral method
Implementing a time management plan; where possible, making life changes to eliminate stressors

Physical method
Progressive relaxation training, exercise, meditation

Few formal presentations in business and the professions are given without the aid of presentation software—a computer software package used to display information in the form of a slide show. PowerPoint was launched in 1990 as part of the Microsoft Office suite. It has since been continuously revised. There are multiple alternatives to PowerPoint each with strengths (e.g., Keynote, Slides, SOHO Docs, Google Slides, Emaze, Visme, Fuze, Prezi). As of 2012, though, various versions of PowerPoint had 95% of the presentation software market share, with installations on at least 1 billion computers; and an estimated 350 PowerPoint presentations are given each second across the globe. As a result, there are many resources available to assist with its use.

Presentation software is filled with wonderful features. Slides, electronic screen shows, overheads, handouts, and speaker notes can all be generated from a single file. Special effects, sound, photography, and animation are easily incorporated. Once created, presentations can be converted into HTML, Java, Flash, auto-run CDs, DVDs, PDFs, or QuickTime movies for reuse. PowerPoint slides can also serve as the centerpiece of Web-conferencing presentations and virtual collaborations.

Two important resources for learning how to use PowerPoint are Microsoft's PowerPoint Site (http://www.microsoft.com/powerpoint) and Presentations Magazine (http://www.presentations.com). Two additional ones are http://www.indezine.com (an amazing repository of information on all things related to PowerPoint, including links, articles, templates, techniques, tutorials, books, product reviews, and a never-ending flow of new ideas) and http://www.presentation-pointers.com (a site that features a compilation of articles on communicating more effectively with PowerPoint in professional situations such as sales pitches, formal presentations, informal meetings, and media presentations).

As you will discover, if you have not already, PowerPoint is easy to learn and use. With it, you can build presentations in a very short amount of time. This ease of use, however, makes it equally easy to misuse it or not use it effectively. Here are some general guidelines that you can stretch or violate as you develop more experience with using the software.

(x) **Start simple**

Don't overuse special effects. While these can be powerful, you don't want your audience to focus on the "gee whiz" aspects of your presentation to the exclusion of your content. Think carefully before using animations, sound, video, and special effects. If used sparingly, they'll have greater impact.

(x) **Be consistent**

Stick with the same backgrounds, styles, and transition effects throughout your presentation. As you choose them, think of the room where the presentation will be made. While light text on a dark background is a good choice for a dark or slightly darkened room, for example, in a brightly lit room the dark background may look so faded that the light text may not show up well.

(x) **Avoid overcrowded Slides**

You want your audience to focus on the content of your presentation and on you as the presenter of that content. Limit your points on a slide to three to five points. When you need more, break the points into separate slides. Crowded slides will turn off your audience and obscure your main points.

(x) **Use a font size and style that are readable**

Put yourself in the audience and ask what they will be seeing. Do the font style and size make the text easily readable?

(x) **Find your own style**

PowerPoint gives you lots of style options. Use only those that you are comfortable with. Play with the templates and "wizards" that walk you through a set of choices for the format of your slides. Be observant when others use PowerPoint. If you like the colors or textures you see, find out what they are. If someone has a way of doing things you like, learn from it and use or modify it.

(x) **Practice and prepare**

Your success depends on how comfortable you are with using the program, so practice giving the speech while running the presentation. Anyone who has attended multiple presentations knows how easy it is for things to go wrong, so ask if there is a technical person assigned to your presentation who can troubleshoot for you. Most important, if at all possible get to the room early and get everything set up and tested. Do not subject your audience to a long delay when technology fails. Have a back-up plan to rely on if necessary.

12.8: Develop an Introduction and a Conclusion

12.8 Report the importance of a proper introduction and conclusion in a presentation

Up to this point, we have worked through basic principles for creating the body of a message—clarifying and focusing on the purpose, identifying and researching the main ideas, and using supporting materials. We now turn to the front and back sections of the message—the introduction and the conclusion.

12.8.1: The Introduction

As you think about how to begin a presentation, consider a similar situation: the first meeting of a class. When you took your seat on the first day of this class, for example, what was it that you wanted to know? If you are at all like other students we have asked, there were at least three categories of information you wanted to learn: course coverage (what will be the content and focus of the course?), course requirements (what is required to complete this course?), and course instructor (what kind of person will this teacher turn out to be?). These questions fall into three general categories: issues of *orientation* (what's happening?), *motivation* (what's in it for me?), and *rapport* (will I like and respect this instructor?). Although you may already have obtained partial answers to these questions before the first class session (from friends, former class members, and so forth), the questions most likely still remained, and you and the instructor probably spent at least a portion of the first meeting answering them.

The **introduction** to a presentation serves similar functions. It informs the listener what the message is about (orientation), why the listener should attend to it (motivation), and why the speaker is a credible source for the message (rapport). As the speaker thinks through the introduction, he or she should consider which of these issues requires attention and what kind.

ORIENTATION One method of orienting the audience is to state the topic to be discussed, give the thesis statement, explain the presentation's title, or review the purpose of the presentation. A speaker at a business fundraiser for local arts groups may begin: "Some of you may wonder why this presentation is titled 'Give; Don't Give Up.' I'm here today to tell you why it's more important now, in the face of difficult economic times, than ever before to contribute to cultural organizations."

Another method of orienting the audience is to preview the structure of the message: "Cultural organizations provide three vital services to our community: they expand our view of the world and each other, they raise issues that we need to discuss, and they enrich our lives and our children's lives."

The speaker may also explain why the topic was narrowed as it was: "When I was asked to give a fundraising presentation to you, business leaders in the community, my first question was 'What can you do for us?' I soon realized that I needed to tell you what *we* are doing—and hope to continue to do—for *you*."

MOTIVATION Motivational strategies include linking the topic and thesis statement to listeners' lives: "How many of you have attended a cultural event in our community in the recent past? Think of how our city would be diminished if these events were no longer held."

Showing how the topic has affected or will affect the audience's past, present, or future is another motivational strategy. A speaker may begin a presentation by saying: "You may not have realized it, but tourism generated $34 million for our city last year. Surveys showed that many of these visitors came to participate in our numerous cultural

events, and in the process they bolstered the profits of your businesses."

Demonstrating how the topic is linked to a basic need or goal of the audience is a third method of motivating an audience to listen. This can be done by saying: "Cultural events are an important part of making our community vital and prosperous, and I'm sure that all of us want to keep it that way."

RAPPORT Building rapport can take several forms. Language that demonstrates competence, such as citing important and respected people, noting relevant events, or describing your expertise on the topic, increases the audience's receptivity to your message.

Trustworthiness, another important factor in building rapport, can be demonstrated by showing that your present behavior is consistent with your past behavior on the topic under discussion, giving time to opposing points of view, and being consistent with verbal and nonverbal behavior. Nonverbal behavior that shows confidence and enthusiasm for the topic—such as a strong voice, direct eye contact with members of the audience, and a measured delivery—promotes an image of trustworthiness.

Complimenting the audience and using humor are additional techniques for developing rapport. Doing so shows that you identify with people in the audience, respect them, and can laugh with them.

In considering introductory strategies, you are wise to remember that many of the most effective strategies contribute to multiple functions. For example, a story can provide both orientation and motivation, and humor can enhance both motivation and rapport. Thus, when you are developing an introduction, make it as compact as possible and as effective as possible in fulfilling the audience's needs for orientation, motivation, and rapport.

WRITING PROMPT

When you are listening to a speech, which of the forms of support (explanations, examples, statistics, testimony, visual aids) seem to have the most effect on you, and why? Would your answer differ depending on general purpose (inform, persuade, motivate, celebrate)? Why or why not?

 The response entered here will appear in the performance dashboard and can be viewed by your instructor.

Submit

12.8.2: The Conclusion

The **conclusion** seeks to provide a sense of completeness and closure. It is often signaled by the phrases "in conclusion" or "in summary" and is accomplished by reminding the audience of the highlights of the presentation and reemphasizing their significance. The conclusion not only helps the audience remember what you have said (people often remember best what they heard last); it also allows you to reinforce the cohesion and importance of the message.

In addition to summarizing the main ideas of the message, you can use the conclusion to reestablish the connection of the topic to the larger context and to provide psychological closure by reminding audience members how the topic affects their lives. Both functions can be achieved by tying the conclusion of the speech to the introduction—bringing both together by reference to and elaboration of quotations, illustrations, or questions that were used in the beginning.

Because the conclusion serves as a summary and an ending, it should be brief and decisive; it should not trail off. When the audience hears a concluding phrase, it will—and is entitled to—believe that the presentation has reached an end. Thus, use your conclusion to reinforce the thesis for your audience, to place that thesis in the larger context known to your audience, and to provide, if possible, a "clincher" (a telling quotation, illustration, or question). Then sit down.

12.9: The Outline

12.9 Report the three basic types of outlines

Now that we have identified all the pieces of the presentation—the main ideas, the supporting materials, the introduction, and the conclusion—the time has come to put them together. The **outline**, a visual, schematic summary of the message, shows the order of the ideas and the general relationships among them.

12.9.1: Types of Outlines

There are basically three types of outlines: **a complete-sentence outline**, which lists each head and subhead in complete-sentence form; a **topic outline**, which reduces the sentences to brief phrases or single words; and a **speaker's outline**, which includes only key words and important quotations or statistics written on index cards.

All three forms are useful for different purposes. The complete-sentence outline allows others to study the organizational structure and to give feedback on its strengths and weaknesses. For this reason, teachers who ask students to hand in outlines usually ask for this format. The topic outline allows the speaker to consider and reconsider organizational choices while working on the presentation. Once those choices have been made, the speaker creates a speaker's outline to aid or trigger her or his memory during the actual presentation. Since each method has different advantages, the speaker should work first with a complete-sentence outline and later reduce it to a speaker's outline for the actual presentation.

12.9.2: Basic Principles

For both complete-sentence and topic outlines, there are four major conventions for writing the outline.

APPROPRIATE NUMBERING SYSTEMS The most widely used numbering system alternates letters and numbers, as shown in the following outline. The main heads are placed at the left margin, and subheads are indented, forming a clearly identifiable column. Heads or subheads that run more than a single line are further indented so that the content portion of the entry aligns with the content above it. Figure 12.1 illustrates this basic format.

Figure 12.1 Basic Outline Format

Introduction (methods for establishing orientation, motivation, rapport)

Conclusion (methods for summarizing, linking, and clinching)

HEADS OF EQUAL IMPORTANCE The main points (Roman numerals I, II, and III) are the main divisions of the presentation and should be of equal importance to the topic. Similarly, the first subdivision of these heads (capital letters A and B) designates logical and equally important divisions of the first main point. This principle also applies to the other subdivisions represented by Arabic numerals and lowercase letters.

CONSISTENCY IN FORM A complete-sentence outline uses complete sentences throughout and does not lapse into topic heads; by contrast, a topic outline uses topic heads, not sentences. In the sentence outline, the punctuation follows written conventions (e.g., use of periods); by contrast, no punctuation is needed at the end of lines in a topic outline.

BALANCE IN FORM Because a topic is not "divided" unless there are at least two parts, an outline normally has at least two subheads under any main head. Even though exceptions are possible, normally for every heading marked I there is at least a II, and for every A there is at least a B.

POINTS AND SUBPOINTS In the outline above, the "speech" contains three main **points** (I, II, and III). These are the major ideas that the speaker wishes the audience to understand and accept. Say, for example, the speaker using this outline is giving a speech suggesting that there are three behavioral commitments involved in being a leader in an organization: (I) confronting and changing the status quo, (II) inspiring a shared vision, and (III) enabling others to act.

In order to make these main points vivid, easily remembered, convincing, and so forth, the speaker needs to use a variety of forms of support (e.g., explanations, examples, statistics, testimony, and/or visual aids). These forms of support become **subpoints** in the outline, of which there can be multiple levels. In terms of the first main point, for example, our hypothetical speaker argues two subpoints in support of (I): (A) an effective leader searches out challenging opportunities to change, grow, innovate, and improve, and (B) an effective leader experiments, takes risks, and learns from the accompanying mistakes. To "support" the first subpoint (A), our speaker develops two additional subpoints (or sub-subpoints): (1) testimony from an acknowledged effective leader and (2) an example of a leader who has done so.

While, in principle, a speech (and the outline of it) can have points, subpoints, sub-subpoints, sub-sub-subpoints, and so forth, the speaker is advised to keep the attention span of the audience in mind and provide no more levels of support than are absolutely necessary to help an audience understand and accept the main points of the presentation.

12.9.3: Transitions

When an audience member listens to the presentation you have outlined, he or she lacks the advantages possessed by the reader of a book or the viewer of a video. That is, the audience member can neither reread a selection—using punctuation as a clue to meaning—nor rewind the video to discover what was missed. If the listener misses your point, he or she has missed it completely. Thus, you must do what you can to guide your listeners through a presentation by providing clear transitions.

Transitions link the various elements of the outline, showing why and how each element relates to the other elements. Transitions help the audience understand the logical relationships among the main points and their subpoints, and they explain how the introduction, body, and conclusion fit together. In short, transitions serve as "signposts" that help listeners understand where you are going, where you are, and where you have been.

The speaker might, for example, forecast the purpose and structure of the message toward the end of the introduction ("Today, I will talk about five behaviors that characterize effective leaders. They are . . ."). As the speech proceeds, the speaker might use internal previews and summaries to review a main point and anticipate the next one ("Having described why leaders need to challenge the process, let's turn now to the need to inspire a shared vision"). The conclusion of the speech might include a final summary ("I've talked today about five behaviors that characterize effective leaders. Effective leaders . . ."). Transitions need not be elaborate, although they should be frequent and well spaced throughout the message. The

transition from one point to the next should be smooth and obvious. When listeners find it difficult to follow your organizational structure, they rapidly lose interest and will neither remember nor accept the thesis of your message.

12.10: Present the Message Competently

12.10 **Scrutinize the need to deliver an effective presentation appropriate for the message, audience, and occasion**

Having generated a message and put it into a standard presentation format, a presenter is now in a position to think about effective methods for delivering the message to listeners. This stage of the presentation relates to the third component of strategic communication, communication competence. The speaker must be able to identify and employ a delivery that is both effective and appropriate for the message, audience, and occasion.

Support for a balanced emphasis on content and delivery is provided in the research literature on nonverbal communication. Judee Burgoon, David Buller, and Gill Woodall summarize approximately one hundred studies on channel reliance—which channels or codes most influence listeners as they assign meaning to communication events.[8] They conclude that adults place greater reliance on nonverbal cues (which include issues of delivery) than on verbal cues (issues of content) in determining meaning. They also conclude that 60 to 65 percent of the meaning in a communication exchange is conveyed nonverbally.

This general pattern, the authors suggest, has several qualifiers:

1. young children place greater reliance on verbal cues (the words) than adults do

2. reliance on nonverbal cues is greatest when there is a conflict between the verbal and nonverbal channels

3. "verbal content is more important for factual, cognitive, abstract, and persuasive interpretations, while nonverbal context is more important for judging emotional and attitudinal expressions, relational communication, and impression formation"

4. there are individual differences in channel dependence (some people rely on nonverbal channels, some typically rely on verbal content, and others adapt their channel choice to the situation)[9]

12.10.1: Types of Delivery

Given these findings on channel reliance, a presenter must carefully consider the choices available for the presentation of a message. She or he must choose an appropriate method of delivery early on. To do this, he or she must decide if the presentation will be developed on the spot (impromptu), given from brief notes (extemporaneous), written out and read (manuscript), or memorized word for word and recited (memorized).

IMPROMPTU **Impromptu speaking** is best avoided when possible. If the presenter knows or anticipates being called on to make some remarks, the message should be prepared in advance. This preparation will increase the likelihood that the message is not weak in terms of organization, forms of support, quality of word choice, or effectiveness of delivery. Nevertheless, there will be times when the presenter is given little, if any, chance to prepare. For example, the presenter may be told to make a brief presentation to a committee at work, asked to say a few words on a topic about which she or he is knowledgeable, or asked on the spot to answer a question or describe a policy or procedure.

EXTEMPORANEOUS **Extemporaneous speaking** encourages thorough preparation and adaptability to the particulars of the situation. The presenter starts with a full-sentence outline and then reduces it to a speaker's outline for rehearsal and actual presentation. Rehearsal helps the presenter to use a style similar to normal conversation. However, because she or he is working from ideas and key words rather than from complete sentences, the message is never delivered exactly the same way twice. The wording of the ideas remains flexible to let the presenter better adapt the message to the audience. With extemporaneous speaking, segments of the message can be expanded or reduced, depending on audience response.

MANUSCRIPT When the situation requires precise wording (e.g., a technical or research report where exact wording is crucial) or exact timing (e.g., a television presentation of exactly nine minutes), the appropriate mode of presentation may be **manuscript speaking**. In this mode, the speaker prepares an organized and easily readable manuscript that has an oral, conversational style. Starting with a full-sentence outline, the speaker writes out the whole message. To ensure that the final product is conversational, the speech is rehearsed orally (perhaps with a recorder) before it is written on paper. Once the message has been developed into its final form, the manuscript is prepared for reading (e.g., triple-spaced and marked for special emphases) and the speaker rehearses until she or he feels very comfortable with the delivery. In some situations, speakers will read their prepared speech from a TelePrompTer, which is a screen on which the speech is projected and scrolled as the speech is delivered. TelePrompTers enable a speaker to avoid having to look down at the written speech. A successful speech delivery looks and sounds as if the speech were being given extemporaneously—that is, the delivery is conversational and unforced and includes eye contact with audience members.

What delivery method has this speaker selected (e.g., impromptu, extemporaneous, manuscript, memorized)? What considerations do you think led him to this choice? What can he do to enhance the effectiveness of her choice?

SOURCE: Zoran Mladenovic/123rf

MEMORIZED Except for a lack of something to place on the lectern, podium, or TelePrompTer, **memorized speaking** is really no different from manuscript speaking. Thus, approaches to preparation and use overlap for these two modes of delivery.

The memorized speech is frequently used in situations in which reading a manuscript appears inappropriate. In creating such a presentation, the speaker's goal is to make the speech sound as if it were being delivered extemporaneously.

Memorized presentations lack the security of a manuscript to which the speaker can refer, so the speaker anticipates and rehearses for the possibility of a memory block. If a block occurs, the speaker focuses on key words until he or she is able to click back into the memorized phrases of the presentation.

12.10.2: Characteristics of Effective Delivery

Regardless of the delivery method you choose, its function remains the same—to aid listeners in understanding, accepting, and retaining what you have said. Although there are multiple ways to achieve **effective delivery**, they all involve the application of four general criteria.[10]

EFFECTIVE DELIVERY IS INTELLIGIBLE Before audience members will accept a message, they must hear it. Thus, you have to practice speaking with adequate volume and appropriate rate. When you are using a microphone, this means keeping the proper distance away from it. With a standard podium mike, this is about six inches or a little closer. If you get too close to the mike, however, some sounds (e.g., the letter *P*) become overemphasized and create an annoying sound for audiences.

In addition to volume and rate, intelligibility also requires that you pay attention to articulation and pronunciation. Not only will mispronunciation inhibit clarity; it will also lead listeners to make negative judgments about your credibility. Thus, whenever you have the slightest doubt about proper pronunciation, it is worth the effort to consult a dictionary. Recording a rehearsal version of the presentation or having a friend listen and comment is useful for evaluating how understandable your message is.

EFFECTIVE DELIVERY IS CONVERSATIONAL In ordinary conversation participants use a great deal of variation in the pitch and volume of their voices. They also indicate their involvement in and commitment to the dialogue via body orientation and eye contact, and they reinforce the points they make with gestures and physical movement.

In short, variations in voice and physical action are used naturally and unconsciously to focus attention on and reinforce the content of a conversation. These variations provide an excellent model for a public presentation. The presenter should attempt to talk with, rather than at, a group of listeners. Good delivery can be characterized as a conversation with an audience.

EFFECTIVE DELIVERY IS DIRECT Good delivery signals to listeners that the speaker truly cares about communicating with them. In our culture, respect for and interest in an audience are communicated primarily with eye contact. Sustaining appropriate eye contact with listeners also helps the presenter discover how the message is being received.

Achieving these goals requires eye contact with all segments of the audience. A practical strategy for achieving this is to start the presentation by locating a small number of listeners in different parts of the room who are responding positively with smiles and head nods. Establishing eye contact with these people can help a speaker to gain confidence during the first moments of a speech. As the presentation proceeds, the speaker can then widen eye contact to include the total audience by moving her or his gaze randomly and smoothly, rather than systematically, throughout the room and looking directly into the eyes of individual listeners.

EFFECTIVE DELIVERY IS UNOBTRUSIVE Good delivery focuses attention on the speaker's message, not on the speaker. The three principles we have just discussed—being intelligible, conversational, and direct—promote this goal. You can also try to eliminate distracting mannerisms such as playing with note cards, rocking back and forth while standing in one place, locking both hands on the lectern or in your pants pockets, or using pauses excessively (such as repeating "uh" or "you know").

You may not even be aware of your tendencies to exhibit these or similar mannerisms. One way to recognize them is to videotape yourself or to watch others. Simply identifying distracting behaviors is often the greatest part of eliminating them. You can also engage in *negative practice*—consciously overemphasize the distracting mannerism while rehearsing the delivery of your presentation. This exercise allows you to become hyperaware of the behavior while you are speaking, thus making it easier to eliminate it from your presentation.

12.10.3: Develop a Strategy for Rehearsal

You can make your presentation effective with self-analysis and rehearsal. Every speaker finds her or his own method of practicing. Some take advantage of the privacy of their bathroom, with its mirrors and great acoustics. Some record their practices on video- or audiotape. A few inflict their rehearsals on friends and family. Find what fits your needs, but you should practice. You need to time your speech, get used to the material, become accustomed to your audiovisual aids, and make the message your own so that your presentation sounds like you and is consistent with your personality.

Whatever your practice strategy, consider methods of collecting relevant data that provide answers to questions such as the following:

- Are the general purpose (inform, persuade, motivate, or celebrate) and specific purpose both clear to and relevant for your audience?

- Have you selected the three to five main points that will best lead your audience to understand and accept your specific purpose?

- Have you included a variety of supporting materials (explanations, examples, statistics, testimony, visual aids) that your audience will understand and find compelling?

- Does the introduction to your speech provide appropriate orientation, motivation, and rapport?
- Is the organizational structure of the body of your speech easy for your audience to follow? Have you used transitions well?
- Does your choice of language aid (rather than distract from) the accomplishment of your purpose?
- Does your conclusion provide a sense of completeness and closure?
- Is your choice of delivery mode (impromptu, extemporaneous, manuscript, or memorized) the best choice?
- Is the delivery of your speech intelligible, conversational, direct, and unobtrusive?

12.10.4: Other Considerations

In addition to the four general principles of effective delivery, there are several additional considerations worthy of comment.

APPEARANCE   First impressions of another person are to a large degree the result of physical appearance cues. In a presentation, this means that audiences use natural elements—such as the speaker's height, weight, and body shape—and planned cues—such as clothing, accessories, or cosmetics—as bases for making judgments about the speaker's credibility that affect the development of their subsequent impressions.

You are wise to analyze your appearance in terms of how you will be viewed by a particular audience. Ask yourself how the audience may react to your dress, accessories, neatness, or degree of formality in your clothing choice. What are audience members likely to conclude on the basis of this assessment? What judgments are they likely to form about you? An awareness of such issues increases your sensitivity to audience perceptions. Many speakers, for example, choose to dress slightly more formally when speaking than they normally do. This can boost your confidence and can also suggest to the audience that you care about the speech and the speaking situation.

Your appearance and delivery, however, must be comfortable for you. Efforts to completely change your natural style of speaking, dress, appearance, or even gesturing are likely to result in audience perceptions of incongruity and inconsistency. Although you can improve your style, an all-out attempt to "be someone else" during a presentation will likely decrease your rapport with the audience.

USE OF VISUAL AIDS   Visual aids should be prepared early enough to allow you to practice with them until you can use them quickly and smoothly. Important points to remember during both practice and the actual presentation include the following.

⊗ Visual aids must be easily seen by every member of the audience.

In many rooms, a projection screen may need to be set up, or a large, blank, light wall can be used. In addition, there are often hooks and clips at the front of the room where visual aids can be hung. When this is not the case, it is usually possible to place them on an easel. Wherever they are placed, the goal is to locate them high enough so that every member of the audience can see them quickly and easily. This situation requires both thinking about placement and rehearsing the actual placement of the visual aids ahead of time.

⊗ Talk to the audience rather than to the visual aid.

Listeners want your attention, and you have to be able to see their reactions to your message. Neither is possible if you are talking to the visual aid. Thus, help listeners to understand your visual by telling them what you want them to see, hear, and understand. At the same time, maintain eye contact with them to determine whether this understanding is taking place.

⊗ Display the visual aid only when it is being used.

Visual aids are intended to enhance understanding, not compete for the audience's attention. Keep aids from being seen until you are ready to use them, and remove them when you have finished with them. For this reason, avoid passing visual aids (such as handouts) through the audience while you are speaking. There is no surer way to lose the attention of portions of your audience!

TIMING YOUR PRESENTATION   In many situations, particularly when there exists a program with multiple speakers, you may be asked to keep your remarks limited to a set time. Good speakers use several techniques to ensure they finish on time:

⊗ Use a clock or watch.

Ideally, you will be able to see a wall clock in the back of the room. If you have a lectern, you can set a small clock on it (or set your wristwatch there) where it is easily visible. Avoid looking down at your wrist or showing obvious concern about time. As you begin to speak, take note not of the current time but of where the minute hand should be when you are to stop. If you are nervous, jot down the number where you can see it.

⊗ Have a collaborator in the audience.

A well-placed collaborator in the audience can be very useful. A collaborator can tell you if your voice is projecting sufficiently to fill the room, for example, or can jump-start a question-and-answer session with a prepared question. In situations where time is of the essence, the collaborator should have signs indicating "5 minutes left" and "1 minute left" to cue you when to wrap up.

⊗ Practice your presentation aloud.

Rehearsal is essential to most successful presentations. Just remember that a speech—that is, a presentation that is not to be interrupted by questions—is likely to be a bit longer when it is delivered before an audience than when you practice it alone.

12.11: How to Field Audience Questions

12.11 **Report the need to prepare for fielding audience questions**

In most situations, questions are postponed until the end of the presentation. This doesn't have to be the case, however, and you should decide in advance whether questions will be handled during or after the speech. In either case, a small number of guidelines can contribute to a smooth and effective questioning period.

REPEAT QUESTIONS FROM THE AUDIENCE In some situations—for example, with a large theater-seated group in which members don't have access to a microphone— audience members are unable to hear the questions asked by other members. In these cases, repeating questions from the audience helps everyone hear the questions. Repetition also allows you to buy time when hit with a surprise question for which there is no ready answer or to clarify confusing or unclear questions.

TREAT ALL QUESTIONS WITH RESPECT Some questions—those that are difficult, rude, or hopelessly naïve— are a challenge to answer gracefully. Many speakers dread the possibility of a hostile question or critical remark during the question-and-answer session. This doesn't have to be the case. For example, a simple, yet effective, method for coping with critical comments without getting into arguments or being locked into a defensive position is to compliment the questioner on her or his insight and respond to any points of truth or areas of agreement that you can find.[11] Difficult questions requiring complex answers— particularly if you are running long and are near the end of your presentation—may best be left for discussion with the audience member afterward. Lastly, no matter what the question, never try to be humorous at the expense of the questioner.

FINDING A POINT OF AGREEMENT OR TRUTH Although looking for a point of agreement or truth may contradict your natural desire to argue and defend yourself, it is very effective to be flexible and open-minded. By doing so, you can better understand the issue and increase your credibility with the audience. Consider the following example:

> AUDIENCE MEMBER: Your ideas about this new business proposal sound far-fetched to me. I think that we need to solidify our regional market before we try to expand abroad.
>
> SPEAKER: You have a good point—our regional sales have traditionally been the backbone of this

company. But we need to expand so that we can avoid slumps if the regional economy takes a downturn.

When you do not have an answer, punt.
Occasionally, you will receive a question for which you have no ready answer. When you are not able to answer, choose an alternative approach to the question so you don't lose control of the questioning period. There are several ways to do this:

- Rephrase the question into one that you can answer— for example, by narrowing it to an area of your expertise or relating it to the main idea of the presentation.

- Redirect the question by saying, "That's a good point. What do *you* think we should do?" or "We just happen to have an expert on that topic in our audience. Dr. Stone, what do you think we should do?"

- Acknowledge that you do not have an answer at this time and promise to get back to the questioner at a later date.

- Whatever the choice, implement it smoothly and confidently, just as you delivered the main body of your presentation.

ANTICIPATE LIKELY QUESTIONS As you think about your topic and audience, anticipate potential questions. Are there points that may be confusing? Are there points that may produce disagreement? Just as students must anticipate and prepare for teachers' questions at examination time, speakers can and should prepare responses to the questions they anticipate receiving from the audience.

Audience Challenge

Ethical Issues

Jim Cordoni has just finished his presentation. A member of the audience who has developed a reputation among his peers for such behavior belittles Jim's conclusions in a combative manner and, in doing so, misrepresents the data on which Jim has based his conclusions. Jim is tempted to make this person look foolish for asking the question. He even suspects the audience would approve. How might he do this? Should he do it? Why or why not? Can you think of other strategies Jim might employ (for example, using humor, asking for clarification, or asking the audience member to "come and talk with me afterwards")? What are the advantages and disadvantages of the alternative strategies you've identified? Which one would you advise Jim to use?

Strategic Scenario Wrap Up
Develop and Deliver Effective Presentations

The B. J. Turock Art Museum Museum is a university museum founded in 1903. It occupies a 70,000-square foot facility on the university's main campus and houses over 90,000 works of art. Particular strengths exist in American 19th and 20th century art, Russian and Soviet Art, and glass art. The Museum's Director of Education, Danielle Bechta, trains and coordinates a group of approximately 40 docents who provide tours of the museum's collections and special exhibitions. In addition to educating the docents on the art itself, she works with them on how to best present the information to small groups of visitors. Danielle has decided to offer two trainings: 1) an all-day workshop on developing presentations skills, and 2) certification training on the permanent and temporary exhibitions. She must clarify her specific purposes and goals and structure each of her presentations accordingly.

Danielle Bechta, Director of Education for the B.J. Turock Museum of Art, has decided to put together an all day workshop for docents, developing their ability to make presentations that are engaging and effective for individuals taking an art museum tour. She will begin by focusing on the content to be mastered by the docents:

1. How to welcome visitors to the Museum and briefly describe it (when it was founded, its current status, its mission)
2. How to describe the exhibition (what's in it, how it was selected, the contributions of the exhibition to the world of art), and

3. How to conclude the tour (summarizing the tour, inviting the visitors to return).

In working with the docents on presenting the content they create, Danielle will make a number of points:

1. Docents represent the Museum. They need to think carefully about the image they will present.
2. Tours are normally an hour or less to accommodate attention span. Content should be presented in an interactive mode.
3. In addition to talking, docent should ask lots of questions that involve visitors and get them thinking about the museum and the art in the exhibition.

Danielle allows some time for questions and answers from the group before she gives the docents their assignments.

WRITING PROMPT

What two assignments can Danielle give the docents to help them practice their presentation skills? The assignments should be brief but comprehensive.

 The response entered here will appear in the performance dashboard and can be viewed by your instructor.

Submit

Summary

Develop and Deliver Effective Presentations

- **Presentations are vital to successful communication** in business. If they are not assigned or determined by context, their topic and purpose can be generated through brainstorming, mapping, or library and online research.
- **Communication apprehension** can be caused by lack of skills, conditioned anxiety, and/or negative cognitive appraisal.

- Ways to get over **fear of public speaking** include practicing the speech, employing relaxation and deep-breathing techniques, and trying cognitive restructuring of irrational, negative self-statements.
- The **topic and specific purpose** correspond to the communication goals for the presentation.
- After these goals are set, a thorough **audience analysis**, which covers several categories, can provide the presenter with situational knowledge and insight into how to target the message to best achieve her or his goals.

- For the body of the presentation, main ideas can be identified by the **topical system**, which includes sixteen themes common to most subjects.

- The speaker should generally limit the presentation to three, four, or five of the **themes that best suit** the audience and the occasion.

- These **main ideas** can then be researched through a variety of resources, including informational interviews, reference books, databases, and queries to a reference librarian.

- **Supporting materials** can be drawn from research on the topic and can include explanations, examples, statistics, testimony, and visual aids.

- The purpose of supporting materials is to make the presentation varied and exciting for the audience and to **increase the speaker's credibility**.

- The **introduction and the conclusion** are prepared after the bulk of the presentation is complete.

- The **introduction** serves to orient, motivate, and build rapport between the audience and the speaker.

- The **conclusion** provides a summary and a sense of the significance of the presentation so that listeners will leave with a clear understanding and recollection of the main ideas discussed.

- The **outline** is the standard format for organizing the three parts (introduction, body, and conclusion) of a presentation.

- A **full-sentence outline, topic outline, and speaker's outline** serve different purposes but follow the same basic principles.

- **Basic outline principles** include using a correct numbering system for outline entries, choosing headings of equal importance, maintaining consistency in the form of outline entries, striving for balance in entries so that every heading has at least two subheadings, and appropriately supporting main points with subpoints.

- When it comes to **delivering the presentation**, the speaker can choose from several delivery styles—impromptu, extemporaneous, manuscript, and memorized—depending on the circumstances.

- The **choice of a delivery style** should be considered early in the process of preparing the presentation as each makes different demands on the speaker's level of preparation, skill, and choice of material.

- **Effective delivery** focuses attention on the speaker's message rather than on the speaker and should be comfortable and natural rather than formal or forced.

SHARED WRITING: DEVELOP AND DELIVER EFFECTIVE PRESENTATIONS

Ken is a 25-year-old marketing executive and works for a pharmaceutical company. He has to give a presentation about a new product to be launched at the company's annual launch event in three weeks. He has been told that the audience will come with varied cultural backgrounds. In addition, they will be diverse in age and work experience. Based on this, what additional information should Ken gather about the audience for a successful presentation, and for what purpose? How will his audience research help him tie his speech together: what common thread can he weave in that will reach the diverse audience?

▶ A minimum number of characters is required to post and earn points. After posting, your response can be viewed by your class and instructor, and you can participate in the class discussion.

Post   0 characters | 140 minimum

Chapter 12 Quiz: Develop and Deliver Effective Presentations

Chapter 13
Informative Presentations

⌄ Learning Objectives

13.1 Tell about the basic functions of informative presentations

13.2 Report the different situations where informative presentations may be used

13.3 Examine the modern-day phenomenon of having access to more information than can be assimilated

13.4 Express the goals of informative presentations

13.5 Show methods of organizing the three major categories of speech

13.6 Describe the basic settings of giving informative presentations

13.7 Evaluate the basic guidelines to be followed for ensuring successful presentations

13.8 Analyze the use of the video, television, and big screen projections in presentations

13.9 Explain how to develop some of the skills necessary for communication competence

13.10 Analyze how to manage anxiety about giving a presentation through practice and knowledge

Strategic Scenario: Invitation to Inform

Julia Tulovsky is the curator of the Russian Collection for the B. J. Turock Museum of Art. One of her tasks as curator is to create exhibitions for the museum using the permanent collection, collections from other museums, or both. Next week the museum will open a new exhibition, *Leonid Sokov: Ironic Objects,* which will be on display for six months. At the exhibit's opening reception, Julia will be making a twenty-minute presentation on the artist, the art, and the exhibition itself to between 50 and 75 individuals who have accepted the museum's invitation to attend. After this presentation, there will be a reception and tours of the art. What goals should Julia focus on? What medium should she use to present the information to a group of this size?

As you read this chapter, think about the skills that Julia will need to build and present an engaging informative presentation. At the end of the chapter, we will return to this scenario with some solutions.

13.1: Overview
Informative Presentations

13.1 Tell about the basic functions of informative presentations

Developing effective presentations involves (1) identifying the main points to be shared with an audience and researching them; (2) developing supporting materials to make those main points believable and credible; (3) organizing and outlining the total message, including introduction, body, transitions, and conclusion; and (4) selecting an appropriate type of delivery and developing a strategy for rehearsal that will make the delivery of the presentation both comfortable and effective. In this chapter, we build on this analysis and elaborate it in terms of informative presentations.

Every time you give a presentation in a business or a professional context, you have a general purpose and a specific purpose. Whereas specific purposes vary widely, general purposes can usually be classified as either informative or persuasive. The dominant purpose of informative presentations is to share adequate, accurate information with an audience in ways that are interesting and understandable. The dominant purpose of persuasive presentations is to convince an audience to believe an idea or perform a task. In this chapter, we discuss the importance of informative presentations, along with guidelines and resources for you as a speaker.

13.2: The Range of Informative Presentations

13.2 Report the different situations where informative presentations may be used

Organizational life is filled with informative presentations, and the range of possible uses for **informative presentations** in a corporate office is a wide one. Just consider the following situations:

Reviewing quarterly sales figures

Introducing a new policy for recruiting personnel

Explaining market research findings on the feasibility of introducing a new product line

Briefing executives on departmental performance goals

Training people to use new computer software

Reviewing a feasibility study for the purchase of new equipment

Demonstrating new machinery or equipment

What do all of these presentations have in common? They are informative! Their purpose is to tell listeners something they do not already know or to supplement or reinforce their existing knowledge.

The fact that informative presentations are a regular part of organizational life in business and the professions alone justifies their study and importance. Nevertheless, there are many additional reasons that exhibiting skill in informative speaking is critical to your professional success.

13.3: Accumulation of Information

13.3 Examine the modern-day phenomenon of having access to more information than can be assimilated

In today's organizations, more information and more sources of information are available than at any previous time. People have access to more information than they can possibly digest. There is no indication that this trend will do anything but continue to accelerate.

The scientific literature alone, not counting all other information domains, is huge—and growing at a rate of over 5% on an annual basis. According to the *World List of Scientific Journals,* 59,961 journals are published throughout the world (in sixty-five languages), in which about 1 million articles appear yearly; and some 300,000 scientific monographs are published each year, along with 15,000 conference proceedings. According to Louis Martin, associate editor of the Association of Research Libraries, "If an average reader tried to catch up with one year's output of learned publications in the sciences, it would take about 50 years of reading at 24 hours a day for seven days a week."[1]

In addition, some of the now-common methods by which we send and receive information did not even exist a short time ago. People receive information online through the Web and through any number of computer retrieval sources, through satellite transmission sources, and of course through newspapers, magazines, and books (both print and online), television, radio, and cellular and land-line phone systems.

Fast-moving developments in information access support the conclusion that the presentation of information is both important and challenging for people in today's organizations. To meet this challenge, a speaker must be knowledgeable about what informative presentations are and how best to give them.

All Sides of the Issue

Ethical Issues

In deciding how much information to present, do you have an ethical responsibility to present all sides of an issue? For example, does a district attorney have a responsibility to tell a grand jury about all known facts of a case? Should a sales representative for a drug manufacturer tell doctors about the side effects of a drug? Should an army recruiter tell potential recruits about both the advantages and disadvantages of military life? Include the criteria you would use to arrive at answers to these questions in your personal consideration or discussion.

13.4: Functions of Informative Presentations

13.4 Express the goals of informative presentations

The presentation's **function** is the answer to the question "What does this presentation do?" The function of a successful informative presentation is sharing information and ideas, shaping perceptions, and setting agendas.

13.4.1: Share Information and Ideas

One of the goals of many informative presentations is to share information and ideas. Speakers throughout organizations are called on to share with groups of coworkers ideas about new methods, new directions, and proposed changes. Other presentations share the latest information on status quo affairs within the organization, such as sales figures, employee absenteeism, results from market research studies, and budgeting procedures.

13.4.2: Shape Perceptions

Most people who listen to informative presentations are not simply taking what the speaker says at face value. As the speaker talks, they constantly react to the material in their own minds. What the speaker says may produce questions, new thoughts, alternative ideas, and disagreement, among other responses. When a listener's perception is altered by a presentation, the speaker has been persuasive. Many informative presentations shape listeners' perceptions by narrowing down possibilities or by defining an issue in a particular way, even though standard persuasion techniques are not used.

13.4.3: Set Agendas

In addition to sharing information and ideas and shaping perceptions, informative presentations set agendas for the organization or for subdivisions of it. In order to accomplish this, an informative presentation gives listeners the knowledge they need to set priorities, order their goals, and put ideas in context.

PRACTICING BUSINESS COMMUNICATION

Best Western International, Inc.

Best Western's crown logo has long been a familiar feature along America's highways—symbolizing a place for vacation lodging, meetings, and stopovers during trips. From humble beginnings as an informal referral system for motels back in 1946, the company later removed the term *motel* from its corporate communications, began to compete head-to-head with other full-service hotel lodging chains, and soon expanded into Europe, the Caribbean, the Pacific, and elsewhere. Today, Best Western is the world's largest hotel chain, with more than 4,000 hotels in more than 100 countries and territories (including 310,000 hotel rooms and more than 400,000 guests each night). Best Western is not a hotel franchise. It's a group of member hotel owners who are committed to quality. Each Best Western–branded hotel is independently owned and operated. This arrangement lends a unique feel to the company's culture—the feel of an extended family in which each member has an equal, valued, and experienced voice in the governance of the brand.

Best Western's brand continually receives industry recognition. In 2014, the organization won more than 60 awards from AAA/CAA, the Hospitality Sales & Marketing Association International, TripAdvisor®, Business Travel News, Travel Click and others.

⊗ A Brand with Heritage

The chain includes many second- and third-generation members who build the traditions that form Best Western's organizational culture today, and they have a deep, personal investment in the brand. For example, during the chain's half-century celebration in 1996, members tracked down and displayed Best Western memorabilia such as old travel guides, correspondence, and postcards.

⊗ Informative Presentations

Although over the years there have been important changes in the membership's composition and in technology and marketing, one of the founding principles of Best Western's corporate culture—a democratic, nonprofit structure—remains basically unchanged. Monthly Board meetings, an annual series of seven district meetings, an annual convention, and a variety of regional meetings in Europe, Africa, South and Central America, Asia, and the Pacific Rim all serve to reinforce this structure.

At events such as these, members join corporate staff to develop policies and informational programs to help hotels drive greater revenue and take more market share. A standard of values is maintained through a *Code of Business Conduct and Ethics* that applies to the Best Western Board of Directors and a separate *Code of Business Conduct and Ethics* that applies to corporate staff. Hoteliers are required to conduct business in a high ethical standard as stated in the *Best Western Rules and Regulations*.

⊗ Communication Power

An early adopter of Web-based communication, Best Western introduced its first hotel listings on its Web site bestwestern.com in 1995. Complete information on all member properties, including photographs, became instantly available to anyone with access. Over the years the value and popularity of the site has increased. For example, in 2014 the site had more than 71 million unique visitors.

Best Western's Web site was completely redesigned in 2012 to enhance its navigability and improve its overall look and feel. It includes TripAdvisor® ratings and reviews, enhanced account management for members of the brand's Best Western Rewards® loyalty program, a more streamlined booking process, and more. More recently, bestwestern.com has been leveraging innovative Google Business Photos technology to enable consumers to digitally visit a hotel before they decide to book. The company rolled out free high-speed Internet access in every guest room in its North American hotels as early as 2004.

⊗ Person-to-Person

Direct communication plays a central role in the Best Western organization, a logical result of its corporate culture and guest-service orientation. Hotel owner-operators are kept abreast of brand developments through in-person presentations, workshops, roundtables, working groups, and educational sessions at district meetings, co-op meetings, Governors' meetings, and the annual convention. These traditional venues also offer ample opportunities for industry experts to present to members in attendance.

Worth noting, Best Western's Education and Training department offers a full slate of informative programs all year long at the corporate headquarters, at district meetings, during the annual convention, and online. These deal with a host of issues from revenue management to expanding market share and enhancing individual hotel Web sites. A centerpiece of this training program is Best Western's I Care initiative, aimed at ensuring that every guest experience is outstanding.

⊗ Varied Channels

Corporate employees utilize a number of communications channels to keep members in the loop about the latest promotions, online tools, trainings, and marketing programs to help them deliver outstanding guest care and boost their profitability. Among these channels: a weekly newsletter that is faxed and emailed to the hotels, the member intranet (mybestwestern.com), regular email updates following Board meetings, emails keyed to specific initiatives or announcements of importance, special departmental newsletters, and more.

Communication at Best Western is an active and challenging combination of the traditional and the innovative. Technology will continue to assist in improving service and information sharing, but Best Western remains focused on person-to-person relationships—one person serving another.

You can visit Best Western International, Inc., online at http://www.bestwestern.com.

WRITING PROMPT

Explain the communications strategy Best Western uses to create a cohesive group environment for its independent hotel owners. Why do you think informative presentations play such a big role within this strategy?

▶ The response entered here will appear in the performance dashboard and can be viewed by your instructor.

Submit

13.5: Organize the Presentation

13.5 Show methods of organizing the three major categories of speech

The pattern by which an informative presentation is organized can help the audience members grasp its content much more readily. The speaker's goal is to choose a method of organization that corresponds to the function of the presentation and the content of the material to be presented.

Informative speeches generally fall into one of three major categories: descriptive presentations, demonstrative presentations, or explanatory presentations. In the next sections, we provide suggestions and examples for preparing each type.

13.5.1: Description

Informative presentations that focus on **description** satisfy the audience members' need for facts, figures, or other data. They answer *what* questions such as these:

> What government regulations currently affect our operations?
>
> What are the demographics of our membership?
>
> What company library resources are checked out most frequently by our employees?

What types of company-sponsored programs do employees want to participate in?

When a speaker has researched the topic and collected the necessary data for the presentation, he or she must choose a pattern of organization that will enhance the audience members' comprehension and retention of the message. Although there are many ways that one might organize descriptive information, two structural patterns that work especially well for such presentations are the topical pattern and the chronological pattern.

TOPICAL PATTERN With a **topical pattern,** the main points of the message are organized as parallel elements of the topic itself. Perhaps the most common pattern for organizing presentations, it is useful when describing components of persons, places, things, or processes. Thus, for example, a speaker might use a topical pattern in a presentation on the various departments (such as sales, production, and human resources) that comprise a business organization, on the characteristics of an effective supervisor, or on reasons for giving a charitable contribution to the United Way.

When using a topical pattern, the sequence of topics is quite important. Presentations that begin with the most important topic and end with the least important topic may lose some audience members' interest along the way. On the other hand, a presentation that begins with the least important topic will have an exceedingly slow start and may fail to catch the audience's interest at all. The most successful topical arrangement is to choose the two most important topics and to begin and end with them—doing so creates immediate interest and provides a sense of closure and significance as well. While that is a good arrangement of topics under ideal circumstances, if time is a factor—as when you are the last speaker in a program that is running long—you should touch on all your important points first to make sure they get covered.

To illustrate the application of the topical pattern to the task of presenting descriptive information, consider the following outline of a presentation responding to the question "What types of company-sponsored programs do our employees want to participate in?"

Thesis:

My audience will know the five categories of programs that they want the company to sponsor, as indicated by their response to a survey.

Introduction:

Orient the audience briefly by describing the employee survey

Motivate their interest by noting that we plan to act on the information gathered

Build rapport by telling a story about various difficulties you encountered while conducting the survey.

First main point:

The survey results showed that many of you would like programs on the history and current status of the organization.

⊗ Sequence of topics:

A. These topics were ranked highest by survey respondents:
   1. Visual aid: Display survey results (see Strategic Skills, 13.5.2).
   2. Your answers have alerted us to the need to keep all lines of communication open.

B. In response, we are planning exhibits, discussion groups, and more coverage of these issues in company publications.
   1. Our goal is to increase your understanding of where the organization has been and where it is going.
   2. We also hope to provide an open environment in which to discuss issues of importance to all of us.

Second main point:

You also said you wanted programs on educational topics.

⊗ Sequence of topics:

A. One possibility is a symposium featuring the managers of various departments.
   1. Some topics for symposiums might include (a) conducting performance reviews, (b) determining when new employees should be hired, and (c) improving quality control.

2. Symposiums will allow you to compare how routine tasks are accomplished in other departments.

B. Another suggestion is to have outside experts speak on such topics as health, safety, nutrition, and eldercare.

Third main point:

Finally, many of you are interested in getting to know our CEO better.

⊗ Sequence of topics:

A. We would like Georgette Smith to give more frequent presentations to the employees, especially in a small-group format.

B. We are looking into other activities, such as a "Breakfast with the Boss," to promote this interaction.

Conclusion:

Briefly summarize survey results and describe the next step in the process of implementing such programs.

State the significance of the programs for the company as well as for individual employees.

CHRONOLOGICAL PATTERN   A second organizational pattern that is well suited to providing description is known as a **chronological pattern.** When using this construction, the presenter organizes the main points of the message in a time-related sequence. The sequence could be highly generalized, for example:

Thesis:

My audience will understand our company's past, present, and future approaches to conducting appraisal interviews.

   I. Describe the organization's past use of management by objectives as an approach to conducting appraisal interviews.
   II. Describe the present method of conducting appraisal interviews.
   III. Describe the future plans for revising the organization's approach to appraisal interviews.

The sequence may also be highly specific:

   I. On December 1, the reports came in.
   II. The alterations detailed in the reports were completed and in place by December 4.
   III. We sent out the replacement parts on December 5.

The chronological pattern is also useful when analyzing a process step by step. Thus, a presentation on how to use an automobile driver's seat might be organized using a chronological pattern, as the following outline shows:

Thesis:

My audience will be able to position an automobile driver's seat in a way that maximizes safety.

ⓧ Main points in chronological pattern:

I. The goal is to position the driver's seat so that you can wear the seat belt correctly, while being as far away from the front airbag as possible.

II. Sit upright with both feet on the floor and the seat back reclined no more than 30 degrees.

III. Make sure that you can easily reach the pedals and that your arms are slightly bent when holding the steering wheel.

IV. Your chest should be at least 10 inches from the center of the airbag cover.

V. Place the shoulder section of the seat belt mid-way between your neck and your shoulder.

VI. Fit the lap section of the belt tightly across your hips, not across your stomach.

To illustrate how the chronological pattern may be used for a descriptive informative presentation, consider the following outline of a presentation that compares company sales performance over the last five years.

Thesis:

My audience will know the five-year sales trends for our company.

Introduction:

Orient the audience by briefly summarizing the time period to be covered in the presentation, and build motivation and rapport by complimenting the audience members on their hard work and demonstrated success.

First main point:

Five years ago, we held only 13 percent of the market for specialized testing equipment.

ⓧ Subpoints in chronological pattern:

A. Our major market entry was a portable unit to measure air quality.

B. We sold an average of 23,000 units per year.

Second main point:

Three years ago, we expanded our product line to include water-testing equipment and a new unit to test auto emissions.

ⓧ Subpoints in chronological pattern:

A. Our market share increased to 18 percent.

B. We opened a regional office in the Northwest.

Third main point:

Two years ago, we began to phase out all harmful chemicals used in our equipment and manufacturing processes as well as to search for environmentally safe alternatives.

ⓧ Subpoints in chronological pattern:

A. At the same time, we maintained our strong sales by benefiting from an increased interest in home water-testing.

B. We sold more than 30,000 home testing unit.

Fourth main point:

Last year, we had a record $56 million in sales.

ⓧ Subpoints in chronological pattern:

A. Our profit margin increased 8 percent.

B. We were named one of the top ten small businesses in the region by a major business journal.

C. We predict even better results for next year based on a new unit to test for chemicals in the groundwater supply that will be purchased by municipalities.

Conclusion:

State the significance of the presentation by summarizing that the company has built its success on developing new products to meet emerging needs. Provide closure by reviewing the outlook for the next year.

In preparing a descriptive presentation, the speaker's purpose is not to persuade, motivate, or change the audience members' minds. The purpose of an informative presentation is to do just that: inform! The speaker should present the data at hand in as straightforward a manner as possible.

13.5.2: Demonstration

A **demonstration** answers *how* questions, such as "How does this work?" or "How does someone or something move from point A to point B?" Consider, for example, a demonstrative presentation given by a member of the U.S. Postal Service to a group of business leaders who had made complaints about the quality of local mail delivery and handling.

In his presentation, the postal worker demonstrated the numerous checkpoints and distribution centers through which a piece of mail travels before it reaches its destination. He supplemented the demonstration with maps, flowcharts, and even photographs of the various locations. He followed the presentation with a question-and-answer session.

A demonstrative presentation has the potential to work in persuasive ways in the minds of listeners. You can probably see how this presentation, although technically informative, may have shaped the perspective of the audience. The speaker did not announce that he intended to vindicate the postal service, but by demonstrating the many quality checks, special distribution centers, and trained personnel staffing the post offices, he may well have changed some of the audience members' minds about their postal service.

Presenting Statistics Visually

Strategic Skills

When using visual aids to present statistics during informative presentations, ensure that percentages add to 100 and that numbers and categories are easily readable. The visual shown here supports the presentation on new employee programs.

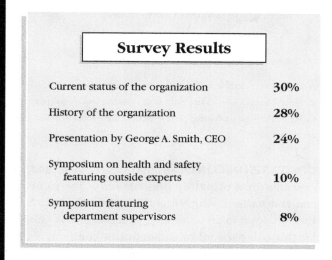

Survey Results	
Current status of the organization	30%
History of the organization	28%
Presentation by George A. Smith, CEO	24%
Symposium on health and safety featuring outside experts	10%
Symposium featuring department supervisors	8%

When planning and organizing a demonstrative presentation, a **spatial or geographical pattern** of organizing ideas works well. A geographical pattern organizes main points in terms of their physical locations, especially in relation to each other. For example, the terms *north, south, east,* and *west* might be used in a presentation showing the physical layout of a business or the location of famous landmarks, such as the Mall in Washington, D.C.

A spatial pattern shows the physical layout of an object's parts, frequently through such directional cues as *top, bottom, outside, inside, left,* or *right*. When presenting a demonstration to an audience, the speaker is often involved in a range of communication from *tell* to *show*, as he or she describes where the part is located and then shows the location through a visual aid. Successful spatial demonstrations are often hands-on.

The following excerpt from a presentation given in a computer-training workshop uses a spatial pattern to describe how to create a comfortable environment for using a computer. The emphasis is on the relationships between and among the pieces of computer equipment and the user.

Thesis:

I want my audience to understand basic principles for creating a comfortable computer workspace.

Introduction:

Many factors go into creating a comfortable workspace, including proper placement and adjustment of furniture and equipment, good light, and other environmental considerations. Today I will share some suggestions that can make your work more comfortable. Comfort is very personal, though, and only you can judge what works best for you.

First main point:

Furniture and posture.

ⓧ Subpoints in demonstration pattern:

A. Adjust the height of your chair and desk so that your body is comfortably aligned.
B. Have your knees slightly lower than your hips, so that the angle of your torso and thighs is more than 90 degrees.
C. Let your chair support you. Support your lower back with your chair's backrest.

Second main point:

Keyboard and mouse.

ⓧ Subpoints in demonstration pattern:

A. Place your keyboard and mouse so that your forearms are parallel or almost parallel to the floor. Your wrist should not be extremely flexed or extended.
B. Your hands and wrists should be in roughly the same neutral position as when your arms are loosely hanging by your sides. Your wrist should not be bent too much to one side or the other.
C. You should not have to reach or stretch to use either the keyboard or the mouse.

Although spatial and geographical patterns are most useful when showing how things or places relate to each other in physical space, the pattern of organization for a presentation should be chosen based on the goal of the speech. For example, if the speaker at the computer workshop wants to inform the audience of possible uses for computers, he or she might choose a topical pattern rather than a geographical pattern. If the goal of the presentation is to inform the audience of the technological advances in a particular component that have occurred over the last three years, he or she might choose a chronological pattern.

13.5.3: Explanation

The third type of informative presentation addresses *why* questions, such as these:

Why is our market share declining?

Why are we restructuring the department?

Why do we need to raise membership dues 15 percent by the end of the year?

Each of these topics challenges the speaker to inform the audience and to justify the actions or decisions in question. *Why* questions frequently address controversial issues, and the audience may be predisposed to hostility, anger, or skepticism. Thus, one benefit of an explanatory presentation is to calm the audience. Once the audience members know why a condition exists or why an action is being taken, they are more likely to consider it in a rational and calm manner. If an audience is informed, for example, of the specific factors that led to a 15 percent increase in membership dues, they are more likely to accept the increase.

Two patterns of organization are especially well suited to the goal of providing explanation: the cause/ effect pattern and the comparison/contrast pattern. Once again, however, we emphasize that the pattern chosen should reflect the speaker's goal, the audience, and the occasion.

CAUSE/EFFECT PATTERN With a **cause/effect pattern** of organization, the presenter organizes the message around the origins and the results of a series of events. For example, a presentation on the cost of air travel might employ a cause/effect pattern by first noting the rapid rise in the cost of fuel over the winter, resulting in higher operating costs for airlines and thus causing higher ticket prices.

The presenter might also choose to begin with a description of present conditions (the effects) and then identify and explore the possible causes of the effects. The choice between these approaches can be made based on which element (the cause or the effect) is most familiar to the audience. To illustrate how a cause/effect pattern might be used to explain an event, consider the following excerpt from an outline of a presentation on why membership dues for an organization must be raised 15 percent by the end of the year.

Thesis:

My audience will both understand the rationale for and accept a membership dues increase of 15 percent.

Introduction:

Orient the audience by giving a brief overview of the problem, and build rapport by explaining your long involvement with and belief in the organization.

First main point (cause):

The costs of running the organization continue to rise, and we have had no dues increases for the past two years.

(×) Subpoints in cause/effect pattern:

A. The costs of producing our journal have risen dramatically.

B. Administrative costs for operating the office have also increased.

C. We estimate that our total costs have increased by more than 50 percent.

Second main point (additional cause):

We have implemented as many cost-cutting measures as possible during the last two years, allowing us to keep dues at the same amount.

(×) Subpoints in cause/effect pattern:

A. Budgets have been strictly monitored.

B. We have also eliminated unnecessary spending.

Third main point (effect):

In light of our increased costs, and having reduced expenditures and eliminated unnecessary spending, it is now necessary to find other ways to keep the organization out of debt.

(×) Subpoints in cause/effect pattern:

A. A 15 percent increase in dues will cover our outstanding costs.

B. We will begin a membership drive to increase our total dues revenue.

C. We will explore fundraising ideas to increase the amount of money in our operating budget.

COMPARISON/CONTRAST PATTERN A second way to organize an explanatory presentation is the **comparison/ contrast pattern,** which identifies a familiar situation and then relates it to an unfamiliar situation that is either similar (for comparison) or different (for contrast). Consider the following outline of a presentation given to a group of management trainees in a large retail store.

Thesis:

My audience will see their management training program as similar in function to the experience of their first few weeks of college.

Introduction:

Orient the audience by briefly describing your role in the training process; provide rapport by noting that you went through the training program four years ago.

First main point (familiar situation):

Many of you are recent college graduates. Think back to your first few weeks of school.

(×) Subpoints in comparison/contrast pattern:

A. You probably didn't know many other students.

B. You probably got lost on campus more than a few times.

C. Slowly you learned how to get around, study, organize your time, and set priorities.

Second main point (comparison):

You will find many similarities to your initial college experiences as new employees here at Martingale Company.

(×) Subpoints in comparison/contrast pattern:

A. As the training program progresses, you will learn skills.

1. Seminars on public speaking and interviewing are offered.

2. Specialized training programs for the international department will be given.

B. You will also get to know the other trainees and supervisors.

1. Do not hesitate to ask questions.

2. You can learn a lot through informal communication as well as through the training program.

Conclusion:

Emphasize the significance of the training program and provide closure by thanking the audience for attending.

As you can see, the organization of an informative speech is an important tool to ensure that the audience members understand and remember your presentation. A logical and appropriate pattern boosts the impact of any informative presentation.

Comparative Statistics

Strategic Skills

Comparative statistics are most effective when presented graphically, as this bar graph illustrates. Graph headings should be simple and eye-catching.

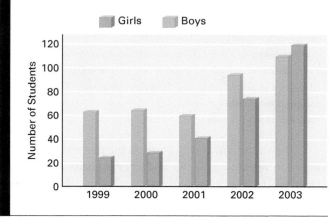

13.6: Typical Formats

13.6 **Describe the basic settings of giving informative presentations**

Formats are the structures or settings in which informative presentations are given. The format may reflect the setting, the audience's needs, the speaker's goal, or a combination of the three. Formats for informative presentations are meant to maximize the efficient transmission of information to audience members.

Briefings are relatively short presentations that inform an audience about a particular event. The White House press secretary provides frequent briefings for the press about the activities of the president.

Reports simply give an account of the status quo. Presentations that provide data such as the amount of money remaining in the budget and profit and loss figures are good examples of reports.

Training presentations educate listeners to help them to gain or improve on specific skills. Presentations that train as a format typically provide listeners with background information, introduce specific principles, and then follow through with skills practice, which the listeners perform.

Routine and regularly scheduled meetings: The weekly meeting follows a *telling format,* wherein the supervisor, boss, or executive shares information that is to be transmitted down the chain of command or presents new goals for the week. The monthly meeting is often a formal meeting that attempts to present positive messages and summary reports by specific ad hoc or permanent committees or work groups. (*Ad hoc,* which translates literally as "to this," refers to a group set up for a specific purpose, which disbands when the purpose is fulfilled.)

For each of these formats, the presentation is only as good as the preparation that precedes it. A strong presentation depends on the *inside* (an appropriate pattern and effective supporting materials, introduction, and conclusion) as well as the *outside* (the format).

13.7: Guidelines for a Successful Presentation

13.7 **Evaluate the basic guidelines to be followed for ensuring successful presentations**

Now that you have an understanding of patterns and formats for informative presentations, it is important to attend to situational details.

Advance planning and preparation are the greatest defense against elements in the situation that can adversely affect your presentation. Think about some of the *worst* possible things that could happen to you during a presentation. What could you do in advance to prevent them from ruining your presentation? You probably came up with as good a list as we did. Nevertheless, here are some guidelines for ensuring successful presentations that we think are particularly worth considering.

13.7.1: Analyze Potential Sources of Noise

Noise is anything that interferes with the communication process. Noise can occur at any time in the process. For purposes of illustration, let us look at three potential levels on which noise can occur:

1. In the transmission of information from speaker to listener (e.g., does the listener even receive or hear the information?)

2. In the comprehension of information (e.g., once the information is received and heard, does the listener understand the information the same way the speaker intended?)

3. In the pragmatics of information (e.g., once the information is heard and understood, does the listener do what the speaker wants?).

A speaking setting actually has three potential sources of noise—physical, physiological, and psychological. **Physical noise** refers to distractions in the environment of the presentation. Does the room in which you will speak require a microphone for you to be heard clearly? Are there windows that will invite listeners to daydream or not pay attention to you? These are just two possible sources of physical noise.

There is no reason to find out about these problems in the midst of your presentation. Scouting out the room before you start and making appropriate adjustments are well worth your time.

Physiological noise comes from competing personal needs the listener may have. For example, is the listener too hot or too cold? Thirsty? Tired? Think of times when you have been uncomfortable as an audience member. Did you really pay attention to the speaker? All you probably thought about was when the next break was scheduled.

By satisfying the listeners' physiological needs as much as possible, the speaker can increase the listeners' attention. Adjusting the temperature in the room the night before you are to present can be helpful. Arranging for pitchers of water and snacks such as fresh fruit or candy can alleviate thirst or hunger. Planning breaks at strategic times can enable listeners to digest what they have just heard and ready themselves for the information to come.

Psychological noise includes internal distractions within the mind of the listener. For example, if the listener is concerned about what he is wearing tonight, what she may say when she has to speak tomorrow, or whether the spouse picked up the kids from school on time, that person is not listening to you!

The best way to overcome psychological noise is to make sure that your presentation is more interesting and captivating than anything else the listener may prefer to think about. This is no easy task. But by using a range of voice inflections and pacing, providing a variety of supporting materials, and incorporating visual aids, you will have a much better chance of obtaining and maintaining the audience's attention.

The general point is that you as the presenter can and should control the circumstances in which you speak. Planning in advance and overcoming barriers that can create noise are crucial for your success as a speaker.

13.7.2: Adapt to Your Listeners

One common mistake made by beginning speakers is to assume that the *same speech* can be given to different audiences. Although the same *topic* can be presented to many audiences, speakers can quite easily fail if they do not adapt the material from group to group because the audience will not perceive their presentations as relevant.

Adaptation does not mean starting over. The same main points, basic premises, and even data or evidence may be quite applicable in every group with which you talk. But examples, illustrations, case studies, or incidents usually require adaptation to the particular group. For example, Ali, who works for a multinational corporation, will speak on the same topic to two groups, but he has adapted his speech for his extended family and work partners in Saudi Arabia and his fellow workers in the United States.

⊕ Who are you talking to?

Consider these situations: An example that employees in an accounting department may find relevant and understandable may make no sense to employees in personnel. A brief reference to an incident (such as the Korean War) that is relevant to a group whose ages coincide with that conflict may be meaningless to an audience composed of younger people. Discussing the merits of investing in company stocks and bonds may be exciting to a group of executives but depressing to a group of hourly workers whose every dollar is spent even before it is made.

The successful speaker adapts the material of the presentation according to the audience's needs and requirements. There are actually three levels of adaptation: knowledge, interest, and acceptance. In terms of the **knowledge level,** the two basic extremes are audiences whose members are well informed versus those whose members are entirely uninformed. The differences in adaptation between these two audiences may be obvious to you. With an uninformed audience, you are obliged to provide more background material, define terms carefully, and link the material in the presentation to material already known. With an informed audience, you can assume more and de-emphasize the three preceding factors. Indeed, if you emphasize background material, term definition, and linkage of material with an informed audience, the participants may feel insulted or bored!

The **interest level** ranges from high initial interest to no interest at all. Some listeners, for example, may find any topic related to microcomputers fascinating but be completely uninterested in topics related to plant safety. Uninterested listeners will not meet any of your objectives for the presentation, whether they are to discover, learn, laugh, or review. If audience members are not interested, they will not listen; if they do not listen, they will not understand; and if they do not understand, your objective will not be met.

What are some ways that you can facilitate audience interest? Look at some of these lines from actual speeches given in businesses and organizations. Would they capture your interest? (If not, what are some that would?)

> "Have you ever wondered how successful people choose which stocks and bonds to buy?"

> "If I could tell you how to get a day's worth of work finished in half a day, would you be interested?"

> "In the next ten minutes, I will outline a new program that will significantly increase almost all the benefits that you as an employee of this company can receive."

Successful informative presentations have one characteristic in common. They all give audience members a reason to listen. They connect with needs or values of audience members and motivate their curiosity.

13.7.3: Shared Perspectives

In every informative presentation, the data come from somewhere. Sharing with your listeners the origins of these data and providing a perspective on them are good ways to reduce unanswered questions in listeners' minds. Specific ways of doing this vary with topic and context, but they include sharing with your audience how certain numbers were figured, the source from which information was derived, how certain conclusions were drawn, where some possible problems are, and so forth.

A shared perspective benefits from including listeners' experiences and viewpoints as well. The more you link your message with what the audience already knows, the more successful you will be.

Shared perspective benefits from frequent use of analogies. **Analogies** compare two items and in essence argue that what is true in one case is also true in the other. You have heard speakers draw analogies between two time periods, two states, two presidential administrations, and even two families.

Analogies are quite useful in an informative presentation. If the audience is knowledgeable in one subject area and you are introducing new material, you can use an analogy from that area to explain how the new information is "just like what you have already heard before" or "very similar to the way we have discussed this in the past."

Shared perspective is also increased by avoiding jargon as much as possible. For example, communication specialists call a student who has a great deal of anxiety about giving a public presentation "high comm apps." To those who have not taken a communication course, communication specialists' use of this term—which means "high communication apprehensive"—may conjure up any number of confusing images. Confusion, misunderstanding, and resentment can result when jargon is introduced to listeners. If you must use jargon, define it so that you ensure audience understanding. A shared perspective

facilitates the transfer and acceptance of information between speaker and listener.

Coping with Murphy's Law
Strategic Skills

A public speaker has to cope with a variety of unusual events. Murphy's Law famously states *that what can go wrong will go wrong*. The following situations can happen, therefore at least some of them will happen. Use this list as a reminder to be ready for anything.

- Pillars in the room prevent some audience members from seeing the visuals you are presenting.
- When you arrive you are asked to speak for an hour instead of thirty minutes because a second speaker has canceled.
- You take out your speaking notes but, just as you are being introduced to the audience, discover that some notes are missing.
- A technology glitch prevents you from showing your slides.
- Someone in the audience interrupts you to say that you are not speaking on the subject the audience has come to hear about.
- Someone in the audience begins laughing uncontrollably.
- The preceding speaker covers all of your material.
- Your introducer undermines your credibility with some caustic remarks.
- Nonverbal clues from your audience suggest that many listeners do not understand your supporting examples.
- No one laughs at the joke you just told to support a key idea.
- At the end of your speech, someone yells, "Keep going!"
- Handouts are accidentally distributed ahead of schedule and the audience stops paying attention to your speech.
- Movements and facial expressions of the audience signal boredom, and you have just begun to speak.
- A couple of audience questions can be interpreted as hints that your idea development is not sophisticated enough.

SOURCE: Reprinted with permission from the National Communication Association: http://www.natcom.org.

13.8: Situational Knowledge and Technology

13.8 Analyze the use of the video, television, and big screen projections in presentations

Are you used to seeing video clips and animations that enhance the presentation of information on both small and large screens? Chances are the video made the material more interesting. Have you ever found yourself in a large conference or lecture hall and were happy to see the speaker's image on a large monitor? That way you had clear knowledge of who was speaking when. Video and television technology greatly enhance professional presentations in many situations. Knowing where, when, and how to use this technology is essential.

13.8.1: Video

Many businesses and professions make extensive use of video. Medical schools record residents examining patients. Organizations such as Miles Laboratories provide videos of seminars in which physicians learn how to improve their credibility with patients and their public presentations. Professional organizations for attorneys and teachers use videos for in-service training, continuing education, and certification training. Manufacturing and service businesses and government agencies require employees to attend seminars and workshops at which instructional and informational videos are shown. The range of applications of video technology has expanded dramatically in the last ten years. Annual reports, product demonstrations, and training sessions are just three of the many uses of video in business and the professions.

Many of the skills and techniques of video production are similar to those required for live or taped television productions.

What would you identify as the three most significant challenges for this individual making a big screen presentation? Were you the presenter, how would you meet them?

SOURCE: Maxim Blinkov/Shutterstock

13.8.2: Television

Our discussion focuses on speeches given in one room and piped to different locations on multiple television monitors, speeches that are presented live to large audiences and that incorporate a big-screen monitor to aid the audience's view of the speaker, and speeches that are recorded for playback on a monitor at a later time. Although we do not directly address interviews, debates, or panel discussions, these are televised on a regular basis, and many of the principles we refer to apply to them.

In business and the professions, speeches are often projected on a big screen. You may have attended conferences or conventions where this technique was used, especially for major or keynote presentations. You may also have attended concerts or sporting events where the audience's view of the star or the action was enhanced by big-screen technology. Television cameras project the speaker's image onto a big screen that is raised for all to see.

Of course, the big screen creates some difficulties for the speaker. Tiny variables are captured by the camera. Facial expressions such as raised eyebrows, smiles, frowns, or pauses with the mouth held slightly open are greatly emphasized. The screen reveals nervous tics as readily as it does friendly, conversational gestures such as upward palms to signal openness or downward pointing to indicate concreteness. Also, the speaker must restrict her or his body movement. Most speeches delivered through the big-screen medium are scripted and read from a prompter (a screen showing a large-type copy of the speech that can be seen by the speaker but not by the audience). It is difficult, if not impossible, for a speaker to read a presentation from a prompter if he or she is moving around the stage. In addition, the speaker's microphone is generally placed on the podium, and movement away from it causes her or his voice to fade. A lavaliere or lapel microphone (which is attached to the speaker's clothing and sometimes is wireless) can help to prevent fadeout.

The challenge for you as a speaker is to minimize the problems and take advantage of the benefits that the big screen offers. Television has the potential to reveal your confidence, forcefulness, and emotion much more readily than any other medium.

13.9: Camera Skills and Special Occasions

13.9 Explain how to develop some of the skills necessary for communication competence

Communication competence for technology and special occasions depends on practice. Video and television presentations and special occasion speeches require the acquisition of skills through specific effort and situational knowledge.

13.9.1: Practice

Many people are frightened by the prospect of making a televised presentation because they have never done so before. If you were told that your presentation would be broadcast, would you have some of these concerns?

- "I'll look funny."
- "I won't sound like myself on television."
- "My lips will quiver, my voice will shake, and my tongue will stick to my teeth."
- "I don't want someone to be able to replay my speech."
- "Anything I wear will look unflattering on camera."

If you are prone to such negative self-assessments, you are not alone. These are natural feelings that cause apprehension. Remember that giving a speech in public is the behavior most feared by most adults. Having a presentation aired over television only heightens that apprehension, whether the speech is a live big-screen presentation, a live television appearance, or a taped presentation that will be distributed for viewing.

We cannot alleviate all your concerns. Nor do we believe that you should be totally calm when delivering your presentation. Some apprehension provides the adrenaline needed to keep you excited and energetic. Our goal is to help you to manage the additional apprehension caused by the televised medium. The following comments address some of the on-camera delivery skills that you will need.

The red light on one of the cameras signals that your presentation is being taped, broadcast, or both. Where should you look? Should you look directly at the camera? Should you look only at the camera whose red light indicates that it is operating? Should you ignore the camera and focus on the audience (even if you cannot see the audience because of the lights shining in your eyes)? If no audience is present, should you pretend that there is one and talk to it?

The answers to these questions are difficult to provide because many variables can affect individual televised performances. We offer the following general guidelines as a starting point for performing in some of the most common television setups.[2]

If you are speaking from a prompter that is located above or on the camera, you necessarily must look at that camera to read your manuscript. Getting the words right is your primary concern and should be emphasized over placement of eye contact.

If prompters are located to the left and right of the podium, you can alternate eye contact from one to the other (and to the audience seated in front of you) without losing focus on your manuscript. The camera operator will follow your gaze as you alternate between the TelePrompTers.

If you are not using a prompter, your notes or speaker's outline should be prepared on small blue or green note cards to avoid causing camera glare or distracting the audience. If a live audience is present, focus on the audience and let the cameras find you. Awkward changes in eye contact are likely to occur as you glance from one camera to another. If a live audience is not present, decide to whom you want to direct the presentation. Looking directly at the camera gives those who watch the presentation on a monitor the impression that you are speaking directly to them. If you want to convey the impression that you are actually speaking to an audience and that viewers are eavesdropping on the presentation, speak to the room and let the camera find you.

13.9.2: Appearance

What about your appearance? There are ways to optimize your appearance in a televised presentation.[3] While these are basics, we hope you take time to consider the particular needs of your own presentation.

COSMETICS   A speaker's features often appear flat on television, and other distortions may occur as well. During the Nixon-Kennedy presidential debates of 1960, Richard Nixon refused to wear makeup. People who listened to the debate on radio thought Nixon beat John Kennedy. But viewers of the televised version saw Nixon's pallor and five-o'clock shadow and believed that Kennedy won the debate. Cosmetics, especially eyeliner and blush, restore the natural dimensions of the face. In professional settings, listen to the experts. If you lack access to professional guidance, try various types of cosmetics and make test videos. (Do not, however, expect to change your on-camera appearance radically through makeup!) Powder can reduce the glare and reflection produced by hot lights. If you are not skilled in applying powder, blush, or other cosmetics, have someone on hand to help you. Remember always to check yourself on a monitor to see how you look. The picture on the television monitor is the most accurate indicator of your appearance.

Both men and women should be aware of their hair. Neither should lapse into bad habits such as nervously brushing their hair. Because nonverbal behavior is clearly seen on screen, practice avoiding nervous habits.

CLOTHING   On television and in formal settings in videos, men are generally requested to wear traditional suits for business and for most other professions. The context, of course, is the final determination. Both men and women should avoid white, although new lighting developments have made white less problematic. When men or women are seated during a presentation and they are wearing suit jackets, they should sit on the bottom of their jackets to avoid bunching at the back of the neck or shoulder area. Some suit jackets look better buttoned when the wearer is seated; others need to be unbuttoned. Experiment for the best results.

If men are to sit at a table without a curtain in front of it or in interview chairs like those the morning talk shows use, they should wear long dark socks to avoid a gap between the top of their socks and the beginning of their pants leg. U.S. culture dictates that credible speakers do not expose that inch of bare skin!

Like men, women can have particular problems with clothing. Short skirts create difficulties for fashion-conscious female broadcasters. If you are an occasional video or television presenter, you might choose to wear a longer skirt to avoid the "struggle with the skirt" syndrome that causes female interviewers and interviewees to be uncomfortable on camera during long shots.

When you are choosing clothing for a televised presentation, consider the background against which you will be speaking. Be sure to find out from the director what the background is before you begin the session. Dark clothing against a dark background or light clothing against a light background will cause problems for the studio engineers. In most cases, cool colors such as blue, gray, or pastels are preferable to black, and white should be avoided because it causes camera glare. The guiding principle is to avoid major color contrasts within your outfit or against the background. Avoid stripes, checks, and polka dots because they blur on camera. Minimize or avoid wearing jewelry; it can cause glare and distract the audience from your presentation.

By following these general principles, you can improve your appearance, self-confidence, and delivery on camera.

The Informative Speech

Strategic Skills

Full preparation for an informative speech starts with defining the purpose and runs all the way through rehearsal. Use this checklist to make sure you have everything covered.

(×) Checklist:

- Do you have a clear purpose in mind?
- Is your speech best described as descriptive, demonstrative, or explanatory?

- Given a clear purpose, what are the three to five main points that the audience will need to understand and accept if you are to achieve it?
- What forms of support (e.g., explanations, examples, statistics, testimony, and visual aids) will make your main points most informative, interesting, relevant, clear, and acceptable?
- Would some form of information technology be most useful in making your presentation?
- What organizational pattern for your speech will best accommodate both your purpose and your forms of support: topical, chronological, spatial/geographical, cause/effect, or comparison/contrast?
- How can you best achieve the functions of the introduction (orientation, motivation, and rapport) and conclusion (completeness and closure) of your speech?
- Which type of delivery (impromptu, extemporaneous, manuscript, or memorized) is likely to be most effective in accomplishing your purpose?
- Independent of type of delivery, how can you make your delivery intelligible, conversational, direct, and unobtrusive?
- How will you prepare to field questions from the audience?
- How will you prepare to deal with the anxiety you are likely to experience?
- How will you rehearse your presentation?

13.9.3: Multimedia Technology and Presentations

This rapidly expanding area of technology changes almost daily. Advances include the use of interactive computer programs in business and in education; videophones, which incorporate computer-generated hardcopy messages with real-time pictures and the voices of both sender and receiver; and video scanners, which through digitalization produce real-life pictures, an addition to the existing technology of simulation and graphics. Scanners that transform hard-copy documents and photographs into computer files have been available for some time, but scanners for videotape and film are still relatively new to the market. These are just a few of the current advancements. As you enter the work force, be aware that technology is changing rapidly. It is to your advantage to keep current.

13.10: Manage Anxiety Through Practice and Knowledge

13.10 Analyze how to manage anxiety about giving a presentation through practice and knowledge

Practice is the key to reducing anxiety. When you become accustomed to cameras running, bright lights shining in your face, microphones clipped to your clothing, and eye contact with the camera, your level of apprehension will decrease. Only time and repetition of the experience will allow a televised presentation to seem like a natural behavior.

Nevertheless, there are ways to combat anxiety in your very first televised presentation. Watch yourself on tape with a critical but constructive eye. Do not say, "I look awful." Watch the tape and ask, "What actions can I take to improve my appearance during this presentation?" Are there some things you are wearing, ways you are standing, and so forth, that you could change?

Concentrate on the way you sound as well as on the way you look. If your microphone is on the podium, speak over the microphone rather than into it to avoid popping sounds. If you are using a lavaliere microphone, avoid excessive rustling and fidgeting, which will cause static or interference.

If possible, show your practice video to someone else for his or her comments. This person does not have to be an expert to offer you a constructive opinion. If you do not have access to video equipment before the presentation, practice in front of a mirror or with a friend. Doing so can go a long way toward reducing your anxiety when you actually have to perform on camera.

Translating ideas into clear and attractive forms is an increasingly important challenge for members of the business community.

In addition to the techniques already presented, here are some other general hints for increasing your confidence and skill level as a speaker.[4]

ⓧ **Hints:**

1. When you are speaking informatively, think of how you became interested in your topic and build your audience's motivation to listen by recapturing for them your own initial experience.

2. Oral rehearsal is especially important in an informative speech because you can never be really sure that you understand a concept until you hear yourself explain it.

3. Do not become overly specific too early in an informative speech because listeners forget foreign details easily; concentrate on explaining one central feature of your concept.

4. Try to recall the specific sequence of events that caused you suddenly to understand the topic you will be discussing; try leading listeners down the same path you took.

5. Dictionary definitions of key terms are rarely helpful in an informative speech because listeners need more fully amplified and more colorful explanations of a concept.

6. Long quotations from expert sources may be lacking in flair and clarity; oftentimes, you will have to supplement such remarks with your own better-adapted paraphrases.

7. Each major section of a speech outline should contain a minimum of one extended example and two or more brief examples if a concept is to be truly clarified for others.

8. We strongly advise preparing a sentence outline for every speech you make, although you may choose to use a shorter version of this outline when actually delivering your speech.

9. Put the burden of proof on the use of visual aids (that is, carefully assess their potential to enhance your presentation) because their distracting capacities can outweigh their helpfulness in clarifying ideas.

10. Remember this proposition above all others: if there is any chance that listeners can misunderstand you, they will.

Strategic Scenario Wrap-Up

Informative Presentations

ⓧ Strategic Scenario

Julia Tulovsky is the curator of the Russian Collection for the B. J. Turock Museum of Art. One of her tasks as curator is to create exhibitions for the museum using the permanent collection, collections from other museums, or both. Next week the museum will open a new exhibition, Leonid Sokov: Ironic Objects, which will be on display for six months. At the exhibit's opening reception, Julia will be making a twenty-minute presentation on the artist, the art, and the exhibition itself to between 50 and 75 individuals who have accepted the museum's invitation to attend. After this presentation, there will be a reception and tours of the art. What goals should Julia focus on? What medium should she use to present the information to a group of this size?

Julia Tulovsky, the B. J. Turock Museum's curator of Russian Art, has just curated and installed an exhibition called *Leonid Sokov: Ironic Objects*. She had two primary goals in mind:

1. To remind the audience of the importance of the Russian collection to the museum

2. To explain how she created an exhibition to demonstrate the importance of Leonid Sokov's significant contributions to that collection

To achieve her goals, Julia put together a PowerPoint presentation of Sokov's life and work. The presentation covered this content:

1. Consisting of 80 pieces of art, 40 from the Turock collection and 40 from private collectors, the exhibition showcases the museum's strength in Russian and Soviet art.

2. Leonid Sokov (b. 1941) is one of the leading figures in Soviet underground and Russian–American contemporary art. The artist, who started his career in Moscow, and immigrated to the United States in 1980, lives and works in New York.

3. This exhibition is a survey of his career from the 1960s to 2000. It highlights themes and developments in his art, which often combines well-known literary and visual references to Russian culture with ideas of Western modernism (for example, combining images of Joseph Stalin and Marilyn Monroe).

To close her presentation, Julia invited the audience to ask questions as they toured the exhibit.

Summary

Informative Presentations

- **Informative speaking** is a common form of presentation and one that most businesspeople will have to engage in at one time or another.
- The successful informative presentation **shares traits with other kinds of presentations**: it identifies the main points to be shared with an audience, it uses supporting materials to elaborate these points and increase their credibility, it presents a total message, and it is delivered in a style appropriate to the audience and its concerns.
- An informative presentation usually has one (or more) of **three functions**: to share information and ideas, shape perception, or set agendas.
- Likewise, the **pattern of a presentation reflects its function**: Is the presentation designed to describe, demonstrate, or explain?
- **Possible patterns** include topical, chronological, spatial/geographical, cause/effect, and comparison/contrast.
- Presentations also take **different formats**; among these are briefings, reports, and training sessions.
- Once a speaker has decided on the appropriate function, organization, and format of the presentation, the work of **ensuring the success of the presentation** begins.
- To do so, the speaker is wise to follow several principles. First, **analyze and prepare** for potential sources of noise (physical, physiological, and psychological). Second, **adapt to your listeners**. Successful adaptation requires discovery of each audience's knowledge, interest, and acceptance levels. Third, work toward a **shared perspective** with audience members by disclosing where information came from and using analogies to reach the listeners.
- A speaker can also **increase his or her confidence and skill level** by rehearsing the speech, avoiding simplistic dictionary definitions that are neither colorful nor

broad enough, giving sufficient examples of major points, and using visual aids in ways that will minimize their capacity to distract the audience.
- Although these techniques do not guarantee that every speaker will finally come to public speaking with ease and self-assurance, they can help all potential public speakers realize the **extent of their own resources** and how to use them.
- **Video, television, and multimedia presentations** are parts of the ongoing and dramatic changes in presentations in business and in the professions.
- It is important to develop your **audio-presentation skills** as increasingly sophisticated technology becomes common in the workplace.
- Competent speakers can take **advantage of technology** to enhance their contact with and appeal to the audience.
- Understanding and practicing with **broadcast technology** can decrease anxiety and ensure a successful presentation.

Chapter 13 Quiz: Informative Presentations

Chapter 14

Persuasive and Special Presentations

 Learning Objectives

14.1 Review situations when persuasive and special presentations may be used

14.2 Interpret the four basic functions of persuasive presentations

14.3 Describe the three most popular formats of persuasive or special presentations

14.4 Examine the basic resources of persuasion

14.5 Express some of the strategies that may be employed in the process of persuasion

14.6 Examine nine types of special occasion presentations

Strategic Scenario: Fifteen Minutes

Michael Martello is the director of development at the B. J. Turock Museum of Art. Michael and his assistants are charged with friend- and fund-raising for the Museum. While the university provides funds for the museum, they are only a fraction of what the museum needs for operating expenses and collection preservation and development. Michael's task is to raise funds for the museum by multiple means: producing an annual gala; soliciting donations via letters, emails, phone calls, meetings; writing grants, and so on. Michael works with the Museum's Advisory Board on these tasks. Advisory Board members are selected at least partially because they

have the ability to make major donations or influence others to make them. Michael meets with the Board four times a year. They will be meeting next week and Michael has fundraising as the number one item on the agenda. This said, there is only 15 minutes set aside on the agenda for his presentation to the Board. What is the most efficient and effective way that he can use this short amount of time?

As you read this chapter, think about the skills, competencies, and credibility that Michael needs to call upon to be persuasive. At the end of the chapter, we will return to this scenario and present some solutions.

14.1: Overview

Persuasive and Special Presentations

14.1 **Review situations when persuasive and special presentations may be used**

As important as informative presentations are in the business world, persuasive presentations are even more prevalent. Persuasive presentations identify and promote ideas and options to guide listeners toward the course of action desired by the speaker. One reason for their frequency is that many persuasive presentations occur informally.

Employees further their views, ideas, or suggestions in meetings, in one-to-one discussions with a supervisor, or even in social groups, in addition to making formal presentations. Nevertheless, the basic resources for persuasion remain constant, although they must be adapted to the particular audience or setting.

Persuasive presentations incorporate the skills needed to prepare an informative presentation. Although the goal of a persuasive presentation may be to reinforce (or change) the audience members' beliefs or to act on the speaker's suggestions, informing the audience is one component of that process.

Special presentations, which are made on special occasions or at ceremonial events, include introductions, the presentation of an award to an honored guest, the acceptance of an honor or award, and tributes and "roasts." Such presentations share many similarities. At the end of this chapter we compare and contrast the demands that are made on you as a speaker at such events. The model of strategic communication can guide your endeavors as you use technology and make presentations at special occasions.

14.2: Functions of Persuasive Presentations

14.2 Interpret the four basic functions of persuasive presentations

Your goal for your persuasive speech should be related to the function, the audience, and the setting. This discussion is related to persuasion for U.S. audiences. Persuasion, like other communication processes, is closely tied to the culture in which it occurs. The function of a persuasive presentation should determine the pattern used to organize the information. The function and the pattern of organization become tools in achieving the presenter's goal and in meeting the audience's expectations.

Persuasive presentations perform one or more of the following functions:

1. *reinforce* the listeners' beliefs, attitudes, or values
2. *refute,* or disprove, an idea or belief held by the listeners
3. *change* the listeners' beliefs, actions, or values
4. *call* the listeners to action

As with informative presentations, the pattern used to organize the information in a persuasive presentation is itself a tool for achieving the presenter's goal.

The lines separating these four persuasive functions (as well, for that matter, as the line separating informing and persuading) are more permeable than solid. It is not uncommon for a speaker to discover that the audience considers the speaker's informative thesis to be a persuasive one (or vice versa). The audience, for example, may perceive a speaker's informative speech on a vegetarian lifestyle as an attempt to either reinforce or change their lifestyle (persuasive). While speakers should try to anticipate such problems, it is not always possible to avoid them, and the speaker needs to be prepared to adapt.

In the current case of the four functions of persuasive presentations, it is often the case that a presentation includes multiple functions—for example, the speaker may wish to refute some ideas or beliefs while reinforcing others; or the speaker may attempt to change the audience's beliefs or values before asking them to take a particular action. Thus, while in the next sections we pair

function and pattern, the reality is seldom that simple. More frequently, the speaker will need to create a presentation by mixing and matching the options we present.

14.2.1: Reinforce

Many persuasive presentations are designed to maintain the status quo by reinforcing audience members' decisions, actions, or opinions, especially if the presenter believes that these things are under attack or are in danger of being changed or rendered obsolete. To make such a presentation persuasive, the speaker must show that existing favorable conditions are in danger of becoming nonexistent or unfavorable.

This approach can be used to achieve a variety of goals: alerting a sales force to the need to reverse a trend toward providing less personalized service to clients, recommending that a planning committee "get back to basics" and concentrate on core markets, or even petitioning a school board to back away from a proposed change in the process of textbook selection. When organizing the presentation, the speaker must first show the benefits of the present condition, then describe the threat to the status quo, and finally reemphasize the worth and viability of the present condition.

The following example shows how these steps are accomplished. It is an outline of a presentation made by a teacher to a school board that was considering legislation that would allow parents and community officials to participate in the process of selecting books for the school system. After each main point in the outline (and in other outlines in the chapter), we suggest options for locating and incorporating appropriate supporting materials.[1]

Thesis:

My audience will agree that the school system's current textbook selection process should be retained.

Introduction:

Motivate the audience to listen by recounting a similar situation in Fargo, North Dakota; orient the audience by stating your opinion that book selection should be the responsibility of teachers and school officials; build rapport by describing your experience as a teacher in the school system.

First main point:

Although selecting textbooks has always been the duty of school officials, parental and community intervention in book selection is gradually increasing.

⊗ Subpoints to reinforce:

A. Testimony: A quotation from an urban history or history of education textbook can be used to describe the historical role of teachers and school officials in textbook selection.

B. Statistics: Statistics from a contemporary newspaper or journal such as *USA Today* can provide evidence that intervention in the selection process is increasing.

Second main point:

The problem with such intervention is that parents and community leaders often cannot agree (with one another or with the school board) on the proper curricula and objectives for students.

ⓧ Subpoints to reinforce:

A. Example: Use an illustration from a news magazine, newspaper, or education journal to highlight a similar situation in another city.
B. Example: Provide a contrasting example of a city that has successfully avoided the problem.

Third main point:

Parental and community interference in the selection process may potentially limit learning.

ⓧ Subpoints to reinforce:

A. Statistics: Cite research done in this area, which may be found in an academic journal such as *Educational Psychologist or American Educational Research Journal.*
B. Visual: Use Power Point or large chart to represent graphically the effect of interference on the student (Figure 14.1).

Fourth main point:

Parental input into textbook selection restricts student exposure to a variety of viewpoints.

ⓧ Subpoints to reinforce:

A. Explanation: Explain what "restriction" means in terms of a well-rounded education.
B. Testimony: Quote a well-known and well-respected educational leader who disagrees with restrictions on learning.

Figure 14.1 Visual Impact
This visual enhances the impact of the speaker's words by using familiar images to represent the negative effect of a change in the status quo.

Conclusion: Ask for the school board to reject legislation (maintain the status quo) based on these arguments. State the significance of doing so by noting that one role of education is to give students the means and information to decide among a variety of divergent perspectives. Close with testimony: Quote students from your classes who are eager to learn and explore.

14.2.2: Refute

A second type of persuasive presentation works to show listeners that a belief, event, or situation is misunderstood or misconceptualized so that the audience will accept a new or different interpretation of it. By effectively *refuting,* or arguing against, the existing perception, the speaker can correct or clarify the audience members' thinking on the subject and persuade them to accept her or his interpretation of it.

A refutative presentation generally begins by exposing the misunderstanding or incorrect assumption, then provides several points that disprove it or show that it is at best a partial truth. The following outline of a presentation given by a financial analyst to a consumer group shows how this can be achieved.

Thesis:

My audience will understand that the causes of inflation are multiple and complex rather than singular and simple.

Introduction:

Orient the audience members by welcoming them to the presentation; motivate the audience by reading a quote about inflation from a news magazine; build rapport by explaining that the purpose of the presentation is to help audience members understand that many interrelated factors cause inflation.

First main point:

Many Americans blame the government for spiraling inflation.

ⓧ Subpoints to refute:

A. Statistics: Use statistics (which can be located through indexes such as the *Gallup Index*) to show that the public thinks the government is responsible for causing inflation.
B. Example: Give an account of government spending on seemingly obscure or wasteful projects, such as studying methane production in cows.

Second main point:

In reality, one of the major causes of inflation is consumers' erratic spending patterns.

ⓧ Subpoints to refute:

A. Testimony: Quote a respected economist on the subject.
B. Visual: Use a graph or chart to show the relationship between consumer spending and inflation during the past ten years.

Third main point:

> Demands for higher wages without strong growth in the gross national product (GNP) may contribute to inflation as well.

(×) Subpoints to refute:

A. Statistics: Cite the recent slowdown in growth of the GNP. A newspaper such as the *Wall Street Journal* can provide statistics on the GNP.
B. Example: Journals such as the *Journal of Human Resources* and the *Industrial and Labor Relations Review* may provide examples of wage negotiations in a range of industries.

Fourth main point:

> Unwise investment, both by individuals and by banking institutions, is another problem.

(×) Subpoints to refute:

A. Testimony: Quote from noted financial analysts to show that many investments offering quick, high returns are deceptive and possibly fraudulent.
B. Explanation: Provide a brief explanation of investment practices in the savings and loan industry and their results.

Conclusion: Summarize the complex nature of inflation; state the significance by noting that understanding is the first step toward tackling the problem; ask for questions.

14.2.3: Promote Change

Persuasive presentations that call for a change in audience members' beliefs, attitudes, actions, or values go one step further than those that refute existing beliefs or values. The speaker attempts to *redirect* the course of the listeners' thoughts or behavior.

When organizing the presentation, the presenter first shows the prevalent belief or action. The successive main points provide reasons audience members should adopt a new belief or change their behavior. The presenter does this by citing the advantages of the new belief/behavior or the disadvantages that will occur by holding on to the old belief/behavior. The following example is excerpted from an outline of a presentation given to several groups of executives at a small department store.

Thesis:

My audience will agree that our current policy of monthly promotional sales needs to be changed.

Introduction:

Orient the audience to the reason for the presentation by citing declining sales revenues; motivate the audience to listen by telling the story of a customer who was surprised to find an item *not* included in a promotional sale; build rapport by noting your recent participation in a national promotional convention where alternative techniques for promotional sales were discussed.

First main point:

> We currently hold promotional sales in practically every department of our stores on a monthly basis.

(×) Subpoints to promote change

A. Statistics: Describe the practice of monthly promotional sales.
B. Explanation: Use an article from the company newsletter to summarize why we have adhered to the policy.

Second main point:

> We need to change our policy for several reasons. One is that promotional sales do not necessarily increase customer traffic.

(×) Subpoints to promote change

A. Statistics: Specialized periodicals such as *Sales Promotion Monitor* and *Shopper Report* may contain research data in this area.
B. Example: Describe an informal study you did over the last three months that showed nearly constant traffic, regardless of the promotional sales.

Third main point:

> Frequent promotional sales generally do not increase a store's sales revenues.

(×) Subpoints to promote change

A. Visual: Display a key quote from a professional journal such as *Ad Review* that supports this position.
B. Statistics: Note that statistics provided by our accounting department show that volume varies seasonally, but the pattern is not influenced by our promotional sales.

Fourth main point:

> We should consider changes in our promotional sales policy that will help us achieve the goal of promotional sales—more customers making more purchases.

(×) Subpoints to promote change

A. We need to take advantage of natural trends in buying (such as seasonal trends).
B. We need to hold less frequent, better advertised promotional sales at strategic points throughout the year.

Note that the fourth main point *restates the need for change* while *providing suggestions* to accomplish the change. Such an ending is more effective than simply giving the listeners several reasons why their current belief or practice is not the best one. By providing an alternate belief or plan of action, the speaker primes the audience to act on her or his suggestion, as we will discuss in the next section.

14.2.4: Call to Action

The main purpose of many persuasive presentations is to get listeners to act on the advice or direction of the speaker.

This type of presentation differs slightly from one in which the speaker's goal is to bring about a change in the audience members' actions—an effective approach for *initiating* audience action differs from one meant to *modify* it.

The first main point of a presentation that calls listeners to action identifies the problem or shortcoming that exists. The second main point, however, demonstrates that the problem has not or apparently cannot be solved or that no attempt is being made to solve it at the current time. In the remaining points, the speaker presents her or his proposed solution and urges the audience to act on the suggestion.

The following example shows an outline of a presentation made by the payroll director at a large company to groups of employees who had enrolled in a series of seminars on investment. Because the employees had little previous experience with the various options for investment, this presentation, the first of the series, begins with the basics.

Thesis:

My audience will accept savings bonds as a good investment and buy them.

Introduction:

Orient the audience by giving a brief overview of what each lecture will contain and a specific preview of this first lecture; motivate and build rapport by giving some examples of how listeners will benefit from acting on what they learn during this presentation.

First main point:

The number of savings bonds purchased has steadily declined, costing the country billions of dollars in liquid capital.

⊗ Subpoints for a call to action:

A. Explanation: Describe what a savings bond is and how it works.
B. Explanation: Give a definition of "liquid capital" in mainstream terms.

Second main point:

Due to widespread misconceptions about the nature of savings bonds, investors often overlook them.

⊗ Subpoints for a call to action:

A. Example: Illustrate the misconceptions held by our own work force by giving several brief examples of employees' attitudes toward savings bonds.
B. Testimony: Cite an expert, such as a federal banking official, on reasons for the declining interest in savings bonds and the potential negative results for the economy.

Third main point:

Savings bonds provide a good yield at low risk, contribute to national growth and stability, and have always been an excellent way to start investing.

⊗ Subpoints for a call to action:

A. Explanation: Define "yield" and "risk" in mainstream terms.
B. Visual: Show an old advertisement for savings bonds to demonstrate their role in building the country.
C. Statistics: A financial journal or periodical such as the *Wall Street Journal* may be a source for statistics on comparing yields and calculating risks.

Fourth main point:

Buying savings bonds is easy—act now to prepare for the future!

⊗ Consider these options to call the listeners to action:

A. Pick up one of the forms I've provided explaining how to buy savings bonds.
B. Make an appointment with me to discuss options for similar investments.

Conclusion: Reemphasize the significance of starting a savings plan now and the ease of starting with savings bonds; provide closure by thanking the audience members for their attention and offering to make appointments to answer specific questions.

The last point in the presentation gives listeners directions for taking the action recommended by the speaker. This tactic is very effective because by providing listeners with the direct means to act on your suggestions, you greatly increase the chances that they will do so.

14.3: Persuasive Formats

14.3 **Describe the three most popular formats of persuasive or special presentations**

Persuasive presentations in a business or organizational context can take a number of forms. Any of the purposes we have just discussed can be realized through these forms. Three of the most commonly used formats are sales presentations, proposals, and motivational sessions, and a fourth format involves crisis situations.

14.3.1: Sales Presentations

Selling products, services, or ideas occupies a great deal of time in organizational life. In addition to one-on-one selling opportunities, in many cases sales presentations are formal events in which a speaker in the front of a room gives a presentation utilizing visual aids and the audience is seated in an organized fashion.

Note that in sales presentations the speaker may be required to reinforce a belief in his or her product if the organization is about to discontinue using it. The speaker may need to change the attitude of a group of buyers toward the product line. Or the speaker may attempt to close a sale at the time of the presentation by convincing the audience to purchase the product. Thus, a sales presentation frequently will incorporate several major functions of persuasion.

PRACTICING BUSINESS COMMUNICATION

Connections in a Global Media Company

Pearson is an international media and education company with businesses in education, business information, and consumer publishing, and 374,000 employees in more than 60 countries. It is a large family of businesses that share the same aim: a focus on making the reading and learning experience as enjoyable and as beneficial as it can possibly be.

Pearson started life as a very different company, however. Founded by Samuel Pearson in 1844 as S Pearson and Son, the company began as a small building firm in Yorkshire, England. Under the leadership of Weetman Pearson (later known as Lord Cowdray), Pearson became one of the world's largest building contractors working across Europe, China, and Latin America at a time when the industry controlled development of the transportation, trade, and communication links that fueled world economies.

Pearson's publishing interests began in the 1920s, with the purchase of Westminster Press, a group of provincial newspapers in the United Kingdom. Some thirty years later, Pearson acquired the Financial Times, and Longman publishing was added to the portfolio in 1968. Penguin was acquired just two years later, and math and science publisher Addison-Wesley was purchased and merged with Longman in 1988. Ten years later, Pearson Education was founded. In 2013, Penguin Random House was created through a merger with Bertelsmann and Pearson.

Pearson is organized into three major publishing groups with many smaller groups and imprints: Pearson Education, The Financial Times, and Penguin Random House.

Pearson Education

Pearson Education is the world's leading education company, from preschool to high school, early learning to professional certification. Pearson's textbooks, multimedia learning tools, and testing programs help to educate more than 100 million people worldwide—more than any other private enterprise. Pearson products are present in over 50,000 schools of the 100,000 schools in the US.

Financial Times Group

The Financial Times group, one of the world's leading business information companies, provides a broad range of business information and multimedia services to the growing audience of internationally minded business people.

The Penguin Group

According to its Web site, Penguin Random House LLC is the world's largest English-language general trade book publisher. Its many publishing groups and their imprints publish fiction and nonfiction, both original and reprints, by prominent and popular writers. Its worldwide roster ranges from novels and classics to cookbooks, bestsellers and classics, children's books and illustrated reference treasure chests.

Core Values

At the heart of the company's culture are three core values: bravery, decency, and imagination. These define the organization and have always underpinned the way it does business.

Bravery has always distinguished Pearson's publishing businesses. Penguin was the proud publisher of *Lady Chatterley's Lover* and *The Satanic Verses;* Pearson Education stands up for its authors every year in the face of special interest groups who seek to influence the content of school books; and the Financial Times formidable reputation is built on the impartiality, accuracy, and integrity of its reporting.

Pearson believes that its role is to help people reach their potential. In return, it expects employees to show a high level of personal motivation and commitment, as well as a willingness to take responsibility and pride in their work.

Like all large companies, Pearson considers it important for employees to share information. Pearson likes to bring people together on a regular basis and has seen many great new ideas spring from face-to-face gatherings.

Pearson works hard to be a diverse company—a company that reflects the societies in which it operates. It attracts the very best candidates, at all levels, regardless of race, gender, age, physical ability, religion, or sexual orientation.

The terms corporate *social responsibility and sustainability mean different things to different companies, but at Pearson, the goal is simple: to be a socially responsible company that has a positive impact on society.*

You can visit Pearson online at http://www.pearson.com/.

Also see
http://www.pearsoned.com/
https://pearsoneducationservices.com/mediakit.php
http://www.pearsoned.co.uk/Imprints/FTPublishing/
http://www.penguinrandomhouse.biz/ourpublishers/

WRITING PROMPT

Imagine you are a sales representative with any of the main publishing groups, and you are attending a Pearson sales meeting. Choose one of the three core values (bravery, decency, and imagination) and write a brief outline for a presentation emphasizing how reinforcing that value will increase sales of a specific book (real or imaginary). You are speaking to fellow sales representatives.

> The response entered here will appear in the performance dashboard and can be viewed by your instructor.

Submit

14.3.2: Proposals

Businesses and professional organizations are frequently inundated with proposals that must be acted upon. The choice of action often depends on the persuasiveness with which a proposal's backer presents it. Even when the speaker succeeds, proposals are often modified from their original form before they are accepted.

Here are a few examples of proposals that might be presented to business and professional audiences:

- A plan to upgrade all personal computers in the corporate headquarters office
- A budget for a ten-day "outward bound" training program for corporate executives at a remote site
- A schedule for moving the home office of a company from one building to another
- A method by which an employee's grievance may be settled without incurring costly court proceedings
- A plan to employ a work force with greater multicultural diversity

Proposals can be designed to reinforce beliefs, change beliefs, or induce action. For example, a presentation by a marketing manager may be designed to reinforce a plan to print new brochures despite some disagreement or criticism of the plan. A presentation by a personnel administrator may attempt to persuade audience members to reverse their decision on allocating funding for professional travel. Or a presentation may call for the listeners to sign their benefits contracts or to return borrowed equipment.

14.3.3: Motivational Sessions

Persuasive presentations can certainly be motivational. You may be familiar with some of the great motivational speakers of our time, including Melanie "Mel" Robbins, American television host, CNN Contributor, life coach, author, and syndicated radio host of *The Mel Robbins Show*; Louis Leo "Lou" Holtz, a college football analyst for ESPN as well as a former football coach (New York Jets); Ilyasah Shabazz, the third daughter of Malcolm X and Betty Shabazz and an author, most notably of a memoir *Growing Up X*; Tony Robbins, American life coach and self-help author who became well known through his infomercials and self-help books such as *Unleash the Power Within*; and Kenneth Hartley Blanchard, an American author and management expert whose book, *The One Minute Manager*, has sold over 13 million copies and has been translated into 37 languages. Each of these speakers is enthusiastic and has a strong delivery, as demonstrated by the ways they vary inflection, emphasis, rate, volume, and gestures. Furthermore, their messages are typically upbeat and filled with inspiring words that instill confidence in the listener.

Many motivational speakers use persuasion to convince an audience to change its attitude so that each person becomes better, healthier, or happier. Some attempt to convince listeners to lose weight, invest money, perform a task better, manage employees differently, or be more enthusiastic communicators.

14.3.4: Crisis Situations

Times of crisis occur in all organizations. Corporate takeovers, consolidation of large industries, downsizing of companies, scandals in management, and erroneous administrative decisions in major U.S. companies are just a few examples of crises in business. In the medical, academic, government, and legal professions, societal changes and financial upswings and downturns have created controversial and unproductive climates. Within these organizations and professions, managers, employees, and outside consultants have used persuasive presentations to make transitions, facilitate change, and placate irate or displaced employees.

14.4: Basic Resources for Persuasion

14.4 Examine the basic resources of persuasion

Persuasion is not just form and content; successful presentations in businesses and professional organizations take advantage of resources. We now turn our attention to some of the resources that are available to you as a persuasive speaker.

14.4.1: The Listeners' Perspective

As in informative presentations, audience analysis and adaptation are the key to success in a persuasive presentation. Nevertheless, the audience is considered from a slightly different angle. The power in a persuasive presentation resides in an analysis of what makes the listeners "tick"; knowing what triggers the listeners is crucial. Table 14.1 shows a variety of methods for connecting with listeners, as opposed to

Table 14.1 Speaker Versus Listener Perspective

Speaker Perspective	Listener Perspective
Speaker uses arguments and appeals that are pleasing to him or her.	Speaker uses arguments and appeals that are pleasing to the audience. ⟳
Speaker uses style and delivery that are natural for him or her.	Speaker uses style and delivery that will be effective and liked by the audience. ⟳
Speaker says what makes him or her feel better.	Speaker says what will bring the desired response from the audience. ⟳
Speaker views the situation from his or her point of view.	Speaker views the situation from the audience's point of view. ⟳
Speaker selects sources and authorities that are his or her favorites.	Speaker selects sources and authorities that are likely to be acceptable to the listeners. ⟳
Speaker dresses to please himself or herself.	Speaker dresses in accordance with the tastes and preferences of the audience. ⟳
Speaker assumes others share his or her beliefs, attitudes, and values.	Speaker searches for the beliefs, attitudes, and values that are held by the audience. ⟳

Hide All Cells	Show All Cells

focusing on the speaker's needs and personal interests. Even more than just sharing a perspective, as in an informative presentation, a persuasive presenter must take the listeners' perspective because the presenter is asking more of the audience, be it a change in beliefs or a call to action.

After winning the 2008 election, President Barack Obama took the stage in Chicago, Illinois, to address the public, emphasizing the unlikeliness of his victory, the hope for change, and the hard work ahead. What follows is the last portion of that speech.[2] What does Obama do in this speech to connect with his listeners?

> This election had many firsts and many stories that will be told for generations. But one that's on my mind tonight is about a woman who cast her ballot in Atlanta. She's a lot like the millions of others who stood in line to make their voice heard in this election except for one thing—Ann Nixon Cooper is 106 years old.
>
> She was born just a generation past slavery; a time when there were no cars on the road or planes in the sky; when someone like her couldn't vote for two

reasons—because she was a woman and because of the color of her skin.

> And tonight, I think about all that she's seen throughout her century in America—the heartache and the hope; the struggle and the progress; the times we were told that we can't, and the people who pressed on with that American creed: Yes we can.
>
> At a time when women's voices were silenced and their hopes dismissed, she lived to see them stand up and speak out and reach for the ballot. Yes we can.
>
> When there was despair in the dust bowl and depression across the land, she saw a nation conquer fear itself with a New Deal, new jobs and a new sense of common purpose. Yes we can.
>
> When the bombs fell on our harbor and tyranny threatened the world, she was there to witness a generation rise to greatness and a democracy was saved. Yes we can.
>
> She was there for the buses in Montgomery, the hoses in Birmingham, a bridge in Selma, and a preacher from Atlanta who told a people that "We Shall Overcome." Yes we can.
>
> A man touched down on the moon, a wall came down in Berlin, a world was connected by our own science and imagination. And this year, in this election, she touched her finger to a screen, and cast her vote, because after 106 years in America, through the best of times and the darkest of hours, she knows how America can change. Yes we can.
>
> America, we have come so far. We have seen so much. But there is so much more to do. So tonight, let us ask ourselves—if our children should live to see the next century; if my daughters should be so lucky to live as long as Ann Nixon Cooper, what change will they see? What progress will we have made?
>
> This is our chance to answer that call. This is our moment. This is our time—to put our people back to work and open doors of opportunity for our kids; to restore prosperity and promote the cause of peace; to reclaim the American Dream and reaffirm that fundamental truth—that out of many, we are one; that while we breathe, we hope, and where we are met with cynicism, and doubt, and those who tell us that we can't, we will respond with that timeless creed that sums up the spirit of a people:
>
> Yes We Can. Thank you, God bless you, and may God Bless the United States of America.

When a speaker encounters an unsympathetic, or even hostile, audience, other adaptations are necessary. Some of the actions a speaker can take are (1) to appeal to the audience for a chance to explain his or her side of the story; (2) to begin the presentation with points that reflect shared values, attitudes, and beliefs on which to base later points of disagreement; (3) to minimize the differences and maximize the similarities in opinion between speaker and audience; and (4) to shorten the gap between points, thus rendering it more difficult for the audience to interrupt or to react in unfavorable ways. When Edward M. Kennedy, the late U.S. Senator of Massachusetts, offered to speak at Liberty University in October of 1983 after receiving a membership solicitation letter from Jerry Falwell's Moral Majority, he certainly needed to go further than merely sharing his perspective on the separation of church and state to the attendees. Note how Kennedy began his speech:[3]

> I have come here to discuss my beliefs about faith and country, tolerance and truth in America. I know we begin with certain disagreements; and I strongly suspect that at the end of the evening some of our disagreements will remain. But I also hope that tonight and in the months and years ahead, we will always respect the right of others to differ, that we will never lose sight of our own fallibility, and that we will view ourselves with a sense of perspective and a sense of humor. After all, in the New Testament, even the Disciples had to be taught to look first to the beam in their own eyes, and only then to the mote in their neighbor's eyes.

14.4.2: Motivators

Motivators are a second valuable resource for persuasion. Discovering what motivates people is a topic that has been discussed since the beginning of time. Abraham Maslow, who established five levels of human needs, wrote the classic work on motivation and persuasion.[4] He ranked the needs in order of their importance:

1. *Basic needs* include access to air, food, water, sex, sleep, and elimination of waste.
2. *Security needs* relate to freedom from threats to one's physical well-being.
3. *Love and belonging needs* include sympathy, friendship, and acceptance.
4. *Esteem needs* are needs for pride, honor, duty, reputation, recognition, loyalty, and competition.
5. *Self-actualization needs* include adventure and fulfillment of one's potential.

Maslow's hierarchy of needs is based on the argument that lower-level needs must be satisfied before higher-level needs can be motivating factors. According to Maslow, once a lower-level need has been satisfied, it no longer serves as a motivating force. When this scheme is applied to persuasion, the speaker's task becomes to identify audience needs and then to phrase appeals that will fulfill those needs.

Let us look at an example of how this works in a presentation. A developer is planning a strategy to persuade members of a community group to invest funds to build a marina in their town. The appeal that the developer uses in her presentation is determined by her assessment of the listeners' needs.

The developer decides to appeal to the group's esteem needs by arguing that "this is the best contribution to the community your group can make; with this marina, your town will gain visibility and prestige and, of course, community members would have prime access to boat slips." The appeal could be successful if the community group members have all fulfilled their belonging and safety needs. But suppose that the group has an ongoing problem with

vandalism and vagrancy in its neighborhood and that some residents do not feel safe on the streets at night. The esteem appeal will not be motivating for the group if lower-level needs are still wanting. To be persuasive, the developer will have to pitch an appeal to a need that is still unfulfilled.

Without knowing the context in which this photo was taken, where on Maslow's hierarchy of needs would you place the three individuals? Why?

SOURCE: Riza Ozel/Getty Images

The key to motivational resources is identifying the threshold level at which audience needs are fulfilled. Having identified that point, the speaker may then phrase an appeal that targets those needs that are still unfulfilled.

14.4.3: Opinion Leaders

Opinion leaders are people who are capable of influencing others' decisions, attitudes, and behavior. Their judgments, taste, and background are respected. They are credible sources for you on a wide range of topics. As such, they are a powerful resource for persuasive presentations.

Practically every organized group has at least one opinion leader; some have several. Importantly, opinion leaders are not necessarily those who are high in rank within a business or organization; some very knowledgeable and respected individuals can be found within the "ranks." In the House of Representatives, for example, there are influential opinion leaders who will never be the Speaker of the House or even the chairperson of a committee. Yet their years of service and loyal constituent base make them influential. The same is true of business settings. Influence in an organization does not always follow the patterns outlined on an organizational chart. In many offices, for example, a key secretary may be the most influential opinion leader for many important issues.

Identifying opinion leaders in an audience can be an important resource for effective persuasion. Linking your message to a person whom the audience respects is a means of bringing about instant acceptance. Aligning your ideas to coincide with those of an individual whom the listeners already believe in or admire can be critical to persuasion as well.

Who are your opinion leaders? Compare your ideas with the ideas of others in your class, and discuss the reasons for your choices.

If you want to use the influence of opinion leaders for your presentations, you cannot be shy about doing so. Remember that audience members rarely draw links for themselves. You must do this for them. Listeners will probably not think, "That sounds just like what Mr. Peters would say." If Mr. Peters is an opinion leader for this audience, overtly claim his support of the idea you wish your listeners to accept. To make effective use of opinion leaders, reference their names clearly and frequently, demonstrate ways in which your ideas are similar to their ideas, and give credit to their accomplishments through liberal use of examples, incidents, illustrations, or case studies.

14.4.4: Critical Thinking and Persuasion

Critical thinking skills—analysis, reasoning, interpretation, and evaluation—play a vital role in persuasive presentations. Strong use of evidence (supporting materials) and reasoning enables the speaker to create a message that is logically sound and well argued and that can withstand questions or attacks. A presentation that incorporates logical reasoning, analysis, and interpretation works persuasively in the minds of listeners as they apply their own critical thinking skills to it.

14.4.5: Source Credibility

That a speaker can be persuasive because he or she is credible was recognized in ancient times by Greek and Roman scholars who labeled this concept **ethos**. In *Rhetoric*, Aristotle wrote:

> Persuasion is achieved by the speaker's personal character when the speech is so spoken as to make us think him credible. We believe good men more fully and more readily than others: this is true generally whatever the question is, and absolutely true where exact certainty is impossible and opinions are divided.... His character may almost be called the most effective means of persuasion he possesses.[5]

In essence, when we talk about credibility, we mean that an audience can be persuaded on the basis of who the speaker is or what he or she has to say. There are two sources that yield credibility in a presentational context and are thus important for persuasion: the speaker and his or her supporting materials. The audience perceives credibility in the speaker by what it knows about him or her before the presentation or learns about him or her during the presentation. The speaker, in turn, derives credibility from sources, whether they are quotations, testimonies, statistics from studies, or other evidence.

In American society, people are very influenced by source credibility. Why do people buy a name brand can of green beans instead of a store-label version? What is so magical about a car with "Ltd." after its name? Is a professor with a Ph.D. more credible than one with an M.S. or an M.A.?

Think for a moment. Who is the most credible source that you can think of? This person is instantly believable to you: if he or she says something, it must be right! We all have someone who is credible to us, whether it be our father or mother, a physician, a minister, an instructor whose courses we have taken several times, or a writer or broadcaster from the media. Indeed, the media also contain sources that have more or less credibility than others. Would you be more likely to believe something you read in *The New York Times* or *National Enquirer*?

Note, however, that credibility is based solely on the audience's perception; it does not exist in any absolute or tangible sense. As a speaker in a business or professional organization, you have control over the information you allow an audience to have, and you therefore can shape how the audience evaluates your character and grants you credibility.

Early studies on source credibility demonstrated its significance. In this research, investigators typically varied the credibility of the source while holding the message constant and using equivalent audiences. In one such study,[6] two audiences heard a recorded persuasive speech on zero population growth. The two audiences had been pretested for their attitudes about family planning, and they were roughly equivalent before the speech was given.

Nobel Peace Laureate and Myanmar opposition leader Aung San Suu Kyi met with students prior to receiving her honorary doctorate from the Australian National University in Canberra, Australia. If you had been one of the students who met her, how do you think your credibility would be enhanced?

SOURCE: Stefan Postles/Getty Images

Both audiences heard the same presentation. One was told that the speaker was a "nationally famous expert on family planning." The other audience was told that the speaker was a "student at the University of Michigan."

Post-testing revealed that the people who thought they were hearing a national expert changed their minds significantly more than the other audience did. Given that the speaker's background was the only variant, credibility obviously produced the difference.

There is no sensible reason not to enhance credibility during a presentation wherever possible. "If no other reason exists for seeking high credibility, being liked and respected is more pleasant than suffering the opposites."[7]

COMPONENTS OF CREDIBILITY   Three primary components make up source credibility for presenters: trustworthiness, competence, and dynamism.[8] These factors are what audiences consider when they label a speaker or a source as either credible or not credible.

Trustworthiness refers to the way that a source is perceived as being honest, friendly, warm, agreeable, or safe, instead of dangerous or threatening. When Brian Williams, *NBC Nightly News* anchor, received a six-month suspension for lying about riding in a military helicopter that was hit by a rocket-propelled grenade during the Iraq War, network executives were concerned that Williams had lost trustworthiness.

The second dimension, **competence,** is based on the source's expertise, training, experience, skill, ability, authoritativeness, and intelligence. Many people believe that competence is the single most important factor in determining the degree to which a source has credibility. Thus, when a speaker's competence to speak on a topic is suspect, a major effort is required to remedy this perceived defect.

Finally, **dynamism** is composed of a speaker's energy, liveliness, boldness, activity, forcefulness, and frankness. Many competent speakers who would otherwise be perceived as quite credible damage this assessment because they fail to be dynamic. Some research has shown that speakers who demonstrate high levels of dynamism are likely to be perceived as more competent and believable than speakers who fail to do this.

OCCURRENCES OF CREDIBILITY   You may ask, "Where does credibility come into play during a presentation?" The answer is that it comes into play at all stages of the process. Audiences are more likely to attend presentations by and pay attention to speakers they consider credible, making credibility an important pre-presentation concern. Credibility is also an important factor during the presentation, as audience members are more likely to accept what they hear from someone they consider credible. Finally, audience members are more willing to carry out a commitment urged by a credible speaker.

Audiences can learn about a speaker's credibility before he or she even utters a word. Because this learning occurs outside of the presentation the speaker gives, it is called extrinsic credibility. There are many ways that extrinsic credibility can be built. Words about how "good" or "bad" a speaker is can float down from other people who have previously heard the speaker. A listener can also read about a speaker in the newspaper or company newsletter. And prior experience with the speaker lets audience members know what they can expect in the presentation to follow.

One of the most important ways that extrinsic credibility is communicated to an audience is through the introduction of the speaker immediately before the presentation. Items such as the speaker's qualifications, membership in groups, past or present positions, and recent accomplishments can be given to bolster the speaker's credibility with the audience. Remember, however, that the audience decides whether credibility exists. If listeners do not understand a speaker's qualifications or do not have any admiration for the groups in which the speaker holds membership, her or his credibility will not be enhanced.

Credibility also plays an intrinsic role within the presentation itself. Here the audience learns about a speaker from listening, observing, and inferring. Factors such as the speaker's preparedness, seriousness, sincerity, poise, evenhandedness, firmness, dress, and appearance all give information to listeners that can affect their judgments of her or his credibility.

Extrinsic and intrinsic credibility can work well together. What a listener has heard about a speaker extrinsically can either be strengthened or weakened when assessments of intrinsic credibility are made. If a listener has heard that a speaker is "wonderful" (extrinsic) and he or she falls short on some of the factors just discussed (intrinsic), the listener's judgment of the speaker's credibility will be worsened. If, however, the listener has heard that a speaker is "not worth hearing" (extrinsic) but he or she does well in the speech (intrinsic), the listener's assessment will be favorably changed.

Vested Interests

Ethical Issues

Imagine that you are trying to persuade your employer to buy a particular Brand X portable computer for employees to use for business trips. You are to make a presentation to a management committee, and you want to give members convincing evidence for your recommendation. You also want to make the presentation in an ethical fashion.

You like the selected model for a variety of reasons, including the fact that your spouse works part-time for Brand X and has told you a lot of good things about it.

- As you think through the presentation, what, if any, ethical issues will you encounter? What are some possible ways of dealing with them? Which would you choose?
- Would your answer change if you or your family owned stock in Brand X? Why or why not?
- Can you imagine other situations that would make ethical issues more or less salient for your situation?

As a speaker, you can build your own credibility as well as the credibility of your sources by providing their qualifications, accomplishments, company or university affiliations, or academic degrees wherever necessary. If you are citing a research study as part of your evidence, build up the quality of the study by explaining the circumstances under which it was done and the methodology, the timeliness, or any other information that will lend credence to the findings.

WRITING PROMPT

Consider the credibility components of trustworthiness, competence, and dynamism. When your audiences vary among peers, colleagues (either at work or as fellow students), and people whom you want to impress (whether in business or daily life) does your credibility change? Why or why not? How would you adjust to the similarities and differences in these three audiences when giving a presentation?

▶ The response entered here will appear in the performance dashboard and can be viewed by your instructor.

[Submit]

14.5: The Persuasion Process

14.5 Express some of the strategies that may be employed in the process of persuasion

We now turn to the process through which persuasion occurs and to some strategies you may be called on to use when speaking to, for, or within your business or professional organization.[9]

The **process of persuasion** has five distinct stages: awareness, interest, evaluation, trial, and adoption. If anywhere along the line the listener withdraws from the process, persuasion will not result. Listeners must first be aware that a proposal exists. They then have to be interested in hearing more. After learning more about the topic, listeners then evaluate the feelings or reactions that they have formed. In many cases, there is a trial period to assess the feasibility of the proposal. If the outcome of the trial is favorable, they then adopt the proposal and put it into practice or action.

Here is an example of how these five stages work, as applied to a presentation in which junior executives are proposing to senior management that they be allowed to travel on sales incentive trips. In this company, the trips are reserved only for top management.

Awareness: "Junior executives at our organization should be permitted to travel on sales incentive trips." (The management group may not have even known that competing companies offered trips to their junior executives.)

Interest: "The long-term results of sending junior executives on these trips are beneficial to the company."

(The management group may want to know what these results are.)

Evaluation: "Think of the large return on such a small investment." (The management group may ponder this benefit.)

Trial: "Give this plan a chance for one year to see how it works." (The management group may consider a shorter period to assess results.)

Adoption: "If the trial period yields results that meet or exceed expectations, the activity will become permanent policy."

Of course, the process is not infallible. Think about how many times you have listened to a persuasive presentation and have withdrawn at some point in the process. It happens regularly. You may be made aware of an issue, become convinced of its logic, and even think it is a good idea, but you just do not want to implement it. As a result, you are not persuaded. Strategies that can help speakers prevent persuasion dropouts are covered in the next two sections.

Additional Hints for Persuasive Presentations

Strategic Skills

Some of your most challenging presentations in the business world will be persuasive in nature. To stay confident and effective when facing the challenge of a persuasive presentation, consider the following hints:

⊗ **Hints for having a persuasive presentation**

1. In persuasion, try to give listeners the feeling that the proposal you are advocating is a natural extension of directions in which they are tending.

2. Because people agree more readily about abstract matters than about concrete matters, be especially selective about the specific examples you use early in your speech.

3. Even though all of us identify with certain reference groups, few of us like to admit such "dependence"; therefore, do not make careless attributions about your listeners in their presence.

4. Do not be glib when presenting large-scale statistical information; always try to show the "local consequences" of such data.

5. Even though it is good to have several reasons to support your thesis, using too many will cause your audience to be suspicious of your selectivity.

6. Never underestimate candor; looking at your audience directly and admitting that you disagree with them on some issue can be a prudent course of action.

7. When you speak to a hostile audience, never save your proposal until the conclusion lest you be viewed as a coward.

8. Do not underestimate the power of careful phrasing; language has great power to color ideas. Sometimes, the elimination of bothersome bits of jargon or hackneyed expressions can open up listeners' minds.

9. When you are dealing with a hostile audience, do not allow your voice to become shrill, even though your frustration at the audience's resistance may push you in that direction.

SOURCE: R. P. Hart, G. W. Friedrich, and B. Brummett, Public Communication, 2nd ed. (New York: Harper & Row, 1983), p. 286. Reprinted with permission of Barry Brummett and Rod Hart.

14.5.1: Order Effects

Every persuasive presentation has some arguments that are stronger than others. The question frequently facing a speaker is "In what order should I present my arguments?"[10] The speaker can usually choose from one of three options.

In a **climax order,** the weakest argument is presented first and the strongest last; this organization provides a recency effect, meaning that the audience will most likely remember the last (and strongest) argument. In an **anticlimax order,** the strongest argument is presented first, and weaker arguments follow; this plan gives a primacy effect (audience members are immediately struck by the strength of the argument). In a **pyramidal order,** the speaker places the strongest argument between two weaker ones.

The decision of which to employ is up to you. If you are planning to give the presentation more than once, you may wish to experiment until you are comfortable with the ordering of your ideas. Research shows that arguments presented early and late are more effective than those presented in the middle. If you have high credibility in the mind of the audience, you will find it better to present strong arguments early in the speech.

14.5.2: One-Sided Versus Two-Sided Presentations

In what circumstances should you bring up the other side's position in your presentation? If you present only your position, the presentation is one-sided; if you bring up the other side's arguments and then refute them, the presentation is two-sided. Research shows the following:

- Two-sided presentations are best if the weight of evidence is on your side.
- Two-sided presentations are best for better-educated listeners.
- Two-sided presentations are best when the listeners initially disagree with your position.
- Two-sided presentations are preferable when you believe the listeners will be exposed to the other side following your own presentation.
- One-sided presentations are best when the listeners already agree with you, provided that they are not likely to be influenced by later opposing arguments.

The Persuasive Speech

Strategic Skills

- Do you have a clear purpose in mind?
- Is the purpose of your speech best described as reinforcing, refuting, promoting change, or calling to action?
- Does your presentation fit into one of the following formats: sales presentation, proposal, motivational session, or crisis situation?
- Given a clear purpose, what are the three to five main points that the audience will need to understand and accept if you are to achieve it?
- What forms of support (e.g., explanations, examples, statistics, testimony, and visual aids) will make your main points most informative, interesting, relevant, clear, and persuasive?
- Are any of the following resources for persuasion relevant to your speech: the listeners' perspective, motivators, opinion leaders, critical thinking, source credibility, order effects, or one-sided versus two-sided presentation?
- Would some form of information technology be most useful in making your presentation?
- How can you best achieve the functions of the introduction (orientation, motivation, and rapport) and conclusion (completeness and closure) of your speech?
- Which type of delivery (impromptu, extemporaneous, manuscript, or memorized) is likely to be most effective in accomplishing your purpose?
- Independent of type of delivery, how can you make your delivery intelligible, conversational, direct, and unobtrusive?
- How will you prepare to field questions from the audience?
- How will you prepare to deal with the anxiety you are likely to experience?
- How will you rehearse your presentation?

14.6: Special Occasion Presentations

14.6 Examine nine types of special occasion presentations

Special occasion or ceremonial speeches play a variety of roles in business. Their function is to bring people together to recognize growth, celebrate achievement, support tradition, and reinforce organizational values. These occasions may also be used to boost employee morale or to strengthen commitment to the organization.

All cultures have special occasions. In the United States, special occasion speaking represents a broad spectrum of activities. Each of them has unspoken cultural rules that set boundaries for you as the speaker. These rules govern

(1) length of speech, (2) purpose, (3) behavior, (4) appearance, (5) use of humor, (6) seriousness, and (7) language use.

14.6.1: Types of Presentations

Most special occasions are formal. If you are unsure of the appropriate standards, ask. It is better to overdress than to underdress; underdressing may offend some participants. Understanding such issues as dress codes should help you meet the cultural expectations of the people who are in your audience. We will briefly discuss nine types of special occasion presentations.

INTRODUCTIONS   Guest speakers who address business and professional groups or are invited to make presentations on university campuses are formally introduced to their audience. The selection of the person who gives the introduction depends on the status of the speaker. For example, Wilma Mankiller, then chief of the Cherokee Nation, spoke in April 1994 in South Bend, Indiana, at a YWCA luncheon for 1,200 people honoring women of achievement. The person deemed most appropriate to introduce Chief Mankiller was the highest-ranking woman tribal official in the local Potawatomie Nation. At other times the head of ceremonies or moderator, the person responsible for bringing the speaker to the group, or a close colleague may be selected to give the introduction.

Introductions should be brief (from three to five minutes) and should not be used to call attention to the introducer. The focus must be on the guest. The introduction should make the speaker feel welcome, indicate that the group feels privileged to have the person as the speaker, build credibility for the speaker by mentioning facts from his or her biography or résumé (usually supplied by the speaker or his or her public relations representative), announce the title or the subject of the presentation, and set an appropriate tone or mood.

Choose only pertinent facts from the biography or résumé to include in the introduction—information that will raise the credibility of the speaker. A few of your choices are the title of current or past positions held, academic degrees earned, honorary degrees earned, offices held in organizations, awards or honors received, places traveled to, books or other materials published, programs or panels participated in, outstanding career achievements, and personal achievements or interests (family, hobbies, skills). Obviously, not all of these should be included in the introduction, and other particulars may be more pertinent. Make your selection carefully.

PRESENTATION OF AN HONOR OR AWARD   Like an introduction, the presentation of an award should be brief. Inform the audience of the importance and perhaps give a brief history of the honor or award, demonstrate why the person is worthy of the award, and call the person to the front to accept the award.

ACCEPTANCE OF AN HONOR OR AWARD   Because honors or awards are sometimes given without previous notice, you may be surprised to be named as the recipient. Naturally, your expressions of surprise and pleasure are to be expected and respected in your impromptu remarks. In such cases (and in instances when you *are* aware of the honor ahead of time), you should thank the people or organization responsible for giving the award, express appreciation to a few individuals (be very selective), make a final expression of appreciation and gratitude, and leave the stage or podium with aplomb.

TRIBUTES AND "ROASTS"   A tribute is sometimes given to a person who has achieved greatness or success over a lifetime. Nobel Prizes, Pulitzer Prizes, and Academy Awards—as well as countless awards by corporations honoring long-term employees—are some examples of recognizing lifetime achievement. A tribute may also be for a single heroic act, a stellar performance, or a record-breaking sales month. The person giving the tribute should explain the purpose of the tribute, detail the achievement, and identify the recipient. These particulars can be arranged according to the context or to the speaker's preference.

"Roasts" are occasions at which a person is honored for her or his craft, career, or personal life through humorous and occasionally insulting speeches, skits, and entertainment performed by her or his peers and friends. The Friars Club in New York City has a long history of roasts that some consider to be a wonderful tradition and others view as controversial.

Roasts can be good-natured and enjoyable or vicious and damaging. The tone and content of your contribution to a roast should reflect your sense of ethics and the context of the event.

PROMOTION OF GOODWILL   Many organizations support or promote positive interaction among members and create positive rhetorical perspectives in public presentations. Not-for-profit service groups sometimes have luncheons or dinners designed to promote goodwill. Some companies promote activities that allow for presentations that encourage positive reactions. The division of education at a major southwestern university, for example, has a picnic on the first Friday afternoon after the beginning of the fall semester. All students, staff, faculty, and administrators are invited. The dean of the division gives a five-minute speech welcoming newcomers; honoring current students, staff, and faculty; and stating positive projections for the school year. Then, everyone eats and socializes in the park.

MEMORIALS   Presentations that memorialize individuals sometimes occur in response to tragic events. Such presentations should be solemn and respectful and should present a positive perspective for the event. A eulogy is given at funerals or memorial services. The brevity of your presentation will be appreciated by the audience, but your presentation should include the following: identification of positive facts about the person, short anecdotes that reveal the personality of the person, gentle humor that can uplift spirits, and a conclusion that helps to heal the human spirit.

CELEBRATIONS When organizations experience success or an individual has a success that reflects on the group, appropriate celebrations encourage, enhance the status of, and support all members of the organization. A presentation at such an event should include the reasons for the celebration, the names of individuals or groups responsible for the success, and rhetoric that moves listeners to efforts that will result in more celebratory events.

ENTERTAINMENT Of all the speaking occasions, this one has the greatest potential for disaster for the speaker. We think of entertainment in public speaking as being comedy. Many presentations are comedic, but unfortunately very few public speakers can successfully present a sustained humorous presentation.

If you are called upon to give an entertaining speech—usually after a breakfast, lunch, or dinner meeting—examine the context carefully. Instead of relying on old jokes and anecdotes, use myths and stories about the organization that are interesting or entertaining, relate experiences that make you (rather than other people) the object of humor, keep your remarks ethical and appropriate for public gatherings (avoid slang, sexual innuendo, inflammatory remarks, and curses), and keep your speech brief.

RETIREMENT If you are introducing or honoring a retiree, review the preceding material on presenting honors and on tributes and roasts. Additional suggestions are to avoid age-deprecating humor, derogatory jokes about retirement, and supposedly humorous slurs on the person's career.

If you are the retiree, review the section on accepting honors. Graciously accept the accolades, gifts, and comments of your supervisors, peers, and employees. This is not an occasion to right old wrongs or to criticize the organization. If your primary reaction to the company or organization has been negative, try to convince the organization not to have a retirement gathering for you.

These special occasions all require the following: brevity; appropriateness of purpose, behavior, appearance, humor, mood, and language use; and effective delivery skills. Each presentation will be affected by the local culture and by taken-for-granted styles. As in all public speaking situations, analyze the audience demographics, the reasons for the audience's presence, the organizational culture, and the environmental dynamics. Your behavior, your appearance, and the content of your presentation will determine your success.

TECHNOLOGY TOOLS

Great Speeches Online

One can learn a great deal about speechmaking by reading, watching, and listening to important speeches by well-known speakers. A resource that facilitates this is *American Rhetoric: The Power of Oratory in the United States*. This Web site includes (a) a database of and index to 5,000+ full-text, audio, and video versions of public speeches, sermons, legal proceedings, lectures, debates, interviews, and other recorded media events; (b) a full-text, audio, and video database of the 100 most significant American political speeches of the twentieth century according to 137 leading scholars of American public address; (c) 200+ short audio and video clips illustrating stylistic figures of speech ranging from alliteration to synecdoche; and (d) many additional public speaking resources.

ⓧ Read more

Another resource, under development, is *The National Gallery of the Spoken Word*, a fully searchable digital library of spoken-word collections spanning the twentieth century. The National Science Foundation funded this project under Digital Library Initiative II.

Important current addresses made by recognized leaders are collected and published in *Vital Speeches of the Day* and *Vital Speeches International*. Both are monthly publications of speeches by influential business executives, politicians, educators, and other opinion leaders and are available either by subscription or in the library.

In addition to building public speaking skills by mining important speeches of well-known speakers, the Internet can be used to locate information on special occasion presentations. Using your Web browser to locate, for example, "speeches of introduction" or "tributes and roasts" will produce a wealth of suggestions and examples.

WRITING PROMPT

Name someone you admire. Which of the categories listed in the last paragraph of the section describing speeches of introduction would you use to build credibility when introducing this person? For each category you choose, briefly explain why in relation to that person.

▶ The response entered here will appear in the performance dashboard and can be viewed by your instructor.

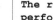

Strategic Scenario Wrap-Up

Persuasive and Special Presentations

ⓧ Strategic Scenario

Michael Martello is the director of development at the B. J. Turock Museum of Art. Michael and his assistants are charged with friend- and fund-raising for the Museum. While the university provides funds for the museum, they are only a fraction of what the museum needs for operating expenses and collection preservation and development. Michael's task is to raise funds for the museum by multiple means: producing an annual gala; soliciting donations via letters, emails, phone calls, meetings; writing grants, and so on. Michael works with the Museum's Advisory Board on these tasks. Advisory Board members are selected at least partially because they have the ability to make major donations or influence others to make them. Michael meets with the Board four times a year. They will be meeting next week and Michael has fund-raising as the number one item on the agenda. This said, there is only 15 minutes set aside on the agenda for his presentation to the Board. What is the most efficient and effective way that he can use this short amount of time?

Michael Martello, the B. J. Turock Museum of Art's Director of Development, had a meeting with the museum's Advisory Board to ask them to help him raise funds for the institution's acquisition fund. Michael put together a concise and information-rich presentation that connected the Board's role to the Museum's success. His three main goals were:

1. To remind the four-person Advisory Board of their important role in the success of the museum and thank them for their contributions in the past

2. To illustrate the historic importance of the acquisition fund

3. To ask Board members for their suggestions for raising additional funds to acquire art

To accomplish these goals, Michael emphasized what it will take for the museum to remain successful, while allowing some "wiggle room" for Board members to follow their personal interests in choosing how they contribute. As he presented each of the following points, he handed the Board members a printed sheet containing a corresponding:

1. Overview of which of last year's activities were most successful in terms of raising funds

2. Chart showing exact funds needed for three levels of success: a) funds needed to maintain the collections; b) funds needed to moderately expand, and c) a "wish list" of funds ultimately desired to expand acquisitions into new areas in the future

3. Information on which collections could use the most development from a content perspective

He finished by asking for specific fund-raising suggestions, which the members could feel free to make at that time, or later, after they had more time to look over the summarized information.

WRITING PROMPT

Why did Michael choose to start with a review of the most successful fund-raising activities of the year before? Do you think handing printed material at the moment he brought up each topic saved Michael time? Why or why not?

   The response entered here will appear in the performance dashboard and can be viewed by your instructor.

Submit

Summary

Persuasive and Special Presentations

- **Persuasive presentations,** regardless of their setting and audience, usually have one of four functions: to reinforce listeners' beliefs or values, to refute these beliefs or values, to change these beliefs or values, or to move the listeners to action.

- **Reinforcement and refutative presentations** can be used to rebuild listeners' original beliefs or prove that these beliefs are untrue.

- From the latter use, it follows that **change presentations** seek to go one step further and to convince listeners to change a particular attitude, value, or belief.

- A **call to action** intends to get listeners to do something, such as sign a petition or donate money to a charitable cause, that they would not have done had they not heard the presentation.

- Persuasive presentations can take a **variety of formats** that reflect the speaker's approach and use of supporting materials.

- **Sales presentations, proposals, and motivational sessions** are three of the most common formats for persuasive presentations.

- To **deliver a successful persuasive presentation,** a speaker is wise to **concentrate** on the particular demands made on the audience.

- The **effective presentation** takes the listeners' perspective, discovering what makes listeners tick and whether they are likely to be favorably disposed toward a particular message.

- **Presentational strategies** differ, of course, depending on whether the audience is sympathetic or suspicious.

- A **persuasive speaker** benefits from addressing his or her appeals to the appropriate need level of the audience.

- An **audience** whose basic needs (for food, water, shelter) are not met is not likely to **respond** to a message geared toward higher-level needs.

- To work, persuasive messages **have to be pitched to needs that are unfulfilled, not ones that are satisfied.**

- The **successful presentation** also takes into account the opinion leaders in the audience and directs its appeals to or references them.

- The importance of **opinion leaders** also suggests the larger issue of credibility.

- A speaker **who is not credible,** or who uses sources that are not credible, is **not likely to get very far** in his or her persuasive efforts.

- Because credibility is in the eye of the beholder—it resides with the audience—the speaker is wise to **present himself or herself** in such a way as to **signal trustworthiness, competence, and dynamism.**

- The credibility gained in the process is called **intrinsic credibility.**

- **Extrinsic credibility,** however, is communicated through the introduction of the speaker and through other external sources of information about the speaker.

- Apart from the previously mentioned components, **persuasion is also a process,** and the effective speaker knows how to use each stage in the process to her or his advantage.

- In the **first phase,** listeners become aware that a message exists.

- In the **second phase,** they become interested in hearing more.

- In the **third phase,** they evaluate what they have heard and what they feel about what they have heard.

- In the **fourth phase,** they set aside a trial period to judge the feasibility of the message.

- In the **fifth phase,** they adopt the message and put it into practice.

- Not all persuasive presentations **work out quite so neatly.**

- A speaker may have to deal with the necessity of **choosing among several options for ordering arguments** (arguments presented early or late get audience attention more than do those presented in the middle) and with deciding whether to give **both sides** of the argument.

- But if the speaker **employs candor, careful phrasing, respect for the audience, and equanimity,** he or she is much more likely to achieve the objectives of the persuasive presentation.

- **Nine types of special occasion or ceremonial speaking** were discussed: introductions, the presentation of an award to an honored guest, the acceptance of an honor or award, tributes and roasts, the promotion of goodwill, memorials, celebrations, entertainment, and a retirement speech for or by a retiree.

- Each requires **understanding of the cultural context, the audience, and the setting.** And once again, your **delivery skills** and **your content** determine your success.

SHARED WRITING: PERSUASIVE AND SPECIAL PRESENTATIONS

Who are your opinion leaders? Compare your ideas with the ideas of others in your class, and discuss the reasons for your choices.

▶
> A minimum number of characters is required to post and earn points. After posting, your response can be viewed by your class and instructor, and you can participate in the class discussion.

Post   0 characters | 140 minimum

Chapter 14 Quiz: Persuasive and Special Presentations

Glossary

Adaptation tailoring the message and material of the presentation to the audience's needs and requirements

Adaptive learning understanding how goals, policies, procedures, and other people's actions conform to the dynamics of the workplace

Adaptors actions that reveal psychological or physical needs

Advocacy presentation of competing views on a controversial issue

Affect displays unintentional movements that reflect the sender's true emotions

Affinity group a group consisting of eight to twelve members in a sponsoring organization that meet on a regular basis to exchange information, ideas, opinions, and experiences on a variety of issues in a safe and supportive atmosphere, resulting in personal and professional growth

Agenda a guide that specifies what is to be discussed, when, in what order, and for how long

Analogies comparison of two items, with the argument that what is true in one case is also true in the other

Analysis the process of tearing apart an issue and examining its component parts to see how they relate to the whole

Analytical listening encompasses a concentration on the content and includes understanding, interpreting, and analyzing a message

Anticlimax order the strongest argument is presented first, and the weaker arguments follow

Anxiety management the ability to control nervousness, fear, stress, and worries

Apathy lack of emotional involvement in the job

Appraisal interviews interviews to evaluate employees' performances over a certain period of time, generally specified by company policy

Appreciative listening used to judge the aesthetic value of what is heard

Argumentativeness an inclination to argue or a fondness for arguing

Attention the cognitive ability that allows us to select certain types of information for processing and ignore others

Attitudes a person's learned likes and dislikes

Audience analysis gathering information about an audience (i.e., audience type, audience characteristics, and environmental characteristics) so that the speaker can adapt the speech to the situation at hand

Auditorium setup setup with chairs, but no tables; chairs are lined up in straight rows with a center aisle between them

Authoritarian decision making style of decision making in which a leader hands down a decision to the group

Beliefs a person's judgments about right and wrong

BFOQs short for bona fide occupational qualifications, these are the concrete requirements—including necessary experience, educational background, and skills—for performing a job

Bibliography a detailed list of all the books, articles, interviews, and abstracts you have reviewed in the course of your research

Briefings relatively short presentations that inform an audience about a particular event

Causal reasoning type of reasoning that asserts that one factor is strong enough to produce an effect in another factor; asks the question, "Why did that happen?"

Cause/effect pattern structural pattern of organization in which the message is organized around the origins and the results of a series of events

Ceremonial presentations presentations that share many of the elements found in informative, persuasive, and motivational presentations; include introduction, acceptance, tribute, goodwill, inspiration, and celebration presentations

Channel the medium that carries a message once it is encoded by a source

Channel richness the ability of a communication channel to handle information or convey the meaning contained in a message

Channels the media that carry messages to receivers

Charismatic authority authority structure that results from the personal qualities (expertise, knowledge, vision, values) of a leader

Chronemics the use of time as each culture determines it to be appropriate

Chronological pattern structural pattern of organization in which the main points of the message are organized in a time-related sequence

Classical theory describes an organization that functions like a machine and is management-oriented

Classroom arrangement setup that uses tables and chairs; tables are lined up in straight rows with a center aisle separating them

Climax order the weakest argument is presented first, and the strongest argument is presented last

Closed question a question that gives the interviewee minimal choice in terms of form of response

Closed systems systems that deliberately shut themselves off from the outside environment

Closing ending an interview by performing functions such as concluding, summarizing, and supporting

Coaching phase phase of situational leadership in which the leader can instruct, act as a role model, and nurture group members

Cohesiveness the degree to which a group hangs together

Coldness a lack of enthusiasm for the job

Communication apprehension the fear of speaking in public; also termed *reticence, shyness,* and *unwillingness to communicate*

Communication climate an aspect of an organization's character that is a function of the interactions and social processes that occur in the workplace

Communication competence the ability to communicate both appropriately and effectively with other people

Communication competence the strengths and weaknesses you possess in any conflict situation

Comparative reasoning type of reasoning that pulls together two examples and assumes that what is true in the first case must be true in the second case

Comparison/contrast pattern   structural pattern of organization that identifies a familiar situation and then relates it to an unfamiliar situation

Competence   a component of credibility that is based on the source's expertise, training, experience, skill, ability, authoritativeness, and intelligence

Competitive strategies   attempts to maximize one's own position at the expense of the adversary

Complete-sentence outline   an outline that lists each head and subhead in complete-sentence form

Conceptual skills   the ability to see your job in its relationship to the entire organization and to recognize how the organization interacts with its environment

Concession   giving up some goals to obtain something in return

Conclusion   the ending of a speech, which provides a sense of completeness and closure

Conference arrangement   all members are seated around the same table

Conflict   "an expressed struggle between at least two interdependent parties who perceive incompatible goals, scarce rewards, and interference from the other party in achieving their goals"

Conflict escalation   heightened tensions in conflict situations due to poor communication or misunderstandings

Conformity   agreement with or correspondence to a set of ideas, rules, or principles

Congruity   the parallel between what a leader says and what a leader does

Consensus   unanimous agreement among group members concerning a particular decision

Constancy   the ability to stay on course, to remain focused on the vision and goals regardless of setbacks

Content element   what you are trying to communicate

Content goals   the apparent issues or obvious reasons for a dispute

Context   the situation or setting in which communication occurs

Controlling   using authority and power to ensure that a plan succeeds

Cooperative strategies   open, honest, and upfront attempts at objective and productive problem solving

Corrective feedback   feedback that attempts to alter negative or inappropriate behavior

Cross-cultural communication   communication between people from two cultures

Culture   a broad term that explains why people from various nations and co-cultures (groups different from mainstream populations in those countries) act and speak as they do

Decoding   the process that recipients go through to make sense of the message they receive

Deductive reasoning   type of reasoning that moves from general truths to specific conclusions

Delegating phase   phase of situational leadership in which the leader directly or indirectly moves responsibility for group tasks, creativity, solutions, and decisions to group members

Delphi technique   technique that uses questionnaires to collect opinions and judgments from experts, who usually remain anonymous

Demonstration   type of informative presentation that aims to explain the *how* of an issue

Description   type of informative presentation that satisfies the audience members' needs for facts, figures, and other data

Devil's advocate   the group member who introduces dissent into decision-making processes

Directed question   a question that either subtly (leading) or blatantly (loaded) clues the respondent to the expected answer

Directing phase   phase of situational leadership in which a leader must provide a great deal of guidance to the group

Directive interview   a situation in which the interviewer controls the purpose, structure, and pacing of the interview

Discrimination   favoritism or negative differences in treatment of individuals because of the attributes of diversity that set them apart from others

Discriminative listening   involves drawing inferences from auditory cues and evaluating reasons for the message

Distributive   the bargainer's assumption that a gain for her or his side equals a loss to the other side

Diversity   one of the many terms used to explain how people differ by gender, age, ethnicity, physical abilities, religious affiliation, and sexual orientation

Downward communication   messages from superiors to subordinates

Dyadic discourse   two parties engaged in a conversation; each party may consist of more than one person

Dynamism   a component of credibility that refers to a speaker's energy, liveliness, boldness, activity, forcefulness, and frankness

Effective delivery   delivery that is intelligible, conversational, direct, and unobtrusive

Emblems   body movements that substitute for words

Empathic listening   concentrates on the feelings or attitudes of the speaker, rather than on the message, and is employed to discover the feelings of the speaker

Empathy   the act of sharing the feelings of another person

Empowerment   giving people the opportunity to think and act for themselves within the guidelines of the shared values and vision of the organization

Encoding   the physical process of organizing elements of the message for transmission to the receivers

Environment   includes the political, economic, and social characteristics of society that affect the way an organization operates

Ethnocentrism   belief in the superiority of one's own culture

Ethos   the audience's perception of a speaker's character, intelligence, and goodwill

Euphemisms   agreeable, neutral, or indirect phrases used to describe unpleasant events

Evaluation   the process of making judgments about information or data

Evaluative response   a response indicating that the interviewer has judged the relative goodness, appropriateness, effectiveness, or rightness of the interviewee's response

Example reasoning   type of reasoning based on collecting specific cases and then making a generalization based on them

Examples   illustrations that connect the main ideas of a presentation with a real or an ideal state envisioned by the speaker

Explanation   the act or process of making a subject plain or comprehensible

Extemporaneous speaking   given from brief notes, this type of situation encourages thorough preparation and adaptability to the particulars of the situation at hand

External communication   messages that are exchanged between the organization and its environment

Feedback any response, verbal or nonverbal, that a receiver makes to a message

Flat organizations organizations with few hierarchical levels

Formal bargaining process that develops when recurring issues require deliberation and confrontation over time

Function what the presentation accomplishes or aims to accomplish

Functional leadership style of leadership in which groups rise to an occasion and perform needed leadership functions

Funnel sequence a sequence in which the interviewer starts with broad, open questions and moves toward narrower, closed questions

General purpose the basic goal of a presentation, that is, to inform, to persuade, to motivate, or to celebrate

Glass ceiling a barrier that is not visible but is real enough to keep women from top-management positions in many businesses and professions

Globalization the trend toward increasing business transactions between foreign countries, which requires recognition of work-force diversity and changing technologies

Goal setting an important feature of manager-employee relation-ships in ensuring coordination

Good speech topics topics the speaker is knowledgeable about and/or interested in, are relevant for the audience, and meet the requirements of the assignment or situation

Group goals goals that serve the mission and purpose of the group itself

Groupthink the tendency of group members to seek agreement solely for agreement's sake

Hasty generalizations conclusions based on small or nonrepre-sentative samples of data

Hearing an automatic process in which sound waves stimulate nerve impulses to the brain

Horizontal communication messages exchanged at the same hier-archical level in an organization

Hostile environment a sexual harassment situation in which work-place conditions are sexually offensive, intimidating, or hostile and affect an individual's ability to perform his or her job

Human relations messages messages that help employees fully realize their potential in the organization

Human skills the ability to work with people to accomplish goals

Humanistic theory focuses on the needs of labor rather than on the structure of management

Illustrators body movements that amplify, accent, or supplement what is being said orally

Impromptu speaking situation in which a presentation is de-veloped and prepared "on the spot," with little or no time for preparation

Individual goals goals that group members have in addition to the group's stated goals

Inductive reasoning type of reasoning that moves from specific statements to general conclusions

Informal bargaining process that involves spontaneous situations that are seldom repeated

Informational dimension of group evaluation concerned with the task that the group is working on

Informative presentation presentations that tell listeners some-thing they do not already know, or that supplement or reinforce listeners' existing knowledge

Informative presentations presentations that provide ideas, alter-natives, data, or even opinions and that provide credible, reliable information to back up major points

Integration bringing people together so that their varied talents and skills can be complementary and mutually supportive, giving employees a sense of cooperation

Integrity keeping promises and commitments and refusing to make promises that compromise the well-being of coworkers and the organization

Interactive communication communication in which each person taking part listens and responds to the others

Interdependency the concept of relatedness within systems theory

Interest level level of adaptation that is based on how much or little an audience is interested in your message and material

Interethnic cultural communication communication between people who identify themselves as members of different ethnic groups

Internal communication or intra-organizational communication messages that are sent and received within the organizational boundaries of the company

International cultural communication communication between representatives of different nations

Interpersonal dimension of group evaluation in which the emphasis is on how well the members of the group work with one another

Interpretation an extension of causal reasoning in which you ask not only "Why did that happen?" but also "What does it mean?"

Interpretative response a response indicating that the inter-viewer's intent is to teach or tell the interviewee what the response means

Interracial cultural communication communication between peo-ple with physical differences

Interview planned, dyadic, interactive discourse

Intimate zone the zone where people interact at the closest dis-tance, ranging from skin contact to eighteen inches

Introduction the beginning of a speech, which informs the listener about the topic of the speech (orientation), the reason for attending to the speech (motivation), and the credibility of the source deliver-ing the message (rapport)

Inverted-funnel sequence a sequence in which the interviewer begins the questioning with a closed question and gradually moves toward broad, open questions

Involvement getting people working on activities other than their daily tasks, giving employees a sense of importance in the organization

Jargon the specialized language that professionals use to communi-cate efficiently with one another

Kinesics the study of gestures and body movement that can be intentional or unintentional

Knowledge level level of adaptation that is based on how much or little an audience knows about your message and material

Laissez-faire decision making style of decision making in which there is minimal involvement by the group leader

Language culture the means by which we represent ourselves and the means by which we interpret others

Leader the member of a group who speaks the most, speaks the most to the group as a whole, is spoken to the most, and directs communication in the group to productive levels

Leadership style the behaviors that leaders use when interacting with group members

Listening   a voluntary process that goes beyond simply reacting to sounds and includes understanding, analyzing, evaluating, and responding

Maintenance messages   messages that keep the organization in working order so that tasks can be performed

Manager   coordinates and organizes activities

Manuscript speaking   situation in which a speech is written out and read verbatim; used when a situation requires precise wording or exact timing

Maslow's hierarchy of needs   theory of motivation based on the argument that lower-level needs must be satisfied before higher-level needs can become motivating factors; includes basic needs, security needs, love and belonging needs, esteem needs, and self-actualization needs

Maturity   a combination of a group's willingness and ability to perform a task

Memorized speaking   situation in which a speech is memorized word for word and then recited

Mentor   experienced, mature, and successful employees who give help and guidance to protégés in many areas, including knowledge, skills, and appropriate attitudes and behavior

Message   the content of communication with others—the ideas people wish to share

Motivating   generating commitment and support for a plan

Motivational presentations   presentations that employ persuasion but rely extensively on stimulating the emotions and feelings of listeners as a method of inducing action

Negative listening   takes place when the receiver is listening to find fault with the sender or is listening to attack what is being said

Negotiation   a planned and structured process of communication in which two or more people with different goals exchange communication to produce a mutually desirable outcome

New business   new issues that have to be addressed

Noise   anything that interferes with the communication process; can occur at any time in the process

Nominal group technique (NGT)   technique that allows groups to discuss problems and solutions in a relatively structured setting

Nondirective interview   a situation in which the interviewer cedes control of the purpose, structure, and pacing of the interview to the interviewee

Nonverbal communication   any message—other than spoken or written words—that attempts to convey meaning

Norms   recurring patterns that define accepted behavior

Oculesics   the movement of the eyes and how they are focused on other people and objects

Open question   a question that allows the interviewee a wide range of choice in terms of form of response

Open systems   systems that allow free movement of energy, information, ideas, data, people, and so on, across organizational boundaries

Opening   initial moments of an interview in which issues of credibility, orientation, and motivation may be addressed

Openness   a receiver-oriented concept that focuses on being receptive and responsive to information from others

Opinion leaders   people who are capable of influencing your decisions, attitudes, and behaviors

Organizational communication   the exchange of oral, written, and nonverbal messages among people working to accomplish common tasks and goals

Organizational culture   the social or normative glue that holds an organization together, consisting of values and beliefs that are shared by some groups or organizational members

Organizational goals   goals that are set at upper levels of an organization's hierarchy and describe pathways to excellence

Organizational structure   the actual environment where the organization is located

Organizing   the process of accumulating and coordinating the human and capital resources necessary to undertake a plan

Outline   a visual, schematic summary of the message that shows the order of ideas and the general relationships among them

Paralanguage   voice qualities or characteristics of speech, such as pitch, tempo, volume, rhythm, and articulation

Participative decision making   style of decision making in which the leader makes decisions with the group

Passive listening   takes place when the receiver is not concentrating on the message and consequently loses much of its meaning

Perception   the process of creating meaning based on experience

Personal zone   ranging from eighteen inches to four feet, this zone is usually reserved for interactions that are personal or private

Persuasive presentations   presentations that perform one or more of the following functions: (1) *reinforce* the listeners' beliefs, attitudes, or values, (2) *refute*, or disprove, an idea or belief held by listeners, (3) *change* the listeners' beliefs, actions, or values, and (4) *call* the listeners to action

Persuasive presentations   presentations that change or reaffirm existing attitudes about important topics, strive to gain audience commitment, and motivate action

Physical noise   distractions in the environment of the presentation

Physiological noise   competing personal needs of the listeners

Planning   setting goals and outlining steps to achieve those goals

Point   the major ideas that a speaker wishes the audience to understand and accept

Positioning   moving the focus of the negotiation to issues that are important to you

Prejudice   a negative preconception about people, activities, or places based upon personal experience, hearsay, or other incomplete data

Primary question   a question that introduces a new topic or area of questioning

Probing response   a response indicating that the interviewer's intent is to seek further information or to provoke further discussion

Problem solving   the process of defining a problem and generating solutions

Procedural   dimension of group evaluation that looks at how well the group's activities and communication are coordinated

Process goals   goals that attempt to improve the working of the group itself

Process of persuasion   process characterized by five distinct stages: awareness, interest, evaluation, trial, and adoption

Protégé   a newer employee who is guided by a mentor

Proxemics   the study of personal space

Proximity   a measure of physical closeness among officemates

Pseudolistening   faking attention; pretending to listen

Psychological noise   internal distractions within the mind of the listener

Public zone   the largest zone, ranging from twelve feet and beyond

Pyramidal order the speaker places the strongest argument between two weaker ones

Quality circles groups of employees who meet on a regular basis during work time to improve quality control and job methods

Quid pro quo a sexual harassment situation in which an employee is offered a reward or is threatened with punishment based upon his or her participation in sexual activity

Quintamensional plan a special sequence of questions designed by George Gallup, it consists of five steps: awareness of the topic, uninfluenced attitudes, specific attitudes, reasoning behind the attitudes, and intensity of feelings

Quorum number of members required to be present for a group to conduct business officially

Rational-legal authority authority structure that grows out of rules, policies, procedures, laws, or other legalistic avenues of conferring power

Reading the minutes summarization of what took place in previous meetings of the group

Reasoning the ability to pull various data together and draw sound conclusions from them

Receiver the destination of the message

Reception the physical process of hearing aural and seeing visual stimuli

Reflective thinking a five-step process whose success depends on each group member's willingness to participate

Regulators nonverbal, usually automatic acts that help to maintain the flow of a conversation

Relational consequences the way in which a message will influence future communication with the receiver

Relational element how you feel about the person with whom you are communicating

Relational goals "define each party's importance to the other, the emotional distance they wish to maintain, the influence each is willing to grant the other, the degree to which the parties are seen as a unit, or the rights each party is willing to grant to the others"

Reliability a leader's support of employees and coworkers in times of need, whether personal, organizational, or professional

Reports informative accounts of the status quo

Robotism rigid and inflexible behavior

Role behavior or expectations for behavior within a group

Roll call an attendance check

Satellite tables an innovative arrangement that gives considerable room for the leader to roam around the room while conducting the session; participants sit around individual tables that occupy independent spaces in the room

Secondary question a question that develops a topic or area that has already been introduced by a primary question

Self-managing teams small groups of employees who share the responsibility for a significant task

Sexual harassment this includes (1) inappropriate demands made on an employee by a fellow worker or supervisor, and (2) the development of uncomfortable and unprofessional work environments

Shared meaning the mutual understanding that results when the sender and all intended receivers interpret the message in the same way

Sign reasoning type of reasoning that draws conclusions from simple observations

Situational factors elements in the conflict that affect the nature of conflict and the styles you select to deal with them

Situational knowledge the information or facts you use in devising an effective communication strategy

Situational leadership leadership style that involves adapting behaviors to the situation at hand rather than relying on one "best" style in all situations

Social zone ranging from four to twelve feet, this zone is used a great deal in business settings

Source the person who creates a message

Spatial or geographical pattern structural pattern of organization in which main points are organized in terms of their physical locations, especially in relation to each other

Speaker's outline an outline that includes only key words and important quotations or statistics written on index cards

Special committees temporary subgroups created to look into short-term or specific problems

Specific purpose purpose derived from the general purpose, identifying what the presenter wants the audience to think, believe, feel, or do as a result of listening to the presentation

Standing committees permanent subgroups that concentrate on long-term developments in broad areas

Statistics descriptions of the result of collecting, organizing, and interpreting numerical data

Subpoint forms of support for the main ideas

Supporting materials explanations, examples, statistics, testimony, and visual aids used to give credibility to your main ideas and to make the message more informative, interesting, relevant, clear, and acceptable

Supporting phase phase of situational leadership in which the leader is in the role of peer and gives compliments, reassures, minimizes doubts, and encourages productivity

Supportive feedback feedback that encourages desirable behavior

Supportive response a response indicating that the interviewer's intent is to reassure, pacify, or reduce the interviewee's intensity of feeling

Syllogism a three-part argument containing a general truth, a related claim, and a conclusion

Sympathy identification with others' feelings

Synergy the phenomenon whereby the combined and integrated talents, energies, abilities, and knowledge of organizational members are greater than the sum of the isolated efforts of individuals

Systems theory acknowledges the interrelationship of an organization's environment, labor, and management

Tall organizations organizations characterized by a large number of hierarchical levels

Task messages messages intended to make others accomplish specific goals

Technical skills the ability to use data, information, innovations, and techniques

Telecommuters employees who maintain regular communication with their organizations through email, phones, fax, pagers, and the Internet

Territoriality the behaviors or actions associated with the use, maintenance, or defense of physical space so as to indicate ownership

Testimony a statement by a credible person (source) that lends weight and authority to the speaker's presentation

Thesis statement a single declarative sentence that summarizes the main ideas to be presented to the audience

Topic outline an outline that reduces the sentences of a speech to brief phrases or single words

Topical pattern structural pattern of organization in which the main points of the message are organized as parallel elements of the topic itself

Topical system method that uses a small set of headings or topics to identify standard ways of thinking and talking about any subject

Traditional authority authority structure that results from the recognition of and adherence to power produced by history, succession, or norms

Training presentations informative presentations that educate listeners to help them gain or improve on specific skills

Traits the personalities, physical appearances, or behaviors of people in a group

Transaction occurs when each party gives up something in exchange for something else

Transitions "signposts" that link the various elements of the outline, showing why and how each element relates to the other elements

Trust a characteristic resulting from a strong commitment to ethical behavior within the organization's system of values

Trustworthiness a component of credibility that refers to the way that a source is perceived as being honest, friendly, warm, agreeable, or safe, instead of dangerous or threatening

Tunnel sequence a sequence in which the interviewer uses a series of questions at a similar level of openness or closedness

U-shaped setup tables and chairs are arranged so that participants sit adjacent to or directly across from one another; designed for full-room interaction

Understanding a characteristic resulting from listening to others, using clear and respectful language, and relying on appropriate techniques for behavior control

Understanding response a response indicating that the interviewer's intent is to find out whether he or she correctly understands what the interviewee is saying

Unfinished business topics that were not agreed on at earlier meetings

Upward communication messages from subordinates to superiors

Values the principles and ideas that people or organizations strongly believe in and consider important

Verbal aggressiveness the tendency to attack other people instead of other points of view

Verbal communication all messages composed of words, either spoken or written

Virtual organization an organization structured through telecommunications connections

Endnotes

Chapter 1

1. "Employers Cite Communication Skills, Honesty/Integrity as Key for Job Candidates," *Job Outlook 2007 Survey*, March 15, 2007, National Association of Colleges and Employers: http://www.naceweb.org/press/display.asp?year=2007&prid=254 (accessed April 25, 2007); H. Meverson (2009), Communication—Seven-Verbal-Communication-Skills-That-Improve-Workplace-Management-Effectiveness: http://ezinearticles.com/?Communication—Seven-Verbal-Communication-Skills-That-Improve-Workplace-Management-Effectiveness&id=2148192 (accessed June 19, 2009); *Equipped for the Future: 21st Century Skills Standards for the New Economy*, Yardley, PA: Technology Based Solutions: http://www.askTBS.com (accessed June 20, 2009).

2. G. Braud, "Ready for the Worst," *Communication World* (March–April 2009): 48.

3. W. Bennis and R. Thomas, "Crucibles of Leadership," *Harvard Business Review* (September 2002): 39–45.

4. O. Wiio, *Wiio's Laws—and Some Others* (Espoo, Finland: Welin-Göös, 1978).

5. F. Taylor, *The Principles of Scientific Management* (New York: Harper, 1911).

6. M. Weber, *The Theory of Social and Economic Organizations* (New York: Free Press, 1947).

7. G. Morgan, *Images of Organizations* (Newbury Park, CA: Sage, 1986).

8. E. Mayo, *The Human Problems of an Industrial Civilization* (New York: Macmillan, 1933).

9. E. Mayo, *The Social Problems of an Industrial Civilization* (Andover, MA: Andover Press, 1945), p. 22.

10. D. McGregor, *The Human Side of Enterprise* (New York: McGraw-Hill, 1960).

11. L. von Bertalanfy *General Systems Theory: Foundations, Development, and Applications* (New York: Braziller, 1960).

12. R. H. Kilmann, *Managing Beyond the Quick Fix* (San Francisco: Jossey-Bass, 1989).

13. T. Deal and A. Kennedy, *Corporate Culture: The Rights and Rituals of Corporate Life* (Reading, MA: Addison-Wesley 1982); T. Peters and R. Waterman, *In Search of Excellence: Lessons from America's Best-Run Companies* (New York: Warner Books, 1982).

14. Morgan, *Images of Organizations*.

Chapter 2

1. M. Tonello, *Revisiting Stock Market Short-Termism* (New York: The Conference Board, 2006).

2. A. V. Laskin, "A Descriptive Account of Investor Relations Profession," *Journal of Business Communication* 46 (2009): 208–33; Tonello, *Revisiting*.

3. Information from http://www.wrf.com/publication_newsletters.cfm?sp=newsletter&year=2004&ID=17&publication_id=10204&keyword=; http://www.usatoday.com/money/industries/telecom/2003-06-10-worldcom_x.htm; http://judiciary.senate.gov/member_statement.cfm?id=846&wit_id=51.

4. "*Bernard Madoff gets 150 years behind bars for fraud scheme,*" CBC News, June 29, 2009, http://www.cbc.ca/money/story/2009/06/29/madoff-ponzi-fraud-sentence564.html (accessed July 9, 2009).

5. Laskin, "A Descriptive Account."

6. "Timeline of Enron's Collapse," *Washingtonpost.com,* September 30, 2005, http://www.washingtonpost.com/wp-dyn/articles/A25624-2002Jan10.html (accessed May 18, 2006).

7. Floyd Norris, "History Gives Other Cases of G.M.'s Behavior," *New York Times*, March 27, 2014, http://nyti.ms/1|7iWa4 (Accessed January 20, 2014).

8. Kristen Hays, "Former Merrill Execs Sentenced," *WashingtonPost.com*, April 22, 2005, http://www.washingtonpost.com/wp-dyn/articles/A8069-2005April21.html (accessed May 18, 2006).

9. M. W. Seeger, "Organizational Communication Ethics: Directions for Critical Inquiry and Application," in *Key Issues in Organizational Communication*, ed. D. Tourish and O. Hargie, 220–33 (New York: Routledge, 2004): 227; W. S. Howell, *The Empathic Communicator* (Belmont, Calif.: Wadsworth, 1982), 192.

10. S. P. Golen, C. Powers, and M. A. Titkemeyer, "Ethics," in *Methods of Teaching Selected Topics in Business Communication*, ed. S. P. Golen, 3–8 (Urbana, Ill.: Association for Business Communication, 1986).

11. C. M. Kelly, *The Destructive Achiever* (Reading, Mass.: Addison-Wesley, 1988), 196–97.

12. (© 2014 Ethics Resource Center) http://www.ethics.org/nbes/

13. G. Baker, "The Effects of Synchronous Collaborative Technologies on Decision Making: A Study of Virtual Teams," *Information Resource Management Journal* 15 (2002): 79–94; P. R. Monge and N. Contractor, *Theories of Communication Networks* (New York: Oxford University Press, 2003); P. Monge, B. M. Heiss, and D. B. Margol, "Communication Network Evolution in Organizational Communities," *Communication Theory* 18 (2008): 449–77; D. B. Roebuck, S. J. Brock, and D. R. Moodie, "Using a Simulation to Explore Challenges of Communication in Virtual Teams," *Business Communication Quarterly* 67 (2004): 359–67.

14. Information from http://www.networkworld.com/news/2002/0520nw500.html; http://www.house.gov/ed_workforce/hearings/106th/oi/telework102899/edwards.htm; http://telecommutect.com/content/itacsurvey2004.htm; http://www.businesswire.com/webbox/bw.022801/210590161.htm.

15. Roebuck, Brock, and Moodie, "Using a Simulation."

16. S. Wilson, "Forming Virtual Teams," *Quality Progress* 36 (2003): 36–41.

17. D. Jude-York, L. D. Davis, and S. L. Wise, *Virtual Teaming* (Menlo Park, CA: Crisp Learning, 2000).

18. C. B. Gibson and J. A. Manuel, "Building Trust," in *Virtual teams that work,* ed. C. B. Gibson and S. G. Cohen, 59–86 (San Francisco: Jossey-Bass, 2003).

19. J. H. Waldeck, D. R. Seibold, and A. J. Flanagin, "Organizational Assimilation and Communication Technology Use," *Communication Monographs,* 71 (2004): 161–83.

20. F. M. Jablin, "Organizational Entry, Assimilation, and Exit," in *The New Handbook of Organizational Communication*, ed. F. M. Jablin and L. L. Putnam, 732–818 (Thousand Oaks, CA: Sage, 2001).

21. Kevin Freiberg and Jackie Freiberg, *Nuts! Southwest Airlines Crazy Recipe for Business and Personal Success* (New York: Broadway Books, 1998).

22. Jablin, "Organizational Entry"; K. K. Myers and J. G. Oetzel, "Exploring the Dimensions of Organizational Assimilation: Creating and Validating a Measure," *Communication Quarterly* 51 (2003): 438–57.

23. P. Shrivesta in R. L. Daft and G. P. Huber, "How Organizations Learn: A Communication Framework," *Research in the Sociology of Organizations* 5 (1987): 1–36.

24. F. Jablin, "Organizational Communication: An Assimilation Approach," in *Social Cognition and Communication*, ed. M. Rolof and C. Berger, 255–86 (Newbury Park, Calif.: Sage, 1982).

25. P. Frost, "Power, Politics, and Influence," in *Handbook of Organizational Communication*, ed. F. Jablin, L. Putnam, K. Roberts, and L. Porter (Newbury Park, Calif.: Sage, 1987), 518.

26. P. Fleming and A. Spicer, *Contesting the Corporation* (Cambridge, UK: Cambridge University Press, 2007).

27. P. Fleming and A. Spicer, "Working at Cynical Distance: Implications for Subjectivity, Power, and Resistance," *Organization* 10 (2003): 157–79; P. Fleming and A. Spicer, "Beyond Power and Resistance: New Approaches to Organizational Politics," *Management Communication Quarterly* 21 (2008): 301–11.

28. Frost, "Power, Politics, and Influence," 504–48.

29. R. E. Reidenbach and D. P. Robin, *Ethics and Profits* (Englewood Cliffs, N. J.: Prentice Hall, 1989).

30. http://books.google.com/books?hl=en&lr=&id=HOPKAgAAQ BAJ&oi=fnd&pg=PR5&dq=organizational+communication+cli mate+2015&ots=MHviEWB-L-&sig=kF8E3-vtkPBnkNVwJG5oY GUxJ8A#v=onepage&q&f=false

31. C. Redding, *Communication within the Organization: An Interpretive Review of Theory and Research* (New York: Industrial Communication Council, 1972). Reprinted with permission.

32. D. Rogers, "The Development of a Measure of Perceived Communication Openness," *Journal of Business Communication* 24 (1987): 53–61. Reprinted by permission of the author.

33. Rogers, "The Development of a Measure."

34. E. A. Locke, D. Chah, S. Harrison, and N. Lustgarten, "Separating the Effects of Goal Specificity from Goal Level," *Organizational Behavior and Human Decision Making* 43 (1989): 270–87.

35. E. A. Locke, K. N. Shaw, L. M. Saari, and G. P. Latham, "Goal Setting and Task Performance: 1969–1980," *Psychological Bulletin* 90 (1981): 125–52.

36. Locke et al., "Separating the Effects of Goal Specificity"; Locke et al., "Goal Setting and Task Performance."

37. Locke et al., "Separating the Effects of Goal Specificity"; Locke et al., "Goal Setting and Task Performance."

38. L. Sussman, A. J. Adams, F. E. Kuzmits, and L. E. Raho, "Organizational Politics: Tactics, Channels, and Hierarchical Roles," *Journal of Business Ethics* 41 (2002): 313–29.

39. D. Katz and R. Kahn, *The Social Psychology of Organizations* (New York: Wiley, 1966).

40. J. Koehler and G. Huber, "Effects of Upward Communication on Managerial Decision Making" (paper presented at the annual meeting of the International Communication Association, New Orleans, 1974).

41. Postmes, Tanis, and De Wit, "Communication and Commitment."

42. T. Daniels and B. Spiker, *Perspectives on Organizational Communication* (Dubuque, Iowa: Brown, 1987).

43. Sussman, Adams, Kuzmits, and Raho, "Organizational Politics."

44. J. Main, "Betting on the 21st Century Jet," *Fortune*, April 20, 1992, 102–17.

45. J. R. Katzenbach and D. K. Smith, *The Wisdom of Teams* (Boston: Harvard Business School Press, 1993).

46. G. Goldhaber, *Organizational Communication* (Dubuque, Iowa: Brown, 1990).

47. T. Kelleher and B. M. Miller, "Organizational Blogs and the Human Voice: Relational Strategies and Relational Outcomes." *Journal of Computer-Mediated Communication* 11, no. 2 (2006), article 1, http://jcmc.indiana.edu/vol11/issue2/ kelleher.html.

48. R. L. Daft and R. H. Lengel, "Organizational Information Requirements, Media Richness, and Structural Design," *Management Science* 32 (1986): 554–71; R. L. Daft and G. P. Huber, "How Organizations Learn: A Communication Framework," *Research in the Sociology of Organizations* 5 (1987): 1–36; G. P. Huber and R. L. Daft, "The Information Environments of Organizations," in *Handbook of Organizational Communication*, ed. F. Jablin, L. Putnam, K. Roberts, and L. Porter, 130–64 (Newbury Park, Calif.: Sage, 1987).

49. S. C. D'Urso and S. A. Rains, "Examining the Scope of Channel Expansion: A Test of Channel Expansion Theory with New and Traditional Communication Media," *Management Communication Quarterly* 21 (2008): 486–508.

50. E. Shiu and A. Lenhart, *How Americans use instant messaging* (Washington, DC: Pew Internet and American Life Project, 2004), http://www.pewinternet.org/Reports/2004/How- -Americans-Use-Instant-Messaging.aspx (accessed July 9, 2009); L. C. Tidwell and J. B. Walther, "Computer-Mediated Communication Effects on Disclosure, Impressions, and Interpersonal Evaluations," *Human Communication Research* 28 (2002): 317–48.

51. D'Urso and Rains, "Examining the Scope"; Shiu and Lenhart, *How Americans Use*; Tidwell and Walther, "Computer-Mediated Communication Efforts."

52. Daft and Lengel, "Organizational Information Requirements."

53. Daft and Huber, "How Organizations Learn"; Sussman, Adams, Kuzmits, and Raho, "Organizational Politics."

54. D'Urso and Rains, "Examining the Scope"; adapted from D. A. Level and W. P. Galle, *Business Communication: Theory and Practice* (Dallas: Business Publications, 1980); A. J. Melcher and R. Beller, "Toward a Theory of Organization Communication: Considerations in Channel Selection," *Academy of Management Journal* 10 (1967): 39–52; Shiu and Lenhart, *How Americans Use*; Tidwell and Walther, "Computer-Mediated Communication Efforts."

55. P. Pace, *Organizational Communication: Foundations for Human Resource Development* (Englewood Cliffs, N. J.: Prentice Hall, 1983).

56. A. H. Buss, *Self-Consciousness and Social Anxiety* (San Francisco: Freeman, 1980); J. Daly and J. L. Hailey, "Putting the Situation into Writing Research: Situational Parameters of Writing Apprehension as Disposition and State," in *New Directions in Composition Research*, ed. R. E. Beach and L. Bidwell (New York: Guilford, 1983).

57. V. P. Richmond and J. C. McCroskey, Communication: Apprehension, Avoidance, and Effectiveness (Scottsdale, Ariz.: Gorusch, Scarisbrick, 1985). Judge, W., & Elenkov, D. (2005). Organizational capacity for change and environmental performance: an empirical assessment of Bulgarian firms. Journal of Business Research, 58, 893–901.

Chapter 3

1. A. L. Nagata, "Promoting Self-Reflexivity in Intercultural Education," *Journal of Intercultural Communication* 8 (2005):140-41.

2. Information from http://www.usahistory.info/timeline/ (accessed September 1, 2009).

3. Centers for Disease Control, Latino or Hispanic Populations, http://www.cdc.gov/omh/populations/HL/HL.htm (accessed April 25, 2006; updated April 26, 2006).

4. Information from http://www.ehow.com/how_18311_cope_with_gender.html.

5. Orbe and Harris, *Interracial Communication: Theory Into Practice* (Thousand Oaks, CA: Sage, 2008).

6. H. Laube, K. Massoni, J. Sprague, and A. L. Ferber, "The Impact of Gender on the Evaluation of Teaching: What We Know and What We Can Do," *NWSA Journal* 19(3) (2007): 87–104.

7. B. McMahon, R. Roessler, P. Rumrill, J. Hurley, S. West, F. Chan, and L. Carlson (2008), "Hiring Discrimination against People with Disabilities under the ADA: Characteristics of Charging Parties," *Journal of Occupational Rehabilitation* 18 (2008): 122–32.

8. L. Dixon Shaver, "The Relationship between Language Cultures and Recidivism Among Women Offenders," in *Women Offenders: A Forgotten Population*, ed. B. Fletcher, L. Dixon Shaver, and D. Moon, 119–34 (Westport, CT: Praeger, 1993).

9. C. Bantz, *Understanding Organizations: Interpreting Organizational Communication Cultures* (Columbia: University of South Carolina Press, 1993); U. Eco, *The Limits of Interpretation* (Bloomington: Indiana University Press, 1990); Y. Lotman, *Universe of the Mind: A Semiotic Theory of Culture* (Bloomington: Indiana University Press, 1990); J. Potter and M. Wetherell, *Discourse and Social Psychology: Beyond Attitudes and Beliefs* (Beverly Hills, CA: Sage, 1987); P. Shaver and L. Dixon, "'Icons' of Bureaucratic Therapy: An Application of Eco's Semiotic Methodology," *Intercultural Communication Studies* 8(2) (1998): 115–30; L. Dixon and P. Shaver, "The Cultural Perspective of a Public Health Facility for Oklahoma American Indians: Architectural Changes as Organizational Rhetoric," in *Rhetoric in Intercultural Contexts: International and Intercultural Communication Annual NCA 22*, ed. A. Gonzalez & D. Tanno (Thousand Oaks, CA: Sage, 2000); L. Weisman, *Discrimination by Design: A Feminist Critique of the Man-Made Environment* (Chicago: University of Illinois Press, 1992).

10. P. Shaver and L. D. Shaver, "Applying Perspectival Rhetorical Analysis in Intercultural Consulting: The Chromosomal Bivalency Mode," *Intercultural Communication Studies* 2(2) (1992): 1–22.

11. This discussion of personality traits incorporates ideas from these sources: L. Barna, "Stumbling Blocks in Intercultural Communication," in *Intercultural Communication: A Reader,* 6th ed., ed. R. Samovar and L. Porter, 345–52 (Belmont, CA: Wadsworth, 1991); C. Dodd, *Dynamics of Intercultural Communication,* 3rd ed. (Dubuque, IA: Brown, 1991); M. Lustig and J. Koester, *Intercultural Competence: Interpersonal Communication Across Cultures* (New York: HarperCollins, 1993); B. Spitzberg, "Intercultural Communication Competence," in *Intercultural Communication: A Reader,* 6th ed., ed. R. Samovar and L. Porter, 353–65 (Belmont, CA: Waveland Press, 1991).

12. The CAI was developed by L. Dixon.

13. The SPEF was developed by L. Dixon.

14. R. Gesteland, *Cross-Cultural Business Behavior: Negotiating, Selling, Sourcing and Managing across Cultures* (Copenhagen, Denmark: Copenhagen Business School Press, 2005).

15. D. Conklin, *Cases in the Environment of Business: International Perspectives* (Thousand Oaks, CA: Sage Publications, 2006).

16. P. Shaver and L. Dixon Shaver, "Applying Perspectival Rhetorical Analysis."

Chapter 4

1. W. Brown, "Listen Up," *Professional Safety* 54 (2009): 8.

2. Interview with Captain Robert Dunford, Boston Police Department, December 10, 1990.

3. J. Patterson, "Better Listening for Business and Personal Success" http://www2.pvc.maricopa.edu/~patterson/listening .doc (accessed September 19, 2003).

4. S. Reese, "Are You Listening?" *Techniques Magazine* (April 2009): 10–11.

5. B. Goss, *Processing Communication* (Belmont, CA: Wadsworth, 1982).

6. J. Keyton, *Communication in Groups*, 3rd ed., 33–34 (New York: Oxford University Press, 2006).

7. B. Hannon, "Listen Up: Tips on Being a Better Listener from People Whose Jobs Depend on It," *St. Joseph News-Press* (March 29, 2009).

8. D. L. Strayer, F. A. Drews, and W. A. Johnston, "Cell Phone Failures of Visual Attention During Simulated Driving," *Journal of Experimental Psychology: Applied* 9(23)(2003): 23–32. http://www.psych.utah.edu/AppliedCognitionLab/JEP_Applied.pdf.

9. B. Goss and D. O'Hair, *Communicating in Interpersonal Relationships* (New York: Macmillan, 1998).

10. J. Haas and C. Arnold, "An Examination of the Role of Listening in Judgments of Communication Competence in Co-workers," *Journal of Business Communication* 32 (1995): 123 ff: http://www.questia.com (accessed September 21, 2003).

11. W. Pauk and R. Owens, *How to Study in College* (Wadsworth, 2007).

12. T. Harris, "Listen Carefully," *Nation's Business* (June 1989): 78.

13. A. Wolvin and C. Coakley, *Listening* (Dubuque, IA: Brown, 1988).

14. S. Lucas, *The Art of Public Speaking*, 9th ed. (Boston: McGraw-Hill, 2005).

15. M. Whitefield, "Listen Up—Your Job Could Depend on It," *Miami Herald* (April 20, 2009).

16. M. Fitch-Hauser, D. Barker, and A. Hughes, "Receiver Apprehension and Listening Comprehension: A Linear or Curvilinear Relationship?" *Southern Communication Journal* 56 (1990): 62–71.

17. P. Schrodt and L. Wheeless, "Aggressive Communication and Informational Reception Apprehension: The Influence of Listening Anxiety and Intellectual Inflexibility on Trait Argumentativeness and Verbal Aggressiveness," *Communication Quarterly* 49 (2001): 53 ff: http://www.questia.com (accessed September 22, 2003).

18. C. Bowers, B. Chew, M. Bowers, C. Ford, C. Smith, and C. Herrington, "Interdisciplinary Synergy: A Partnership between Business and Library Faculty and Its Effects on Students' Information Literacy," *Journal of Business and Finance Librarianship* 14 (2009): 110–27.

Chapter 5

1. J. Neuliep, *Intercultural Communication: A Contextual Approach,* 2nd ed. (Boston: Houghton Mifflin, 2008).

2. B. Glassman, G. Krugg, and M. Menefee, "Improving Organizational Communication: The Use of the MCR Media Model," *International Journal of Intercultural Information Management* 1(3) (2009): 213–32.

3. E. Mohlina and M. Johannesson, "Communication: Content or Relationship?" *Journal of Economic Behavior & Organization* 65(3–4)(2008): 409–19.

4. S. Mohrman and C. Worley, "Dealing with Rough Times: Capabilities Development Approach to Surviving and Thriving," *Human Resource Management* 48(3) (2009): 443–45.

5. E. T. Hall, *The Hidden Dimension* (Garden City, NY: Doubleday, 1966).

6. F. S. Steingold, *The Employer's Legal Handbook* (Berkeley, CA: Nolo Publishing, 2005).

7. A. Nelson and S. K. Golant, *You Don't Say: Navigating Nonverbal Communication between the Sexes* (Saddle Creek, NY: Prentice Hall, 2004).

8. D. Gerson and D. Gerson, *Modern Rules of Business Etiquette* (Chicago: American Bar Association, 2008).

9. K. L. Ashcraft and D. K. Mumby, *Reworking Gender: A Feminist Communicology of Organization* (Thousand Oaks, CA: Sage, 2003).

10. M. L. Knapp and J. A. Hall, *Nonverbal Communication in Human Interaction,* 6th ed. (Belmont, CA: Thomson-Wadsworth, 2006).

11. R. Harper, A. Wiens, and J. Matazzaro, *Nonverbal Communication: The State of the Art* (New York: Wiley, 1978), 173.

12. Knapp and Hall, *Nonverbal Communication.*

13. C. Kennedy and C. Camden, "A New Look at Interruptions," *Western Journal of Speech Communication* 47 (1982): 45–58.

14. D. Tannen, "Power Talk," interview by L. Lusardi, *Working Women,* July 1990, 92–94.

15. M. L. Hecht, S. Ribeau, and J. K. Alberts, "An Afro-American Perspective on Interethnic Communication," *Communication Monographs* 56 (December 1989), 386–399.

16. M. Lustig and J. Koester, *Intercultural Competence: Interpersonal Communication across Cultures,* 5th ed. (Boston: Allyn and Bacon, 2006).

17. E. M. Rogers and D. L. Kincaid, *Communication Networks, Toward a New Paradigm for Research* (New York: Free Press, 1981).

Chapter 6

1. P. G. Northouse, *Leadership: Theory and Practice,* 3rd ed. (Thousand Oaks, CA: Sage, 2004).

2. P. Hersey and K. Blanchard, *Management of Organizational Behavior: Utilizing Human Resources* (Englewood Cliffs, NJ: Prentice Hall, 1982).

3. Ibid.

4. R. Likert, *New Patterns of Management* (New York: McGraw-Hill, 1961).

5. R. Blake and J. Mouton, "Managerial Facades," *Advanced Management Journal* 31 (July 1966): 30–7.

6. V. Vroom and P. Yetton, *Leadership and Decision-Making* (Pittsburgh: University of Pittsburgh Press, 1973).

7. K. Kuhnert and P. Lewis, "Transactional and Transformational Leadership: A Constructive Development Analysis," *Academy of Management Review* 12 (1987): 648–57.

8. J. M. Burns, *Leadership* (New York: Harper & Row, 1978); J. Kouzes and B. Posner, *The Leadership Challenge* (San Francisco: Jossey-Bass, 1987).

9. This is an often-used quote of Peter Drucker.

10. G. Terry, *Principles of Management,* 3d ed. (Homewood, IL: Irwin, 1960); R. Tannenbaum, I. Weschler, and F. Massarik, *Leadership and Organization: A Behavioral Science Approach* (New York: McGraw-Hill, 1959); H. Koontz and C. O'Donnell, *Principles of Management,* 2nd ed. (New York: McGraw-Hill, 1959); J. Kotter, *The Leadership Factor* (New York: Free Press, 1988).

11. Kouzes and Posner, *The Leadership Challenge,* 336.

12. B. Posner, J. Kouzes, and W. H. Schmidt, "Shared Values Make a Difference: An Empirical Test of Corporate Culture," *Human Resource Management* 3 (1985): 293–310.

13. W. Bennis and B. Nanus, *Leaders: The Strategies for Taking Charge* (New York: Harper & Row, 1985), p. 89.

14. Information from http://www.economist.com.

15. Information from http://www.nintendo.com/corp/history.jsp.

16. Kotter, *The Leadership Factor;* W. Lee and K. Krayer, *Organizing Change* (San Francisco: Pfeiffer, 2003).

17. T. Peters and R. Waterman, *In Search of Excellence: Lessons from America's Best-Run Companies* (New York: Warner Books, 1982).

18. Information from http://www.writer4business.com/bosses_blogs.htm (accessed August 3, 2006).

19. K. R. Andrews, "Ethics in Practice," *Harvard Business Review* (September–October 1989): 103.

20. S. Kerr, "Integrity in Effective Leadership," and R. Harrison, "Quality of Service: A New Frontier for Integrity in Organizations," in *Executive Integrity: The Search for High Human Values in Organizational Life,* ed. S. Shrivastva (San Francisco: Jossey-Bass, 1988), pp. 122–139, 45–67; C. C. Walton, *The Moral Manager* (Cambridge, MA: Ballinger, 1988). M. Sharifi, G. McCombs, L. Fraser, & R. McCaabe (2009). "Structuring a Competency-Based Accounting Communication Course at the Graduate Level," *Business Communication Quarterly* 72: 177–99.

21. W. Bennis, *On Becoming a Leader* (Reading, MA: Addison-Wesley, 1989).

22. Kouzes and Posner, *The Leadership Challenge.*

23. J. K. Van Fleet, *The 22 Biggest Mistakes Managers Make and How to Correct Them* (West Nyack, NY: Parker, 1982), p. 147.

24. D. Gouran, "Communication Skills for Group Decision Making," in *Handbook of Communication and Social Interaction Skills,* ed. J. Greene and B. Burleson, 835–70 (Mahwah, NJ: Erlbaum, 2003).

25. R. Hart, *Verbal Style and the Presidency* (Orlando, FL: Academic Press, 1984).

26. Example from *INC. Magazine,* August 1993, p. 28.

27. D. Seibold and B. C. Shea, "Participation and Decision Making," in *The New Handbook of Organizational Communication,* ed. F. Jablin and L. Putnam, 664–703 (Thousand Oaks, CA: Sage, 2001).

28. Kouzes and Posner, *The Leadership Challenge,* p. 67.

29. Van Fleet, *The 22 Biggest Mistakes.*

Chapter 7

1. C. Warren, "Monster Managers," *American Way Magazine,* June 1, 2003, 62–63.

2. Adapted from www.humanresourcemanagement.co.uk/idealboss.htm (accessed October 13, 2003). Also adapted from www.staff.pl/ (accessed October 16, 2003).

3. For further reference, see F. M. Jablin, "Superior-Subordinate Communication: The State of the Art," *Psychological Bulletin* 8 (1979): 1201–22; G. Goldhaber, *Organizational Communication* (Dubuque, Iowa: Brown, 1990); E. Dansereau and S. E. Markham, "Superior-Subordinate Communication: Multiple Levels of Analysis," in *Handbook of Communication Science,* ed. F. Jablin et al., 343–88 (Beverly Hills, CA: Sage, 1987); R. Klauss and R. Bass, *Interpersonal Communication in Organizations* (New York: Academic Press, 1982).

4. W. C. Redding, *Communicating within the Organization: An Interpretive Review of Theory and Research* (New York: Industrial Communication Council, 1972); T. L. Albrecht, "The Role of

Communication in Perceptions of Organizational Climate," in *Communication Yearbook 3*, ed. D. Nimmo, 343–57 (New Brunswick, NJ: Transaction Books, 1979); Dansereau and Markham, "Superior-Subordinate Communication."

5. H. P. Sims and C. C. Manz, "Observing Leader Verbal Behavior: Toward Reciprocal Determinism in Leadership Theory," *Journal of Applied Psychology* 69 (1984): 222–32.

6. G. Fairhurst, "Dualisms in Leadership Research, in *The New Handbook of Organizational Communication*, ed. F. Jablin and L. Putnam, 379–439 (Thousand Oaks, CA: Sage, 2001).

7. J. Kouzes and B. Z. Posner, *The Leadership Challenge* (San Francisco: Jossey-Bass, 1987).

8. Ibid., p. 162.

9. Ibid., p. 175.

10. M. Tossi, "Labor Force Projections to 2020: A More Slowly Growing Workforce," *Monthly Labor Review* (January 2012): 43-64. http://www.bls.gov/opub/mlr/2012/01/art3full.pdf

11 F. Newport, "Americans Still Prefer Male Bosses; Many Have No Preference," *Gallup* (September 8, 2011); http://www.gallup.com/poll/149360/Americans-Prefer-Male-Bosses-No-Preference.aspx

12. From "Mission for Mail," at http://www.star.net.uk/star/home/media_centre/library/articles/mission_for_mail.stml. The authors of the survey are the Institute of Directors, with the communication firm Avaya.

13. N. Smith, "Digital Overload: Too much Technology Takes a Toll" Business New Dailey (November 8, 2010). http://www.businessnewsdaily.com/379-digital-overload-too-much-data-costs-businesses-billions.html

14. This outline was partially developed from material in A. J. Di Brin, *Effective Business Psychology*, 2nd ed. (Reston, VA: Reston Publishing, 1985); Kouzes and Posner, *The Leadership Challenge*.

15. R. A. Noe, "Women and Mentoring: A Review and Research Agenda," *Academy of Management Review* 13 (1988); 65–78; K. E. Kram, *Mentoring at Work: Development Relationships in Organizational Life* (Glenview, IL: Scott, Foresman, 1985); R. J. Burke and C. A. McKeen, "Developing Formal Mentoring Programs in Organizations," *Business Quarterly* 53 (1989): 76–79.

16. R. M. Kanter, *The Change Masters* (New York: Simon & Schuster, 1984).

17. J. Kotter, *Power and Influence* (New York: Free Press, 1985).

18. Noe, "Women and Mentoring"; T. Daniels and B. Spiker, *Perspectives on Organizational Communication* (Dubuque, Iowa: Brown, 1987); E. A. Fagenson, "The Mentor Advantage Perceived Career/Job Experiences of Protégés vs. Nonprotégés," *Journal of Organizational Behavior* 10 (1989): 309–20.

19. J. Lawrie, "How to Establish a Mentoring Program," *Training and Development Journal* 41 (1987): 25–27.

20. Noe, "Women and Mentoring."

21. Ibid.; Burke and McKeen, "Developing Formal Mentoring Programs."

22. Reprinted with permission of *Business Quarterly*.

23. G. Haight, "Managing Diversity," *Across the Board* (March 1990): 22–29.

24. Noe, "Women and Mentoring."

25. Burke and McKeen, "Developing Formal Mentoring Programs."

26. J. P. Dillard and K. I. Miller, "Intimate Relationships in Task Environments," in *Handbook of Personal Relationships*, ed. S. Duck, 449–65 (Sussex, England: Wiley, 1988).

27. Ibid.

28. Dillard and Miller, "Intimate Relationships"; R. E. Quinn, "Coping with Cupid: The Formation, Impact, and Management of Romantic Relationships in Organizations," *Administration Science Quarterly* 22 (1977): 30–45; Witteman, "Organizational Romance."

29. S. Heathfield, "Tips about Dating, Sex, and Romance at Work." http://humanresources.about.com/cs/workrelationships/a/workromance.htm (accessed September 20, 2006).

30. Quinn, "Coping with Cupid"; C. Anderson and P. Hunsaker, "Why There's Romance in the Office and Why It's Everyone's Problem," *Personnel* 62 (1985): 57–63; J. P. Dillard and S. M. Broetzman, "Romantic Relationships at Work: Perceived Changes in Job-Related Behaviors as a Function of Participant's Motive, Partner's Motive, and Gender" (paper presented at the annual meeting of the Western Speech Communication Association, San Diego, February 1988).

31. J. Keyton, P. Ferguson, and S. C. Rhodes, "Cultural Indicators of Sexual Harassment," *Southern Communication Journal* 67 (2001): 33–50.

32. H. Witteman, "The Interface Between Sexual Harassment and Organizational Romance," in *Sexual Harassment: Communication Implications*, ed. G. Kreps (Cresskill, NJ: Hampton Press, 1994).

33. L. L. Jansma, "Sexual Harassment Research: Integration, Reformulation, and Implications for Mitigation Efforts," in *Communication Yearbook 23*, ed. M. Roloff, 163–225 (Thousand Oaks, CA: Sage, 2000).

34. This section is influenced by C. Berryman-Fink, "Preventing Sexual Harassment Through Male-Female Communication Training," in Kreps, *Sexual Harassment*.

35. *From Completeness: Quality for the 21st Century*, by P. B. Crosby. Copyright © 1992 by P. B. Crosby.

36. K. Albrecht, *At America's Service: How Corporations Can Revolutionize the Way They Treat Their Customers* (Homewood, IL: Dow Jones-Irwin, 1988).

37. T. Peters and R. Waterman, *In Search of Excellence: Lessons from America's Best-Run Companies* (New York: Warner Books, 1982).

38. Albrecht, *At America's Service*.

39. D. Finkelman and T. Goland, "The Case of the Complaining Customer," *Harvard Business Review* (May–June 1990): 9–21.

Chapter 8

1. P. F. Drucker, "How to Be an Employee," *Fortune*, May 1952, reprinted in N. B. Sighand and D. N. Bateman, *Communicating in Business* (Glenview, IL: Scott, Foresman, 1981), 454.

2. Personnel Interviewers' Perceptions of The Importance And Adequacy Of Applicants' Communication Skills. Marshalita Sims Peterson. *Communication Education* Vol. 46, 1997, pp. 287–291.

3. D. B. Curtis, J. L. Winsor, and R. D. Stephens, "National Preferences in Business and Communication Education," *Communication Education* 38 (1989): 6–14.

4. A. P. Carnevale, L. J. Gainer, and J. Villet, *Training in America: The Organization and Strategic Role of Training* (San Francisco: Jossey-Bass, 1990).

5. P. Page and S. Perelman, *Basic Skills and Employment: An Employer Survey* (Madison: University of Wisconsin System, Interagency Basic Skills Project, 1980).

6. B. Burgess-Wilkerson, "Selection and Interview Procedures at a Multi-National Company," *Business Communication Quarterly* 71 (2008): 100–21; C. Goldberg and D. J. Cohen, "Walking the Walk and Talking the Talk: Gender Differences in the Impact of Interviewing Skills on Applicant Assessment," *Group and Organizational Management* 29 (2004): 369–72; M. P. Joyce, "Interviewing Techniques Used in Selected Organizations Today," *Business Communication Quarterly* 71 (2008): 376–80.

7. R. Fidgeon, "Online Interviewing Tool Boosts Recruitment at Proximity London," *Strategic Human Resources Review* 7 (2008): 36–48.

8. U. Johnson-Smaragdi, "Media Use Styles among the Young," in *Children and their Changing Media Environment. A European Comparative Study,* ed. S. Livingstone and M. Bovill, 113–41 (Mahwah, N.J.: Lawrence Erlbaum, 2001); H. Kim, G. J. Kim, H. W. Park, and R. E. Rice, "Configurations of Relationships in Different Media: Face-to-Face, Email, Instant Messages, Mobile Phone, and SMS," *Journal of Computer-Mediated Communication* 12 (2007): 1183–207; C. Licoppe and Z. Smoreda, "Are Social Networks Technically Embedded? How Networks Are Changing Today with Changes in Communication Technology," *Social Networks* 27 (2005): 317–35; B. Nardi, "Beyond Bandwidth: Dimensions of Connection in Interpersonal Communication," *Computer-Supported Cooperative Work* 14 (2005): 91–130; A. Quan-Haase and B. Wellman, "Hyperconnected Network," in *The Firm as a Collaborative Community: Reconstructing Trust in the Knowledge Economy,* ed. C. Heckscher and P. Adler, 281–333 (New York: Oxford University Press, 2006).

9. C. Stewart and W. Cash, *Interviewing: Principles and Practices,* 9th ed. (Burr Ridge, IL: The McGraw-Hill Companies, Inc. 2000), p.103; http://career-advice.monster.com/job-interview/Interview-Preparation/Successfully-Closing-the-Interview/article.aspx; http://hrweb.berkeley.edu/guides/managing-hr/recruiting-staff/employment/interviewing/closing; http://www.roberthalf.com/how-to-close-an-interview.

10. S. L. Payne, *The Art of Asking Questions* (Princeton, N.J.: Princeton University Press, 1951).

11. S. L. Payne, "Thoughts About Meaningless Questions," *Public Opinion Quarterly* 14 (1950): 687–96.

12. S. L. Payne, "Case Study in Question Complexity," *Public Opinion Quarterly* 13 (1949): 653–58.

13. Stewart and Cash, *Interviewing.*

14. G. Gallup, "The Quintamensional Plan of Question Design," *Public Opinion Quarterly* 11 (1947): 385.

15. Carl Rogers's research is discussed in D. W. Johnson, *Reaching Out: Interpersonal Effectiveness and Self-Actualization* (Englewood Cliffs, N.J.: Prentice Hall, 1972), 117–140.

16. Understanding responses point is paraphrased from Johnson, *Reaching Out,* p. 125.

17. Burgess-Wilkerson, "Selection and Interview Procedures."

18. Workforce 2020: The Looming Talent Crisis. http://www.successfactors.com/content/dam/successfactors/en_us/resources/white-papers/sap-workforce2020-executive-summary.pdf

19. M. P. Joyce, "Interviewing Techniques"; R. Knight, "Don't Panic—Help Is at Hand; Casualties of the Crunch Are Turning to Alma Maters for Emotional and Practical Support in Navigating the Job Market," *Financial Times* (London, UK), October 6, 2008, p. 17; M. Massue, "Hiring the Best," *Training & Development* (July 2006): 76–78.

20. M. P. Joyce, "Interviewing Techniques"; H. Z. Levin, "Supervisory Selection Systems," *Personnel* 63 (1986): 61–65.

21. M. Massue, "Hiring the Best."

22. A. Finder, "For Some, Online Persona Undermines a Résumé," *NYTimes.com* (June 11, 2006), http://www.nytimes.com/2006/06/11/us/11recruit.html?ei=5090&en=ddfbe1e3b386090b&ex=1307678400&pagewanted=all.

23. Johnson-Smaragdi, "Media Use Styles"; Kim, Kim, Park, and Rice, "Configurations of Relationships"; Licoppe and Smoreda, "Are Social Networks Technically Embedded?"; Nardi, "Beyond Bandwidth"; Quan-Haase and Wellman, "Hyperconnected Network."

24. Finder, "For Some, Online Persona."

25. "Recruiters Dig Up Dirt on Potential Employees Online," ABC7.com, http://abclocal.go.com/kabc/story?section=seenon&id=4308602 (accessed Aug. 21, 2006).

26. B. J. Jansen, K. J. Jansen, and A. Spink, "Using the Web to Look for Work: Implications for Online Job Seeking and Recruiting," *Internet Research* 15 (2004): 49–67.

27. P. Capelli, "Making the Most of Online Recruiting," *Harvard Business Review* 79 (2001): 139–46; A. Spink and B. J. Jansen, *Websearch: Public Searching of the Web* (New York: Kluwer Academic/Plenum, 2004).

28. Jansen, Jansen, and Spink, "Using the Web to Look for Work"; Spink and Jansen, *Websearch.*

29. L. Bowes, *No One Need Apply* (Boston: Harvard Business School Press, 1990).

30. B. E. Bostwick, *Résumé Writing: A Comprehensive How-to-Do-It,* 4th ed. (New York: Wiley, 1990).

31. J. A. Kerekes, "Winning an Interviewer's Trust in a Gatekeeping Encounter," *Language in Society* 35 (2006): 27–57.

32. "Job Hunters, Get Found: Build an Online Brand 'You,'" *PR Newswire* (June 25, 2009).

33. Tom Rosenstiel, Amy Mitchell, Kristen Purcell, and Lee Rainie September 26, 2011. How People Learn About Their Local Community Part 5: The Role Of The Internet. September 26, 2011. Accessed at http://Www.Pewinternet.Org/2011/09/26/Part-5-The-Role-Of-The-Internet/

34. K. Hutchinson and D. Brefka, "Personnel Administrators' Preferences for Résumé Content: Ten Years After," *Business Communication Quarterly* 60 (1997): 67ff. Retrieved from Questia, October 15, 2003.

35. Résumé formats based on J. T. Bostwick, *The Perfect Resume* (New York: Doubleday, 1990).

36. S. E. Needleman, "Thanks for the Interview; Tailored Follow-Up Note Can Make a Difference in Landing the Job," *Wall Street Journal* (Eastern Edition), December 6, 2005, p. B10.

37. "Job Hunters."

38. Goldberg and Cohen, "Walking the Walk."

39. E. P. Kelly and R. J. Alberts, "Americans with Disabilities Act: Undue Hardship for Private Sector Employers?"*Labor Law Journal* 41 (1990): 675–84.

40. K. E. Buckner, H. S. Field, and W. H. Holley, "The Relationship of Legal Case Characteristics with the Outcomes of Personnel Selection Court Cases," *Labor Law Journal* 41 (1990): 31–40.

41. C. S. Atwood and J. M. Neel, "New Lawsuits Expand Employer Liability," *HRMagazine* 35 (1990): 74–75.

42. M. Orey, "Fear of Firing," *Business Week,* April 23, 2007, pp. 52–62.

43. K. G. Lamude, J. Scudder, and D. Simmons, "The Influence of Applicant Characteristics on Use of Verbal Impression Management Tactics in the Employment Selection Interview," *Communication Research Reports* 20 (2003): 299–307.

44. T. DeGroot, and J. Gooty, "Can Nonverbal Cues Be Used to Make Meaningful Personality Attributes in Employment Interviews?" *Journal of Behavior and Psychology* 24 (2009): 179–93.

45. B. Russell, "Interviews," *Liverpool Daily Post & Echo,* July 21, 2007, p. 9.

46. L. R. Weber and A. I. Carter, *The Social Construction of Trust* (New York: Kluwer Academic/Plenum, 2003).

47. Kerekes, "Winning an Interviewer's Trust."

48. S. M. Ralston, W. G. Kirkwood, and P. A. Burant, "Helping Interviewees Tell Their Stories," *Business Communication Quarterly* 66 (2003): 8–22.

49. C. K. Stevens and A. L. Kristof, "Making the Right Impression: A Field Study of Applicant Impression Management during the Interviews," *Journal of Applied Psychology* 80 (1995): 587–606, p. 596.

50. M. S. Weisel, "Employer's Burden of Proof in 'Mixed Motive' Title VII Litigation and Available Remedies: *Hopkins v. Price Waterhouse* One Year Later," *Labor Law Journal* 42 (1991): 45–51.

51. Needleman, "Thanks for the Interview."

52. K. Kellerman and H. S. Park, "Situational Urgency and Conversational Retreat: When Politeness and Efficiency Matter," *Communication Research* 28 (2001): 3–47.

53. K. Weber, M. M. Martin, and J. L. Cayanus, "Student Interest: A Two-Way Re-Examination of the Concept," *Communication Quarterly* 53 (2005): 71–86.

54. T. R. Kurtzberg, L. Y. Belkin, and C. E. Naquin, "The Effect of Email on Attitudes towards Performance Feedback," *International Journal of Organizational Analysis* 14 (2006): 4–21.

55. Michael E. Gordon and Lea P. Stewart. Conversing About Performance: Discursive Resources for the Appraisal Interview. Management Communication Quarterly, Vol. 22, No. 3, 473–501 (2009).

56. C. W. Downs, G. P. Smeyak, and E. Martin, *Professional Interviewing* (New York: Harper & Row, 1980).

57. C. J. Stewart and W. B. Cash, *Interviewing: Principles and Practices;* 5th ed. (Dubuque, IA: Brown, 1988); Downs, Smeyak, and Martin, *Professional Interviewing;* J. P. Zima, *Interviewing: Key to Effective Management* (Chicago: Science Research Associates, 1983).

58. H. Karp, "The Lost Art of Feedback," in *1987 Annual: Developing Human Resources,* ed. J. W. Pfeiffer (ed.), 14–24 (San Diego, CA: University Associates, 1987); A. Gabor, "Catch a Falling Star System," *U.S. News & World Report,* June 5, 1984, pp. 43–45.

59. L. V. Imundo, *Employee Discipline: How to Do It Right* (Belmont, Calif.: CA: Wadsworth, 1985).

60. G. H. Morris, S. C. Gaveras, W. L. Baker, and M. L. Coursey, "Aligning Actions at Work: How Managers Confront Problems of Employee Performance," *Management Communication Quarterly* 3 (1990): 303–33; M. L. McLaughlin, M. J. Cody, and H. D. O'Hair, "The Management of Failure Events: Some Contextual Determinants of Accounting Behavior," *Human Communication Research* 9 (1983): 208–24.

61. Kellerman and Park, "Situational Urgency"; Weber, Martin, and Cayanus, "Student Interest."

Chapter 9

1. K. Lewin, *Field Theory in Social Science* (New York: Harper & Row, 1951).

2. N. Romano, Jr. and J. Nunamaker, Jr., *Meeting Analysis: Findings from Research and Practice,* in *Proceedings of the 34th Hawaii International Conference on System Sciences* (Los Alamitos, CA: IEEE Press, 2001).

3. G. A. Yukl, *Leadership in Organizations,* 2nd ed. (Englewood Cliffs, NJ: Prentice Hall, 1989).

4. M. Argyle, "Five Kinds of Small Social Groups," in *Small Group Communication: A Reader,* 5th ed., ed. R. S. Cathcart and L. A. Samovar, 33–41 (Dubuque, IA: Brown, 1988).

5. R. K. Kanter, *Evolve!* (Boston: Harvard Business School Press, 2001).

6. M. E. Shaw, *Group Dynamics: The Psychology of Small Group Behavior,* 2nd ed. (New York: McGraw-Hill, 1976).

7. D. Scheerhorn and P. Geist, "Social Dynamics in Groups," in *Managing Group Life: Communicating in Decision-Making Groups,* ed. L. R. Frey and J. K. Barge (Boston: Houghton Mifflin, 1997), p. 92.

8. L. B. Rosenfeld, *Human Interaction in the Small Group Setting* (Columbus, OH: Merrill, 1973). This section is based on many works including K. D. Benne and P. Sheats, "Functioning Roles in Group Members," *Journal of Social Issues* 4 (1948): 41–9; C. M. Anderson, B. L. Riddle, and M. M. Martin, "Socialization in Groups," in *Handbook of Group Communication Theory and Research,* ed. L. Frey, D. Gouran, and M. Poole, 139–63 (Thousand Oaks, CA: Sage, 1999); A. J. Salazar, "An Analysis of the Development and Evolution of Roles in the Small Group," *Small Group Research* 27 (1996): 475–503.

9. Cass R. Sunstein, "The Law of Group Polarization," *Journal of Political Philosophy* 10(2)(2002): 175–95: http://uchicagolaw.typepad.com/faculty/2006/02/deliberation_da.html.

10. J. Longley and D. G. Pruitt, "Groupthink: A Critique of Janis's Theory," in *Review of Personality and Social Psychology,* vol. 1, ed. L. Wheeler, 74–93 (Beverly Hills, CA: Sage, 1980).

11. I. L. Janis, *Victims of Groupthink: A Psychological Study of Foreign-Policy Decisions and Fiascoes* (Boston: Houghton Mifflin, 1972); D. M. Schweiger, W. R. Sandberg, and R. J. Ragan, "Group Approaches for Improving Strategic Decision Making: A Comparative Analysis of Dialectical Inquiry, Devil's Advocacy, and Consensus," *Academy of Management Journal* 29 (1986): 51–71.

12. From Irving L. Janis, *Groupthink,* 2nd ed. Copyright © 1982 by Houghton Mifflin Company.

13. Information from http://www.cnn.com/2003/TECH/space/08/26/sprj.colu.shuttle.report/index.html; http://www.cnn.com/2003/TECH/space/02/03/sprj.colu.shuttle.investigation/index.html.

14. Janis, *Groupthink.*

15. Ibid.

16. C. R. Schwenk, *The Essence of Strategic Decision Making* (Lexington, MA: Lexington Books, 1988), p. 87.

17. Ibid.

18. Ibid.

19. C. R. Schwenk and R. A. Cosier, "Effects of the Expert, Devil's Advocate, and Dialectical Inquiry Methods on Prediction Performance," *Organizational Behavior and Human Performance* 26 (1980): 409–24.

20. R. A. Mason, "A Dialectical Approach to Strategic Planning," *Management Science* 15 (1969): 403–14; Schwenk, *Essence;* Schwenk and Cosier, "Effects."

21. Schwenk and Cosier, "Effects."

22. E. Mabry, "The Systems Metaphor in Group Communication," in *The Handbook of Group Communication Theory and Research,* ed. L. Frey, 71–91 (Thousand Oaks, CA: Sage, 1999); B. Haslett and J. Ruebush, "What Differences Do Individual Differences in Groups Make? The Effects of Individuals, Culture, and Group Composition," in *Handbook,* ed. Frey, 115–38.

23. K. Barge and R. Hirokawa, "Toward a Communication Competency Model of Group Leadership," *Small Group Behavior* 20 (1989): 167–89.

24. R. M. Stogdill, "Personal Factors Associated with Leadership: A Survey of the Literature," *Journal of Psychology* 25 (1948): 35–71.

25. J. Jaworkski, "The Attitude and Capacities Required of the Successful Leader," *Vital Speeches of the Day* (August 1982): 68–70.

26. J. G. Geier, "A Trait Approach to the Study of Leadership in Small Groups," *Journal of Communication* 17 (1967): 316–23.

27. R. Blake and J. S. Mouton, *The Managerial Grid* (Houston: Gulf, 1964).

28. P. Hersey and K. H. Blanchard, *Management of Organizational Behavior: Utilizing Human Resources,* 5th ed. (Englewood Cliffs, NJ: Prentice Hall, 1988).

29. F. E. Fiedler, "The Leadership Game: Matching the Man to the Situation," *Organizational Dynamics* 4 (1976): 6–16.

30. D. A. Romig, *Breakthrough Teamwork: Outstanding Results Using Structured Teamwork* (Chicago: Irwin, 1996).

31. D. C. Kinlaw, *Developing Superior Work Teams* (San Diego: Lexington Books, 1991).

32. Information from http://www.msnbc.msn.com/id/14062437 (accessed July 24, 2006).

33. Information from http://www.melancon.house.gov/SupportingFiles/documents/AnalysisofBrownEmails.pdf.

34. G. A. Yukl, *Leadership in Organizations* (Englewood Cliffs, NJ: Prentice Hall, 1981), p. 203.

35. F. G. Elias, M. E. Johnson, and J. B. Fortman, "Task-Focused Self-Disclosure: Effects on Group Cohesiveness, Commitment to Task, and Productivity," *Small Group Behavior* 20 (1986): 87–96.

36. M. L. Marks, P. H. Mirvis, E. J. Hackett, and J. F. Grady, "Employee Participation in a Quality Circle Program: Impact on Quality of Work Life, Productivity, and Absenteeism," *Journal of Applied Psychology* 71 (1986): 61–69; Elias, Johnson, and Fortman, "Task-Focused Self-Disclosure."

37. B. Dumaine, "Who Needs a Boss?" *Fortune* (May 7, 1990): 52–60.

38. Ibid., p. 52.

39. L. Moran and E. Musselwhite, "Self-Directed Workteams: A Lot More Than Just Teamwork" (paper presented to the national conference of the American Society for Training and Development, Dallas, 1988); H. P. Sims and J. W. Dean, Jr., "Beyond Quality Circles: Self-Managing Teams," *Personnel* 62 (1985): 25–32.

Chapter 10

1. H. M. Robert, *Robert's Rules of Order,* 11th ed. (Cambridge, MA: Da Capo Press, 2011).

2. This section is based on a review of research by S. Ketrow, "Nonverbal Aspects of Group Communication," in *The Handbook of Group Communication Theory and Research*, ed. L. Frey, 251–87 (Thousand Oaks, CA: Sage, 1999).

3. D. Forsyth, *Group Dynamics*, 6th ed. (Belmont, CA: Wadsworth Cengage Learning, 2013)

4. R. Y. Hirokawa and D. S. Gouran, "Facilitation of Group Communication: A Critique of Prior Research and an Agenda for Future Research," *Management Communication Quarterly* 3 (1989): 71–92.

5. B. J. Broome and D. B. Deever, "Next Generation Group Facilitation," *Management Communication Quarterly* 3 (1989): 107–27.

6. F. G. Smith, "Defining Managerial Problems: A Framework for Prescriptive Theorizing," *Management Science* 35 (1989): 963–81.

7. C. H. Moore, *Group Techniques for Idea Building* (Newbury Park, CA: Sage, 1987).

8. G. Corey, *Group Techniques*, 4th ed. (Stamford, CT: Brooks/Cole Cengage Learning, 2015).

9. J. K. Brilhart, "Observing and Evaluating Discussion," in *Small Group Communication*, ed. R.S. Cathcart and R.S. Samovar, p. 559. (Dubuque, IA: W.C Brown, 1979).

10. A. C. Kowitz and T. J. Knutson, *Decision Making in Small Groups: The Search for Alternatives* (Boston: Allyn & Bacon, 1980).

11. L. A. Samovar and S. W. King, *Communication and Discussion in Small Groups* (Scottsdale, AZ: Gorsuch-Scarisbrick, 1981).

Chapter 11

1. D. A. Infante, *Arguing Constructively* (Prospect Heights, IL: Waveland Press, 1988), p. 7.

2. D. A. Infante and W. I. Gorden, "Superiors' Argumentativeness and Verbal Aggressiveness as Predictors of Subordinates' Satisfaction," *Human Communication Research* 12 (1985): 117–25.

3. D. A. Infante and C. J. Wigley, "Verbal Aggressiveness: An Interpersonal Mode and Measure," *Communication Monographs* 53 (1986): 61.

4. Infante, *Arguing Constructively*.

5. D. A. Infante and A. S. Rancer, "A Conceptualization and Measure of Argumentativeness," *Journal of Personality Assessment* 46 (1982): 72–80. Reported in D. De Wine, A. M. Nicotera, and D. Parry, "Argumentativeness and Aggressiveness: The Flip Side of Gentle Persuasion," *Management Communication Quarterly* 4 (1991): 386–411.

6. Infante, *Arguing Constructively*, p. 21.

7. Ibid.

8. The distinction between bargaining and negotiation is not enough to quibble over. See L. L. Putnam and M. S. Poole, "Conflict and Negotiation," in *Handbook of Organizational Communication*, ed. F. Jablin, L. Putnam, K. Roberts, and L. Porter, 549–99 (Beverly Hills, CA: Sage, 1987); D. F. Womack, "Assessing the Thomas-Kilmann Conflict MODE Survey," *Management Communication Quarterly* 1 (1988): 321–49; O. Marey, "Agents' Uncertainty in Argumentation-based Negotiation: Classification and Implementation," *Procedia Computer Science* 32 (2014): 61–8; The 5th International Conference on Ambient Systems, Networks and Technologies (ANT-2014), the 4th International, Conference on Sustainable Energy Information Technology (SEIT-2014): http://www.sciencedirect.com/science/article/pii/S1877050914005985.

9. M. A. Rahim, *Managing Conflict in Organizations*, 3rd ed. (Westport, CN: Greenwood Publishing Group, 2001).

10. Michael Fitzmoser, "Multidimensional analysis of negotiation processes," *Group Decision and Negotiation* GDN (2014): https://books.google.com/books?hl=en&lr=&id=gA_GBgAAQBAJ&oi=fnd&pg=PA8&dq=dimensions+of+negotiation&ots=xKyDQ2EisY&sig=AvV4TW6-G2J8fOoJ1c1-kM6emmw#v=onepage&q=dimensions%20of%20negotiation&f=false; L. L. Putnam and T. S. Jones, "Reciprocity in Negotiations: An Analysis of Bargaining Interaction," *Communication Monographs* 49 (1982): 171–91.

11. Putnam and Poole, "Conflict and Negotiation."

12. W. A. Donahue, M. E. Deiz, and M. Hamilton, "Coding Naturalistic Interaction," *Human Communication Research* 10 (1984): 403–26.

13. Stephanie Cammarata, "Strategies of Cooperation in Distributed Problem Solving," *Readings in Distributed Intelligence* (2014): https://books.google.com/books?hl=en&lr=&id=jp6jBQAAQBAJ&oi=fnd&pg=PA102&dq=cooperative+strategies+in+communication&ots=0oZH_TeI8T&sig=8dZfkFYCUNVyzkApg-2hlghVGWQ#v=onepage&q=cooperative%20strategies%20in%20communication&f=false; R. E. Walton and R. E. McKersie, *A Behavior Theory of Labor Negotiations: An Analysis of a Social Interaction System* (New York: McGraw-Hill, 1965); Putnam and Jones, "Reciprocity in Negotiations"; Putnam and Poole, "Conflict and Negotiation."

14. W. A. Donahue, "An Empirical Framework for Examining Negotiation Processes and Outcomes," *Communication Monographs* 45 (1978): 247–57; L. L. Putnam and T. S. Jones, "The Role of Communication in Bargaining," *Human Communication Research* 8 (1982): 262–80.

15. J. L. Hocker and W. W. Wilmot, *Interpersonal Conflict*, 3rd ed. (Dubuque, IA: Brown, 1991), p. 12.

16. M. Afzalur Rahim, *Managing Conflict in Organizations*, 4th ed. (New Brunswick, NJ: Transaction Publishers, 2011).

17. Rahim, 2011; Hocker and Wilmot, *Interpersonal Conflict*.

18. Ibid., p. 48.

19. M. L. Knapp, L. L. Putnam, and L. J. Davis, "Measuring Interpersonal Conflict in Organizations: Where Do We Go from Here?" *Management Communication Quarterly* 1 (1988): 414–29.

20. M. A. Rahim, "A Measure of Styles of Handling Interpersonal Conflict," *Academy of Management Journal* 26 (1983): 368–76; M. A. Rahim, *Managing Conflict in Organizations* (New York: Praeger, 1986).

21. T. L. Lee, "The serial reproduction of conflict: Third parties escalate conflict through communication biases," *Journal of Experimental Social Psychology*; H. Deutsch, "Cooperation and Competition," in *The Handbook of Conflict Resolution*, ed. M. Deutsch and P. Coleman, 21–40 (San Francisco: Jossey-Bass, 2000).

Chapter 12

1. P. R. Evans, "'Tense' Is Good for You!" *This Week Magazine*, July 9, 1967, p. 4.

2. "The 14 Worst Human Fears," *Detroit Free Press*, June 7, 1977.

3. G. Friedrich and B. Goss, "Systematic Desensitization," in *Avoiding Communication: Shyness, Reticence, and Communication Apprehension*, ed. J. A. Daly and J. C. McCroskey, 173–87 (Beverly Hills, CA: Sage, 1984).

4. S. E. Berry and R. J. Garnston, "Become a State-of-the-Art Presenter," *Training and Development Journal* 41 (1987): 19–26.

5. G. A. Market, "Many Executives Must Learn How to Speak," *Marketing News* 22 (1988): 8–10.

6. Wilson et al., Public Speaking as a Liberal Art, "Topical System for Generating Thoughts," pp. 112–113, © 1990 Pearson Education. Reproduced by permission of Pearson Education, Inc.

7. T. Cothran, "The Value of Visuals," *Presentation Technologies*, (July 1989), pp. 6–7.

8. B. Parks, "Death to PowerPoint!", Bloomberg Businessweek, businessweek.com, retrieved 3 April 2015.

9. J. Burgoon, D. Buller, and W. G. Woodall, *Nonverbal Communication: The Unspoken Dialogue* (New York: Harper & Row, 1989), pp. 154–61.

10. Ibid., p. 158.

11. R. P. Hart, G. W. Friedrich, and B. Brummett, *Public Communication*, 2nd ed. (New York: Harper & Row, 1983), pp. 183–85.

12. Based on D. Burns, *The Feeling Good Handbook* (New York: William Morrow, 1989), pp. 311–12.

Chapter 13

1. J. Fiala, "Citation Analysis Controls the Information Flood," *Thermochimica Acta* 110 (1987): 11.

2. Some of this summary is taken from these sources: S. Hyde, *Television and Radio Announcing*, 6th ed. (Boston: Houghton Mifflin, 1990); S. Bension, *Producer's Masterguide, 1990: The International Production Manual for Motion Pictures, Broadcast Television, Commercials, Cable, and Videotape Industries*, 10th ed. (New York: N.Y. Production Manual, 1990); Hyatt Research Corporation Staff, *The Executive's Guide to Network Media* (Fairfax, VA: DataTrends Publications, 1990).

3. P. H. Lewis, "New Camera Simplifies Computer Processing of Images," *South Bend (Indiana) Tribune*, June 9, 1994, p. A11.

4. R. P. Hart, G. W. Friedrich, and B. Brummett, *Public Communication*, 2nd ed. (New York: Harper & Row, 1983), p. 141.

Chapter 14

1. This outline and others in this chapter are adapted from K. J. Krayer, *Basic Speech Communications Workbook* (Dallas: Bellwether Press, 1987).

2. Barack Obama. Remarks on Election Night (November 4, 2008). Retrieved from http://millercenter.org/president/obama/speeches/speech-4424 on April 7, 2015.

3. Edward M. Kennedy, *Faith, Truth and Tolerance in America*, speech at Liberty University, October 1983.

4. A. H. Maslow, *Motivation and Personality* (New York: Harper & Row, 1954).

5. Aristotle, *Rhetoric* (New York: Modern Library, 1954).

6. E. P. Bettinghaus, *Persuasive Communication*, 2nd ed. (New York: Holt, Rinehart & Winston, 1973).

7. W. N. Thompson, *The Process of Persuasion: Principles and Readings* (New York: Harper & Row, 1975), p. 72.

8. J. L. Whitehead, Jr., "Factors of Source Credibility," *Quarterly Journal of Speech* 54 (1968): 59–63.

9. Bettinghaus, *Persuasive Communication*, pp. 248–72.

10. H. Gulley and D. K. Berlo, "Effects of Intercellular and Intracellular Speech Structure on Attitude Change and Learning," *Speech Monographs* 23 (1956): 288–97.

Credits

Chapter 1 **Excerpt** on p. 2: Based on W. Bennis and R. Thomas, "Crucibles of Leadership," Harvard Business Review (September 2002), 39–45; **Figure 1.1**, p. 3: © Pearson Education Inc; **Excerpt** on p. 4: O. Wiio, Wiio's Laws—and Some Others (Espoo, Finland: Welin-Göös, 1978); **Figure 1.2**, p. 8: © Pearson Education Inc; **Excerpt** on p. 9: E. Mayo, The Social Problems of an Industrial Civilization (Andover, MA: Andover Press, 1945), p. 22; **UnBox 1.1**, p. 5: Based on D. Fallows (2007), "Spam 2007" Pew Internet: http://www.pewinternet.org/reports/2007/spam=2007.aspx (accessed may 20, 2009). "Spam: How Much Do We Get?": http://www.silicon.com/news/165–500001/1/4618.html (accessed July 30, 2003), "U.S. Workers Spared Junk E-mails": http://news.bbc.co.uk/2/hi/technology/2558113.stm (accessed July 30, 2003), "Managing the Email Explosion": http://CNN.com/2000/TECH/computing/09/06/email.management.idg.index.html (accessed September 7, 2000). S. Robbins (2004). "Tips for Mastering E-mail Overload": http://hbswk.hbs.edu/item.jhtml?id=4438&t=srobbins (accessed March 12, 2006); **UnBox 1.2**, p. 9: Based on "Employee Monitoring: Is There Privacy in the Workplace?": http://www.privacyrights.org/fs/fs7-work.htm (accessed March 13, 2006), "Trying to Measure Your Surfing at Work": http://www.cnn.com/2001/CAREER/trends/08/14/employee.net.use.idg/(accessed July 31, 2003); B. Petersen (May 26, 2008), "Employee Monitoring: It's Not Paranoia—You Really Are Being Watched!"; http://www.pcmag.com/article2/0,2817,2308369,00.asp; **Table 1.1**, p. 10: © Pearson Education Inc.; **Figure 1.2**, p. 10: © Pearson Education Inc.; **Table 1.2**, p. 11: © Pearson Education Inc.; **Excerpt** on p. 12: Inter IKEA Group, management vision; **Excerpt** on p. 12: IKEA, Business goal for IKEA employees **Excerpt** on p. 12: IKEA Timeline; **Excerpt** on p. 11: R. H. Kilmann, Managing Beyond the Quick Fix (San Francisco: Jossey-Bass, 1989).

Chapter 2 **Figure 2.1**, p. 16: © Pearson Education Inc.; **Figure 2.2** p. 20: © Pearson Education Inc.; **Excerpt** on p. 18: M. W. Seeger, "Organizational Communication Ethics: Directions for Critical Inquiry and Application," in Key Issues in Organizational Communication, ed. D. Tourish and O. Hargie, 220–33 (New York: Routledge, 2004): 227; **Excerpt** on p. 21: P. Shrivesta in R. L. Daft and G. P. Huber, "How Organizations Learn: A Communication Framework," Research in the Sociology of Organizations 5 (1987): 1–36; **Excerpt** on p. 23: P. Frost, "Power, Politics, and Influence," in Handbook of Organizational Communication, ed. F. Jablin, L. Putnam, K. Roberts, and L. Porter (Newbury Park, Calif.: Sage, 1987), 504–48; **Excerpt** on p. 23: R. E. Reidenbach and D. P. Robin, Ethics and Profits (Englewood Cliffs, N. J.: Prentice Hall, 1989); **Excerpt** on p. 23: C. Redding, Communication within the Organization: An Interpretive Review of Theory and Research (New York: Industrial Communication Council, 1972). Reprinted with permission; **Figure 2.3**, p. 26: Based on Locke et al., "Goal Setting and Task Performance: 1969–1980." Psychological Bulletin (90), 1981; pp. 125–152. Copyright © 1981 by The American Psychological Association and Edwin A. Locke. Adapted with permission from The American Psychological Association and Edwin A. Locke; **Excerpt** on p. 26: Based on E. A. Locke, K. N. Shaw, L. M. Saari, and G. P. Latham, "Goal Setting and Task Performance: 1969–1980," Psychological Bulletin 90 (1981): 125–52; **Excerpt** on p. 29: D. Katz and R. Kahn, The Social Psychology of Organizations (New York: Wiley, 1966); **Figure 2.4**, p. 30: © Pearson Education Inc.; **Excerpt** on p. 30: T. Daniels and B. Spiker, Perspectives on Organizational Communication (Dubuque, Iowa: Brown, 1987); **Excerpt** on p. 30: L. Sussman, A. J. Adams, F. E. Kuzmits, and L. E. Raho, "Organizational Politics: Tactics, Channels, and Hierarchical Roles," Journal of Business

Ethics 41 (2002): 313–29; **Excerpt** on p. 30: J. R. Katzenbach and D. K. Smith, The Wisdom of Teams (Boston: Harvard Business School Press, 1993); **Figure 2.5**, p. 31: © Pearson Education Inc.; **Excerpt** on p. 31: G. Goldhaber, Organizational Communication (Dubuque, Iowa: Brown, 1990); **Figure 2.6**, p. 32: © Pearson Education Inc.; **Excerpt** on p. 33: "Sources: Based on D'Urso and Rains, "Examining the Scope"; adapted from D. A. Level and W. P. Galle, Business Communication: Theory and Practice (Dallas: Business Publications, 1980); A. J. Melcher and R. Beller, "Toward a Theory of Organization Communication: Considerations in Channel Selection," Academy of Management Journal 10 (1967): 39–52; Shiu and Lenhart, How Americans Use; Tidwell and Walther, "Computer-Mediated Communication Efforts; **Excerpt** on p. 34: "Sources: Based on A. H. Buss, Self-Consciousness and Social Anxiety (San Francisco: Freeman, 1980); J. Daly and J. L. Hailey, "Putting the Situation into Writing Research: Situational Parameters of Writing Apprehension as Disposition and State," in New Directions in Composition Research, ed. R. E. Beach and L. Bidwell (New York: Guilford, 1983); **Excerpt** on p. 33: P. Pace, Organizational Communication: Foundations for Human Resource Development (Englewood Cliffs, N. J.: Prentice Hall, 1983).

Chapter 3 **Table 3.1**, p. 39: www.bls.gov/cps/cpsrace2013.pdf; **Excerpt** on p. 48: P. Shaver and L. D. Shaver, "Applying Perspectival Rhetorical Analysis in Intercultural Consulting: The Chromosomal Bivalency Mode," Intercultural Communication Studies 2(2) (1992): 1–22; **Figure 3.1**, p. 53: © Pearson Education Inc.

Chapter 4 **Table 4.1**, p. 59: From Communication Works, 8th ed. by Teri Gamble et al., p. 193. © 2005 by The McGraw-Hill Companies, Inc. Reprinted with permission; **Excerpt** on p. 60: B. Goss, Processing Communication (Belmont, CA: Wadsworth, 1982); **Figure 4.1**, p. 60: © Pearson Education Inc.; **UnBox 4.2**, p. 63: Based on You can visit Ball Aerospace online at www.ballaerospace.com; **UnBox 4.1**, p. 64: Based on B. Lampton, "What Good Listeners Do: Becoming the Company Others Love to Keep!" Expert Magazine (2003) [online]. Available: http://www.expertmagazine.com/artman/publish/article_309.shtml. C. Reid, "How to Promote OSH," OSH Promotion in the Workplace (1998) [online]. Available: http://www.safetyline.wa.gov.au/institute/level1/course7/lecture26/126_02.asp; **Table 4.2**, p. 68: © Pearson Education Inc.; **Table 4.3**, p. 69: © Pearson Education Inc.; **Table 4.4**, p. 69: © Pearson Education Inc.; **Table 4.5**, p. 70: © Pearson Education Inc.; **UnBox 4.3**, p. 71: Reprinted with permission from the National Communication Association: www.natcom.org. All Rights Reserved.

Chapter 5 **Table 5.1**, p. 78: © Pearson Education Inc.; **Table 5.2**, p. 86: K. L. Ashcraft and D. K. Mumby, Reworking Gender: A Feminist Communicology of Organization (Thousand Oaks, CA: Sage, 2003); **Excerpt** on p. 87: R. Harper, A. Wiens, and J. Matazzaro, Nonverbal Communication: The State of the Art (New York: Wiley, 1978), 173.; **Excerpt** on p. 90: E. M. Rogers and D. L. Kincaid, Communication Networks, Toward a New Paradigm for Research (New York: Free Press, 1981).; **Table 5.3**, p. 91: © Pearson Education Inc.; **Table 5.4** p. 91: © Pearson Education Inc.

Chapter 6 **Figure 6.1**, p. 96: © Pearson Education Inc.; **Excerpt** on p. 96: Based on R. Likert, New Patterns of Management (New York: McGraw-Hill, 1961); **Table 6.1**, p. 97: © Pearson Education Inc.; **Excerpt** on p. 98: Peter Drucker, and Warren Bennis, as quoted in Seven Habits of Highly Effective People (1989) by Stephen R. Covey, p. 101; **Table 6.2**, p. 99: For a more thorough comparison of leadership theories from a communication perspective, we highly recommend Gail Fairhurst's chapter in The New Handbook of Organizational Communication. G. Fairhurst, "Dualisms in Leadership Research," in F. Jablin and L. Putnam (eds.), The New Handbook of Organizational Communication (Thousand Oaks, CA: Sage, 2001), pp. 379–439; **Excerpt** on p. 100: W. Bennis and B. Nanus, Leaders: The Strategies for Taking Charge (New York: Harper & Row, 1985), 89; **Excerpt** on p. 100: Edwin H. Friedman quoted in Greg Robinson with Mark Rose, A Leadership Paradox: Influencing Others by Defining Yourself (AuthorHouse, 2004); **Figure 6.2**, p. 101: © Pearson Education Inc.; **Excerpt** on p. 101: John F. Kennedy, Remarks Prepared for Delivery at the Trade Mart in Dallas, TX, November 22, 1963; **Excerpt** on p. 102: T. Peters and R. Waterman, In Search of Excellence: Lessons from America's Best-Run Companies (New York: Warner Books, 1982); **Excerpt** on p. 103: © Pearson Education, Inc.; **Excerpt** on p. 104: K. R. Andrews, "Ethics in Practice," Harvard Business Review (September–October 1989): 103; **Excerpt** on p. 104: J. K. Van Fleet, The 22 Biggest Mistakes Managers Make and How to Correct Them (West Nyack, NY: Parker, 1982), 147; **Excerpt** on p. 104: R. Hart, Verbal Style and the Presidency (Orlando, FL: Academic Press, 1984); **Excerpt** on p. 105: Warren Bennis (1999) Managing People Is Like Herding Cats. p. 89; **Excerpt** on p. 106: J. Kouzes and B. Posner, The Leadership Challenge (San Francisco: Jossey-Bass, 1987). p. 67; **Figure 6.3**, p. 106: © Pearson Education Inc.

Chapter 7   Table 7.1, p. 111: © Pearson Education Inc.; **Figure 7.1**, p. 111: © Pearson Education Inc.; **Excerpt** on p. 112: J. Kouzes and B. Z. Posner, The Leadership Challenge (San Francisco: Jossey-Bass, 1987). p. 162; **Excerpt** on p. 112: J. Kouzes and B. Z. Posner, The Leadership Challenge (San Francisco: Jossey-Bass, 1987). p. 175; **Excerpt** on p. 115: From "Mission for Mail," at http://www.star.net. uk/star/home/media_centre/library/articles/mission_for_mail. stml. The authors of the survey are the Institute of Directors, with the communication firm Avaya; **Excerpt** on p. 116: N. Smith, "Digital Overload: Too much Technology Takes a Toll'" Business New Dailey (November 8, 2010). http://www.businessnewsdaily. com/379-digital-overload-too-much-data-costs-businesses-billions. html; **Excerpt** on p. 117: J. Kotter, Power and Influence (New York: Free Press, 1985); **Excerpt** on p. 117: E. A. Fagenson, "The Mentor Advantage Perceived Career/Job Experiences of Protégés vs. Nonprotégés," Journal of Organizational Behavior 10 (1989): 309–20; **UnBox 7.1**, p. 117: R. A. Noe, "Women and Mentoring: A Review and Research Agenda," Academy of Management Review 13 (1988), 65–78; **UnBox 7.2**, p. 121: Summarized by H. Witteman, "The Interface between Sexual Harassment and Organizational Romance," in Sexual Harassment: Communication Implications, ed. G. Kreps (Cresskill, N.J.: Hampton Press, 1994); **Excerpt** on p. 122: From Completeness: Quality for the 21st Century, by P. B. Crosby. Copyright © 1992 by P. B. Crosby; **UnBox 7.3**, p. 122: Reprinted with permission from Joann Keyton, North Carolina State University, 2009; **UnBox 7.4**, p. 123: This list is adapted from D. Finkelman and T. Goland, "The Case of the Complaining Customer," Harvard Business Review, May–June 1990, pp. 9–21.

Chapter 8   Excerpt on p. 127: P. F. Drucker, "How to Be an Employee," Fortune, May 1952, reprinted in N. B. Sighand and D. N. Bateman, Communicating in Business (Glenview, IL: Scott, Foresman, 1981), 454; **Excerpt** on p. 127: Personnel interviewers' perceptions of the importance and adequacy of applicants' communication skills. Marshalita Sims Peterson. Communication Education Vol. 46, 1997 pp. 287–281; **Table 8.1**, p. 128: © Pearson Education Inc.; **Excerpt** on p. 128: A. P. Carnevale, L. J. Gainer, and J. Villet, Training in America: The Organization and Strategic Role of Training (San Francisco: Jossey-Bass, 1990); **Table 8.2**, p. 130: "Adapted from R. S. Goyer, W. C. Redding, and J. T. Rickey, Interviewing Principles & Techniques. Published by Wm. C. Brown Group, 1968; **Excerpt** on p. 132: Based on S. L. Payne, "Thoughts About Meaningless Questions," Public Opinion Quarterly 14 (1950): 687–96; **Figure 8.1**, p. 134: © Pearson Education Inc.; **Figure 8.2**, p. 134: © Pearson

Education Inc.; **Table 8.3**, p. 134: © Pearson Education Inc.; **Table 8.4**, p. 135: © Pearson Education Inc.; **Excerpt** on p. 135: Based on G. Gallup, "The Quintamensional Plan of Question Design," Public Opinion Quarterly 11 (1947): 385; **Excerpt** on p. 136: Carl Rogers's research is discussed in D. W. Johnson, Reaching Out: Interpersonal Effectiveness and Self-Actualization (Englewood Cliffs, N.J.: Prentice Hall, 1972), 117–140; **Excerpt** on p. 138: A. Finder, "For Some, Online Persona Undermines a Résumé," NYTimes.com (June 11, 2006), http://www.nytimes.com/2006/06/11/us/11recruit.html?ei=5090 &en=ddfbe1e3b386090b&ex=1307678400&pagewanted=all; **Excerpt** on p. 138: A. Finder, "For Some, Online Persona Undermines a Résumé," NYTimes.com (June 11, 2006), http://www.nytimes. com/2006/06/11/us/11recruit.html?ei=5090&en=ddfbe1e3b386090 b&ex=1307678400&pagewanted=all; **Excerpt** on p. 138: "Recruiters Dig Up Dirt on Potential Employees Online," ABC7.com, http:// abclocal.go.com/kabc/story?section=seenon&id=4308602 (accessed Aug. 21, 2006); **Excerpt** on p. 140: Based on K. Hutchinson and D. Brefka, "Personnel Administrators' Preferences for Résumé Content: Ten Years After," Business Communication Quarterly 60 (1997): 67ff. Retrieved from Questia, October 15, 2003; **Figure 8.3a**, p. 141: Résumé formats based on J. T. Bostwick, The Perfect Resume (New York: Doubleday, 1990); **Figure 8.3b**, p. 141: Résumé formats based on J. T. Bostwick, The Perfect Resume (New York: Doubleday, 1990); **Figure 8.4**, p. 142: © Pearson Education Inc.; **Figure 8.5**, p. 144: © Pearson Education Inc.; **Table 8.5**, p. 145: © Pearson Education Inc.; **Figure 8.6**, p. 148: © Pearson Education Inc.

Chapter 9   Excerpt on p. 154: G. A. Yukl, Leadership in Organizations, 2d ed. (Englewood Cliffs, NJ: Prentice Hall, 1989); **Figure 9.1**, p. 155: From Moorhead/Griffin. Organizational Behavior, 2E. © 1989 South-Western, a part of Cengage Learning, **Inc.** Reproduced by permission. www.cengage.com/permissions; **Excerpt** on p. 156: M. E. Shaw, Group Dynamics: The Psychology of Small Group Behavior, 2d ed. (New York: McGraw-Hill, 1976); **Excerpt** on p. 156: D. Scheerhorn and P. Geist, "Social Dynamics in Groups," in Managing Group Life: Communicating in Decision-Making Groups, ed. L. R. Frey and J. K. Barge (Boston: Houghton Mifflin, 1997), 92; **Excerpt** on p. 158: Cass R. Sunstein, "The Law of Group Polarization," Journal of Political Philosophy 10(2) (2002): 175–95, http://uchicagolaw.typepad.com/faculty/2006/02/ deliberation_da.html; **Figure 9.2**, p. 159: © Pearson Education Inc.; **Excerpt** on p. 159: From Irving L. Janis, Groupthink, 2d ed. Copyright © 1982 by Houghton Mifflin Company; **Excerpt** on p. 159: Columbia Accident Investigation Board Excerpts by SPACE.com, August 26, 2003; **Excerpt** on p. 159: Information from http://www.cnn. com/2003/TECH/space/08/26/sprj.colu.shuttle.report/index.html; **Excerpt** on p. 159: From Irving L. Janis, Groupthink, 2d ed. Copyright © 1982 by Houghton Mifflin Company; **Excerpt** on p. 160: C. R. Schwenk, The Essence of Strategic Decision Making (Lexington, MA: Lexington Books, 1988), 87; **Excerpt** on p. 161: C. R. Schwenk and R. A. Cosier, "Effects of the Expert, Devil's Advocate, and Dialectical Inquiry Methods on Prediction Performance," Organizational Behavior and Human Performance 26 (1980): 409–24; **Excerpt** on p. 164: D. C. Kinlaw, Developing Superior Work Teams (San Diego: Lexington Books, 1991); **UnBox 9.1**, p. 165: Adapted from D. O'Hair, M. Wiemann D. Mullin, and J. Tevon, Real Communication, 3rd ed. (New York: Bedford/St. Martin's Press, 2015); "Dealing with Different Types of Participants," http://www.wi-scd.org (accessed June 19, 2001); R. Schwartz, The Skilled Facilitator (San Francisco: Jossey-Bass, 1994); D. O'Hair, R. Stewart, H. Rubenstein, A Speaker's Guidebook, 6th ed. (Boston: Bedford/St. Martins, 2015); **Excerpt** on p. 165: Information from http://www.msnbc.msn.com/id/14062437 (accessed July 24, 2006); **Excerpt** on p. 165: Information from http://www.melancon.house.gov/-SupportingFiles/documents/ AnalysisofBrownEmails.pdf; **Excerpt** on p. 166: G. A. Yukl, Leadership in Organizations (Englewood Cliffs, NJ: Prentice Hall, 1981), 203; **Table 9.1**, p. 167: © Pearson Education Inc.; **Table 9.2** p. 169: © Pearson Education Inc.

Chapter 10 **Figure 10.1**, p. 172: © Pearson Education Inc.; **Figure 10.2**, p. 174: © Pearson Education Inc.; **Figure 10.3**, p. 175: © Pearson Education Inc.; **Excerpt** on p. 179: B. J. Broome and D. B. Deever, "Next Generation Group -Facilitation," Management Communication Quarterly 3 (1989), 107–27; **Excerpt** on p. 179: F. G. Smith, "Defining Managerial Problems: A Framework for Prescriptive Theorizing," Management Science 35 (1989); 963–81; **Figure 10.4**, p. 182: © Pearson Education Inc.; **Table 10.1**, p. 184: © Pearson Education Inc.; **UnBox 10.1**, p. 185: You can visit Creative Communication Network online at http://www.creativecommnet.com; **Excerpt** on p. 185: J. K. Brilhart, "Observing and Evaluating Discussion," in Cathcart and Samovar, Small Group Communication, p. 559; **Figure 10.5**, p. 187 From L. A. Samovar and S. W. King, Communication and Discussion in Small Groups (Scottsdale, AZ: Gorsuch-Scarisbrick, 1981). Reprinted with permission of the authors; **Figure 10.6**, p. 188: From L. A. Samovar and S. W. King, Communication and Discussion in Small Groups (Scottsdale, AZ: Gorsuch-Scarisbrick, 1981). Reprinted with permission of the authors.

Chapter 11 **Excerpt** on p. 191: D. A. Infante, Arguing Constructively (Prospect Heights, IL: Waveland Press, 1988), p. 7; **Excerpt** on p. 191: D. A. Infante and C. J. Wigley, "Verbal Aggressiveness: An Interpersonal Mode and Measure," Communication Monographs 53 (1986): 61; **UnBox 11.2**, p. 192: Reprinted with permission from the National Communication Association. All Rights Reserved; **UnBox 11.3**, p. 194: You can visit Tootsie Roll Industries, Inc., online at http://www.tootsie.com; **Excerpt** on p. 197: W. A. Donahue, "An Empirical Framework for Examining -Negotiation Processes and Outcomes," Communication Monographs 45 (1978): 247–57; L. L. Putnam and T. S. Jones, "The Role of Communication in Bargaining," Human -Communication Research 8 (1982): 262–80; **Excerpt** on p. 198: J. L. Hocker and W. W. Wilmot, Interpersonal Conflict, 3rd ed. (Dubuque, IA: Brown, 1991), p. 12; **Excerpt** on p. 199: Rahim, 2011. J. L. Hocker and W. W. Wilmot, Interpersonal Conflict, 3rd ed. (Dubuque, IA: Brown, 1991), p. 48.

Chapter 12 **Excerpt** on p. 208: P. R. Evans, "Tense' Is Good for You!" This Week Magazine, July 9, 1967, p. 4; **UnBox 12.1**, p. 213: You can visit the American Red Cross online at http://www.redcross.org; **Excerpt** on p. 214: Wilson et al., Public Speaking as a Liberal Art, "Topical System for Generating Thoughts," pp. 112–113, © 1990 Pearson Education. Reproduced by permission of Pearson Education, Inc.; **Excerpt** on p. 222: J. Burgoon, D. Buller, and W. G. Woodall, Nonverbal Communication: The Unspoken Dialogue (New York: Harper & Row, 1989), p. 158.

Chapter 13 **Excerpt** on p. 230: J. Fiala, "Citation Analysis Controls the Information Flood," Thermochimica Acta 110 (1987): 11; **UnBox 13.2**, p. 239: Reprinted with permission from the National Communication Association. All Rights Reserved.

Chapter 14 **Figure 14.1**, p. 247: © Pearson Education Inc.; **UnBox 14.1**, p. 250 (c) Pearson Education Inc.; **Table 14.1**, p. 252: © Pearson Education Inc.; **Excerpt** on p. 253: Edward M. Kennedy, Faith, Truth and Tolerance in America, the late U.S. Senator of Massachusetts, offered to speak at Liberty University in October of 1983; **Excerpt** on p. 253: A. H. Maslow, Motivation and Personality (New York: Harper & Row, 1954); **Excerpt** on p. 254: Aristotle, Rhetoric (New York: Modern Library, 1954); **Excerpt** on p. 255: W. N. Thompson, The Process of Persuasion: Principles and Readings (New York: Harper & Row, 1975), p. 72; **UnBox 14.2**, p. 256: R. P. Hart, G. W. Friedrich, and B. Brummett, Public Communication, 2nd ed. (New York: Harper & Row, 1983), p. 286. Reprinted with permission of Barry Brummett and Rod Hart; **Excerpt** on p. 257: H. Gulley and D. K. Berlo, "Effects of Intercellular and Intracellular Speech Structure on Attitude Change and Learning," Speech Monographs 23 (1956): 288–97.

Index